California
Real Estate License
Preparation

TWELFTH EDITION

California Real Estate License Preparation

William H. Pivar
Professor Emeritus
College of the Desert

Dennis J. McKenzie
Real Estate Coordinator and Instructor
College of the Redwoods

THOMSON

SOUTH-WESTERN

Australia · Canada · Mexico · Singapore · Spain · United Kingdom · United States

THOMSON
™
SOUTH-WESTERN

California Real Estate License Preparation, 12e

William H. Pivar and Dennis J. McKenzie

VP/Editorial Director:
Jack W. Calhoun

Executive Publisher:
Dave Shaut

Sr. Acquisitions Editor:
Scott Person

Developmental Editor:
Jennifer Warner

Marketing Manager:
Mark Linton

Production Editor:
Colleen A. Farmer

Manufacturing Coordinator:
Charlene Taylor

Design Project Manager:
Rik Moore

Internal Designer:
Lisa Albonetti

Cover Designer:
Trish Knapke, Rik Moore

Cover Photo:
Source: PhotoDisc, Inc.

Production House:
Pine Tree Composition, Inc.

Printer:
Westgroup

For permission to use material from
this text or product, contact us by
Tel (800) 730-2214
Fax (800) 730-2215
http://www.thomsonrights.com

For more information
contact South-Western,
5191 Natorp Boulevard,
Mason, Ohio, 45040.
Or you can visit our Internet site at:
http://www.swlearning.com

Contents

Introduction

This book was written to prepare readers to take and pass the California real estate salesperson and broker examinations. The book can be used by itself or in conjunction with a California real estate principles text.

The chapter outline carefully follows the best-selling seventh edition of *California Real Estate Principles*, published by South-Western and written by Dennis McKenzie, Lowell Anderson, Frank Battino, and Cecilia Hopkins. Used together, these books not only meet the prelicensing requirements of real estate principles but also focus the information for examination success.

Included in this book is a comprehensive glossary of real estate terms and phrases. It is strongly recommended that students read through the glossary at least once during each week of study.

Note: At times the Department of Real Estate will test on material we do not consider to be of significant importance. Such material might not be covered in the chapter text material, but we have tried to include this material within the chapter and review examinations.

How to Study

You should designate a period of time every day, seven days a week, for study. When you study for short periods over a longer period of time, your retention will be far greater than if you study the same total length of time, but over a one- or two-day period. When you study for a long period, your mind tends to wander. The longer you study, the less productive your study time is. For greater retention, study in short spurts. Take a break every 30 or 45 minutes. Do something else for a while. Your first goal will be to understand the vocabulary and text material. When you are proficient in this area, you should concentrate on the examinations in this text. Periodically review all the material. You will find that each time you will learn something new. The complete glossary should be reviewed on a regular basis.

Your first task in each chapter should be to scan the material quickly (five minutes should be sufficient). This will give you a general idea of what you will be learning. When you have a general idea of what you will be learning before you read the material, you'll have far greater retention. Next, read the chapter slowly. After each paragraph, close your eyes and ask yourself what you just read. If you can paraphrase the material in your own words, your retention will increase tremendously. We recommend that you repeat this reading and self-questioning technique with two slow readings. If your place of study allows it, consider reading aloud. Many students find this helpful. Once a week you should spend an hour quickly reviewing previous chapters. This will help you to integrate the material learned.

Because of the sheer volume of new material to be digested, expect to be confused. Confusion is normal. In fact, most students don't really begin to gain confidence in themselves until they are in the review process.

When learning vocabulary, many people find that writing down terms on three-by-five-inch cards and looking at them whenever they have a chance during the day aids them greatly in understanding these vocabulary words and terms. If you are using this text without benefit of an instructor, you might find it advisable to procure a *real estate reference book* from the department of real estate in order to study further any area where you are encountering difficulty.

Many students find that *underlining* helps them in their reading. The use of yellow accent pens can also be helpful. Your text is a tool, and if notes, underlining, or accents help you, then by all means use these methods. One danger with underlining or accent pens is that *too much* special emphasis makes the special emphasis practically worthless.

Use the examination techniques explained in this section in taking the text examinations. Take each examination at a single sitting and use a separate answer sheet. Do not mark the correct answers in your book; this will reduce the effectiveness of later reviews. After taking an examination you should check not only whether you have the correct answers, but also whether you are right for the right reason. Some material on the examinations is not fully covered in the text material. Normally you should be able to deduce the correct answer by reasoning. The material so presented is likely of lesser importance than material fully covered in the text.

Study the material before class to obtain maximum comprehension and reinforcement from the lecture. Take notes of changes in the law and new material not covered in the text. Do not copy down what is already in your text.

In the back of the book is a complete glossary. Because it includes terms occasionally found on real estate examinations but not included in the text material, we recommend that you review the glossary at least once during each week of study, as well as before taking the state examination. Studying the glossary also helps to bring the material together into an understandable whole rather than a group of separate elements.

The California Examination

The Department of Real Estate keeps a test bank of an estimated 3,500 to 3,600 real estate questions. Questions that fewer than 25 percent of license applicants pass are dropped from the bank, as are questions that over 85 percent of license applicants pass. Therefore, new questions are constantly being added. The difficulty level for questions on the broker's exam is slightly greater than on the salesperson's exam. A major difference is that to pass the salesperson's exam, a score of only 70 percent is needed, as opposed to 75 percent for the broker's exam. The Department of Real Estate keeps a history on each question. Questions are not designed to be tricky, but they must be carefully read. One of the major sources for questions is the *Real Estate Reference Book,* published by the Department of Real Estate, although texts such as this one and *California Real Estate Principles* are also used as sources.

A good question stays practically forever and will be repeated time and again. Questions will often be changed slightly to call for a "negative" rather than a "positive" answer. Other times a question will be used identically, but the answers will be changed. The examinations are apparently formulated so that the Department of Real Estate can predict a particular passing rate.

The Real Estate Commissioner has decided that most examinations will include a purchase contract and/or a listing form. There will be at least two questions on fair housing, and each examination will cover real estate licensing law. Generally no more than 10 of the examination questions on a given test will be on math.

The salesperson's examination consists of 150 multiple-choice questions and lasts three hours and 15 minutes. The broker's examination consists of 200 multiple-choice questions, and five hours are allowed—2 1/2 hours in the morning and 2 1/2 hours in the afternoon. The examinations contain specific California requirements as well as multi-state or general material.

The California salespersons and brokers examinations cover 7 areas with weight as shown:

Area 1–Property Ownership and Land Use Controls and Regulations
Approximately 18% of sales exam & 15% of broker exam

- Classes of property
- Property characteristics
- Encumbrances
- Types of ownership
- Descriptions of property
- Government rights in land
- Public controls
- Environmental hazards and regulations
- Private controls
- Water rights
- Special categories of land

Area 2–Laws of Agency
Approximately 12% of sales exam & 12% of broker exam

- Law, definition and nature of agency relationships, types of agencies, and agents
- Creation of agency and agency agreements
- Responsibilities of agent to seller/buyer as principal
- Disclosure of agency
- Disclosure of acting as principal or other interest
- Termination of agency
- Commission and fees

Area 3–Valuation and Market Analysis
Approximately 12% of sales exam & 11% of broker exam

- Value
- Methods of estimating value

Area 4–Financing
Approximately 13% of sales exam & 13% of broker exam

- General concepts
- Types of loans
- Sources of financing
- How to deal with lenders
- Government programs

- Mortgages/deeds of trust/notes
- Financing/credit laws
- Loan brokerage

Area 5–Transfer of Property
Approximately 9% of sales exam & 10% of broker exam

- Title insurance
- Deeds
- Escrow
- Reports
- Tax aspects
- Special processes

Area 6–Practice of Real Estate and Mandated Disclosures
Approximately 24% of sales exam & 27% of broker exam

- Trust account management
- Fair housing laws
- Truth in advertising
- Record keeping requirements
- Agent supervision
- Permitted activities of unlicensed sales assistants
- DRE jurisdiction and disciplinary actions
- Licensing, continuing education requirements and procedures
- California Real Estate Recovery Fund
- General ethics
- Technology
- Property management/landlord-tenant rights
- Commercial/industrial/income properties
- Specialty areas
- Transfer disclosure statement
- Natural hazard disclosure statements
- Material facts affecting property value
- Need for inspection and obtaining/verifying information

Area 7–Property Ownership and Land Use Controls and Regulations
Approximately 18% of sales exam & 15% of broker exam

- General
- Listing agreements

- Buyer broker agreements
- Offers/purchase contract
- Counteroffers/multiple counteroffers
- Leases
- Agreements
- Promissory notes/securities

After all necessary qualifications are submitted, the waiting period to take the examination is usually around four weeks but may be as short as two weeks in some locations; therefore, be prepared for your examination when sending in your application. The real estate salesperson's and broker's examinations are given weekdays (as needed) in Fresno, Los Angeles, Sacramento, San Diego, and Oakland. Examination results are now being sent out within five working days from the date of your examination. You can obtain examination results within three working days by using a touch-tone phone and calling (916) 227–0899.

TAKING THE EXAMINATION

Knowing how to take an examination can make the difference between passing and failing. Many people fail the examination before they enter the examination room. People are nervous at test time. Fear can be contagious. Don't listen to the expert who knows the ropes because he or she has taken the exam five times. Keep calm. Sit toward the front of the room; that way you will be less likely to be distracted by other students.

The examination is multiple-choice and provides four answers for each question. Generally, the Department of Real Estate gives two answers that are known as *detractors*. They are completely wrong. By carefully reading the question, you can usually spot and eliminate the detractors. Between the other two answers, in some instances one may be more correct than the other, in which case you should choose the one that is always correct.

Many people fail the examination simply because they read what they expect the question to say and not what it actually states. As an example, they may have seen "almost" the same question before, perhaps in this book, but the question may be slightly changed so that it calls for a different answer. *Read carefully:* the Department of Real Estate likes to rewrite questions. The question may now ask for the incorrect or negative answer. Don't speed-read. If an answer is partially false, treat it as always being false. Watch out for absolute words such as *must* or *always*. When words like this are used, if there are any exceptions, the obvious answer is not correct.

If you are right-handed, keep the answer sheet to the right of your examination booklet. In this way your hand will not cross over the answer sheet, which could cause you to lose your place. Because you are using an answer sheet separate from your examination book, be very careful that you are checking the correct answer on the examination sheet. If you decide not to answer a question, you can get thrown off sequence and end up answering every question wrong. People who leave questions until later usually end up not putting in any answer at all, so answer as you go along. If you are really in doubt about an answer, make a note to check the question later on the edge of the sheet of scratch paper furnished. Do not allow yourself to get bogged down by one question. Since all questions count the same, you cannot allow one difficult question to slow you down so that you find you haven't enough time to finish the examination. However, most students will find that time is not a significant problem.

For math questions, we advise you to draw a *T-bar* on the piece of scratch paper provided (See Chapter 6). It will keep you straight as to which formula to use to determine the answers.

Before you work a math problem, try to estimate the answer in your head. If your mental guess is far off from the calculated answer, you should do your calculations again to make certain that you divide into the right number and your decimal points were in the proper place. Wrong answers given on your test are likely based on common wrong answers such as dividing into the wrong number, not carrying out the problem to a final step or misplacing a decimal point. Just because your answer agrees exactly with an answer given does not mean it is the *correct* answer.

Since you are allowed to use a simple electronic calculator, take one with you, but be sure you know how to use it. While you can use a sophisticated financial calculator, all you really need is a simple one that costs less than $10, with addition, subtraction, multiplication, and division capabilities. You may not use a calculator that makes an audible sound or one that allows you to store data, or has an alphabetic keyboard or printout capabilities.

Never change the wording of a question. Go along with the assumption being made, even if you believe the assumption is incorrect. *Don't* argue with the question. Answer the question as it is written.

On your purchase contract or listing form, you should read the questions first, and then read the purchase contract or listing form. In this way, the answers will seem to "pop out" at you as you read the receipt form.

Occasionally during an examination, you may notice that you have answered a large number of questions in the same column, say "d." You may feel that something is wrong and that you have a mental block, and you may want to change an answer just to break the pattern. *Beware!* You will often find a great number of questions answered in the same column. You will also find that frequently the answers to some questions are found in later questions on the examination.

Read all the answers carefully. Often the first one is correct, but as you read on, you will sometimes find that two or three answers are correct and the real correct answer would be "all of the above" or "both a and b." You may find a math question in which none of the answers is correct. In this case choose the closest answer, unless one of the answers is "none of the above." There may be a few questions where you will have to take a guess. If there are two answers with the same wording except for one or two words, then one of them is usually the correct answer. If you are unsure between two answers, the answer that is much longer or much shorter than the others tends to be the correct answer. If a question is an incomplete sentence and the answer is supposed to complete the sentence, then any answer that is not grammatically correct is usually a wrong answer. When two answers appear correct you should reread the question. It may be asking for an *incorrect* answer.

After you finish the examination, you must fight the urge to turn in your examination immediately. Use your full allotted time. First, go back over those questions you were unsure of, then start reading through the entire examination slowly. Remember: Don't change answers for change's sake, as your first answer is usually correct. But if by rereading you find errors caused by misreading the question the first time, then change the answers. Everyone makes some foolish errors. Try to find them. If you have to erase an answer, erase it completely; otherwise it may be marked as wrong (two checked answers). Mark firmly. Make a solid black line in the column indicated, using the marking pencil provided. *Don't use your own pen.*

As simple as these instructions may seem, by following them you can expect to pick up a few vital points. Practice these examination techniques in reviewing your chapter examinations in this text. Take every quiz as if it were a licensing examination. Some material covered in the chapter quizzes is not fully covered in the text. This is done to include material of relatively less importance without making the text cumbersome. This is another reason why you should review the glossary on a regular basis.

California
Real Estate License
Preparation

Introduction to Real Estate

A BRIEF HISTORY OF CALIFORNIA REAL ESTATE

California's first inhabitants were Indians. They had a crude form of land ownership. Tribes had areas that were considered theirs for hunting purposes. These divisions of land were generally respected, but when they were violated, conflicts arose.

In 1513, Balboa claimed the land washed by the Pacific Ocean for Spain, but it wasn't until 1542 that Cabrillo discovered and explored California. Other than a few garrisons (**presidios**) and villages (**pueblos**), there was negligible development until the mission era.

The mission era came quite a bit later in California history. The first mission was established in 1769. The period really ended with Mexican independence in 1822 and the subsequent secularization of the missions. There was thus a span of only about 55 years in which Spanish missions influenced California history.

Under Spanish civil law, all of the land in California belonged to the king of Spain. Spain made comparatively few land grants. The grants that were made generally were not grants of title, but rather of the right to use the land for a particular purpose, such as grazing land for cattle.

After gaining independence in 1822, Mexico realized that without colonization of California it would not be able to hold its land. In order to colonize California, Mexico gave **land grants.** Most of what are frequently referred to as "Spanish land grants" in California are actually "Mexican land grants." Mexico gave 675 land grants (known as **ranchos**) between 1822 and the start of the Mexican War in 1846.

These land grants were not filed or recorded. The only evidence of title was the actual paper giving the grant. Therefore, loss of the paper would result in an inability to prove title. In the closing days of the Mexican War, many grants were given out to keep the land from being claimed by United States citizens.

In 1848, the Mexican War was ended by the Treaty of Guadalupe Hidalgo. Under this treaty, the United States agreed to recognize existing land rights of the Mexican people including the concept of community property. The Mexican period in California was thus quite limited—from 1822 to 1848.

Everything probably would have been quite peaceful as to land rights, except for the discovery of gold in California in 1848. Since land grants were huge and there were many hungry people, land and property that could not be defended were seized. Miners and squatters showed little respect for the property rights of the land grantees. At this point in history, there still was not a system whereby an individual could record the deed to a property and be protected as to his or her land rights.

In 1850, California came into the Union as a state. One of the first acts of the state legislature was to provide for a system of recording rights in real estate. The **Torrens system** was an early system of recording land titles that we no longer use. Under the Torrens system, a title was entered into a register kept by a registrar. A **recording system** is a method whereby a person's claim to land or property is placed on public record; destruction of the deed will not affect the title.

In 1851, Congress appointed a Board of Land Commissioners. These commissioners were to bring about the correction of any conflicting claims as to land ownership. It was an attempt by the United States to live up to its obligations under the **Treaty of Guadalupe Hidalgo.**

The Board of Land Commissioners was characterized by lengthy procedures. Twenty-year litigation was common. Because of deaths and the return of families to Mexico, expensive legal proceedings, and poor evidence of title, many land grants were lost in the process.

When California came into the Union, the state became owner of the tidelands, but the federal government retained as public land all land not previously owned under land grants or by cities and towns. The original conveyances of land from the government to individuals were known as **government patents.** Much of this federal land passed to individuals through the Homestead Act, timber culture laws, the Timber and Stone Act, and other legislation. However, approximately half of California land is still held by the federal and state governments today.

Most of our real estate law has come from **English common law,** which is unwritten and derived from custom and previous decisions (**stare decisis**). Spanish **civil law,** on the other hand, was elaborately written law. California has written laws, not common law.

PROPERTY

Property is divided into two categories—**real property** and **personal property.**

Real Property

Real property consists of land and that which goes with the land, such as buildings, fences, trees, water rights, mineral rights, shares in a mutual water company, and easements. Real property is generally considered immovable. Things that "go with the land" are **appurtenances.** Mobile homes on permanent foundations are generally regarded as real property, while mobile homes on wheels are considered personal.

Personal Property

Personal property (also known as **chattel**) is defined as anything that is not real property. Property can change its character. As an example, a board would be personal property, but if used as siding for a house it becomes real property.

While real property would be transferred by a **deed,** personal property is transferred by a **bill of sale.**

Chattel Real   A **chattel real** is an interest in real property, such as a lease, trust deed, or mortgage. Chattels real are, however, personal property.

Emblements   **Emblements** are cultivated crops, which the tenant can remove after the lease expires if they were the fruits of his or her labor. Cultivated annual crops (**fructus industriales**) are considered personal property. Uncultivated naturally growing trees and plants (**fructus naturales**) are considered real property. Unless specified otherwise, growing crops would transfer with the real estate.

Constructive Severance   According to the **doctrine of constructive severance,** when growing crops are sold or mortgaged, they are considered separated from the land, even though they have not been severed from the land. If constructively severed, they would not transfer with the sale of the land.

Fixtures

These are items of personal property that have become affixed to real property so that they are considered to be part of the real property and pass with the land.

Three Primary Tests of Fixtures

1. **Intent** (most important test)—what the parties intended.
2. **Method of attachment**—how it is attached. The degree of permanence is important.
3. **Adaptability**—if it is essential for the normal use of the property, it is probably a fixture.

Other Indications of Fixtures

1. **Agreement between the parties**—there is no problem if the parties agree as to the nature of the property. The agreement would govern.
2. **Relationship between the parties**—other factors being equal, the law favors the buyer over the seller, the tenant over the landlord, and the lender over the borrower.

Not all the tests of a fixture have to be met in order for a court to decide that an item is a fixture.

Trade Fixtures   The tenant may remove, prior to the expiration of his or her lease, anything affixed for the purpose of trade or manufacture, if removal can be made without permanent injury to the premises. Tenant must repair any damage. Trade fixtures remain personal property.

OWNERSHIP

All rights incidental to ownership, such as the right to use, exclude, encumber, sell, or lease, are known as the **bundle of rights.** Historically, ownership was considered to be from the center of the earth reaching to the highest heavens. The contemporary view is that ownership includes only a reasonable air space.

LATERAL SUPPORT

Owners have the right to **lateral support**—to have their land supported by the land of their neighbors. An owner must notify his or her neighbors at least 30 days before excavating below their footings to allow the neighbor time to protect the property. Failure to notify them would result in liability for damages even if the excavator was not negligent. When an owner excavates more than nine feet down from the curb and is below neighbors' footings, the excavator must actually protect the neighboring structures.

   Subjacent support is support from underneath the surface and would apply to parties mining or taking fluids or gas from below the surface.

WATER RIGHTS

California Department of Water Resources   Handles disputes involving water use. (Its decisions are subject to court approval.)

Riparian Rights   The right of a landowner to the *reasonable use* of water flowing through, adjoining, or under his or her property.

Littoral Rights   The right of a landowner to the reasonable use of water from an adjacent lake, sea, or ocean (a nonflowing body of water).

Right of Correlative User   The right of a landowner to the reasonable use of underground percolating water.

Right of Prior Appropriation   The right by which the first user of riparian rights obtains priority over later users. A nonriparian rights holder can obtain the right to use water based on his or her historical use of the water.

Accretion   The buildup of land by the action of water.

Avulsion The sudden tearing away of land by the action of water (for example, land loss caused by a river changing course). The former owner can reclaim the land.

Alluvium Land Land formed by buildup or the action of water. It belongs to the owner of the land to which it is added.

Dereliction or Reliction Land formed when water recedes. The owner of the waterfront gets the added land.

Surface Water Water that has no defined channel. A landowner may not obstruct or divert flow so as to flood the land of another.

Flood Water Water overflowing a defined channel. A landowner may dam against such water.

Flood related terms include
- **Inundation**—covering an area with water.
- **Flood Plain**—land adjoining waterways prone to flooding.
- **Sheet Flooding**—storm runoff down an incline but not in a water course.
- **Ponding**—depressions in level areas where pools of water accumulate.

National Flood Insurance Act Flood insurance is available to residents of communities that have initiated approved flood protection systems. The Department of Housing and Urban Development (HUD) subsidizes the premiums of the policies, which are written with private insurance carriers.

Dams A landowner may not divert or dam water in a defined channel without the permission of the local flood control district.

Porter-Cologne Water Quality Control Act A statewide program for control of water quality. The state can stop development if water quality is not met. Drinkable water is considered **potable.**

Mutual Water Company An incorporated (nonprofit) group of users in a water district. The stock is appurtenant to the land and cannot be sold separately.

Irrigation District A **quasi-public** corporation (a public corporation for a municipal purpose). Bonds are issued (voted on by residents). These are formed primarily for agricultural purposes.

Public Utilities Private corporations subject to the control of the Public Utilities Commission.

CHAPTER 1 QUIZ

1. Appurtenances are things going with the land. Which of the following are *not* appurtenances?
   a. fences
   b. buildings
   c. shares in a mutual water company
   d. none of these

2. An item of personal property may be called a:
   a. freehold   b. fee   c. chattel   d. tenancy

3. Most of California real estate law originally comes from:
   a. Spanish law
   b. Mexican law
   c. English common law
   d. the Commissioner's regulations

4. To determine if property is real or personal, consider as a test:
   a. cost   b. size   c. movability   d. location

5. As to real and personal property, which of the following is false?
   a. Growing crops go with real property unless sold or mortgaged.
   b. Real property is generally considered to be immovable.
   c. Personal property can become real property.
   d. None of the above.

6. Real property would *not* include a(n):
   a. leasehold interest
   b. appurtenant easement
   c. air space
   d. fence

7. All of these are real property except:
   a. air space above a house
   b. ground under a house
   c. growing trees
   d. trade fixtures

8. Property is:
   a. real if it is an estate
   b. personal if it is a fixture
   c. personal if it is not real
   d. all of these

9. The doctrine of constructive severance applies to:
   a. removal of fixtures
   b. sales of growing crops
   c. removal of trade fixtures
   d. moving of buildings

10. Which of the following is considered personal property?
    a. land
    b. physical improvements
    c. growing trees
    d. a trust deed

11. A landowner can legally protect his or her property against flood damage by:
    a. diverting water flow
    b. building a dam without approval
    c. building a dike against flood water
    d. any of these

12. The right of reasonable use of water flowing on, under, or adjacent to a property is called a:
    a. right-of-way
    b. riparian right
    c. right of eminent domain
    d. right of appropriation

13. *Riparian rights* are best described as:
    a. reasonable use of adjacent water
    b. absolute use of adjacent water
    c. reasonable use of nonadjacent water
    d. absolute use of nonadjacent water

14. To dam or divert water, a landowner must have the approval of:
    a. the local flood control district
    b. the state water and power commission
    c. all adjoining land users
    d. all of these

15. A nonriparian rights owner may get the right to use surplus water from a lake by:
    a. appropriation   b. avulsion   c. dereliction   d. accretion

16. To check what riparian rights he or she has in a property, a landowner should check:
    a. the deed
    b. the policy of title insurance
    c. the county records
    d. none of these

17. *Emblements* refers to:
    a. landscaping   b. crops   c. fixtures   d. none of these

18. Community property laws:
    a. are based on English common law
    b. are based on the Canons of Ethics of the American Bar Association
    c. are based on Spanish law accepted by the Treaty of Guadalupe Hidalgo
    d. none of these

19. The contemporary view of property ownership is ownership of:
    a. usable land and infinite air space   c. land only
    b. infinite land and infinite air space   d. none of these

20. A mobile home on wheels would be considered:
    a. a chattel real   c. personal property
    b. an emblement   d. real estate

21. The right to use, exclude, encumber, sell, or lease refers to:
    a. chattels real   c. emblements
    b. the bundle of rights   d. riparian rights

22. After his or her lease has expired, a former tenant may enter the property and remove:
    a. fixtures   b. emblements   c. fences   d. none of these

23. The most important test of a fixture is:
    a. adaptability   b. cost   c. method of attachment   d. intent

24. The right to take adjacent nonflowing water is called:
    a. littoral rights   c. the right of a correlative user
    b. riparian rights   d. reliction

25. Land is added to a waterfront lot when a lake recedes because of:
    a. avulsion   b. reliction   c. appropriation   d. a correlative user

26. Which of the following would be regarded as real property?
    a. crops that have been sold but have not been harvested
    b. growing crops that have been mortgaged
    c. riparian rights
    d. trees that have been cut down

27. Which of the following would run with the land?
    a. riparian rights
    b. littoral rights
    c. shares in a mutual water company
    d. all of the above

28. A lease would be a:
    a. freehold interest   c. chattel real
    b. fee simple interest   d. reversionary interest

29. Cropland is sold with no provision for the growing crops. Who has the greatest rights to the crops?
    a. buyer   c. State of California
    b. seller   d. buyer and seller equally

30. A problem with personal property that makes ownership rights difficult to ascertain can occur because personal property can:
    a. be alienated   c. become real property
    b. be hypothecated   d. all of the above

31. Which of the following would be personal property?
    a. an easement   c. water rights
    b. a trade fixture   d. mineral rights

32. According to the classical definition of ownership of land:
    a. One owns all the land below and some of the air space above.
    b. One owns all the sky above and some of the land below.
    c. One owns all the sky above and the land below to the center of the earth.
    d. One owns some of the land below and some of the sky above.

33. A landowner obtains the right to take water from another property by:
    a. riparian rights   b. appropriation   c. avulsion   d. alluvium

34. *Potable* refers to:
    a. drinkable   b. plumbing metal   c. septic tanks   d. indebtednesss

35. The real estate law comes from:
    a. regulations of the real estate commissioner   c. Mexico
    b. the state legislature   d. Spain

36. Crops produced by labor are known as:
    a. emblements   b. annuals   c. fixtures   d. encumbrances

37. You acquire property by accession. Most likely you get the property by:
    a. accretion   c. adverse use
    b. grant deed   d. eminent domain

38. The following is not appurtenant to real estate:
    a. growing trees   b. buildings   c. fences   d. trade fixtures

39. *Bundle of rights* refers to:
    a. mineral and water rights   c. government rights
    b. tenant rights   d. all beneficial rights in property

40. When a river or lake permanently recedes, the land created belongs to the owner of the bank by:
    a. reliction   b. avulsion   c. accretion   d. eminent domain

41. The opposite of *avulsion* is:
    a. accretion   c. ponding
    b. correlative users   d. reliction

42. *Emblements* are:
    a. perennial crops   c. fructus naturales
    b. annual crops   d. none of the above

43. Which of the following is misspelled?
    a. emblements   c. appurtenance
    b. accreation   d. avulsion

44. In an area with many abandoned mines, a developer would be primarily concerned with:
    a. adjacent support   c. lateral support
    b. subacent support   d. inundation

45. Floodwater accumulating in depressions, is known as:
    a. inundation   c. ponding
    b. sheet flooding   d. flood plain

ANSWERS—CHAPTER 1 QUIZ

1. d. All go with the land.
2. c.
3. c.
4. c.
5. d.
6. a. This is a chattel real.
7. d. They remain personal property.
8. c. Always true (while a leasehold is an estate, it is personal property).
9. b. They are considered severed if sold. (Also trees)
10. d. This is a chattel real.
11. c. Can dike but can't divert.
12. b. Flowing adjacent water.
13. a. A reasonable right to use.
14. a.
15. a. By prior appropriation (use).
16. d. Rights are to reasonable use of adjacent flowing water.

17. b. Regarded as personal property.
18. c.
19. d. Land plus reasonable air space.
20. c. It does not go with the land.
21. b. All beneficial rights of ownership.
22. b. Crops that were the fruit of his or her labor.
23. d. Was the intent to make it part of realty?
24. a. Lakes or seas.
25. b.
26. c. They go with the land.
27. d. All are real property.
28. c. Personal property.
29. a. Unless sold or mortgaged.
30. c. By attachment—fixture.
31. b. Trade fixtures remain personal property.

32. c. "Classical," not contemporary.
33. b. Prior appropriation.
34. a. Fit for consumption.
35. b. Statutory law.
36. a.
37. a. Being joined to.
38. d. They don't transfer with the realty.
39. d.
40. a.
41. a. Avulsion is rapid tearing away of soil but accretion is a gradual buildup.
42. b. Planted annual crops.
43. b. accretion
44. b. Underneath support.
45. c.

2

CHAPTER

Legal Descriptions, Methods of Acquiring Title, Deeds, Estates, and Methods of Holding Title

LAND DESCRIPTIONS

Recorded Lot, Block, and Tract Systems

An example would be "Lot 17, Block 3 in Jones's second addition to the City of Podunk recorded on pages 2 and 3 of Volume 1 of the official records of the County of Podunk." This method merely identifies the lot by the subdivider's identification. Most urban property is described by this method.

Metes and Bounds

This method measures land by measurements and boundaries and shows the boundary lines by their terminal points and angles. The starting point for a metes and bounds description is the **point of beginning (POB).** The description must entirely enclose the described property, setting the boundary lines, and must end at the point of begining. As an example, "Starting at the NW corner of the Ted Jones farm, four miles east of Podunk, proceed in a straight line N 500 feet to an iron stake, thence 257 feet SE to the large red rock, thence S 80 feet to an iron stake, thence in a straight line to the point of beginning." Distances and directions are measured. Actual angles may be given. Angles are measured from a north and south line, and are expressed east and west in degrees and minutes (1/60 of a degree). Metes and bounds are given clockwise. Measuring points are known as **monuments. Natural monuments** would include rivers, rocks, trees, and so on, while **artificial monuments** include nonnatural objects such as stakes, roads, and fences. Whenever a boundary is a road, the owner of the land abutting it is presumed to own to the center of the road, unless otherwise indicated. If a nonnavigable river is a boundary, the boundary line would be the center of the river. For navigable rivers, the boundary would be the average low-water mark. If a boundary is the ocean, the boundary line would be the middle (**mesne**) high-tide line.

10

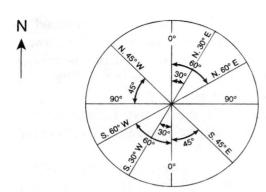

There are 360° in a circle.
There are 180° in a half-circle.
There are 90° in a quarter-circle (right angle).
Each degree is divided into 60 minutes.
Each minute is divided into 60 seconds.
The point of beginning is at the intersection of the two lines (or the center of the circle). The **bearing** of a course is described by measuring easterly or westerly from the north and south lines.

Government Survey

This method measures land from the intersections of principal surveying lines going east and west, which are called **base lines.** Those going north and south are called **meridians.**

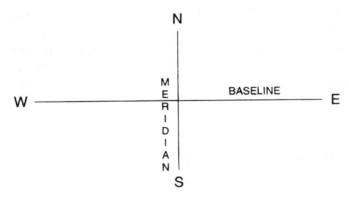

Land in California is measured from three sets of these base lines and meridians:

In Southern California—San Bernardino Base Line and Meridian.
In Central California—Mt. Diablo Base Line and Meridian.
In Northern California—Humboldt Base Line and Meridian.

Horizontal rows of townships are known as **tiers.**

Vertical rows of townships are known as **ranges.**

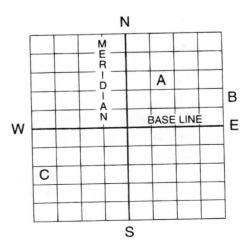

11

From the intersections of the base lines and meridians, land is measured in **townships.** Townships are six miles square and contain 36 square miles. The township marked A is three tiers north of the base line and two ranges east of the meridian line. It would thus be designated Tier 3 North, Range 2 East, or T3N, R2E, San Bernardino Base Line and Meridian (or appropriate reference).

Township B is two tiers above or north of the base line and five ranges east of the meridian; thus, it would be Tier 2 North, Range 5 East, or T2N, R5E (with reference to the appropriate base line and meridian).

Township C is three tiers south of the base line and four ranges west of the meridian; thus, it would be described as T3S, R4W (with reference to the appropriate base line and meridian).

Correction Lines

Correction lines are surveyors' lines run so as to compensate for the curvature of the earth. They are run every 24 miles east and west of the principal meridian (**guide meridians**) and every 24 miles north or south of the principal base line (**standard parallels**). They result in the sections along the north and west boundaries of each township being slightly smaller (11 sections per township are so affected). The 24-mile-square areas formed by the correction lines are known as **checks** or **quadrangles.**

26	25	30	29	28	27	26	25	30	29
35	36	31	32	33	34	35	36	31	32
2	1	6	5	4	3	2	1	6	5
11	12	7	8	9	10	11	12	7	8
14	13	18	17	16	15	14	13	18	17
23	24	19	20	21	22	23	24	19	20
26	25	30	29	28	27	26	25	30	29
35	36	31	32	33	34	35	36	31	32
2	1	6	5	4	3	2	1	6	5
11	12	7	8	9	10	11	12	7	8

The north and south boundary lines of each township are known as **township lines,** which run east and west. The east and west boundary lines of townships are known as **range lines,** which run north and south.

Each township contains 36 sections. Each section is one mile square and contains 640 acres. Land is normally described by its location within a specific section. Sections in a township are always numbered as shown. You will note that numbering starts in the upper right-hand (NE) corner, and you can draw a snake line through the sections in numerical order.

Also note that townships are not isolated; they adjoin other townships. As an example, north of Section 1 would be Section 36 of an adjoining township.

Whenever you attempt to find a description from a government survey reference, try putting down your directions on your work paper so that simple errors will be avoided.

N
W   **E**
S

The northwest quarter (NW 1/4) of a section would be as follows:

Since a section contains 640 acres, the NW 1/4 would contain 160 acres.

Deciphering a description is not always as simple as finding a quarter section. Suppose the description is "the S 1/2 of the NW 1/4 of the SE 1/4 of Section 27, T8N, R17W, SBBL&M (San Bernardino Base Line and Meridian)." First, find the township by counting 8 north from the base line and 17 west from the meridian. Find the section by the numbering as previously explained.

To find the described area, look at the description and go backward: the S 1/2 of the NW 1/4 of the SE 1/4.

First: Find the SE 1/4.
Second: Find the NW 1/4 of the first area.
Third: Find the S 1/2 of the second area

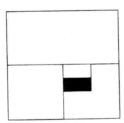

As another example, find the SW 1/4 of the NE 1/4 of the NE 1/4 of the SE 1/4 of the section shown.

Go backward!
First: Find the SE 1/4.
Second: Find the NE 1/4 of the first area.
Third: Find the NE 1/4 of the second area.
Fourth: Find the SW 1/4 of the third area.

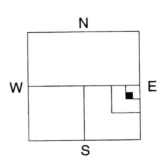

In the *first* step above, you found 160 acres: 1/4 of a section
In the *second* step you found 40 acres: 1/4 of 160 acres
In the *third* step you found 10 acres: 1/4 of 40 acres
In the *fourth* step you found 2 1/2 acres: 1/4 of 10 acres

Actually, you can find the acreage from a legal description without bothering to draw it out. Just go backward:

the S 1/2	of the NW 1/4	of the SE 1/4	of the NW 1/4	of the SW 1/4
1 1/4	2 1/2	10	40	160

So the parcel described contains 1 1/4 acres.

Government monuments and **benchmarks** are surveyors' markers showing elevation and location in relation to longitude and latitude.

Know These Measurements

One township = 36 square miles

One section = 640 acres

One mile = 5,280 feet or 320 rods

One acre = 43,560 square feet

Commercial acre = (less than an acre). Land that is left for development after taking out land for roads, walks, etc.

One square acre = approximately 208.7 feet square

One rod = 16.5 linear feet

One chain = 66 linear feet (4 rods)

One board foot = 144 cubic inches of wood

One cubic yard = 27 cubic feet

One square yard = 9 square feet

Informal Descriptions

Informal methods of describing property are by simple street address or owner's name. These methods are not considered legal descriptions but can be used on a deed. Title companies will not insure a title without a legal description (recorded lot, block and tract, metes and bounds, or government survey), however. Informal descriptions based on the property's relationship to other properties are known as **physical descriptions.**

Area

A right triangle contains half of the square footage of a square.

The square contains 10,000 square feet (length × width), 100 feet × 100 feet, so the right triangle contains 5,000 square feet.

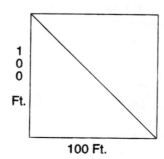
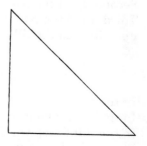

100 Ft.

You may occasionally have to use this principle in finding the acreage in a plot of land. For example:

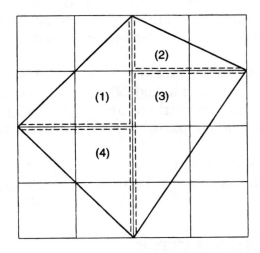

To find out how many acres are contained inside the figure within a section, we would first find approximate right triangles and squares.

Triangles marked with (1) and (4) each contain 80 acres, since they each contain half of a 160-acre quarter section. The triangle marked (2) contains half of 80 acres (two 40-acre squares), so it contains 40 acres. The triangle marked (3) contains half of 240 acres, or 120 acres.

Triangles (1) and (4)	160 acres
Triangle (2)	40 acres
Triangle (3)	120 acres
Total	320 acres

So the figure contains 320 acres; since there are 640 acres in a section, there are 320 acres outside the figure.

Sometimes, because of angles, it is necessary to find the number of acres outside the parcel within the section and deduct this amount from 640 acres in order to find the acreage of the parcel, as in the following example:

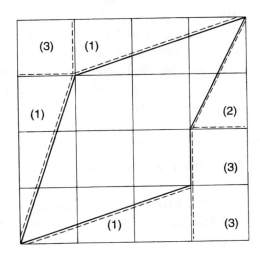

Because of the angles in the northeast and southwest corners of the section, you will need to find the acreage outside the parcel to find out how many acres the parcel contains. The triangles marked (1) contain half of 120 acres, or 60 acres, each. The triangle marked (2) contains half of 80 acres, or 40 acres. The squares marked (3) are each one-quarter of a quarter section, or 40 acres.

3 triangles marked (1)	180 acres
1 triangle marked (2)	40 acres
3 squares marked (3)	120 acres
Outside of parcel	340 acres
Total section	640 acres
Minus outside of parcel	−340 acres
Size of parcel	300 acres

METHODS OF ACQUIRING TITLE

Adverse Possession

This is the act of taking title to land based on use. A landowner may obtain an easement, which is a right of way, by prescription (adverse use), but obtains title by adverse possession.

Requirements for Adverse Possession

1. Open and notorious occupancy.
2. Occupancy that is hostile to the owner's interest.
3. Occupancy under some claim of right or color of title. (It can be based on defective or forged documents or simply upon physical possession.)
4. Continuous uninterrupted use for five years.
5. The claimant must have paid real property taxes for five years.

The adverse user does not have to live on the land; fencing the land or using the land for business or agriculture is enough. Differences between obtaining an easement by prescription and obtaining title by adverse possession are that to obtain title, the adverse user must pay taxes and must have exclusive use of the property (for an easement, the use need not be exclusive and taxes need not be paid).

Adverse possession does not result in marketable (saleable) title. To obtain marketable title, the adverse user needs either:

1. A **quitclaim deed** from the former owner giving up all rights.
2. A **quiet title action** (to determine who has title).

The five-year period of occupancy can be based on one person occupying the property for three years and transferring his or her interest to another, who occupies it for two years (**tacking on**).

A person cannot take title from the government, a minor, or an insane person by adverse possession. Also, one cannot get greater rights by adverse possession than the person he or she took the property from. (If the original owner did not have mineral rights, the adverse user does not get mineral rights.)

Permission of the owner defeats a claim for adverse possession, because use is not hostile.

Preventing adverse use any time prior to the expiration of the 5-year period would require the user to start again on a new 5-year period.

Accession

Title can also be obtained by **accession,** or the joining of property to property. As an example, fixtures were once items of personal property that became part of the real estate by being joined to it. If an improvement is made on the land of another because of error on the part of the improver, the court might allow the improver to remove the improvement, but the improver would be liable for damages caused by the removal. In addition, the buildup of soil by accretion or avulsion gives title to the landowner. When there has been a sudden tearing away or loss of land, such as when a river changes its course, an owner could lose title to the land taken unless the owner reclaims it by use within one year.

Probate

Probate is a legal procedure for disposing of the estate of a deceased person. Its purpose is to carry out the wishes of the deceased and to protect the creditors of the deceased. Probate proceedings commence with a **petition for probate** or **letters of administration** (if there is no will). Notice is given to creditors, who have four months to file claims. **Distribution** is the division of the estate to the heirs.

Superior Court   Handles probates.

Administrator/Administratrix   A man (or woman) appointed by the court to administer the estate of a person who dies **intestate** (without a will). (Words ending in *-trix* indicate women.)

Executor/Executrix   One appointed by a will to administer an estate (the deceased died leaving a will, so he or she died **testate**).

Testator/Testatrix   One who makes a will.

Will   A testament. It is considered to be an **ambulatory document,** since it can be changed by the testator any time prior to death.

Codicil   An amendment to a will. It requires the same formalities as the will itself.

Witnessed Will   A formal written document. It must be signed by the testator and by two witnesses in each other's presence (three signatures). A witness may not be a beneficiary of the will.

Holographic Will An entirely handwritten and signed will (no witnesses are required).

Nuncupative Will An oral will. Such a will is no longer valid in California.

Bequest and Legacy Gifts of personal property (a legacy usually consists of money). The legatee is the recipient of a legacy.

Devise A gift of real property by will.

Devisor One who gives real property by will. (Words ending in -*or* indicate givers.)

Devisee One who receives real property by will. (Words ending in -*ee* indicate receivers.)

Domiciliary and Ancillary Probate Real estate is probated in the state where it is located. If a California resident dies in this state and leaves real property here, the probate is **domiciliary.** If a resident of another state dies and leaves property in California, the probate in California would be **ancillary.**

Testate A person who dies having a will dies **testate,** as opposed to **intestate** if there is no will.

Intestate Succession If a person dies without leaving a will, his or her property goes to his or her heirs according to the law of intestate succession.

Community Property All community property goes to the surviving spouse (if it is not disposed of by the will). While normally a spouse can will community property to another, title can be held as **community property with the right of survivorship.** This property is like joint tenancy in that it cannot be willed. It passes on death immediately to the surviving spouse.

Separate Property If there is no will, separate property is divided as follows:

Surviving Heirs	Share of Property
Spouse, 1 child	Spouse gets 1/2, child gets 1/2
Spouse, 2 or more children	Spouse gets 1/3, children share equally in the other 2/3
Spouse, no children, surviving parent	Spouse gets 1/2, parent gets 1/2

Unless there is a premarital agreement, a surviving spouse never gets less than 1/3 of separate property. If any child is deceased and leaves children, the children share equally in the share their parent would have had by right of representation, or **per stirpes.** In other situations, inheritance is by degree of kinship, established by common ancestors.

Simultaneous Death   If both spouses die in a common accident, the property goes to the heirs of each spouse as if he or she were the survivor.

Escheat   If a person dies without a will (intestate) and without heirs, his or her property goes to the state after five years. When the state disposes of property acquired by escheat, it gives a **state comptroller's deed.**

Probate Sales

Real property may have to be sold in probate in order to carry out the wishes of the deceased or to pay expenses. Property must be appraised and may be sold at a private sale or auction.

Offers must be at least 90 percent of the appraised value. When an offer has been accepted by the representative of the estate, the court must then approve the sale. Before approving a sale, the court will ask if there are any higher bids. At this time anyone can step forward. Any late bids, to be considered, must be at least 10 percent higher on the first $10,000 and 5 percent higher on the balance. For example, suppose the highest bid is $90,000. A late bid must be 10 percent higher on the first $10,000, or $1000, and 5 percent higher on the balance of $80,000, or $4,000. The late bid must be at least $95,000. (As a simple rule, the late bid must be 5 percent greater plus $500).

The broker's commission may be subject to court approval in probate sales. The court may make its own determination of the commission to be paid. (If another broker brings in a late high bid, the court will ordinarily order the commission split between the two brokers, but the broker representing the purchaser cannot receive more than one-half of the difference between the opening bid and the accepted bid.)

The court may authorize 90 days of exclusive listings of probate property if it is a matter of necessity or an advantage to the estate. All other listings in probate are open listings.

Eminent Domain

Eminent domain is the power of condemnation, by which land may be taken for public use. Property owners are entitled to fair market value at the time the property is taken. Tenants are entitled to the value of their leasehold.

Eminent domain is *not* the exercise of police power, since there is no compensation for loss under exercise of police power. Police power is exercised for health, safety, morals and general welfare purposes. Police power cannot generally be delegated, but eminent domain not only can be used by governmental units but also is delegated to public utilities and to schools. In some instances it can be given to a private individual.

A property owner can obtain an easement over the land of another for utilities by eminent domain.

Dedication   A transfer of real property to a governmental unit for a public purpose without any consideration.

DEEDS

Deeds convey interest in real estate. A deed is used only once. When a person buys real estate, he or she receives a deed from the seller. When that buyer later sells the property, he or she gives a new deed. (A transfer of an interest is an **alienation.**)

Grantor   A person who gives a deed.

Grantee   A person who receives a deed.

Requirements of a Deed

Delivery   A deed must be delivered to the grantee or his or her agent to be a valid conveyance. (Mailing constitutes delivery.) Intent to pass title immediately determines delivery. A recorded deed is presumed to have been delivered. A deed is presumed to be delivered as of the date of the deed. An undated deed is presumed to be dated on the date of delivery. (**Recording** is entering the document in the public records of the county recorder.)

Acceptance   A deed must be accepted by the grantee. Acceptance can be shown by words or conduct of the grantee. An exception to the requirement of acceptance is a beneficial grant to a minor or mentally incompetent person.

Words of Conveyance   A deed must have a granting clause (words indicating that title is to pass immediately).

A Written Document   A deed must be in writing (per the Statute of Frauds).

Description   The property must be properly described so that boundaries can be ascertained. A legal description is not required to convey title, but is required if title insurance is to be obtained.

Competent Grantor   The grantor must be capable of conveying (must have mental and legal capacity). The grantee need not be capable of contracting to receive a deed (see "Gift Deed" later in this chapter). A deed by an unemancipated minor or a person declared incompetent would be void.

Definite Grantee   The grantee must be definite. The grantor may convey property to a real person using a fictitious name, but not to a fictitious (nonexistent) person.

Signature   The deed must be signed by the grantor. (The grantee does not sign the deed.) A forged deed is void and does not transfer any interest; the same is true for a deed altered after signing to include property other than what was originally granted. A deed cannot be signed in blank as completing it would be an alteration.

20

Not Required for a Deed

Seal No seal is required, although corporations may use them. A seal may be shown by the letters "LS" or "(Seal)." A corporate seal on a document is a presumption that the person signing has the authority to convey.

Habendum Clause (To Have and to Hold Clause) A **habendum clause** is the granting clause of a deed that describes the extent of the estate granted. In California, the absence of this clause in a deed conveys title in fee simple (see "Estates" covered later in this chapter).

Consideration A deed is a conveyance and does not require consideration (such as in a gift deed). A promise to give a deed, however, would require consideration to be enforceable.

Witnesses A deed need not be witnessed (unless the grantor signs with an "X").

Acknowledgment **Acknowledgment** is the grantor's formal declaration before a notary or an officer of the court that he or she is the person who signed the deed. The grantor need not acknowledge the deed for it to be valid, but it must be acknowledged to be recorded. An instrument recorded but not acknowledged still gives constructive notice, but only after one year. The notary public must affix a seal that includes the state seal, the name of the notary, and the words "notary public." A notarization by a party to the transaction is void, although an employee or officer of a corporation can notarize documents signed by another corporate representative. A notary public can insist on official identification. The right thumbprint is now required of the person executing a deed for the notary record. The notary must keep a record of every notarization and the identification used.

Date A valid deed need not be dated. It takes effect as of the date of delivery.

Recording As between the grantor and the grantee, a deed need not be recorded to be valid. An instrument is considered recorded when it is deposited with the proper person in the recorder's office and marked "filed for record." Recording must be with the County Recorder in the county where the property is located in order to affect the property. Recording gives constructive notice to a third person of the grantee's interest. For example: Suppose Albert deeds a parcel of land to Belinda. The deed is not recorded. Then Albert deeds the same parcel of land to Charlie; however, the deed to Charlie is recorded. By law, Charlie gets the property, since Charlie had no notice of Belinda's interest. If Belinda had taken possession prior to the sale to Charlie, then Charlie would have had **constructive notice** of Belinda's interest and Belinda would prevail (since occupancy also serves as constructive notice of a person's interest). However, the recording of a gift deed would not give the grantee priority over a prior unrecorded deed given for value to a good-faith purchaser. In addition, if a grantee has actual knowledge of a prior unrecorded interest, then recording of the instrument would also not give the grantee priority over the prior unrecorded interest.

If a deed is recorded without acknowledgment the deed would not provide constructive notice of the grantee's interest until one year after recordation.

The County Recorder must keep a **grantor/grantee alphabetical index.** Anyone has the right to check the recorder's records without supervision. If a grantor or grantee's name is spelled wrong, so that a diligent search of the records would not reveal the document, then the recording would not provide constructive notice.

A **purchase-money trust deed,** financing the purchase of property, takes priority over recorded liens against the grantee, even if the liens are said to attach as soon as the grantee takes title. (A purchase-money trust deed would take priority over prior recorded judgments against the grantee.)

There is no time limit as to recording, but there is no constructive notice until the deed is recorded.

In a sale in which a deed of trust is used to secure the lien, the broker must see that the deed of trust is recorded within one week of closing or delivered to the beneficiary with the recommendation of recording. Delivering the signed deed to escrow satisfies this requirement.

Name and Address for Tax Purposes If a deed does not contain the name and address where tax statements are to be sent, the deed will not be recorded.

Documentary Transfer Tax This will be covered in Chapter 13. This tax must be paid in order for the deed to be recorded.

Types of Deeds

Grant Deed This is the most common deed in California. It is normally used in conjunction with a policy of title insurance. It contains two warranties:

1. The grantor has not previously conveyed the property.
2. The estate is free from undisclosed encumbrances made by the grantor.

The grant deed is the only deed that conveys **after-acquired title.** If, after giving a grant deed, the grantor gets better title (easement released, etc.), the prior grant deed serves to convey the later acquired interest.

Quitclaim Deed With a quitclaim deed, the grantor gives whatever rights he or she may have in a property without making any claims to having any rights. There are no express or implied warranties. A quitclaim deed is frequently used to remove clouds on title or to give up an easement. Of course, if the grantor has good title, the quitclaim deed conveys whatever he or she has.

Warranty Deed This deed is not generally used in California. The grantor personally warrants good title and will defend the grantee's title if it is challenged.

Sheriff's Deed A **write of execution** is the court order for the sheriff to sell the property to satisfy a judgment claim. A **certificate of sale** is given upon the sheriff's sale. After the **one-year period of redemption,** a **sheriff's deed** is given. It carries no warranties or representations, and gives only the interest that was fore-closed. (The property could still have encumbrances.)

Tax Deed   This is given at a tax sale.

Gift Deed   This is any type of deed given for love and affection. The grantee is not required to have contractual capacity. A gift deed can be voided if it is given to de-fraud creditors.

Special Clauses and Language

Exception   A clause that excludes part of the property from the deed. The word *sans* in a deed means "without."

Reservation   A clause that retains for the grantor some right, such as an easement.

Et ux.   A Latin phrase meaning "and wife."

Et al.   A Latin phrase meaning "and others."

ESTATES (DEGREES OF OWNERSHIP)

Fee Simple Absolute   This is the highest possible degree of ownership. It lasts forever (there is no time limitation), and it can be transferred or inherited freely.

Fee   An estate of inheritance. There can be more than one fee in the same prop-erty, such as separate ownership of mineral rights and land.

Life Estate   This is an estate in property for the life of some person. Suppose An-drea gives property to Bernard for life. Bernard has a life estate. On Bernard's death, the property reverts back to Andrea. Andrea has a **reversionary interest.**

If Andrea gives the property to Bernard for life and then to Carmen, Carmen has a **remainder interest.** Since Bernard must someday die, we know that Car-men, or her heirs, will get the property. Therefore, Carmen has a **vested remain-der.** If the estate goes from Andrea to Bernard for life and then to Carmen, providing Carmen is still alive, Carmen has an interest contingent on her outliving Bernard, or a **contingent remainder.** Remainder- and reversionary-interest hold-ers have **inchoate interest,** which means their interest is not perfected until some-thing happens (the death of the holder of the life estate).

A life estate can be established for the life of a third person that has no interest in the property (**pur autre vie**). As an example, Albert could give a life estate to Baker for the life of Charlie. If Baker died, Baker's heirs would be entitled to the property as long as Charlie was alive.

The life tenant cannot encumber the life estate beyond his or her lifetime, so leases cease with his or her death. The life tenant must also make repairs and pay taxes; he or she may not commit **waste.** Lenders will sometimes lend on the life tenant's interest but will require him or her to take out a policy of life insurance in favor of the lender, since the life tenant cannot encumber the property beyond his or her lifetime. In California life estates are created either by grant or by will.

Defeasible Estate (Fee Simple Defeasible)   This is a qualified estate that may be lost on the happening of some event or **condition subsequent.** For example: Suppose a property is deeded with the condition that it is never to be used for the sale of alcoholic beverages. If the new owner opens a tavern, the property reverts back to the original owner.

Freehold Estate   This is a fee simple or life estate.

Nonfreehold Estate   This is a leasehold interest. Leasehold estates are considered to be personal property. They are covered in Chapter 11.

METHODS OF HOLDING TITLE

There are various ways a person can own property. (*Note:* **Tenancy** refers to the form of ownership.)

Tenancy in Severalty

This means separate ownership by one person alone. (It does not mean ownership by several people.)

Joint Tenancy

This is two or more people holding title with an **undivided interest** (each has an interest in the entire property, which is not divided) with the **right of survivorship** (upon the death of any joint tenant, his or her interest immediately passes to the surviving joint tenants and not to his or her heirs). To create a joint tenancy, four **unities** are required:

1. **Time**—all must obtain their interest at the same time. (However, an owner in severalty can convey property to himself or herself and others, with all parties as joint tenants.)
2. **Title**—all must obtain their interest by the same document.
3. **Interest**—each joint tenant has an equal share in ownership.
4. **Possession**—each joint tenant has an equal right of possession.

A joint tenant cannot will his or her share of the property, as it passes immediately upon death to the survivors. There is no probate. The survivors record a court decree of death or a copy of a death certificate, an affidavit that the deceased was a joint tenant, and an inheritance-tax release.

Surviving joint tenants are not liable to personal creditors of the deceased joint tenant. The property passes free and clear as to the personal debts of the deceased, as well as to any encumbrances that the deceased joint tenant placed against his or her interest without the other joint tenants.

To create a joint tenancy, the parties must clearly indicate that there is a joint tenancy, or the courts will declare it to be a tenancy in common. For example:

1. Arthur, Beverly, and Claude are joint tenants (1/3 interest each). Arthur dies. Beverly and Claude remain joint tenants (1/2 interest each).

2. Arthur, Beverly, Claude, and Daphne are joint tenants. Daphne sells her share to Eduardo. Arthur, Beverly, and Claude remain joint tenants, but Eduardo is a tenant in common, since he did not obtain his interest at the same time by the same document.

Voluntary or involuntary transfer terminates the joint tenancy as to the interest transferred. A **partition action** may also be brought by a joint tenant to break the joint tenancy (and may also be brought to break up any other undivided ownership).

Tenancy in Common

This is an undivided interest by two or more people without the right of survivorship. When property is conveyed to two or more people (other than husband and wife) and it is not specified how title shall vest, it is considered to be a tenancy in common. Since there is no survivorship upon the death of a tenant in common, his or her interest passes to his or her heirs and not to the surviving tenants.

Not all of the four unities of joint tenancy are present in a tenancy in common:

1. The parties do not have to acquire their interest at the same time.
2. The parties need not acquire title by the same document.
3. The interests of the parties need not be equal (one can have a one-half interest and the other five can have only a one-tenth interest each).
4. The only one of the four unities present is possession. All tenants in common have equal rights of possession.

A tenant in common can sell or encumber his or her own interest without the consent of the other tenants in common, but cannot place an encumbrance against the entire property without the concurrence of all of the cotenants. A tenant in common need not pay rent to the other tenants in common for use, but if a tenant in common receives rents or royalties from a third person, then all of the tenants in common have a right to the proceeds. Tenants in common who make necessary repairs or tax payments have the **right of contribution** from the other tenants in common. (These also apply to joint tenancy.)

Community Property

Community property law is a result of the **Treaty of Guadalupe Hidalgo** ending the Mexican War, in which we agreed to respect property rights of inhabitants. (Community property was a Spanish concept, adopted by Mexico.) All property acquired by the husband or the wife during the marriage is regarded as community property.

They each have an equal interest in this property. Only a husband and wife can hold property as community property. In the absence of any statement to the contrary, a deed to both spouses conveys title as community property.

The husband and the wife have equal control over community property. Neither spouse alone can sell or give community property or his or her share of the community property to another. Therefore, agreements to sell as well as conveyances of community property should be signed by both husband and wife.

Either spouse can will his or her one-half interest in the community property to anyone. However, should either spouse die intestate (without a will), his or her share automatically goes to the surviving spouse. The surviving spouse can elect to take title to community property by a simplified procedure without going through probate.

Exceptions to Community Property (Separate Property)

1. Property acquired by the husband or the wife prior to marriage.
2. Property acquired by gift or inheritance of either spouse.
3. Rents or profits of separate property.
4. Earnings of spouses while they are separated.
5. Damages awarded either spouse for personal injury (accident).
6. Property conveyed from one spouse to the other as a gift.
7. Property acquired with separate property.

Separate property may become community property if it becomes so commingled that it cannot be separated. Separate property or earnings of either spouse are not liable for debts incurred by the other spouse prior to marriage.

Community Property with Right of Survivorship (CPRS)

It is now possible to create a CPRS but it must be expressly declared in the deed. When a spouse dies, the surviving spouse is treated as if he or she were a joint tenant and takes title regardless of any will.

Prior to death, both spouses can terminate the tenancy by executing and recording a new deed as to their interests.

Living Trusts

Many couples hold title in a revocable living trust. They hold the property as joint trustees for their benefit. Upon the death of one spouse, the other spouse would hold the title as trustee and upon that spouse's death, it would pass to the beneficiaries. The benefits of a living trust are that, like community property and joint tenancy, probate is avoided. However, living trusts can be written to allow the federal inheritance tax deduction to be doubled. This is very important for property owners who would have an estate that would otherwise be subject to estate taxes.

Trusts

Besides living trusts used for estate planning, real estate can be held in trust with title held in a trustee's name for the benefit of a beneficiary. There are many charitable trusts.

Tenancy in Partnership (General Partnership)

This consists of two or more co-owners of a business for profit. A partnership is created by agreement, but the agreement need not be in writing. However, for the parties to hold title in a partnership name, the partnership agreement must be signed, acknowledged, and recorded. Sharing of profit is evidence that a partnership exists. Title to property may be taken in the name of the partnership.

A partner's interest in the partnership is not subject to attachment for the personal debts of a partner. Partners have equal rights to use partnership property for partnership purposes, and, in the absence of any agreement to the contrary, they share equally in the profits. Partners can transfer title without their spouses' signatures. While a partner cannot sue the partnership (because this would involve suing himself or herself), a stockholder in a corporation can sue the corporation, which is a separate legal entity. A partnership requires consent, so a general partner cannot transfer his or her partnership interest to another.

Partners' Liability General partners (who are active in the partnership) are personally liable for the debts of the partnership (creditors of the partnership can reach the personal assets of the partners). Any partner can contractually bind other partners.

Partners' liability is considered to be **joint and several** which means a creditor can bring action against all the partners or a single partner for a partnership debt.

Limited Partnership An exception to the unlimited liability of partners is a limited partnership. There must be one **general partner** (can be a corporation), but the other partners would have limited liability in that they would have no liability beyond their investment and pledges. Their personal assets cannot be reached to pay partnership debt.

Limited partners contribute only money (they are not active in the business, and their names are not associated with it). Their personal assets cannot be reached when partnership debts exceed partnership assets. Limited partners are entitled to an accounting from the general partner(s) and in some cases can oust a general partner for misconduct.

Limited partnership names must end with the words "A Limited California Partnership." Limited partnership agreements, to be effective as to limited liability, must be in writing, and the partners must file a Certificate of Limited Partnership with the California secretary of state.

Death of a Partner The estate of a deceased general partner has no right in the assets of the partnership. It does have a right to the deceased's share of undistributed profits and surplus (assets minus liabilities). The right to continue to conduct business vests in the surviving partners, who, of course, must account to the estate. **Partnership insurance** pays insurance to the partners of the deceased so that they have funds to pay off the estate of the deceased without dissolving the business. (Limited partners' interests may be inherited since they are financial only and have no management duties or responsibilities.)

Joint Venture

This is an association for a single endeavor (a partnership is broader—it is formed to carry on a business). It is treated for most purposes as a partnership, although spouses must join in conveyances of real property.

Corporation

This is an artificial person created by law. Since a corporation does not die, it cannot hold title in joint tenancy. Shareholders are not personally liable for the debts of the corporation. If a corporation has a seal, then the use of the seal is a presumption that the document was authorized by the corporation.

A **foreign corporation** (one not incorporated in California, as opposed to a **domestic corporation**) may get permission to operate in California, but must have an agent upon whom process can be served (in the event of a lawsuit against the corporation) or must consent to service of process upon the California secretary of state.

Equity capital of the corporation comes from the sale of stocks and retained earnings. **Corporate bonds** are corporate debts (**debt capital**) that must be repaid. A corporation is subject to double taxation in that the corporate profit is taxed to the corporation, and dividends paid to stockholders are taxed to the stockholders, although the dividends are taxed at a preferential rate.

When a person dealing with a corporation is in doubt as to the authority of an officer, he or she should ask to see the bylaws.

S Corporation

A small, closely held corporation (75 or fewer investors) can elect to be taxed as a partnership (all earnings are taxed to the shareholders) and thus no corporate taxes are paid.

Limited Liability Company (L.L.C.)

Offering the limited liability of corporations, limited liability companies have minimum requirements and less regulation than S corporations. Two or more members must file articles of organization with the secretary of state. They must also provide annual statements. Limited liability companies can be used to engage in any lawful business.

Unincorporated Nonprofit Association

An unincorporated association can hold title in the organization's name, but property not essential to the group's purpose cannot be held for more than 10 years. Members are personally liable only for leases or purchase agreements if they agree to be liable in writing.

Note: Syndicates, Securities and Real Estate Investment Trusts are covered in Chapter 8.

CHAPTER 2 QUIZ

1. The blackened area in the section is:
   a. the NW 1/4 of the NE 1/4
   b. the NE 1/4 of the NW 1/4
   c. the NE 1/4 of the NE 1/4
   d. none of these

2. The SE 1/4 of the SW 1/4 of the NW 1/4 of the NE 1/4 of a section contains:
   a. 2 1/2 acres
   b. 10 acres
   c. 1 1/4 acres
   d. 40 acres

3. Which of the following is larger than an acre?
   a. 209′ × 209′
   b. 100′ × 420′
   c. 1 mile × 5′
   d. none of these

4. Section 19 in a township is located where in the township?
   a. NW 1/4
   b. SW 1/4
   c. SE 1/4
   d. NE 1/4

5. The largest area among the following is:
   a. 2,000 acres
   b. 1/12 of a township
   c. three sections
   d. two square miles

6. The W 1/2 of the SW 1/4 of the NE 1/4 of a section contains how many acres?
   a. 40 acres
   b. 20 acres
   c. 1 1/4 acres
   d. 10 acres

7. A square 40-acre parcel contains on each side:
   a. 1,320 feet
   b. 2,640 feet
   c. 5,280 feet
   d. none of these

8. Which of the following is the largest?
   a. three sections
   b. 1/10 of a township
   c. 1,000 acres
   d. 5,000 feet × 15,000 feet

9. The distance between the north and south boundaries of a township is:
   a. 1 mile
   b. 6 miles
   c. 36 miles
   d. 24 miles

10. Lydia owns the NW 1/4 of the NW 1/4 of a section. A road runs along the north section line. What is the maximum number of square one-acre parcels she can create fronting on this road?
    a. 10
    b. 4
    c. 6
    d. 12

11. The description, "the NW 1/4 of the SW 1/4 of Section 13, Tier 8 North, Range 7 East," is not complete. Which of the following is not included?
    a. a reference to the base line and meridian
    b. the lot number
    c. the recording number
    d. a plat book

12. Multiplying the number of acres in the NW 1/4 of the SE 1/4 of a section by the number of miles of fencing it would take to fence this parcel gives:
    a. 40
    b. 80
    c. 160
    d. 320

13. The number of principal base lines and meridians in California is:
    a. infinite
    b. 36
    c. 3
    d. 1

14. Which of the following would be the least desirable reference point for a metes and bounds description?
    a. a corner of a section
    b. a township line
    c. a corner of a quarter section
    d. a riverbank

15. A lot contains 73,000 square yards. In acres it contains:
    a. 29 acres
    b. 14.7 acres
    c. 10 acres
    d. 15.1 acres

16. Horizontal rows of townships are known as:
    a. ranges
    b. tiers
    c. layers
    d. base lines

17. Vertical rows of townships are known as:
    a. ranges
    b. tiers
    c. layers
    d. meridians

18. The Humboldt Base Line runs:
    a. northwest and southeast
    b. north and south
    c. east and west
    d. north-northeast and south-southwest

19. A township contains how many acres?
    a. 640
    b. 23,040
    c. 36
    d. 6 on each side

20. On a map, east is usually to the:
    a. right
    b. left
    c. top
    d. bottom

21. To fence a township requires how much fencing?
    a. 6 miles
    b. 36 miles
    c. 24 miles
    d. 4 miles

22. To fence a quarter section requires how much fencing?
    a. 1 mile
    b. 2 miles
    c. 4 miles
    d. 1/2 mile

23. The maximum number of 50' × 75' lots that can be made from one acre (any shape) is:
    a. 10
    b. 12
    c. 11
    d. 13

24. The number of linear feet around a section is:
    a. 5,280
    b. 21,120
    c. 640
    d. 4

25. The southeast corner of the intersection of 1st and A streets is:
    a. the SE corner of lot 1
    b. the NE corner of lot 1
    c. the NW corner of lot 1
    d. none of these

26. The darkened portion of the section shown would be described as follows:
    a. the NW 1/4 of the SE 1/4
    b. the NW 1/4 of the NW 1/4
    c. the SW 1/4 of the NW 1/4
    d. the SE 1/4 of the NW 1/4

27. The section east of Section 13 of a township would be:
    a. Section 18
    b. Section 14
    c. Section 12
    d. none of these

28. A township contains:
    a. 640 acres
    b. 6 square miles
    c. 6 sections
    d. none of these

29. Which of the following is larger than a section?
    a. sixteen 40-acre parcels
    b. 1,000 feet × 4 miles
    c. 1/36 of a township
    d. 6,000 feet square

30. Which of the following is always true?
    a. Every section contains 640 acres.
    b. Every township contains 36 square miles.
    c. There are 5,280 linear feet in a mile.
    d. all of these

31. The number of feet around a square one-acre parcel is closest to:
    a. 210 feet
    b. 1,320 feet
    c. 43,560 feet
    d. 840 feet

32. Assume the following to be a proper metes-and-bounds description: "Starting at the SW corner of a designated section, thence in a straight line to the center of said section, thence in a straight line to a point midway between the SW and SE corners of said section, thence in a straight line to the point of beginning." How many acres are in the described parcel?
    a. 80
    b. 160
    c. 320
    d. none of these

33. The distance between Section 3 and Section 34 in a township is:
    a. 31 miles
    b. 3 miles
    c. 4 miles
    d. 5 miles

34. A quarter section is:
    a. 1/2 mile by 1/2 mile
    b. 1/4 mile by 1/4 mile
    c. 1/2 mile by 1 mile
    d. 1/2 mile by 1/4 mile

35. Land is commonly sold in California in all of the following ways except by:
    a. the foot
    b. the square foot
    c. metes and bounds
    d. the acre

36. A rectangular lot 1,320' × 2,640' contains:
   a. 40 acres
   b. 80 acres
   c. 120 acres
   d. 320 acres

37. An acre is:
   a. 43,560 square feet
   b. 264' × 165'
   c. 198' × 220'
   d. any of these

38. Artificial monuments are:
   a. streets and canals
   b. rocks and trees
   c. rivers and canals
   d. trees and fences

39. The boundary of an oceanfront lot would be the:
   a. high-tide line
   b. low-tide line
   c. mesne high-tide line
   d. mesne low-tide line

40. The maximum number of townships possible in an area 29 miles square is:
   a. 6
   b. 12
   c. 16
   d. none of these

41. Probate matters would be handled by:
   a. the referee in probate
   b. the superior court
   c. the municipal court
   d. none of these

42. A man who handles an estate by direction of the court rather than the testator is a(n):
   a. testatrix
   b. executor
   c. administrator
   d. none of these

43. A resident of Utah dies in Utah, leaving real property in California. The probate for this property would be handled:
   a. in California
   b. in Utah
   c. in California or Utah
   d. in federal court

44. A person who dies intestate normally has his or her property:
   a. escheat to the state
   b. distributed to his or her heirs
   c. go according to his or her will
   d. none of these

45. When no heirs claim property, it reverts to the State of California by:
   a. will
   b. grant deed
   c. comptroller deed
   d. escheat

46. There is no such thing as a typed:
   a. will
   b. grant deed
   c. codicil
   d. holographic will

47. A man appoints his wife to administer his will. She would be an:
   a. administratrix
   b. administrator
   c. executrix
   d. executor

48. A holographic will may not be:
   a. written in pencil
   b. signed with an "X"
   c. both a and b
   d. neither a nor b

49. A man dies. In his safe is his will with a signed and acknowledged deed to his home, giving it to his church. No mention is made of this in his will, which gives everything to his son.
   a. Whichever instrument was dated later would govern.
   b. Since the deed was not delivered, the son gets the house.
   c. The church gets the property, since acknowledgment is a presumption of delivery.
   d. None of these are true.

50. A will is ambulatory:
   a. when it is made at the time of the testator's last illness
   b. upon the death of the testator
   c. because it can be changed
   d. none of these

51. Which of the following is not a requirement of a formal will?
   a. a signature
   b. witnesses
   c. an acknowledgment
   d. none of these

52. A property in probate is appraised at $96,000. At auction the highest bid is $90,000. For the court to consider any other offer, it would have to be at least:
   a. $90,000.01
   b. $99,000.00
   c. $100,000.00
   d. $95,000.00

53. A valid deed must have certain requirements, but it need not:
    a. have the signature of the grantor
    b. have two competent parties
    c. contain an adequate description
    d. name the grantee

54. As to an acknowledgment to a deed, which of the following is true?
    a. It may not be notarized by the grantee.
    b. The notary must have a seal.
    c. The notary must keep a record of identification of the person acknowledging the deed.
    d. all of these

55. A man dies testate, leaving a wife and one child. His estate is distributed:
    a. to his heirs by right of representation
    b. one-half to his wife and one-half to his child
    c. one-third to his wife and two-thirds to his child
    d. in accordance with his will

56. The most important requirement of adverse possession is:
    a. actual physical possession
    b. some claim of title
    c. five years' use by one party
    d. all of these are equally important

57. Elaine acquires property by accession. Most likely she got the property by:
    a. accretion
    b. grant deed
    c. adverse use
    d. eminent domain

58. Which of the following does not have to be recorded to have effect:
    a. a mechanic's lien
    b. a grant deed
    c. a judgment
    d. a homestead declaration

59. A deed is recorded and indexed:
    a. by location
    b. by recording day and time
    c. by grantor and grantee names alphabetically
    d. all of these

60. Stan gives a life estate to Carter. Stan's retained interest is:
    a. leasehold
    b. reversionary
    c. personal property
    d. remainder

61. A recorded deed:
    a. must have been acknowledged
    b. gives constructive notice
    c. creates a presumption of delivery
    d. all of these

62. Conrad gives a deed to Fiona with the following instructions: Fiona should return the deed on demand, but if Conrad dies, then Fiona should give the deed to Conrad's son. The problem is one of:
    a. recording
    b. acknowledgment
    c. delivery
    d. acceptance

63. The person making an acknowledgment on a deed would be:
    a. the maker
    b. the recorder
    c. the purchaser
    d. a notary public

64. To be recorded, a deed must have:
    a. the signature of the grantee
    b. a recitation of consideration
    c. a seal
    d. a name and address where tax bills are to be sent

65. After buying property and receiving a recorded deed, the buyer and the seller decide to rescind the deal. The buyer should:
    a. return the deed in exchange for the consideration
    b. give a deed of reconveyance
    c. file a cancellation
    d. give a new grant deed to the original seller

66. A county recorder must keep:
    a. microfilm records
    b. a phonetic index
    c. a documentary tax stamp ledger
    d. an adequate index system

67. A reservation in a deed:
    a. voids the deed
    b. is a retention of an interest
    c. creates a fee simple
    d. none of these

68. A valid deed requires:
    a. witnesses
    b. recording
    c. acknowledgment
    d. a clear description of the property

69. A deed transfers title at the time of:
    a. signing
    b. acknowledgment
    c. recording
    d. delivery

70. Quitclaim deeds convey:
    a. only easements
    b. after-acquired title
    c. any interest the grantor has
    d. none of these

71. A gift deed may be voided by:
    a. the grantor
    b. debtors of the grantor
    c. creditors of the grantor
    d. none of these

72. An exception in a grant deed:
    a. voids the deed
    b. is the same as a reservation
    c. excludes part of the property from the grant
    d. none of these

73. A deed would not contain:
    a. a description of the property
    b. a date
    c. the signature of the grantee
    d. a granting clause

74. The W 1/2 of the SE 1/4 of the SW 1/4 of the NW 1/4 of a section contains:
    a. 2 1/2 acres
    b. 5 acres
    c. 10 acres
    d. 20 acres

75. The most important element of proper delivery of a deed is:
    a. recording
    b. intent
    c. physical transfer
    d. witnesses

76. Ramon sells property to Kate, with the provision in the deed that if the property were ever used as a tavern, it would revert back to Ramon. This would be best described as a:
    a. restriction
    b. condition precedent
    c. condition subsequent
    d. covenant

77. Alicia deeds a property to Bud. The deed is never recorded. How can Bud transfer title back to Alicia?
    a. destroy the deed
    b. hand the deed back as a reconveyance
    c. write "canceled" across the face of the deed, sign and date it, then return it to Alicia
    d. none of these

78. A disadvantage of joint tenancy is that:
    a. it avoids probate
    b. interest passes free of debts of the deceased
    c. once established, it cannot be broken even if all of the owners wish to end it
    d. an interest can be transferred without the knowledge or approval of other joint tenants

79. A brother and sister would never hold property as:
    a. joint tenants
    b. tenants in common
    c. tenants in partnership
    d. community property

80. Mabel and Edgar have three children. They have $100,000 in community property. Edgar dies intestate (without a will). Each of the children receives:
    a. 1/3
    b. 1/5
    c. 1/3 of the remaining 2/3 interest
    d. nothing

81. The only one of four unities required for joint tenancy that is also required for tenancy in common is:
    a. possession
    b. ownership
    c. interest
    d. time

82. A person having an interest as community property may not:
    a. will that interest to another
    b. sell his or her half-interest to another
    c. both a and b
    d. neither a nor b

83. Property cannot be held in joint tenancy by:
    a. nonrelated parties
    b. brothers and sisters
    c. more than three people
    d. corporations

84. Tom leases to John for 20 years. Two years later Tom dies. John discovers that Tom had a life estate.
    a. The owner now has a remainder interest.
    b. The owner now has a reversionary interest.
    c. The lease is still valid for 18 years.
    d. The lease is terminated.

85. Under a tenancy in common:
    a. interests must be equal
    b. there is a right of survivorship
    c. a tenant can sell his or her interest without consent of other tenants
    d. none of these

86. A brother and sister hold land as joint tenants. The sister conveys one-half of her interest to her husband.
    a. The brother and sister are joint tenants and the husband is a tenant in common.
    b. The brother, sister, and her husband are joint tenants.
    c. All are tenants in common.
    d. None of these are true.

87. A husband alone, without his wife's consent, may:
    a. give away community property
    b. sell community property
    c. buy real estate
    d. sell household furniture

88. By will a spouse may dispose of:
    a. all of the community property
    b. a tenancy-in-common interest
    c. a joint-tenancy interest
    d. a and b

89. Which of the following cannot be a "less than freehold" estate?
    a. a life estate
    b. an estate for years
    c. a periodic tenancy
    d. an estate at sufferance

90. When the word *fee* is used in connection with real estate, it means:
    a. a commission
    b. a charge for conveyance
    c. an estate of inheritance
    d. the price of land

91. Chang and Jerome, both single men, wish to take title together with undivided equal interests without the right of survivorship. The granting clause in the deed would read:
    a. Chang, a single man, and Jerome, a single man, as tenants in common
    b. Chang, a single man, and Jerome, a single man, in severalty
    c. Chang, a single man, and Jerome, a single man, as joint tenants
    d. Chang, a single man, and Jerome, a single man, as community property

92. In accordance with her deceased husband's will, Roberta can collect the rents from an apartment house for her lifetime, after which the apartment house goes to their church. Roberta has a:
    a. periodic tenancy
    b. tenancy at will
    c. life estate
    d. fee simple

93. A corporation seal on a deed:
    a. is required by law
    b. must be notarized
    c. can be affixed only by the corporate treasurer
    d. is evidence that the person signing for the corporation has authority to sign

94. In taking an offer from a corporate representative, a broker should be sure to check the representative's authority. This would be found most likely in the:
    a. state Corporation Code
    b. corporation charter
    c. corporation bylaws
    d. Business and Professions Code

95. Which of the following is true regarding an estate in real estate?
    a. It is always forever.
    b. It must vest immediately.
    c. It must be the result of a deed.
    d. More than one estate can exist as to one property at the same time.

96. It is normally best to have:
    a. a life estate
    b. an estate for years
    c. a fee simple
    d. none of these

97. Joint tenancy:
    a. involves only real property
    b. involves only personal property
    c. is an inheritable estate
    d. is a single estate

98. A husband and wife own Greenacres as community property. The husband dies, leaving a will specifying that all his interest goes to his son.
    a. The wife and son own Greenacres as joint tenants.
    b. The wife and son own Greenacres as tenants in common.
    c. The wife and son own Greenacres as community property.
    d. The wife gets all of Greenacres, since community property passes to the surviving spouse.

99. Which of the following pairs of terms do not match?
    a. joint tenancy and right of survivorship
    b. tenancy in common and undivided interest
    c. estate for years and freehold estate
    d. fee simple and perpetuity

100. Alfonso and Boyd, both single men, inherit a farm as joint tenants. They each later marry. Alfonso dies without a will, leaving a wife and three children.
    a. Alfonso's wife and children are joint tenants.
    b. Alfonso's wife and Boyd are tenants in common.
    c. Alfonso's wife and children do not get the farm.
    d. Alfonso's wife and children are tenants in common with Boyd.

101. A husband cannot legally object if his wife does which of the following without his consent?
    a. sells community property
    b. leases community property for more than one year
    c. buys an apartment building using community property funds
    d. none of these

102. John gives property to Paul for the life of Albert. Paul dies.
    a. The property goes to John.
    b. The property goes to Albert.
    c. The property goes to Paul's heirs.
    d. None of these are true.

103. One joint tenant borrowed on her interest.
    a. The loan terminated the joint tenancy.
    b. The tenancy is now a tenancy in common.
    c. Both a and b are true.
    d. Neither a nor b is true.

104. An elderly husband and wife (no children) with total savings of $25,000, are buying a $150,000 home through a real estate office. They ask the broker how they should take title. The broker should tell them:
    a. as tenants in common
    b. as community property
    c. as joint tenants
    d. to see an attorney

105. A limited partner may:
    a. use his or her name in the partnership
    b. request an accounting from the partnership
    c. serve as an advisor
    d. make management decisions

106. Which of the following cannot be owned in fee simple?
    a. a house owned as community property
    b. a house owned in joint tenancy
    c. a house owned in severalty
    d. none of these

107. A deed in California is made out to a husband and wife but does not specify how title is to be taken. Title would be:
    a. as community property
    b. as tenants in common
    c. in joint tenancy
    d. in severalty

108. Creditors can access your personal assets for the debts of:
   a. a general partnership
   b. a limited partnership
   c. a corporation
   d. all of these

109. An undivided interest without the right of survivorship constitutes:
   a. tenancy in severalty
   b. tenancy in common
   c. joint tenancy
   d. none of these

110. A limited partner is:
   a. limited as to the hours he or she can work
   b. treated the same as an active partner
   c. liable without limits
   d. limited as to liability for debts

111. A married man owns a lot by himself as his separate property. He most likely owns the lot:
   a. as a tenant in common
   b. as community property
   c. as a joint tenant
   d. in severalty

112. An S corporation:
   a. is taxed as a partnership
   b. is limited as to shareholders
   c. passes tax liability to shareholders
   d. all of these

113. Which of the following groupings gives the greatest and most complete interest in real estate?
   a. freehold, fee simple, life estate
   b. estate for years, defeasible estate
   c. estate at will, estate on condition subsequent
   d. estate for years, nonfreehold estate

114. As to a fee estate, which of the following is false?
   a. It can be freely transferred.
   b. It is of definite duration.
   c. It can be inherited.
   d. none of these

115. A deed that would convey after-acquired property would be a:
   a. bargain-and-sale deed
   b. quitclaim deed
   c. grant deed
   d. tax deed

116. A life estate:
   a. cannot exceed 99 years
   b. can exist with another estate
   c. can be leased by a life tenant beyond his or her life
   d. is illegal in California because of the rule against perpetuities

117. In California, life estates are not created by:
   a. gift
   b. will
   c. grant
   d. action of law

118. Some maps show topographical lines. These lines show:
   a. rivers
   b. contours
   c. boundaries
   d. soil conditions

119. A grantor conveys less than her fee estate. The interest she retains would be a(n):
   a. reversionary interest
   b. remainder interest
   c. leasehold
   d. easement

120. Normally in California a buyer wants a(n):
   a. warranty deed
   b. abstract of title
   c. grant deed coupled with title insurance
   d. quitclaim deed

121. The four unities of joint tenancy are:
   a. time, title, interest, and possession
   b. title, time, ownership, and liability
   c. title, interest, possession, and liability
   d. time, interest, possession, and liability

122. A user with only 3 years adverse use was able to obtain title by adverse possession because:
   a. of the 4 unities
   b. he was a minor
   c. of possession
   d. of tacking on

123. *Partition action* refers to:
    a. a subdivision
    b. a court proceeding to break up a joint tenancy
    c. a construction project
    d. none of these

124. *Pur autre vie* refers to:
    a. water quality
    b. an estate of inheritance
    c. personal property
    d. the life of another person

125. Three buyers take title to a property as joint tenants. There would be:
    a. three deeds
    b. only one deed
    c. no right of survivorship
    d. separate one-third ownerships

126. *Alienation* refers to:
    a. angering another
    b. transfer of an estate
    c. giving possession but keeping title
    d. using a property as security for a loan

127. Which of the following is an estate of inheritance?
    a. life estate
    b. leasehold interest
    c. fee simple
    d. all of the above

128. A grant deed that contains no limitations would grant:
    a. a fee simple
    b. a license
    c. possessory interest only
    d. a nonfreehold estate

129. Which of the following does not describe a fee simple interest?
    a. free of encumbrances
    b. inheritable
    c. without time limit
    d. transferable

130. A corporation buys property and takes title in the corporate name. They would hold title:
    a. in joint tenancy
    b. in tenancy in common
    c. as limited partners
    d. in severalty

131. Jones has a life estate in a farm, and Smith desires an easement over a private road crossing the farm. As to the easement:
    a. only the owner of the reversionary interest can grant it
    b. since no one has a fee simple interest, an easement cannot be given
    c. Jones can grant it
    d. an easement may only be granted by Jones giving Smith a quitclaim deed

132. The owner of a paramount legal title alienated property but retained a future right based on a contingency. What did she convey?
    a. fee simple absolute
    b. fee simple defeasible
    c. estate for years
    d. a nonfreehold interest

133. The holder of a life estate cannot:
    a. sell it
    b. lease it
    c. will it
    d. borrow against it

134. A proper legal description is least likely to be obtained from a:
    a. deed
    b. policy of title insurance
    c. preliminary title report
    d. property tax bill

135. A recorded deed was not acknowledged. The deed:
    a. is void
    b. would only provide constructive notice after one year
    c. is treated in the same manner as an alteration
    d. none of the above

136. Most urban property would have what type of legal description?
    a. tax assessor's number
    b. metes and bounds
    c. recorded lot, block, and tract
    d. government survey

137. Range lines are lines:
    a. going north and south
    b. going east and west
    c. four miles apart
    d. showing agricultural zoning

138. 320 rods equal one:
    a. section
    b. township
    c. chain
    d. mile

139. A husband and wife owned property together that could not be transferred by will. They owned the property:
    a. without the right of possession
    b. as tenants in common
    c. as community property
    d. as community property with right of survivorship

140. A purchased property from B. He did not get title since B had prevoiusly sold the property to C who had recorded the deed. The effect of the prior recording was:
    a. constructive notice
    b. to insure C's title is free of encumbrances
    c. to prevent later fraud
    d. to extablish homestead rights

ANSWERS—CHAPTER 2 QUIZ

1. c.
2. a. Go backwards from 640.
3. a. A square acre is approx. 208.7′ × 208.7′.
4. b.
5. a. Over 3 sections.
6. b.
7. a. 1/4 mile.
8. b. 3.6 sections.
9. b. 6 miles square.
10. c. 1320′ ÷ 208.7.
11. a.
12. a. 40 × 1.
13. c. San Bernardino, Mt. Diablo, and Humboldt.
14. d. It could change.
15. d. 1 sq. yd. = 9 sq. ft. 73,000 × 9 divided by 43,560.
16. b. Think of a cake.
17. a.
18. c. All baselines run east and west.
19. b. 36 sections × 640.
20. a.
21. c. 6 miles × 4 sides.
22. b. 1/2 mile each side.
23. c. 50′ × 75′ = 3,750, 43,560 ÷ 3,750.
24. b. 5,280 × 4.
25. c.
26. d.
27. a. Of the adjoining township.
28. d. 6 miles square, or 36 square miles.
29. d. Section is 5,280′ square.
30. c. The curvature of the earth causes discrepancies.
31. d. 208.7′ each side.
32. a. 1/2 of 160 acres. (Triangle)
33. c.
34. a.
35. a. This is a linear measurement.
36. b.
37. d. All equal one acre. (43,560 square feet)
38. a. Both are manmade.
39. c. *Mesne* means mean or middle.
40. c. Since by definition a township is 6 miles square, the maximum number on a side is 4.
41. b. As are most real estate matters.
42. c. An executor is appointed by will.
43. a. Ancillary probate.
44. b. Generally there are heirs.
45. d. After five years.
46. d. Handwritten by definition.
47. c. She is a woman appointed by will.
48. b. Since it is handwritten, the maker would be literate and sign his or her name.
49. b.

50. c.
51. c. It must be signed and witnessed.
52. d. 10 percent higher on the first $10,000, 5 percent on the balance.
53. b. The grantee on a gift deed need not be competent.
54. d.
55. d.
56. a.
57. a. Being joined to.
58. b. It is valid between the parties without recording.
59. c.
60. b. It reverts back to him after the death of Carter.
61. d.
62. c. The deed is not delivered; it is part of Conrad's estate.
63. a. The maker acknowledges the deed before a notary.
64. d.
65. d. A deed is only used once.
66. d. Usually a grantor/grantee index.
67. b.
68. d. The description must be unambiguous.
69. d.
70. c. Without claiming an interest.
71. c. If the grantor was insolvent at the time of the gift.
72. c.
73. c. The grantee need not sign.
74. b. Work backwards from 640 acres.
75. b. Intent for present transfer.
76. c. The property reverts on the happening of a condition.
77. d. Bud must give Alicia a new deed.
78. d. Breaking the joint tenancy.
79. d. Requires marriage.
80. d. All to the surviving spouse.
81. a. Equal rights of possession.
82. b. Both parties must convey.
83. d. Since corporations don't die.
84. d. A life tenant cannot encumber the property beyond his or her life.
85. c. The buyer becomes a tenant in common.
86. c. The unities are no longer present.
87. c.
88. b. He can will only one-half of community property.
89. a. It is a freehold estate.
90. c.
91. a.
92. c. The church has a remainder interest.

93. d.
94. c. Rules governing a corporation.
95. d. Such as a fee simple and a leasehold interest.
96. c. This is the highest form of ownership.
97. d. In which each owner has an undivided interest.
98. b.
99. c. An estate for years is a non-freehold estate.
100. c. The property goes to the surviving joint tenant.
101. c. Either spouse can commit community property funds.
102. c. For as long as Albert lives.
103. d. But her survivors would receive it free of the loan.
104. d. Otherwise it is unauthorized practice of law.
105. b. A limited partner cannot be or appear active.
106. d. All can be held in fee simple, which is the degree of ownerships not the form of ownership.
107. a.
108. a. Unlimited liability.
109. b.
110. d. To the extent of his or her investment.
111. d.
112. d.
113. a. All are freehold estates.
114. b. Indefinite duration.
115. c.
116. b. Such as a remainder interest.
117. d. Some states have dower (widow's life estate).
118. b. Land elevations.
119. a. Returns to grantor.
120. c.
121. a.
122. d. To a prior adverse user.
123. b. Or tenancy in common.
124. d. For life estates.
125. b.
126. b.
127. c. Freehold interests that passes to heirs.
128. a.
129. a. It usually has some encumbrances.
130. d. As sole owner.
131. c. But it ends with Jones's death.
132. b. Can obtain title if condition breached.
133. c. It is only for life.
134. d. Uses assessor numbers.
135. b.
136. c.
137. a.
138. d.
139. d.
140. a. Of C's interest.

CHAPTER 3

Encumbrances, Liens, and Homesteads

ENCUMBRANCES

An **encumbrance** is a claim, liability, or restriction on use of a property. Some encumbrances affect title, such as mechanic's liens and mortgages, while others affect the physical nature of the property, such as easements, encroachments, and use restrictions. A **beneficial restriction** on use that helps maintain value can nevertheless be an encumbrance. **Liens,** which are claims against real estate, can be foreclosed and result in the loss of the property. While all liens are also encumbrances, not all encumbrances are liens.

Easements

An **easement** is a **nonpossessory** real property interest. It is an irrevocable right or interest one person has in the land of another. A typical easement is a right-of-way one person has in the land of another for purposes of ingress or egress.

Alan Dominant Tenement (Use dominates land of another)	Bob Servient Tenement (Serves land of another)	R O A D
	Easement	

Alan has an easement over Bob's land. Alan has the **dominant tenement** (his land is using or dominating the land of another). Bob has the **servient tenement** (his land is being used by another or serves the land of another). Since the easement benefits Alan's land and transfers with the land, it is **appurtenant** to Alan's land (**easement appurtenant**). Since the easement restricts Bob's use of the land, it is an **encumbrance** to Bob's land. The easement holder, Alan, has the duty to maintain the easement.

An easement is classified as either an **affirmative** easement or a **negative** easement. An easement is considered real property but is not an estate.

Affirmative Easement   The right to use someone's land.

Negative Easement   The right to prevent the owner of the land from doing some act he or she otherwise could do, such as building a fence that might interfere with the easement holder's right of light or view.

Profit a Prendre   A type of easement whereby the easement holder can take profits from the land (right to crops, minerals, gas, oil, etc.).

Conservation Easement   An easement whereby the landowner must retain the land in a natural or agricultural state. A conservation easement is normally purchased by a nonprofit organization.

Creation of an Easement

1. **By grant** (deed) or by reservation in a deed (by the landowner either conveying the easement or conveying the land and retaining the easement).
2. **By implication.**
3. **By necessity.**
4. **By dedication** (giving the easement to the city or county for public use).
5. **By prescription.**
6. **By eminent domain.**
7. **By estoppel,** when the owner by words or actions leads another to believe there is an easement and the other party acts to his or her own detriment based on this belief. As an example, an easement by estoppel is created when a user improves a right-of-way based on the assertion of the landowner that an easement exists.

Easement by Implication   An easement implied by law although not actually expressed. For example, when a grantor conveys land that is landlocked by other land belonging to the grantor, an easement to the grantee is implied of a reasonable right-of-way across the land of the grantor for access purposes. Owners of mineral, oil, and gas rights have an implied easement to enter and mine or drill. When a subdivider sells lots based on a map showing access, there is an implied easement over the access even if it was not actually granted. Although there is no implied easement as to light or air in California, the Solar Shade Act provides an implied easement of light in specified cases involving solar collectors.

Easement by Necessity A form of implied easement. When there is no other possible means of access, the courts will allow an easement by necessity providing that at one time both the dominant and servient tenements were under a common ownership. This easement ends when any other means of access becomes available.

Easement by Prescription An easement obtained by *use*.

Elements of an Easement by Prescription

1. Open and notorious use (not secretive).
2. Continuous use for five years. (If the landowner stops the user, then a new five-year period must begin.) Prior use of a previous owner will count toward the five years (**tacking on**).
3. Hostile and adverse use. (If permission is given by the owner, then the user has a **license,** or revocable privilege, as use is not hostile.)
4. Use under some claim of right.

Until an easement by prescription is obtained, the user is a trespasser and can be ejected.

By prescription a person obtains use, but title insurance as to the use cannot be obtained unless the user brings a **quiet title action** to make his or her right a matter of court record.

Easement in Gross An easement in which there is no dominant tenement (for example, a right to place billboards on the land of another). An easement in gross is a personal right. Because there is no dominant tenement, it does not run with the land. It is therefore personal to the easement holder although it can be assigned to another.

Terms of Easements

1. An easement lasts forever, unless stated otherwise.
2. An easement terminates upon **merger,** or when one person acquires title to both the dominant and the servient tenement (an owner can't have an easement to use his or her own land).
3. An easement by prescription is the only kind of easement lost by nonuse (five years).
4. Destruction of the servient tenement terminates an easement.
5. An easement created for a particular purpose would end with the end of the purpose.
6. Agreement. The parties may agree to discontinue the easement (for example, a quitclaim deed from the holder of the dominant tenement would end the easement).
7. Prescriptive use or adverse possession by the holder of the servient tenement (that is, if the servient tenement holder uses the right-of-way for another purpose for five years).

License

A **license** is permissive use. It is personal in nature and cannot be assigned. It gives no right to the user of the land and can be canceled by the landowner. Because the use is permissive, not hostile, the user can get no rights by prescription or adverse use.

CC&Rs

Covenants, conditions, and restrictions (restrictive covenants) are restrictions based on agreement of the parties rather than governmental control. CC&Rs are **private restrictions,** as opposed to zoning, which is a **public restriction.** Private restrictions are generally beneficial in that they tend to maintain property values. If zoning and other restrictions are in conflict, the more restrictive provisions prevail.

Restrictions are generally in the form of **covenants** (promises) in deeds and are created by grantors. Restrictions may also be placed on property or removed by the agreement of all the affected property owners. The CC&Rs may provide for a percentage of owners who must agree to change or remove them. The covenants generally run with the land. Action for breach normally is **injunction** or **money damages.** The Statute of Limitations for enforcement of restrictions is five years from discovery or when it should have been known.

Restrictions go on forever unless a fixed period is stated. Courts will refuse to enforce restrictions that have become unreasonable because of a change in conditions, as well as restrictions that unreasonably restrain **alienation** (conveyance). (For example, a prohibition against "For Sale" signs would be an unreasonable **restraint on alienation.**) Although racial restrictions are unenforceable (*Shelly* v. *Kraemer,* U.S. Supreme Court, 1948), they would not invalidate a transfer.

Homeowner associations are required to remove racially restrictive covenants in their CC&Rs, and real estate brokers must stamp or place a cover sheet on CC&Rs provided to a buyer that indicates in bold face, red type that the racial restrictions are void.

Merger of ownership can also end restrictions. As an example, if one person acquired all the property covered by the restrictions, that person would not be subject to the restrictions because of the merger of interests.

Declaration of Restrictions

Subdividers can record a declaration setting forth restrictions prior to the first sale. Each deed includes the phrase "subject to the conditions of record," so that the restrictions, while not set forth in individual deeds, are incorporated by reference.

Condition

This is a qualification of an estate placed by a grantor. The penalty for breach is reversion to the grantor. (The courts do not favor forfeiture, so conditions are usually treated as covenants.)

Encroachment

An **encroachment** is trespass in the placing of improvements on or over the land of another. A permanent improvement is considered a permanent trespass, and the owner of the land must bring action to remove the improvement within three years or his or her rights are lost. A good-faith encroacher can remove the encroachment, but would be liable for damages. When the encroachment was due to an excusable mistake and the value of the improvements is great, the court may readjust the boundaries and award money damages.

Ejectment   An action to remove an encroachment or oust a trespasser.

Nuisance   A **nuisance** is a use that detracts from others enjoying their property. It is a trespass to the senses. Examples include noise, vibrations, smells and unsightly conditions.

An **abatement action** can be brought to abate the nuisance (have it cease).

Injunction   A court order to cease an activity or use.

LIENS

A **lien** is a charge or debt against a property. A **voluntary lien,** such as a mortgage, is placed against a property by the owner. Judgments and tax liens are **involuntary liens.** A **specific lien** applies to a specific property, such as a tax lien or mortgage. A judgment would be a **general lien** that could apply to all the property owned by a debtor. Liens for property taxes and special assessments take priority over all other liens. They are covered in detail in Chapter 13.

Mechanic's Liens

These specific liens are **statutory liens** (civil code) upon real property for labor and materials used in construction or improvement. An unlicensed contractor cannot file a mechanic's lien although a laborer working for a contractor can file a lien. However, a real estate broker acting as a property manager does not need a contractor's license to file a mechanic's lien nor does an architect.

For priority purposes, all mechanic's liens are dated from the date the work actually starts. If work starts June 1, and a bank loan is taken out on June 5, a painter who finishes up on October 1 has priority over the bank, since his priority goes back to June 1. (Some work must be apparent to constitute a work start date. Commencement of work could be demolition of an old structure, clearing of a site, delivery of materials, etc.) Multiple mechanic's liens share the same priority. Mechanic's liens must be verified and recorded to have any effect.

A lender that does not have priority over mechanic's liens can file a bond of 75 percent of the loan. The loan then takes priority over all work performed subsequent to the filing of the bond.

Preliminary Notice   In order to file a lien, a mechanic or materials supplier must first give to the owner, within 20 days after commencement of supplying services, materials, or equipment, a written preliminary notice that the work is subject to a lien. A late preliminary notice would cover the work and material only for the prior 20 days.

When Liens Are Filed   If a **notice of completion** is filed, the prime contractor has 60 days to file a lien; subcontractors have 30 days to file. If no notice of completion is filed, all contractors have 90 days from the date the work was actually completed to file liens. (The purpose of a notice of completion is to set the time of completion.)

Notice of Cessation   If work stopped but was not completed and a notice of cessation was filed, the prime contractor has 60 days to file a lien, and subcontractors have 30 days to file. If no notice of cessation is filed, everyone has 90 days to file. (**Cessation** means no work for 60 days.) Liens that are not filed in a timely manner are lost (although the debt still remains, there is no longer a security interest in the property).

Notice of Nonresponsibility   If work is done without the owner's knowledge (for example, by a tenant or vendee under a land contract) the owner must, *within 10 days* of finding out about such work (if he or she wishes to avoid responsibility):

1. Post a notice of nonresponsibility on the premises.
2. Record a copy of said notice with the county recorder.

If the owner or vendor requires the tenant or vendee to make the repairs or improvements, then recording a notice of nonresponsibility would not protect the owner or vendor from mechanic's liens.

Verification   A statement in which the lienholder swears as to the correctness of the facts covering the lien under penalty of perjury (required to file a mechanic's lien).

Affirmation   A solemn statement made before a court by a person whose religion prohibits him or her from taking an oath.

Affidavit   A written statement of facts given under oath.

After Lien   The lienholder must bring an action to foreclose the property to enforce the lien within 90 days or the lien is lost.

Stop Notice   Given by a subcontractor to a lender, it requires a preliminary notice. It requires the lender to hold out funds for the subcontractor (to be used, it also requires a 20-day preliminary notice). If the validity of the claim is questioned, the contractor can get the funds released by posting a bond of 125% of claimed amount.

Lien Release   An owner can get a disputed mechanic's lien released by posting a bond of 1 1/2 times the amount claimed.

Lis Pendens

A notice of a pending lawsuit involving a claimed real estate interest. When it is recorded, it is constructive notice to a subsequent purchaser of an interest another claims in the property.

Attachment Seizing property before a judgment. An attachment is a lien on real property for three years after the date of levy, but a court can extend the lien for another two years. A hearing must be held prior to an attachment. Attachment is limited to claims arising from the conduct of a business, trade, or profession.

Judgment The final order of a court that an amount is due. When it is recorded, a judgment becomes a general lien on all real property of the debtor in the county where it is recorded. A judgment is good for 10 years and may be renewed. (An **abstract of judgment** may be recorded in more than one county.)

A judgment is enforced by a **writ of execution.** The sheriff may carry out the judgment by seizing property of the debtor and selling it to satisfy the judgment.

A purchaser receives a sheriff's deed. While an action to set aside a judgment must be commenced within 90 days of sale (where the purchaser is a judgment creditor), owner redemption is possible within one year of sale.

DECLARATION OF HOMESTEAD

The California constitution provides for homestead rights. A **homestead declaration** protects the home of the debtor from being foreclosed to satisfy claims of unsecured creditors. Homestead property need not be owned. A life tenant, a tenant on a lease for 30 years or more, or a buyer under a real property purchase contract can file a homestead.

A declaration of homestead, to be valid, must be recorded in the county where the homestead is located. The declaration must be recorded prior to judgment by an unsecured creditor, since once a judgment is recorded, it becomes a lien on all property of the debtor in the county where filed. A declaration of homestead is *not* an encumbrance. To have a declaration of homestead, it makes no difference how the property is held (joint tenancy, community property, etc.).

Requirements of a Valid Homestead Declaration

1. A statement that the claimant is the head of the family (if applicable).
2. The name of the claimant's spouse (if he or she is married).
3. A statement that the claimant is residing on the premises. (It can be any type of building used as a residence, but cannot be a vacant lot.)
4. A description of the property.

A person may have an unlimited number of homesteads, but only one at a time. Either spouse may file a valid homestead declaration on jointly owned property or upon property separately owned by the homesteading spouse.

The amount of the homestead exemption is:

Family units	$ 75,000
Persons over 65 and persons unable to work because of mental or physical disabilities as well as certain low-income persons over 55	$125,000
All other persons	$ 50,000

This exemption applies to the declarant's equity, so:

Home worth	$150,000
First trust deed	−69,000
Second trust deed	−25,000
Debtor's equity	$56,000

Assuming a family unit deduction of $75,000, the equity of $56,000 could not be touched by creditors. In the event that the debtor's equity is over $75,000, a judgment creditor can force a sale through the superior court. The sale proceeds would go as follows:

1. To all existing lienholders (trust deeds, etc., in order of their priority).
2. To the debtor in the amount of his or her exemption. (The head of the household would get $75,000 cash. The money can be reinvested in another homestead and cannot be touched by creditors for six months—**six-month rule.**)

   If the homeowner sells the property, the homestead exemption applies to the proceeds of the sale for six months. If proceeds are invested in a new residence, then the new residence would be protected by the exemption.
3. To the judgment claimants.
4. The balance, if any, to the debtor.

A declaration of homestead does *not* protect a debtor against:

1. A judgment filed prior to the declaration.
2. Mechanic's liens.
3. Mortgages and trust deeds.
4. Homeowners' association assessments.

Homesteads Are Lost:

1. By filing a **declaration of abandonment.**
2. By selling the property (moving out does not abandon the homestead).

(In cases of bankruptcy and foreclosure of a judgment lien, the court will automatically provide for homestead exemption even though a homestead declaration was not filed.)

Bankruptcy

Bankruptcy is provided for in the United States Constitution. It may be voluntary or involuntary.

The title to a bankrupt's nonexempt property goes to a trustee. A person may not go bankrupt more than once every seven years. All unsecured creditors' rights are wiped out by bankruptcy providing the debt was identified prior to filing the petition for bankruptcy. If a bankrupt wishes to be absolved of secured debts, then he or she must give up the secured property.

Chapter 7 bankruptcy is the most common form of bankruptcy. Chapter 11 bankruptcy allows a business to continue to operate with protection from creditors. Chapter 13 bankruptcy is a wage-earner plan whereby the wage earner pays off creditors in accordance with an agreed-upon schedule.

CHAPTER 3 QUIZ

1. A water company's rights to run a water line through a person's property would most likely be:
   a. riparian rights
   b. the right of a correlative user
   c. an easement in gross
   d. a servient tenement

2. A property owner pays the prime contractor and obtains his or her lien waiver.
   a. The owner is protected against any liens.
   b. The owner may be liable for unpaid material supplies and subcontractors.
   c. The owner is protected if the lien waiver and contract were recorded.
   d. The owner is protected as to labor liens, but not as to material suppliers.

3. Mechanic's liens can be filed by:
   a. general contractors
   b. subcontractors
   c. materials suppliers
   d. all of these

4. An action is started against David, so he files a declaration of homestead as head of a family. The creditor obtains a $20,000 judgment. David sells the house for $100,000. He has a first trust deed for $29,000. The judgment creditor hears of the sale before escrow has closed. He or she can obtain:
   a. nothing
   b. $19,000
   c. $20,000
   d. $1,000

5. A sale of real estate would not affect:
   a. restrictive covenants
   b. easements by reservation
   c. rights of mechanic's lien holders
   d. any of these

6. Wendell, a single man, files a declaration of homestead on a home where he lives alone. The home is worth $190,000. Wendell owes $150,000 against it. Julian, an unsecured creditor, obtains a $50,000 judgment against Wendell.
   a. Julian cannot touch Wendell's home.
   b. Julian can foreclose against Wendell and get his equity.
   c. Wendell has no exemption since he is not head of a household.
   d. Julian can collect the amount of the homestead exemption.

7. An instrument that would be incorporated by reference in a deed would most likely be:
   a. an easement by prescription
   b. a declaration of restrictions
   c. a formal will
   d. a notice of completion

8. By mistake, Sheila builds a shed encroaching on her neighbor's property.
   a. After five years, Sheila gets title to the property.
   b. Sheila's neighbor owns her shed.
   c. Sheila can remove the shed but is liable for any damages to her neighbor's property.
   d. None of these are true.

9. A married person cannot file a declaration of homestead on property he or she owns:
   a. in severalty
   b. as a tenant in common
   c. as a joint tenant
   d. none of these

10. Quentin buys an unfinished house and intends to complete the work himself. He should be concerned with:
    a. whether he has an extended policy of title insurance or merely a standard policy
    b. whether a notice of cessation was filed
    c. whether the seller provided lien waivers from all mechanics and material suppliers
    d. all of these

11. Which of the following is not an encumbrance?
    a. a homestead declaration
    b. a mechanic's lien
    c. an easement
    d. none of these

12. Leroy sells the back half of his 10-acre parcel to Virginia, granting to Virginia a 10-foot right-of-way along the south boundary. Virginia dies 40 years later. Virginia's son decides to build on the

parcel. Leroy's son has recently fenced the entire front portion of his property. Virginia's son asks Leroy's son to remove the fence so he can have access.

    a. Leroy's son should remove the fence.

    b. The son has no right, as the easement is personal.

    c. The easement was lost by 5 years' nonuse.

    d. The easement was lost by 20 years' nonuse.

13. A homestead cannot be obtained by a(n):

    a. unmarried person

    b. husband on a vacant 10-acre parcel

    c. wife without her husband's permission

    d. person over 65 years of age

14. Action for removal of a permanent encroachment must be taken:

    a. against the original encroacher

    b. within 3 years of the encroachment

    c. within 10 years of the encroachment

    d. none of these

15. Jackie cleans and grades a lot for construction. The lot owner then obtains a loan and builds. Troy, a painter, is the last one to finish the job and is unpaid.

    a. Troy may obtain a lien for his services, but it would be secondary to the lender's lien.

    b. Troy has no lien on the property.

    c. If Troy files a lien, his rights are superior to those of the lender.

    d. Troy may not obtain a lien if he does not complete work within 90 days of the start of the job.

16. Darrell sells Emily a farm, reserving the mineral rights. Darrell wishes to tap a pool of oil under the middle of the farm.

    a. Darrell has an implied easement to enter and drill.

    b. Darrell can take oil only by slant-drilling from a point outside the land.

    c. Darrell cannot get the oil unless, coupled with the oil rights, he has an easement to drill through or enter the land.

    d. None of these are true.

17. Once a person files a homestead, he or she is protected against:

    a. prior unsecured creditors who have recorded judgments

    b. prior secured creditors

    c. subsequent claims by mechanics for work on the property

    d. none of these

18. Anne gives an easement over her land to Boris so Boris can get to his land. The easement is recorded. Boris then buys Anne's land and sells it to Carole, making no mention of the easement. Boris does not use the easement for five years; but when he later wishes to use it, Carole objects.

    a. Carole must allow Boris access.

    b. The easement was lost by five years' nonuse.

    c. The easement was lost when Boris purchased Anne's land.

    d. None of these are true.

19. A covenant in Norman's deed prohibits him from keeping more than three dogs. Norman builds a commercial kennel. His neighbor would most likely:

    a. cause Norman to forfeit his property

    b. sue Norman for damages because of the effect on the value of his property

    c. obtain an injunction

    d. have criminal charges brought against Norman

20. Homesteaded property is sold by court order. The first disbursement would be:

    a. cash in the amount of the homestead exemption to the principal owner

    b. to the unsecured creditors who forced the sale

    c. to the holder of the senior encumbrance secured by the home

    d. equal distribution to the creditors based on the dollar value of their claims

21. CC&Rs are most likely to be found in:

    a. deeds

    b. easements

    c. zoning

    d. homestead declarations

22. An unrecorded homestead declaration is:
   a. illegal   b. valid   c. voidable   d. void

23. Land having a servient tenement has:
   a. an encumbrance   c. an appurtenance
   b. a cloud on its title   d. none of these

24. A wife files a declaration of homestead on community property as head of the family without her husband's knowledge or consent.
   a. The declaration of homestead is good.
   b. The declaration applies to only half of the property.
   c. The declaration would protect her only to $50,000, since she was not, in fact, the head of the household.
   d. The declaration is void.

25. Deed restrictions are created by:
   a. zoning   c. county or city planning commissions
   b. grantors   d. all of these

26. A valid mechanic's lien by an electrical contractor must be:
   a. acknowledged and recorded   c. made by a licensed contractor
   b. verified and recorded   d. both b and c

27. A person can lose his or her homestead by:
   a. leaving the state   c. selling it
   b. renting it to tenants   d. any of these

28. A lien that covers all the property of a person is:
   a. a specific lien   c. a general lien
   b. a mechanic's lien   d. none of these

29. A search of records would always show:
   a. a grant deed   c. zoning
   b. a mechanic's lien   d. easements

30. An easement by prescription:
   a. can be lost by five years' nonuse
   b. does not require permission
   c. requires five years' open and hostile continuous use under some claim of right
   d. all of these

31. A neighbor feeds pigeons and has attracted hundreds to the area so you are unable to enjoy your patio. An action you might consider would be to ask the court for a(n):
   a. replevin   b. writ of execution   c. injunction   d. attachment

32. Which of the following is spelled wrong?
   a. appurtenance   b. devisee   c. encumbrence   d. acknowledgment

33. Generally, the final payment on a construction loan would be given to the builder on:
   a. occupancy   c. the date specified in the loan
   b. acceptance   d. the expiration of the lien period

34. To remove an easement, the servient tenement holder could:
   a. obtain a quitclaim deed from the holder of the dominant tenement
   b. sell by quitclaim deed
   c. sell the property without reference to the easement
   d. all of these

35. Six inches of the eaves of José's new house hang over his neighbor's land. This is:
   a. an encroachment   c. an appurtenance
   b. an easement by prescription   d. an encumbrance to the neighbor's land

36. A man is injured in his neighbor's swimming pool. He sues the neighbor for negligence and obtains a lien. The lien is:
   a. a specific lien   c. both a and b
   b. a mechanic's lien   d. neither a nor b

37. Deed restrictions based on race are:
    a. illegal
    b. voidable
    c. valid if there is no state law to the contrary
    d. void

38. As to encumbrances, which of the following is true?
    a. Encumbrances do not affect value.
    b. Beneficial restrictions can be encumbrances.
    c. All encumbrances must be recorded.
    d. None of these.

39. Restrictions binding all owners in a subdivision cannot be placed by:
    a. the owner of a subdivision unilaterally prior to first sale
    b. agreement by the majority of owners in the absence of any agreement
    c. agreement of all owners
    d. none of these

40. A lien on property can be created by:
    a. an easement
    b. a zoning restriction
    c. a restrictive covenant
    d. an improver of property for the value of his or her improvements

41. Angela files a declaration of homestead as head of a household on a house. The house burns to the ground. Angela rebuilds the house for rental purposes. Brent obtains a judgment against Angela for $20,000. The house is free of encumbrances and is worth $75,000.
    a. Brent cannot force sale of the house.
    b. If Angela fails to refile, the homestead is lost.
    c. The homestead is lost because it is now rental property.
    d. Destruction of property destroys the homestead rights.

42. To get rid of a nuisance, a homeowner would ask a court for a(n):
    a. abatement
    b. attachment
    c. execution
    d. judgment

43. Rhonda's lawn is dug up by a pipeline company that obtained an easement from a previous owner (two years ago). Although it was recorded, she was never told about it. The easement:
    a. has expired because of the Statute of Limitations
    b. is void as to subsequent purchasers
    c. is void since there has been no notification
    d. is valid

44. Gilbert would post a notice of nonresponsibility if:
    a. his wife brings action for dissolution
    b. his tenant makes repairs
    c. he no longer wishes to be bound by an instrument
    d. he wishes to be protected against claims of trespassers

45. A subcontractor must file his or her lien within _____ days if there is no notice of completion:
    a. 15   b. 30   c. 60   d. 90

46. The difference between mechanic's liens and judgment liens is:
    a. mechanic's liens must be recorded to be valid
    b. a mechanic's lien that is not enforced within a particular period of time is lost
    c. mechanic's liens are based upon statutory rights
    d. none of these

47. An easement created by reservation:
    a. is not lost by nonuse
    b. has no time limitation unless stated
    c. neither a nor b
    d. both a and b

48. The phrase "to be recorded it must be verified" refers to a:
    a. trust deed   b. judgment   c. mechanic's lien   d. grant deed

49. The priority of mechanic's liens over trust deeds in foreclosure situations would be determined by:
    a. date and time of recording
    b. date of completion of work
    c. date of commencement of work
    d. none of these

50. An easement that is personal would be:
    a. an appurtenance
    b. a license
    c. an easement by necessity
    d. an easement in gross

51. To obtain an easement by prescription, one must:
    a. live on the property
    b. live on and use the property
    c. use the property
    d. none of these

52. As to restrictions, which of the following is true?
    a. Zoning restrictions are public restrictions.
    b. Restrictive covenants are private restrictions.
    c. Restrictions may be created by a subdivider.
    d. all of these

53. A person may not file a declaration of homestead if:
    a. the property is encumbered
    b. his or her spouse refuses to sign
    c. the premises are not occupied at the time of filing
    d. the value is more than $100,000

54. An easement by prescription would be lost by:
    a. nonuse for five years
    b. merger of ownership of the easement and property interests
    c. a quitclaim deed granted by the holder to the servient tenement owner
    d. all of these

55. As to easements, which of the following is false?
    a. Easements must be recorded for the holder to have any rights against subsequent purchasers.
    b. All easements are encumbrances, yet not all encumbrances are easements.
    c. An easement doesn't necessarily run forever.
    d. all of these

56. A property owner pays a general contractor in full and files a notice of completion.
    a. There is no possibility of a mechanic's lien.
    b. The owner should have filed a notice of nonresponsibility.
    c. The owner should have filed a notice of cessation of work.
    d. Unpaid subcontractors, workers, and materials suppliers can file their liens up to 30 days after the owner files a notice of completion.

57. After filing notice of completion, a property owner should wait _____ days before paying the prime contractor.
    a. 15   b. 30   c. 60   d. 90

58. The homestead declaration of a 70-year-old single woman living alone would protect her property up to:
    a. $50,000   b. $60,000   c. $75,000   d. $125,000

59. Ralph sold his homestead without filing a declaration of abandonment. He then filed a homestead declaration on another home. The second homestead was:
    a. illegal   b. unenforceable   c. void   d. valid

60. A homestead was inadvertently filed in the wrong county. The:
    a. homestead is still valid
    b. homestead declaration is void
    c. owner has 60 days to correct the filing
    d. owner has 90 days to correct the filing

61. Which of the following is not a conservation easement?
    a. a solar easement
    b. a prohibition against future development
    c. a requirement that the land remain in its present state
    d. a negative easement that prohibits a landowner from change in land use

62. Alex uses Barbara's land continuously and exclusively for 30 years, with Barbara's permission.
    a. Alex can get title by quiet title action.
    b. Alex can get an easement by quiet title action.
    c. Both a and b are true.
    d. Neither a nor b is true.

63. Mechanic's liens are based on:
    a. the California Civil Code
    b. common law
    c. the Real Estate Law
    d. federal law

64. The easement of a utility company that prohibits a property owner from building over a gas line would be:
    a. personal and affirmative
    b. in gross and negative
    c. in gross and affirmative
    d. appurtenant and affirmative

65. Restrictive covenants based on which of the following would be most difficult to enforce?
    a. square-foot minimum
    b. lot size
    c. value of improvements
    d. height restrictions

66. Henry has the right to cross Kate's land to get to his home. He most likely has:
    a. a license
    b. a dominant tenement
    c. a servient tenement
    d. an easement in gross

67. The maximum possible homestead exemption that a person can claim, would be:
    a. $50,000   b. $75,000   c. $100,000   d. $125,000

68. The sheriff's seizure of property prior to a judgment is known as:
    a. a seizure action
    b. a sheriff's execution
    c. an attachment
    d. a prejudgment levy

69. An attachment is a lien on property for:
    a. forever
    b. 10 years
    c. 3 years from the date of levy
    d. 90 days

70. Which of the following is the proper order of events?
    a. execution, judgment, attachment
    b. judgment, attachment, execution
    c. attachment, judgment, execution
    d. judgment, execution, attachment

71. Which of the following would be an encumbrance?
    a. mechanic's lien
    b. trust deed
    c. restrictive covenant
    d. all of the above

72. While a person does not have an estate, she has the right to use property of another. She would have a(n):
    a. license
    b. lease
    c. easement
    d. nonfreehold interest

73. A deed provided for an easement for access but failed to locate the easement. In this case:
    a. the deed is invalid
    b. the deed is valid but there is no easement
    c. the servient tenement holder can specify a particular area
    d. the dominant tenement holder can use any area for access

74. A 90-year-old, low-income, single, totally disabled homeowner filed a homestead exemption. His maximum exemption would be:
    a. $50,000
    b. $75,000
    c. $125,000
    d. $375,000

75. Albert filed a homestead exemption, then built an addition to his house. Albert did not pay Baker, his contractor. If Baker files a lien:
    a. the lien would be unenforceable because of the homestead exemption
    b. the lien is enforceable only if the value of the property exceeds the homestead exemption
    c. the lien is enforceable
    d. the lien cannot be foreclosed but remains until the property can be sold

ANSWERS—CHAPTER 3 QUIZ

1. c. Since there is no dominant tenement.
2. b. Unless the period for filing has expired.
3. d. Contractors must be licensed.
4. a. David's $71,000 equity is protected by his $75,000 exemption. He has six months to invest the sale proceeds in another homestead.
5. d. They go with the land.
6. a. Wendell has $40,000 equity and a $50,000 exemption.
7. b. Recorded by the developer and referenced in deeds.
8. c. Sheila is an innocent improver.
9. d. Can file regardless of form of ownership.
10. d.
11. a.
12. a. An easement by grant is not lost by nonuse.
13. b. Must reside on the property.
14. b. After that period, it can remain.
15. c. All liens go back to the commencement of work.
16. a.
17. d. A homestead protects against unsecured liens.
18. c. Lost by merger.
19. c. An order to cease.
20. c. Secured creditors are paid first.
21. a. Covenants, conditions, and restrictions.

22. d. Homesteads, judgments, and mechanic's liens must be recorded.
23. a. Subject to use by another.
24. a.
25. b. In their grants.
26. d.
27. c. A homestead is lost by sale.
28. c. Such as a judgment lien.
29. b. Must be recorded.
30. d.
31. c. To cease the activity.
32. c.
33. d.
34. a. Which gives up all rights.
35. a.
36. d. A judgment is a general lien.
37. d. They have no effect.
38. b. Such as CC&Rs.
39. b. All must agree.
40. d. Mechanic's lien.
41. a. The homestead is still valid.
42. a. Abate a nuisance.
43. d. It goes with the land.
44. b. Within 10 days of discovery.
45. d. If there is a notice of completion—30 days.
46. c. Judgments are based on court decision.
47. d.
48. c. The lienholder swears to the truth of the facts.
49. c. All go back to the first work.
50. d. It doesn't go with the land.

51. c. The person does not have to occupy the property.
52. d.
53. c.
54. d.
55. a. An easement by prescription is not recorded.
56. d.
57. b. Subcontractors have 30 days to file.
58. d. Over 65.
59. d. The sale ended the original homestead.
60. b. Same as not recorded.
61. a.
62. d. Alex has a license.
63. a. Statutory law.
64. b. It has no dominant tenement and is prohibitive.
65. c. Might be subjective.
66. b. Since he has a right.
67. d. Over 65.
68. c.
69. c.
70. c.
71. d.
72. c. A right; a license is a privilege.
73. c. Must be reasonable.
74. c. Maximum exemption.
75. c. Homestead does not protect against voluntary liens.

4

Real Estate Agency

AGENCY

An **agency** is a contractual relationship in which an **agent** acts as a representative of a **principal.** An agency can be created in several ways:

Expressly, by a written or verbal statement. In real estate, the agency is normally created by a listing agreement.

By **implication,** where an agency is implied by the actions of the parties.

By **ratification,** where the principal approves a previously unauthorized act.

By **estoppel,** by which a party will not be allowed to deny that an agency existed if his or her words or actions caused another person to act to his or her detriment on the belief that an agency existed. Such an agent would be an **ostensible agent.** (An **express agent** would have been expressly appointed.)

The principal is liable for the acts and torts of the agent or employee committed within the course of an agency. (A **tort** is a wrongful injury.) The principal is not liable for acts or torts of independent contractors. (An **independent contractor** is distinguished from an agent in that the principal exercises no control over the acts of the independent contractor.)

Power of Attorney

This is a written agency whereby a person authorizes another to act for him or her. A person acting under a power of attorney is said to be an **attorney-in-fact.** A **general power of attorney** allows an attorney-in-fact to do anything the principal could do, whereas a **specific power of attorney** is for specified acts only.

Equal Dignities Rule

If the **Statute of Frauds** requires an act to be in writing, then the appointment of an agent to perform the act must also be in writing. (Buying or selling real property must be in writing, so the appointment of an agent or listing must, therefore, be in writing.)

Broker as Agent

The broker may represent the seller or buyer exclusively or have a **dual agency** representing both seller and buyer. The broker's primary duty is to his or her principal; however, the broker also has a duty to other parties of full and honest disclosure of any detrimental facts known.

The real estate salespeople are generally regarded as employees of the broker (despite contracts that might provide otherwise). Salespersons have duties to the principal equivalent to the duties owed by the real estate broker. Each salesperson is required to have a contract with his or her broker. The broker's duty to supervise salespeople includes establishing policies, rules and procedures, and systems of review; overseeing; and managing. While a broker may use other salespersons or brokers within his or her office to help supervise salespeople, the broker bears the responsibility for supervision. Formerly the broker had five days to review instruments prepared by a salesperson. This has been replaced by a reasonable supervision policy.

Real estate contracts specifying that salespeople are independent contractors are used because the IRS will treat salespeople as independent contractors and relieve the broker of withholding taxes and contributing to Social Security if:

1. The salesperson is properly licensed.
2. Pay is related to sales success, not to hours worked.
3. There is a written contract stating that the salesperson shall be treated as an independent contractor for tax purposes.

The IRS treatment of salespersons as independent contractors does not change the employer/employee relationship recognized by the Department of Real Estate or agency responsibilities.

Unemployment Insurance Contributions by the employer for unemployment benefits. (Real estate brokers and salespeople paid by commission are exempt.)

Workers' Compensation Paid by the employer. This fund provides weekly benefits to employees unable to work because of job-related injuries or illness. It also pays medical expenses.

Types of Agency

Three types of broker agency are possible:

1. **Seller's Agent.** Represents the seller only. A property listing agent as well as the selling agent can elect to be solely a seller's agent.
2. **Dual Agent.** Representing both buyer and seller. Both the listing agent and the selling agent can separately elect to be dual agents with agency duties to both parties.
3. **Buyer's Agent.** A selling agent can elect to be a buyer's agent only. A listing agent has a duty to the seller so cannot elect to be a buyer's agent.

Even though a broker may not have agency duties to a party to a transaction, the broker still would have a duty of fair and honest dealing.

Agency Representation Disclosure

If an agent leads a purchaser to believe that he or she is being represented by that agent, then the agent could be held to have full agency responsibilities to both buyer and seller. It is not necessary for the agent to be paid by both buyer and seller for a dual agency to exist. To avoid a dual agency, the agent must make certain that the buyer fully understands the representation of the agent if the agent is to be the sole agent of the seller.

A broker who acts for more than one party to a transaction without the knowledge and consent of all parties could be subject to disciplinary action. The contract would also be subject to being voided by a party who did not know of the dual agency. The broker could be required to return commissions received when the seller did not know that the agent also represented the buyer.

The agent is required to provide written and oral disclosure to both buyers and sellers as to agency representation as soon as possible. Prior to making or presenting an offer, the agency elected must be confirmed. (Study the Disclosure Regarding Real Estate Agency Relationships form that is shown.)

Agency disclosure is a three-step process:

1. **Disclosure** of agency relationships that are possible.
2. **Elect** This is the decision as to the type of agency elected by the parties.
3. **Confirm** This is the written confirmation of the election. It is usually part of the purchase contract. Confirmation must be given and agreed to by both buyer and seller.

Fiduciary Responsibility

Both the broker and the salesperson have a fiduciary responsibility to the owner. This is a responsibility of financial trust that requires good-faith dealing.

1. The broker must inform the owner of all pertinent facts concerning the property as he or she becomes aware of them.
2. The broker must not make any **secret profit.**
3. The broker must act in the principal's best interest.

CALIFORNIA ASSOCIATION OF REALTORS®

DISCLOSURE REGARDING REAL ESTATE AGENCY RELATIONSHIPS

(As required by the Civil Code)
(C.A.R. Form AD-11, Revised 10/01)

When you enter into a discussion with a real estate agent regarding a real estate transaction, you should from the outset understand what type of agency relationship or representation you wish to have with the agent in the transaction.

SELLER'S AGENT

A Seller's agent under a listing agreement with the Seller acts as the agent for the Seller only. A Seller's agent or a subagent of that agent has the following affirmative obligations:
To the Seller:
    A Fiduciary duty of utmost care, integrity, honesty, and loyalty in dealings with the Seller.
To the Buyer and the Seller:
    (a) Diligent exercise of reasonable skill and care in performance of the agent's duties.
    (b) A duty of honest and fair dealing and good faith.
    (c) A duty to disclose all facts known to the agent materially affecting the value or desirability of the property that are not known to, or within the diligent attention and observation of, the parties.

An agent is not obligated to reveal to either party any confidential information obtained from the other party that does not involve the affirmative duties set forth above.

BUYER'S AGENT

A selling agent can, with a Buyer's consent, agree to act as agent for the Buyer only. In these situations, the agent is not the Seller's agent, even if by agreement the agent may receive compensation for services rendered, either in full or in part from the Seller. An agent acting only for a Buyer has the following affirmative obligations:
To the Buyer:
    A fiduciary duty of utmost care, integrity, honesty, and loyalty in dealings with the Buyer.
To the Buyer and the Seller:
    (a) Diligent exercise of reasonable skill and care in performance of the agent's duties.
    (b) A duty of honest and fair dealing and good faith.
    (c) A duty to disclose all facts known to the agent materially affecting the value or desirability of the property that are not known to, or within the diligent attention and observation of, the parties.

An agent is not obligated to reveal to either party any confidential information obtained from the other party that does not involve the affirmative duties set forth above.

AGENT REPRESENTING BOTH SELLER AND BUYER

A real estate agent, either acting directly or through one or more associate licensees, can legally be the agent of both the Seller and the Buyer in a transaction, but only with the knowledge and consent of both the Seller and the Buyer.

In a dual agency situation, the agent has the following affirmative obligations to both the Seller and the Buyer:
    (a) A fiduciary duty of utmost care, integrity, honesty and loyalty in the dealings with either the Seller or the Buyer.
    (b) Other duties to the Seller and the Buyer as stated above in their respective sections.

In representing both Seller and Buyer, the agent may not, without the express permission of the respective party, disclose to the other party that the Seller will accept a price less than the listing price or that the Buyer will pay a price greater than the price offered.

The above duties of the agent in a real estate transaction do not relieve a Seller or Buyer from the responsibility to protect his or her own interests. You should carefully read all agreements to assure that they adequately express your understanding of the transaction. A real estate agent is a person qualified to advise about real estate. If legal or tax advice is desired, consult a competent professional.

Throughout your real property transaction you may receive more than one disclosure form, depending upon the number of agents assisting in the transaction. The law requires each agent with whom you have more than a casual relationship to present you with this disclosure form. You should read its contents each time it is presented to you, considering the relationship between you and the real estate agent in your specific transaction.

This disclosure form includes the provisions of Sections 2079.13 to 2079.24, inclusive, of the Civil Code set forth on the reverse hereof. Read it carefully.

I/WE ACKNOWLEDGE RECEIPT OF A COPY OF THIS DISCLOSURE.

BUYER/SELLER _____ Date _____ Time _____ AM/PM

BUYER/SELLER _____ Date _____ Time _____ AM/PM

AGENT _____ By _____ Date _____
           (Please Print)   (Associate-Licensee or Broker Signature)

THIS FORM SHALL BE PROVIDED AND ACKNOWLEDGED AS FOLLOWS (Civil Code §2079.14):
•When the listing brokerage company also represents the Buyer, the Listing Agent shall give one AD-11 form to the Seller and one to the Buyer.
•When Buyer and Seller are represented by different brokerage companies, then the Listing Agent shall give one AD-11 form to the Seller and the Buyer's Agent shall give one AD-11 form to the Buyer and one AD-11 form to the Seller.

SEE REVERSE SIDE FOR FURTHER INFORMATION

Published and Distributed by:
R E B S **I N C** REAL ESTATE BUSINESS SERVICES, INC.
a subsidiary of the CALIFORNIA ASSOCIATION OF REALTORS®
525 South Virgil Avenue, Los Angeles, California 90020

Reviewed by _____
Broker or Designee _____ Date _____

EQUAL HOUSING OPPORTUNITY

AD-11 REVISED 10/01 (PAGE 1 OF 1)   **Print Date**

Reprinted with permission, CALIFORNIA ASSOCIATION OF REALTORS®. Endorsement not implied.

CHAPTER 2 OF TITLE 9 OF PART 4 OF DIVISION 3 OF THE CIVIL CODE

2079.13 As used in Sections 2079.14 to 2079.24, inclusive, the following terms have the following meanings: **(a)** "Agent" means a person acting under provisions of title 9 (commencing with Section 2295) in a real property transaction, and includes a person who is licensed as a real estate broker under Chapter 3 (commencing with Section 10130) of Part 1 of Division 4 of the Business and Professions Code, and under whose license a listing is executed or an offer to purchase is obtained. **(b)** "Associate licensee" means a person who is licensed as a real broker or salesperson under Chapter 3 (commencing with Section 10130) of Part 1 of Division 4 of the Business and Professions Code and who is either licensed under a broker or has entered into a written contract with a broker to act as the broker's agent in connection with acts requiring a real estate license and to function under the broker's supervision in the capacity of an associate licensee. The agent in the real property transaction bears responsibility for his or her associate licensees who perform as agents of the agent. When an associate licensee owes a duty to any principal, or to any buyer or seller who is not a principal, in a real property transaction, that duty is equivalent to the duty owed to that party by the broker for whom the associate licensee functions. **(c)** "Buyer" means a transferee in a real property transaction, and includes a person who executes an offer to purchase real property from a seller through an agent, or who seeks the services of an agent in more than a casual, transitory, or preliminary manner, with the object of entering into a real property transaction. "Buyer" includes vendee or lessee. **(d)** "Dual agent" means an agent acting, either directly or through an associate licensee, as agent for both the seller and the buyer in a real property transaction. **(e)** "Listing agreement" means a contract between an owner of real property and an agent, by which the agent has been authorized to sell the real property or to find or obtain a buyer. **(f)** "Listing agent" means a person who has obtained a listing of real property to act as an agent for compensation. **(g)** "Listing price" is the amount expressed in dollars specified in the listing for which the seller is willing to sell the real property through the listing agent. **(h)** "Offering price" is the amount expressed in dollars specified in an offer to purchase for which the buyer is willing to buy the real property. **(i)** "Offer to purchase" means a written contract executed by a buyer acting through a selling agent which becomes the contract for the sale of the real property upon acceptance by the seller. **(j)** "Real property" means any estate specified by subdivision (1) or (2) of Section 761 in property which constitutes, or is improved with one to four dwelling units, any leasehold in this type of property exceeding one year's duration, and mobilehomes, when offered for sale or sold through an agent pursuant to the authority contained in Section 10131.6 of the Business and Professions Code. **(k)** "Real property transaction" means a transaction for the sale of real property in which an agent is employed by one or more of the principals to act in that transaction, and includes a listing or an offer to purchase. **(l)** "Sell," "sale," or "sold" refers to a transaction for the transfer of real property from the seller to the buyer, and includes exchanges of real property between the seller and buyer, transactions for the creation of a real property sales contract within the meaning of Section 2985, and transactions for the creation of a leasehold exceeding one year's duration. **(m)** "Seller" means the transferor in a real property transaction, and includes an owner who lists real property with an agent, whether or not a transfer results, or who receives an offer to purchase real property of which he or she is the owner from an agent on behalf of another. "Seller" includes both a vendor and a lessor. **(n)** "Selling agent" means a listing agent who acts alone, or an agent who acts in cooperation with a listing agent, and who sells or finds and obtains a buyer for the real property, or an agent who locates property for a buyer or who finds a buyer for a property for which no listing exists and presents an offer to purchase to the seller. **(o)** "Subagent" means a person to whom an agent delegates agency powers as provided in Article 5 (commencing with Section 2349) of Chapter 1 of Title 9. However, "subagent" does not include an associate licensee who is acting under the supervision of an agent in a real property transaction.

2079.14 Listing agents and selling agents shall provide the seller and buyer in a real property transaction with a copy of the disclosure form specified in Section 2079.16, and, except as provided in subdivision (c), shall obtain a signed acknowledgement of receipt from that seller or buyer, except as provided in this section or Section 2079.15, as follows: **(a)** The listing agent, if any, shall provide the disclosure form to the seller prior to entering into the listing agreement. **(b)** The selling agent shall provide the disclosure form to the seller as soon as practicable prior to presenting the seller with an offer to purchase, unless the selling agent previously provided the seller with a copy of the disclosure form pursuant to subdivision (a). **(c)** Where the selling agent does not deal on a face-to-face basis with the seller, the disclosure form prepared by the selling agent may be furnished to the seller (and acknowledgment of receipt obtained for the selling agent from the seller) by the listing agent, or the selling agent may deliver the disclosure form by certified mail addressed to the seller at his or her last known address, in which case no signed acknowledgement of receipt is required. **(d)** The selling agent shall provide the disclosure form to the buyer as soon as practicable prior to execution of the buyer's offer to purchase, except that if the offer to purchase is not prepared by the selling agent, the selling agent shall present the disclosure form to the buyer not later than the next business day after the selling agent receives the offer to purchase from the buyer.

2079.15 In any circumstance in which the seller or buyer refuses to sign an acknowledgement of receipt pursuant to Section 2079.14, the agent, or an associate licensee acting for an agent, shall set forth, sign, and date a written declaration of the facts of the refusal.

2079.17 (a) As soon as practicable, the selling agent shall disclose to the buyer and seller whether the selling agent is acting in the real property transaction exclusively as the buyer's agent, exclusively as the seller's agent, or as a dual agent representing both the buyer and the seller. This relationship shall be confirmed in the contract to purchase and sell real property or in a separate writing executed or acknowledged by the seller, the buyer, and the selling agent prior to or coincident with execution of that contract by the buyer and the seller, respectively. **(b)** As soon as practicable, the listing agent shall disclose to the seller whether the listing agent is acting in the real property transaction exclusively as the seller's agent, or as a dual agent representing both the buyer and seller. This relationship shall be confirmed in the contract to purchase and sell real property or in a separate writing executed or acknowledged by the seller and the listing agent prior to or coincident with the execution of that contract by the seller.
(c) The confirmation required by subdivisions (a) and (b) shall be in the following form:

_____ is the agent of (check one): ☐ the seller exclusively; or ☐ both the buyer and seller.
(Name of Listing Agent)

_____ is the agent of (check one): ☐ the buyer exclusively; or ☐ the seller exclusively; or
(Name of Selling Agent if not the same as the Listing Agent)   ☐ both the buyer and seller.

(d) The disclosures and confirmation required by this section shall be in addition to the disclosure required by Section 2079. 14.

2079.18 No selling agent in a real property transaction may act as an agent for the buyer only, when the selling agent is also acting as the listing agent in the transaction.

2079.19 The payment of compensation or the obligation to pay compensation to an agent by the seller or buyer is not necessarily determinative of a particular agency relationship between an agent and the seller or buyer. A listing agent and a selling agent may agree to share any compensation or commission paid, or any right to any compensation or commission for which an obligation arises as the result of a real estate transaction, and the terms of any such agreement shall not necessarily be determinative of a particular relationship.

2079.20 Nothing in this article prevents an agent from selecting, as a condition of the agent's employment, a specific form of agency relationship not specifically prohibited by this article if the requirements of Section 2079.14 and Section 2079.17 are complied with.

2079.21 A dual agent shall not disclose to the buyer that the seller is willing to sell the property at a price less than the listing price, without the express written consent of the seller. A dual agent shall not disclose to the seller that the buyer is willing to pay a price greater than the offering price, without the express written consent of the buyer. This section does not alter in any way the duty or responsibility of a dual agent to any principal with respect to confidential information other than price.

2079.22 Nothing in this article precludes a listing agent from also being a selling agent, and the combination of these functions in one agent does not, of itself, make that agent a dual agent.

2079.23 A contract between the principal and agent may be modified or altered to change the agency relationship at any time before the performance of the act which is the object of the agency with the written consent of the parties to the agency relationship.

2079.24 Nothing in this article shall be construed to either diminish the duty of disclosure owed buyers and sellers by agents and their associate licensees, subagents, and employees or to relieve agents and their associate licensees, subagents, and employees from liability for their conduct in connection with acts governed by this article or for any breach of a fiduciary duty or a duty of disclosure.

4. The broker must present all offers received to the principal.

5. The broker cannot represent more than one party to the transaction without the consent of all parties.

Subagency

When the seller authorizes an agent to work with other agents, these other agents may elect to be subagents of the owner in seeking buyers for the property. A subagent owes the same fiduciary duties to the owner as the listing agent.

Licensee as a Principal

Since licensees are presumed to be acting as agents, if they act as principals they must notify any party they deal with that they are licensees acting as principals.

If a buyer is a licensee and shares in the commission, the licensee would be acting in an agency capacity and would have a duty of full disclosure to the seller.

Liability of Agent

If the owner supplies the broker with false information and the broker repeats the information to the buyer, then the broker is not liable to the buyer unless he or she knew or ought to have known that the information was false. (Although only the seller would be liable, the buyer would normally sue both the seller and the broker.) Of course the agent is liable for all of his or her wrongful acts. The agent is personally liable if the agent exceeds the agency authority.

Trust Funds

Deposits received by a broker acting as an agent may be handled in one of three ways. By the third business day following receipt, they must either be:

1. Deposited into a trust account (on the third business day following receipt).
2. Given to the principal.
3. Deposited directly into escrow.

A broker may hold a deposit check uncashed in the following circumstances:

1. Under written instructions of the buyer prior to acceptance.
2. Under written instructions of the seller after acceptance. When the broker receives a deposit, he or she is doing so for his or her principal. If a broker returns a buyer's deposit to the buyer without the principal's consent, he or she could be liable to the principal.

Trust Accounts

It is not always necessary for a broker to have a trust account. Deposits could be made out directly to his or her principal or to an escrow. However, if the broker does have a trust account:

1. The account must be open for inspection.

2. The broker must keep columnar or cash receipt and cash disbursement journals of each beneficiary and transaction (showing dates, check numbers, etc.). The trust account record includes checks made out directly to escrow or the title company that are never deposited in the account as well as checks held uncashed. Records may be maintained on computers. Journals need not be maintained for checks of $1,000 or less that are received but made out directly to service providers.

3. The account must be balanced daily.

4. The broker must **reconcile** the trust account with his or her bank statement monthly.

5. Separate records must be kept of each beneficiary and transaction.

6. Deposits must be placed in the trust account within three business days of receipt.

The broker must retain his or her records (copies of listings, deposit receipts, canceled checks, trust account records, etc.) for three years. The broker may keep up to $200 of his or her own funds in the trust account (to cover check fees, etc.); there is no minimum amount required. Earned commissions may remain in the trust account no longer than 30 days.

If requested by the principal, trust money may be kept in a federally insured interest-bearing account. Trust accounts for taxes and insurance for one to four residential units may also be kept in insured interest-bearing accounts. Other trust accounts must be demand accounts (no interest and no notice required for withdrawal). The broker may not benefit by interest received; it belongs to the person owning the funds.

A real estate broker may not disburse trust funds without the written consent of all owners of funds in the account if the disbursement will reduce the balance in the trust account below the liability of the broker to all other fund owners in the trust account. (This would preclude the broker from returning a deposit from the trust account when the deposit had not cleared the bank.)

If two or more parties claim entitlement to trust funds, a broker could commence an **interpleader action,** asking the court to decide. Withdrawals from the trust account may be made by a person other than the broker, with the broker's approval. If the person is not a licensee, then that person must be bonded. For a corporate broker, withdrawals from the trust fund require the signature of the broker through whom the corporation is licensed.

A broker who mixes personal funds with deposits received is guilty of **commingling.** A broker who appropriates deposits for his or her own use is guilty of **conversion.** A broker may not withhold trust funds as an offset against another debt owed him or her by the owner or buyer.

Duty to Purchaser

In the case of *Easton* v. *Strassburger* (Court of Appeals, 1984), the court held that an agent has an affirmative duty to find out detrimental facts and make those facts known to the purchaser (the decision applies to one to four residential units). The legislature has limited the duty to a visual inspection of accessible areas. It does not include off-site areas or public records. The legislature has also set a statute of limitations of two years from close of escrow to bring action against an agent.

The agent should be watchful for **red flags,** which are indications of a possible problem. As an example, watermarks on a ceiling could indicate a roof leak, and cracks in the foundation or walls and floors that are not level could indicate structural problems.

An agent need not disclose the fact that a resident of the property was infected with or died of AIDS. After three years, an agent need not disclose the cause of death of a prior occupant from any other cause (such as murder or suicide). If a buyer directly asks about any known death or case of AIDS concerning a property, the agent should be truthful. An agent need not disclose the location of a residential group home for one to six persons.

Sellers also have a duty of disclosure. A seller of one to four residential units (including mobile homes) must provide the buyer with a written disclosure of the defects (Real Estate Transfer Disclosure Statement). The form is not required for sales requiring a public report, transfers by court order (probate and bankruptcy sales), foreclosure sales, or sales between co-owners or spouses. Carefully review the Real Estate Transfer Disclosure Statement shown. (Note that this form provides for agent as well as seller disclosure.) The buyer cannot waive the receipt of this form.

"As is" provisions in a purchase contract are not fair to a purchaser unless the purchaser is fully informed as to the condition of a property. For residential sales, the courts will enforce "as is" provisions only if the condition is **patent** (obvious) or the buyer has been fully informed. "As is" provisions will generally not protect sellers and agents if the condition was known and was **latent** or not discoverable by a reasonable inspection of the property.

REAL ESTATE COMMISSION

The principal purpose of the Real Estate Commission is to protect the public. The Real Estate Commissioner, who must have been a broker for five years or have related experience, is appointed by the governor and serves at his or her pleasure. The Department of Real Estate is part of the Business, Transportation, and Housing Agency.

The Real Estate Commissioner appoints a **Real Estate Advisory Commission** to meet and consult with him or her regarding the policies of the Department of Real Estate. The Advisory Commission consists of 10 members, 6 of whom are licensed real estate brokers and 4 of whom are public members. They meet four times a year in different California cities. The Commissioner is the only paid member; others get expenses only.

The Real Estate Commissioner does not make law. Only the state legislature can make law. The Real Estate Law is part of the Business and Professions Code and is an exercise of the **police power** of the state (safety, comfort, health, and morals). The Real Estate Commissioner makes reasonable regulations to enforce the

CALIFORNIA ASSOCIATION OF REALTORS®

REAL ESTATE TRANSFER DISCLOSURE STATEMENT
(CALIFORNIA CIVIL CODE 1102, ET SEQ)
(C.A.R. Form TDS, Revised 10/01)

THIS DISCLOSURE STATEMENT CONCERNS THE REAL PROPERTY SITUATED IN THE CITY OF _____
_____, **COUNTY OF** _____, **STATE OF CALIFORNIA,**
DESCRIBED AS _____.
THIS STATEMENT IS A DISCLOSURE OF THE CONDITION OF THE ABOVE DESCRIBED PROPERTY IN COMPLIANCE WITH SECTION 1102 OF THE CIVIL CODE AS OF (date) _____. **IT IS NOT A WARRANTY OF ANY KIND BY THE SELLER(S) OR ANY AGENT(S) REPRESENTING ANY PRINCIPAL(S) IN THIS TRANSACTION, AND IS NOT A SUBSTITUTE FOR ANY INSPECTIONS OR WARRANTIES THE PRINCIPAL(S) MAY WISH TO OBTAIN.**

I. COORDINATION WITH OTHER DISCLOSURE FORMS

This Real Estate Transfer Disclosure Statement is made pursuant to Section 1102 of the Civil Code. Other statutes require disclosures, depending upon the details of the particular real estate transaction (for example: special study zone and purchase-money liens on residential property).

Substituted Disclosures: The following disclosures have or will be made in connection with this real estate transfer, and are intended to satisfy the disclosure obligations on this form, where the subject matter is the same:

☐ Inspection reports completed pursuant to the contract of sale or receipt for deposit.

☐ Additional inspection reports or disclosures: _____
_____

II. SELLER'S INFORMATION

The Seller discloses the following information with the knowledge that even though this is not a warranty, prospective Buyers may rely on this information in deciding whether and on what terms to purchase the subject property. Seller hereby authorizes any agent(s) representing any principal(s) in this transaction to provide a copy of this statement to any person or entity in connection with any actual or anticipated sale of the property.

THE FOLLOWING ARE REPRESENTATIONS MADE BY THE SELLER(S) AND ARE NOT THE REPRESENTATIONS OF THE AGENT(S), IF ANY. THIS INFORMATION IS A DISCLOSURE AND IS NOT INTENDED TO BE PART OF ANY CONTRACT BETWEEN THE BUYER AND SELLER.

Seller ☐ is ☐ is not occupying the property.

A. The subject property has the items checked below (read across)

☐ Range	☐ Oven	☐ Microwave
☐ Dishwasher	☐ Trash Compactor	☐ Garbage Disposal
☐ Washer/Dryer Hookups		☐ Rain Gutters
☐ Burglar Alarms	☐ Smoke Detector(s)	☐ Fire Alarm
☐ T.V. Antenna	☐ Satellite Dish	☐ Intercom
☐ Central Heating	☐ Central Air Conditioning	☐ Evaporator Cooler(s)
☐ Wall/Window Air Conditioning	☐ Sprinklers	☐ Public Sewer System
☐ Septic Tank	☐ Sump Pump	☐ Water Softener
☐ Patio/Decking	☐ Built-in Barbecue	☐ Gazebo
☐ Sauna		
☐ Hot Tub ☐ Locking Safety Cover*	☐ Pool ☐ Child Resistant Barrier*	☐ Spa ☐ Locking Safety Cover*
☐ Security Gate(s)	☐ Automatic Garage Door Opener(s)*	☐ Number Remote Controls _____
Garage: ☐ Attached	☐ Not Attached	☐ Carport
Pool/Spa Heater: ☐ Gas	☐ Solar	☐ Electric
Water Heater: ☐ Gas	☐ Water Heater Anchored, Braced, or Strapped*	☐ Private Utility or
Water Supply: ☐ City	☐ Well	Other _____
Gas Supply: ☐ Utility	☐ Bottled	
☐ Window Screens	☐ Window Security Bars ☐ Quick Release Mechanism on Bedroom Windows*	

Exhaust Fan(s) in _____ 220 Volt Wiring in _____ Fireplace(s) in _____
☐ Gas Starter _____ ☐ Roof(s): Type: _____ Age: _____ (approx.)
☐ Other: _____

Are there, to the best of your (Seller's) knowledge, any of the above that are not in operating condition? ☐ Yes ☐ No. If yes, then describe. (Attach additional sheets if necessary): _____
_____

(*see footnote on page 2)

Buyer and Seller acknowledge receipt of a copy of this page.

Buyer's Initials (_____)(_____)
Seller's Initials (_____)(_____)

EQUAL HOUSING OPPORTUNITY

Reviewed by _____
Broker or Designee _____ Date _____

TDS-11 REVISED 10/01 (PAGE 1 OF 3) **Print Date**

REAL ESTATE TRANSFER DISCLOSURE STATEMENT (TDS-11 PAGE 1 OF 3)
Reprinted with permission, CALIFORNIA ASSOCIATION OF REALTORS®. Endorsement not implied.

Property Address: _____ Date: _____

B. Are you (Seller) aware of any significant defects/malfunctions in any of the following? ☐ Yes ☐ No. If yes, check appropriate space(s) below.

☐ Interior Walls ☐ Ceilings ☐ Floors ☐ Exterior Walls ☐ Insulation ☐ Roof(s ☐ Windows ☐ Doors ☐ Foundation ☐ Slab(s)
☐ Driveways ☐ Sidewalks ☐ Walls/Fences ☐ Electrical Systems ☐ Plumbing/Sewers/Septics ☐ Other Structural Components
(Describe:_____
_____)
If any of the above is checked, explain. (Attach additional sheets if necessary):_____
_____
_____

*This garage door opener or child resistant pool barrier may not be in compliance with the safety standards relating to automatic reversing devices as set forth in Chapter 12.5 (commencing with Section 19890) of Part 3 of Division 13 of, or with the pool safety standards of Article 2.5 (commencing with Section 115920) of Chapter 5 of Part 10 of Division 104 of, the Health and Safety Code. The water heater may not be anchored, braced, or strapped in accordance with Section 19211 of the Health and Safety Code. Window security bars may not have quick release mechanisms in compliance with the 1995 Edition of the California Building Standards Code.

C. Are you (Seller) aware of any of the following:
1. Substances, materials, or products which may be an environmental hazard such as, but not limited to, asbestos, formaldehyde, radon gas, lead-based paint, mold, fuel or chemical storage tanks, and contaminated soil or water on the subject property . . . . ☐ Yes ☐ No
2. Features of the property shared in common with adjoining landowners, such as walls, fences, and driveways, whose use or responsibility for maintenance may have an effect on the subject property . . . . ☐ Yes ☐ No
3. Any encroachments, easements or similar matters that may affect your interest in the subject property . . . . ☐ Yes ☐ No
4. Room additions, structural modifications or other alterations or repairs made without necessary permits . . . . ☐ Yes ☐ No
5. Room additions, structural modifications, or other alterations or repairs not in compliance with building codes . . . . . . ☐ Yes ☐ No
6. Fill (compacted or otherwise) on the property or any portion thereof . . . . ☐ Yes ☐ No
7. Any settling from any cause, or slippage, sliding, or other soil problems . . . . ☐ Yes ☐ No
8. Flooding, drainage or grading problems . . . . ☐ Yes ☐ No
9. Major damage to the property or any of the structures from fire, earthquake, floods, or landslides . . . . ☐ Yes ☐ No
10. Any zoning violations, nonconforming uses, violations of "setback" requirements . . . . ☐ Yes ☐ No
11. Neighborhood noise problems or other nuisances . . . . ☐ Yes ☐ No
12. CC&R's or other deed restrictions or obligations . . . . ☐ Yes ☐ No
13. Homeowners' Association which has any authority over the subject property . . . . ☐ Yes ☐ No
14. Any "common area" (facilities such as pools, tennis courts, walkways, or other areas co-owned in undivided interest with others) . . . . ☐ Yes ☐ No
15. Any notices of abatement or citations against the property . . . . ☐ Yes ☐ No
16. Any lawsuits by or against the seller threatening to or affecting this real property, including any lawsuits alleging a defect or deficiency in this real property or "common areas" (facilities such as pools, tennis courts, walkways, or other areas, co-owned in undivided interest with others) . . . . ☐ Yes ☐ No

If the answer to any of these is yes, explain. (Attach additional sheets if necessary): _____
_____
_____

Seller certifies that the information herein is true and correct to the best of the Seller's knowledge as of the date signed by the Seller.

Seller_____ Date _____

Seller_____ Date _____

TDS-11 REVISED 10/01 (PAGE 2 OF 3) **Print Date**

Buyer and Seller acknowledge receipt of a copy of this page.
Buyer's Initials (_____)(_____)
Seller's Initials (_____)(_____)

Reviewed by
Broker or Designee _____ Date _____

EQUAL HOUSING OPPORTUNITY

REAL ESTATE TRANSFER DISCLOSURE STATEMENT (TDS-11 PAGE 2 OF 3)

Reprinted with permission, CALIFORNIA ASSOCIATION OF REALTORS®. Endorsement not implied.

Property Address: _____ Date: _____

III. AGENT'S INSPECTION DISCLOSURE
(To be completed only if the Seller is represented by an agent in this transaction.)

THE UNDERSIGNED, BASED ON THE ABOVE INQUIRY OF THE SELLER(S) AS TO THE CONDITION OF THE PROPERTY AND BASED ON A REASONABLY COMPETENT AND DILIGENT VISUAL INSPECTION OF THE ACCESSIBLE AREAS OF THE PROPERTY IN CONJUNCTION WITH THAT INQUIRY, STATES THE FOLLOWING:

☐ Agent notes no items for disclosure.

☐ Agent notes the following items: _____
_____
_____
_____
_____

Agent (Broker Representing Seller) _____ By _____ Date _____
                               (Please Print)   (Associate-License or Broker Signature)

IV. AGENT'S INSPECTION DISCLOSURE
(To be completed only if the agent who has obtained the offer is other than the agent above.)

THE UNDERSIGNED, BASED ON A REASONABLY COMPETENT AND DILIGENT VISUAL INSPECTION OF THE ACCESSIBLE AREAS OF THE PROPERTY, STATES THE FOLLOWING:

☐ Agent notes no items for disclosure.

☐ Agent notes the following items: _____
_____
_____

Agent (Broker Obtaining the Offer) _____ By _____ Date _____
                               (Please Print)   (Associate-License or Broker Signature)

V. BUYER(S) AND SELLER(S) MAY WISH TO OBTAIN PROFESSIONAL ADVICE AND/OR INSPECTIONS OF THE PROPERTY AND TO PROVIDE FOR APPROPRIATE PROVISIONS IN A CONTRACT BETWEEN BUYER AND SELLER(S) WITH RESPECT TO ANY ADVICE/INSPECTIONS/DEFECTS.

I/WE ACKNOWLEDGE RECEIPT OF A COPY OF THIS STATEMENT.

Seller _____ Date _____   Buyer _____ Date _____

Seller _____ Date _____   Buyer _____ Date _____

Agent (Broker Representing Seller) _____ By _____ Date _____
                                                (Associate-License or Broker Signature)

Agent (Broker Obtaining the Offer) _____ By _____ Date _____
                                                (Associate-License or Broker Signature)

SECTION 1102.3 OF THE CIVIL CODE PROVIDES A BUYER WITH THE RIGHT TO RESCIND A PURCHASE CONTRACT FOR AT LEAST THREE DAYS AFTER THE DELIVERY OF THIS DISCLOSURE IF DELIVERY OCCURS AFTER THE SIGNING OF AN OFFER TO PURCHASE. IF YOU WISH TO RESCIND THE CONTRACT, YOU MUST ACT WITHIN THE PRESCRIBED PERIOD.

A REAL ESTATE BROKER IS QUALIFIED TO ADVISE ON REAL ESTATE. IF YOU DESIRE LEGAL ADVICE, CONSULT YOUR ATTORNEY.

REAL ESTATE TRANSFER DISCLOSURE STATEMENT (TDS-11 PAGE 3 OF 3)

Reprinted with permission, CALIFORNIA ASSOCIATION OF REALTORS®. Endorsement not implied.

Real Estate Law. These regulations have the force and effect of law and are part of the California Administrative Code.

The Real Estate Commissioner can investigate complaints and hold formal hearings in accordance with the **Administrative Procedures Act** and can revoke, suspend, or deny a license after such a hearing. He or she can bring an action (injunction) to enjoin acts believed to violate statutes. The first step in a hearing is an **accusation.** Disciplinary actions may be appealed to the courts, but they will be reversed only if they are arbitrary or unreasonable.

The California attorney general is the legal advisor to the Commissioner. When a licensee commits an offense against the law, he or she is prosecuted by the district attorney of the county where the offense was committed. The Real Estate Commissioner has no power to adjudicate commission disputes. Licensees must go to the courts to enforce these agreements.

REAL ESTATE RECOVERY FUND

This fund, a separate account in the Real Estate Fund, is sustained by license fees collected. If a person deals with a licensee and obtains a judgment against the licensee because of fraud, misrepresentation, deceit, or conversion of trust funds, and the judgment is uncollectable, then that person can recover up to $20,000 from the fund (the liability of the fund as to any single transaction is $20,000 and for any one licensee shall not exceed $100,000). If the fund must pay for a licensee, that person's license is automatically suspended and will not be reinstated until the fund is repaid plus interest. Bankruptcy does not discharge the obligation to repay the fund. An illegal alien is not entitled to benefit from the recovery fund.

Disciplinary action may be taken against a licensee for any of the following reasons:

1. Procuring or attempting to procure or renew a license for anyone by fraud.
2. Entering a guilty plea or being found guilty of a crime involving moral turpitude.
3. Publication or false statement concerning business or property offered for sale.
4. Willful violation of the Real Estate Law.
5. Willful use of the term **REALTOR®** by a broker who is not a REALTOR®, or the term **Realtist** by a broker who is not a Realtist.
6. Any action that would have warranted denial of a license application.
7. Demonstrated negligence or incompetence.
8. Failure to supervise salespeople.
9. Violation of confidentiality of information received while serving in a governmental capacity.
10. Any conduct constituting fraud or dishonest dealing.
11. Violation of any terms in an order granting a restricted license.

12. Inducing of panic selling, leasing, or listing based on loss of value, increase in crime, etc., caused by entry into the neighborhood of people of another race, color, religion, ancestry, or national origin.

13. Violation of any provision of the Franchise Investment Law.

14. Violation of any provision of the Corporation Code.

15. Any substantial misrepresentation.

16. Any false promise to influence another.

17. A continued and flagrant course of misrepresentation.

18. Acting for more than one party to a transaction without the knowledge or consent of all parties.

19. Commingling funds.

20. Claiming a fee for an exclusive listing that does not contain a definite termination date.

21. Making a secret profit.

22. Exercising an option to purchase in a listing without full disclosure of profit and written consent of the owner as to the amount of profit.

23. Using a send-out slip without written authorization of the owner.

24. Accepting a referral fee from an escrow agent, title insurer, structural pest control firm, or home protection company.

25. Discrimination based on race, color, sex, religion, ancestry, physical disability, marital status, or national origin in sales, rentals, solicitations, or other dealings relating to sales or rentals.

26. Denial, revocation, or suspension of a real estate license by the licensing agency of another state.

27. Employing or compensating an unlicensed person for acts requiring a real estate license.

28. A final judgment in a civil suit on grounds of fraud, misrepresentation, or deceit.

29. Failure to disclose to the buyer an ownership interest in property being sold, leased, or exchanged.

The penalty for paying a commission to a nonlicensee for services for which a license is required is a fine of up to $100. The penalty for receiving said compensation is a fine of up to $10,000 and/or up to six months in jail. (For a corporation, the fine is up to $50,000.)

Memory Tool $100 give, $10,000 receive, and/or six months in jail. *It is better to give than to receive.*

If licensee is found guilty of making a false statement about anything in real estate, he or she can be find up to $1000 and/or sentenced up to one year in jail.

Action must be initiated within one year of discovery of the licensee's action or within three years from the occurrence unless the act involves fraud, misrepresentation, or a false promise, in which case the time period in which an action must be filed is within one year of the date of discovery or three years of the action, whichever is later.

A licensee delinquent in child support payments will be given 150 days to make arrangements to cure the deficiency. If the licensee fails to do so, the license will be suspended.

Sherman Anti-Trust Act

The Sherman act applies to real estate brokers as well as other businesses. Violations can result in a fine, prison or triple the damages suffered by an injured party.

Violations include:

- **Price Fixing.** Agreements by two or more brokers to set commission rates.
- **Market Allocation.** Agreement among firms to divide a market between them so as not to compete.
- **Group Boycotts.** Agreements among brokers not to cooperate with another broker or business.
- **Tie-In Agreements.** Requirement that in order to obtain desired services the party agree to obtain other goods or services from the service provider. An example would be requiring a buyer to agree to insure a property through the broker's insurance agency as a condition before showing the buyer a property.

CHAPTER 4 QUIZ

1. Use of the term *REALTOR*® by a licensee not authorized to do so could result in:
   a. suit by the National Association of REALTORS®
   b. suspension of license
   c. revocation of license
   d. any of these

2. A property owner suffers a loss because of the fraudulent misrepresentation of a broker. The owner should:
   a. immediately file a claim with the Real Estate Commissioner
   b. immediately file a claim with the Real Estate Education Research and Recovery Fund
   c. sue the broker for damages
   d. none of these

3. Commingling is the reason more licenses are revoked than any other. Which of the following is an example of commingling?
   a. holding a deposit check uncashed prior to acceptance at the direction of the buyer
   b. holding a deposit check uncashed after acceptance at the direction of the seller
   c. holding a deposit check uncashed at your own discretion
   d. all of these

4. A broker who is on the city planning commission tells some friends about an advantageous deal based on confidential plans to change the zoning. The broker does not personally benefit in any way. The broker's action:
   a. is unethical
   b. places his license in jeopardy
   c. both a and b
   d. neither a nor b

5. The Real Estate Commission conducts hearings in accordance with the:
   a. Real Estate Law
   b. Public Procedures Act
   c. Commissioner's regulations
   d. Administrative Procedures Act

6. Under the Business and Professions Code, which of the following is not grounds for revocation of license?
   a. making a single false promise of a character likely to induce a buyer
   b. acting for more than one party to a transaction with the consent of all parties
   c. commingling one's own funds with money of others held by him or her
   d. none of these

7. The first action of the Real Estate Commissioner, prior to disciplinary action against a licensee, would be:
   a. notification to the attorney general
   b. an accusation
   c. suspension of license activity
   d. an injunction

8. The Real Estate Law comes from:
   a. the Real Estate Commissioner
   b. the National Association of Real Estate Brokers
   c. the state legislature
   d. the federal government

9. The Commissioner's regulations:
   a. are the Real Estate Law
   b. have the effect of law
   c. are part of the Corporation Code
   d. must be approved by the governor

10. The Real Estate Law is part of:
    a. the Corporation Code
    b. the Business and Professions Code
    c. the Statute of Limitations
    d. none of these

11. The court decision that requires the agent to make a reasonable visual inspection of the premises is:
    a. *Easton* v. *Strassburger*
    b. *Brown* v. *Board of Education*
    c. *Charley* v. *Vogel*
    d. *Shelley* v. *Kraemer*

12. The maximum amount that a person can recover from the Real Estate Education Research and Recovery Fund after he or she has obtained a judgment against a licensee is:
    a. no limit—the amount of his or her loss
    b. $500
    c. $5,000
    d. $20,000

13. Penny sues a licensee for damages resulting from dishonest conduct in a real estate dealing. The maximum she can collect is:
    a. $5,000
    b. $7,500
    c. $20,000
    d. none of these

14. Commingling is the opposite of:
    a. subrogation
    b. mixing
    c. subordination
    d. separation

15. A real estate broker is guilty of conversion. He or she most likely:
    a. commingled funds
    b. acted for both parties to a transaction without their approval
    c. split his or her commission with an unlicensed party
    d. used trust funds for personal use

16. How long does a broker have to deposit a check received made out to the broker's trust account?
    a. 24 hours
    b. one business day
    c. two business days
    d. three business days

17. A property owner tells the broker that the house is connected to the sewer. The broker relays this information to the buyer, who later finds that the house has a septic system in need of repair. The buyer would probably sue:
    a. the broker and the owner
    b. no one, since he or she should have checked
    c. the broker
    d. the owner

18. A majority of the Real Estate Commission is:
    a. six members
    b. four members
    c. three members
    d. two members

19. A country real estate broker's office is in his home. His sign reads "John Jones—REALTOR®." He lives 25 miles from a bank and makes trips twice a month to deposit funds in his trust account. He keeps deposits in his office safe until then. He does not belong to any professional organizations, but he pays a 17-year-old boy $5 for each listing. Jones is guilty of all but which of the following?
    a. commingling funds
    b. paying an unlicensed person to solicit listings
    c. an illegal sign
    d. a zoning violation

20. The Business and Professions Code comes from:
    a. the state legislature
    b. the Real Estate Commission
    c. the National Association of REALTORS®
    d. the California Association of Real Estate Brokers

21. An attorney-in-fact cannot:
    a. sell real estate of his or her principal
    b. take a mortgage on his or her principal's property
    c. record a notarized power of attorney
    d. any of these

22. The written contract between an employing broker and an employed salesperson is required by:
    a. Real Estate Commission regulations
    b. the Real Estate Board
    c. the Business and Professions Code
    d. none of these

23. A salesperson, in selling listings of another broker, would be directly responsible to:
    a. his or her broker
    b. the multiple listing service
    c. the listing broker
    d. the owner

24. The primary purpose of the Real Estate Law is to:
    a. limit competition
    b. protect the public
    c. protect commissions
    d. none of these

25. A valid agency requires a(n):
    a. written agreement
    b. express agreement
    c. attorney-in-fact
    d. none of these

26. A listing broker may not be:
    a. the sole agent of the owner
    b. the sole agent of the buyer
    c. a dual agent
    d. none of these

27. An agency relationship would not be created by:
    a. a verbal agreement
    b. ratification
    c. implication
    d. subornation

28. A broker may never:
    a. accept commissions from the buyer and the seller
    b. sell his or her own property to a customer
    c. act as an escrow
    d. none of these

29. A contract for the sale of residential property includes a general "as is" provision. This provision:
    a. is valid on *caveat emptor* theory
    b. applies only to matters of record
    c. applies only to visible and observable conditions
    d. can be ignored, since it takes away the right to a habitable dwelling

30. A broker exceeds his authority and without the owner's knowledge tells the buyer that the house will be repainted.
    a. The broker is liable.
    b. The owner alone is liable as the broker was her agent.
    c. Neither the owner nor the broker is liable if it wasn't in writing.
    d. None of these are true.

31. A real estate salesperson is to his or her broker as:
    a. an independent contractor is to a principal
    b. a principal is to a principal
    c. an employee is to an employer
    d. an agent is to a principal

32. A principal would not be liable for torts of:
    a. an independent contractor within the scope of the contract
    b. an independent contractor outside the scope of the contract
    c. an agent outside the scope of the contract
    d. any of these

33. A salesperson's relationships to an owner-client of the broker would be most nearly that of:
    a. independent contractor
    b. employee
    c. subagent
    d. principal

34. As to money held in trust, which of the following is true?
    a. Records must be kept of checks held uncashed.
    b. Trust funds for taxes and insurance may bear interest.
    c. Trust accounts must be reconciled monthly.
    d. all of these

35. A broker sells an apartment building to a syndicate of which the broker is a member without informing the seller of this interest. Before closing, the owner discovers the broker's interest and refuses to sell. In a suit to collect a commission, the result would probably be:
    a. revocation of the broker's license
    b. that no commission would be paid
    c. that the broker would get the commission
    d. that the buyer would obtain specific performance

36. When is a broker engaged in dual agency?
    a. When the broker represents the seller and the buyer
    b. When the broker buys a property he or she listed
    c. When the broker lists a property he or she previously sold
    d. When the broker represents the seller and another broker represents the buyer

37. A seller sold property "as is." The broker knew the plumbing was in bad repair but did not inform the buyer. The buyer can sue:
    a. no one, since the sale was "as is"
    b. no one, since "as is" is really notice of problem
    c. the broker
    d. none of these

38. A broker buys a property he has listed.
    a. He must inform the owner that the offer is his.
    b. He has violated the Real Estate Law.
    c. He violated his agency.
    d. all of these

39. A broker acts as an undisclosed agent for both the buyer and seller in a transaction. The buyer does not want to go through with the purchase although the price she agreed to pay is fair.
    a. The buyer may withdraw without penalty.
    b. The buyer could be subject to liquidated damages.
    c. The buyer could be subject to actual damages.
    d. Either a or b is true.

40. An agency agreement does not require:
    a. mutual consent
    b. a competent principal
    c. consideration
    d. any of these

41. When may a broker accept a commission from both a buyer and a seller?
    a. if he or she provided service to both parties
    b. if the total commission received does not exceed $500
    c. if both parties consent
    d. never

42. The agency between a real estate broker and an owner would not be:
    a. an executed agreement
    b. an implied agency
    c. an express agency
    d. a formal document

43. Upon acceptance of an offer, a broker may never:
    a. deposit earnest money into escrow
    b. deposit earnest money into a trust account
    c. turn earnest money over to the seller
    d. none of these

44. The agency formed by an exclusive listing is:
    a. an ostensible agency
    b. an express agency
    c. an implied agency
    d. none of these

45. A broker is selling his own rental unit. He collects the rent on the first day of the month, which is the same day he receives a deposit with an offer to purchase giving him three days to accept. He should:
    a. put the rent and purchase deposit in his usual trust account
    b. open two new trust accounts, one for the rent and one for the deposit
    c. put the rent in a new trust account and the deposit in the usual trust account
    d. none of these

46. A Real Estate Transfer Disclosure Statement is **NOT** required for the sale of:
    a. a residence sold "as is"
    b. a non-owner occupied duplex
    c. a home where the sale price is less than $300,000
    d. a commercial property

47. As to a broker's trust accounts, which of the following is true?
    a. Every broker must have one.
    b. It must be audited yearly.
    c. A record must be kept of funds received that are deposited directly into escrow.
    d. none of these

48. As to a broker's trust accounts, which of the following is true?
    a. Every broker must have one.
    b. A broker must maintain a minimum balance.
    c. A broker may not have any of his or her own money in the account.
    d. none of these

49. A real estate broker can be disciplined for:
    a. failure to supervise salespeople
    c. violating the Franchise Investment Law
    b. making a secret profit
    d. any of these

50. If a principal allows his or her agent to appear to have authority, the principal may not later deny an act of the agent, because of:
    a. ratification
    b. subrogation
    c. the Unruh Act
    d. estoppel

51. If an agent is guilty of a tort, the:
    a. principal is liable for all torts of an agent
    b. agent is liable, even if the tort is committed at the principal's direction
    c. principal is liable only if the tort is outside the scope of the agency
    d. agent is liable only if the tort is outside the scope of the agency

52. A buyer claims that a seller and a broker failed to reveal many defects known to them that made the property unsuitable for the purpose stated.
    a. The buyer does not have a case.
    b. The broker could be subject to discipline.
    c. The broker should have stated "as is" in the deposit receipt.
    d. The broker should have stated "as is condition" in the deposit receipt.

53. Balancing a bank statement with a trust account is known as:
    a. reconciliation
    b. trial balance
    c. auditing
    d. none of these

54. Which of the following does not need any special knowledge of law?
    a. a real estate broker
    c. an attorney-in-fact
    b. a real estate salesperson
    d. none of these

55. A person may give a power of attorney to:
    a. list real estate
    c. sign a grant deed
    b. accept an offer on real estate
    d. any of these

56. A listing broker can have any of the following agencies *except:*
    a. seller's agent
    c. dual agent
    b. buyer's agent
    d. b and c

57. A selling agent can elect to be:
    a. seller's agent
    c. dual agent
    b. buyer's agent
    d. any of these

58. The three steps of agency disclosure, in the proper chronological order, are:
    a. disclose–elect–confirm
    b. elect–confirm–disclose
    c. confirm–elect–disclose
    d. disclose–confirm–disclose

59. The Sherman Act prohibits all *except* agreements to:
    a. divide a market geographically
    b. refrain from cooperation with another broker
    c. set minimum commission
    d. split commission

60. An agent failed to reveal to the seller that she was acting in a dual agency capacity. Therefore, the agent:
    a. could be subject to disciplinary action
    b. cannot enforce the collection of a commission from the seller
    c. has placed the seller in a position where he can recind the contract
    d. all of the above

ANSWERS—CHAPTER 4 QUIZ

1. d. It is a trade name.
2. c. If a judgment is entered into and it is uncollectable, then the owner can go to the Recovery Fund.
3. c.
4. c.
5. d.
6. b. With consent is OK.
7. b.
8. c.
9. b. Their purpose is to carry out the law.
10. b.
11. a.
12. d. $20,000 for a single transaction.
13. d. There is no limit as to what she can obtain from the licensee—the limit is the liability of fund.
14. d.
15. d. Conversion is theft.
16. d.
17. a. Although the broker may not be liable.
18. a. There are 10 members plus the commissioner (11 total).
19. d. The other violations are clear.

20. a. State law.
21. b. Inconsistent with agency duties.
22. a.
23. a. To the employing broker.
24. b.
25. d. It may be verbal or implied.
26. b. The broker may be the seller's agent or a dual agent.
27. d. Means inducing perjury.
28. d. All are proper with disclosure.
29. c.
30. a.
31. c. According to the DRE.
32. d. The principal is liable for the agent's torts within the scope of the agency.
33. c.
34. d.
35. b. The broker violated fiduciary duty.
36. a.
37. c. "As is" applies to observable defects.
38. a.
39. a. Since there is an undisclosed dual agency.
40. c. The agreement may be gratuitous.

41. c.
42. b. Listings must be in writing.
43. d.
44. b. Since it is stated.
45. d. Since the broker is a principal, not an agent.
46. d. For 1–4 residential units only.
47. c.
48. d.
49. d.
50. d. The principal is estopped from denial.
51. b. And the principal is liable if the tort is within the scope of the agency or directed by the principal.
52. b. The broker failed to reveal a material defect.
53. a.
54. c. Person acting under power of attorney.
55. d. A person may give power of attorney for any legal purpose.
56. b Seller's agent or dual agent.
57. d.
58. a.
59. d.
60. d.

CHAPTER 5

Real Estate Contracts

CONTRACTS

A **contract** is an enforceable promise.

A **valid contract** must fulfill four requirements:

1. **Competent parties:** Insane people cannot contract. Minors (people under 18) can contract only for necessities. Minors cannot contract for real property. Restrictions can also be placed on prisoner contract rights for the security of the prison and to protect the public, however, the Department of Corrections can prohibit or restrict sales for business purposes. Prisoners can contract, other than those under a life imprisonment or death sentence. An **emancipated minor** is allowed to contract. To be emancipated, the minor must:

   a. be married, widowed, or divorced—an unmarried minor can contract since unmarried means formerly married (widowed or divorced);

   b. be in military service; or

   c. have received a declaration of emancipation from the court.

   Contracts entered into by a minor may be voided within a reasonable period of time after the minor reaches the age of 18.

2. **Mutual agreement:** There must be enough certainty so that a reasonable person would say there was an actual "meeting of the minds" as to what was agreed upon.

   If a contract is based on a mutual mistake of fact, there is no agreement. However, in the absence of fraud, a unilateral mistake by one party would not void the contract.

3. **Consideration:** In order for a promise to be binding upon a party, he or she must have received something of value (an unsupported promise to make a gift is generally unenforceable). Generally, it is not necessary for the consideration to be fair, just that it have some value. Grossly inadequate consideration might, however, be evidence of fraud or undue influence.

4. **Legal purpose:** A contract that requires laws to be broken is void.

If any one of these four requirements is not met, the contract is generally *void*. If the contract is void it is also, of course, **unenforceable.** (Contracts dealing in real estate must also be in writing.)

Voidable Contracts

These are contracts in which only one party has the right to void (or can elect to be bound by the contract). Contracts entered into because of **duress, menace, undue influence, fraud,** or **misrepresentation** are voidable at the option of the injured party.

Duress   Force.

Menace   Threat of force.

Undue Influence   Influence based on the relationship of the parties that deprives one party of freedom of will (for example, a doctor-patient or parent-child relationship).

Fraud   Fraud may consist of any of the following:

1. The suggestion as fact of that which is not true by one who does not believe it to be true.
2. Positive assertion as fact of that which is not true when not warranted by information known.
3. Suppression of fact.
4. A promise made without any intention of performance.
5. Any other deceitful act.

While fraud to induce a person to contract makes the contract voidable, fraud as to the **inception** of the contract, whereby the person is deceived as to the nature of the agreement being signed, makes the contract void.

Misrepresentation   A false statement to induce a contract. Unlike fraud, intent is not required. It makes a contract voidable at the option of the injured party.

Puffing   A statement of opinion such as, "This is a great deal." It is not a basis to void a contract.

Contracts are either **bilateral** or **unilateral.**

Bilateral Contract   A promise for a promise; mutual promises supported by each other. (Example: "I promise to pay $5,000 for your lot and you promise to sell me the lot for $5,000.")

Unilateral Contract A promise for an act; one party makes a promise but receives no promise in return. A contract is formed by the other party performing the required act. (Example: "I will give you $50 if you trim my fruit trees." The party to whom the offer was made can, by trimming the trees, accept the offer, making a binding contract.)

Contracts are either **executed** or **executory.**

Executed Contract A fully performed contract with nothing left to be done.

Executory Contract A contract that has yet to be performed. A mutual agreement for the sale of a lot next week would be a **bilateral executory contract.**

Contracts are either **express** or **implied.**

Express Contract A contract in which the terms are either written or stated but specifically agreed to.

Implied Contract A contract in which the terms are not actually agreed to, but a contract results from the conduct of the parties. (Example: Ordering a termite report may involve no specific agreement to pay a particular price, but reasonable payment is implied by the conduct of the parties.)

Offers

An offer by an offeror is not a contract until it is accepted by the offeree. Acceptance must be in the manner specified; but if not specified, it can be in any reasonable manner. It is accepted when the offeror is informed of the acceptance. Mailing an acceptance is considered an acceptance as of the time of mailing.

Generally, an offer can be withdrawn at any time prior to acceptance, and the death or insanity of the offeror prior to acceptance also revokes the offer. An offer is generally considered withdrawn when the offeree is notified of the withdrawal. Mailing of a notice that an offer is revoked is not effective until it is received (acceptance takes place upon mailing, but revocation takes place upon receipt). Death of the offeror or the offeree after a binding contract is entered into does not affect the contract; it would be binding on the estate of the deceased party.

Novation

The substitution of a new contract for an old one. (Example: "Instead of selling you a lot for $500, we agree that you will buy a different lot for $700.") A novation can also be a substitution of one party for another.

Accord and Satisfaction

An agreement to accept a different consideration than was previously agreed upon. (Example: "Instead of giving you $1,000 for your lot as previously agreed to, I will give you $750 plus some lumber as payment in full.") An accord and satisfaction generally results from a disagreement as to the acceptability of performance.

Interpretation of Contracts

If ambiguous, a contract is generally interpreted against the party drafting it. Since a contract is interpreted in accordance with the intent of the parties, in case of ambiguities, a typed portion takes precedence over a printed portion and a handwritten portion takes precedence over a typed portion. If numbers are written out as words, they take precedence over numerals. A later agreement takes precedence over an earlier agreement in case of any ambiguity.

Assignment of Contracts

Generally, contracts can be assigned unless they specifically prohibit assignment. An exception is that contracts calling for purely personal services cannot be assigned (for example, an artist cannot assign to another artist a contract to paint a portrait).

Statute of Frauds

This statute is derived from English common law requiring certain contracts to be in writing. In California:

1. A contract dealing in real estate, other than a lease of one year or less, must be in writing (so verbal, short-term leases are valid).
2. An agreement that cannot by its terms be performed within one year must be in writing. (Therefore, a 6-month lease starting in 7 months would take 13 months to perform, so it must be in writing.)
3. An agreement to answer for the debt of another must be in writing.
4. An agreement for the sale of personal property involving $500 or more must be in writing.

Parol Evidence Rule

Oral evidence may not be admitted to modify a written contract that appears complete. Oral evidence may be admitted to clarify an ambiguity or to prove fraud or undue influence, and may also be admitted to show a later modification of a written contract.

Estoppel

A party can be prevented (**estopped**) from raising the defense of the Statute of Frauds if the other party made improvements to the property based on an oral promise to sell.

Laches

If one party delays in bringing action and another party acts based on the delay so that allowing the action now would be inequitable, then the action would be barred by **laches.** (Example: Assume you knew that I was building a house for you in a location other than the one specified in our contract. It would not be equitable to allow you to wait until I finished the house and then demand that it be relocated. Your delay caused me to act to my detriment. You would be barred from enforcing the agreement as written because of laches.)

Statute of Limitations

This stipulates a period in which legal action must be brought after a cause for action arises. Legal action pertaining to a written contract must be brought within four years or rights are lost. (Example: A note written today is due in five years. If it is not paid when due, there are four years to start action. So action must be brought within nine years from today or the right to recover would be lost.) Therefore, while a contract may be valid, it could nevertheless be unenforceable because of the Statute of Limitations. The Statute of Limitations for verbal contracts is 2 years; for judgments, 10 years.

REMEDIES FOR BREACH OF CONTRACT

Compensatory Damages   Money to compensate the injured party for his or her actual cash loss. (Example: A buyer breaches an agreement to buy a lot for $5,000. If the lot can be resold for only $4,500, then the seller's damages are $500.)

Specific Performance   Forcing the defaulting party to perform when money damages are not adequate. Since every piece of real estate is unique, specific performance is available to force parties to sell as agreed. Specific performance will not be granted if the court determines that the consideration was not adequate.

Punitive or Exemplary Damages   Damages assessed beyond the actual compensatory amount because an injury was willful. They are awarded as a way of punishing the wrongdoer.

Nominal Damages   Where a party violates the rights of another but there is no real financial loss, the court may award a small token sum. (Note: The term *nominal amount* may also refer to the amount stated or named in a contract.)

Liquidated Damages   Damages are agreed to prior to any breach. They will be enforced if reasonable. Unreasonable damages would be considered a penalty and would be unenforceable. An example of liquidated damages would be an agreement that the buyer will forfeit a deposit if he or she breaches the contract.

LISTINGS

A listing is a contract whereby a principal (owner) employs an agent (broker) to sell his or her property (gives authorization to sell). Prospective buyers could also give a listing to an agent for the purpose of locating property. Since listings deal in real estate, they must be in writing (per the Statute of Frauds). However, property management contracts need not be in writing unless they authorize a manager to enter into a lease for more than one year.

Listings as agency agreements are personal contracts. The death of either the agent or the principal terminates the listing. (Of course, if an offer is received and accepted prior to the death of either the agent or the principal, the contract would be binding on the estate of the deceased.) If the owner or broker is a corporation, the death of an officer would not end the listing, since a corporation never dies.

Because an agency requires consent, an owner can generally terminate a listing. However, termination without cause could subject the principal to damages. An exception to the principal's right to terminate would be an **agency coupled with an interest.** For example, assume a broker advances an owner funds to stop a foreclosure action, in consideration of which the owner agrees to list the property for sale and to repay the funds advanced upon the sale. In this case the agency is coupled with an interest in the property, so it cannot be unilaterally canceled by the owner.

Exclusive-Right-to-Sell Listing

This listing gives the broker the exclusive right to sell; the broker is entitled to a commission if the property is sold by anyone, including the owner or another broker. Listings accepted by a multiple listing service (MLS) are normally a form of exclusive-right-to-sell listings (but MLS listings can also be exclusive-agency or open listings). Neither brokers nor appraisers can be excluded from MLS access. Because the broker is assured of a commission if the property is sold, the broker is more likely to advertise this type of listing.

Study the Residential Listing Agreement (Exclusive Authorization and Right to Sell.) The following numbered items relate to the paragraphs on the listing:

1. This paragraph names the seller and gives the broker an exclusive right to sell. It has a definite termination date (required on all exclusive listings) and describes the property. While a legal description is not required, it must be clear and unambiguous.

2. This paragraph provides that fixtures and fittings are included in the sale but personal property is excluded. Space is provided for additional items that are to be included or excluded. By being specific, it avoids later misunderstandings.

3. The list price and any terms are set forth.

4. The statement that commissions are negotiable must be set forth in boldface print in the listing.

   A. Subparagraph (1) makes it clear that by accepting an offer at any price, the broker becomes entitled to a commission.

   Subparagraph (2) is known as the **Safety Clause.** If, within a designated period of time after the listing expires, a sales agreement is reached with everyone who physically entered and was shown the premises by an agent, or who submitted an offer and whose name was provided in writing to the owner (within 3 calendar days after the listing expired, then the broker is entitled to a commission).

   The Safety Clause protects brokers from buyers and owners delaying a purchase to avoid paying a commission.

Subparagraph (3) provides that the broker is entitled to a commission if property is withdrawn from the market or made unmarketable by a voluntary act of the owner (such as entering a long-term lease).

B. If completion of the sale is prevented by buyer's action, compensation shall be due the broker if the seller collects damages. The commission shall be 1/2 of the damages recovered after costs or the commission agreed in the listing, whichever amount is less.

C. Provides for any additional broker fees.

D. The broker is authorized to cooperate with other agents and could set forth commission splits. Without this authorization, the broker could not delegate any agency duties by allowing others to show the property.

E. This is an irrevocable assignment of the commission rights from escrow. Without this assignment, an owner could notify the escrow not to pay the agent but pay all of the proceeds to the owner.

F. The owner warrants that he or she has not entered into any other listings, unless disclosed, and has no obligation to pay any other broker a commission unless sold to named individuals (See Para. 4A(2)). If a sale is made to any named individuals and the owner is obligated to pay the commission to another agent, the listing agent shall not be entitled to a commission.

5. The seller(s) warrant that they are the owner(s) and have the authority to execute this agreement and to sell the property.

6. This authorizes the broker to provide information on the listing to an MLS service as well as to Internet sites.

7. The seller indicates that he or she is unaware of delinquent payments, foreclosure action or other proceedings affecting the property as well as government investigations, proposed special assessments, etc., that affect the property. The seller agrees to notify the broker if he or she receives such information.

8. By agreeing to exercise a reasonable effort to sell the property, the listing becomes a bilateral contract (promise for a promise). The owner agrees to cooperate in the sale and to hold the broker harmless from claims arising from incorrect information supplied by the seller or from known material facts not conveyed to the broker.

9. The broker is authorized to accept a deposit. Without this authorization, a deposit taken would be as an agent of the buyer.

10. A. This paragraph points out if the property is 1–4 residential units, the owner will receive a Disclosure Regarding Agency Relationships.

B. This points out that the agent will represent the seller.

C. This points out situations where there will be a dual agency.

D. The owner is informed that the broker will also be handling similar property for other owners.

E. The owner is informed that final agency confirmation will be prior or concurrent with seller's execution of the purchase agreement.

11. Owner is informed that the broker is not responsible for loss or damage to personal or real property. The seller is advised to take reasonable steps to protect valuables and to obtain insurance to cover risks.

12. The owner can check a box that a lockbox is not authorized. Otherwise the broker can install a lockbox.

13. The broker is authorized to place a "For Sale" sign on the property. The owner by checking a box can indicate that a sign is not authorized.

14. The property is offered in compliance with all antidiscrimination laws. The broker cannot discriminate.

15. If there are legal proceedings between seller and broker, the prevailing party will be entitled to reasonable attorney fees (this helps reduce frivolous lawsuits.)

16. Space is provided for additional terms.

17. This clause gives the broker the right to cancel this agreement within 5 days, by giving written notice, if an associate licensee (salesperson or broker-associate) entered into the agreement.

18. The agreement is binding on the seller and seller's successors or assigns.

19. A. The parties agree to mediate any dispute before legal action or arbitration (they don't have to resolve the problem.)

    B. By initialing, the broker and seller agree to binding arbitration as to any dispute (they give up the right to court action.)

20. The parties agree that this document is their entire agreement and no prior or contemporaneous expressions made can contradict this agreement.

21. By signing, the seller(s) state(s) that they have read and understand the agreement and that they have received a copy of it. (Sellers must receive copy of any exclusive listing.)

The broker or associate also signs the listing.

Exclusive-Agency Listing

Under this type of listing, the broker is the only one who can act as agent. If the broker or any other agent sells the property, the listing broker is entitled to a commission. If the owner sells the property without the agent's help, then the broker is not entitled to a commission (this type of listing excludes sales personally made by the owner from the listing).

Exclusive listings are bilateral contracts (a promise for a promise). The owner agrees to pay a commission if the property is sold, and the agent agrees to use diligence in finding a buyer.

The agent must give a copy of any exclusive listing to the persons signing at the time of signing. All exclusive listings must have a definite termination date. It is not enough to state "valid until canceled." Failure to give an owner a copy or to include a termination date in an exclusive listing is grounds for disciplinary action by the Commissioner. In the absence of a termination date, an agent cannot collect a commission on an exclusive listing.

CALIFORNIA
ASSOCIATION
OF REALTORS®

RESIDENTIAL LISTING AGREEMENT
(Exclusive Authorization and Right to Sell)
(C.A.R. Form LA, Revised 10/02)

1. EXCLUSIVE RIGHT TO SELL: _____ ("Seller")
hereby employs and grants _____ ("Broker")
beginning (date) _____ and ending at 11:59 P.M. on (date) _____ ("Listing Period")
the exclusive and irrevocable right to sell or exchange the real property in the City of _____,
County of_____, California, described as: _____
_____ ("Property").

2. ITEMS EXCLUDED AND INCLUDED: Unless otherwise specified in a real estate purchase agreement, all fixtures and fittings that
are attached to the Property are included, and personal property items are excluded, from the purchase price.
ADDITIONAL ITEMS EXCLUDED: _____.
ADDITIONAL ITEMS INCLUDED: _____.
Seller intends that the above items be excluded or included in offering the Property for sale, but understands that: **(i)** the purchase
agreement supersedes any intention expressed above and will ultimately determine which items are excluded and included in the sale;
and **(ii)** Broker is not responsible for and does not guarantee that the above exclusions and/or inclusions will be in the purchase agreement.

3. LISTING PRICE AND TERMS:
    A. The listing price shall be: _____
        _____ Dollars ($ _____).
    B. Additional Terms: _____
        _____.

4. COMPENSATION TO BROKER:
**Notice: The amount or rate of real estate commissions is not fixed by law. They are set by each Broker
individually and may be negotiable between Seller and Broker (real estate commissions include all
compensation and fees to Broker).**
    A. Seller agrees to pay to Broker as compensation for services irrespective of agency relationship(s), either ☐ _____ percent
        of the listing price (or if a purchase agreement is entered into, of the purchase price), or ☐ $ _____,
        AND _____, as follows:
        (1) If Broker, Seller, cooperating broker, or any other person procures a buyer(s) who offers to purchase the Property on the
            above price and terms, or on any price and terms acceptable to Seller during the Listing Period, or any extension.
        (2) If Seller, within _____ calendar days after the end of the Listing Period or any extension, enters into a contract to sell,
            convey, lease or otherwise transfer the Property to anyone ("Prospective Buyer") or that person's related entity: **(i)** who
            physically entered and was shown the Property during the Listing Period or any extension by Broker or a cooperating broker;
            or **(ii)** for whom Broker or any cooperating broker submitted to Seller a signed, written offer to acquire, lease, exchange or
            obtain an option on the Property. Seller, however, shall have no obligation to Broker under paragraph 4A(2) unless, not later
            than **3 calendar days** after the end of the Listing Period or any extension, Broker has given Seller a written notice of the
            names of such Prospective Buyers.
        (3) If, without Broker's prior written consent, the Property is withdrawn from sale, conveyed, leased, rented, otherwise
            transferred, or made unmarketable by a voluntary act of Seller during the Listing Period, or any extension.
    B. If completion of the sale is prevented by a party to the transaction other than Seller, then compensation due under paragraph
        4A shall be payable only if and when Seller collects damages by suit, arbitration, settlement or otherwise, and then in an amount
        equal to the lesser of one-half of the damages recovered or the above compensation, after first deducting title and escrow
        expenses and the expenses of collection, if any.
    C. In addition, Seller agrees to pay Broker: _____.
    D. **(1)** Broker is authorized to cooperate with and compensate brokers participating through the multiple listing service(s)
        ("MLS"): **(i)** in any manner; **OR (ii)** (if checked) by offering MLS brokers: either ☐ _____ percent of the purchase
        price, or ☐ $ _____.
        (2) Broker is authorized to cooperate with and compensate brokers operating outside the MLS in any manner.
    E. Seller hereby irrevocably assigns to Broker the above compensation from Seller's funds and proceeds in escrow. Broker may
        submit this agreement, as instructions to compensate Broker pursuant to paragraph 4A, to any escrow regarding the Property
        involving Seller and a buyer, Prospective Buyer or other transferee.
    F. **(1)** Seller represents that Seller has not previously entered into a listing agreement with another broker regarding the Property,
        unless specified as follows: _____.
        (2) Seller warrants that Seller has no obligation to pay compensation to any other broker regarding the Property unless the
        Property is transferred to any of the following individuals or entities: _____
        _____.
        (3) If the Property is sold to anyone listed above during the time Seller is obligated to compensate another broker: **(i)** Broker is
        not entitled to compensation under this agreement; and **(ii)** Broker is not obligated to represent Seller in such transaction.

LA REVISED 10/02 (PAGE 1 OF 3) Print Date

Seller acknowledges receipt of a copy of this page.
Seller's Initials (_____)(_____)

| Reviewed by _____ Date _____ |

EQUAL HOUSING
OPPORTUNITY

RESIDENTIAL LISTING AGREEMENT-EXCLUSIVE (LA PAGE 1 OF 3)

Property Address: _____ Date: _____

5. **OWNERSHIP, TITLE AND AUTHORITY:** Seller warrants that: **(i)** Seller is the owner of the Property; **(ii)** no other persons or entities have title to the Property; and **(iii)** Seller has the authority to both execute this agreement and sell the Property. Exceptions to ownership, title and authority are as follows: _____.

6. **MULTIPLE LISTING SERVICE:** Information about this listing will (or ☐ will not) be provided to the MLS of Broker's selection. All terms of the transaction, including financing, if applicable, will be provided to the selected MLS for publication, dissemination and use by persons and entities on terms approved by the MLS. Seller authorizes Broker to comply with all applicable MLS rules. MLS rules allow MLS data to be made available by the MLS to additional Internet sites unless Broker gives the MLS instructions to the contrary.

7. **SELLER REPRESENTATIONS:** Seller represents that, unless otherwise specified in writing, Seller is unaware of: **(i)** any Notice of Default recorded against the Property; **(ii)** any delinquent amounts due under any loan secured by, or other obligation affecting, the Property; **(iii)** any bankruptcy, insolvency or similar proceeding affecting the Property; **(iv)** any litigation, arbitration, administrative action, government investigation or other pending or threatened action that affects or may affect the Property or Seller's ability to transfer it; and **(v)** any current, pending or proposed special assessments affecting the Property. Seller shall promptly notify Broker in writing if Seller becomes aware of any of these items during the Listing Period or any extension thereof.

8. **BROKER'S AND SELLER'S DUTIES:** Broker agrees to exercise reasonable effort and due diligence to achieve the purposes of this agreement. Unless Seller gives Broker written instructions to the contrary, Broker is authorized to order reports and disclosures as appropriate or necessary and advertise and market the Property by any method and in any medium selected by Broker, including MLS and the Internet, and, to the extent permitted by these media, control the dissemination of the information submitted to any medium. Seller agrees to consider offers presented by Broker, and to act in good faith to accomplish the sale of the Property by, among other things, making the Property available for showing at reasonable times and referring to Broker all inquiries of any party interested in the Property. Seller is responsible for determining at what price to list and sell the Property. **Seller further agrees to indemnify, defend and hold Broker harmless from all claims, disputes, litigation, judgments and attorney fees arising from any incorrect information supplied by Seller, or from any material facts that Seller knows but fails to disclose.**

9. **DEPOSIT:** Broker is authorized to accept and hold on Seller's behalf any deposits to be applied toward the purchase price.

10. **AGENCY RELATIONSHIPS:**
    A. **Disclosure:** If the Property includes residential property with one-to-four dwelling units, Seller shall receive a "Disclosure Regarding Agency Relationships" form prior to entering into this agreement.
    B. **Seller Representation:** Broker shall represent Seller in any resulting transaction, except as specified in paragraph 4F.
    C. **Possible Dual Agency With Buyer:** Depending upon the circumstances, it may be necessary or appropriate for Broker to act as an agent for both Seller and buyer, exchange party, or one or more additional parties ("Buyer"). Broker shall, as soon as practicable, disclose to Seller any election to act as a dual agent representing both Seller and Buyer. If a Buyer is procured directly by Broker or an associate licensee in Broker's firm, Seller hereby consents to Broker acting as a dual agent for Seller and such Buyer. In the event of an exchange, Seller hereby consents to Broker collecting compensation from additional parties for services rendered, provided there is disclosure to all parties of such agency and compensation. Seller understands and agrees that: **(i)** Broker, without the prior written consent of Seller, will not disclose to Buyer that Seller is willing to sell the Property at a price less than the listing price; **(ii)** Broker, without the prior written consent of Buyer, will not disclose to Seller that Buyer is willing to pay a price greater than the offered price; and **(iii)** except for (i) and (ii) above, a dual agent is obligated to disclose known facts materially affecting the value or desirability of the Property to both parties.
    D. **Other Sellers:** Seller understands that Broker may have or obtain listings on other properties, and that potential buyers may consider, make offers on, or purchase through Broker, property the same as or similar to Seller's Property. Seller consents to Broker's representation of sellers and buyers of other properties before, during and after the end of this agreement.
    E. **Confirmation:** If the Property includes residential property with one-to-four dwelling units, Broker shall confirm the agency relationship described above, or as modified, in writing, prior to or concurrent with Seller's execution of a purchase agreement.

11. **SECURITY AND INSURANCE:** Broker is not responsible for loss of or damage to personal or real property, or person, whether attributable to use of a keysafe/lockbox, a showing of the Property, or otherwise. Third parties, including, but not limited to, appraisers, inspectors, brokers and prospective buyers, may have access to, and take videos and photographs of, the interior of the Property. Seller agrees: **(i)** to take reasonable precautions to safeguard and protect valuables that might be accessible during showings of the Property; and **(ii)** to obtain insurance to protect against these risks. Broker does not maintain insurance to protect Seller.

12. **KEYSAFE/LOCKBOX:** A keysafe/lockbox is designed to hold a key to the Property to permit access to the Property by Broker, cooperating brokers, MLS participants, their authorized licensees and representatives, authorized inspectors, and accompanied prospective buyers. Broker, cooperating brokers, MLS and Associations/Boards of REALTORS® are **not** insurers against injury, theft, loss, vandalism or damage attributed to the use of a keysafe/lockbox. Seller does (or if checked ☐ does not) authorize Broker to install a keysafe/lockbox. If Seller does not occupy the Property, Seller shall be responsible for obtaining occupant(s)' written permission for use of a keysafe/lockbox.

13. **SIGN:** Seller does (or if checked ☐ does not) authorize Broker to install a FOR SALE/SOLD sign on the Property.

14. **EQUAL HOUSING OPPORTUNITY:** The Property is offered in compliance with federal, state and local anti-discrimination laws.

15. **ATTORNEY FEES:** In any action, proceeding or arbitration between Seller and Broker regarding the obligation to pay compensation under this agreement, the prevailing Seller or Broker shall be entitled to reasonable attorney fees and costs from the non-prevailing Seller or Broker, except as provided in paragraph 19A.

16. **ADDITIONAL TERMS:** _____
    _____
    _____

17. **MANAGEMENT APPROVAL:** If an associate licensee in Broker's office (salesperson or broker-associate) enters into this agreement on Broker's behalf, and Broker or Manager does not approve of its terms, Broker or Manager has the right to cancel this agreement, in writing, within 5 days after its execution.

18. **SUCCESSORS AND ASSIGNS:** This agreement shall be binding upon Seller and Seller's successors and assigns.

Seller acknowledges receipt of a copy of this page.
Seller's Initials (_____)(_____)

Copyright © 1991-2002, CALIFORNIA ASSOCIATION OF REALTORS®, INC.
LA REVISED 10/02 (PAGE 2 OF 3)

| Reviewed by _____ Date _____ |

RESIDENTIAL LISTING AGREEMENT-EXCLUSIVE (LA PAGE 2 OF 3)

Reprinted with permission, CALIFORNIA ASSOCIATION OF REALTORS®. Endorsement not implied.

Property Address: _____ Date: _____

19. DISPUTE RESOLUTION:

A. MEDIATION: Seller and Broker agree to mediate any dispute or claim arising between them out of this agreement, or any resulting transaction, before resorting to arbitration or court action, subject to paragraph 19B(2) below. Paragraph 19B(2) below applies whether or not the arbitration provision is initialed. Mediation fees, if any, shall be divided equally among the parties involved. If, for any dispute or claim to which this paragraph applies, any party commences an action without first attempting to resolve the matter through mediation, or refuses to mediate after a request has been made, then that party shall not be entitled to recover attorney fees, even if they would otherwise be available to that party in any such action. THIS MEDIATION PROVISION APPLIES WHETHER OR NOT THE ARBITRATION PROVISION IS INITIALED.

B. ARBITRATION OF DISPUTES: (1) Seller and Broker agree that any dispute or claim in Law or equity arising between them regarding the obligation to pay compensation under this agreement, which is not settled through mediation, shall be decided by neutral, binding arbitration, including and subject to paragraph 19B(2) below. The arbitrator shall be a retired judge or justice, or an attorney with at least 5 years of residential real estate law experience, unless the parties mutually agree to a different arbitrator, who shall render an award in accordance with substantive California Law. The parties shall have the right to discovery in accordance with Code of Civil Procedure §1283.05. In all other respects, the arbitration shall be conducted in accordance with Title 9 of Part III of the California Code of Civil Procedure. Judgment upon the award of the arbitrator(s) may be entered in any court having jurisdiction. Interpretation of this agreement to arbitrate shall be governed by the Federal Arbitration Act.

(2) EXCLUSIONS FROM MEDIATION AND ARBITRATION: The following matters are excluded from mediation and arbitration hereunder: **(i)** a judicial or non-judicial foreclosure or other action or proceeding to enforce a deed of trust, mortgage, or installment land sale contract as defined in Civil Code §2985; **(ii)** an unlawful detainer action; **(iii)** the filing or enforcement of a mechanic's lien; and **(iv)** any matter that is within the jurisdiction of a probate, small claims, or bankruptcy court. The filing of a court action to enable the recording of a notice of pending action, for order of attachment, receivership, injunction, or other provisional remedies, shall not constitute a waiver of the mediation and arbitration provisions.

"NOTICE: BY INITIALING IN THE SPACE BELOW YOU ARE AGREEING TO HAVE ANY DISPUTE ARISING OUT OF THE MATTERS INCLUDED IN THE 'ARBITRATION OF DISPUTES' PROVISION DECIDED BY NEUTRAL ARBITRATION AS PROVIDED BY CALIFORNIA LAW AND YOU ARE GIVING UP ANY RIGHTS YOU MIGHT POSSESS TO HAVE THE DISPUTE LITIGATED IN A COURT OR JURY TRIAL. BY INITIALING IN THE SPACE BELOW YOU ARE GIVING UP YOUR JUDICIAL RIGHTS TO DISCOVERY AND APPEAL, UNLESS THOSE RIGHTS ARE SPECIFICALLY INCLUDED IN THE 'ARBITRATION OF DISPUTES' PROVISION. IF YOU REFUSE TO SUBMIT TO ARBITRATION AFTER AGREEING TO THIS PROVISION, YOU MAY BE COMPELLED TO ARBITRATE UNDER THE AUTHORITY OF THE CALIFORNIA CODE OF CIVIL PROCEDURE. YOUR AGREEMENT TO THIS ARBITRATION PROVISION IS VOLUNTARY."

"WE HAVE READ AND UNDERSTAND THE FOREGOING AND AGREE TO SUBMIT DISPUTES ARISING OUT OF THE MATTERS INCLUDED IN THE 'ARBITRATION OF DISPUTES' PROVISION TO NEUTRAL ARBITRATION."

Seller's Initials _____ / _____   Broker's Initials _____ / _____

20. ENTIRE CONTRACT: All prior discussions, negotiations and agreements between the parties concerning the subject matter of this agreement are superseded by this agreement, which constitutes the entire contract and a complete and exclusive expression of their agreement, and may not be contradicted by evidence of any prior agreement or contemporaneous oral agreement. If any provision of this agreement is held to be ineffective or invalid, the remaining provisions will nevertheless be given full force and effect. This agreement and any supplement, addendum or modification, including any photocopy or facsimile, may be executed in counterparts.

By signing below, Seller acknowledges that Seller has read, understands, accepts and has received a copy of this agreement.

Seller _____ Date _____
Address _____ City _____ State _____ Zip _____
Telephone _____ Fax _____ E-mail _____

Seller _____ Date _____
Address _____ City _____ State _____ Zip _____
Telephone _____ Fax _____ E-mail _____

Real Estate Broker (Firm) _____
By (Agent) _____ Date _____
Address _____ City _____ State _____ Zip _____
Telephone _____ Fax _____ E-mail _____

THIS FORM HAS BEEN APPROVED BY THE CALIFORNIA ASSOCIATION OF REALTORS® (C.A.R.). NO REPRESENTATION IS MADE AS TO THE LEGAL VALIDITY OR ADEQUACY OF ANY PROVISION IN ANY SPECIFIC TRANSACTION. A REAL ESTATE BROKER IS THE PERSON QUALIFIED TO ADVISE ON REAL ESTATE TRANSACTIONS. IF YOU DESIRE LEGAL OR TAX ADVICE, CONSULT AN APPROPRIATE PROFESSIONAL.

This form is available for use by the entire real estate industry. It is not intended to identify the user as a REALTOR®. REALTOR® is a registered collective membership mark which may be used only by members of the NATIONAL ASSOCIATION OF REALTORS® who subscribe to its Code of Ethics.

Published and Distributed by:
REAL ESTATE BUSINESS SERVICES, INC.
a subsidiary of the CALIFORNIA ASSOCIATION OF REALTORS®
525 South Virgil Avenue, Los Angeles, California 90020

Reviewed by _____ Date _____

LA REVISED 10/02 (PAGE 3 OF 3)

RESIDENTIAL LISTING AGREEMENT-EXCLUSIVE (LA PAGE 3 OF 3)

Reprinted with permission, CALIFORNIA ASSOCIATION OF REALTORS®. Endorsement not implied.

Open Listing

This is a written memorandum (frequently just a letter) that authorizes the broker to act as agent in a sale. Usually no time limit is specified (an open listing requires no termination date). Open listings can be given concurrently to more than one agent. The commission is earned by the broker who first finds a buyer ready, willing, and able to buy according to the terms of the listing, or who submits an offer accepted by the owner. All other open listings are automatically canceled by the sale. It is not necessary for the broker to give the owner a copy of the open listing at the time of signing since it is often merely a letter or note. (Both the owner and the broker must sign exclusive listings, but the owner alone can sign an open listing.) Open listings are unilateral contracts in that the agent accepts the owner's offer by performance in finding a buyer.

Net Listing

In this type of listing, compensation is not definite; the broker gets all over a set amount. If the net listing is for $10,000 and the broker obtains a buyer at $12,000, the commission would be all that is received over the $10,000 net amount, or $2,000. If the sale is for $10,000 or less, the broker would get nothing. Net listings are legal; however, the broker must reveal to the owner the amount of the commission prior to or at the time the principal binds himself or herself. (The penalty for failure to do so is suspension or revocation of the broker's license.) Because of the disclosure requirement, net listings are used very seldom.

A net listing can be an exclusive-agency listing, an exclusive-right-to-sell listing, or an open listing. The word *net* applies only to the means of determining the commission.

Buyer Listing

A listing authorizing the agent to help a buyer to acquire property can be an exclusive right to acquire, exclusive agency, open and even a net listing. The listing can provide that the agent's share in the commission paid by a seller will be the agent's compensation. Who pays the agent does not determine the agency.

Procuring Cause

Procuring cause becomes important in the case of open listings and exclusive-agency listings in which the owner makes the sale without the agent. If the agent initiated an uninterrupted course of events that led directly to the sale, then the agent is the procuring cause and is entitled to a commission. For an exclusive-right-to-sell listing, the listing agent need not be the procuring cause to be entitled to a commission.

Retention of Records

Listings, deposit receipts, canceled checks, trust records, etc., must be retained for three years from the date of closing. If the property is not sold, they must be retained for three years from the date of the listing. Broker-salesperson agreements must be retained by the broker for three years from termination of the salesperson's employment.

Loan broker records (Chapter 7) must be retained for 4 years although copies of the Mortgage Loan Disclosure Statetment need only be retained for 3 years.

Listings are the property of the broker, not the salesperson who obtained them. If the salesperson leaves the broker's employ, the listings remain with the broker. The broker must initial a copy of a listing taken by a salesperson within a reasonable period.

Listings may *not* be recorded, as they don't give the broker an interest in the land.

Options

An *option* is a contract to make a contract (a right given to one party to buy or lease at an agreed price within a stated period of time).

Optionor   The owner who gives the option.

Optionee   The party who gets the option.

Time is of the essence as to an option; it must be exercised within the time stated. To have a valid option, there must be valuable consideration. It is not enough to state "for good and valuable consideration." The consideration must also have actually changed hands from the optionee to the optionor or his or her agent. An option in a lease would also be regarded as a covenant or promise.

Right of First Refusal   The **right of first refusal** is not an option, but the right to buy at the price and under the terms that the owner is willing to accept from another. If the owner does not wish to sell, the right cannot be exercised.

Personal Option   If part of the purchase price for exercising the option is personal, such as a note from the optionee, then the option cannot be assigned to another person. (The optionor agrees to take a note from a particular party he or she knows, not a note from someone who might not be as trustworthy.) Options other than personal options may be assigned by the optionee to others.

Options may be recorded to give purchasers constructive notice of the optionee's interest. If the optionee is in possession of the property, then his or her possession, of course, is constructive notice of his or her interest.

Listings Containing Options   A broker may take a listing in combination with an option; however, prior to exercising such an option, the broker must reveal in writing to the owner the full amount of his or her profit and obtain the written consent of the owner to the amount of said profit. Therefore, few listing-and-option combinations are used. If a broker thinks a property is a good deal, he or she normally buys it outright or takes an option alone. In an option the licensee deals as a principal, but in a listing the licensee deals as an agent.

Advertising

In advertising a property, the licensee must indicate that he or she is a broker or agent. A salesperson can advertise without using the broker's name, but the ad must indicate that the salesperson is acting as a licensee. If the broker is buying or selling his or her own property, he or she must disclose to the buyer that he or she is a licensee. (The agent must let the other party know that he or she is an expert.)

Commission

A commission is earned by the broker when the broker finds a buyer who is ready, willing, and able to buy in accordance with the terms of the listing or who submits an offer accepted by the owner. It makes no difference that the seller can't or won't deliver title or that the seller refuses the buyer. The broker still has earned a commission. However, commission is normally paid at the close of escrow. (The offer must be in accordance with the listing, so a broker has not earned a commission if, for example, the seller wants 29 percent down and the buyer wants to pay cash.) The commission on a listing is by agreement between the parties. There is no minimum or maximum commission. A broker may split a commission with other agents.

Signatures on the Listing

Both husband and wife have equal rights to control community property. Although the signature of either spouse can bind the community property as to a commission, the broker should obtain both signatures. Of course, both must sign the deed.

Time of Listing

If a listing is for a specified number of days, every day counts in determining when the listing expires. For example, a three-day listing signed at 10 P.M. on Tuesday would expire at midnight on Thursday (Tuesday, Wednesday, Thursday = three days).

Refusal to Sell

A listing is a contract between the owner and the broker. A buyer is not a party to the listing, so he or she cannot collect damages or demand specific performance should the seller refuse to sell at the listing price.

REAL ESTATE PURCHASE CONTRACTS

A real estate purchase contract, also known as a *deposit receipt,* is more than a receipt for money because, when accepted, it becomes a binding contract in which the buyer agrees to buy and the seller agrees to sell under the terms stated. It should be a complete understanding. The purchase contract shown also covers joint escrow instructions.

The buyer normally makes the offer in the form of an executed real estate purchase contract and is the **offeror.** The **offeree,** or seller, by accepting the offer, forms a binding bilateral contract.

Acceptance takes place when the buyer is notified of the seller's acceptance. This is usually done by delivering a copy of the purchase contract executed by the seller to the buyer. An acceptance is also binding on the buyer when the seller mails him or her the signed copy.

Prior to acceptance, the buyer may revoke the offer at any time. This is true even when he or she agreed in writing to keep the offer open for a particular time period. Unless there is consideration for a promise to keep an offer open (which would make it an option), it can be withdrawn.

The buyer's revocation of an offer is not binding until received by the seller. If the buyer mails a revocation and the seller mails an acceptance at the same time, then a binding contract is formed.

Study the California Residential Purchase Agreement (and Joint Escrow Instructions) that follows. The following list explains the paragraphs in the form.

1. A. Identifies the document as an offer and identifies the offeror.

   B. The property to be acquired is identified (a legal description is not necessary but it must be a clear unambiguous description).

   C. The purchase price is set forth.

2. Finance terms are given and the offer is made contingent on obtaining any stated loans unless subparagraph K or L is checked.

   A. The amount of deposit is shown (a deposit is not required for a valid offer but usually an offer without a deposit will not be seriously considered). The deposit, if by personal check, will remain uncashed until acceptance and then deposited within 3 business days either with an escrow or into the broker's trust account (as checked).

   B. This paragraph provides for the deposit to be increased within a stated period of acceptance. An agreement to increase would make a seller feel more secure, especially if the initial deposit was small.

   C. This paragraph sets forth specifications of a new loan that the offer is contingent on.

   D. Space is provided for additional financing terms.

   E. Provides that the balance of the purchase price will be deposited in a timely manner.

   F. Totals the down payment and new loans to show the full purchase price.

   G. The buyer agrees to show that the buyer's loan application has been evaluated and has been prequalified for a loan as specified in paragraph 2C.

   H. Seller agrees to verify he or she has funds for the down payment and closing costs.

   I. The seller agrees to remove the loan contingency or cancel the agreement within a stated period after acceptance. If the appropriate block is checked, the loan contingency shall remain in effect until funded.

   J. By checking the appropriate block, the offer is not contingent on the appraisal being no less than the purchase price. If the block is not checked, the contingency stands.

   K. If checked, the loans specified in 2C and 2D are not a contingency of the offer.

   L. If checked, this is an all cash offer and no loan is needed.

91

3. A. By checking, the buyer states that he or she does not intend to occupy the premises as a principal residence. If the buyer intends it as a principal residence, then liquidated damages are limited. (See paragraph 16.)

   B. This paragraph provides when occupancy shall be given to the buyer. If not at close of escrow, the buyer and seller are advised to enter into a written occupancy agreement.

   C. If the property is tenant occupied, this paragraph indicates if and when the property will be vacated or if tenant is to remain in possession.

   D. Seller agrees to assign any transferable warranties to the buyer at close of escrow.

4. This paragraph specifies who is to pay for reports, inspections, tests and services specified.

   A. Pest inspection.

   B. Other inspections (listed).

   C. Government requirements (smoke detectors, water heater bracing).

   D. Escrow and title insurance costs.

   E. Other listed costs.

5. Statutory Disclosures.

   A. Lead Based Paint Disclosure. The seller of residential property built prior to 1978, must deliver to the buyer a booklet explaining the dangers of lead in a home. The seller must also disclose known lead paint hazards, Real Estate Transfer Disclosure Statement (Chapter 4), Natural Hazards Disclosure Statement, knowledge release of illegal controlled substances, notice of special tax or assessments, Mello-Roos Bonds, and military ordnance location disclosure.

   B. Natural and Environmental Hazards Disclosure.

   C. A database disclosure must be made as to the ability to obtain information as to sex offenders in the area (Megan's Law).

6. For condominium developments, several disclosures are required.

   A. Within 7 days after acceptance, seller must disclose to buyer if the property is located in a common interest development.

   B. If the property is in a common interest development, the seller shall request copies of Homeowner Association documents required by law, disclosure of claims pending against the Homeowner Association, copies of the last 12 months of Homeowner Association minutes and names of contact persons.

7. Conditions affecting property.

   A. Property is sold in present condition (unless specified otherwise) subject to buyer's investigative rights. The property is to be maintained in the substantially same condition and debris and personal property not included in the sale are to be removed.

   B. Seller shall disclose known material facts and defects (Transfer Disclosure Statement) and make other disclosures required by law.

C. Buyer is advised to conduct investigations of entire property.

D. Seller is advised that buyer has inspection rights and based on discoveries, may request repairs or that the agreement be cancelled.

8. Items included and excluded in the sale are specified.

9. A. Buyer's right of inspection is a contingency of this agreement. Sets forth particulars of inspection that shall be at buyer's expense.

   B. Buyer shall give seller copies of inspection at no cost.

10. Repairs shall be completed in a workmanlike manner. Seller shall obtain receipts for repairs (protection against mechanics' liens).

11. Buyer shall keep property free from liens and will hold owner harmless for any claims resulting from the inspections.

12. A. Buyer shall be provided a preliminary title report.

    B. Title shall be in present condition unless agreed otherwise. Monetary liens shall be paid off unless assumed.

    C. Seller shall disclose all matters affecting title.

    D. A grant deed shall be given at close of escrow. The purchaser is notified that the manner of taking title can have significant legal and tax consequences and a professional should be consulted.

    Note: It is illegal practice of law for a broker to recommend the manner in which title shall be taken.

    E. A Homeowner Policy of Title Insurance shall be issued to the buyer.

13. If block is checked, the sale is contingent on the sale of another property.

14. The time periods for reports, disclosures, contingency removals, etc., are set forth.

    If the contract is cancelled, the release of funds requires a release signed by both parties.

    Failure to sign, in the absence of a good-faith dispute, could subject a party to a civil penalty of $1,000.

15. Buyer has the right to final inspection to confirm the property has been maintained and seller's obligations such as repairs, have been fulfilled.

16. If the buyer intends to occupy premises as principal residence (paragraph 3A), then liquidated damages are limited to 3 percent of the purchase price. Any excess must be returned to buyer. A separate liquidated damages agreement will be signed if there is any increased deposit.

17. A. The buyer and seller agree to mediation of any dispute (the parties are not required to reach an agreement).

    B. By initiating, the buyer and seller agree to binding arbitration of any dispute, giving up their rights to pursue a claim in court.

18. Parties agree to prorate taxes and other items. Proration shall be based on a 30-day month (360-day year).

19. Seller and buyer agree to comply with FIRPTA (Foreign Investment in Real Property Tax Act), as well as California-required withholding.

20. Brokers are authorized by the parties to report the terms of the sale to the MLS service (without this authorization, the terms would be confidential).

21. The property is being sold in compliance with antidiscrimination laws.

22. In the event of any dispute, the prevailing party shall be entitled to reasonable attorney fees.

23. Buyer and seller are informed that the broker does not guarantee performance of any service provider referred by the broker, and parties are free to select any provider.

24. The "time is of the essence" clause indicates that times as stated will not be waived. The paragraph also indicates this agreement is the full and final agreement and cannot be contradicted by prior agreements or contemporaneous statements.

25. Other terms and conditions may be set forth.

26. Terms used in the agreement are defined.

27. Buyer and seller acknowledge receipt of Disclosure Regarding Real Estate Agency Relationships and the possibility of multiple representation. The agency elected is confirmed in this agreement.

28. This paragraph indicates that portions of this purchase agreement shall be the joint escrow instructions and shall be delivered to the escrow. The only interest the brokers shall have in the escrow are in the commission, which has been assigned to the brokers.

29. If a buyer is paying a commission, it shall be by a separate broker/buyer agreement.

30. Paragraph 30 reiterates that this is an offer to purchase and initialed paragraphs are part of this agreement. If only one party initials a paragraph, then it is considered to be a counteroffer.

31. A definite date is set for expiration of the offer.

32. Broker compensation shall be at close of escrow (in accordance with listing agreement).

33. Acceptance clause indicates seller is the owner and agrees to accept the offer unless the counteroffer block is checked. The counteroffer would be attached. A confirmation of delivery of acceptance is included. (Note that acceptance does not take place until the offerer is notified of acceptance.)

Blocks are included for real estate selling broker and listing broker agreement as to commissions and for escrow to acknowledge receipt of a copy of the joint escrow instructions.

Counteroffers

When the seller changes the terms of an offer, it is really a *counteroffer*. If a seller states in his or her acceptance, "Accepted providing..." and then makes material changes to the offer, it is not an acceptance, but a counteroffer. A counteroffer is a rejection of the original offer and a new offer by the seller. It must now be accepted by the buyer to form a contract. Since the counteroffer serves as a rejection of the original offer, the original offer is "dead" and cannot be revived by any acceptance thereafter.

When the buyer makes an offer and when the seller accepts the offer, the broker must give them copies of the instrument they signed (the first copy to the buyer when he or she makes the offer, the second copy to the seller when he or she accepts, the third copy showing the acceptance to the buyer, and the fourth copy to the broker). Remember, the sale is not complete until the third copy showing the acceptance is delivered to the buyer. At any time prior to receiving the acceptance, the buyer may revoke the offer and would be entitled to the return of any earnest money deposit made.

"As Is" Provisions

"As is" provisions in a purchase contract are not fair to a buyer unless the buyer is fully informed as to the condition of a property. For residential sales, courts will enforce "as is" provisions only if the condition is patent (obvious) or the buyer has been fully informed. "As is" provisions will generally not protect sellers and agents if the condition was known and was latent or not discoverable by a reasonable inspection of the property.

Home Equity Sales Contracts

A homeowner may rescind a transaction with an **equity purchaser** (a purchaser of the owner's interest) within two years of recording if the equity purchaser took unconscionable advantage of the owner. (This is the result of dealers placing pressure on owners in foreclosure.) The right of rescission is lost if the buyer resells. An equity purchaser who takes unconscionable advantage of an owner in foreclosure is subject to a fine of up to $10,000 and/or one year's imprisonment.

A seller in foreclosure has five days after signing a sales contract to rescind. This rescission right exists even if the buyer did not take improper advantage of the seller.

In order to represent a buyer in purchasing a foreclosure property, the agent must:

1. Have a real estate license.
2. Post a surety bond for twice the fair market value of the property being purchased.

Because of these restrictions, most agents elect to be the seller's agent only, rather than the buyer's agent or a dual agent, when handling foreclosure sales.

Return of Deposit

If an offer is not accepted, the buyer is entitled to a return of deposit. If the offer is accepted and the sale is not completed, both buyer and seller will have to agree to the disposition of the deposit. If a party fails to agree to the disposition of funds when there is not a good faith dispute, that party can be liable for treble damages of not less than $100 or more than $1,000.

**CALIFORNIA
RESIDENTIAL PURCHASE AGREEMENT
AND JOINT ESCROW INSTRUCTIONS**
For Use With Single Family Residential Property — Attached or Detached
(C.A.R. Form RPA-CA, Revised 10/02)

Date _____, at _____, California.
1. **OFFER:**
   A. **THIS IS AN OFFER FROM** _____ ("Buyer").
   B. **THE REAL PROPERTY TO BE ACQUIRED** is described as _____
   _____, Assessor's Parcel No. _____, situated in
   _____, County of _____, California, ("Property").
   C. **THE PURCHASE PRICE** offered is _____
   _____ Dollars $ _____.
   D. **CLOSE OF ESCROW** shall occur on _____ (date)(or ☐ _____ **Days** After Acceptance).
2. **FINANCE TERMS:** Obtaining the loans below **is a contingency** of this Agreement unless: **(i)** either 2K or 2L is checked below; or **(ii)** otherwise agreed in writing. Buyer shall act diligently and in good faith to obtain the designated loans. Obtaining deposit, down payment and closing costs **is not a contingency.** Buyer represents that funds will be good when deposited with Escrow Holder.
   A. **INITIAL DEPOSIT:** Buyer has given a deposit in the amount of ....$ _____
   to the agent submitting the offer (or to ☐ _____
   (or ☐ _____), made payable to _____), by personal check
   which shall be held uncashed until Acceptance and then deposited within **3** business days after
   Acceptance (or ☐ _____),
   Escrow Holder, (or ☐ into Broker's trust account).
   B. **INCREASED DEPOSIT:** Buyer shall deposit with Escrow Holder an increased deposit in the amount of ...$ _____
   within _____ **Days** After Acceptance, or ☐ _____.
   C. **FIRST LOAN IN THE AMOUNT OF** ....$ _____
   (1) NEW First Deed of Trust in favor of lender, encumbering the Property, securing a note payable at
   maximum interest of _____% fixed rate, or _____% initial adjustable rate with a maximum
   interest rate of _____%, balance due in _____ years, amortized over _____ years. Buyer
   shall pay loan fees/points not to exceed _____. (These terms apply whether the designated loan
   is conventional, FHA or VA.)
   (2) ☐ FHA ☐ VA: (The following terms only apply to the FHA or VA loan that is checked.)
   Seller shall pay _____% discount points. Seller shall pay other fees not allowed to be paid by
   Buyer, ☐ not to exceed $_____. Seller shall pay the cost of lender required Repairs
   (including those for wood destroying pest) not otherwise provided for in this Agreement, ☐ not to
   exceed $_____. (Actual loan amount may increase if mortgage insurance premiums,
   funding fees or closing costs are financed.)
   D. **ADDITIONAL FINANCING TERMS:** ☐ Seller financing, (C.A.R. Form SFA); ☐ secondary financing, ...$ _____
   (C.A.R. Form PAA, paragraph 4A); ☐ assumed financing (C.A.R. Form PAA, paragraph 4B)
   _____
   _____
   E. **BALANCE OF PURCHASE PRICE** (not including costs of obtaining loans and other closing costs) in the amount of ...$ _____
   to be deposited with Escrow Holder within sufficient time to close escrow.
   F. **PURCHASE PRICE (TOTAL):** ....$ _____
   G. **LOAN APPLICATIONS:** Within **7 (or ☐ _____) Days** After Acceptance, Buyer shall provide Seller a letter from lender or mortgage loan broker stating that, based on a review of Buyer's written application and credit report, Buyer is prequalified or preapproved for the NEW loan specified in 2C above.
   H. **VERIFICATION OF DOWN PAYMENT AND CLOSING COSTS:** Buyer (or Buyer's lender or loan broker pursuant to 2G) shall, within **7 (or ☐ _____) Days** After Acceptance, provide Seller written verification of Buyer's down payment and closing costs.
   I. **LOAN CONTINGENCY REMOVAL: (i)** Within **17 (or ☐ _____) Days** After Acceptance, Buyer shall, as specified in paragraph 14, remove the loan contingency or cancel this Agreement; **OR (ii)** (if checked) ☐ the loan contingency shall remain in effect until the designated loans are funded.
   J. **APPRAISAL CONTINGENCY AND REMOVAL:** This Agreement is **(OR,** if checked, ☐ is NOT) contingent upon the Property appraising at no less than the specified purchase price. Buyer shall, as specified in paragraph 14, remove the appraisal contingency or cancel this Agreement when the loan contingency is removed (or, if checked, ☐ within **17 (or ☐ _____) Days** After Acceptance).
   K. ☐ **NO LOAN CONTINGENCY** (If checked): Obtaining any loan in paragraphs 2C, 2D or elsewhere in this Agreement is NOT a contingency of this Agreement. If Buyer does not obtain the loan and as a result Buyer does not purchase the Property, Seller may be entitled to Buyer's deposit or other legal remedies.
   L. ☐ **ALL CASH OFFER** (If checked): No loan is needed to purchase the Property. Buyer shall, within **7 (or ☐ _____) Days** After Acceptance, provide Seller written verification of sufficient funds to close this transaction.
3. **CLOSING AND OCCUPANCY:**
   A. Buyer intends (or ☐ does not intend) to occupy the Property as Buyer's primary residence.
   B. **Seller-occupied or vacant property:** Occupancy shall be delivered to Buyer at _____ AM/PM, ☐ on the date of Close Of Escrow; ☐ on _____; or ☐ no later than _____ **Days** After Close Of Escrow. (C.A.R. Form PAA, paragraph 2.) If transfer of title and occupancy do not occur at the same time, Buyer and Seller are advised to: **(i)** enter into a written occupancy agreement; and **(ii)** consult with their insurance and legal advisors.

RPA-CA REVISED 10/02 (PAGE 1 OF 8) Print Date

Buyer's Initials (_____)(_____)
Seller's Initials (_____)(_____)

Reviewed by _____ Date _____

CALIFORNIA RESIDENTIAL PURCHASE AGREEMENT (RPA-CA PAGE 1 OF 8)

Property Address: _____ Date: _____

C. Tenant-occupied property: (i) Property shall be vacant at least 5 (or ☐ _____) **Days** Prior to Close Of Escrow, unless otherwise agreed in writing. **Note to Seller: If you are unable to deliver Property vacant in accordance with rent control and other applicable Law, you may be in breach of this Agreement.**

OR (ii) (if checked) ☐ Tenant to remain in possession. The attached addendum is incorporated into this Agreement (C.A.R. Form PAA, paragraph 3.);

OR (iii) (if checked) ☐ This Agreement is contingent upon Buyer and Seller entering into a written agreement regarding occupancy of the Property within the time specified in paragraph 14. If no written agreement is reached within this time, either Buyer or Seller may cancel this Agreement in writing.

D. At Close Of Escrow, Seller assigns to Buyer any assignable warranty rights for items included in the sale and shall provide any available Copies of such warranties. Brokers cannot and will not determine the assignability of any warranties.

E. At Close Of Escrow, unless otherwise agreed in writing, Seller shall provide keys and/or means to operate all locks, mailboxes, security systems, alarms and garage door openers. If Property is a condominium or located in a common interest subdivision, Buyer may be required to pay a deposit to the Homeowners' Association ("HOA") to obtain keys to accessible HOA facilities.

4. **ALLOCATION OF COSTS** (If checked): Unless otherwise specified here, this paragraph only determines who is to pay for the report, inspection, test or service mentioned. If not specified here or elsewhere in this Agreement, the determination of who is to pay for any work recommended or identified by any such report, inspection, test or service shall be by the method specified in paragraph 14.

   A. WOOD DESTROYING PEST INSPECTION:

   (1) ☐ Buyer ☐ Seller shall pay for an inspection and report for wood destroying pests and organisms ("Report") which shall be prepared by _____, a registered structural pest control company. The Report shall cover the accessible areas of the main building and attached structures and, if checked: ☐ detached garages and carports, ☐ detached decks, ☐ the following other structures or areas _____. The Report shall not include roof coverings. If Property is a condominium or located in a common interest subdivision, the Report shall include only the separate interest and any exclusive-use areas being transferred and shall not include common areas, unless otherwise agreed. Water tests of shower pans on upper level units may not be performed without consent of the owners of property below the shower.

   OR (2) ☐ (If checked) The attached addendum (C.A.R. Form WPA) regarding wood destroying pest inspection and allocation of cost is incorporated into this Agreement.

   B. OTHER INSPECTIONS AND REPORTS:
   (1) ☐ Buyer ☐ Seller shall pay to have septic or private sewage disposal systems inspected _____.
   (2) ☐ Buyer ☐ Seller shall pay to have domestic wells tested for water potability and productivity _____.
   (3) ☐ Buyer ☐ Seller shall pay for a natural hazard zone disclosure report prepared by _____.
   (4) ☐ Buyer ☐ Seller shall pay for the following inspection or report _____.
   (5) ☐ Buyer ☐ Seller shall pay for the following inspection or report _____.

   C. GOVERNMENT REQUIREMENTS AND RETROFIT:
   (1) ☐ Buyer ☐ Seller shall pay for smoke detector installation and/or water heater bracing, if required by Law. Prior to Close Of Escrow, Seller shall provide Buyer a written statement of compliance in accordance with state and local Law, unless exempt.
   (2) ☐ Buyer ☐ Seller shall pay the cost of compliance with any other minimum mandatory government retrofit standards, inspections and reports if required as a condition of closing escrow under any Law. _____.

   D. ESCROW AND TITLE:
   (1) ☐ Buyer ☐ Seller shall pay escrow fee _____.
   Escrow Holder shall be _____.
   (2) ☐ Buyer ☐ Seller shall pay for **owner's** title insurance policy specified in paragraph 12 _____.
   Owner's title policy to be issued by _____.
   (Buyer shall pay for any title insurance policy insuring Buyer's **lender**, unless otherwise agreed in writing.)

   E. OTHER COSTS:
   (1) ☐ Buyer ☐ Seller shall pay County transfer tax or transfer fee _____.
   (2) ☐ Buyer ☐ Seller shall pay City transfer tax or transfer fee _____.
   (3) ☐ Buyer ☐ Seller shall pay HOA transfer fee _____.
   (4) ☐ Buyer ☐ Seller shall pay HOA document preparation fees _____.
   (5) ☐ Buyer ☐ Seller shall pay the cost, not to exceed $ _____, of a one-year home warranty plan,
   issued by _____
   with the following optional coverage: _____.
   (6) ☐ Buyer ☐ Seller shall pay for _____.
   (7) ☐ Buyer ☐ Seller shall pay for _____.

5. **STATUTORY DISCLOSURES (INCLUDING LEAD-BASED PAINT HAZARD DISCLOSURES) AND CANCELLATION RIGHTS:**
   A. (1) Seller shall, within the time specified in paragraph 14, deliver to Buyer, if required by Law: **(i)** Federal Lead-Based Paint Disclosures and pamphlet ("Lead Disclosures"); and **(ii)** disclosures or notices required by sections 1102 et. seq. and 1103 et. seq. of the California Civil Code ("Statutory Disclosures"). Statutory Disclosures include, but are not limited to, a Real Estate Transfer Disclosure Statement ("TDS"), Natural Hazard Disclosure Statement ("NHD"), notice or actual knowledge of release of illegal controlled substance, notice of special tax and/or assessments (or, if allowed, substantially equivalent notice regarding the Mello-Roos Community Facilities Act and Improvement Bond Act of 1915) and, if Seller has actual knowledge, an industrial use and military ordnance location disclosure (C.A.R. Form SSD).
   (2) Buyer shall, within the time specified in paragraph 14, return Signed Copies of the Statutory and Lead Disclosures to Seller.
   (3) In the event Seller, prior to Close Of Escrow, becomes aware of adverse conditions materially affecting the Property, or any material inaccuracy in disclosures, information or representations previously provided to Buyer of which Buyer is otherwise unaware, Seller shall promptly provide a subsequent or amended disclosure or notice, in writing, covering those items. **However, a subsequent or amended disclosure shall not be required for conditions and material inaccuracies disclosed in reports ordered and paid for by Buyer.**

Buyer's Initials (_____)(_____)
Seller's Initials (_____)(_____)

Reviewed by _____ Date _____

CALIFORNIA RESIDENTIAL PURCHASE AGREEMENT (RPA-CA PAGE 2 OF 8)

Property Address: _____ Date: _____

(4) If any disclosure or notice specified in 5A(1), or subsequent or amended disclosure or notice is delivered to Buyer after the offer is Signed, Buyer shall have the right to cancel this Agreement within **3 Days** After delivery in person, or **5 Days** After delivery by deposit in the mail, by giving written notice of cancellation to Seller or Seller's agent. (Lead Disclosures sent by mail must be sent certified mail or better.)

(5) Note to Buyer and Seller: Waiver of Statutory and Lead Disclosures is prohibited by Law.

B. NATURAL AND ENVIRONMENTAL HAZARDS: Within the time specified in paragraph 14, Seller shall, if required by Law: **(i)** deliver to Buyer earthquake guides (and questionnaire) and environmental hazards booklet; **(ii)** even if exempt from the obligation to provide a NHD, disclose if the Property is located in a Special Flood Hazard Area; Potential Flooding (Inundation) Area; Very High Fire Hazard Zone; State Fire Responsibility Area; Earthquake Fault Zone; Seismic Hazard Zone; and **(iii)** disclose any other zone as required by Law and provide any other information required for those zones.

C. DATA BASE DISCLOSURE: NOTICE: The California Department of Justice, sheriff's departments, police departments serving jurisdictions of 200,000 or more and many other local law enforcement authorities maintain for public access a data base of the locations of persons required to register pursuant to paragraph (1) of subdivision (a) of Section 290.4 of the Penal Code. The data base is updated on a quarterly basis and a source of information about the presence of these individuals in any neighborhood. The Department of Justice also maintains a Sex Offender Identification Line through which inquiries about individuals may be made. This is a "900" telephone service. Callers must have specific information about individuals they are checking. Information regarding neighborhoods is not available through the "900" telephone service.

6. CONDOMINIUM/PLANNED UNIT DEVELOPMENT DISCLOSURES:

   A. SELLER HAS: 7 (or ☐ _____) Days After Acceptance to disclose to Buyer whether the Property is a condominium, or is located in a planned unit development or other common interest subdivision.

   B. If the Property is a condominium or is located in a planned unit development or other common interest subdivision, Seller has **3 (or ☐ _____) Days** After Acceptance to request from the HOA (C.A.R. Form HOA): **(i)** Copies of any documents required by Law; **(ii)** disclosure of any pending or anticipated claim or litigation by or against the HOA; **(iii)** a statement containing the location and number of designated parking and storage spaces; **(iv)** Copies of the most recent 12 months of HOA minutes for regular and special meetings; and **(v)** the names and contact information of all HOAs governing the Property (collectively, "CI Disclosures"). Seller shall itemize and deliver to Buyer all CI Disclosures received from the HOA and any CI Disclosures in Seller's possession. Buyer's approval of CI Disclosures is a contingency of this Agreement as specified in paragraph 14.

7. CONDITIONS AFFECTING PROPERTY:

   A. Unless otherwise agreed: **(i) the Property is sold (a) in its PRESENT physical condition as of the date of Acceptance and (b) subject to Buyer's Investigation rights; (ii)** the Property, including pool, spa, landscaping and grounds, is to be maintained in substantially the same condition as on the date of Acceptance; and **(iii)** all debris and personal property not included in the sale shall be removed by Close Of Escrow.

   B. SELLER SHALL, within the time specified in paragraph 14, **DISCLOSE KNOWN MATERIAL FACTS AND DEFECTS affecting the Property, including known insurance claims within the past five years, AND MAKE OTHER DISCLOSURES REQUIRED BY LAW.**

   C. NOTE TO BUYER: You are strongly advised to conduct investigations of the entire Property in order to determine its present condition since Seller may not be aware of all defects affecting the Property or other factors that you consider important. Property improvements may not be built according to code, in compliance with current Law, or have had permits issued.

   D. NOTE TO SELLER: Buyer has the right to inspect the Property and, as specified in paragraph 14, based upon information discovered in those inspections: **(i)** cancel this Agreement; or **(ii)** request that you make Repairs or take other action.

8. ITEMS INCLUDED AND EXCLUDED:

   A. NOTE TO BUYER AND SELLER: Items listed as included or excluded in the MLS, flyers or marketing materials are **not** included in the purchase price or excluded from the sale unless specified in 8B or C.

   B. ITEMS INCLUDED IN SALE:

   (1) All EXISTING fixtures and fittings that are attached to the Property;

   (2) Existing electrical, mechanical, lighting, plumbing and heating fixtures, ceiling fans, fireplace inserts, gas logs and grates, solar systems, built-in appliances, window and door screens, awnings, shutters, window coverings, attached floor coverings, television antennas, satellite dishes, private integrated telephone systems, air coolers/conditioners, pool/spa equipment, garage door openers/remote controls, mailbox, in-ground landscaping, trees/shrubs, water softeners, water purifiers, security systems/alarms;

   (3) The following items: _____

   _____

   (4) Seller represents that all items included in the purchase price, unless otherwise specified, are owned by Seller.

   (5) All items included shall be transferred free of liens and without Seller warranty.

   C. ITEMS EXCLUDED FROM SALE: _____

   _____

9. BUYER'S INVESTIGATION OF PROPERTY AND MATTERS AFFECTING PROPERTY:

   A. Buyer's acceptance of the condition of, and any other matter affecting the Property, is a contingency of this Agreement as specified in this paragraph and paragraph 14. Within the time specified in paragraph 14, Buyer shall have the right, at Buyer's expense unless otherwise agreed, to conduct inspections, investigations, tests, surveys and other studies ("Buyer Investigations"), including, but not limited to, the right to: **(i)** inspect for lead-based paint and other lead-based paint hazards; **(ii)** inspect for wood destroying pests and organisms; **(iii)** review the registered sex offender database; **(iv)** confirm the insurability of Buyer and the Property; and **(v)** satisfy Buyer as to any matter specified in the attached Buyer's Inspection Advisory (C.A.R. Form BIA). Without Seller's prior written consent, Buyer shall neither make nor cause to be made: **(i)** invasive or destructive Buyer's Investigations; or **(ii)** inspections by any governmental building or zoning inspector or government employee, unless required by Law.

   B. Buyer shall complete Buyer Investigations and, as specified in paragraph 14, remove the contingency or cancel the Agreement. Buyer shall give Seller, at no cost, complete Copies of all Buyer Investigation reports obtained by Buyer. Seller shall make the Property available for all Buyer Investigations. Seller shall have water, gas, electricity and all operable pilot lights on for Buyer's Investigations and through the date possession is made available to Buyer.

Buyer's Initials (_____)(_____)
Seller's Initials (_____)(_____)

RPA-CA REVISED 10/02 (PAGE 3 OF 8)

| Reviewed by _____ Date _____ |

EQUAL HOUSING OPPORTUNITY

CALIFORNIA RESIDENTIAL PURCHASE AGREEMENT (RPA-CA PAGE 3 OF 8)

Property Address: _____ Date: _____

10. **REPAIRS:** Repairs shall be completed prior to final verification of condition unless otherwise agreed in writing. Repairs to be performed at Seller's expense may be performed by Seller or through others, provided that the work complies with applicable Law, including governmental permit, inspection and approval requirements. Repairs shall be performed in a good, skillful manner with materials of quality and appearance comparable to existing materials. It is understood that exact restoration of appearance or cosmetic items following all Repairs may not be possible. Seller shall: **(i)** obtain receipts for Repairs performed by others; **(ii)** prepare a written statement indicating the Repairs performed by Seller and the date of such Repairs; and **(iii)** provide Copies of receipts and statements to Buyer prior to final verification of condition.

11. **BUYER INDEMNITY AND SELLER PROTECTION FOR ENTRY UPON PROPERTY:** Buyer shall: **(i)** keep the Property free and clear of liens; **(ii)** Repair all damage arising from Buyer Investigations; and **(iii)** indemnify and hold Seller harmless from all resulting liability, claims, demands, damages and costs. Buyer shall carry, or Buyer shall require anyone acting on Buyer's behalf to carry, policies of liability, workers' compensation and other applicable insurance, defending and protecting Seller from liability for any injuries to persons or property occurring during any Buyer Investigations or work done on the Property at Buyer's direction prior to Close Of Escrow. Seller is advised that certain protections may be afforded Seller by recording a "Notice of Non-responsibility" (C.A.R. Form NNR) for Buyer Investigations and work done on the Property at Buyer's direction. Buyer's obligations under this paragraph shall survive the termination of this Agreement.

12. **TITLE AND VESTING:**
    A. Within the time specified in paragraph 14, Buyer shall be provided a current preliminary (title) report, which is only an offer by the title insurer to issue a policy of title insurance and may not contain every item affecting title. Buyer's review of the preliminary report and any other matters which may affect title are a contingency of this Agreement as specified in paragraph 14.
    B. Title is taken in its present condition subject to all encumbrances, easements, covenants, conditions, restrictions, rights and other matters, whether of record or not, as of the date of Acceptance except: **(i)** monetary liens of record unless Buyer is assuming those obligations or taking the Property subject to those obligations; and **(ii)** those matters which Seller has agreed to remove in writing.
    C. Within the time specified in paragraph 14, Seller has a duty to disclose to Buyer all matters known to Seller affecting title, whether of record or not.
    D. At Close Of Escrow, Buyer shall receive a grant deed conveying title (or, for stock cooperative or long-term lease, an assignment of stock certificate or of Seller's leasehold interest), including oil, mineral and water rights if currently owned by Seller. Title shall vest as designated in Buyer's supplemental escrow instructions. THE MANNER OF TAKING TITLE MAY HAVE SIGNIFICANT LEGAL AND TAX CONSEQUENCES. CONSULT AN APPROPRIATE PROFESSIONAL.
    E. Buyer shall receive a CLTA/ALTA Homeowner's Policy of Title Insurance. A title company, at Buyer's request, can provide information about the availability, desirability, coverage, and cost of various title insurance coverages and endorsements. If Buyer desires title coverage other than that required by this paragraph, Buyer shall instruct Escrow Holder in writing and pay any increase in cost.

13. **SALE OF BUYER'S PROPERTY:**
    A. This Agreement is NOT contingent upon the sale of any property owned by Buyer.
OR B. ☐ (If checked): The attached addendum (C.A.R. Form COP) regarding the contingency for the sale of property owned by Buyer is incorporated into this Agreement.

14. **TIME PERIODS; REMOVAL OF CONTINGENCIES; CANCELLATION RIGHTS: The following time periods may only be extended, altered, modified or changed by mutual written agreement. Any removal of contingencies or cancellation under this paragraph must be in writing (C.A.R. Form RRCR).**
    A. **SELLER HAS: 7 (or ☐ _____) Days** After Acceptance to deliver to Buyer all reports, disclosures and information for which Seller is responsible under paragraphs 4, 5A and B, 6A, 7B and 12.
    B. (1) **BUYER HAS: 17 (or ☐ _____) Days** After Acceptance, unless otherwise agreed in writing, to:
        (i) complete all Buyer Investigations; approve all disclosures, reports and other applicable information, which Buyer receives from Seller; and approve all matters affecting the Property (including lead-based paint and lead-based paint hazards as well as other information specified in paragraph 5 and insurability of Buyer and the Property); and
        (ii) return to Seller Signed Copies of Statutory and Lead Disclosures delivered by Seller in accordance with paragraph 5A.
        (2) Within the time specified in 14B(1), Buyer may request that Seller make repairs or take any other action regarding the Property. Seller has no obligation to agree to or respond to Buyer's requests. (C.A.R. Form RR)
        (3) By the end of the time specified in 14B(1) (or 2I for loan contingency or 2J for appraisal contingency), Buyer shall, in writing, remove the applicable contingency (C.A.R. Form RRCR) or cancel this Agreement. However, if the following inspections, reports or disclosures are not made within the time specified in 14A, then Buyer has **5 (or ☐ _____) Days** after receipt of any such items, or the time specified in 14B(1), whichever is later, to remove the applicable contingency or cancel this Agreement in writing: **(i)** government-mandated inspections or reports required as a condition of closing; or **(ii)** Common Interest Disclosures pursuant to paragraph 6B.
    C. **CONTINUATION OF CONTINGENCY OR CONTRACTUAL OBLIGATION; SELLER RIGHT TO CANCEL:**
        (1) **Seller right to Cancel; Buyer Contingencies:** Seller, after first giving Buyer a Notice to Buyer to Perform (as specified below), may cancel this Agreement in writing and authorize return of Buyer's deposit if, by the time specified in this Agreement, Buyer does not remove in writing the applicable contingency or cancel this Agreement. Once all contingencies have been removed, failure of either Buyer or Seller to close escrow on time may be a breach of this Agreement.
        (2) **Continuation of Contingency:** Even after the expiration of the time specified in 14B(1), Buyer retains the right to make requests to Seller, remove in writing the applicable contingency or cancel this Agreement until Seller cancels pursuant to 14C(1). Once Seller receives Buyer's written removal of all contingencies, Seller may not cancel this Agreement pursuant to 14C(1).
        (3) **Seller right to Cancel; Buyer Contract Obligations:** Seller, after first giving Buyer a Notice to Buyer to Perform (as specified below), may cancel this Agreement in writing and authorize return of Buyer's deposit for any of the following reasons: **(i)** if Buyer fails to deposit funds as required by 2A or 2B; **(ii)** if the funds deposited pursuant to 2A or 2B are not good when deposited; **(iii)** if Buyer fails to provide a letter as required by 2G; **(iv)** if Buyer fails to provide verification as required by 2H or 2L; **(v)** if Seller reasonably disapproves of the verification provided by 2H or 2L; **(vi)** if Buyer fails to return Statutory and Lead Disclosures as required by paragraph 5A(2); or **(vii)** if Buyer fails to sign or initial a separate liquidated damage form for an increased deposit as required by paragraph 16. **Seller is not required to give Buyer a Notice to Perform regarding Close of Escrow.**
        (4) **Notice To Buyer to Perform:** The Notice to Buyer to Perform (C.A.R. Form NBP) shall: **(i)** be in writing; **(ii)** be signed by Seller; and **(iii)** give Buyer at least **24 (or ☐ _____) hours** (or until the time specified in the applicable paragraph, whichever occurs last) to take the applicable action. A Notice to Buyer to Perform may not be given any earlier than **2 Days** Prior to the expiration of the applicable time for Buyer to remove a contingency or cancel this Agreement or meet a 14C(3) obligation.

Buyer's Initials (_____)(_____)
Seller's Initials (_____)(_____)

| Reviewed by _____ Date _____ |

RPA-CA REVISED 10/02 (PAGE 4 OF 8)

CALIFORNIA RESIDENTIAL PURCHASE AGREEMENT (RPA-CA PAGE 4 OF 8)

D. EFFECT OF BUYER'S REMOVAL OF CONTINGENCIES : If Buyer removes, in writing, any contingency or cancellation rights, unless otherwise specified in a separate written agreement between Buyer and Seller, Buyer shall conclusively be deemed to have: **(i)** completed all Buyer Investigations, and review of reports and other applicable information and disclosures pertaining to that contingency or cancellation right; **(ii)** elected to proceed with the transaction; and **(iii)** assumed all liability, responsibility and expense for Repairs or corrections pertaining to that contingency or cancellation right, or for inability to obtain financing.

E. EFFECT OF CANCELLATION ON DEPOSITS: If Buyer or Seller gives written notice of cancellation pursuant to rights duly exercised under the terms of this Agreement, Buyer and Seller agree to Sign mutual instructions to cancel the sale and escrow and release deposits, less fees and costs, to the party entitled to the funds. Fees and costs may be payable to service providers and vendors for services and products provided during escrow. **Release of funds will require mutual Signed release instructions from Buyer and Seller, judicial decision or arbitration award. A party may be subject to a civil penalty of up to $1,000 for refusal to sign such instructions if no good faith dispute exists as to who is entitled to the deposited funds (Civil Code §1057.3).**

15. FINAL VERIFICATION OF CONDITION: Buyer shall have the right to make a final inspection of the Property within **5 (or _____) Days** Prior to Close Of Escrow, **NOT AS A CONTINGENCY OF THE SALE,** but solely to confirm: **(i)** the Property is maintained pursuant to paragraph 7A; **(ii)** Repairs have been completed as agreed; and **(iii)** Seller has complied with Seller's other obligations under this Agreement.

16. LIQUIDATED DAMAGES: If Buyer fails to complete this purchase because of Buyer's default, Seller shall retain, as liquidated damages, the deposit actually paid. If the Property is a dwelling with no more than four units, one of which Buyer intends to occupy, then the amount retained shall be no more than 3% of the purchase price. Any excess shall be returned to Buyer. Release of funds will require mutual, Signed release instructions from both Buyer and Seller, judicial decision or arbitration award.
BUYER AND SELLER SHALL SIGN A SEPARATE LIQUIDATED DAMAGES PROVISION FOR ANY INCREASED DEPOSIT. (C.A.R. FORM RID)

Buyer's Initials _____ / _____	Seller's Initials _____ / _____

17. DISPUTE RESOLUTION:

A. MEDIATION: Buyer and Seller agree to mediate any dispute or claim arising between them out of this Agreement, or any resulting transaction, before resorting to arbitration or court action. Paragraphs 17B(2) and (3) below apply whether or not the Arbitration provision is initialed. Mediation fees, if any, shall be divided equally among the parties involved. If, for any dispute or claim to which this paragraph applies, any party commences an action without first attempting to resolve the matter through mediation, or refuses to mediate after a request has been made, then that party shall not be entitled to recover attorney fees, even if they would otherwise be available to that party in any such action. THIS MEDIATION PROVISION APPLIES WHETHER OR NOT THE ARBITRATION PROVISION IS INITIALED.

B. ARBITRATION OF DISPUTES: (1) Buyer and Seller agree that any dispute or claim in Law or equity arising between them out of this Agreement or any resulting transaction, which is not settled through mediation, shall be decided by neutral, binding arbitration, including and subject to paragraphs 17B(2) and (3) below. The arbitrator shall be a retired judge or justice, or an attorney with at least 5 years of residential real estate Law experience, unless the parties mutually agree to a different arbitrator, who shall render an award in accordance with substantive California Law. The parties shall have the right to discovery in accordance with California Code of Civil Procedure §1283.05. In all other respects, the arbitration shall be conducted in accordance with Title 9 of Part III of the California Code of Civil Procedure. Judgment upon the award of the arbitrator(s) may be entered into any court having jurisdiction. Interpretation of this agreement to arbitrate shall be governed by the Federal Arbitration Act.
(2) EXCLUSIONS FROM MEDIATION AND ARBITRATION: The following matters are excluded from mediation and arbitration: **(i)** a judicial or non-judicial foreclosure or other action or proceeding to enforce a deed of trust, mortgage or installment land sale contract as defined in California Civil Code §2985; **(ii)** an unlawful detainer action; **(iii)** the filing or enforcement of a mechanic's lien; and **(iv)** any matter that is within the jurisdiction of a probate, small claims or bankruptcy court. The filing of a court action to enable the recording of a notice of pending action, for order of attachment, receivership, injunction, or other provisional remedies, shall not constitute a waiver of the mediation and arbitration provisions.
(3) BROKERS: Buyer and Seller agree to mediate and arbitrate disputes or claims involving either or both Brokers, consistent with 17 A and B, provided either or both Brokers shall have agreed to such mediation or arbitration prior to, or within a reasonable time after, the dispute or claim is presented to Brokers. Any election by either or both Brokers to participate in mediation or arbitration shall not result in Brokers being deemed parties to the Agreement.

"NOTICE: BY INITIALING IN THE SPACE BELOW YOU ARE AGREEING TO HAVE ANY DISPUTE ARISING OUT OF THE MATTERS INCLUDED IN THE 'ARBITRATION OF DISPUTES' PROVISION DECIDED BY NEUTRAL ARBITRATION AS PROVIDED BY CALIFORNIA LAW AND YOU ARE GIVING UP ANY RIGHTS YOU MIGHT POSSESS TO HAVE THE DISPUTE LITIGATED IN A COURT OR JURY TRIAL. BY INITIALING IN THE SPACE BELOW YOU ARE GIVING UP YOUR JUDICIAL RIGHTS TO DISCOVERY AND APPEAL, UNLESS THOSE RIGHTS ARE SPECIFICALLY INCLUDED IN THE 'ARBITRATION OF DISPUTES' PROVISION. IF YOU REFUSE TO SUBMIT TO ARBITRATION AFTER AGREEING TO THIS PROVISION, YOU MAY BE COMPELLED TO ARBITRATE UNDER THE AUTHORITY OF THE CALIFORNIA CODE OF CIVIL PROCEDURE. YOUR AGREEMENT TO THIS ARBITRATION PROVISION IS VOLUNTARY."

"WE HAVE READ AND UNDERSTAND THE FOREGOING AND AGREE TO SUBMIT DISPUTES ARISING OUT OF THE MATTERS INCLUDED IN THE 'ARBITRATION OF DISPUTES' PROVISION TO NEUTRAL ARBITRATION."

Buyer's Initials _____ / _____	Seller's Initials _____ / _____

Buyer's Initials (_____)(_____)
Seller's Initials (_____)(_____)

Reviewed by _____ Date _____

CALIFORNIA RESIDENTIAL PURCHASE AGREEMENT (RPA-CA PAGE 5 OF 8)

Reprinted with permission, CALIFORNIA ASSOCIATION OF REALTORS®. Endorsement not implied.

Property Address: _____ Date: _____

18. **PRORATIONS OF PROPERTY TAXES AND OTHER ITEMS:** Unless otherwise agreed in writing, the following items shall be PAID CURRENT and prorated between Buyer and Seller as of Close Of Escrow: real property taxes and assessments, interest, rents, HOA regular, special, and emergency dues and assessments imposed prior to Close Of Escrow, premiums on insurance assumed by Buyer, payments on bonds and assessments assumed by Buyer, and payments on Mello-Roos and other Special Assessment District bonds and assessments that are now a lien. The following items shall be assumed by Buyer WITHOUT CREDIT toward the purchase price: prorated payments on Mello-Roos and other Special Assessment District bonds and assessments and HOA special assessments that are now a lien but not yet due. Property will be reassessed upon change of ownership. Any supplemental tax bills shall be paid as follows: **(i)** for periods after Close Of Escrow, by Buyer; and **(ii)** for periods prior to Close Of Escrow, by Seller. TAX BILLS ISSUED AFTER CLOSE OF ESCROW SHALL BE HANDLED DIRECTLY BETWEEN BUYER AND SELLER. Prorations shall be made based on a 30-day month.

19. **WITHHOLDING TAXES:** Seller and Buyer agree to execute any instrument, affidavit, statement or instruction reasonably necessary to comply with federal (FIRPTA) and California withholding Law, if required (C.A.R. Forms AS and AB).

20. **MULTIPLE LISTING SERVICE ("MLS"):** Brokers are authorized to report to the MLS a pending sale and, upon Close Of Escrow, the terms of this transaction to be published and disseminated to persons and entities authorized to use the information on terms approved by the MLS.

21. **EQUAL HOUSING OPPORTUNITY:** The Property is sold in compliance with federal, state and local anti-discrimination Laws.

22. **ATTORNEY FEES:** In any action, proceeding, or arbitration between Buyer and Seller arising out of this Agreement, the prevailing Buyer or Seller shall be entitled to reasonable attorney fees and costs from the non-prevailing Buyer or Seller, except as provided in paragraph 17A.

23. **SELECTION OF SERVICE PROVIDERS:** If Brokers refer Buyer or Seller to persons, vendors, or service or product providers ("Providers"), Brokers do not guarantee the performance of any Providers. Buyer and Seller may select ANY Providers of their own choosing.

24. **TIME OF ESSENCE; ENTIRE CONTRACT; CHANGES:** Time is of the essence. All understandings between the parties are incorporated in this Agreement. Its terms are intended by the parties as a final, complete and exclusive expression of their Agreement with respect to its subject matter, and may not be contradicted by evidence of any prior agreement or contemporaneous oral agreement. If any provision of this Agreement is held to be ineffective or invalid, the remaining provisions will nevertheless be given full force and effect. **Neither this Agreement nor any provision in it may be extended, amended, modified, altered or changed, except in writing Signed by Buyer and Seller.**

25. **OTHER TERMS AND CONDITIONS,** including attached supplements:
    A. ☑ Buyer's Inspection Advisory (C.A.R. Form BIA)
    B. ☐ Purchase Agreement Addendum (C.A.R. Form PAA paragraph numbers: _____)
    C. _____
       _____
       _____
       _____

26. **DEFINITIONS:** As used in this Agreement:
    A. **"Acceptance"** means the time the offer or final counter offer is accepted in writing by a party and is delivered to and personally received by the other party or that party's authorized agent in accordance with the terms of this offer or a final counter offer.
    B. **"Agreement"** means the terms and conditions of this accepted California Residential Purchase Agreement and any accepted counter offers and addenda.
    C. **"C.A.R. Form"** means the specific form referenced or another comparable form agreed to by the parties.
    D. **"Close Of Escrow"** means the date the grant deed, or other evidence of transfer of title, is recorded. If the scheduled close of escrow falls on a Saturday, Sunday or legal holiday, then close of escrow shall be the next business day after the scheduled close of escrow date.
    E. **"Copy"** means copy by any means including photocopy, NCR, facsimile and electronic.
    F. **"Days"** means calendar days, unless otherwise required by Law.
    G. **"Days After"** means the specified number of calendar days after the occurrence of the event specified, not counting the calendar date on which the specified event occurs, and ending at 11:59PM on the final day.
    H. **"Days Prior"** means the specified number of calendar days before the occurrence of the event specified, not counting the calendar date on which the specified event is scheduled to occur.
    I. **"Electronic Copy"** or **"Electronic Signature"** means, as applicable, an electronic copy or signature complying with California Law. Buyer and Seller agree that electronic means will not be used by either party to modify or alter the content or integrity of this Agreement without the knowledge and consent of the other.
    J. **"Law"** means any law, code, statute, ordinance, regulation, rule or order, which is adopted by a controlling city, county, state or federal legislative, judicial or executive body or agency.
    K. **"Notice to Buyer to Perform"** means a document (C.A.R. Form NBP), which shall be in writing and Signed by Seller and shall give Buyer at least 24 hours **(or as otherwise specified in paragraph 14C(4))** to remove a contingency or perform as applicable.
    L. **"Repairs"** means any repairs (including pest control), alterations, replacements, modifications or retrofitting of the Property provided for under this Agreement.
    M. **"Signed"** means either a handwritten or electronic signature on an original document, Copy or any counterpart.
    N. **Singular and Plural** terms each include the other, when appropriate.

Buyer's Initials (_____)(_____)
Seller's Initials (_____)(_____)

Reviewed by _____ Date _____

CALIFORNIA RESIDENTIAL PURCHASE AGREEMENT (RPA-CA PAGE 6 OF 8)

Property Address: _____ Date: _____

27. AGENCY:

    A. DISCLOSURE: Buyer and Seller each acknowledge prior receipt of C.A.R. Form AD "Disclosure Regarding Real Estate Agency Relationships."

    B. POTENTIALLY COMPETING BUYERS AND SELLERS: Buyer and Seller each acknowledge receipt of a disclosure of the possibility of multiple representation by the Broker representing that principal. This disclosure may be part of a listing agreement, buyer-broker agreement or separate document (C.A.R. Form DA). Buyer understands that Broker representing Buyer may also represent other potential buyers, who may consider, make offers on or ultimately acquire the Property. Seller understands that Broker representing Seller may also represent other sellers with competing properties of interest to this Buyer.

    C. CONFIRMATION: The following agency relationships are hereby confirmed for this transaction:
Listing Agent _____ (Print Firm Name) is the agent of (check one): ☐ the Seller exclusively; or ☐ both the Buyer and Seller.
Selling Agent _____ (Print Firm Name) (if not same as Listing Agent) is the agent of (check one): ☐ the Buyer exclusively; or ☐ the Seller exclusively; or ☐ both the Buyer and Seller. Real Estate Brokers are not parties to the Agreement between Buyer and Seller.

28. JOINT ESCROW INSTRUCTIONS TO ESCROW HOLDER:

    A. The following paragraphs, or applicable portions thereof, of this Agreement constitute the joint escrow instructions of Buyer and Seller to Escrow Holder, which Escrow Holder is to use along with any related counter offers and addenda, and any additional mutual instructions to close the escrow: 1, 2, 4, 12, 13B, 14E, 18, 19, 24, 25B and C, 26, 28, 29, 32A, 33 and paragraph D of the section titled Real Estate Brokers on page 8. If a Copy of the separate compensation agreement(s) provided for in paragraph 29 or 32A, or paragraph D of the section titled Real Estate Brokers on page 8 is deposited with Escrow Holder by Broker, Escrow Holder shall accept such agreement(s) and pay out from Buyer's or Seller's funds, or both, as applicable, the Broker's compensation provided for in such agreement(s). The terms and conditions of this Agreement not set forth in the specified paragraphs are additional matters for the information of Escrow Holder, but about which Escrow Holder need not be concerned. Buyer and Seller will receive Escrow Holder's general provisions directly from Escrow Holder and will execute such provisions upon Escrow Holder's request. To the extent the general provisions are inconsistent or conflict with this Agreement, the general provisions will control as to the duties and obligations of Escrow Holder only. Buyer and Seller will execute additional instructions, documents and forms provided by Escrow Holder that are reasonably necessary to close escrow.

    B. A Copy of this Agreement shall be delivered to Escrow Holder within **3** business days after Acceptance (or ☐ _____). Buyer and Seller authorize Escrow Holder to accept and rely on Copies and Signatures as defined in this Agreement as originals, to open escrow and for other purposes of escrow. The validity of this Agreement as between Buyer and Seller is not affected by whether or when Escrow Holder Signs this Agreement.

    C. Brokers are a party to the escrow for the sole purpose of compensation pursuant to paragraphs 29, 32A and paragraph D of the section titled Real Estate Brokers on page 8. Buyer and Seller irrevocably assign to Brokers compensation specified in paragraphs 29 and 32A, respectively, and irrevocably instruct Escrow Holder to disburse those funds to Brokers at Close Of Escrow or pursuant to any other mutually executed cancellation agreement. Compensation instructions can be amended or revoked only with the written consent of Brokers. Escrow Holder shall immediately notify Brokers: **(i)** if Buyer's initial or any additional deposit is not made pursuant to this Agreement, or is not good at time of deposit with Escrow Holder; or **(ii)** if Buyer and Seller instruct Escrow Holder to cancel escrow.

    D. A Copy of any amendment that affects any paragraph of this Agreement for which Escrow Holder is responsible shall be delivered to Escrow Holder within **2** business days after mutual execution of the amendment.

29. BROKER COMPENSATION FROM BUYER: If applicable, upon Close Of Escrow, **Buyer** agrees to pay compensation to Broker as specified in a separate written agreement between Buyer and Broker.

30. TERMS AND CONDITIONS OF OFFER:

This is an offer to purchase the Property on the above terms and conditions. All paragraphs with spaces for initials by Buyer and Seller are incorporated in this Agreement only if initialed by all parties. If at least one but not all parties initial, a counter offer is required until agreement is reached. Seller has the right to continue to offer the Property for sale and to accept any other offer at any time prior to notification of Acceptance. Buyer has read and acknowledges receipt of a Copy of the offer and agrees to the above confirmation of agency relationships. If this offer is accepted and Buyer subsequently defaults, Buyer may be responsible for payment of Brokers' compensation. This Agreement and any supplement, addendum or modification, including any Copy, may be Signed in two or more counterparts, all of which shall constitute one and the same writing.

Buyer's Initials (_____)(_____)
Seller's Initials (_____)(_____)

Reviewed by _____ Date _____

RPA-CA REVISED 10/02 (PAGE 7 OF 8)

CALIFORNIA RESIDENTIAL PURCHASE AGREEMENT (RPA-CA PAGE 7 OF 8)

Property Address: _____ Date: _____

31. EXPIRATION OF OFFER: This offer shall be deemed revoked and the deposit shall be returned unless the offer is Signed by Seller and a Copy of the Signed offer is personally received by Buyer, or by _____, who is authorized to receive it by 5:00 PM on the third calendar day after this offer is signed by Buyer (or, if checked) ☐ by _____ (date), at _____ AM/PM).

Date _____ Date _____

BUYER _____ BUYER _____

_____ _____
(Print name) **(Print name)**

_____
(Address)

32. BROKER COMPENSATION FROM SELLER:
    A. Upon Close Of Escrow, **Seller** agrees to pay compensation to Broker as specified in a separate written agreement between Seller and Broker.
    B. If escrow does not close, compensation is payable as specified in that separate written agreement.
33. ACCEPTANCE OF OFFER: Seller warrants that Seller is the owner of the Property, or has the authority to execute this Agreement. Seller accepts the above offer, agrees to sell the Property on the above terms and conditions, and agrees to the above confirmation of agency relationships. Seller has read and acknowledges receipt of a Copy of this Agreement, and authorizes Broker to deliver a Signed Copy to Buyer.
    ☐ (If checked) **SUBJECT TO ATTACHED COUNTER OFFER, DATED** _____.

Date _____ Date _____

SELLER _____ SELLER _____

_____ _____
(Print name) **(Print name)**

_____
(Address)

(_____/_____) **CONFIRMATION OF ACCEPTANCE:** A Copy of Signed Acceptance was personally received by Buyer or Buyer's authorized
(Initials) agent on (date) _____ at _____ AM/PM. **A binding Agreement is created when a Copy of Signed Acceptance is personally received by Buyer or Buyer's authorized agent whether or not** confirmed in this document. Completion of this confirmation is not legally required in order to create a binding Agreement; it is solely intended to evidence the date that Confirmation of Acceptance has occurred.

REAL ESTATE BROKERS:
A. Real Estate Brokers are not parties to the Agreement between Buyer and Seller.
B. Agency relationships are confirmed as stated in paragraph 27.
C. If specified in paragraph 2A, Agent who submitted the offer for Buyer acknowledges receipt of deposit.
D. **COOPERATING BROKER COMPENSATION:** Listing Broker agrees to pay Cooperating Broker (**Selling Firm**) and Cooperating Broker agrees to accept, out of Listing Broker's proceeds in escrow: **(i)** the amount specified in the MLS, provided Cooperating Broker is a Participant of the MLS in which the Property is offered for sale or a reciprocal MLS; or **(ii)** ☐ (if checked) the amount specified in a separate written agreement (C.A.R. Form CBC) between Listing Broker and Cooperating Broker.

Real Estate Broker (Selling Firm) _____
By _____ Date _____
Address _____ City _____ State _____ Zip _____
Telephone _____ Fax _____ E-mail _____

Real Estate Broker (Listing Firm) _____
By _____ Date _____
Address _____ City _____ State _____ Zip _____
Telephone _____ Fax _____ E-mail _____

ESCROW HOLDER ACKNOWLEDGMENT:
Escrow Holder acknowledges receipt of a Copy of this Agreement, (if checked, ☐ a deposit in the amount of $ _____),
counter offer numbers _____ and _____, and agrees to act as Escrow Holder subject to paragraph 28 of this Agreement, any supplemental escrow instructions and the terms of Escrow Holder's general provisions.

Escrow Holder is advised that the date of Confirmation of Acceptance of the Agreement as between Buyer and Seller is _____

Escrow Holder _____ Escrow # _____
By _____ Date _____
Address _____
Phone/Fax/E-mail_____
Escrow Holder is licensed by the California Department of ☐ Corporations, ☐ Insurance, ☐ Real Estate. License # _____

THIS FORM HAS BEEN APPROVED BY THE CALIFORNIA ASSOCIATION OF REALTORS® (C.A.R.). NO REPRESENTATION IS MADE AS TO THE LEGAL VALIDITY OR ADEQUACY OF ANY PROVISION IN ANY SPECIFIC TRANSACTION. A REAL ESTATE BROKER IS THE PERSON QUALIFIED TO ADVISE ON REAL ESTATE TRANSACTIONS. IF YOU DESIRE LEGAL OR TAX ADVICE, CONSULT AN APPROPRIATE PROFESSIONAL.
This form is available for use by the entire real estate industry. It is not intended to identify the user as a REALTOR®. REALTOR® is a registered collective membership mark which may be used only by members of the NATIONAL ASSOCIATION OF REALTORS® who subscribe to its Code of Ethics.

SURE·TRAC Published by the
The System for Success™ California Association of REALTORS®

 EQUAL HOUSING OPPORTUNITY

RPA-CA REVISED 10/02 (PAGE 8 OF 8)   Reviewed by _____ Date _____

CALIFORNIA RESIDENTIAL PURCHASE AGREEMENT (RPA-CA PAGE 8 OF 8)

Reprinted with permission, CALIFORNIA ASSOCIATION OF REALTORS®. Endorsement not implied.

Disclosures

A number of disclosures must be made in a real estate transaction.

A **Natural Hazards Disclosure Statement** requires seller disclosure as to the property being in a:

- Special flood hazard area. Special flood hazard areas are designated on Federal Emergency Management Area (FEMA) maps.

- Areas of potential flooding. Areas of potential flooding may be shown on a dam-failure inundation map.

- Very high fire severity zone. A high-fire severity zone designation would subject the owners to property maintenance requirements.

- Wildland area that may contain substantial fire risks and hazards. Unless the Department of Forestry enters into a cooperative agreement, the state is not responsible for fire protection services within the wildland area.

- Earthquake fault zone.

- Seismic hazard zone. Seismic hazards could include areas prone to landslides as well as soil liquification resulting from seismic activity.

The above information is to be supplied based on the seller's knowledge and maps drawn by the state or FEMA. The location of maps for natural hazards disclosures are posted at the county recorder, country assessor and planning agency.

- The existence of **Mello-Roos Bonds** to pay for area improvements must be disclosed.

- A **Megan's Law** disclosure would indicate where a buyer can obtain information as to known sex offenders in the area.

- A **Homeowner's Guide to Earthquake Safety** must be given to buyers of one to four residential units built before 1960 and an Earthquake Safety Disclosure Statement must be filled out and signed by the buyer and seller.

- **Agency disclosure, election and confirmation** must be given to both buyers and sellers. (Chapter 4)

- **Real Estate Transfer Disclosure Statement** with seller disclosures as well as Agent's Inspection Disclosure (Chapter 4) must be provided.

- A copy of the booklet *Environmental Hazards: A Guide for Homeowners, Buyers, and Landlords and Tenants* specifies environmental hazards and the seller or seller's agent need not furnish any further information unless the seller or agent has knowledge of environmental hazards concerning the property.

- Sellers must disclose if they know of the **presence of or release of hazardous waste** material on the premises.

- **Hazardous Material Notice** This notifies the buyer that structure may contain material known to be hazardous or that may in the future be designated as a hazard and that removal might be required. The current, past, and future owners might be liable for cleanup costs.

- For one to four residential units built prior to 1978, a federal disclosure is required. *Protect Your Family from Lead in Your Home* booklet must be provided, and the California booklet entitled, *Environmental Hazards: A Guide For Homeowners, Buyers, Landlords and Tenants* meets the federal disclosure requirement.

- Known lead-based paint must be disclosed.

- **Military ordnance locations** within one mile that may contain potentially explosive substances must be disclosed.

- In **common interest developments,** purchaser is entitled to receive:
  - the booklet *Common Interest Development General Information;*
  - copies of covenants, conditions and restrictions;
  - Homeowners Association bylaws and articles of incorporation;
  - Homeowners Association financial statement, operating budget, current assessments, late charges, plans as to change in assessments, as well as pending legal actions.

- **Seller Financing Disclosure.** This disclosure is required if seller financing is involved. (Chapter 7)

- **Elder Abuse.** California's elder abuse law requires real estate agents to report any instance where they feel that abuse, fraud or undue influence is being used against an elderly person.

- **Importance of Home Inspection Notice.** For the sale of one to four residential units involving FHA financing, the borrower must sign a notice, *Importance of a Home Inspection.*

- **Smoke Detector Notice.** A buyer of a single-family home must be given a statement that the property is in compliance with California law as to smoke detectors.

- **Window Security Bars.** The presence of security bars and any safety release mechanism must be disclosed to buyer.

- **Water Heater Bracing.** Seller must provide buyer with certification that water heater is properly braced.

- **Septic System Disclosure.** This disclosure relates to the fact that a property is not currently connected to a sewer and that the owner may be required to connect to a sewer at a later date at the owner's expense. This disclosure also warns the purchaser that septic system problems may not be known or disclosed by an inspection.

- **Affiliated Business Arrangement Disclosure.** The broker must disclose to the parties any ownership or interests in a service provider recommended and that services can be obtained from other providers.

CHAPTER 5 QUIZ

1. Amy agreed to buy Bert's horse for $100. Bert agreed to sell it for $100. Bert delivered the horse to Amy and Amy paid Bert $100. This is an:
   a. executory bilateral contract
   b. executed bilateral contract
   c. executory unilateral contract
   d. executed unilateral contract

2. Clark leases Francine's store under an oral, one-year lease. After three months, Clark finds a less expensive rental.
   a. Since the lease was not in writing, Clark can get out of it immediately.
   b. Even though the lease was not binding because it was verbal, Clark is bound, since he treated the lease as being valid for three months.
   c. Clark must give notice, as in periodic tenancy.
   d. Clark is liable on the entire lease.

3. Which of these contracts must be in writing in accordance with the Statute of Frauds?
   a. a lease for one year
   b. the sale of growing crops
   c. a contract that is not to be performed for 13 months
   d. all of these

4. Albert agrees to buy Boswell's "corner lot in Block 4 of College Heights" for $30,000. Boswell thinks the sale is for Lot 18, but Albert thinks it is for Lot 32, which is another corner lot in the same block that is also owned by Boswell.
   a. Albert gets Lot 18
   b. Albert gets Lot 32
   c. Albert has a choice of Lot 18 or 32
   d. there is no contract

5. A contract to sell real estate by a 17-year-old unemancipated girl is:
   a. illegal   b. valid   c. enforceable   d. unenforceable

6. Failure to perform as agreed under a contract is known as:
   a. novation   b. illegal act   c. breach   d. damages

7. Losing a right due to failure to assert it in a timely fashion is called:
   a. laches   b. subrogation   c. satisfaction   d. dereliction

8. The essential elements of an enforceable contract are:
   a. express, consideration, mutuality, lawful object
   b. mutuality, written, competent parties, lawful object
   c. communicated, written, competent parties, lawful object
   d. competency, mutual consent, lawful object, consideration

9. A verbal agreement to sell real estate would be enforceable where:
   a. it involves unimproved land
   b. the purchase price is less than $500
   c. the parties swear to the agreement on a Bible
   d. the buyer takes possession, makes a down payment, and improves the property

10. As to contracts, which of the following is true?
    a. Printed text takes precedence over typed text.
    b. In a printed contract, the printed form takes precedence over handwritten text.
    c. Printed and handwritten notations carry the same weight and the court decides that meaning.
    d. The handwritten portion takes precedence over the printed portion in the event of any differences.

11. Coercion and duress are applied to one party in a contract. The contract is:
    a. void   b. voidable   c. illegal   d. unenforceable

12. Armand contracts to sell some land to Brenda and thereafter refuses to perform. Brenda wants the land, so she should bring suit against Armand for:
    a. recision
    b. novation
    c. compensatory damages
    d. specific performance

13. Mutual consent is usually evidenced by:
    a. offer and acceptance   b. fraud   c. duress   d. none of these

14. A minor inherits land. While still a minor, she deeds the land to the church, which puts a building on it. After reaching majority, she changes her mind and wants the land back.
    a. If it was a charitable gift, she cannot get it back.
    b. She must pay the church the value of the structure.
    c. She can get the land back.
    d. All of these are true.

15. After agreeing verbally to lease a house for six months starting the following month, a tenant notifies the owner that he has found a more suitable place to move. The contract is:
    a. unenforceable
    b. not valid for lack of writing
    c. binding
    d. illegal

16. An offer usually has to be accepted:
    a. in writing
    b. in the manner specified in the offer
    c. within 10 days
    d. none of these

17. All of the following are essential elements of a contract except:
    a. an offer   b. acceptance   c. consideration   d. performance

18. Which of the following would not have to be in writing to be enforceable?
    a. sale of a lot for $100
    b. sale of a residence
    c. sale agreement for a prize bull for $600
    d. none of these

19. A broker sold a home under an oral listing and was paid a commission. As to this:
    a. the broker has placed her license in jeopardy
    b. the sale is voidable
    c. the compensation must be returned
    d. none of these

20. Antonio enters into a contract with Bess through the chicanery of a broker who induced the contract through fraud. The contract is:
    a. unenforceable   b. void   c. valid   d. voidable

21. Which of the following is true?
    a. An illegal contract can be an enforceable contract.
    b. A valid contract can be an unenforceable contract.
    c. A void contract can be enforced by one party only.
    d. "Voidable" means "void unless validated."

22. April signed a contract to buy Byron's property. Byron obtained April's signature by representing that the sale agreement was a petition to the city for street improvement. The purchase agreement would be:
    a. voidable at April's option
    b. voidable at April's or Byron's option
    c. void
    d. valid

23. Two brokers agree verbally to split a commission. The agreement is:
    a. enforceable
    b. void because of the Statute of Frauds
    c. unenforceable
    d. voidable

24. All contracts require all of the following *except:*
    a. a proper writing
    b. an offer and acceptance
    c. a legal purpose
    d. consideration

25. A listing entered into on March 12, expiring at midnight on April 12, is for _____ days:
    a. 30   b. 31   c. 32   d. 33

26. All four copies of a purchase agreement would most likely be signed by the:
    a. buyer
    b. seller
    c. buyer and seller
    d. buyer, seller, and broker

27. A broker receives a full-price offer on a house she has listed in accordance with the terms of the listing. Before she can present the offer, another broker brings in an offer for $500 less but slightly better terms. The listing broker should:
    a. refuse to accept the second offer
    b. present both offers at the same time
    c. tell the other broker the property has been sold
    d. present both offers in the order received

28. A broker has a standard CAR Residential Listing Agreement. During the listing, the owner signs a two-year lease without the consent of the broker.
    a. No consent is ever needed.
    b. The owner owes the broker a commission.
    c. The owner owes the broker half the commission.
    d. None of these are true.

29. The seller defaults on an executed purchase contract. The broker is:
    a. not entitled to a commission
    b. entitled to a commission on default
    c. entitled to a commission only on close of escrow
    d. entitled to half of the deposit after expenses

30. An owner signs open listings on a parcel of land with five different brokers.
    a. Each broker has an opportunity to earn the entire commission.
    b. The brokers will split a commission five ways if any of them sell the property.
    c. The owner must pay a full commission to each of the brokers if the property is sold.
    d. The owner must pay the broker of the first listing entered into if the owner procures a buyer.

31. A real estate commission is normally based on the:
    a. listing price   b. selling price   c. owner's equity   d. cash involved

32. A broker obtains a $1,200 down payment on a $20,000 full-price offer on her exclusive 6 percent listing. After acceptance, the seller releases the buyer from his obligation. The broker should:
    a. return the $1,200 to the buyer
    b. leave the $1,200 in escrow
    c. keep the $1,200 as her commission
    d. ask the local real estate board to arbitrate

33. A young couple indicates to a broker that the down payment is beyond their means. While showing them a property, the broker overhears them discussing taking out a personal loan for the down payment. The broker should:
    a. tell them not to buy if they must borrow
    b. point out the appreciation advantages of real estate
    c. explain that real estate ownership is well worth a temporary hardship
    d. caution the purchasers as to the danger of overextending themselves

34. Ashley gives her broker, Bob, an exclusive-agency listing. Ashley's cousin, a broker in another town, finds a buyer and takes a reduced commission.
    a. Ashley owes Bob a commission
    b. Ashley does not have to pay Bob
    c. Ashley's cousin must split his commission with Bob
    d. Ashley's cousin has placed his license in jeopardy

35. An offer would be terminated by:
    a. rejection by the offeror
    b. rejection by the offeree
    c. revocation by the offeree
    d. a request for an extension by the offeree

36. The authority of the broker to accept a deposit is provided for in the:
    a. escrow instructions
    b. listing
    c. deposit receipt
    d. all of these

37. The provision in a deposit receipt calling for forfeiture by the buyer of a deposit is known as:
    a. punitive damages
    b. liquidated damages
    c. forfeiture clause
    d. none of these

38. Listings of real estate must be in writing because of the:
    a. Commissioner's regulations
    b. Statute of Frauds
    c. NAR
    d. none of these

39. An owner dies one week after giving a six-month exclusive-right-to-sell listing. His administrator does not wish to sell the property.
    a. The administrator is liable for the commission.
    b. The estate is liable for the commission.
    c. The heirs are liable for the commission.
    d. None of these are true.

40. On an exclusive listing, a broker can be disciplined for:
   a. failure to attach a tax statement
   b. failure to give a copy to the owner
   c. failure to include a definite termination date
   d. both b and c

41. A broker lists a property for $20,000. He discovers that the holder of a $5,000 second trust deed will discount it 50 percent. A prospective buyer will pay $17,500 for the property, but the seller indicates her price is firm. The broker should:
   a. find another buyer
   b. buy the trust deed himself
   c. inform the seller that the trust deed can be discounted
   d. tell the buyer to offer $20,000 and assume the second trust deed

42. A listing cannot be terminated by the principal when:
   a. the agent has not breached the agreement
   b. the agent has an interest coupled with the agency
   c. the listing has not expired
   d. both a and c

43. An option cannot be assigned:
   a. if the option period is over three months
   b. if purchase consideration is an unsecured note
   c. in any instance
   d. both a and b

44. The instrument most likely to state that "time is of the essence" is a(n):
   a. real estate purchase contract
   b. exclusive-agency listing
   c. open listing
   d. exclusive-right-to-sell listing

45. On a dwelling having four units, one of which the buyer intends to occupy as a residence, liquidated damages cannot exceed:
   a. the amount of the sales commission
   b. actual expenses
   c. 3 percent of the sale price
   d. none of these

46. Anita signs a real estate purchase contract as a buyer. The contract states that it is good for three days. One day later, Anita wishes to revoke her unaccepted offer.
   a. Anita may revoke but is liable for the commission.
   b. Anita is bound because the offer is irrevocable.
   c. Anita may revoke and recover her deposit.
   d. Anita may revoke but will forfeit her deposit.

47. Three people own a piece of property. A broker takes an exclusive listing to each of their places of business to get it signed. The broker must:
   a. give a copy to the first one who signs
   b. give a copy to each when he or she signs
   c. give one copy to any of the owners
   d. get them to sign at the same time

48. A broker finds a buyer for his listed property at more than the listing price. He therefore buys the property himself and resells it. This is a:
   a. violation of Article V
   b. secret profit
   c. violation of Article VI
   d. violation of Article VII

49. A safety clause in a listing requires the broker to submit names of people with whom she negotiated to the owner prior to the expiration of the listing. The broker inadvertently left out Edwin's name. One week after the listing expires, the owner sells to Edwin.
   a. Edwin is liable for the commission.
   b. The owner is liable for full commission.
   c. The owner is liable for half of the commission.
   d. The owner is not liable for any commission.

50. After agreeing verbally to split a commission with a selling broker, the listing broker now refuses to do so. The selling broker should:
   a. notify the state labor commissioner
   b. sue the listing broker
   c. contact the Real Estate Commission
   d. none of these—the agreement was verbal

51. A buyer gives an offer to purchase on February 1, requiring acceptance within 10 days.
    a. The buyer cannot withdraw before February 10.
    b. The buyer cannot withdraw prior to February 11.
    c. The buyer cannot withdraw prior to February 12.
    d. None of these are true.

52. A real estate purchase contract is:
    a. an agency
    b. a unilateral contract
    c. a bilateral contract
    d. none of these

53. Alan, a broker, obtains an offer from Bridget to buy Carl's house. After Carl accepts and the escrow instructions have been signed, both Bridget and Carl die.
    a. Alan has earned his commission, but the deal cannot be completed.
    b. The agreement is binding on the estates of both Bridget and Carl.
    c. The agency and executory contract were canceled by death.
    d. None of these are true.

54. If a buyer wishes to give a promissory note as a deposit with an offer:
    a. the broker cannot accept without the owner's permission
    b. the broker can never accept a note
    c. the broker can accept the note but must inform the principal that the deposit is in the form of a note
    d. none of these

55. An owner refuses to convey property after signing her acceptance on a purchase contract. Specific performance can be enforced by:
    a. the purchaser   b. the broker   c. either a or b   d. neither a nor b

56. An owner signs an exclusive listing. He refuses a full-price offer. Specific performance can be enforced by:
    a. the purchaser
    b. the broker
    c. both the purchaser and the broker
    d. neither the purchaser nor the broker

57. After an offer is accepted, the seller dies. The seller's wife inherits the property.
    a. The offer is terminated.
    b. The offer is voidable.
    c. The wife can be forced to sell.
    d. None of these are true.

58. An election of remedies would most likely appear in:
    a. a listing
    b. escrow instructions
    c. a deed
    d. a purchase agreement

59. An option provides for a consideration of one dollar. The option is:
    a. void because of the inadequacy of the consideration
    b. valid as long as the option stated a consideration
    c. valid if the consideration has been paid
    d. none of these

60. In accordance with the safety clause in a listing, the broker notifies the owner verbally of a prospective buyer. The day after the listing expires, the buyer purchases the property.
    a. The broker is entitled to a commission based on the listing price.
    b. The broker is entitled to a commission based on the selling price.
    c. The amount of the commission would be decided by the Real Estate Commission.
    d. The broker is not entitled to any commission.

61. A seller accepts an offer but changes the escrow period. The broker notifies the buyer of acceptance.
    a. A bilateral contract has been made.
    b. A unilateral contract has been made.
    c. No contract has been made.
    d. The buyer must submit a counteroffer.

62. A broker lists property owned by a corporation. Before expiration of the exclusive listing, all of the officers of the corporation die.
    a. The listing is terminated automatically.
    b. The listing remains in full effect.
    c. The listing must be reaffirmed by new offers.
    d. The listing is suspended.

63. Inadvertently, a deposit receipt is not filled in as to who pays for the standard policy of title insurance. The person responsible would then be:
    a. the broker
    b. the buyer
    c. the seller
    d. determined by local custom

64. A broker fails to give the owner a copy of the open listing or to include a termination date. The broker then obtains an offer which is accepted by the owner.
    a. The broker is entitled to her commission.
    b. The broker has not done anything wrong.
    c. Both a and b are true.
    d. Neither a nor b is true.

65. Burt, a broker, shows houses on which he has listings to Don and Wilma Smith. They don't like any of them. When Don is away, Burt shows a house to Wilma. She likes it and gives a deposit. On the purchase contract form, what would be appropriate to write after "received from"?
    a. Wilma Smith
    b. Don and Wilma Smith
    c. Don and Wilma Smith as joint tenants
    d. Don and Wilma Smith, husband and wife

66. A listing dated June 1995 states "cash and assume a loan at _____ percent interest per annum with balance due in December 2010."
    a. The listing is okay.
    b. The salesperson who wrote it is subject to discipline.
    c. The listing is illegal.
    d. The existing loan is illegal.

67. Which of the following may be recorded?
    a. an exclusive-right-to-sell listing
    b. an exclusive-agency listing
    c. contracts of sale
    d. all of these

68. An exclusive-right-to-sell listing contract shows the expiration of the listing as 12 noon on December 3. At 3 P.M. on December 3, Adam, the original listing broker, produces a buyer. The owner gave an exclusive listing on the property at 2 P.M. on December 3 to Bernadine, another broker.
    a. Adam is entitled to a commission.
    b. Adam has placed his license in jeopardy.
    c. Bernadine is entitled to a commission.
    d. None of these are true.

69. A broker is least likely *not* to get in trouble by:
    a. failing to put a termination date in an open listing
    b. forgetting to give a copy of an exclusive listing to the person signing it
    c. taking a net listing
    d. taking an option with a listing

70. A seller sold property "as is." The broker knew the plumbing was in bad repair but did not inform the buyer. The buyer can sue:
    a. no one since the sale was "as is"
    b. no one since "as is" is really notice of a problem
    c. the broker
    d. none of these

71. Payment of a commission orally agreed to without subsequent written ratification is:
    a. illegal
    b. legal
    c. contrary to real estate rules and regulations
    d. both a and b

72. Harvey gives Jonas, a broker, an exclusive-agency listing for three months. After one week, Harvey notifies Jonas in writing that he is terminating the agreement. The next day, Harvey signs an open listing with Keith, another broker. Lee, a salesman working for Keith, brings in an offer, which Harvey accepts. As to the commission, which of the following is true?

a. Jonas is not entitled to a commission because Harvey canceled the listing.

b. Harvey was not entitled to list with Keith because the other listing had not expired.

c. Harvey is liable to Jonas and Keith for the commission.

d. Only Keith gets the commission.

73. Escrow is unable to close because the seller cannot deliver marketable title. The buyer can get his deposit back but is:

a. liable for one-half of the escrow costs

b. liable for costs incurred

c. liable for the broker's commission

d. none of these

74. Marlene offers to buy Sean's farm. The accepted offer was contingent on Marlene's getting an $85,000 first trust deed on the farm. The best loan Marlene can get is $83,500.

a. Marlene is obligated to go through with the purchase, as the loan is in substantial agreement with the offer.

b. Marlene is not required to make the purchase.

c. Marlene would be obligated if Sean takes a $1,500 second trust deed.

d. Both b and c are true.

75. A buyer defaults on a purchase contract. The seller notifies the buyer that he has elected to rescind their agreement. Under these circumstances:

a. the buyer is entitled to the return of his deposit

b. the seller may retain the deposit as liquidated damages

c. the seller should sue for both actual and punitive damages

d. the seller should hold the deposit until the property is resold, when damages can be determined

76. A buyer makes an accepted offer conditioned upon the approval of the buyer's spouse. Prior to the spouse's approval, this is a(n):

a. illusory contract

b. void contract

c. illegal contract

d. binding contract

77. Unknown to the seller, the buyer dies 10 minutes before the seller accepts the purchase offer. The contract is:

a. illegal

b. voidable

c. valid

d. unenforceable

78. An ordinary exclusive-right-to-sell listing in a broker's inventory is an:

a. executed unilateral contract

b. executed bilateral contract

c. executory unilateral contract

d. executory bilateral contract

79. A broker takes a listing that does not include an authorization to take a deposit.

a. The authorization is implied.

b. The broker cannot take a deposit.

c. If the broker takes a deposit, he does so as the agent of the buyer.

d. None of these are true.

80. Abby, a broker, has a listing from Bruce, who has been declared insane, unknown to Abby, who acted in good faith. The listing is:

a. void

b. voidable

c. illegal

d. all of these

81. A listing that does not require a broker to use diligence in obtaining a purchaser is:

a. void

b. illegal

c. a bilateral contract

d. not an exclusive listing

82. A broker obtains an exclusive 6 percent listing for $40,000. The broker brings in an offer of $16,000. The offer angers the owner, who then leases the property for five years prior to the expiration of the listing. The broker is:

a. entitled to a $900 commission

b. entitled to a $1,200 commission

c. entitled to a $2,400 commission

d. not entitled to a commission

83. Under an exclusive-agency listing, a broker advertises a home. The owner sells the home prior to the expiration of the listing. The broker is entitled to:

a. nothing

b. her full commission

c. half of her commission

d. her expenses

84. A purchase agreement signed by Mr. Jones alone calls for the title to be in Mr. and Mrs. Jones's names as community property. The purchase agreement is:

a. valid

b. unenforceable

c. illegal

d. void

85. The broker who has most likely earned his or her commission has:
    a. received an offer on listed property
    b. received the seller's acceptance of the offer
    c. notified the buyer of the seller's acceptance
    d. any of these

86. A $500 deposit is received on a $20,000 offer. The seller accepts with a 6 percent commission agreement. The buyer backs out before close of escrow. Assuming the CAR standard-form purchase contract was used, how much does the broker get if expenses were $130?
    a. $500   b. $250   c. $200   d. $185

87. A broker locates a buyer ready, willing, and able to buy accepting the exact terms of an exclusive-right-to-sell listing. The seller refuses to sell because the buyer has been arrested and convicted on a morals charge.
    a. The owner can refuse the offer without penalty.
    b. The owner must accept the offer.
    c. The owner does not have to accept.
    d. The broker has violated his agency.

88. An offer based on a $10,000 loan assumption was made and accepted. During escrow, it developed that the loan was for $9,000, not $10,000.
    a. The buyer must come up with $1,000 more in cash.
    b. The seller must accept the buyer's note of $1,000.
    c. The buyer can void the contract.
    d. The seller must reduce the price by $1,000.

89. The broker's agreement to use diligence in finding a purchaser:
    a. makes the listing a unilateral contract   c. makes the listing a bilateral contract
    b. makes the listing revocable by the owner   d. none of these

90. The rate of commission for selling a business is determined by:
    a. real estate regulations
    b. Code of Commissions of the NAR
    c. the agreement between the broker and the owner
    d. the Real Estate Law

91. The listing price is most likely:
    a. a low market value   c. a high market value
    b. an average market value   d. not related to market value

92. Brokers earn their commissions:
    a. at the time that they list properties
    b. by finding buyers ready, willing, and able to buy
    c. on close of escrow
    d. none of these

93. A lot is listed for $37,800 with 29 percent down. The broker brings in a full-price cash offer. The owner refuses. The broker is entitled to:
    a. half of her commission   c. her full commission less expenses
    b. her full commission   d. nothing

94. According to the CAR standard real estate purchase contract, if the seller fails to deliver title:
    a. the broker is liable for damages   c. the buyer forfeits his or her deposit
    b. the buyer can terminate   d. none of these

95. An option set forth in a lease would be a(n):
    a. restriction   b. encumbrance   c. appurtenance   d. covenant

96. The only provision an exclusive listing contains for termination is upon the owner giving two-hour notice to the broker.
    a. The provision as to early notice has no effect.
    b. The listing is a unilateral contract.
    c. There is nothing wrong with the broker's action.
    d. The broker is subject to disciplinary action.

97. To take a valid option on real property, which of the following is not required?
    a. a real estate license
    b. written agreement
    c. valuable consideration
    d. transfer of consideration to the optionor

98. *Optionor* best describes a(n):
    a. broker
    b. owner
    c. prospective buyer
    d. lender

99. An astute broker would least likely spend his or her advertising dollars on:
    a. radio advertising
    b. billboards
    c. newspaper ads on open listings
    d. ads in the Yellow Pages

100. Angelo lists his farm on July 1 with Benita, a broker. The listing is for 30 days. On August 2, Benita finds a full-price buyer who makes a deposit directly into escrow (no purchase contract is signed).
    a. Benita is not legally entitled to a commission.
    b. The escrow must pay the commission to Benita.
    c. The buyer owes the commission.
    d. Angelo must pay Benita the commission.

101. After a house on which Paula, a broker, had an exclusive-agency listing has been sold by another broker, she finds out about it. The selling broker received a full commission. Paula should make a demand on the:
    a. selling broker for full commission
    b. selling broker for half commission
    c. owner for full commission
    d. owner for half commission

102. A broker has a combination of a listing and an option. She exercises the option without disclosing that she has a buyer at a higher price. The broker:
    a. is guilty of fraud
    b. has made a secret profit
    c. represented two parties without permission
    d. is not guilty of wrongdoing

103. As to an offer to purchase, which of the following is true?
    a. The broker has the option of submitting the offer.
    b. Structural inspection and clearance is required.
    c. It must include a deposit.
    d. none of these

104. A purchaser wishes to make a full-price offer, but not a deposit with it. The broker should:
    a. inform the purchaser that an offer without a deposit is not valid
    b. inform the purchaser that to take such an offer would violate the Real Estate Law
    c. take the offer, but inform the offeror that it cannot be presented until a deposit is made
    d. take the offer and inform the owner that there is no deposit

105. A broker has an exclusive listing on a property that also provides the broker with an option to buy that property. The broker wishes to exercise the option. The broker:
    a. should forget it as he has violated his fiduciary duty
    b. must obtain the approval of the Department of Real Estate
    c. must obtain the seller's approval in writing
    d. must publish his intent for 30 days prior to exercising the option

106. Sandra, a broker, had 40 houses listed when she passed away. Her daughter, also a broker, inherits the business. She must:
    a. renegotiate the 40 listings
    b. seek judgment in court to get the commissions
    c. inform the 40 sellers as to what happened and that all the listings belong to her
    d. tell the 40 sellers that she is taking over and that as far as they are concerned there is no change

107. A contract that allows a real estate agent to be an agent of all of the parties to a transaction would be a(n):
    a. exclusive-right-to-sell listing
    b. exchange agreement
    c. open listing
    d. seller disclosure statement

108. Alec gives Betty an option to buy his farm for $50,000 within 30 days. Betty gives Alec $50 for this option. Alec notifies Betty 25 days later that he is withdrawing the option. Two days later Betty tenders the full option price to Alec for the farm.
    a. Alec must accept or he can be sued for damages or specific performance.
    b. Alec does not have to sell, since the option was properly canceled.

c. Alec must return the $50 to Betty.

d. Both b and c are true.

109. A sale falls apart and both the buyer and the seller make demands on the broker for the buyer's deposit. A wise broker would:

a. give it to the owner

b. give it to the broker

c. file an interpleader action

d. take it out of his commission

110. In taking a listing it is proper for the broker to:

a. accept the listing at whatever price the owner wants

b. raise the owner's asking price to include the commission

c. agree to accept a listing at a greater price than that suggested by a competitor

d. ascertain the seller's reason for listing

111. Archie, a broker, listed a property. Conrad, a salesperson working for Beryl, another broker, received an offer. Diana, a salesperson working for Archie, got the offer accepted. Who earned the commission?

a. Archie
b. Beryl
c. Conrad
d. Diana

112. A broker repeated rent information he received from his client to a purchaser. After the sale, it was discovered the information was false. The new buyer went to an attorney. Most likely she would sue:

a. the seller

b. the broker

c. the seller and the broker

d. none of these, because of *caveat emptor*

113. The listing offering the greatest chance for the listing broker to earn a commission is a(n):

a. net listing

b. open listing

c. exclusive-right-to-sell listing

d. exclusive-agency listing

114. A statement that commissions are negotiable need not be included in:

a. a listing of a single-family home

b. a listing of a five-unit apartment building

c. both a and b

d. neither a nor b

115. A salesperson obtains a listing on her brother's house. Immediately thereafter, she changes brokers.

a. The listing belongs to her previous broker.

b. The listing belongs to the salesperson.

c. The listing belongs to her new broker.

d. The listing is terminated by the change.

116. Alice, a broker, submits a listing to an MLS based on a phone conversation with the owner, who indicates he will give Alice the listing. Bart, another broker, obtains a full-price offer, but the owner refuses to sell.

a. The owner is liable to Alice for a commission.

b. Alice is liable to Bart for his commission.

c. Bart is not entitled to any reimbursement.

d. The owner is liable to Bart only.

117. A broker informs an owner that a listing is really an open listing, when in fact it is an exclusive-agency listing.

a. The broker is entitled to a commission, no matter who sells the property.

b. The doctrine of *caveat emptor* prevails.

c. The broker has placed her license in jeopardy.

d. None of these are true.

118. The function of board arbitration is to:

a. set standard closing costs for buyers and sellers

b. settle disputes regarding closing costs

c. settle disputes between agents

d. none of these

119. A husband signs a contract to sell community real estate without his wife's signature. The contract would be:

a. valid
b. illegal
c. unenforceable
d. void

120. A purchase contract signed because of duress is:
    a. void   b. voidable   c. illegal   d. all of these

121. Sherman agrees to pay $100,000 for Ray's lot. During escrow, Ray learns that Sherman has an offer to sell the lot for $300,000 and that Sherman had privileged information about this buyer before he made his offer. Ray sues Sherman for his profit.
    a. Because it was a secret profit, Ray will prevail.
    b. Ray is liable to both Sherman and his buyer.
    c. Ray has no valid claim against Sherman's profit.
    d. Sherman can obtain specific performance but no money damages.

122. The agreement between a broker and a salesperson as to commission splits would normally be:
    a. an express contract   c. an agency agreement
    b. an implied contract   d. none of these

123. As to an option, which of the following is true?
    a. It is illegal if the option price is not money.
    b. The optionor must exercise it.
    c. The optionee must exercise it.
    d. none of these

124. All of the following are ways by which an offer to purchase real estate would be terminated, *except:*
    a. failure to accept the offer within a prescribed period
    b. a conditional acceptance of the offer by the offeree
    c. failure to communicate notice of revocation before the other party has communicated acceptance
    d. death or insanity of the offeror or offeree, regardless of the notice thereof

125. An example of an illegal earnest money deposit would be:
    a. a personal check   b. a promissory note   c. cash   d. none of these

126. A minor cannot:
    a. pay income taxes   c. appoint an agent
    b. contract for purchase of personal property   d. any of these

127. Arbitration under the CAR purchase contract shall be in accordance with:
    a. the Administrative Procedures Act
    b. the Real Estate Commissioner's regulations
    c. the rules of the American Arbitration Association
    d. none of these

128. An option is a(n):
    a. fiduciary agreement   c. offer to enter into a contract
    b. voluntary lien   d. contract to keep an offer open

129. Enthusiasm of a licensee often results in painting an overly optimistic picture. This is known as:
    a. fraud   b. misrepresentation   c. puffing   d. coercion

130. A broker has an exclusive-agency listing on a property and inadvertently states 6 cents rather than 6 percent as his commission on the listing. If the owner sells the property, the broker is entitled to:
    a. 6 percent of the sale price
    b. the amount determined by the Commissioner
    c. 6 cents
    d. nothing

131. As to options, which of the following is true?
    a. There is a fiduciary duty between the optionor and the optionee.
    b. The optionee is entitled to the return of his or her consideration if the option is not exercised.
    c. Consideration does not actually have to change hands as long as the option says it has.
    d. none of these

132. A broker under an exclusive-right-to-sell listing had her license revoked. In order to collect a commission, she must prove all but which of the following?
    a. She was licensed at the time the commission was earned.
    b. The parties agreed to the sale before the listing expired.

c. The broker was the procuring cause of the sale.

d. The listing was properly executed.

133. Which of the following may be recorded?

a. an exclusive-right-to-sell listing

b. an open listing

c. an option

d. none of these

134. The Alquist-Priolo Act deals with:

a. lead paint disclosure

b. military ordnance locations

c. special-studies zones

d. toxic waste

135. The buyer would sign a receipt for a booklet dealing with:

a. environmental hazards

b. unhealthy air

c. nonconforming use

d. "as is" sale condition

136. An offer to perform in accordance with contractual obligations would be:

a. completion

b. consideration

c. tender

d. performance

137. An owner instructed her broker that she did not want to see any offer that did not include a deposit of at least 5 percent of the price offered. The broker received an offer without any deposit. The broker should:

a. inform the buyer that a deposit is required by law

b. return the offer to the buyer

c. present the offer

d. use trust funds to make up a deposit

138. An agent had a listing that authorized the agent to accept deposits. The agent received a $50,000 cash deposit. The agent and the deposit cannot be located. Who is responsible for the loss?

a. the recovery fund

b. the agent only

c. the buyer since the offer was not accepted

d. the owner since her agent took the money

139. Entering into a contract with a person you did not know and had no reason to know had been declared incompetent would make the contract:

a. void   b. voidable   c. voidable by either party   d. valid

140. Broker Elsie listed a property owned by Widow Jones. The listing called for a 12 percent commission. After the sale was completed and the commission paid, Widow Jones discovered that Elsie charged other owners 6 percent for sales of similar property. As to this transaction:

a. Elsie has placed her license in jeopardy

b. Jones is entitled to the return of the entire commission paid

c. Jones is entitled to the return of half of the commission

d. none of the above

141. Megan's Law deals with:

a. water quality   b. waste disposal   c. sex offenders   d. military ordnance

142. The lead paint information booklet must be given to buyer of one to four residential units contructed prior to:

a. 1978   b. 1980   c. 1988   d. 1992

143. A buyer must be notified about a military ordnance location that may contain explosives if within _____ mile(s) of the property.

a. 1   b. 2   c. 5   d. 8

144. A buyer of a common interest development is entitled to receive all *except*:

a. copies of the CC&Rs

b. Homeowner Association bylaws

c. Homeowner Association financial statement

d. one year buyer warranty

145. A buyer of a single-family home is entitled to certification that:

a. window security bars have been installed

b. water heater is properly braced

c. the home is in compliance with smoke detector laws

d. both b and c

117

ANSWERS—CHAPTER 5 QUIZ

1. b. Completed mutual promises.
2. d. One-year-or-less exception to the Statute of Frauds.
3. c. The contract will not be performed within one year.
4. d. No "meeting of the minds."
5. d. and void.
6. c.
7. a.
8. d. Real estate requires a written contract.
9. d. Estoppel.
10. d. It more clearly shows intent.
11. b. At the option of the injured party.
12. d. To force performance.
13. a. It shows a "meeting of the minds."
14. c. She can void the transfer. (The church may be allowed to remove improvements.)
15. c. Exception to the Statute of Frauds.
16. b.
17. d. A binding contract can be breached.
18. d. All must be in writing.
19. d. But it was unenforceable prior to performance.
20. d. By the injured party.
21. b. Such as one outlawed by the Statute of Limitations.
22. c. Fraud as to the nature of the instrument.
23. a. Exception to the Statute of Frauds.
24. a. Not all contracts must be written.
25. c. Every day is counted.
26. a. Who is then given a copy.
27. b. Fiduciary duty.
28. b. The owner made the property unmarketable.
29. b. Since the broker performed.
30. a. Open listing.
31. b. Percentage.
32. a. But the seller owes the agent a commission.
33. d.
34. a. Bob was the exclusive agent.
35. b. Or revocation by the offeror.
36. b.
37. b.
38. b.
39. d. The agency is terminated by death.
40. d.
41. c. Fiduciary duty.
42. b.
43. b. The note is personal consideration.

44. a.
45. c.
46. c. No consideration for keeping the offer open.
47. b.
48. b. The broker has a duty to disclose the buyer.
49. d. The broker must submit all names in writing.
50. b.
51. d. The buyer can withdraw anytime prior to acceptance.
52. c. Between the buyer and the seller.
53. b. There is a valid contract.
54. c.
55. a. But not the broker.
56. d. The broker's remedy is money. There is no contract with the buyer.
57. c. Since there is a binding contract.
58. d. Forfeiture of deposit or sue for damages.
59. c. Adequacy is normally not considered.
60. d. The broker must notify the owner in writing.
61. c. The seller gave a counter-offer.
62. b. A corporation doesn't die.
63. d.
64. c. Since it is an open listing.
65. a.
66. a. Interest can be determined. Not essential to listing.
67. c. Listings can't be recorded.
68. c. But she may split it with Adam.
69. b. The double negative means "most likely to."
70. c. "As is" applies only to obvious problems. Broker must disclose defects.
71. b. Payment is legal but the agreement is unenforceable.
72. c. The listing was wrongfully terminated.
73. d. The seller is responsible for costs.
74. b. But Marlene may waive the condition.
75. a. Rescision requires returning the parties to their original positions.
76. a. Since the buyer is not bound.
77. d. No contract—the buyer's death terminated the offer.
78. d. Not yet performed.
79. c.
80. a. The owner lacks competency.

81. d. Open listing—unilateral contract.
82. c. The owner made the property unmarketable.
83. a. Since the listing was exclusive-agency, the owners can sell the property themselves.
84. a. Either spouse can buy community property.
85. c. So the buyer cannot rescind.
86. d. Half after expenses.
87. c. But would owe the broker a commission.
88. c. Or pay the difference.
89. c. A promise for a promise.
90. c. Commissions are negotiable.
91. c.
92. b. In accordance with the listing or acceptable to the owner.
93. d. The offer is not in accordance with the listing.
94. b. And gets his or her deposit back.
95. d. A promise by the lessor.
96. d. The listing needs a definite termination date.
97. a. The optionor is acting as principal.
98. b. The person who gives the option.
99. c. Since others can sell the property.
100. a. Since there is no valid listing.
101. c. Paula is entitled to it.
102. b. She had a disclosure duty.
103. d.
104. d.
105. c.
106. a. Death of the agent terminates the agency.
107. b.
108. a. Alec cannot cancel the option.
109. c. Ask the court to decide.
110. d.
111. a. The listing broker earns it.
112. c. But the broker may not be liable unless he should have known that the information was false.
113. c.
114. b. Only for one to four residential units.
115. a.
116. b.
117. c. Fraud as to the nature of a contract voids the contract.
118. c.
119. c. Both must convey.
120. b. By the injured party.
121. c. Sherman is not an agent.
122. a. Broker-salesperson contracts must be in writing.

118

123. d. The optionee has the option.
124. c. The offer has been accepted prior to revocation.
125. d.
126. c. Lacks capacity.
127. c.
128. d.
129. c. Statement of opinion.
130. d. Since it was an exclusive-agency listing.
131. d.

132. c. Not needed for exclusive right to sell.
133. c. An option is a recordable interest.
134. c.
135. a.
136. c. A tender is an offer to perform.
137. c. Every offer (if not clearly frivolous) must be presented.
138. d. Principal is liable for actions of the agent.

139. a.
140. d. Commissions are negotiable.
141. c. Notify buyer of the registry information for the area.
142. a.
143. a.
144. d.
145. d.

6

Practical Real
Estate Mathematics

Understanding the principles and problems in this chapter will prepare you for the type of mathematics found on the California Real Estate Examinations.

Basic Math

Fractions, Percentages, and Decimals

A fraction such as 1/5 can be converted to a decimal by dividing the numerator by the denominator:

$$1 \div 5 = .2$$

To change a decimal to a percentage, move the decimal point two places to the right:

$$.2 = 20\%$$

To change a percentage to a decimal, move the decimal point two places to the left:

$$20\% = .2$$

Measurement

Square Footage

To find the square footage of a rectangular parcel, multiply length times width (in feet):

$$\text{Length} \times \text{Width} = \text{Square footage}$$

A $60' \times 90'$ lot would therefore contain 5,400 square feet ($60' \times 90' = 5,400$ square feet).

If you know one dimension of a rectangle and its total area in square feet, you can find the other dimension by dividing the known dimension into the total area:

$$\frac{\text{Total area}}{\text{Known dimension}} = \text{Other dimension}$$

Example: If you know that a rectangular lot has $60'$ on one side and a total area of 5,400 square feet, you can find the unknown dimension by dividing:

$$5,400 \div 60 = 90$$

You must be careful to convert square feet to square yards and square yards to square feet when required by a problem. A square yard contains 9 square feet ($3' \times 3'$).

Problem: A rectangular parcel of land has 730 feet of highway frontage. It contains 10 acres. How deep is the parcel?

One acre contains 43,560 square feet. Ten acres would contain 435,600 square feet. Divide the total square footage by the front linear footage to get the depth:

$$435,600 \div 730 = 596.7 \text{ feet}$$

Cubic Footage

To determine cubic footage, multiply length $\times$ width $\times$ depth. Be certain to convert all measurements to the same units (inches or feet).

A cubic yard contains $3' \times 3' \times 3'$, or 27 cubic feet (length $\times$ width $\times$ depth).

A **board foot** is a cubic measure equal to 144 cubic inches, or a board $12'' \times 12'' \times 1''$.

Example: A room $20' \times 12'$ that is $8'$ high contains 1,920 cubic feet:

$$20 \times 12 \times 8 = 1,920$$

Problem: How many board feet are in a beam $6'' \times 18'' \times 36'$?

$6'' \times 18'' \times 432''$ (36×12 to convert to inches) = 46,656 cubic inches

Now divide by 144 to find the number of board feet:

$$46,656 \div 144 = 324 \text{ board feet}$$

Using the T-Bar

This simple T-Bar will take much of the mystery out of math.

$$\frac{\div \text{ Part } \div}{\text{Whole} \mid \text{Rate}}$$

$$\times$$

Using this T-Bar, if we know two of the three (part, whole, and rate) we can determine the unknown third.

If the line between two known numbers is horizontal then we can find the unknown by simple division, dividing the top number by the bottom number.

$$\text{Rate} = \frac{\text{Part}}{\text{Whole}}$$

$$\text{Whole} = \frac{\text{Part}}{\text{Rate}}$$

If the line between the two known numbers is vertical, then you multiply the two known numbers to find the unknown. Therefore:

$$\text{Part} = \text{Whole} \times \text{Rate}$$

Finding the Rate (Percentage)

Problem: If the interest on $6,000 for 1 year is $720, we could find the rate of interest by the T-bar formula:

$$\text{Rate} = \frac{\text{Part}}{\text{Whole}}$$

$720 is the Part (interest earned) and $6,000 is the Whole:

$$\text{Rate} = \frac{720}{6,000}$$

Rate = .12 or 12% rate of interest.

122

Problem: If $1,050 was earned on an investment of $14,000 for one year, what was the interest rate that was earned?

    The part (interest earned) was $1050 and the whole (amount invested) is $14,000, so:

$$\text{Rate} = \frac{1,050}{\$1,4000}$$

Rate = .075 or 7 1/2% interest earned.

Problem: **Finding the Whole.** To find the amount of principal (the whole) when the interest earned for 1 year at 12% is $720, we would use the formula from the T-bar:

$$\text{Whole} = \frac{\text{Part}}{\text{Rate}}$$

The part is $720 and the rate is 12% so:

$$\text{Whole} = \frac{720}{.12}$$

Whole = $6,000

Problem: If a property sells for $10,000, which is 80% of its list price, what is the list price?

    The same formula would apply:

$$\text{Whole} = \frac{\text{Part}}{\text{Rate}}$$

The part is $10,000 and the rate is 80% or. 80, therefore:

$$\text{Whole} = \frac{10,000}{.80}$$

Whole = $12,500

Finding the Part

Problem: What is the interest earned on $140,000 at 8% for one year? The formula would be:

Part = Rate × Whole
Part = .08 × $140,000
Part = $11,200 interest earned

Problem: If the problem above asked for the interest earned on $140,000 for one month, then you would divide the interest earned for 1 year, $11,200 by 12 since it is 1/12 of a year:

$$\frac{11,200}{12} = \$933.33$$

Finding the Time

If the rate of interest, the amount of interest earned and the principal are known, you can determine the period of the loan by the simple formula:

$$\text{Time} = \frac{\text{Interest Earned}}{\text{Principal} \times \text{Rate}}$$

Assume $720 was earned on a $6,000 investment at 12% interest:

$$\text{Time} = \frac{720}{6000 \times .12}$$

$$\text{Time} = \frac{720}{720}$$

$$\text{Time} = 1 \text{ Year}$$

Percentage of Return

To find a percentage of return, divide the item on which you want to know the percentage of return into the net income.

Problem: The down payment is $5,000. The net income of the property is $750. What percentage of return is obtained on the down payment?

$$\text{Net (\$750)} \div \text{Down payment (\$5,000)} = .15 = 15\%$$

Problem: A property cost $120,000. Its net income is $10,000. What percentage is the return on the cost?

$$\text{Net (\$10,000)} \div \text{Cost (\$120,000)} = .0833 = 8.33\%$$

Problem: I have $67,000 equity in an apartment, giving me $6,300 per year net income. What percentage is my return on my equity?

$$\text{Net (\$6,300)} \div \text{Equity (\$67,000)} = .094 = 9.4\%$$

Problem: A house originally cost $80,000 and sells for $120,000. What is the percentage of profit on the sale? The profit was $40,000. To find the percentage of the profit, based on cost, divide the profit by the original cost:

$$\text{Net (\$40,000)} \div \text{Cost (\$80,000)} = .5 = 50\%$$

Taxes

Taxes are generally expressed per $100 of evaluation although the rate could apply to each dollar of evaluation.

Example: If the tax rate per $100 is 1.671 (1 dollar 67 cents and 1 *mill*) and a property is assessed at $72,000, the taxes would be:

$$720 \times \$1.671 = \$1,203.12$$

Note: One mill is 1/10 cent, or $0.001.

Commission

A commission is generally a percentage of the sale price. A 6 percent commission on an $80,000 sale price would be:

$$.06 \times \$80,000 = \$4,800 \text{ (Part = Rate} \times \text{Whole)}$$

Problem: A house sold for $163,800. This was 9 percent less than the price at which it was listed. The commission was 6 percent. What would the commission have been if the house had sold at the listed price?

Since the house sold for 9 percent less than list price, it sold for 91 percent of its list price:

$$\text{Whole (list price)} = \frac{\text{(Part) } 163,800}{\text{(Rate) } .91}$$

$$\text{List price} = \$180,000$$

(*Proof:* 91 percent of $180,000 equals $163,800.)

The property was originally listed at $180,000. Thus, if it had sold at the list price, the commission would have been:

$$\$180,000 \times .06 = \$10,800 \text{ (Part = Rate} \times \text{Whole)}$$

Problem: A seller says he wants $235,000 plus the broker's commission. The broker accepts the seller's price and lists the property to give a 6 percent commission. At what price do you list the property?

If $235,000 is to be left after the 6 percent commission is taken out, then $235,000 is 94 percent of the list price:

$$\text{Whole (list price)} = \frac{\text{(Part) \$235,000}}{\text{(Rate) .94}}$$

$$\text{List price} = \$250,000$$

(*Proof:* $250,000 minus 6 percent of $250,000 equals $235,000.)

Thus, the broker would list at $250,000 for the seller to get $235,000 after the commission of 6 percent.

Income

Problem: A property has an income of $22,000. It has a 25 percent vacancy factor. If it had a zero vacancy factor, what would its income be?

Since the property is 25 percent vacant and the current income is $22,000, the $22,000 income represents 75 percent of the maximum possible income:

$$\text{Maximum Income (Whole)} = \frac{\$22,000 \text{ (Part)}}{.75 \text{ (Rate)}}$$

$$\text{Maximum Income} = \$29,333$$

(*Proof:* 75 percent of $29,333 equals $22,000.)

Thus, the maximum income of the property when it is fully rented is $29,333.

Investment

Problem: A woman earns $2,830 on an investment. This gives her a 9 percent return on her investment. What was her investment?

$2,830 is equal to 9 percent of the amount of the investment:

$$\text{Investment (Whole)} = \frac{\$2,830 \text{ (Part)}}{.09 \text{ (Rate)}}$$

$$\text{Investment} = \$31,444$$

(*Proof:* 9 percent of $31,444 equals $2,830.)

Home Sale

Problem: A house sells for $129,000, which is 18 percent less than it cost three years earlier. How much of a loss does the seller take?

Since the house sells for 18 percent less than it cost, it sells for 82 percent of its cost:

$$\text{Original Cost (Whole)} = \frac{\$129,000 \text{ (Part)}}{.82 \text{ (Rate)}}$$

$$\text{Original Cost} = \$157,317$$

(*Proof:* 82 percent of $157,317 equals $129,000.)

$$\$157,317 \text{ (Original cost)} \div \$129,000 \text{ (Selling price)} = \$28,317$$

Thus, the seller takes a loss of $28,317.

Problem: One house sold for $9,500 less than another house. The combined price for both houses was $198,000. What did each house sell for?
  Deduct $9,500 from $198,000 to eliminate the difference in price:

$$\$198,000 - \$9,500 = \$188,500$$

Divide by 2 to determine the cost of the first (cheaper) house:

$$\$188,500 \div 2 = \$94,250$$

Add the difference in price to determine the cost of the second (more expensive) house:

$$\$94,250 + \$9,500 = \$103,750$$

(*Proof:* $94,250 + $103,750 = $198,000.)

Inheritance

Problem: By will, a man gives 37 percent of his estate to his son, 27 percent to his daughter, 8 percent to his church, and 28 percent to his wife. The church receives $10,000. How much did his son, his daughter, and his wife receive?
  The amount the church receives, $10,000, is 8 percent of the entire estate:

$$\text{Entire Estate (Whole)} = \frac{\$10,000 \text{ (Part)}}{.08 \text{ (Rate)}}$$

$$\text{Entire Estate} = \$125,000$$

(*Proof:* 8 percent of $125,000 equals $10,000.)
  Thus, the family's shares of the estate are as follows:

Son	$.37 \times \$125,000 = \$46,250$
Daughter	$.27 \times \$125,000 = \$33,750$
Wife	$.28 \times \$125,000 = \$35,000$

Proportion of Cost

Problem: There are five units in a condominium complex. They sold for the following prices: $135,000, $148,000, $152,000, $165,000, and $175,000. The annual common maintenance costs for the complex amount to $19,000. Each of the complex owners is supposed to share this cost in proportion to his or her condo unit cost. What is the monthly share of the owner of the $135,000 unit?

First add the costs of all the units, which total $775,000.

Next, find what percentage of the costs the owner of the $135,000 unit would pay:

$$\text{Rate} = \frac{\$135,000 \text{ (Part)}}{\$775,000 \text{ (Whole)}}$$

$$\text{Rate} = 17.42\%$$

$$\text{Annual Maintenance} = \$19,000$$

$$\frac{\$19,000}{12} = 1583.33 \text{ Monthly Cost}$$

$$\text{Part (Assessment for Unit)} = .1742 \text{ (Rate)} \times 1583.33 \text{ (Whole)}$$

$$\text{Monthly Assessment} = \$275.82$$

The problem can also be solved by showing that the ratio of the cost of the $135,000 unit to the cost of all the units ($775,000) is the same as the ratio of that unit's annual maintenance cost to the total annual maintenance costs.

$$\frac{\$135,000}{\$775,000} = \frac{\text{Unit annual maintenance cost}}{\$19,000}$$

To find the unit annual maintenance cost, cross-multiply (after canceling out the zeros in the left-hand fraction):

$$\$775 \times \text{(Unit annual maintenance cost)} = \$135 \times \$19,000$$
$$= \$2,565,000$$
$$\frac{\$775 \times \text{(Unit annual maintenance cost)}}{\$775} = \frac{\$2,565,000}{\$775}$$
$$\text{Unit annual maintenance cost)} = \frac{\$2,565,000}{\$775}$$
$$= \$3,309.67$$
$$\text{Unit monthly maintenance cost} = \$3,309.67 \div 12 = \$275.80$$

Interest

Problem: A $10,000 loan has payments of $100 per month including interest at 8 percent. What is the balance due on the loan immediately after the second payment?

The first month's interest is 1/12 (1 month) of the yearly interest of 8 percent, or $1/12 \times (.08 \times \$10,000)$:

$$\text{Part (Interest)} = .08 \text{ (Rate)} \times 10,000 \text{ (Whole)}$$
$$\text{Part Interest} = \$800 \text{ yearly}$$

$$.08 \div 12 = \$66.66 \text{ (First month's interest)}$$

Since the first month's payment is $100, the amount paid on the principal is:

$$\$100 \text{ (Payment)} - \$66.66 \text{ (Interest)} = \$33.33 \text{ (Payment on principal)}$$

Now you can determine the balance on the principal after the first month's payment:

$$\$10,000 - \$33.33 = \$9,966.67$$

The second month's interest is 1/12 of the yearly interest of 8 percent times $9,966.67:

$$.08 \times \$9,966.67 = \$797.33 \text{ (Yearly interest)}$$
$$\$797.33 \div 12 = \$66.44 \text{ (Second month's interest)}$$

The second month's payment on the principal is:

$$\$100 \text{ (Payment)} - \$66.44 \text{ (Interest)} = \$33.56 \text{ (Payment on principal)}$$

Thus:

Balance on principal after first month's payment	$9,966.67
Second month's payment on principal	− $33.56
Balance on loan after second month's payment	$9,933.11

Principal Plus Interest

Problem: Assume that the preceding problem provided for payments of $100 per month *plus* interest. In this case the entire $100 would be deducted from the principal, since the interest is paid separately. Thus, after two payments of $100 plus interest on a loan of $10,000, the balance on the principal would be $9,800.

Monthly Amortization Table (per $1,000 of the Loan)

No. of Years	11%	11½%	12%	12½%	13%
5	21.74	21.99	22.25	22.50	22.75
10	13.78	14.06	14.35	14.64	14.93
15	11.37	11.68	12.00	12.33	12.65
20	10.32	10.66	11.01	11.36	11.72
25	9.80	10.16	10.53	10.90	11.28

Amortization

Problem: Clarissa borrows $150,000 at 12 percent interest on a 15-year amortized loan. David borrows $150,000 at 13 percent interest on a 25-year amortized loan. David's total interest payments will amount to what percentage of Clarissa's interest payments?

Payments are monthly. Clarissa's loan is for 15 years; therefore, in 15 years she will make 15 × 12 payments, or 180 payments. According to the table, monthly payments at 12 percent for 15 years are $12.00 per $1,000 of the loan. Since the loan is for $150,000, multiply this rate by 150 to find Clarissa's total monthly payment:

$$150 \times \$12.00 = \$1,800$$

Clarissa's monthly payment, therefore, is $1,800. Over the 15 years (180 months), her total payments equal:

$$\$1,800 \times 180 = \$324,000$$

The amount of Clarissa's payments attributable to interest is the amount over $150,000 (the amount of the loan):

$$\$324,000 \text{ (Payments)} - \$150,000 \text{ (Principal)} = \$174,000 \text{ (Interest)}$$

On the other hand, David's loan is for 25 years; therefore, in 25 years he will make 25 × 12 payments, or 300 payments. According to the table, monthly payments at 13 percent for 25 years are $11.28 per $1,000 of the loan. Since the loan is for $150,000, multiply this rate by 150 to find David's total monthly payment:

$$150 \times \$11.28 = \$1,692$$

David's monthly payment, therefore, is $1,692. Over the 25 years (300 months), his total payments equal:

$$\$1,692 \times 300 = \$507,600$$

The amount of David's payments attributable to interest is the amount over $150,000 (the amount of the loan):

$$\$507,600 \text{ (Payments)} - \$150,000 \text{ (Principal)} = \$357,600 \text{ (Interest)}$$

So, Clarissa's total interest is $174,000 and David's total interest is $357,600. Therefore:

$$\$357,600 \div \$174,000 = 2.055$$

David's total interest payments will amount to 205.5 percent of Clarissa's total interest payments.

CHAPTER 6 QUIZ

Main Street

100'	100'	200'	100'	100'
Lot A	Lot B	Lot C	Lot D	Lot E
100'	100'	100'	200'	100'

(100' on left side, 100' on right side)

1. If the lots in the figure sell for $100 per front foot on Main Street, Lot A would sell for:
   a. $1,000   b. $10,000   c. $20,000   d. none of these

2. If the lots in the figure sell for $10 per front foot on Main Street, Lot D would sell for:
   a. $1,000   b. $10,000   c. $20,000   d. none of these

3. If Lot C sells for $1 per square foot, it would sell for:
   a. $1,000   b. $20,000   c. $15,000   d. $10,000

4. Lot E has a building setback of 30 feet from each side. The maximum square footage of a two-story building on Lot E would be:
   a. 20,000 square feet   c. 12,000 square feet
   b. 3,200 square feet   d. 1,600 square feet

5. Oliver sells his house for $14,900. This is 18 percent more than he paid for it. Oliver paid:
   a. $12,627   b. $12,218   c. $17,582   d. $13,100

6. If the buyer's down payment is $12,000 and the property has a net income of $8,300, the buyer's percentage of return on the down payment is:
   a. 14.5 percent   b. 69 percent   c. 70 percent   d. 71 percent

7. If the tax rate is $2.392 per $100 of assessed valuation and a property is assessed at 25 percent of its real value of $47,500, what are the taxes?
   a. $11,875.00   b. $1,136.20   c. $284.05   d. $4,750.00

8. Lance sells a new note at a 4 percent discount. He receives $5,200. The face amount of the note is:
   a. $5,408.00   b. $5,416.66   c. $4,992.00   d. $5,611.27

9. Lucy owes $8,100 on a note. Her next monthly interest payment will be $58.32. Annual interest on the note is:
   a. 1/2 percent   b. 8.64 percent   c. 5 percent   d. 4 1/2 percent

10. A property was purchased for $10,000 and has a gross income of $2,000. The only expense is the owner's interest payment of 9 percent on an $8,000 trust deed. The owner's percentage of return on his equity is:
    a. 11 percent   b. 80 percent   c. 64 percent   d. 280 percent

11. Frank buys a $1,200 trust deed at a 25 percent discount. The trust deed requires payments of $104 per month, including interest for one year. Frank's percentage of return for the year on his investment is:
    a. 4.8 percent   b. 9.6 percent   c. 29.8 percent   d. 38 percent

12. An investment that would pay $100 per month interest at 6 percent would require an investment of:
    a. $1,666.66   b. $20,000.00   c. $10,000.00   d. $12,000.00

13. The easiest way to compute one month's interest at 7.2 percent would be to multiply the principal by:
    a. .072, and divide by 12   b. 7.2   c. .006   d. .06

14. A rectangular parcel 422 feet wide contains 8.3 acres. Its depth is:
    a. 801.11 feet   b. 435.6 feet   c. 856.75 feet   d. 1,187.2 feet

15. A 2" × 8" board 9 feet long would contain how many board feet?
    a. 1   b. 8.3   c. 9   d. 12

16. A board foot of lumber cannot be obtained from a board:
    a. $1'' \times 6'' \times 20''$ b. $1' \times 2' \times 5'$ c. $6'' \times 6'' \times 6''$ d. $5'' \times 12'' \times 12''$

17. Nate has 10 apartments fully rented at $100 per month. He raises his rent 10 percent and experiences a 10 percent vacancy factor.
    a. His yearly income remains the same.
    b. His monthly income increases.
    c. His monthly income decreases.
    d. This is an example of maximization of the net.

18. An 80-acre parcel purchased for $400 per acre is resold in four 20-acre parcels at $1,000 per acre. The percentage of profit based on cost is:
    a. 60 percent   b. 150 percent   c. 200 percent   d. 40 percent

19. In the preceding question, the percentage of profit based on selling price is:
    a. 60 percent   b. 150 percent   c. 200 percent   d. 40 percent

20. To find the square footage of a square 40-acre parcel:
    a. multiply $40 \times 43,560$ feet
    b. multiply $1,320 \times 1,320$
    c. either a or b
    d. neither a nor b

21. A road runs along the south boundary of a section. It contains three acres. Its width is:
    a. 24.7 feet   b. 18.1 feet   c. 50 feet   d. 43 feet

22. Elena sells her home for $40,000, making a 30 percent profit on what she paid for it. Her profit is:
    a. $12,000   b. $30,769   c. $9,231   d. $9,000

23. An owner divides a one-acre parcel into four equal rectangular lots, each 200 feet deep. What is the approximate width of each lot?
    a. 217.8 feet   b. 54.45 feet   c. 87.12 feet   d. 118.3 feet

24. A property owner had an assessed value of $10,000 on his home, with taxes at $8 per $100 assessed valuation, making his taxes $800. The next year, the tax rate went up to $9 per $100, making his taxes $900. The assessed value:
    a. increased 10 percent
    b. increased 12.5 percent
    c. increased 11.1 percent
    d. remained the same

25. The last month's interest on a 6% loan was $739.12. What was the loan balance?
    a. $136,826   b. $147,824   c. $152,316   d. $198,413

26. Claude wishes to pour a concrete patio $40' \times 10'$ and four inches thick. How many cubic yards of concrete are needed?
    a. 45   b. 5   c. 12   d. 3

27. To find the depth of a rectangular parcel when the width and the total area are known:
    a. multiply the width by the area
    b. divide the width by the area
    c. divide the area by the width
    d. none of these

28. Nine cubic yards of concrete is equal to:
    a. 81 cubic feet   b. 27 cubic feet   c. 243 cubic feet   d. 72 cubic feet

29. On a $90' \times 90'$ lot, the building setbacks are $30'$ from the front, and $10'$ from the sides, and $20'$ from rear line. The net building area is:
    a. 2,650 square feet
    b. 1,750 square feet
    c. 2,800 square feet
    d. none of these

30. Jay sells a lot for 20 percent more than he paid for it and invests the entire proceeds in an investment yielding 9 percent per year. His monthly return on his investment is $320. What did Jay originally pay for the lot?
    a. $3,840   b. $28,730   c. $35,555   d. $42,667

31. A mill is expressed as:
    a. .1   b. .01   c. .001   d. .0001

32. In the figure, how many square feet are contained in the living area of the dwelling only?
    a. 2,236
    b. 2,272
    c. 2,476
    d. cannot be computed

33. What percentage of a section is 1/90 of a township?
    a. 10 percent   b. 40 percent   c. 45 percent   d. 38 percent

34. A man purchased three lots for $17,000. Lot 2 sells for $1,500 more than Lot 1, and Lot 3 sells for $2,000 more than Lot 2. What is the full price of Lot 2?
    a. $5,500   b. $4,000   c. $7,500   d. none of these

35. In a cubic yard there are:
    a. 3 linear feet   b. 9 square feet   c. 27 cubic feet   d. all of these

36. On a 25-year lease at $15,000 a year, a broker gets a commission of 7 percent for the first year, 5 percent for the next 4 years, 3 percent for the next 10 years, and 1 percent for the remainder of the lease. How much commission has the broker earned by the end of the 19th year?
    a. $7,350   b. $12,750   c. $9,150   d. $7,950

37. A $10,000 loan requires payments of $100 per month plus interest. As to the monthly payments, the amount of money applying to:
    a. interest will decrease   c. both a and b
    b. principal will increase   d. neither a nor b

38. A 5-foot fence will be built around the perimeter of a 50' × 120' rectangular lot. If the fence will cost $1.80 per linear foot for labor and $.40 per square foot for material, what will be the cost of the fence?
    a. $1,292   b. $1,700   c. $1,824   d. $1,936

39. A lender agrees to make a 90 percent loan on a home selling for $220,000 providing the borrower pays loan costs of 1 1/2 percent. What are the loan costs?
    a. $3,300   b. $2,970   c. $1,980   d. $1,436

40. A 10-acre rectangular parcel is divided into six equal lots, each having a depth of 250'. The width of each lot is approximately how many feet?
    a. 290.4'   b. 348.48'   c. 217.4'   d. 1,742.4'

41. Seller A offers the S 1/2 of the NW 1/4 of the NE 1/4 of Section 21 for sale through Broker B at a list price of $350 per acre. Broker B presents Buyer C's offer of $6,100 to Seller A. Seller A accepts Buyer C's offer provided that the buyer pays the broker 10 percent commission on the offered price. If the buyer accepts this provision, how much less than the original list price did the buyer actually pay?
    a. $270   b. $280   c. $290   d. $330

42. A road runs along the south boundary of the SW 1/4 of the SW 1/4 of a section. If the road contains 2 acres in area, the width of the road would be:
    a. 16 feet   b. 33 feet   c. 47 feet   d. 66 feet

43. An investor purchased two lots at $6,000 each and divided them into three lots, which he sold for $4,800 each. His percentage of profit based on cost was:

    a. 6 percent   b. 12 percent   c. 20 percent   d. 24 percent

44. A rectangular piece of property has 200 feet on one side and an apartment building that is worth $193,600 which is the equivalent of $4.40 per square foot for the lot. What is the front footage?

    a. 110 feet   b. 220 feet   c. 440 feet   d. 880 feet

45. The cost-of-living index increased from 100 to 120. What effect does this have on the purchasing power of the dollar?

    a. lowers it 25 percent   b. lowers it 20 percent   c. lowers it 16 2/3 percent   d. none of these

46. A 10-acre rectangular lot on High Street sold for $60,000. Assuming a depth of 300′, the price paid per front foot is:

    a. $34.14   b. $83.11   c. $344.14   d. $713.23

47. A property was listed to give the owner $41,000 after the 6 percent commission was paid. It was listed at:

    a. $38,640   b. $43,437   c. $43,617   d. $43,918

48. The maximum number of 50′ × 75′ lots that can be made from one acre, would be:

    a. 10   b. 11   c. 12   d. 13

49. If barbedwire weighs one pound per rod, how many pounds of barbedwire will it take to put a single-strand fence around a section?

    a. 211 lbs.   b. 420 lbs.   c. 687 lbs.   d. 1,280 lbs.

50. A 3-strand wire fence around a square 40-acre parcel would require how much wire?

    a. 3 miles   b. 4.5 miles   c. 6 miles   d. none of these

51. A lot is assessed at 25 percent of its $7,500 market value. The tax rate is .02392 per dollar of valuation. Taxes would be:

    a. $11.13   b. $44.85   c. $284.03   d. none of the above

52. A property was purchased for $87,500. The buyer now wishes to sell it. If selling costs will equal 11 percent of any sales price, how much must the property appreciate in value for the seller to break even?

    a. $9,625   b. $9,738   c. $10,815   d. $11,315

53. A woman purchased a property for $15,000 with $2,000 down and no payments or interest for one year. At the end of the year she sold the property at double the purchase price. Each dollar of the original investment is now worth:

    a. $6.50   b. $7.50   c. $8.50   d. $11.00

54. A man owned a rectangular property with an area of 3/4 of an acre and a depth of 110 feet. He purchased the adjoining property, which was 2/3 the size of his own with the same depth, for $1,400. Putting them together into rectangular lots of 82.5′ × 110′ each, he sold the lots for $750 each, which was 50 percent over his cost. How much did he pay for his original property?

    a. $850   b. $1,600   c. $2,800   d. $3,100

55. A man paid off an 8 percent term loan for $800. His total interest cost was $42.66. He paid off the loan in:

    a. 6 months   b. 7 months   c. 8 months   d. 9 months

56. A woman borrowed $5,000 for one year with 6 percent prepaid interest. She received:

    a. $4,700   b. $5,000   c. $5,300   d. none of these

57. Two houses sold together for $49,911. If one was valued $3,176 more than the other, what did the more expensive home sell for?

    a. $26,543.50   b. $28,081   c. $28,730   d. $29,813

58. Given the amount of interest paid, the rate of interest and the time, which formula would you use to find the amount of the principal?

    a. $P = \dfrac{I}{R}$ b. $P = \dfrac{R}{I}$ c. $P = \dfrac{I}{R \times T}$ d. $P = R \times T \times I$

59. You wish to earn $50 per month on a 6 percent investment. How much would you have to invest?
   a. $5,000   b. $6,000   c. $10,000   d. $20,000

60. Mr. Jones had sales of $25,000. His markup was 50 percent of his cost. The merchandise cost him:
   a. $12,500   b. $16,666.66   c. $17,500   d. $18,200

ANSWERS—CHAPTER 6 QUIZ

1. b. $100 \times \$100$.
2. a. $100 \times \$10$.
3. c. It contains 15,000 square feet.
4. b. $40' \times 40' \times 2$.
5. a. $14,900 = 118\%$ of its original cost. Whole = Part ÷ Rate.
6. b. Divide down payment into net.
7. c. $25\% \times 47,500 = \$11,875$; 118.75×2.392.
8. b. $\$5,200 = .96 \times$ the face amount. Whole = Part ÷ Rate.
9. b. $\$58.32 = 1/12$ of interest. Rate = Part ÷ Whole.
10. c. Divide equity ($2,000) into net ($1,280). Net is gross less interest payment.
11. d. Divide investment ($900) into net ($348). Net is gross ($104 × $12) minus cost ($900).
12. b. Principal = Yearly interest: (Part) ÷ Rate.
13. c. $.006 = 1/12$ of 7.2%.
14. c. Divide the area in square feet by the known dimension.
15. d. $2'' \times 8'' \times 108'' = 1728 \div 144$.
16. a. $1'' \times 6'' \times 20'' = 120$ cubic inches.
17. c. Total rent decreased to $990.
18. b. Net ($600) ÷ cost ($400).
19. a. Net ($600) ÷ selling price ($1,000).
20. c.
21. a. Divide the area in square feet by 5,280. (Known dimension.)
22. c. $40,000 = 130\%$ of cost. Cost was $30,769; difference is profit.
23. b. $43,560 \div 200 = 217.8$; $217.8 \div 4$.
24. d. Only the rate changed.
25. b. Whole = Part ÷ Rate. Part is $739.12 and rate is 1/12 of 6% or .005.
26. b. $40' \times 10' = 400$ square feet. Divide by 3 (1/3 foot thick) = 133.33 cubic feet. Divide by 27.
27. c.
28. c. 9×27.
29. c. $40' \times 70'$
30. c. $\$320 \times 12 = \$3,840$ annual return. $\$3,840 = 9\%$ of investment, $42,666 = 120\%$ of lot cost. Whole = Part ÷ Rate.
31. c. 1/10 of a cent.
32. c. (See drawing.)
33. b. $36 \div 90$.
34. a. Lot 1 + (Lot 2 + $1,500) + (Lot 3 + $3,500) = $17,000; 3 lots +

$5,000 = \$17,000$. 3 lots = $12,000. Lot 1 = $4,000, Lot 2 = $5,500, Lot 3 = $7,500.
35. c. $3' \times 3' \times 3'$.
36. c. $7\% \times \$15,000 = \$1,050$, $5\% \times \$15,000 \times 4 = \$3,000$, $3\% \times \$15,000 \times 10 = \$4,500$, $1\% \times \$15,000 \times 4 = \$600$.
37. a. The amount paid on the principal is the same "plus interest."
38. a. $\$1.80 \times 340 = \$612$; $340' \times 5' = 1,700$; $1,700 \times \$.40 = \$680$.
39. b. $.90 \times \$220,000 = \$198,000$; $.015 \times \$198,000$.
40. a. $43,560 \times 10 = 435,600$; $435,600 \div 250 = 1742.4$; $1742.4 \div 6$.
41. c. 20 acres $\times \$350 = \$7,000$ list price. $6,100 offered + 10\% = \$6,710$. $7,000 - \$6,710 = \$290$.
42. d. 40-acre parcel with 1,320' each side. $2 \times 43,560 = 87,120$ square feet. Divide known dimension (1,320) into area (87,120).
43. c. Paid $12,000. Sold $3 \times 4,800 = 14,400$. Net = $2,400. Divide $12,000 into $2,400.
44. b. $193,600 \div 4.40 = 44,000$ square feet. Divide total area by known dimension.
45. c. It now takes $6 to buy what $5 purchased. Each dollar is worth 1/6 less.
46. a. $10 \times 43,560 = 435,600$ square feet. $435,600 \div 300 = 1,452'$ wide. $\$60,000 \div 1,452 =$ price per front foot. Use closest answer.

47. c. $41,000 = .94$ of sale price. Whole = Part ÷ Rate.
48. b. $50 \times 75 = 3,750$. Divide 43,560 by 3,750. (Can't get 12.)
49. d. $5,280 \times 4 = 21,120'$. A rod is 16.5'.
50. a. 1/4 mile each side, so 1 mile around.
51. b. $1,875 assessed value × tax rate.
52. c. $87,500 = 89\%$ of sale price. $98,315 sale price. $98,315 - \$87,500$.
53. c. $7.50 profit per dollar invested "plus" the dollar.
54. a. 3/4 acre = 32,670 square feet. 2/3 of 32,670 = 21,780 square feet. $32,670 + 21,780 = 54,450$ square feet. $82.5 \times 110 = 9,075$ feet. 54,450 divided by 9,075 gives 6 lots. $6 \times \$750 = \$4,500$ sale price. His cost was $2,250. Since he paid $1,400 for second parcel, the first parcel cost $850.
55. c. $\$800 \times 8\% = \$64$ per year or $5.33 per month.
56. a. $\$5,000 \times .06 = \$300$. Interest was deducted.
57. a. 2 homes = $49,911. 2 homes + $3,176 = $49,911. 2 homes = $46,735. 1 home = $23,367.50 less expensive. $23,367.50 + $3,176 = $26,543.50.
58. a. Whole = Part ÷ Rate.
59. c. $\$50 \times 12 = \$600$. $600 = 6\%$ of investment. Divide $600 by .06. Whole = Part ÷ Rate.
60. b. His markup was 1/3 of selling price.

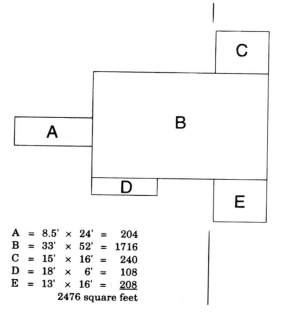

A	= 8.5'	× 24'	=	204
B	= 33'	× 52'	=	1716
C	= 15'	× 16'	=	240
D	= 18'	× 6'	=	108
E	= 13'	× 16'	=	208

2476 square feet

Introduction to Real Estate Finance

NEGOTIABLE INSTRUMENTS

To be negotiable, an instrument must be:

1. An unconditional promise or order to pay.
2. In writing.
3. Signed by the maker.
4. Payable on demand or at a certain time.
5. Payable in money.

Checks and notes are examples of negotiable instruments. Negotiable instruments are bearer paper or order paper.

Bearer Paper   Payable to bearer or cash. No endorsement is necessary to transfer it.

Order Paper   Payable to a particular person. That person must endorse the instrument (sign on back) to transfer it.

A **Holder in due course** is a person who, acting in good faith, gave value for a negotiable instrument before it was past due with no knowledge of any defense that the maker might time.

Assume A gave a note to B:

$$A \to B$$

B could not collect from A if A could prove fraud on the part of B, or prior payment to B. However, if the note was transferred to C, a holder in due course, A could not raise those defenses.

$$A \rightarrow B \rightarrow C$$

C, as a holder in due course, could collect from A even though B, who transferred the note, was precluded from collection by personal defenses that A could raise.

The only defenses that A, the maker, can raise against a holder in due course would be real defenses such as:

- **Forgery** The signature was not that of the maker.
- **Raised Note** The note was altered as to amount due.
- **Incapacity of Maker** Maker lacked legal or mental capacity.
- **Fraud as to the Nature of the Instrument** The party signing did not know it was a negotiable instrument.
- **Discharge in Bankruptcy**
- **Illegality** Instrument was given for an illegal purpose.

Endorsements

If a holder of a negotiable instrument is unable to collect from the maker, the holder can go to any prior endorser of the instrument for payment.

A holder, when transferring a negotiable instrument, may endorse it in several ways:

- **Blank Endorsement** Holder merely signs his or her name. This would turn order paper into bearer paper and further endorsement would not be necessary to transfer the instrument.
- **Special Endorsement** This endorsement would be "Pay to the order of _____." To transfer the instrument, the named party must endorse the instrument.
- **Qualified Endorsement** By adding the words, "without recourse" to the endorsement, the holder is stating that he or she will have no personal liability if the maker defaults on payment. A qualified endorsement avoids any secondary liability.
- **Restrictive Endorsement** A restrictive endorsement would preclude any further endorsement. "Pay to the order of J. Jones Only" means that J. Jones is the only one who can collect on the instrument.

Mortgages

A **mortgage** is a two-party secured loan whereby real estate is **hypothecated.**

Hypothecate   To give something as security without giving up possession.

Given lien (mortgage)

Mortgagor ————————————————————————→ Mortgagee
(borrower)   gives note   (lender or seller)
(retains title) ————————————————————————→ (gets lien only)

Note that two instruments are involved—a lien and a *note*. The note is the primary evidence of the debt. The lien or mortgage is security for the note. To have any effect as to third parties, a mortgage must be recorded, but as between the parties, a mortgage need not be recorded to be valid. A transfer of title for security purposes would be treated by the courts as a mortgage.

Since a mortgage is a lien on the real estate when it is recorded, the mortgagee must give the mortgagor a **Satisfaction of Mortgage** when the note is paid. Recording the satisfaction removes the lien. If the mortgagee refuses to give satisfaction within 21 days of demand by the mortgagor, the mortgagee is liable for a penalty of $300.

Mortgage Foreclosure

At a mortgage foreclosure, the property is sold at auction by a commissioner appointed by the court (20-day posting and publication required). All bidders must bid cash, except the mortgagee, who may bid up to the amount of his or her lien. After the sale, the mortgagor has three months to redeem the property if the proceeds of the sale cover the secured indebtedness; otherwise there is a one-year redemption period, after which the purchaser gets a sheriff's deed.

Mortgagor in Possession

After foreclosure, the mortgagor may retain possession during the redemption period but would be obligated to pay rent. Because of the redemption period, mortgages are not favored in California.

Deficiency Judgment

In some instances, if the amount received at a foreclosure sale is less than the amount due on the note, there may be a deficiency judgment (a judgment against the debtor for the difference between the note amount and the sale price).

Deficiency judgments will not be granted if:

1. Foreclosure is by a sale provision rather than by court action. (If foreclosure is under a sale provision of a trust deed or mortgage, there can be no deficiency judgment. The one-year period of redemption must be present for the lender to obtain the deficiency.)
2. The property is worth more than the debt. (The mortgagee may not bid a low figure in order to get a deficiency judgment.)
3. The mortgage is a **purchase-money loan:**
   a. if the seller financed the buyer.
   b. if the mortgage is an actual cash loan to purchase one to four residential units. (Loans to purchase five or more residential units or nonresidential property can have deficiency judgments.)

Fictitious Mortgage

This is a mortgage that is recorded but is used merely to set forth terms or conditions of a loan. When other mortgages on the property are made, they will incorporate by reference the terms and conditions of the fictitious mortgage. Title companies thus reduce recording costs by removing the boilerplate (standard) clauses and simply recording the first page.

TRUST DEEDS

These are three-party instruments.

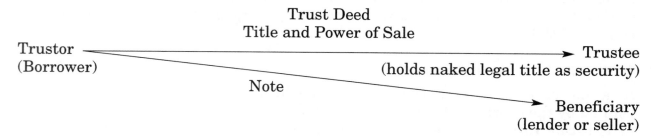

Trust Deed
Title and Power of Sale

Trustor (Borrower) → Trustee (holds naked legal title as security)

Note

→ Beneficiary (lender or seller)

The trust deed is given to the **trustee** to hold as security for the debt (note). Since the **trustor** gives title to the **trustee,** when the note is paid in full the trustee must give the title back by a **deed of reconveyance.** If the trustee fails to deliver a deed of reconveyance within 21 days of the trustor's demand, he or she can be forced to deliver and can be liable for treble damages and a $300 penalty. The fee charged for the deed of reconveyance must be reasonable. A fee not exceeding $65 is presumed to be reasonable. The trustee may be a corporation (escrow company) or an individual, such as an employee of an escrow company.

Satisfaction pertains to a mortgage, whereas a **deed of reconveyance** pertains to a trust deed. Another important distinction is that a trust deed **moves title,** while a mortgage does not.

Trust Deed Foreclosure

If the trustor is in default (failed to make payments, pay taxes, pay insurance, or maintain the property, or used it for an illegal purpose), the beneficiary can order the trustee to foreclose.

Steps in Foreclosure

1. **Three-month notice of default.** (The borrower is notified and notice is recorded. Within 10 days of filing; a copy must be mailed.)
2. **Notice of sale.** (Notice is recorded and published in a newspaper of general circulation after the three-month period and at least 20 days prior to sale.) The trustee is allowed three postponements of the trustee's sale. After three postponements the trustee must readvertise, unless the delay was mutually agreed upon.
3. **Trustee's sale.** The trustee sells the property and gives the trustee's deed to the buyer. The beneficiary may bid the amount of the indebtedness, but all others must bid cash. In the event that the sale brings more than the amount of the foreclosed trust deed, the balance goes first to pay off junior encumbrances, then

to the trustor. It is a crime to fix or restrain bidding at the sale. It is also a violation of the law to take unconscionable advantage of a property owner in default. The trustor must vacate the property immediately after the trustee's sale. The trustee's deed must be recorded to have any effect.

4. **Reinstatement.** The trustor can cure a default up to five business days prior to the sale by making delinquent payments plus paying foreclosure costs. If the sale is postponed more than five days, the trustor again has the right to reinstate the loan up to five business days prior to the trustee's sale. There is no right of redemption after the sale.

A trust deed is considered both a lien and an encumbrance.

No deficiency judgment is possible when a trust deed is foreclosed under its sale provision, but it can be foreclosed as a mortgage by court action, which would give the trustor the one-year period of redemption. If it is foreclosed as a mortgage, a deficiency judgment is possible.

Statute of Limitations

This runs on mortgages so that if the mortgagee does not enforce collection within four years of the debt becoming due, the lien is lost and the debt is not enforceable. The Statute of Limitations on trust deeds is considerably longer (10 years from the due date of the last payment of the obligation, or 60 years from the date of the deed's creation if the due date cannot be ascertained).

Beneficiary Statement

Upon the request of the borrower, the beneficiary must furnish, within 21 days, a written statement of the status of the loan (this rule also applies to mortgages). There is a $300 penalty to the beneficiary if he or she fails to comply. The beneficiary must provide an annual statement if requested, at no charge, but may charge for additional statements ($60 is the maximum charge).

Junior Encumbrances

Time of recording determines whether encumbrances are senior or junior to each other. Should the holder of a trust deed or mortgage foreclose, the foreclosure wipes out encumbrances junior to the foreclosed lien, and the buyer, at foreclosure, takes the property subject to the senior encumbrances.

Since foreclosure wipes out junior liens, the holder of a junior lien can be assured of knowing about a foreclosure through the recording of a request for **notice of default.** Upon notice of the default, a junior lienholder, to protect his or her interest, may make the mortgagor's or trustor's payments and thereby stop foreclosure. The junior lienholder may then foreclose on his or her own lien (based on the amount advanced to the mortgagor or trustor) and take title subject to the prior liens. If the junior lienholder does nothing, he or she will either have to bid cash for the entire purchase price at the foreclosure sale or lose out completely, since foreclosure wipes out all junior liens.

A junior lienholder can be protected against a significant delinquency by requesting **notice of delinquency** from the senior lienholder when the trustor is more than four months behind in payments. The $40 fee for this request is good for five years.

Rent Skimming

It is a felony for a trustor to fail to apply rent collected to mortgage or trust deed payments (applies to five or more properties within two years of purchase). The definition of rent skimming has been expanded to include collecting deposits or rent from property not owed or controlled by the renter (tenant protection).

LAND CONTRACTS (REAL PROPERTY SALES CONTRACTS)

These are sales agreements whereby the seller retains title as security.

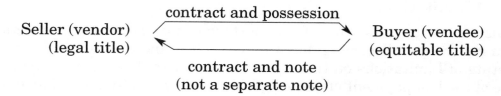

Seller (vendor) (legal title) — contract and possession → Buyer (vendee) (equitable title) — contract and note (not a separate note)

Risk of loss through destruction of the premises rests on the buyer as soon as he or she obtains possession.

Prepayment on land contracts is allowed by law; however, the seller may prohibit or regulate prepayment for a period of 12 months. (The seller does not have to give title for one year.)

In the case of buyer default, foreclosure was formerly comparatively quick, by notice of forfeiture. Now, foreclosure can be complicated, since a quiet title action or an action for ejectment is usually required. Deficiency judgments are not allowed for vendees who default.

Since the buyer has possession and a right to obtain a legal title upon payment (equitable title), if he or she wishes to sell to another, the sale can be by assigning the land contract. A quitclaim deed would also transfer interest.

If the seller under a land contract wishes to sell his or her interest in the contract to a third party, he or she must also convey title to that third person. (Otherwise, when the buyer makes the last payment on the contract, the contract holder will be unable to deliver title.) If a real estate broker negotiates the assignment of the contract, he or she is responsible for recording within 10 working days. The new contract holder must notify the buyer that title has been conveyed (this protects the buyer from continuing to pay the original contract holder).

Every land contract must include:

1. A legal description.
2. A statement of the number of years required to pay it off.

3. The existing encumbrances.

4. The basis upon which the tax estimate was made (if payment includes taxes).

5. A statement that it is in compliance with or an exception to the Map Act (if it involves a division of property).

6. The dollar amount of the contract (unlike trust deeds, a separate note is not used for land contracts).

The seller under a land contract must ensure that when the buyer has paid up the contract he or she can convey title; therefore:

1. The seller may not encumber the property so that the obligation exceeds the buyer's obligation.

2. The seller must first apply the buyer's payments to encumbrances, so that they will be paid off when the land contract is paid up.

3. If the seller receives money from the buyer for taxes and insurance, he or she must hold this money in trust for the purpose designated.

There is a danger in a land contract of the seller not being able to convey good title when the vendee has finished making payments. This danger can be eliminated by delivery of title to a trustee, coupled with title insurance. (This makes a land contract very similar to a trust deed.) Upon request, the seller must supply the buyer with a statement showing money received and disbursements. For violation of the law regarding land contracts, the seller is subject to up to a $10,000 fine and up to one year in jail. (The law protects the purchaser, who otherwise has very little protection under a land contract.)

To be recorded, a land contract must be signed and acknowledged by the seller.

Clauses

Acceleration Clause This clause makes the entire loan due and payable upon the happening of some event. A loan may not be accelerated because of the addition of a junior lien, transfer from one spouse to the other, transfer resulting from dissolution of marriage, or transfer into an *inter vivos* trust in which the borrower is the trust beneficiary.

Alienation or Due-on-Sale Clause The most common type of acceleration clause, this makes a loan payable in full if the property is sold. Property loans with alienation clauses cannot be assumed. On the secondary mortgage market, this type of loan is valued because there is a good chance it will be paid up early. Due-on-sale clauses in loans are fully enforceable.

"Or More" Clause Use of the words "or more," such as in "payments of $100 or more per month," allow prepayment of a loan without penalty.

Prepayment Penalty Clause This sets forth the amount of actual penalty for prepayment. In California, for loans made after January 1, 1980, prepayment penalties are not allowed on residential property of four units or less after the loan has been in force for five years. (For loans made by loan brokers on single-family homes, prepayment penalties are not allowed after seven years.) For loans less than five years old, the borrower cannot be charged more than six months' interest on the prepaid amount. The borrower can also prepay up to 20 percent of the original loan during any 12-month period without penalty. Prepayment penalties are not allowed when loans are accelerated under a due-on-sale clause for owner-occupied properties of one to four units. For tax purposes, prepayment penalties are treated as interest paid.

Prepayment penalties are not allowed on FHA and VA loans (but a penalty is allowed on CAL–VET loans). If the loan is prepaid within five years of its origination date, the purchaser can be charged an amount equal to six months' advance interest on the amount prepaid in excess of 20 percent of the original loan amount. On land contracts for one to four residential units, the seller may prohibit prepayment for 12 months, after which the loan can be prepaid without penalty.

Assignment of Rents An assignment of rents clause in a mortgage provides that should the borrower be in default, the mortgagee (lender) has the right to collect the rents. Otherwise the mortgagor could keep the rents and not pay on the loan until foreclosure.

Defeasance Clause This clause sets forth the provisions for the cancellation of the lien upon payment.

Late Charges The charges for a late payment on a loan secured by a single-family owner-occupied dwelling cannot exceed 6 percent of the principal and interest for the payment due. (Loans made by loan brokers may have a late charge of 10 percent of the loan installment.) A 10-day grace period must be provided and the late charges cannot be pyramided. A $5 minimum late charge is allowed. If a late charge is not specified in the loan, none can be made.

Clause against Recording Provisions against recording in a mortgage, trust deed, or land contract are against public policy, and so are unenforceable. The instrument may be recorded regardless of such a clause.

Subordination Clause This is an agreement in a mortgage or trust deed that the lien will be secondary to later recorded liens. Usually it is on land sales in which the seller, in order to make the sale, agrees to take a trust deed subordinate to a loan for construction purposes.

If a subordination clause states that the loan will be subordinate to another particular loan, then when that particular loan is paid up, the subordinated loan can become the senior encumbrance. However, if the clause states simply that the loan will be subordinate, the subordinated loan will always be last.

144

Subrogation Clause *Do not confuse this with subordination.* This clause allows the original trustor or mortgagor to be released completely from the obligation by the substitution of another party.

Subrogation is also used in conjunction with insurance policies. If a person's insurance carrier pays the insured for damages to his or her car caused by another car, it would then sue the other driver, since it now has the insured's rights by subrogation (substitution).

Lock-In Clause This clause allows prepayment of a loan, but it requires that the interest for the entire loan also be paid (locked in to the interest). Lock-in clauses are not allowed in real estate loans secured by one to four residential units. They are not allowed on loans made or arranged for a fee by loan brokers.

Blanket Encumbrance This is a mortgage or a trust deed covering more than one property. In order to sell a property covered by a blanket encumbrance, there must be a *release clause* allowing the partial release of individual parcels upon payment of a stated sum; otherwise, the entire loan would have to be paid off. A blanket encumbrance must be recorded in all counties where the affected property is located.

Pledge This is giving property as security for a loan. Only personal property can be pledged. Although mortgages and trust deeds are liens on real property, they are considered to be personal property, and so can be pledged.

A pledge is similar to a land contract, in that in both cases possession is given, but title remains with the owner.

Sale with Option to Buy Back This is a sale in which the seller has a right to repurchase. The courts will treat the sale as a loan transaction.

Assuming an Existing Loan The buyer agrees to assume the seller's liability on the loan, so a deficiency judgment is possible. The seller would remain secondarily liable on the loan unless there is a substitution of liability, which would relieve the seller of all liability.

Taking Subject to a Loan The buyer recognizes that the property is encumbered, but since the buyer never agrees to pay the encumbrance, a deficiency judgment is not possible. Of course, if the buyer wishes to keep the property, he or she would have to pay. The seller remains liable on the loan. If a buyer assumes a loan from a seller who had taken subject to a loan then the buyer's liability would be the same as the seller's liability.

Financing Personal Property

A **security agreement** is used for financing personal property. The vendor retains a security interest in the goods.

Under the Uniform Commercial Code (UCC), a **financing statement** is filed with the state secretary of state's office or the appropriate county recorder, giving everyone constructive notice of the vendor's interest. The financing statement is good for five years and can be extended by a **continuation statement.** When the debt is paid in full the creditor files a **termination statement,** which releases the lien. (It is not applicable to consumer goods. Also, for crops or timber the security agreement is filed with the county recorder and not the secretary of state.)

As a result of the filing of the financing statement, the goods remain personal property, even if they are later affixed to real estate.

Under the UCC, security agreements have replaced chattel mortgages and conditional sales. (A security agreement creates a security interest in the goods, while a financing statement gives constructive notice of that interest.)

Loan Terms and Types

Hard-Money Loan   A loan in which cash changes hands (the lender is other than the seller). This type of loan demands the highest market rate of interest.

Soft-Money Loan   A loan in which the seller finances the buyer so cash does not actually change hands.

Purchase-Money Loan   A loan in which the seller finances the buyer. No money changes hands for the amount of the loan. (It may also be a cash loan for purchase of real estate.)

Amortized Loan   An amortized loan pays itself off over the loan period with equal monthly payments. A loan that has one large payment at a due date prior to full amortization is a **partially amortized loan.**

The large payment, if more than twice the smallest regular payment, is known as a **balloon payment.**

Reverse Mortgage   A mortgage that allows the owner to borrow against equity by receiving monthly payments. It provides a means for the elderly to keep their homes.

Rollover or Renegotiable Mortgage   A short-term loan (such as five years) with payments based on a 25- to 30-year period. When due, the loan is rewritten at the then-current interest rate.

Wraparound Loan or All-Inclusive Trust Deed   When higher interest rates make it inadvisable to refinance an existing lower-interest loan, a second trust deed or mortgage may be used for seller financing. The seller, for security purposes, has the loan written for the total of the first and second loans, collects for the total wraparound loan, and makes payments on the first loan. Failure to make purchaser's payments to the underlying loan can subject the seller to up to a $10,000 fine and up to one year in jail.

Graduated-Payment Mortgage (GPM) A mortgage that has lower payments initially; they increase later. This type of mortgage is well suited for young people with rising incomes. The loan may initially have negative amortization.

Growing-Equity Mortgage (GEM) A mortgage in which the payments increase annually to reduce the period of the loan.

Adjustable-Rate Mortgage (ARM) A mortgage in which the interest rate is tied to a changing market rate, Federal Cost of Funds Index, or Libor Rate, and can be raised or lowered. Federal savings and loan institutions have no limitations on their rates, but California-licensed savings and loan institutions' interest rates are linked to the California Cost of Funds Index. The **margin** is the percentage above the **index** at which the loan's interest rate is set (ARM interest rate = Index rate + Margin). The adjustment period, when interest rates are raised and lowered, is also of importance. Most ARMs have **caps.** There may be a cap on the total interest that can be charged, as well as caps upon the amount of any single increase. Some ARMs prohibit **negative amortization,** while others allow it. With negative amortization, the payment is less than the interest, so the loan balance is actually increasing. Lenders frequently have introductory or "teaser" rates less than the Index rate plus the Margin. This lower rate may aid in qualifying a buyer.

California-licensed lenders must notify the borrower at least 50 days prior to a rate increase, and the borrower has the option of paying off the loan within 90 days without penalty. Borrowers must also be given a federally mandated brochure explaining adjustable-rate loans.

Sharing-Appreciation Mortgage (SAM) A mortgage in which the lender agrees to a below-market interest rate in exchange for a percentage of the increased value of the home. These loans usually provide for an appraisal and settlement after a stated period of time. California-regulated lenders may not make SAM loans on one to four residential units.

Home-Equity Loan A loan (other than a purchase-money loan) that is secured by the borrower's home. The creditor must provide a disclosure statement, such as: "This home-equity loan that you are applying for will be secured by your home, and your failure to repay the loan for any reason could cause you to lose your home." Home-equity loans are generally secondary financing.

Open Mortgage A mortgage that can be prepaid without penalty.

Private Mortgage Insurance (PMI) Similar to FHA insurance but issued by private insurance carriers. It is usually required by conventional lenders when the down payment is less than 20 percent. A homeowner may cancel PMI if the mortgage has declined to 75 percent or less of purchase price, payments are current, and there was no more than one late payment in the prior year. For loans made after July 28, 1999, the lender must discontinue PMI coverage when the homeowner's equity reaches 22 percent or when the homeowner's equity reaches 20 percent and the borrowers request that it be dropped.

Mortgage Warehousing Interim financing whereby a mortgage company makes loans to be taken over by a permanent lender. The mortgage company may borrow on its inventory or "warehouse" of such loans. The loan on the mortgages would be said to be **collaterally secured.**

Participation Loans On large projects, lenders sometimes not only insist on getting their interest on the amount loaned, but they also get, as part of the loan, a share of the ownership in the project, so they share in the profits. (They are usually limited partners.)

Packaged Loan A loan covering both real and personal property.

Seasoned Loan A loan with a payment history (usually over 3 years).

Compound Interest This is interest charged on interest. Money deposited in a bank would have compound interest. A real estate loan has simple interest and not compound interest, since interest is paid each month and does not compound.

Legal Rate of Interest The rate charged when it is clearly indicated that interest should be charged but the rate is not stated. In California the legal rate is 7 percent. A 10 percent rate applies to judgments.

Maximum Rate of Interest The rate that the law allows between individuals. In California it cannot exceed 10 percent, or 5 percent above the Federal Reserve Bank of San Francisco rate for advances to member banks, whichever is greater. More than that is **usury.** Licensed lending institutions have higher maximum rates. A seller who finances a buyer by means of a purchase-money loan is not bound by the usury limit. There is no maximum rate for loans arranged or made by a real estate broker.

Points charged by a nonlicensed lender would be considered interest in determining whether a loan is usurious. If a loan provides a usurious rate of interest, then interest cannot be collected. If usurious interest was paid, the borrower can recover the interest paid for the prior two years plus treble damages for the interest paid during the last year. There are also criminal penalties (up to five years' imprisonment).

Open-End Mortgage A mortgage that can be increased up to an agreed ceiling.

Impound Account A trust account of taxes and insurance that are prepaid by the borrower and kept by the lender. The lender cannot require an impound account unless (1) it is required by state or federal law, (2) the loan is 75 percent or more of the sale price, or (3) the borrower has failed to pay two or more tax installments.

For one to four residential units, state-chartered savings and loan associations must pay interest of at least 2 percent on the impound account.

Discounting a Loan Selling an existing loan at less than the face amount due on the note. Second trust deeds are normally discounted if sold.

148

Discount Loan A loan in which interest is taken out in advance.

Construction Loan A short-term commercial loan. Although interest is not charged until funds are disbursed, the repayment period generally starts with the date of the loan. These loans are generally made by commercial banks.

A construction lender might require a completion bond. If the contractor is unable to complete the project, the insurance company that issued the bond has completion responsibiliy.

Obligatory Advance An advance that the lender is obligated to make (usually in construction loans).

Take-Out Loan A permanent loan given to the owner after a building is completed under a construction loan. A commitment for permanent financing is known as a **standby loan commitment.**

Straight Loan An unamortized loan where the borrower pays interest only and must pay the principal at the time the loan is due.

Piggyback Loan A loan shared by two lenders in which one lender takes the bottom portion of the loan and a second lender takes the top portion, which bears greater risk since it is treated like a second mortgage or trust deed should there be a foreclosure. It differs, however, from the use of a second mortgage or trust deed because there is only one loan.

Points Points are percentages of the loan (1 point = 1 percent) and are charged by lenders to make up the difference between the amount of the loan and the value of the loan on the secondary mortgage market. (It makes up for an interest rate that is less than the rate desired by the lender.) On conventional, FHA, and VA loans, points are paid as agreed between parties.

For example: A buyer obtains a new loan for $20,000 that would be worth $18,800 on the secondary mortgage market. This is a discount of $1,200 or 6 percent. The lender would, therefore, demand 6 points, or 6 percent of the loan ($1,200), to make the loan.

As a rule of thumb, each point is considered to be equivalent to 1/8 percent yield on a mortgage. So a loan at 1/2 percent less than an acceptable rate to a lender would require 4 points. (1/2 percent = 4 points, since 1 percent = 8 points.) Points are also called an **origination fee.**

Predatory Loan Predatory lending is prohibited by California law, which provides for disciplinary action against licensees involved and finanial remedies to victims.

Predatory lending involves a number of tactics for a loan that places a lien on the borrower's residence. They include making a loan without regard to the borrower's ability to make payments, refinancing where there is no tangible benefit to the borrower, as well as providing a consumer with a high-cost loan when the consumer would qualify for a less costly financing.

Federal Reserve

The Federal Reserve manages our nation's money supply by:

1. Buying and selling government securities on the open market.
2. Raising and lowering the discount rate (loan rate) to member banks.
3. Raising and lowering the reserve requirements of banks. To fight inflation, the Federal Reserve reduces the money supply by selling securities, raising discount rates, and raising the reserve requirements. An expansionary (as well as inflationary) policy is to buy government securities, lower the discount rate, and lower reserve requirements.

The U.S. government can also affect the economy by increasing or decreasing taxes (increasing taxes to fight inflation or decreasing taxes as an expansionary policy), as well as by increasing or decreasing government spending.

Equal Credit Opportunity Act

This act prohibits discrimination against any applicant for a loan on the basis of sex, marital status, race, color, or public assistance income. The lender cannot arbitrarily reject an applicant because of a second income. If a loan is denied, the reason for the denial must be listed, and the applicant has the right to rebut the reasoning.

California Housing Financial Discrimination Act of 1977 (Holden Act)

This act, which applies to one to four residential units, states that a lender cannot deny a loan or change terms that are not related to the credit of the applicant or the value of the property. They cannot use the neighborhood as a limiting factor. This prohibits the procedure of **redlining,** whereby lenders do not lend in particular areas. This act is enforced by the Business, Transportation, and Housing Agency. The agency can require assistance on nondiscriminatory terms or payment of $1,000 to complainants as relief.

Financial institutions must notify loan applicants of the provisions of this act in bold, 10-point type.

Fair Credit Reporting Act

This act gives a consumer the right to:

1. Notification when adverse action is taken against him or her on the basis of a credit report.

2. Be told of the source of the report.

3. The information contained in the report (not the right to see the actual file).

4. Have the file kept confidential.

5. Have disputed entries reinvestigated.

6. Have obsolete data removed.

7. Receive advance notice if an investigative report is to be made.

Failure to remove information proven false could subject the credit reporting firm to damages. The act does not apply if the report is obtained to extend credit for business purposes. Residential lenders must provide borrowers with a notice of the borrower's right to receive a copy of an appraisal that the borrower paid for within 90 days of loan approval or rejection.

The California Consumer Credit Reporting Agencies Act requires that a credit-reporting agency disclose file information to a consumer upon request. Failure to do so can result in actual damages, up to $5,000 in punitive damages plus attorney's fees.

Real Estate Settlement Procedures Act (RESPA)

This act provides for disclosure of real estate loan costs for federally related primary financing loans (first trust deeds) for one to four residential units, including condominiums and mobile homes (loans made by institutional lenders that have deposits insured by the government or who sell the loans to FNMA, GNMA, etc. are federally related).

A HUD information booklet and **good-faith estimate** of closing costs are provided to the buyer within three business days of the loan application. The borrower has the right to inspect the **uniform settlement statement** one day prior to settlement.

A uniform settlement statement *must* be made to the buyer at or before closing. There must be a justifiable service rendered for every charge made. Limits are placed on the amount of advanced tax and insurance payments that a lender can collect. Excessively large escrow accounts cannot be established or maintained. (Maximum is prorated taxes and insurance plus two months' payment in advance.)

The lender cannot charge for complying with the disclosure requirements of this act. **Kickbacks** or finder's fees for referring services are prohibited. The buyer cannot be required to purchase title insurance from any particular company. The law does not apply to:

1. Refinancing of junior loans (does not apply if there is no change in title).

2. Loans, such as home improvement loans, where there is no change in title.

151

3. Vacant property, unless the loan proceeds are to finance the construction of one to four residential units.

4. A construction loan where the borrower already owns the lot.

5. A loan for property purchased for resale (a dealer loan).

6. Business properties.

7. Assumption of preexisting loans when the assumption fee is less than $50.

8. Loans on 25 or more acres.

9. Land contracts.

Failure to comply with the requirements of the law can result in a fine of up to $10,000 and/or up to one year in jail.

RESPA allows **controlled business arrangements** whereby a broker offers **one-stop shopping** by using businesses that the broker controls. This is permissible as long as the broker's interest is disclosed. The broker-controlled business cannot contract out its services and must act as an independent business. The broker's compensation must be based on the profits of the business, not on the referrals. Referral fees cannot be paid to real estate licensees by the broker-affiliated business.

Truth-in-Lending Law (Regulation Z)

This law, part of the Federal Consumer Credit Protection Act, requires lenders to tell consumers how much they are paying for credit in percentage terms. The law also makes bait-and-switch advertising a federal offense. It applies to real estate loans (without limit) and personal loans under $25,000. The law also applies to creditors who extend credit on real estate transactions more than five times a year. The Federal Trade Commission (FTC) enforces this law. The law does not apply to:

1. Business and agricultural loans (including rental housing).

2. Construction loans.

3. Personal loans over $25,000.

4. Interest-free loans with four or fewer installments.

5. Real estate brokers who arrange credit.

Advertising If an ad includes a **triggering term,** such as the monthly payment, the term of the loan, or the dollar amount of finance charges, then all terms must be included in the ad: the amount of the payments, the amount or percentage of the down payment, the term of the loan, the number of monthly payments, and the **annual percentage rate (APR).** (The APR includes direct and indirect loan costs.) By itself, the annual percentage rate does not trigger the requirement of full disclosure. The APR is larger than the **nominal rate,** which is the rate stated in the note.

Disclosure Statement The lender must furnish a disclosure statement to the borrower (the dollar amount of finance charges is not required on first trust deeds or purchase-money loans). Creditors who extend credit on no more than five real estate transactions a year or no more than 25 consumer credit transactions per year are exempt from this requirement. Charges for appraisals, title insurance, credit reports, and document preparation are not considered finance charges. Escrow costs for taxes and insurance need not be disclosed.

A licensee who receives compensation from a lender in connection with securing financing for a transaction must disclose that fact to all parties.

Right of Rescision   When a loan is secured by the borrower's residence, he or she has the right to rescind until midnight of the third business day following the date the loan is completed (this does not apply to first trust deeds used to purchase property or construction loans). Failure of the lender to inform the borrower of rescision rights extends the rights to up to three years.

Penalty for Violation   The FTC may issue a cease-and-desist order. The penalty for further violations is $10,000 for each day the violation continues. If creditors engage in practices that the FTC has previously determined to be deceptive, a penalty can be assessed of up to $10,000 per violation. Liability to the consumer is twice the amount of the finance charges, with a minimum of $100 and a maximum of $1,000.

Seller Financing Disclosure Law

This law applies to California property of one to four residential units where there is seller financing. The disclosure statement must include:

1. The status of existing loans and loan terms.
2. A warning about any negative amortization that might be possible.
3. Warnings as to any balloon payments.
4. Credit report information.
5. Advice on requesting notice of default.

Holders of balloon-payment notes on one to four owner-occupied residential units must give at least 90 days', but not more than 150 days', notice of balloon payments becoming due. (Loans made prior to January 1, 1984, and loans made where creative financing disclosure was made are exempt.)

Study the Seller Financing Disclosure Statement on pages 154–156.

ARTICLES 5 AND 7 OF THE REAL ESTATE LAW

Article 5

A person who solicits either borrowers or lenders for real property loans must be licensed as a real estate broker. A person who buys eight or more trust deeds in one year for the purpose of resale must be licensed as a broker (a person can handle up

SELLER FINANCING ADDENDUM AND DISCLOSURE
(California Civil Code §§2956-2967)
(C.A.R. Form SFA, Revised 10/02)

This is an addendum to the ☐ Residential Purchase Agreement, ☐ Counter Offer, or ☐ Other _____
_____, ("Agreement"), dated _____,
On property known as _____ ("Property"),
between _____ ("Buyer"),
and _____ ("Seller").
Seller agrees to extend credit to Buyer as follows:

1. **PRINCIPAL; INTEREST; PAYMENT; MATURITY TERMS:** ☐ Principal amount $ _____, interest at _____%
    per annum, payable at approximately $ _____ per ☐ month, ☐ year, or ☐ other _____,
    remaining principal balance due in _____ years.

2. **LOAN APPLICATION; CREDIT REPORT:** Within 5 (or ☐ _____) **Days** After Acceptance: **(a)** Buyer shall provide Seller a completed
    loan application on a form acceptable to Seller (such as a FNMA/FHLMC Uniform Residential Loan Application for residential one to four
    unit properties); and **(b)** Buyer authorizes Seller and/or Agent to obtain, at Buyer's expense, a copy of Buyer's credit report. Buyer shall
    provide any supporting documentation reasonably requested by Seller. Seller may cancel this Agreement in writing if Buyer fails to
    provide such documents within that time, or if Seller disapproves any above item within **5 (or ☐ _____) Days** After receipt of each item.

3. **CREDIT DOCUMENTS:** This extension of credit by Seller will be evidenced by: ☐ Note and deed of trust; ☐ All-inclusive
    note and deed of trust; ☐ Installment land sale contract; ☐ Lease/option (when parties intend transfer of equitable title);
    OR ☐ Other (specify) _____

    **THE FOLLOWING TERMS APPLY ONLY IF CHECKED. SELLER IS ADVISED TO READ ALL TERMS, EVEN THOSE NOT
    CHECKED, TO UNDERSTAND WHAT IS OR IS NOT INCLUDED, AND, IF NOT INCLUDED, THE CONSEQUENCES THEREOF.**

4. ☐ **LATE CHARGE:** If any payment is not made within ____ **Days** After it is due, a late charge of either $ _____,
    or ____% of the installment due, may be charged to Buyer. **NOTE:** On single family residences that Buyer intends to occupy,
    California Civil Code §2954.4(a) limits the late charge to no more than 6% of the total monthly payment due and requires a grace
    period of no less than 10 days.

5. ☐ **BALLOON PAYMENT:** The extension of credit will provide for a balloon payment, in the amount of $ _____
    plus any accrued interest, which is due on _____ (date).

6. ☐ **PREPAYMENT:** If all or part of this extension of credit is paid early, Seller may charge a prepayment penalty as follows (if
    applicable): _____. Caution: California Civil Code
    §2954.9 contains limitations on prepayment penalties for residential one-to-four unit properties.

7. ☐ **DUE ON SALE:** If any interest in the Property is sold or otherwise transferred, Seller has the option to require immediate
    payment of the entire unpaid principal balance, plus any accrued interest.

8.* ☐ **REQUEST FOR COPY OF NOTICE OF DEFAULT:** A request for a copy of Notice of Default as defined in California Civil
    Code §2924b will be recorded. **If Not,** Seller is advised to consider recording a Request for Notice of Default.

9.* ☐ **REQUEST FOR NOTICE OF DELINQUENCY:** A request for Notice of Delinquency, as defined in California Civil Code §2924e,
    to be signed and paid for by Buyer, will be made to senior lienholders. **If not,** Seller is advised to consider making a Request for
    Notice of Delinquency. Seller is advised to check with senior lienholders to verify whether they will honor this request.

10.* ☐ **TAX SERVICE:**
    A. If property taxes on the Property become delinquent, tax service will be arranged to report to Seller. **If not,** Seller is
    advised to consider retaining a tax service, or to otherwise determine that property taxes are paid.
    B. ☐ Buyer, ☐ Seller, shall be responsible for the initial and continued retention of, and payment for, such tax service.

11. ☐ **TITLE INSURANCE:** Title insurance coverage will be provided to **both** Seller and Buyer, insuring their respective interests
    in the Property. **If not,** Buyer and Seller are advised to consider securing such title insurance coverage.

12. ☐ **HAZARD INSURANCE:**
    A. The parties' escrow holder or insurance carrier will be directed to include a loss payee endorsement, adding Seller to
    the Property insurance policy. **If not,** Seller is advised to secure such an endorsement, or acquire a separate
    insurance policy.
    B. Property insurance **does not** include earthquake or flood insurance coverage, unless checked:
    ☐ Earthquake insurance will be obtained; ☐ Flood insurance will be obtained.

13. ☐ **PROCEEDS TO BUYER:** Buyer will receive cash proceeds at the close of the sale transaction. The amount received will be
    approximately $_____, from _____ (indicate source of
    proceeds). Buyer represents that the purpose of such disbursement is as follows: _____

14. ☐ **NEGATIVE AMORTIZATION; DEFERRED INTEREST:** Negative amortization results when Buyer's periodic payments are
    less than the amount of interest earned on the obligation. Deferred interest also results when the obligation does not
    require periodic payments for a period of time. In either case, interest is not payable as it accrues. This accrued interest
    will have to be paid by Buyer at a later time, and may result in Buyer owing more on the obligation than at its origination.
    The credit being extended to Buyer by Seller will provide for negative amortization or deferred interest as indicated below.
    (Check A, B, or C. CHECK ONE ONLY.)
    ☐ **A.** All negative amortization or deferred interest shall be added to the principal _____
    (e.g., annually, monthly, etc.), and thereafter shall bear interest at the rate specified in the credit documents (compound interest);
    OR ☐ **B.** All deferred interest shall be due and payable, along with principal, at maturity;
    OR ☐ **C.** Other _____.

*(For Paragraphs 8-10) In order to receive timely and continued notification, Seller is advised to record appropriate notices and/or to
notify appropriate parties of any change in Seller's address.

Buyer's Initials (_____)(_____)
Seller's Initials (_____)(_____)

Reviewed by _____ Date _____

EQUAL HOUSING
OPPORTUNITY

SELLER FINANCING ADDENDUM AND DISCLOSURE (SFA PAGE 1 OF 3)

Property Address: _____   Date: _____

15. ☐ **ALL-INCLUSIVE DEED OF TRUST; INSTALLMENT LAND SALE CONTRACT:** This transaction involves the use of an all-inclusive (or wraparound) deed of trust or an installment land sale contract. That deed of trust or contract shall provide as follows:
  A. In the event of an acceleration of any senior encumbrance, the responsibility for payment, or for legal defense is: _____ _____ ; OR ☐ **Is not** specified in the credit or security documents.
  B. In the event of the prepayment of a senior encumbrance, the responsibilities and rights of Buyer and Seller regarding refinancing, prepayment penalties, and any prepayment discounts are: _____ ; OR ☐ **Are not** specified in the documents evidencing credit.
  C. Buyer will make periodic payments to _____ (Seller, collection agent, or any neutral third party), who will be responsible for disbursing payments to the payee(s) on the senior encumbrance(s) and to Seller. **NOTE:** The Parties are advised to designate a neutral third party for these purposes.

16. ☐ **TAX IDENTIFICATION NUMBERS:** Buyer and Seller shall each provide to each other their Social Security Numbers or Taxpayer Identification Numbers.

17. ☐ **OTHER CREDIT TERMS** _____ _____

18. ☐ **RECORDING:** The documents evidencing credit (paragraph 3) will be recorded with the county recorder where the Property is located. **If not**, Buyer and Seller are advised that their respective interests in the Property may be jeopardized by intervening liens, judgments, encumbrances, or subsequent transfers.

19. ☐ **JUNIOR FINANCING:** There will be additional financing, secured by the Property, junior to this Seller financing. Explain: _____

20. **SENIOR LOANS AND ENCUMBRANCES:** The following information is provided on loans and/or encumbrances that will be **senior** to Seller financing. **NOTE:** The following are estimates, unless otherwise marked with an asterisk (*). If checked: ☐ A separate sheet with information on additional senior loans/encumbrances is attached

	1st	2nd
A. Original Balance	$ _____	$ _____
B. Current Balance	$ _____	$ _____
C. Periodic Payment (e.g. $100/month):	$ _____	$ _____ /
Including Impounds of:	$ _____	$ _____ /
D. Interest Rate (per annum)	_____ %	_____ %
E. Fixed or Variable Rate:	_____	_____
If Variable Rate: Lifetime Cap (Ceiling)	_____	_____
Indicator (Underlying Index)	_____	_____
Margins	_____	_____
F. Maturity Date	_____	_____
G. Amount of Balloon Payment	$ _____	$ _____
H. Date Balloon Payment Due	_____	_____
I. Potential for Negative Amortization? (Yes, No, or Unknown)	_____	_____
J. Due on Sale? (Yes, No, or Unknown)	_____	_____
K. Pre-payment penalty? (Yes, No, or Unknown)	_____	_____
L. Are payments current? (Yes, No, or Unknown)	_____	_____

21. **BUYER'S CREDITWORTHINESS:** (CHECK EITHER A OR B. Do not check both.) In addition to the loan application, credit report and other information requested under paragraph 2:
  A. ☐ No other disclosure concerning Buyer's creditworthiness has been made to Seller;
OR **B.** ☐ The following representations concerning Buyer's creditworthiness are made by Buyer(s) to Seller:

Borrower _____	**Co-Borrower** _____
1. Occupation _____	1. Occupation _____
2. Employer _____	2. Employer _____
3. Length of Employment _____	3. Length of Employment _____
4. Monthly Gross Income _____	4. Monthly Gross Income _____
5. Other _____	5. Other _____

22. ADDED, DELETED OR SUBSTITUTED BUYERS: The addition, deletion or substitution of any person or entity under this Agreement or to title prior to close of escrow shall require Seller's written consent. Seller may grant or withhold consent in Seller's sole discretion. Any additional or substituted person or entity shall, if requested by Seller, submit to Seller the same documentation as required for the original named Buyer. Seller and/or Brokers may obtain a credit report, at Buyer's expense, on any such person or entity.

Buyer's Initials (_____)(_____)
Seller's Initials (_____)(_____)

Reviewed by _____ Date _____

SELLER FINANCING ADDENDUM AND DISCLOSURE (SFA PAGE 2 OF 3)

Property Address: _____ Date: _____

23. CAUTION:

    A. If the Seller financing requires a balloon payment, Seller shall give Buyer written notice, according to the terms of Civil Code §2966, at least 90 and not more than 150 days before the balloon payment is due if the transaction is for the purchase of a dwelling for not more than four families.

    B. If **any** obligation secured by the Property calls for a balloon payment, Seller and Buyer are aware that refinancing of the balloon payment at maturity may be difficult or impossible, depending on conditions in the conventional mortgage marketplace at that time. There are no assurances that new financing or a loan extension will be available when the balloon prepayment, or any prepayment, is due.

    C. If **any** of the existing or proposed loans or extensions of credit would require refinancing as a result of a lack of full amortization, such refinancing might be difficult or impossible in the conventional mortgage marketplace.

    D. In the event of default by Buyer: (1) Seller may have to reinstate and/or make monthly payments on any and all senior encumbrances (including real property taxes) in order to protect Seller's secured interest; (2) Seller's rights are generally limited to foreclosure on the Property, pursuant to California Code of Civil Procedure §580b; and (3) the Property may lack sufficient equity to protect Seller's interests if the Property decreases in value.

If this three-page Addendum and Disclosure is used in a transaction for the purchase of a dwelling for not more than four families, it shall be prepared by an Arranger of Credit as defined in California Civil Code §2957(a). (The Arranger of Credit is usually the agent who obtained the offer.)

Arranger of Credit - (Print Firm Name) _____ By _____ Date _____

Address _____ City _____ State _____ Zip _____

Phone _____ Fax _____

> BUYER AND SELLER ACKNOWLEDGE AND AGREE THAT BROKERS: (A) WILL NOT PROVIDE LEGAL OR TAX ADVICE; (B) WILL NOT PROVIDE OTHER ADVICE OR INFORMATION THAT EXCEEDS THE KNOWLEDGE, EDUCATION AND EXPERIENCE REQUIRED TO OBTAIN A REAL ESTATE LICENSE; OR (C) HAVE NOT AND WILL NOT VERIFY ANY INFORMATION PROVIDED BY EITHER BUYER OR SELLER. BUYER AND SELLER AGREE THAT THEY WILL SEEK LEGAL, TAX AND OTHER DESIRED ASSISTANCE FROM APPROPRIATE PROFESSIONALS. BUYER AND SELLER ACKNOWLEDGE THAT THE INFORMATION EACH HAS PROVIDED TO THE ARRANGER OF CREDIT FOR INCLUSION IN THIS DISCLOSURE FORM IS ACCURATE. BUYER AND SELLER FURTHER ACKNOWLEDGE THAT EACH HAS RECEIVED A COMPLETED COPY OF THIS DISCLOSURE FORM.

Buyer _____ Date _____
            (signature)

Address _____ City _____ State _____ Zip _____

Phone _____ Fax _____ E-mail _____

Buyer _____ Date _____
            (signature)

Address _____ City _____ State _____ Zip _____

Phone _____ Fax _____ E-mail _____

Seller _____ Date _____
            (signature)

Address _____ City _____ State _____ Zip _____

Phone _____ Fax _____ E-mail _____

Seller _____ Date _____
            (signature)

Address _____ City _____ State _____ Zip _____

Phone _____ Fax _____ E-mail _____

SURE TRAC
The System for Success™

Published by the
California Association of REALTORS®

SFA REVISED 10/02 (PAGE 3 OF 3)

Reviewed by _____ Date _____

EQUAL HOUSING OPPORTUNITY

SELLER FINANCING ADDENDUM AND DISCLOSURE (SFA PAGE 3 OF 3)

to seven transactions per year as a principal without a license). A broker who solicits a borrower or lender for a loan or buys and sells trust deeds:

1. May not accept funds in advance to purchase trust deeds as they become available. (The money accepted must be for specific loans.)
2. May not retain funds from collections for more than 25 days without written authorization.
3. Must have written authorization from the owner to service a loan (handle collections).
4. Must see that all transactions he or she handles are recorded or that the trust deed is delivered to the lender within 10 days of release of the funds, with a written recommendation that the deed be recorded. When an existing land contract or trust deed is assigned, the broker shall see that the assignment is recorded within 10 working days after release of the funds, or shall deliver the land contract or trust deed to the purchaser with a written recommendation that it be recorded immediately.
5. May not use misleading advertising.
6. May not offer to give a gift or premium as an inducement for making a loan.

A person who only makes loan collections on 10 or fewer loans but does not negotiate loans does not require a broker's license. However, a person who makes collections on more than 10 loans or in excess of $40,000 in any calendar year must have either a broker's license or an exemption from the Real Estate Commissioner. (For an exemption, a person must post a bond and agree to comply with the Real Estate Law.)

Article 5 does not apply to loans negotiated by a broker in relation to a sale where the broker acted as an agent. It also does not apply where the broker is the lender or borrower.

Any real estate broker who negotiates or anticipates negotiating or selling 20 or more loans of $2 million or more in any one year must presubmit to the Department of Real Estate for clearance of his or her advertisements dealing with loan terms or the qualifications of the broker. (This does not apply to loans obtained in a sale in which the broker was an agent.)

Brokers must disclose to lenders if they will benefit from funds loaned.

There is a separate Residential Mortgage Lender license for lenders and loan servicers that is administered by the Commissioner of Corporations. Real estate brokers are exempt from this license requirement.

Article 6 dealing with real property securities has been deleted from the statutes. However, the Department of Real Estate still regulates the sale of undivided interests in pools of notes as well as promotional notes. (**Promotional notes** are subordinate notes of three years or less to finance the sale or development of a subdivision.)

A real estate broker can sell up to 10 undivided interests in a note. However, the notice must be filed with the Real Estate Commissioner within 30 days of the first transaction.

Article 7

The purpose of Article 7 is to set maximum charges by a broker for obtaining loans. This article primarily protects the small borrower. The article applies to first trust deeds under $30,000 and second trust deeds under $20,000. The broker must give the borrower a statement setting forth all the conditions of the loan (**Mortgage Loan Disclosure Statement**) and have the borrower sign it. The broker must retain a copy of the loan statement for three years.

The maximum amount of total expenses that can be charged to the borrower shall not exceed 5 percent of the loan or $390, whichever is greater, but in no event shall it exceed $700. (Title charges and recording fees are not included in the expenses that are limited.) For example:

$$\$2,000 \text{ loan} \times .05 \ (5\%) = \$100$$

But loan costs could be up to $390, since the limit is 5 percent or $390, *whichever is greater*. In another example:

$$\$20,000 \text{ loan} \times .05 = \$1,000$$

But the maximum charge is $700, so that is all that can be charged. Use the following table as a memory tool:

Amount of Loan	Maximum Charge
$0–$7,800	$390
$7,801–$13,999	5%
$14,000+	$700

Of course, the borrower can never be charged more than actual costs. For example:

$$\$12,000 \text{ loan} \times .05 = \$600$$

Since the maximum is 5 percent, or $390, whichever is greater, $600 could be charged if actual costs were $600. But if actual costs were only $75, then that is all that could be charged. If the broker charges more than the maximum allowable fees or costs, the borrower can recover three times the excess fees or costs paid. Charges and costs must have in fact occurred and must be reasonable.

Article 7 also sets forth the amount that the broker can charge for his or her services in obtaining a loan (applies to first trust deeds under $30,000 and second trust deeds under $20,000). This is the only time a broker's commission is subject to a statutory limit (although probate sales commissions are subject to court approval). The maximum broker's commissions set forth in Article 7 are as follows:

Type of Loan	Term of the Loan	Maximum Commission
First trust deed	Less than 3 years	5%
	3 years or more	10%
Second trust deed	Less than 2 years	5%
	2 to 3 years	10%
	3 years or more	15%

158

If a broker is to receive compensation for obtaining financing on a transaction, he or she must disclose to the buyer and seller the form, amount, and source of the compensation prior to closing. In addition, if a broker benefits from the loan, either directly or indirectly (other than by fees or commissions), the broker must provide all of the facts to the Department of Real Estate, the lender, and the buyer.

Under Article 7, the broker may not enter into an exclusive agreement to negotiate a loan for a borrower that exceeds 45 days. (The broker may not tie up a borrower for an unreasonable time.)

Loans of six years or less on the borrower's residence (one to three units) may not have balloon payments. For other loans, balloon payments are not allowed for loans of three years or less.

The borrower cannot be charged interest until the loan is available to him or her.

A lender may not condition a loan on the purchase of credit life or credit disability insurance.

Study the Mortgage Loan Disclosure Statement (Borrower) that follows. The broker who has arranged credit is shown on the top of the form. The following list explains the paragraphs in the form.

I. The summary of loan terms includes the principal amount, deductions from the principal amount (fees, costs, and payoffs), and the estimated cash that the borrower will receive.

II. General Information

A. The general information includes the interest rate, number of payments, and the amount of any balloon payment. The borrower is warned in boldface type of the dangers of a balloon payment. (They may have to pay loan costs and fees again to get a loan, and if one is not available, they could face foreclosure.)

B. This explains the security device to be used and the property that will secure the loan.

C. Liens against the property are listed as well as which liens will remain after the loan has been funded. The borrower is warned that if the borrower has wrongfully stated the liens so that it cannot be funded, the borrower will be liable for costs and fees even though no loan is made.

D. The prepayment penalty is set forth. For broker-arranged loans, there cannot be any prepayment penalty after seven years.

E. This paragraph indicates whether there will be late charges.

F. The borrower is informed that the loan is not contingent on purchasing credit life or disability insurance.

G. This indicates whether the loan is on an owner-occupied dwelling. (For owner occupied dwellings, loans under six years may not have a balloon payment.)

III. The deductions from the loan proceeds are indicated. If the fees or costs are paid to the broker, it will be indicated. The broker's commission and fees are set forth as well as payoffs to be made from the loan proceeds.

**CALIFORNIA
ASSOCIATION
OF REALTORS®**

MORTGAGE LOAN DISCLOSURE STATEMENT (BORROWER)

(As required by the Business and Professions Code §10241
and Title 10, California Administrative Code, §2840)

_____
(Name of Broker/Arranger of Credit)

_____
(Business Address of Broker)

I. SUMMARY OF LOAN TERMS
   A. PRINCIPAL AMOUNT . . . . $ _____
   B. ESTIMATED DEDUCTIONS FROM PRINCIPAL AMOUNT
      1. Costs and Expenses (See Paragraph III-A) . . . . $ _____
      *2. Broker Commission/Organization Fee (See Paragraph III-B) . . . . $ _____
      3. Lender Origination Fee/Discounts (See Paragraph III-B) . . . . $ _____
      4. Additional compensation will/may be received from lender not deducted from loan proceeds.
         ☐ YES $ _____ (if known) or ☐ NO
      5. Amount to be Paid on Authorization of Borrower (See Paragraph III) . . . . $ _____
   C. ESTIMATED CASH PAYABLE TO BORROWER (A less B) . . . . $ _____

II. GENERAL INFORMATION ABOUT LOAN
   A. If this loan is made, Borrower will be required to pay the principal and interest at _____% per year, payable
     as follows: _____ payments of $ _____
           (number of payments)   (monthly/quarterly/annually)
     and a **FINAL/BALLOON** payment of $ _____ to pay off the loan in full.

NOTICE TO BORROWER: IF YOU DO NOT HAVE THE FUNDS TO PAY THE BALLOON PAYMENT WHEN IT COMES DUE, YOU MAY HAVE TO OBTAIN A NEW LOAN AGAINST YOUR PROPERTY TO MAKE THE BALLOON PAYMENT. IN THAT CASE, YOU MAY AGAIN HAVE TO PAY COMMISSIONS, FEES AND EXPENSES FOR THE ARRANGING OF THE NEW LOAN. IN ADDITION, IF YOU ARE UNABLE TO MAKE THE MONTHLY PAYMENTS OR THE BALLOON PAYMENT, YOU MAY LOSE THE PROPERTY AND ALL OF YOUR EQUITY THROUGH FORECLOSURE. KEEP THIS IN MIND IN DECIDING UPON THE AMOUNT AND TERMS OF THIS LOAN.

   B. This loan will be evidenced by a promissory note and secured by a deed of trust on property identified as (street
     address or legal description):
     _____
     _____

   C. 1. Liens presently against this property (do not include loan being applied for):

Nature of Lien	Priority	Lienholder's Name	Amount Owing
_____	_____	_____	_____
_____	_____	_____	_____
_____	_____	_____	_____

     2. Liens that will remain against this property after the loan being applied for is made or arranged (include loan
       being applied for):

Nature of Lien	Priority	Lienholder's Name	Amount Owing
_____	_____	_____	_____
_____	_____	_____	_____
_____	_____	_____	_____

NOTICE TO BORROWER: Be sure that you state the amount of all liens as accurately as possible. If you contract with the broker to arrange this loan, but it cannot be arranged because you did not state these liens correctly, you may be liable to pay commissions, fees and expenses even though you do not obtain the loan.

REVISION DATE 10/2000   Print Date
MS-11 (PAGE 1 OF 3)

Borrower acknowledges receipt of copy of this page.
   Borrower's Initials (_____)(_____)

EQUAL HOUSING OPPORTUNITY

Reviewed by
Broker or Designee _____ Date _____

MORTGAGE LOAN DISCLOSURE STATEMENT (MS-11 PAGE 1 OF 3)

Reprinted with permission, CALIFORNIA ASSOCIATION OF REALTORS®. Endorsement not implied.

Property Address: _____ Date: _____

D. If Borrower pays all or part of the loan principal before it is due, a PREPAYMENT PENALTY computed as follows may be charged:

_____
_____
_____

E. Late Charges: ☐ YES, see loan documents or ☐ NO

F. The purchase of credit life or credit disability insurance by a borrower is not required as a condition of making this loan.

G. Is the real property which will secure the requested loan an "owner-occupied dwelling?" ☐ YES____ or ☐ NO____
(Borrower initial opposite YES or NO)

An "owner-occupied dwelling" means a single dwelling unit in a condominium or cooperative or residential building of four or fewer separate dwelling units, one of which will be owned and occupied by a signatory to the mortgage or deed of trust for this loan within 90 days of the signing of the mortgage or deed of trust.

III. DEDUCTIONS FROM LOAN PROCEEDS

A. Estimated Maximum Costs and Expenses of Arranging the Loan to be Paid Out of Loan Principal:

	PAYABLE TO	
	Broker	**Others**
1. Appraisal fee	_____	_____
2. Escrow fee	_____	_____
3. Title insurance policy	_____	_____
4. Notary fees	_____	_____
5. Recording fees	_____	_____
6. Credit investigation fees	_____	_____
7. Other costs and expenses:	_____	_____
	_____	_____
	_____	_____
Total Costs and Expenses	$ _____	

*B. Compensation .... $ _____
1. Brokerage Commission/Origination Fee .... $ _____
2. Lender Origination Fee/Discounts .... $ _____

C. Estimated Payment to be Made out of Loan Principal on Authorization of Borrower

	PAYABLE TO	
	Broker	**Others**
1. Fire or other hazard insurance premiums	_____	_____
2. Credit life or disability insurance premiums (see Paragraph II-F)	_____	_____
3. Beneficiary statement fees	_____	_____
4. Reconveyance and similar fees	_____	_____
5. Discharge of existing liens against property:	_____	_____
	_____	_____
6. Other:	_____	_____
	_____	_____
	_____	_____
Total to be Paid on Authorization of Borrower	$ _____	

If this loan is secured by a first deed of trust on dwellings in a principal amount of less than $30,000 or secured by a junior lien on dwellings in a principal amount of less than $20,000, the undersigned licensee certifies that the loan will be made in compliance with Article 7 of Chapter 3 of the Real Estate Law.

*This loan **may / will / will not** (delete two) be made wholly or in part from broker-controlled funds as defined in Section 10241(j) of the Business and Professions Code.

REVISION DATE 10/2000   Print Date
MS-11 (PAGE 2 OF 3)

Borrower acknowledges receipt of copy of this page.
Borrower's Initials (_____)(_____)

EQUAL HOUSING OPPORTUNITY

Reviewed by
Broker or Designee _____ Date _____

MORTGAGE LOAN DISCLOSURE STATEMENT (MS-11 PAGE 2 OF 3)

Reprinted with permission, CALIFORNIA ASSOCIATION OF REALTORS®. Endorsement not implied.

Property Address: _____ Date: _____

_____	_____
Name of Broker	Broker Representative
_____	_____
License Number	License Number
_____ OR	_____
Signature of Broker	Signature

The Department of Real Estate License Information phone number is _____.

NOTICE TO BORROWER:

DO NOT SIGN THIS STATEMENT UNTIL YOU HAVE READ AND UNDERSTAND ALL OF THE INFORMATION IN IT. ALL PARTS OF THE FORM MUST BE COMPLETED BEFORE YOU SIGN.

Borrower hereby acknowledges the receipt of a copy of this statement.

DATED _____   _____
(Borrower)

_____
(Borrower)

Broker Review: Signature of Real Estate Broker after review of this statement.

DATED _____   _____
Real Estate Broker or Assistant Pursuant to Section 2725

MORTGAGE LOAN DISCLOSURE STATEMENT (MS-11 PAGE 3 OF 3)

For first trust deeds of less than $30,000 and second trust deeds of less than $20,000 the fees and costs are limited by statute.

If the loan is to be made from broker funds, it must be indicated.

A Mortgage Loan Disclosure Statement is not required if the broker represents a commercial lender and charges 2 percent or less for his or her services.

CHAPTER 7 QUIZ

1. A second trust deed can be distinguished from a first trust deed by:
   a. the heading of the instrument
   b. the information contained in the note
   c. the time and date of recording
   d. none of these

2. To *subordinate* means:
   a. to subrogate
   b. to sell
   c. to lease
   d. to be secondary

3. A land contract clause prohibits any prepayment.
   a. The vendee can ignore the clause after one year.
   b. The contract is void, since the clause is illegal.
   c. The vendee cannot prepay.
   d. The vendee can prepay only during the first year.

4. Which of the following is not required when a trust deed is paid up?
   a. the trustor's signature
   b. the trustee's signature
   c. a deed of reconveyance
   d. none of these

5. A mortgage would be released by:
   a. payment in full
   b. a deed of reconveyance
   c. satisfaction of the mortgage
   d. any of these

6. The seller under a real property sales contract may not:
   a. encumber the property
   b. use an address rather than a legal description
   c. sell his or her interest
   d. none of these

7. A release clause would most likely appear in:
   a. a public report
   b. a blanket encumbrance
   c. a subordination statement
   d. a fictitious mortgage

8. A right of possession and equitable title would be held by the:
   a. buyer on a land contract
   b. seller on a land contract
   c. trustee
   d. beneficiary

9. The person who would wish to record a land contract would be the:
   a. trustee
   b. vendor
   c. vendee
   d. beneficiary

10. *Hypothecate* means:
    a. to give a thing as security without giving possession
    b. to sell
    c. to substitute
    d. to pledge

11. A mortgage and a trust deed are similar in that:
    a. neither transfers title
    b. both are personal property
    c. both are three-party documents
    d. none of these

12. A mortgagee foreclosing would first:
    a. publish a notice of foreclosure
    b. give a 90-day notice of default
    c. give three months' notice of default
    d. start an action in court

13. A deed of reconveyance moves title from:
    a. the trustor to the trustee
    b. the trustee to the trustor
    c. the beneficiary to the trustor
    d. none of these

14. A recorded trust deed referred to in other trust deeds is most likely:
    a. a senior encumbrance
    b. a fictitious trust deed
    c. a declaration of restrictions
    d. none of these

15. Who would most likely benefit by a subordination clause in a trust deed?
    a. the beneficiary
    b. the trustor
    c. the trustee
    d. the county tax assessor

16. A statement that says "In the event of sale, the entire balance is due and payable" would be:
    a. a type of acceleration clause
    b. an alienation clause
    c. both a and b
    d. neither a nor b

17. *Naked legal title* refers to a:
    a. beneficiary
    b. trustee
    c. trustor
    d. title insurance company

18. Total foreclosure time under a trust deed most nearly approaches:
    a. one year
    b. 15 months
    c. three months
    d. four months

19. The beneficiary of a trust deed is most likely a:
    a. buyer
    b. bank
    c. trustee
    d. borrower

20. The vendor–vendee relationship under a land contract is most similar to the relationship:
    a. trustor–trustee
    b. trustee–beneficiary
    c. beneficiary–trustee
    d. mortgagee–mortgagor

21. After the three-month notification of default:
    a. the trustee may sell
    b. the publication period begins
    c. foreclosure is completed
    d. the sheriff's sale is made

22. A beneficiary sells a note secured by a trust deed. The beneficiary must:
    a. record the assignment
    b. record the deed of reconveyance
    c. record the trustee's deed
    d. record a satisfaction

23. A trust deed would likely be in default when:
    a. the trustor fails to maintain insurance coverage
    b. the trustor is delinquent in tax payments
    c. the trustor commits waste on the premises
    d. any of these

24. A trust deed is a(n):
    a. encumbrance
    b. lien
    c. both a and b
    d. negotiable instrument

25. A trustor under a trust deed:
    a. holds naked legal title
    b. holds the note
    c. makes the loan
    d. signs the note

26. Real estate used as security for a loan would be:
    a. alienated
    b. hypothecated
    c. pledged
    d. none of these

27. As to trust deeds, which of the following is false?
    a. Trust deeds convey title.
    b. A trust deed is security for a note.
    c. A trust deed may be foreclosed by court action.
    d. none of these

28. As to beneficiary statements, which of the following is true?
    a. There can be a charge up to $60.
    b. Failure to provide a statement within 21 days of receipt can result in $300 damages.
    c. both a and b
    d. neither a nor b

29. A holder of a second trust deed receives notification of default on the first trust deed. He or she would probably:
    a. wait for foreclosure and try to buy the property at a reduced price
    b. make payments on the first trust deed and foreclose on the second trust deed
    c. wait until the publication period to see if the trustor will make the payments
    d. none of these

30. A real property sales contract must show:
    a. the legal description
    b. all existing encumbrances
    c. the number of years required to pay it off
    d. all of these

31. Janet assumes a trust deed from Bill.
    a. Only Janet is liable.
    b. Janet is primarily liable and Bill has secondary liability.
    c. Bill is primarily liable and Janet has secondary liability.
    d. Both Janet and Bill have primary liability.
32. Upon default of a buyer on a land contract, the seller would:
    a. have the trustee foreclose
    b. file a *lis pendens* action
    c. file a quiet title action
    d. sue for damages or specific performance
33. You would find a subordination clause in:
    a. grant deeds
    b. quitclaim deeds
    c. trust deeds
    d. none of these
34. The beneficiary must give consent before the trustor can:
    a. agree to restrictions on land use
    b. grant an easement over the property
    c. settle a boundary dispute
    d. any of these
35. A trustor is to a beneficiary as:
    a. a seller is to a buyer
    b. a trustee is to a buyer
    c. an escrow agent is to a seller
    d. a borrower is to a lender
36. Proceeds from a trustee's sale go to:
    a. the cost of the sale, then the first trust deed, then junior encumbrances, and the balance to the trustor
    b. the first trust deed, and the balance to junior encumbrance holders
    c. the cost of the sale, and the balance to the foreclosing beneficiary
    d. none of these
37. Selling a home under an existing blanket trust deed requires that the trustee give a(n):
    a. new deed of trust
    b. contract of sale
    c. partial reconveyance
    d. assignment of interest
38. In a subdivision, the largest number of properties that can be covered by a trust deed without a blanket encumbrance is:
    a. one   b. two   c. three   d. none of these
39. A disadvantage of a land contract to a buyer is:
    a. continued liability even if interest is transferred
    b. the danger of not obtaining clear title when paid up
    c. difficulty in borrowing on equity
    d. all of these
40. A trust deed is foreclosed by the:
    a. trustee   b. trustor   c. beneficiary   d. sheriff
41. Which of the following is not an element of a mortgage?
    a. alienation   b. a note   c. security   d. redemption
42. A request for notification of default would be most desired by the:
    a. trustor
    b. trustee
    c. beneficiary of a first trust deed
    d. beneficiary of a second trust deed
43. A buyer purchases a $10,000 trust deed for $6,400. The trustor defaults. The most that the buyer of the trust deed can recover at the trustee's sale is:
    a. $6,400
    b. $10,000
    c. nothing
    d. the amount is limited only by the sale price
44. Upon payment of a trust deed in full and on demand of the trustor, the trustee must give a deed of reconveyance:
    a. immediately
    b. within 15 days
    c. within 21 days
    d. within 60 days
45. For a trust deed to be negotiable, it must be:
    a. signed by the trustor
    b. acknowledged
    c. both a and b
    d. neither a nor b

46. After a trustee's sale, there is money left over after paying the beneficiary of the first trust deed. This money would go first to the:
   a. trustor
   b. beneficiary of a second trust deed
   c. state
   d. beneficiary of the first trust deed

47. A trust deed would most likely be discounted by:
   a. the trustor   b. the trustee   c. the beneficiary   d. none of these

48. A prepayment penalty would be inconsistent with:
   a. an alienation clause
   b. an "or more" clause
   c. both a and b
   d. neither a nor b

49. A trust deed foreclosed as a mortgage would be foreclosed by:
   a. the municipal court
   b. the superior court
   c. the court of appeals
   d. none of these

50. When buying a house, a person would not receive:
   a. a grant deed
   b. a quitclaim deed
   c. a reconveyance deed
   d. any of these

51. The basic obligation of a real estate loan in California is evidenced by:
   a. a trust deed   b. the mortgage   c. the note   d. the bill of sale

52. An alienation clause in a trust deed prohibits:
   a. sale of the property
   b. modifying use of the property
   c. prepayment of the trust deed
   d. assumption of the trust deed

53. A land contract is most similar to a:
   a. mortgage   b. trust deed   c. security interest   d. bailment

54. Consideration exists:
   a. among the trustee, the beneficiary, and the trustor
   b. between the trustor and the beneficiary
   c. between the trustor and the trustee
   d. none of these

55. A foreclosure by sale would not involve:
   a. a publication period
   b. a deed of reconveyance
   c. a notice of default
   d. any of these

56. A clause in a trust deed calling for assignment of rents most likely would benefit the:
   a. trustee   b. trustor   c. purchaser   d. beneficiary

57. A clause in a trust deed that allows a trustor to refinance another trust deed without relegating it to a junior priority is a(n):
   a. subordination clause
   b. exculpatory clause
   c. subrogation clause
   d. refinance clause

58. The prepayment penalty on a payoff for a three-year-old conventional residential loan would be based on the:
   a. original purchase price
   b. original loan amount
   c. current loan balance
   d. current loan balance less 20% of the original loan amount

59. The Real Estate Settlement Procedures Act provides for violation penalties of:
   a. a fine of up to $10,000
   b. up to one year in jail
   c. loss of real estate license
   d. both a and b

60. A lender advanced credit to a consumer and took a lien on the consumer's home even though the consumer didn't have sufficient income to pay the debt. This is an example of:
   a. a package mortgage
   b. an open mortgage
   c. subordination
   d. predatory lending

61. The power of sale in a trust deed would be given by:
   a. the trustor to the trustee
   b. the trustee to the beneficiary
   c. the beneficiary to the trustee
   d. the beneficiary to the trustor

62. A blanket encumbrance would have the greatest benefit to the:
    a. lender
    b. trustor
    c. trustee
    d. title insurance company

63. Deficiency judgments are not available to a foreclosing mortgagee if:
    a. the mortgage was a purchase-money mortgage
    b. the value of the property equals or exceeds the amount of the loan
    c. foreclosure is by sale
    d. any of these

64. To be relieved of the primary responsibility of a loan, a seller must find a buyer:
    a. willing to subordinate
    b. who will purchase subject to the loan
    c. who will buy on land contract
    d. who will assume the loan

65. The release clause in a trust deed requires payments higher than they should be considering the value of the property released. Why?
    a. to make certain that the remaining security is adequate
    b. to reduce the danger of default
    c. both a and b
    d. neither a nor b

66. Which gives the most protection to a property owner in default?
    a. mortgage   b. trust deed   c. second trust deed   d. contract of sale

67. Real property would not be:
    a. mortgaged   b. pledged   c. alienated   d. encumbered

68. During the one-year redemption period of a mortgagor in default:
    a. the mortgagee can sue for rent
    b. the mortgagee is not entitled to possession
    c. both a and b
    d. neither a nor b

69. Making biweekly payments on a mortgage of one-half the monthly payment will result in:
    a. increasing the amortization period
    b. 13 monthly payments each year
    c. negative amortization
    d. a final balloon payment

70. Beth, a licensee, sells a real property sales contract for Ricardo, the vendor. Beth is responsible for making certain the contract is recorded:
    a. immediately
    b. within 5 working days
    c. within 10 working days
    d. within 30 days

71. Which of the following constitutes default by a mortgagor?
    a. failure to pay taxes
    b. failure to make monthly payments
    c. failure to pay insurance
    d. all of these

72. A deficiency judgment is possible if there is:
    a. foreclosure by sale provision
    b. foreclosure by court action
    c. a purchase-money mortgage
    d. none of these

73. A basic difference between trust deeds and mortgages is:
    a. subordination   b. amortization   c. acceleration   d. redemption

74. Prepayment penalties are not allowed in California for a home sale:
    a. after five years
    b. after four years
    c. after two years
    d. none of these

75. The payments of the buyer under a land contract include taxes and insurance. The seller:
    a. cannot have a final balloon payment
    b. must keep tax and insurance money in a trust account
    c. can charge up to 5 percent as a collection charge
    d. none of these

76. The person signing an assignment of a land contract is:
    a. the lessor
    b. the vendor
    c. the vendee
    d. both the vendor and the vendee

77. Which of the following clauses can be disregarded by a trustor?
    a. an alienation clause
    b. a clause against recording
    c. an "or more" clause
    d. none of these

78. As to real property sales contracts for land or one to four residential units, which of the following is true?
    a. The seller can prohibit prepayment for up to 12 months following the sale.
    b. The buyer cannot waive his or her right to prepay.
    c. both a and b
    d. neither a nor b

79. When the vendor and vendee sign a real property sales contract:
    a. title passes from vendor to vendee
    b. title passes to the trustee for the benefit of the beneficiary
    c. vendee has no title interest
    d. vendee obtains equitable title

80. Who would sign a request for reconveyance?
    a. the trustor   b. the trustee   c. the beneficiary   d. a new purchaser

81. A borrower makes $100 amortized loan payments.
    a. Each payment has the same amount applying to principal.
    b. There will be a balloon payment.
    c. The amount applying to the principal increases with each payment.
    d. None of these are true.

82. A packaged mortgage is a loan in which:
    a. payment includes principal, interest, taxes, and insurance
    b. personal property is included in the real estate loan
    c. similar loans are given for each home in a subdivision
    d. none of these

83. Large payments to a builder as work progresses would most likely be:
    a. amortized payments
    b. a take-out loan
    c. an open-end loan
    d. obligatory advances

84. By calling in a loan, the lender:
    a. is giving a new loan
    b. shortens the term of the loan
    c. accelerates the loan payments
    d. none of these

85. In the absence of any other economic changes, raising the points to be paid on a loan should:
    a. reduce the risk
    b. increase the risk
    c. reduce the interest
    d. increase the payments

86. Which of the following are synonymous?
    a. obligatory advance, take-out loan
    b. permanent financing, take-out loan
    c. open-end loan, take-out loan
    d. construction loan, take-out loan

87. A broker negotiated a three-year second trust deed for $20,000. He charged a $2,000 fee. The fee is:
    a. usurious   b. voidable   c. both a and b   d. neither a nor b

88. A *straight loan* refers to:
    a. a loan in which only interest is paid, with the principal paid at the due date
    b. an amortized loan
    c. a loan without a balloon payment
    d. a hard-money loan

89. The longer the loan (all other things being equal):
    a. the lower the interest
    b. the higher the interest
    c. the higher the payment
    d. the lower the payment

90. When monthly amortized mortgage payments are equal, the interest charged is:
    a. simple   b. compound   c. accelerated   d. escalated

91. The *nominal* rate of interest would be:
    a. 1 percent or less
    b. the legal rate of interest
    c. the rate stated in the note
    d. none of these

92. When interest rates are high, banks increase points on some loans to:
    a. increase the loan-to-value ratio
    b. stabilize the risks
    c. enhance the competitive position of the loans
    d. stimulate the secondary mortgage market

93. Which of the following are related to each other?
    a. taxes, insurance
    b. points, interest
    c. assessment, book value
    d. interest, taxes

94. The Federal Reserve Board wants to tighten the money supply. What action might it take?
    a. Raise the amount of reserves required for member banks.
    b. Raise the discount rate for member banks.
    c. Sell government bonds on the open market.
    d. all of these

95. A loan amortization table would show:
    a. principal and interest payments
    b. principal, interest, taxes, and insurance payments
    c. principal payments
    d. interest payments

96. In periods of tight money:
    a. interest rates go down
    b. interest rates and money availability are unrelated
    c. interest rates go up
    d. none of these

97. Interest paid on principal and interest is:
    a. compounded interest
    b. simple interest
    c. straight interest
    d. none of these

98. As to points, which of the following is true?
    a. If they cover loan charges for services, they are not a deductible interest expense.
    b. Points that are prepaid interest are deductible to the purchaser.
    c. Points paid by the seller are considered sales costs.
    d. all of these

99. The collection of interest in advance is known as:
    a. loan discountency
    b. a discount loan
    c. usury
    d. an illegal loan

100. Which of the following is false?
    a. The nominal rate of interest is the rate stated.
    b. A normal home loan is not involved with compound interest.
    c. The effective interest rate may be more than stated because of points, discounts, etc.
    d. none of these

101. What is the highest commission a broker can charge in negotiating an $8,000 first trust deed for 2 1/2 years?
    a. 5 percent
    b. 10 percent
    c. 15 percent
    d. there is no limit

102. A financing statement is removed from record by:
    a. final payment of the debt
    b. a reconveyance deed
    c. a notice of abandonment
    d. filing a termination statement

103. Promotional notes, as used in real property securities, do not include a note that has a term of:
    a. 28 months
    b. 24 months
    c. 31 months
    d. 37 months

104. Loan payments based on a 20-year amortization schedule also require that the loan be paid in full within 10 years.
    a. The borrower can disregard the prepayment requirement.
    b. The loan would be considered a term loan.
    c. The loan would be considered a partially amortized loan.
    d. The loan would be considered an open-end mortgage.

105. An individual working for a bank is paid for every real estate loan she arranges. She must:
    a. be a real property security dealer
    b. have a real estate license
    c. both a and b
    d. neither a nor b

106. A broker has a written agreement giving you 60 days to arrange a loan for $1,200.
    a. The broker is in violation of Article 7 of the Real Estate Law.
    b. The deal is all right if the broker is a real property securities dealer.
    c. The broker may not deal in loans under $8,000, in accordance with Article 7.
    d. None of these are true.

107. A broker is the owner of the escrow company that handles most of the office business. As to the escrow company:
    a. It is a controlled business arrangement.
    b. It cannot pay salespersons referral fees.
    c. It must operate as a separate business.
    d. all of the above

108. On an amortized loan, each payment would differ from the previous payment in that:
    a. the amount of the payment would decrease
    b. the amount applying to the interest would increase each month
    c. the amount applying to the principal would decrease each month
    d. none of these

109. A Mortgage Loan Disclosure Statement is for the protection of the:
    a. broker
    b. lender
    c. borrower
    d. Real Estate Commissioner

110. Article 5 of the Real Estate Law does not apply to:
    a. negotiation of a loan in connection with a sale
    b. misleading advertising as to negotiation of loans
    c. gifts as inducements for making loans
    d. transactions in trust deeds

111. A loan that would appeal most to a young person whose income is starting to increase would be:
    a. an ARM   b. a GPM   c. a SAM   d. none of these

112. A broker's commission for negotiating a loan is not subject to Article 7 limitations if the loan is:
    a. a first trust deed of $30,000
    b. a second trust deed of $20,000
    c. both a and b
    d. neither a nor b

113. Points go up when the going interest rate increases above a fixed lending rate. Assume that each percentage point increase in the lending rate equals 6 points. An interest rate increase from 7 1/4 percent to 8 percent would result in what decrease of points?
    a. 4 points   b. 4.5 points   c. 6 points   d. 3 points

114. A borrower receives a monthly check from the lender. This is most likely a(n):
    a. annuity   b. reverse mortgage   c. rollover loan   d. none of these

115. Balloon payments are not allowed for an owner-occupied residence under Article 7:
    a. in all cases
    b. for first trust deeds
    c. for trust deeds of less than six years
    d. for purchase-money loans

116. A straight note would not be:
    a. used in conjunction with a trust deed
    b. amortized
    c. used for a personal loan
    d. none of these

117. A real estate broker made a home loan at 30% interest. The broker:
   a. has violated the usury law
   b. has placed her license in jeopardy
   c. both a and b
   d. neither a nor b

118. You need a permit to:
   a. guarantee a specific yield when selling trust deeds
   b. sell promotional notes
   c. either a or b
   d. neither a nor b

119. Warehousing is becoming extremely important in the field of finance. It refers to:
   a. repossessions
   b. defaulted mortgages
   c. increases in savings accounts
   d. interim financing

120. Regarding financial institutions, deregulation means:
   a. government controls no longer apply to financial institutions
   b. financial institutions can no longer respond to market conditions
   c. the amount of interest paid on savings accounts is no longer regulated
   d. examining and enforcement responsibilities of regulators have been relaxed

121. An adjustable-rate loan is pegged at an interest rate above a loan index. This increase above the index is known as the:
   a. cap
   b. margin
   c. teaser rate
   d. annual percentage rate

122. A loan's index rate is now at 5 1/4%. If the margin is 2.4%, the loan's interest should be:
   a. 2.4%   b. 3.25%   c. 5.25%   d. 7.65%

123. An introductory rate of interest is 3 1/4% less than the index rate of 4.25% and the 2.25% margin indicate. The introductory rate is:
   a. .75%   b. 3.25%   c. 6.5%   d. 7.75%

124. If two lenders share in different portions of the same loan, the loan would be a:
   a. sharing-appreciation loan
   b. participation loan
   c. piggyback loan
   d. take-out loan

125. An adjustable-rate mortgage has an index that has risen from 4.5% to 11% with a margin of 2.5%, but the bank is charging only 12% interest on the loan. This lower interest is due to:
   a. amortization
   b. usury
   c. the interest cap
   d. Article 7

126. RESPA would apply to:
   a. first mortgages
   b. second mortgages
   c. commercial loans
   d. loans on a five-unit apartment building

127. To curb inflation, the government can:
   a. lower FHA and VA rates
   b. lower the prime rate
   c. increase spending for capital improvement
   d. increase taxes

128. The disclosure statement required under the Truth-in-Lending Law is most similar to:
   a. disclosure statements in a public report
   b. a Mortgage Loan Disclosure Statement under Article 7 of the Real Estate Law
   c. an option-listing disclosure
   d. an MOG permit

129. A seasoned loan is:
   a. a loan with a payment history
   b. a long-term loan
   c. a first encumbrance
   d. none of these

130. Equity financing refers to:
   a. purchase-money loans
   b. financing that is fair
   c. cash purchases
   d. borrowing on the difference between property value and liens

131. The Truth-in-Lending Act is part of the:
   a. Business and Professions Code
   b. Federal Consumer Protection Act
   c. Uniform Commercial Code
   d. none of these

132. To pay for an operation, a man obtains a first trust deed on his house. One day after completion of the loan, he wishes to rescind the transaction.
   a. One may never rescind a properly completed loan.
   b. He has up to midnight of the third business day following the loan to rescind.
   c. He may not rescind this loan.
   d. None of these are true.

133. Inflation is best evidenced by a(n):
   a. increase in the cost-of-living index
   b. change in interest rates
   c. tight money market
   d. increase in points by lenders

134. The usury law for individuals does not apply when:
   a. the seller finances the buyer on a home sale
   b. the loan is made through a mortgage loan broker
   c. either a or b
   d. neither a nor b

135. According to Regulation Z, lenders must disclose to borrowers the finance charges. This would not include:
   a. appraisal fees
   b. title insurance
   c. seller's points
   d. any of these

136. A RESPA disclosure statement would least likely be required for a loan made:
   a. by a savings and loan
   b. by a mortgage company to be sold to FNMA
   c. through a licensed California loan broker
   d. for a purchase-money trust deed by a commercial bank

137. As to loan brokers, which of the following is true?
   a. Credit life and disability insurance can be required of borrowers.
   b. Balloon payments are not allowed.
   c. Commissions are regulated for all broker loans.
   d. None of these are true.

138. Discount points are:
   a. considered interest when charged by an individual
   b. raised by lenders when they raise their interest rate
   c. not allowed on VA loans
   d. all of these

139. A trust deed note showed zero interest. The IRS held that the beneficiary should pay taxes as if a reasonable rate of interest had been received. This rate set by the IRS is known as:
   a. the APR
   b. nominal rate
   c. imputed interest
   d. usury rate

140. The Truth-in-Lending Law is enforced by the:
   a. Real Estate Commissioner
   b. Federal Trade Commission
   c. state attorney general
   d. none of these

141. Which party to a mortgage signs the note?
   a. mortgagor
   b. mortgagee
   c. beneficiary
   d. trustee

142. In a sale transaction, which party is most likely responsible for a prepayment penalty?
    a. buyer   b. seller   c. escrow   d. lender

143. A broker advertised the APR but did not include any other financing terms. Was the ad proper?
    a. Yes.
    b. No, it was a RESPA violation.
    c. No because it violated truth in lending.
    d. Yes, if the broker indicated where details as to financing could be obtained.

144. The instrument that is least likely to be recorded is the:
    a. satisfaction of mortgage
    b. note securing a loan given with the trust deed
    c. trustee's deed
    d. land contract

145. The right of rescission under truth-in-lending would apply to a(n):
    a. home equity loan   c. purchase-money loan
    b. agricultural loan   d. none of these

146. RESPA would apply to a:
    a. purchase loan for a five-unit apartment building
    b. loan to refinance a single-family home
    c. purchase-money loan to purchase a duplex
    d. purchase-money loan for a residential lot

147. Which law applies to *federally related* transactions?
    a. Truth-in-Lending Act   c. Fair Credit Reporting Act
    b. RESPA   d. Holden Act

148. An endorsement on a note said "without recourse." What kind of endorsement is it?
    a. blank   b. special   c. restrictive   d. qualified

149. Truth-in-lending disclosure when advertising a graduated payment loan would require the:
    a. schedule of payments
    b. license the lender operates under
    c. property address
    d. name in which title is presently held

150. *Secured collaterally* refers to a:
    a. junior lien
    b. loan secured by personal property
    c. loan secured by another loan
    d. piggyback loan

ANSWERS—CHAPTER 7 QUIZ

1. c.
2. d. To other liens.
3. a. The prohibition is good during the first year.
4. a. The trustee signs a reconveyance.
5. c. Answer b is for a trust deed.
6. b. A legal description is required.
7. b. For a partial release.
8. a. The vendor holds legal title.
9. c. To give constructive notice.
10. a. As in a mortgage.
11. b. They are chattels real.
12. d. A mortgage is foreclosed by court action.
13. b.
14. b. Incorporates terms.
15. b. Can use the seller's equity.
16. c. Due-on-sale clause.
17. b. Has limited powers.
18. d. 3 months plus 20 days.
19. b. The lender or seller.
20. d. A seller and a buyer or lender and borrower.
21. b.
22. a. Or recommend recordation.
23. d.
24. c.
25. d. This note is given to the beneficiary.
26. b. The borrower keeps possession.
27. d.
28. c.
29. b. To protect his or her interests.
30. d.
31. b.
32. c.
33. c. Subordinate's lien.
34. d. All affect loan security.
35. d.
36. a.
37. c. To release the lien.
38. a.
39. d.
40. a. At the beneficiary's request.
41. a. Title is with the mortgagor.
42. d. To protect his or her interest.
43. b. The amount due on the note plus costs.
44. c. Or incur a $300 penalty.
45. d. The note is negotiable, not the trust deed.
46. b. In priority order.
47. c. Sold for less than what is owed.
48. b. Which allows prepayment.
49. b. For most realty suits.
50. c. This is given when a loan is repaid.
51. c. The lien secures the note.
52. d. Due-on-sale clause.
53. d. Title is kept, possession is given.

54. b. The buyer and the lender.
55. d. court foreclosure.
56. d. It gives the lender the rents if the trustor is in default.
57. a.
58. d.
59. d.
60. d.
61. a.
62. a. Greater loan security.
63. d.
64. d. The seller's liability is secondary.
65. c.
66. a. Up to 1 year redemption.
67. b. Personal property is pledged.
68. c.
69. b.
70. c.
71. d.
72. b.
73. d. On a trust deed there is no redemption after sale.
74. a.
75. b.
76. b.
77. b. Not enforceable.
78. c.
79. d. Possession also passes to vendee.
80. c. The request orders the trustee to reconvey.
81. c. And the amount applying to the interest decreases.
82. b.
83. d. Under the construction loan.
84. c. The entire amount is due now.
85. c. Points are prepaid interest.
86. b. The permanent loan replaces the construction loan.
87. d. Since the amount is not under $20,000.
88. a. Also called a *term loan.*
89. d. But more total interest is paid.
90. a. The interest is not compounded.
91. c.
92. c. Increase APR.
93. b. Points are prepaid interest.
94. d. To fight inflation.
95. a.
96. c. Supply and demand.
97. a. Such as on a reverse mortgage.
98. d.
99. b. Usually on a personal loan.
100. d.
101. a. 5 percent; the loan is for less than 3 years.
102. d. On personal property loans.
103. d. Notes over 3 years are excluded.
104. c. Since there is a balloon payment.

105. b. Article 5 requirement.
106. a. 45 days maximum
107. d.
108. d.
109. c. Disclose cost and terms.
110. a.
111. b. Graduated payment mortgage.
112. c. Covers first trust deeds under $30,000 and second trust deeds under $20,000.
113. b. 3/4 of 6 points. (1 percent really equals 8 points.)
114. b.
115. c.
116. b. Payments cover interest only.
117. d. Real estate brokers are exempt from usury limitations.
118. d. Article 6 permit requirements have been deleted from the law.
119. d. Lenders borrowing on their loan inventory.
120. c. Lenders are also less limited as to types of loans they make.
121. b.
122. d. 5.25 + 2.4
123. b. 6.5 − 3.25.
124. c. Top and bottom parts of loan are divided.
125. c. Maximum interest allowed.
126. a. For one to four residential units.
127. d. To decrease the money supply.
128. b. Loan term disclosure.
129. a. A lower-risk loan.
130. d. Owner's equity.
131. b. Under Truth-in-Lending Act.
132. b. Rescission right under the Truth-in-Lending Act.
133. a.
134. c. Both are exemptions.
135. d.
136. c. Not federally related.
137. d.
138. a. Could make loan usurious.
139. c.
140. b.
141. a. The borrower.
142. b. The loan must be paid off.
143. a. APR by itself does not trigger disclosure terms.
144. b. The trust deed is recorded, not the note.
145. a. For nonbusiness purposes.
146. c. Federally related purchase money loans for 1–4 residential units.
147. b.
148. d.
149. a.
150. c. Borrowing on loans.

Real Estate Lenders, FHA, VA, CAL-VET Loans, and the Secondary Mortgage Market

QUALIFYING FOR A LOAN

Lenders are interested in three factors (3C): **collateral** (security for the loan), **capacity** (income to pay off the loan), and **character** (a person's credit history in meeting obligations).

Capacity is customarily measured in **ratios.** The **front-end ratio** is the ratio of PITI (principal, interest, tax, and insurance payments) to the borrower's gross monthly income:

$$\frac{\text{PITI}}{\text{Gross monthly income}} = \text{Front-end ratio}$$

The **back-end ratio** is the ratio of PITI plus long-term debt payments to the borrower's gross monthly income.

$$\frac{\text{PITI} + \text{Debt obligations}}{\text{Gross monthly income}} = \text{Back-end ratio}$$

Generally, lenders will not accept a front-end ratio less than 28 percent and a back-end ratio less than 36 percent, but there are many exceptions.

In determining the income of a borrower for credit purposes, overtime income is generally not considered, and only 50 percent is considered for most stock and rental income. Before the use of ratios, rules of thumb were used, such as: A home should not cost more than 2 1/2 times a buyer's gross yearly income.

Character refers to the will of the borrower to repay the loan. A borrower's credit history will affect the lender's willingness to make the loan and the interest rate that will be charged. Most lenders now utilize **FICO Scores,** which is a credit score devised by Fair Issac and Company.

PRIMARY AND SECONDARY FINANCING

Primary Financing   The first loan on a property, such as a first trust deed.

Secondary Financing   Second trust deeds (junior liens).

Characteristics of Secondary Financing

1. Short period (usually under seven years).
2. Higher interest rate than primary financing.
3. Often made by noninstitutional lenders (primary financing is generally by institutional lenders).
4. Frequently includes a balloon payment (final payment for a large balance).

A loan with a balloon payment is a **partially amortized** loan.

PRIMARY AND SECONDARY MORTGAGE MARKETS

Primary Mortgage Market   The making of loans to a borrower directly by the lender (banks, savings associations, mortgage bankers, and life insurance companies).

Secondary Mortgage Market   The buying and selling of existing loans. **Mortgage loan correspondents** are engaged in the secondary mortgage market, arranging the transfer of existing loans.

CONVENTIONAL LOANS

Conventional loans are loans made by institutional lenders (commercial banks, savings banks and loans, and insurance companies) without government insurance or guarantees. Banks and savings banks and loans are able to attract depositors, despite offering relatively low interest rates, because the accounts are insured up to $100,000 by the FDIC (Federal Deposit Insurance Corporation).

Insurance companies make larger commercial and industrial loans, as well as loans for larger housing complexes (in the primary mortgage market). They also purchase large numbers of government-insured or -guaranteed loans (in the secondary mortgage market). Insurance companies generally will not make loans on older homes (they usually lend only 75 percent of value). While insurance companies may buy groups of home loans, they seldom will make a single home loan.

Banks make construction loans (at 85 percent of value) as well as give permanent financing (which can be up to 90 percent of value, although usually for a lesser amount). Banks also make many home-equity loans (second trust deeds) and business loans. They favor depositors.

Mutual Savings Banks

These are located in northeastern states. They can make government-insured or -guaranteed loans anywhere in the United States. (Depositors are paid dividends rather than interest.)

Noninstitutional Lenders

These include schools, pension funds, trusts, brokers, mortgage companies, and individuals. While institutional lenders take deposits from the general public, non-institutional lenders do not.

Loan Servicing Companies

These are subject to the licensing provisions of the Real Estate Law, unless an exemption is obtained. (To obtain an exemption, a company must pay a $200 annual fee.) Loan servicing companies do not make loans.

Mortgage Bankers (Mortgage Companies)

These companies use their own funds to originate loans, which they then sell in the secondary mortgage market. They differ from mortgage brokers, who seldom use their own funds and who primarily act as go-betweens, putting together lenders and borrowers for a fee. Mortgage bankers are presently the largest source of purchase-money loans for residential property. Mortgage bankers can operate under a real estate broker's license or can be licensed by the Department of Corporations.

Mortgage Brokers

Mortgage brokers are real estate licensees who arrange loans between buyers and sellers. The brokers do not use their own money nor do they service the loans they arrange. They are generally high-cost lenders as to loan costs and interest charged and often deal with subprime borrowers who cannot obtain loans from banks or mortgage bankers. See Article 7 in Chapter 7 for limitation on costs and required disclosures.

GOVERNMENT LOANS

These loans are not made by the government; rather, they are guaranteed or insured by the government. They are made by institutional lenders.

FHA (Federal Housing Administration) Loans

1. Government-insured. A one-time **mortgage insurance premium (MIP),** collected on settlement, protects the lender against the borrower's default (and can be financed by the lender as part of the loan). Depending upon the amount of the down payment, 1/2 percent can be added to mortgage payments for from 5 to 10

years. The maximum insured loan in California for a single-family dwelling varies by region.

2. For housing only (one to four units, including mobile homes).

3. Amortized loans. FHA loans are self-liquidating with equal payments, so they have no balloon payments.

4. High **loan-to-value ratio (LTV).** The low-down-payment requirements eliminate the need for secondary financing. Minimum cash down payment is 3 percent.

5. Floating interest rate.

6. **Minimum property requirements (MPR)** are set by the FHA. Minimum construction standards protect the buyer from shoddy construction and address safety concerns such as handrails for stairs.

7. There is no maximum purchase price but there is a maximum loan amount (in California, the cap on the loan amount limits the use of FHA financing).

8. Secondary financing is not allowed at the time of purchase (although a second trust deed may be placed on the property after purchase). This protects the buyer against becoming overburdened. The FHA will allow the down payment to be borrowed if secured by other than the property, household goods, a car, or trade tools.

9. Long-term loans; therefore, they have lower monthly payments.

10. Taxes and insurance are included in the payments.

11. Require appraisal by an FHA-approved appraiser.

12. No prepayment penalty for early payment.

13. Points are freely negotiable between the lender and the borrower. There is also an FHA application fee, usually 1 percent of the loan, which is paid by the borrower. Closing costs may be financed in the loan.

14. Loans made prior to December 15, 1989, are assumable by anyone. Loans made after December 15, 1989, are assumable only by owner-occupants who qualify for the loan (investors cannot assume these loans). Unless there is a substitution of responsibility, the original borrower remains liable on the loan even when it is assumed.

15. With an eligible buyer, the seller can obtain a **substitution of responsibility** (release of liability), which completely removes the seller from all loan obligations.

16. Structural and pest control inspection is required in areas where termites are found.

17. **Direct endorsement** is possible where a lender is authorized to make the decision whether a loan is to qualify for FHA insurance.

Conditional Commitment An FHA commitment to make a loan for the stated amount to an unknown buyer based on satisfactory credit. The borrower would apply for an FHA loan commitment from a HUD/FHA-approved mortgagee.

Firm Commitment Issued after the conditional commitment to a known party. (FHA commitments are good for six months.)

Title I FHA Act   Authorizes insurance of repair and improvement loans (for up to 15 years).

Title II FHA Act   Covers normal home purchase loans (limited to one to four residential units).

Title III FHA Act   Set up Fannie Mae (Federal National Mortgage Association).

Federal National Mortgage Association (FNMA, or Fannie Mae)   Formerly a government agency; now a private corporation.

FNMA deals in the secondary mortgage market. It buys and sells existing FHA, VA, and conventional loans. Because it creates a marketplace where these loans can be readily sold, lenders are more willing to handle these types of loans. To raise capital, Fannie Mae sells stock as well as participation certificates.

Federal Home Loan Mortgage Corporation (Freddie Mac)   A government-chartered private corporation, Freddie Mac buys FHA, VA, and conventional loans from savings and loan associations. It also sells bonds and participation certificates.

Loans that meet the purchase requirements of Fannie Mae and Freddie Mac are known as **conforming loans.** Currently, the maximum single-family home loan that will be purchased is $322,700. **Jumbo loans** are single-family home loans exceeding $322,700. Because these loans do not conform to the purchase guidelines, they are considered **nonconforming loans** (conforming loan limits are adjusted annually).

Government National Mortgage Association (Ginnie Mae)   An agency of HUD that guarantees securities where other financing is unavailable. Three of its major programs are:

1. **Mortgage-backed securities:** Ginnie Mae guarantees securities backed by pools of mortgages that are issued by private intermediaries. These make it easy for investors to invest in government-guaranteed mortgages. **Pass-through certificates** allow the investors to receive their share of interest and principal payments made on the mortgages.

2. **Special assistance functions:** Under the *Tandem Plan,* Ginnie Mae encourages low-interest home-loan programs for low-income buyers. When Fannie Mae buys the loans at par value, Ginnie Mae reimburses buyers of the loans for the lower market value of the mortgages.

3. **Management and liquidation functions:** Ginnie Mae manages and has the liquidation responsibility for a stock of government-owned mortgages.

Federal Agricultural Mortgage Corporation (Farmer Mac).   Farmer Mac provides a secondary mortgage market for farm and rural housing loans.

VA Loans (Department of Veterans Affairs)

1. The veteran submits his or her military discharge papers and obtains a Certificate of Eligibility.

2. The appraiser certifies the property as to its value and issues a **Certificate of Reasonable Value,** or **CRV.** If the CRV is less than the purchase price, the veteran can get the deposit back or can pay the difference in cash.

3. Loans can be made for a home, farm, or business. If the loan is for a home it must be for personal use, not rental purposes. (Both FHA and VA loans can be obtained for refinance purposes.)

4. An impound account for taxes and insurance is not required by the VA, but lenders generally require them.

5. Loans are made by institutional lenders but are government guaranteed. There is no limit to the amount of the loan, but the VA guarantee is limited as follows: For loans up to $45,000, the guarantee is 50 percent of the loan; for loans between $45,000 and $144,000 the guarantee is 40 percent of the loan with a maximum guarantee of $36,000 and a minimum guarantee of $22,500; for loans more than $144,000, the guarantee is 25 percent of the loan up to a maximum of $60,000.

6. Veterans must pay closing costs (appraisal fees, credit report charges, etc.). They may not be included in the loan amount. The loan amount can include a 1 percent loan origination fee plus a **funding fee** paid to the VA. (The funding fee is up to 2 percent based on the amount of the down payment and may be included in the loan. The veteran may be required to pay additional points.)

7. No down payment is required by the VA for loans up to $240,000, although lenders can require down payments. For manufactured homes, a 5 percent down payment is required.

8. Loans made prior to March 1, 1988, are assumable by anyone. Loans made later can be assumed only if the buyer qualifies for the loan. California antideficiency legislation does not protect a veteran under a VA loan. The veteran is personally liable, even if a subsequent purchaser defaults, unless the veteran is released from liability.

9. There are no prepayment penalties. (For VA loans, any prepayment must not be less than $100 or one installment.)

10. Loans are fully amortized, although payments need not be equal.

11. Structural and pest control inspection is required in areas where termites are found.

12. Secondary financing is not generally allowed at the time of purchase.

13. A veteran can restore eligibility by paying off the loan upon sale. In the case of a sale to another veteran, the seller can ask for a substitution of entitlement.

CAL-VET Loans (California Veterans Farm and Home Purchase Program)

These loans are administered by the California Department of Veterans Affairs. Funds are obtained by bond issues. CAL-VET uses VA standards and forms and also obtains a VA loan guarantee. The borrower must be a resident of California at the time of loan application and must have served honorably during specified wartime periods (90-day minimum service). The Department of Veterans Affairs can set the income level for loan eligibility.

Under a CAL-VET loan, the state takes title and then sells to the veteran under a land contract. (The state holds the title while the veteran gets possession.) CAL-VET loans can now be made through CAL-VET approved lenders.

Loan Limits

House (includes a mobile home sold with a lot): Up to $322,700.

Mobile Home (in a rental park): Up to $70,000.

Farm: $300,000.

The down payment requirements for CAL-VET loans are currently 2 percent of the sale price. There is a 1 percent origination fee as well as a loan guarantee or funding fee of up to 2 percent (based on the down payment).

Secondary financing is allowed on CAL-VET loans, but total financing cannot exceed 90 percent of the appraised value, and the CAL-VET loan must be the priority loan. Special preference is given to wounded veterans and prisoners of war. Vietnam veterans have preference over other veterans.

The loans are for purchase only, not refinancing. (FHA and VA loans can be used for refinancing.)

The interest on a CAL-VET loan can be raised or lowered during the loan period. The interest rate is currently 6.45 percent. The maximum rate is 7.5 percent CAL-VET loans are usually for 30 years. The CAL-VET loan is open-ended in that it can be increased for improvements. The veteran must take out a policy of term life and disability insurance under the CAL-VET loan. The veteran must also purchase flood and earthquake insurance, and must occupy the premises within 60 days of signing a CAL-VET loan contract.

The veteran must continue to reside on the property and cannot rent or sell his or her interest without the consent of the California Department of Veterans Affairs. The department may allow the loan to be assumed. The veteran may assign interest to a spouse if the spouse and children reside on the premises. The veteran can transfer the loan balance to another property with the approval of the Department of Veterans Affairs. If a veteran defaults, the Department of Veterans Affairs can declare a forfeiture, repossess, and resell the property.

CAL-VET loans are reusable loans in that a borrower is not precluded from a loan because he or she had a prior CAL-VET loan.

	FHA (Title II)	**VA**	**CAL-VET**
Source of Loan	Institutional lender	Institutional lender	Bonds issued. Administered by California Department of Veterans Affairs
Type of Loan	First trust deed	First trust deed. Secondary financing is generally not allowed at the time of the loan	Land contract. Secondary financing is now allowed if the total does not exceed 90% of the appraisal

	FHA (Title II)	VA	CAL-VET
Maximum Amount of Loan	Home varies by region	Not more than CRV (Certificate of Reasonable Value)	Home or mobile home with lot—Up to $322,700
		No loan limit but there is a limit on the guarantee	Mobile home—Up to $70,000 for mobile home in rental parks
			Farm—Up to $300,000
Guarantee or Insurance	Insured. Mortgage insurance premium may be added to loan	Guarantee. Maximum guarantee is $50,750	They have a VA guarantee
Down payment	Minimum 3%	None required	2%–3%
	FHA (Title II)	VA	
Loan Purpose	Housing only (does not have to be owner-occupied); 1–4 units	Housing (owner-occupied), farm, business	Home, farm, and mobile home. Housing loans are limited to single-family dwellings
Government Agency Period of Loan	Federal Housing Administration Usually 30 years	Department of Veterans Affairs Home—30 years Farm—40 years Non-real-estate— 10 years	California Department of Veterans Affairs Up to 40 years but usually 30 years
Points and Fees	Negotiable points 1% application fee	Negotiable points 1% origination fee plus funding fee of 1% to 2% Reasonable costs	1.25%–3% (may be financed)
Prepayment Penalty	No penalty	No penalty	Currently, no prepayment penalty but CAL-VET can charge a penalty if prepaid within 5 years
Assumption	Loans made prior to December 15, 1989, are assumable by anyone. Later loans are assumable only by owner-occupants who qualify for the loan.	Assumable by anyone if made prior to March 1, 1988. For loans made after that date, the buyer must qualify for the loan to assume it.	Assumable with California Department of Veterans Affairs approval
Payments	Equal or unequal (under ARM, GEM, or GPM)	Unequal or equal, may be amortized under any recognized plan	Equal

Real Estate Syndicates

A **syndicate** is a group of people operating an investment where some are active in the investment and others are inactive.

Most syndicates are limited partnerships. The advantages of investing in syndicates include limited liability. Real estate syndicates with fewer than 100 members are under the jurisdiction of the Corporations Commissioner (Department of Corporations). Real estate brokers are exempt from licensing as corporate security dealers (syndicates are considered to be securities). Money raised for unspecified properties is known as a **blind pool.**

Real Estate Investment Trust (REIT)

Under federal law, there must be 100 or more investors in a REIT. The trust can be established to invest in mortgages (a mortgage trust), to invest in real property (an equity trust), or a combination of both (a combination trust). It cannot be in the business of buying for resale. Five or fewer investors cannot have more than a 50 percent interest, and investments must account for at least 95 percent of the trust's income, with 75 percent from real estate investments. Trust shares are transferable, and the trust is taxed on retained earnings only, providing it distributes at least 95 percent of its ordinary income. A REIT is considered to be a syndicate.

Securities

Securities are investments in which the investors are inactive in management. Limited partnerships and real estate investment trusts are considered securities, as are purchases of rental units where all management control is kept by others. Intrastate offerings (within California) are exempt from federal security registration, as are sales where the offering is to a limited number of investors. They are still subject to California securities regulations.

CHAPTER 8 QUIZ

1. The functions of Ginnie Mae do not include:
   a. guarantees for mortgage-backed securities
   b. the Tandem Plan for special assistance
   c. management and liquidation functions
   d. insuring housing loans

2. An advantage of FHA financing is *not* that it:
   a. provides for a low down payment
   b. provides long-term loans and thus lower payments
   c. provides loans for people for whom other loans are not possible
   d. protects the buyer with FHA insurance

3. Which of the following loans are assumable by anyone?
   a. CAL-VET
   b. FHA loan made in 1985
   c. VA loan made in 1996
   d. none of these

4. In California most of the real estate syndicates are:
   a. limited partnerships
   b. corporations
   c. real estate investment trusts
   d. general partnerships

5. The lender's best protection would be:
   a. the credit of the borrower
   b. the value of the property
   c. the income of the borrower
   d. a term insurance policy on the life of the borrower

6. Title I FHA loans:
   a. are only for purchases of homes
   b. are property improvement loans
   c. may be used for purchases of multiple units
   d. none of these

7. The major purpose for which the Federal National Mortgage Association (FNMA) was created was to:
   a. make secondary financing more readily available
   b. provide uniformity as to construction standards
   c. encourage lenders to make home loans
   d. provide public housing for low-income people

8. As a general rule, the difference between individual and institutional lenders is that individual lenders:
   a. make larger loans than institutional lenders
   b. charge lower interest
   c. give loans for shorter periods
   d. are more likely to give amortized loans

9. Which of the following is *not* a general characteristic of loan broker-arranged secondary financing?
   a. short term
   b. high interest
   c. amortized
   d. noninstitutional lender

10. In buying a home for rental use, a borrower would not obtain:
    a. an FHA loan b. a VA loan c. a CAL-VET loan d. either b or c

11. On a $45,000 loan, the VA guarantee would be:
    a. 100 percent b. 90 percent c. $22,500 d. $46,000

12. A CRV would be needed for a(n) _____ loan:
    a. VA b. conventional c. FHA d. all of these

13. Term life and disability insurance must be purchased by a borrower under a(n) _____ loan:
    a. conventional b. FHA c. VA d. CAL-VET

14. Which of the following is correct?
    a. The California Department of Veterans Affairs charges a 1 percent penalty for loans prepaid within two years.
    b. The VA prepayment penalty is 1 percent.
    c. The FHA prepayment penalty is 6 percent.
    d. None of these is correct.

15. A lending institution might make a government-insured or -guaranteed loan rather than a conventional loan at higher interest because of:
    a. longer loans   b. easier foreclosure   c. lower risk   d. all of these

16. The primary advantage that an FHA loan offers to an institutional lender over a conventional loan is:
    a. FHA insurance
    b. a higher yield
    c. a shorter maturity date
    d. shorter processing time

17. Title is held under a CAL-VET loan by:
    a. the trustor
    b. the buyer
    c. the Veterans Administration
    d. the State of California

18. After a borrower pays off a CAL-VET loan, he or she receives:
    a. a satisfaction
    b. a deed of reconveyance
    c. a grant deed
    d. none of these

19. Which of the following is *not* a description of FHA loans?
    a. housing only
    b. guaranteed
    c. amortized
    d. high loan-to-value ratio

20. Which of the following is *not* a characteristic of VA loans?
    a. housing or farm property
    b. lower interest rates than conventional loans
    c. rental units allowed
    d. guaranteed

21. An appraisal on a VA loan is less than the purchase-price agreement.
    a. The seller must lower the price.
    b. The buyer must increase the down payment.
    c. Either a or b is true.
    d. The buyer may rescind.

22. In evaluating a man's income for a loan, the least weight would be given to:
    a. his wife's income
    b. his overtime earnings
    c. his investment earnings
    d. his earnings from a part-time job

23. Which type of property has the highest loan-to-value ratio?
    a. improved residential property
    b. unimproved residential lots
    c. commercial property
    d. industrial property

24. Insurance companies, in giving real estate loans:
    a. can lend only within 100 miles of their headquarters
    b. are concerned primarily with secondary financing
    c. generally make only small loans to spread the risk
    d. make large loans

25. A number of people wish to invest money only in a real estate project but wish to limit their liability. They would form a:
    a. limited partnership
    b. corporate syndicate
    c. real estate investment trust
    d. any of these

26. CAL-VET loans are made from:
    a. money received from bonds
    b. state surplus funds
    c. federal grants
    d. federal loans to the state

27. Both FHA and VA loans cover:
    a. farm and home loans
    b. renter- and owner-occupied premises
    c. business and home loans
    d. none of these

28. The property is usually in close proximity; small loans and business loans are preferred; and the past record of the customer is important. What type of lender does the preceding description represent?
    a. savings and loan
    b. insurance company
    c. bank
    d. mortgage company

29. A low loan-to-value ratio would be indicative of:
    a. CAL-VET financing
    b. low buyer equity
    c. a large down payment
    d. a government-insured loan

30. In a period of tight money, which of the following is true?
    a. Purchasers will assume home loans.
    b. The easiest financing to obtain will be FHA or VA.
    c. Loan-to-value ratios will increase.
    d. All of these are true.

31. Under federal law, a real estate trust must have:
    a. 100 or more investors
    b. a corporate charter
    c. under 100 investors
    d. none of these

32. The highest interest rate is most likely to be charged by:
    a. banks
    b. savings and loan associations
    c. insurance companies
    d. individual lenders of cash

33. The amount of a VA loan is limited to:
    a. $22,500   b. $36,000   c. $60,000   d. no limit

34. A lender who often represents other lenders in making loans and likes to sell its inventory would likely be a:
    a. commercial bank
    b. savings and loan
    c. life insurance company
    d. mortgage company

35. As to mortgage brokers and mortgage bankers, which of the following is true?
    a. Neither deal in the primary mortgage market.
    b. Mortgage bankers use their own funds, while mortgage brokers seldom do so.
    c. Both a and b are true.
    d. Neither a nor b is true.

36. An advantage of a government-guaranteed or -insured loan compared with a conventional loan would *not* be a:
    a. lower interest rate
    b. longer term and lower monthly payment
    c. higher loan-to-value ratio
    d. shorter processing time

37. An insurance company is least likely to make a loan on a(n):
    a. shopping center
    b. apartment complex
    c. factory building
    d. older home

38. A construction loan would most likely be made by:
    a. a bank
    b. FNMA
    c. an insurance company
    d. the Veterans Administration

39. A seller insists on $90,000 as a sales price. The buyer can obtain an FHA loan of $82,000 but has only $6,000 down. The broker should:
    a. arrange secondary financing
    b. suggest to the seller that he take a second trust deed from the buyer
    c. take a second trust deed for her commission
    d. forget the deal

40. Which of the following loans is not available for the purchase of a farm?
    a. CAL-VET   b. FHA   c. VA   d. conventional

41. The government is actually the lender of:
    a. an FHA loan   b. a CAL-VET loan   c. a VA loan   d. all of these

42. Which of the following is true?
    a. Secondary financing is normally handled through the secondary mortgage market.
    b. The primary mortgage market is where first trust deeds are sold.
    c. A firm is licensed to deal either in the primary or the secondary mortgage market but not both.
    d. Mortgage loan correspondents deal primarily in the secondary mortgage market.

43. A lender on a note signed by multiple borrowers would prefer that their liability be:
    a. joint   b. several   c. individual   d. joint and several

44. FICO refers to:
    a. mortgage insurance
    b. credit score
    c. front-end ratio
    d. a blind pool

45. A substantial down payment in real estate:
    a. results in less danger of default
    b. normally ensures that the property will be well maintained
    c. results in better loan terms
    d. all of these

46. A broker should direct a buyer on an offer contingent on an FHA loan to:
    a. the FHA
    b. Fannie Mae
    c. Ginnie Mae
    d. a HUD-approved lender

47. Which of the following is an open-end loan?
    a. CAL-VET   b. FHA   c. VA   d. none of these

48. The source of money for most home loans by institutional lenders is:
    a. bond issues
    b. business profits
    c. federal funds
    d. individual and family savings

49. A buyer wishes to obtain a loan on a house and assume the bonded indebtedness. Which of the following would be true?
    a. The existence of the bond would have no effect on the loan.
    b. The maximum loan would be less than if there were no bond.
    c. The maximum loan would be increased because of the bond.
    d. The bond indebtedness could not be assumed.

50. The term *impounds* refers to:
    a. reserves
    b. title insurance
    c. prepayment penalties
    d. late fees

51. Mutual savings banks are located primarily in the _____ part of the United States:
    a. northeastern   b. northwestern   c. southeastern   d. southwestern

52. With a monthly gross income of $3,800, loan payments (PITI) of $1,150, and long term monthly debt obligations of $340, the back-end ratio would be:
    a. 38 percent   b. 39 percent   c. 40 percent   d. 41 percent

53. As to loan brokers, which of the following is true?
    a. Credit life insurance can be required.
    b. Balloon payments are not allowed.
    c. Commissions are regulated for all broker loans.
    d. None of these are true.

54. An advantage of FHA financing to the buyer is:
    a. inclusion of local taxes in the monthly payments
    b. minimum property requirements (MPR)
    c. elimination of short-term financing
    d. all of these

55. Lenders today are generally most interested in the:
   a. condition of the property
   b. transportation in the area
   c. credit history of the borrower
   d. age of the property

56. William, whose credit is good, wants to buy a small business. He is a good customer of the bank where he keeps his account. The business he wants to buy is a reasonable one to make money. Who will most likely be the lender?
   a. a federal savings and loan association
   b. his bank
   c. a mortgage loan company
   d. a state savings and loan bank

57. In considering the liquidity of its mortgage portfolio, a lender would be relating to:
   a. the ratio of performing and nonperforming loans
   b. secondary market sales
   c. the average loan-to-value ratio of the portfolio
   d. the average holding period before loans are refinanced

58. A veteran wishes to refinance her home with a VA loan. The lender is willing but insists on 3 1/2 points.
   a. VA loans are available for purchase, not refinancing.
   b. The veteran can refinance with a VA loan providing there are no points.
   c. The veteran can be required to pay a maximum of 1 point as an origination fee.
   d. The veteran may pay the points.

59. Which of the following is true?
   a. Fannie Mae provides a secondary mortgage market for FHA and VA loans.
   b. FNMA is a private corporation.
   c. Ginnie Mae is involved in federally assisted housing projects and guarantees FNMA securities.
   d. all of these

60. Disintermediation refers to:
   a. a course of logical appraisal
   b. a snap decision not based on fact
   c. a buildup of funds in savings as people cut spending
   d. a sudden withdrawal of savings from lending institutions by depositors

61. A loan-to-value ratio is best described as:
   a. the ratio of the loan to the sale price
   b. the ratio of the loan to the appraisal
   c. the ratio of the loan amount to its selling price on the secondary mortgage market
   d. none of these

62. A veteran is purchasing a home under the California Veterans Farm and Home Purchase Program. Who would be designated the grantee in the grant deed given by the seller?
   a. the Veterans Administration
   b. the California Department of Veterans Affairs
   c. the veteran buyer
   d. the title company

63. A mortgage loan correspondent would be regulated primarily by:
   a. city ordinance
   b. federal regulations
   c. state laws and regulations
   d. the Federal Trade Commission

64. A borrower has a gross monthly income of $3,400. The borrower wishes to obtain a loan in which the mortgage payment including taxes and insurance will be $950. The front-end ratio would be:
   a. 24 percent   b. 26.7 percent   c. 28 percent   d. 35.7 percent

65. In the preceding question, the borrower is making long-term debt payments of $350 per month. The back-end ratio would be:
   a. 34 percent   b. 36 percent   c. 38 percent   d. 40 percent

66. A borrower did not have a sufficient down payment for an FHA loan. The broker loaned the buyer $1,000 on a personal note in order for the buyer to complete this transaction. This loan:
   a. has placed the broker's license in jeopardy
   b. has subjected the broker to criminal penalties
   c. both a and b
   d. neither a nor b

67. A broker aided a buyer in the preparation of fraudulent income statements in order to qualify for a bank loan. This would:
   a. place the broker's license in jeopardy
   b. be a federal crime
   c. both a and b
   d. neither a nor b

68. Who pays for Mutual Mortgage Insurance?
   a. the purchaser under an FHA loan
   b. the purchaser under a VA loan
   c. the purchaser under a CAL-VET loan
   d. all of these

69. When are the premiums paid on the insurance for an FHA loan?
   a. up front   b. with payments   c. both a and b   d. neither a nor b

70. FHA mortgage insured loans are made by:
   a. HUD
   b. mortgage companies, banks, and savings and loans
   c. either a or b
   d. Fannie Mae

ANSWERS—CHAPTER 8 QUIZ

1. d. This is an FHA function.
2. d. The insurance protects the lender.
3. b.
4. a.
5. b. As security for the loan.
6. b.
7. c. It provides a secondary mortgage market.
8. c. Often with balloon payments.
9. c. Partially amortized (balloon payment).
10. d. Buyer occupancy is required.
11. c. 50% up to $45,000.
12. a. Certificate of Reasonable Value.
13. d.
14. d.
15. c. The loan is insured or guaranteed.
16. a. Lower risk.
17. d. The state sells the property on a land contract.
18. c. Since the state held title.
19. b. The FHA insures loans.
20. c. Owner occupancy is required.
21. d. Answers a and b are possible, but not mandatory.
22. b. Next least is answer d.

23. a. Unimproved is the lowest.
24. d.
25. d. All of these provide limited liability.
26. a. Tax-exempt state bonds.
27. d.
28. c.
29. c.
30. a. Where possible.
31. a.
32. d. Hard-money loans.
33. d. The guarantee is limited.
34. d.
35. b.
36. d. A government loan usually takes longer.
37. d.
38. a. Banks prefer the short term and higher interest.
39. d. Or get the seller to lower the price.
40. b. Housing only.
41. b. The state buys the property then resells it to the veteran.
42. d. They handle sales of existing loans.
43. d. Can collect from one or all.
44. b.
45. d.

46. d. Who can directly endorse the loan.
47. a. It can be increased.
48. d. With institutional lenders.
49. b. The bond reduces equity.
50. a. For taxes and insurance.
51. a.
52. b. Divide gross income into PITI + monthly debt payments.
53. d.
54. d.
55. c. Collateral, capacity, and character.
56. b. Banks like business loans.
57. b. Conversion of loans to cash.
58. d. Points are negotiable.
59. d.
60. d. For investments elsewhere.
61. b.
62. b. The state takes title.
63. c.
64. c. 28% of 3,400 = 952.
65. c. 38% of 3,400 = 1,292.
66. c. Federal crime.
67. c. Defrauding a federally insured institution.
68. a.
69. c.
70. b.

Real Estate Appraisal

VALUE

An appraisal is an estimation of value. (This estimation is only as to the value at the particular time it is made; it is not a continuing estimation.) **Value** is defined as worth, or the present worth, of future benefits. Appraisals are concerned with **market value** (that is, the cash price a willing informed buyer will pay to a willing informed seller allowing a reasonable time for a sale).

Other Types of Value

Loan Value   A conservative figure, below market value, that a lender will give, with the property as security.

Insurance Value   Replacement value, which might be greater or less than market value.

Book Value   The value at which a property is carried on a firm's books (its original cost plus the cost of improvements minus depreciation). It bears no relationship to market value.

Exchange Value   A relative value; it is related to the value of the property that can be obtained by an exchange.

Assessed Value   The value placed by the assessor. In California, the assessed value of real estate is set at 100 percent of market value at time of sale.

Subjective Value   The use or utility value a property offers to an owner.

Objective Value   The actual price that will be paid (the market value).

Four Elements of Value

1. **Utility:** The item serves a useful purpose. Even an ornament serves a purpose, but without any purpose there is no value.
2. **Scarcity:** If there are a great many similar items on the market, the value will normally be less than when there are only a few such items available.
3. **Demand:** If no one wants it, there is no value. (Demand must be coupled with purchasing power to be effective.)
4. **Transferability:** If title or possession cannot be transferred, there is little, if any, value.

Utility and demand are the two most important elements as to market value or commercial value. The least important element of value is cost, or price. What the buyer paid does not determine value.

Four Special Factors Influencing Real Estate Value

1. **Physical:**
   a. **Topography:** Steep grades mean greater development costs. Gently rolling terrain breaks the monotony but does not cause excessive costs.
   b. **Size:** Size directly affects value.
   c. **Shape:** Odd-shaped parcels might result in unusable land as well as higher cost.
   d. **Soil:** Load-bearing capabilities are important, but fertility has little importance except for agricultural purposes.
   e. **Location:** The three most important factors as to value are frequently expressed as "location, location, location." Location as to other uses is extremely important.
   f. **Accessibility:** Ingress and egress, as well as traffic in the area, affect value.
2. **Economic:** The national and local economies directly affect value, as do the availability and cost of credit.
3. **Social:** Population changes and movements, attitudes toward recreation, household sizes, etc., all affect value.
4. **Political:** Zoning, building codes, health codes, public housing, growth limitations, and rent control all affect value.

Highest and Best Use   That use of a property that gives it the greatest value. For example: Suppose building a $300,000 apartment on a lot would give the property a value of $450,000. The value of the lot for this purpose would be $150,000. This would not be the highest and best use if $50,000 of improvements for a parking lot would give the property a value of $250,000, or $200,000 attributable to the land. In considering different uses and costs of the improvements, the appraiser in this example is using the *development method*.

Assemblage Taking several small parcels and joining them together to form a larger parcel that has a greater value than the sum of the individual parcels (because of the difficulty of putting together large parcels in areas subdivided or developed by many owners).

Plottage (Plottage Increment) The extent to which the value is increased by assemblage. (Sometimes the terms **plottage** and **assemblage** are used synonymously.)

Amenities The features of a property that give a greater satisfaction in living or pride of ownership. (The elements of utility, convenience, and beauty.)

METHODS OF APPRAISAL

1. Market-comparison (or market data) approach.
2. Cost approach (replacement method).
3. Income-capitalization approach.

Market-Comparison Approach

Used primarily for single-family dwellings, this approach (also known as the **sales-comparison approach**) can also be used for land or other improvements where there are sales that exhibit a high degree of similarity. Actual sale prices, not listing prices, are used. The appraiser, in his or her comparisons, should consider terms of sale (a lower down payment could mean a higher price), added features, quality, location, and other factors in arriving at comparable properties. When properties are not equal, the appraiser must make adjustments to the prices paid for comparable property based on the presence or absence of amenities when compared to the property being appraised. This determines the **adjusted selling price** of comparables. As an example, if the property being appraised had a one-car garage but the comparable being used had a one-and-one-half car garage, a deduction would be made from the sale of the comparable. Similarly, if the property being appraised had 1,600 square feet and the comparable had 1,520 square feet, the sale price of the comparable would be adjusted upward.

The market-comparison approach is the oldest and usually the most easily understood method of appraisal, as well as the most common one in practice. Disadvantages can be the difficulty of locating enough similar properties that have been recently sold to indicate value, as well as the difficulty of adjusting amenities and sale terms.

Principle of Progression Higher value because of more expensive homes in the area.

Principle of Regression Lesser value because of less expensive homes in the area.

Cost Approach

1. Find the cost to replace the improvements (buildings) now.
2. Deduct the amount of accrued depreciation.
3. Add the value of the land (the market value based on highest and best use).

Replacement Cost To determine replacement cost, the appraiser does not consider an exact replica, as this might mean obsolete materials and construction methods. Instead, the appraiser is concerned with the cost of a new building with the same utility value. (Insurance appraisals are generally based on replacement cost.) **Reproduction cost,** on the other hand, applies to an exact duplication of a structure.

Economists say that the value of improved property is the sum of its land, labor, management, and capital. (This is really the cost approach to value.)

Means of Estimating Replacement Cost

1. **Square-foot method:** Multiply square feet times average construction cost per square foot for this type of structure.
2. **Cubic-foot method:** While this method is similar to the square-foot method, it is more accurate because it takes height into consideration.
3. **Quantity-survey method:** All materials and labor are priced separately. This is a detailed appraisal normally used by contractors, not appraisers.
4. **Unit-in-place method:** Costs per unit such as price per room, per outlet, per parking space, etc., are calculated.
5. **Index method:** The original cost is increased or decreased, based on the percentage of increase or decrease in the construction cost index since the structure was built.

Effective Age Not the chronological age, but the age used by an appraiser for the cost approach. If a building is 10 years old but is in exceptionally fine condition, an appraiser might say its effective age is 7 years.

Observed-Condition Method The method for estimating the depreciation based on the building's condition rather than its age. Depreciation is computed based on the replacement costs of the improvement. (Land is not depreciated.) The average building has a useful or economic life of 40 to 50 years. If we assume a building has a 40-year life, then the yearly depreciation would be $100\% \div 40 = 2\ 1/2\%$ per year.

Problem: A parcel of land is worth $170,000 (calculated by the market-comparison method) and contains a 15,000-square-foot building. The cost to build today is $20 per square foot. The building has an economic life of 50 years and an effective age of 8 years. What is the value of the property?

$$15,000 \times \$20 = \$300,000 \text{ to replace}$$
$$50\text{-year life} = 2\% \text{ depreciation per year}$$
$$8 \text{ years} \times 2\% = 16\% \text{ depreciation}$$
$$.16 \times 300,000 = \$48,000 \text{ depreciation}$$

Replacement value	$300,000
Minus depreciation	−48,000
Value of building	$252,000
Plus land	+170,000
Total value	$422,000

In the cost approach we are concerned with present cost to replace, not original cost. The cost approach tends to give us the highest appraisal or *ceiling* on the value.

The cost approach is particularly good for new improvements where the land is utilized at its highest and best use, as well as for service buildings such as schools or libraries. (Since there is no actual market for service buildings, a comparison approach cannot be used.)

The appraiser does not depreciate land or ornamental landscaping. Landscaping is normally appraised separately from the land or building.

Income-Capitalization Approach

This method of appraisal is concerned with the net income that can be derived from a property. (The value is related to net income.) To determine the value, divide the net income by the appropriate **capitalization rate** to obtain the present worth of future benefits (value):

$$\text{Value} = \frac{\text{Net income}}{\text{Capitalization rate}}$$

First Step Start with the scheduled gross income (based on scheduled rents and a 100 percent occupancy factor). Then deduct total annual expenses, including an appropriate vacancy factor and collection loss, to arrive at net income. The appraiser is not as concerned with past income (which is only a guide) as with what the future income will be. (**Forecasting** is the estimation of future income.)

The appraiser is more concerned with **economic rent,** the rent the property should be able to demand based on economic conditions, than the **contract rent,** which is the rent stated in the lease. Contract rent can be greater or less than economic rent.

For expenses, deduct management costs, utilities, taxes, services, repairs, etc. Do not deduct payment on the principal or interest expenses. The management costs are the costs most likely to be overlooked in an appraisal, especially if an owner currently is performing them.

Second Step Select a capitalization rate. (This would be a given percentage on a real estate exam problem.) The capitalization rate is the rate of return an investor would want for the particular property being appraised. (On a new apartment building it may be 8 percent, but for an older rooming house it might be 25 percent.) The higher the risk, the higher the capitalization rate.

The capitalization rate can provide for the return of an investment. For example, assume that the desired rate of return for an investment is 10 percent. Assume also that the asset would have an economic life of 50 years, which would mean a 2 percent depreciation per year. Using a 12 percent capitalization rate provides not only the return *on* the investment (the profit) but the return *of* the investment as well.

Split Rate Separate capitalization rates may be used for land and improvements. The Inwood compound-interest annuity method, the Hoskold sinking-fund-comparison method, and the band-of-investment method are all means of arriving at a capitalization rate.

Band of Investment Method To determine the capitalization rate by the **band of investment method,** multiply the percentage of value of each trust deed times its interest rate, and multiply the percentage of value of the owner's equity times the owner's desired return. Then add the results. *Example:*

	% of Value		Rate		Capitalization
1st trust deed	40%	of	6%	=	2.4%
2nd trust deed	20%	of	9%	=	1.8%
3rd trust deed	10%	of	10%	=	10.0%
Equity	30%	of	12%	=	3.6%
	Capitalization Rate			=	8.8%

Problem: A five-unit apartment building with rentals of $200 per month each has a 10 percent vacancy factor and total expenses of $400 per month. Using a capitalization rate of 8 percent, find the value.

5 × $200	= $1,000 per month gross income
less 10% vacancy factor	= $900 per month
less expenses of $400 per month	= $500 per month net income
12 months × $500	= $6,000 yearly net income

$$\text{Value} = \frac{\text{Net income}}{\text{Capitalization rate}}$$
$$= \frac{\$6,000}{.08}$$
$$= \$75,000$$

The value using the income approach is $75,000. If the capitalization rate is 10 percent:

$$\$6,000 \div .10 = \$60,000$$

If the capitalization rate is 4 percent:

$$\$6,000 \div .04 = \$150,000$$

Therefore:

The value goes up if the rate goes down.

The value goes down if the rate goes up.

If expenses go up, the value goes down (since net income would go down).

If expenses go down, the value goes up.

Deferred Maintenance   Repairs may be postponed by an owner. In this case, an appraiser would deduct the cost of repairs from the value to bring the building up to its proper maintenance level.

Gross Multiplier   This is a variation on the income-capitalization approach in which gross income is multiplied by some given figure. It can be stated as an annual or a monthly multiplier. If the gross annual multiplier is 6 and the gross income is $8,500, then the value would be 6 × $8,500, or $51,000. (Since a building may have unusually high or low expenses, this method determines a "ballpark" figure only.) Dividing the sale price of a similar property by its gross income gives its gross multiplier. This gross multiplier can be applied to the income of the property being appraised to obtain a rough approximation of value.

ECONOMIC LIFE

The economic life of a building is that period of time in which a building contributes to the net income of a property. If a property has a net income of $10,000 and the capitalization rate is 10 percent, the value of the property, of course, would be $100,000. If the land itself is worth $100,000, then the building is not contributing to the net; it has exceeded its economic life.

Age-Life Tables   Show the economic life of various types of buildings. A single-family residence is generally shown as 40 years.

Net Spendable (Cash Flow)   What actually remains in the owner's pocket. (It is not concerned with depreciation, which is a paper expense rather than an actual cash expense.) Net spendable is not the same as net income.

Leverage   Using other people's money (borrowed funds) to make money. For example: A $100,000 property is purchased with 10 percent down. Its value increases by 10 percent. The investment is $10,000. The $10,000 increase gives a 100 percent return on the owner's investment, since the 10 percent increase applies to the entire property. If the owner had paid cash, his or her return would have been only 10 percent, not 100 percent.

Fixed Expenses   Expenses that cannot be changed, as opposed to **variable expenses.** Examples of fixed expenses would be taxes and insurance, while maintenance could be a variable expense as it could be decreased or increased.

DEPRECIATION

Depreciation is a loss in value from any cause. Only improvements to real estate can be depreciated. Land can never be depreciated, although orchards and vineyards (trees and vines) can be depreciated. For tax purposes, depreciation starts on the first day of the month the property is put into service. Salvage value is no longer considered in depreciating assets.

Three Types of Depreciation

1. **Physical deterioration:** Wear and tear from use, negligence, or other causes of actual physical damages. Examples include dry rot, blistering paint, leaking roof, and sagging floors.

2. **Functional or built-in obsolescence:** Loss in value that was built into the structure by poorly designed facilities, outdated equipment or construction methods, or changes in utility demand. Examples include bedrooms without closets, small rooms, massive cornices, and high ceilings. Too expensive (overbuilt) improvements also constitute functional obsolescence. (Functional utility deals with design or layout as to desirability by owners or tenants.)

3. **Economic and social obsolescence:** Loss in value caused by forces outside the property itself. Examples include neighborhood changes and traffic problems. A misplaced improvement is considered economic obsolescence. The statement "more buildings are torn down than wear out" is the result of economic obsolescence. They are not physically worn out, but because of outside factors they are not economical.

Accrued Depreciation   Depreciation that has already accrued.

Remainder Depreciation   Depreciation that will occur in the future.

Curable Depreciation   Depreciation where it is economically feasible to correct the defects. The most difficult depreciation to cure is economic obsolescence, since it is based on factors outside the property itself.

Incurable Depreciation   Depreciation where it is not economically feasible to cure the defects. Economic obsolescence is generally incurable.

While appraisers consider depreciation for all types of property, homeowners may not depreciate that portion of their home used as their residence (only income or business property may be depreciated for tax purposes).

Method of Computing Depreciation for Tax Purposes

Straight-Line Method   An equal sum is deducted each year from the income during the entire economic life of the property. To find the depreciation, divide the cost of the depreciable improvements by the life of the structure. For income tax purposes a 27 1/2-year life is allowed for residential income or investment property; for nonresidential income or investment property, the period is 39 years.

Example: A man owns a residential income property with a 27 1/2-year life and a building cost of $100,000.

$$\$100,000 \div 27.5 \text{ residential rate} = \$3,636 \text{ per year}$$

He could, therefore, subtract $3,636 each year from his net income for tax purposes until he has recaptured the entire cost. (Depreciation is the means by which he can recover his investment.) The straight-line method is the depreciation method that gives the greatest return in the last year. This is the only method of depreciation used for appraisal purposes.

Our tax laws formerly provided accelerated methods of depreciation that allowed owners greater depreciation in the early years of ownership. Present purchasers are now restriced to straight-line depreciation.

Tax Shelter   By showing depreciation as an expense, it is possible to show a paper loss or break-even point but nevertheless have net spendable income. Depreciation can fully shelter the income from an investment. The **passive loss** from depreciation can be used to shelter other income from taxation by taxpayers having an adjusted gross income of $100,000 or less. (Up to $25,000 of active income may be sheltered.) The use of passive losses is phased out between $100,000 and $150,000 of gross income.

Sinking Fund   This is the setting aside and investing of a sum of money each year in an interest-bearing account so that by the time an asset needs replacement, the money set aside will be enough to allow for replacement. For example: Suppose that some of a person's assets will need to be replaced in 10 years. The estimated cost to replace them in 10 years is $10,000. The amount this person needs to set aside each year is less than $1,000, since interest would be compounding. He or she may only have to set aside $750 per year for 10 years to have $10,000 with the interest.

Reserve for Replacement   This is an accounting reserve deducted for tax purposes to replace chattels such as furniture in an apartment. (For example: Suppose the cost is $1,000 and the life is five years; deduct $200 from net income each year.)

LAND EVALUATION

Agricultural Land   Price per acre (also for undeveloped land).

Commercial Lots   Price per front foot or price per square foot.

Industrial Property   Price per square foot or acre.

Residential Lots   Price per lot.

Neighborhood   An area of social conformity (a *homogeneous* area) that has defined boundaries. Boundaries can be natural, such as a river or mountain, or artificial, such as a street, railroad line, or park.

100 Percent Location An idiom meaning the best commercial location in a community.

Corner Influence Added value of a commercial lot because of corner location (traffic on two streets means added window and sign exposure). The value would be less than the front foot value on both streets but more than the front foot value on one street.

Depth Table An appraiser's table showing added value based on added depth to a lot. A lot 600 feet deep would not, however, be worth twice the value of a similar lot 300 feet deep. A simplified means of appraising value by depth is the **4-3-2-1 method,** which assigns 40 percent of the value to the first 25 percent of the depth, 30 percent of the value to the next 25 percent, 20 percent of the value to the third 25 percent, and 10 percent of the value to the back 25 percent of the depth.

Excess Land Land that does not contribute to the property value (too much land for its use).

Abstractive Method (Allocation Method) Site value can be ascertained by determining the value attributable to the improvements and subtracting this amount from the market value of the improved property.

Land-Residual Method Multiply the capitalization rate times the value of the improvements to arrive at the income attributable to the improvements. The balance of the income would be attributable to the land. Capitalize the income attributable to the land to determine the residual land value. (The **building-residual method** is similar and is used when the value of the land is known. The **property-residual method** capitalizes the income for both land and improvements.)

Development Method Deduct the estimated cost of an improvement from the value a property is expected to have when improved to arrive at the land value for that use (this method is used in determining highest and best use).

PROFESSIONAL APPRAISAL DESIGNATIONS

MAI Member of Appraisal Institute

SRA Senior Residential Appraiser (Appraisal Institute)

Appraisal Reports

The first step in an appraisal report is to **define the problem** (identify the property and the object sought). The final step is the conclusion, which sets forth the estimate of value. Every appraisal report should identify the property, be dated, indicate any interest the appraiser might have in the property, include all assumptions, and be signed by the appraiser. If a borrower pays for an appraisal report, the lender must inform the borrower of his or her right to receive a copy of the appraisal if requested within 90 days of loan approval or rejection.

Restricted Appraisal Report   Also known as a letter or letterform report, it is the least comprehensive and least expensive report. It describes the property and gives the appraised value as of an indicated date.

Summary Appraisal Report   Also known as a short-form report, the appraiser checks blocks and fills in blanks on a report. It is commonly used for lender appraisals.

Self-Contained Report   Also known as the narrative report, it is the most comprehensive and expensive report and includes detailed analysis and photographs. It is unlikely to be used for single-family homes.

Certified appraisal   Use of the term **certified appraisal** requires that the written appraisal report be performed within statutory guidelines.

Uniform Residential Appraisal Report   This report form is required by the FHA, the VA, HUD, the Federal Home Loan Mortgage Corporation (Freddie Mac), FNMA (Fannie Mae), and the RECD.

Reconciliation (Correlation or Bracketing)   An appraiser will evaluate the values obtained by each appraisal method and assign different weights to each method to arrive at his or her appraised value (by using all three appraisal methods).

ADDITIONAL REAL ESTATE PRINCIPLES PERTAINING TO APPRAISAL

Economies of Scale   A larger development can be built at a lower cost per unit.

Principle of Diminishing Returns   A point will be reached at which the profit for each additional unit will start to decrease. Continued production will result in lower and lower returns until all profit is eliminated.

Principle of Supply and Demand   The greater the supply of an item, the lower its value; the greater the scarcity of the item, the greater the value.

Principle of Contribution   Maximum values are achieved when improvements return the highest net in relationship to the investment.

Principle of Anticipation   Value is based on anticipated benefits (use and/or income).

Principle of Competition   Where extraordinary profits are being made, competition is created that will increase the supply, thus lowering prices.

Principle of Balance   Value is created and maintained when there is a proper mix of land use so as to obtain the highest and best use for a site.

Principle of Substitution A person will not pay more for a property than it would be necessary to pay for another property of comparable utility and desirability (under the market-comparison approach).

Principle of Surplus or Surplus Productivity After deducting labor costs, value of coordination (management), and capital investment from the value of a property, the remainder should be the value attributed to the land. The principle of surplus assumes that value of property is the sum of land, labor, capital, and management.

Principle of Change Real estate values do not remain constant. An appraiser must consider how changing economic and social conditions affect the value of property.

Principle of Integration and Disintegration Property goes through three phases: development (integration or growth), equilibrium (stable use or maturity), and disintegration (decline or old age). Sometimes there is a fourth stage of rehabilitation.

Principle of Conformity A property will have maximum value when it is in a homogeneous area.

Licensing and Certification Fee appraisers are independent contractors hired to provide an estimation (appraisal) of value. States are required to provide for licensing and certification by the federal Financial Institutions Reform, Recovery, and Enforcement Act (FIRREA). Any loan made by an institution regulated or insured by a federal agency must meet the certification requirements. This includes all loans involving the Federal National Mortgage Association (Fannie Mae), The Federal Home Loan Mortgage Corporation (Freddie Mac), and the Resolution Trust Corporation. State-licensed or -certified appraisers are required for federally related appraisals of $250,000 or more. State-certified appraisers must be used for federally related transactions of $1,000,000 or more, and can be required for transactions less than this amount by the agency involved. Federally related transactions that do not require a certified appraiser require a licensed appraiser. Appraisal licensing and certification in California are administered by the Office of Real Estate Appraisers within the Business, Transportation, and Housing Agency. A nonlicensee can assist in preparing the appraisal report, but the conclusion must be made by a licensed or certified appraiser. The **Uniform Standards of Professional Appraisal Practice (USPAP),** developed by the Appraisal Foundation is the minimum standard of performance for California appraisers. California has four categories of licensees: **trainee, residential, certified residential,** and **certified general.**

1. **Trainee** Can work on any property the supervising appraiser is permitted to appraise.
2. **Residential** Any noncomplex one- to four-family property with a transcation value up to $1 million and nonresidential property with a transaction value up to $250,000.

3. **Certified Residential** Any one- to four-family property without regard to value or complexity and nonresidential property with a transaction value up to $250,000.

4. **Certified General** All real estate without regard to transaction value or complexity.

APPRAISAL ETHICS

It is considered unethical for an appraiser to:

1. Charge a fee based on the appraised amount.
2. Undertake an appraisal beyond his or her ability.
3. Pay a fee for referral.
4. Appraise a property in which the appraiser has an undisclosed interest.
5. Discuss the appraisal with anyone other than the principal for whom the appraisal was performed without permission of the principal.

CHAPTER 9 QUIZ

1. As to capitalization rates, which of the following is true?
   a. Lowering the rate increases the value.
   b. Increasing the rate lowers the value.
   c. Increasing the risk increases the rate.
   d. All of these are true.

2. Rents in an office building became $800 less per month after street parking was made illegal. Assuming a capitalization rate of 8 percent, the building suffered a loss of value of:
   a. $10,000
   b. $120,000
   c. $100,000
   d. zero

3. Loss of value of an expensive home because of a neighborhood of low-price homes is known as:
   a. regression
   b. progression
   c. functional obsolescence
   d. physical depreciation

4. Income minus operating expenses minus principal, interest, and tax payments equals:
   a. effective gross income
   b. net spendable income
   c. net income
   d. net gross

5. An apartment building produces a monthly rent of $1,600. A similar property with monthly rents of $2,100 recently sold for $294,000. Using this as the only data, the appraiser would say that the first apartment building is worth:
   a. $294,000
   b. $224,000
   c. $293,600
   d. $247,500

6. The most difficult depreciation to correct would be:
   a. functional
   b. physical
   c. economic
   d. accelerated

7. An appraisal method wherein electrical work was appraised at a price per outlet would be the:
   a. quantity-survey method
   b. capitalization method
   c. comparison method
   d. unit-in-place method

8. Demand has no effect on value unless there is also:
   a. a need
   b. an adequate supply
   c. a scarcity
   d. purchasing power

9. A property value can be influenced by neighboring property. The value of a home would least likely be influenced by a neighborhood containing:
   a. vacant lots
   b. mixed residential and commercial uses
   c. large homes converted to small apartments
   d. homes of significantly lower value

10. Depth tables would be most likely used in appraising which kind of property?
    a. residential
    b. commercial
    c. industrial
    d. acreage

11. Assemblage is closest to:
    a. contribution
    b. residual value
    c. capitalization
    d. plottage

12. In appraising an income property, an appraiser is concerned with:
    a. the amount of income
    b. the quality of tenants
    c. the continuing prospect of present income
    d. all of these

13. In using the replacement-cost approach, an appraiser would not need:
    a. cost when new
    b. depreciation
    c. effective age
    d. land value

14. The best comparable property for appraising a home would be:
    a. a similar home sold at a foreclosure sale
    b. a similar property sold to a buyer who had a need for that property
    c. a similar home sold by a person wanting to sell to a buyer wanting to buy
    d. a home sold by an unwilling seller to a willing buyer

15. The narrative form of an appraiser's report would include all except:
    a. a description of the property
    b. the data used with analysis
    c. the qualifications of the appraiser
    d. the financial terms

16. The period for which a property can show a return attributable to the improvements is known as the property's:
    a. economic life
    b. chronological life
    c. effective age
    d. depreciation life

17. A major problem in using the cost method to appraise an older apartment building is:
    a. that construction materials have changed
    b. that construction methods have changed
    c. determining accrued depreciation
    d. all of these

18. The oldest method of appraising is:
    a. the gross multiplier   b. cost   c. capitalization   d. comparison

19. An appraiser is going to use the cost method in appraising two houses. One is new and one is 50 years old. The cost method:
    a. has no validity for either appraisal
    b. would be less effective for the 50-year-old house
    c. would be less effective for the new house
    d. would be equally effective for both appraisals

20. In determining economic obsolescence, an appraiser would be interested in knowing whether:
    a. the building has exceeded its economic life
    b. the people in the area are doing well economically
    c. the building is well managed
    d. the building needs repair

21. To offset depreciation, a person may:
    a. combine functional and economic obsolescence
    b. lower the rate of contemplated capitalization
    c. use a reserve-for-replacement method
    d. include the plottage value

22. The most important factor in determining the value of a single-family home is its:
    a. original cost   b. square footage   c. floor plan   d. location

23. In appraising a house for insurance coverage, an appraiser would most likely be concerned with:
    a. income
    b. replacement cost
    c. the selling price of similar homes
    d. the age of the house

24. The conditions of sale will affect the:
    a. price of the subject property
    b. value of the subject property
    c. utility of the subject property
    d. cost basis of the subject property

25. A separate value for the land must be computed for the:
    a. market approach
    b. cost approach
    c. capitalization approach
    d. all of these

26. Which one of these forces is not a force influencing value?
    a. Economic   b. Political   c. Social   d. Demand

27. A property is valued at $300,000 with a 5 percent capitalization rate. If the prospective investor wants an 8 percent return on her money, the property would be valued at:
    a. $187,500   b. $270,000   c. $480,000   d. $420,000

28. In appraising a vacant lot, an appraiser would first determine the:
    a. asking price
    b. highest and best use
    c. price asked for similar lots
    d. original cost and when purchased

29. The cost approach is most appropriate for appraising:
    a. raw land
    b. commercial property
    c. apartments
    d. service buildings

30. Depreciating an apartment building $10,000 in one year would:
   a. increase the book value $10,000
   b. decrease the book value $10,000
   c. increase the market value $10,000
   d. decrease the market value $10,000

31. The principle of substitution is that:
   a. a person will not pay more for a property than the cost of another property of equal utility and desirability
   b. amenities are balanced in appraising
   c. locations can be freely substituted in the market
   d. none of these

32. As to the income capitalization method of appraising, which of the following is true?
   a. It is not a good method for single-family dwellings as it does not consider the amenities of home ownership.
   b. It requires the determination of an applicable capitalization rate.
   c. It is interested in net returns, not gross income.
   d. all of these

33. The period in which a building produces income attributable to the building itself is known as:
   a. depreciation
   b. economic life
   c. replacement period
   d. residual period

34. The factors of value do not include:
   a. cost and age
   b. utility and demand
   c. scarcity and transferability
   d. any of these

35. The value of a commercial lot would be least influenced by factors relating to:
   a. compaction   b. transportation   c. fertility   d. drainage

36. Neighborhood is important in real estate because:
   a. traffic affects desirability
   b. property in a poor neighborhood doesn't sell
   c. real estate is immobile
   d. none of these

37. An 8-year-old apartment building would cost $220,000 to build today. The land is worth $50,000. With a 40-year expected economic life, its net income is $27,000. The gross multiplier is 10. The desired return on this type of property is 8 1/2 percent. Using the most applicable single method to appraise the building, an appraiser would say it is worth:
   a. $270,000
   b. $226,000
   c. $317,647
   d. the average of a, b, and c

38. Each unit in a duplex rents for $400 per month. With a price of $96,000, the monthly gross multiplier would be:
   a. 10   b. 120   c. 240   d. 20

39. To appraise a lot with a worthless, condemned building on it, an appraiser would:
   a. capitalize the value of the entire property and deduct the value of the building
   b. forget about the building
   c. add the appraisal value of the building to the value of the lot
   d. deduct the cost of demolition from the value of the lot

40. An appraiser would most likely have the designation:
   a. AAA   b. MAIA   c. MAI   d. AA

41. Rising interest rates as the only economic change would affect the value of an apartment house in that the:
   a. value would drop
   b. value would rise
   c. rentals would drop
   d. value would remain unchanged

42. Which of the following basic real economic characteristics is the best expression of why real estate has value?
   a. better prospects for speculative growth
   b. maximum utilization of available resources
   c. nearness to high-rent districts
   d. high cost of replacement

43. As to economic life and physical life, which of the following is true?
    a. Economic life is shorter.
    c. Economic life is longer.
    b. Physical life is shorter.
    d. They normally are of the same duration.

44. In finding comparables, an appraiser uses the term *adjusted sale price*. This refers to:
    a. sale price less sale costs
    b. sale cost adjusted for inflation
    c. estimate of sale price when adjusting for characteristics of a particular property
    d. none of these

45. In using the market-data approach in appraising a single-family residence, comparisons should be made as to:
    a. gross multipliers
    c. rental income
    b. cubic footage
    d. the entire property

46. Which of the following is not a factor in appraising a one-family home?
    a. square footage   b. floor plan   c. rent   d. type of construction

47. A lot has three possible uses. Building a kennel would yield a net return of $87,000 on an investment of $65,000. Building an apartment house would yield a $211,000 return on a $2,552,000 investment, and building a supermarket would yield $157,000 on a $520,000 investment. If the capitalization rate for all three investments is 9 percent, then the investment that would yield the highest income attributable to the land alone would be the:
    a. kennel
    c. supermarket
    b. apartment building
    d. cannot be computed from data given

48. Two properties have an appraised value of $100,000 each. One uses a capitalization rate of 10 percent and one a rate of 11 percent. The property using the 11 percent rate has an income:
    a. 10 percent higher than the other property
    b. 10 percent less than the other property
    c. 1 percent higher than the other property
    d. 1 percent less than the other property

49. Utility value would be most nearly equivalent to:
    a. market value   b. cost   c. price   d. use value

50. A building would cost $140,000 to replace, but it is appraised at $90,000. This difference is:
    a. accrued depreciation
    c. the progression factor
    b. remainder depreciation
    d. the conformity factor

51. In order to determine accrued depreciation of a residential property, each year of the economic age of a structure receives:
    a. increasing depreciation
    c. 1/27.5 of the replacement value
    b. decreasing depreciation
    d. equal weight

52. An appraiser would appraise landscaping and fences:
    a. separately
    c. with the building
    b. with the land
    d. none of these

53. Two identical buildings were each leased for 20 years at the same rent. One was leased as a hardware store and one as a post office. At a sale, which building would bring more money?
    a. the hardware store
    c. the value would be the same
    b. the post office
    d. the value would depend on the cost

54. Subtracting vacancy and collection factors from gross income gives:
    a. net   b. net spendable   c. adjusted gross   d. gross profit

55. An appraiser defines the boundaries of a neighborhood by:
    a. social conformity
    c. traffic patterns
    b. geographical status
    d. economic status

56. To obtain depreciation on real estate, the real estate:
    a. must be a single-family dwelling
    c. must be commercial property
    b. must be improved property
    d. none of these

57. In making an appraisal for a bank, an appraiser would be concerned with:
    a. the amount of the loan requested
    b. the purchase price to be paid to the seller
    c. both a and b
    d. none of these

58. A building is in exceptionally good condition. Its effective age is:
    a. less than its actual age
    b. more than its actual age
    c. the same as the actual age
    d. none of these

59. The principle of anticipation relates to the:
    a. gross multiplier
    b. cost approach
    c. income approach
    d. market-comparison approach

60. The best method to appraise a warehouse would be:
    a. income-capitalization
    b. cubic-foot
    c. square-footage
    d. index

61. The appraisal principle that relates to the market approach to value is the principle of:
    a. anticipation   b. substitution   c. conformity   d. competition

62. An accountant and an appraiser are both interested in depreciation.
    a. The accountant would be interested in straight-line depreciation.
    b. The accountant would be interested in accelerated depreciation.
    c. The appraiser would be interested in straight-line depreciation.
    d. All of these are true.

63. Urban blight results from:
    a. mixed property use
    b. deteriorating structures
    c. lower income and educational levels
    d. all of these

64. The least important factor in appraising a home for market value would be:
    a. any special amenities
    b. the tax appraisal
    c. its physical condition
    d. the neighborhood

65. An appraiser would appraise an apartment house by:
    a. capitalizing the past income
    b. capitalizing anticipated future income
    c. using the reproduction method
    d. using the market-comparison method

66. The replacement-cost method of appraising:
    a. is generally the best method for income property
    b. is never used in conjunction with other methods
    c. tends to set the upper limit of value
    d. tends to set the lower limit of value

67. A means of providing for return of your investment is:
    a. depreciation
    b. a sinking fund
    c. a reserve for depreciation
    d. profit

68. The most difficult aspect of utilizing the cost approach is in:
    a. determining adjusted gross income
    b. setting the capitalization rate
    c. determining replacement cost
    d. determining accrued depreciation

69. Allocating a percentage of total value to the land and a percentage to the improvements is known as:
    a. the allocation approach
    b. the ratio of total value to site value
    c. both a and b
    d. neither a nor b

70. A real estate appraisal would customarily be:
    a. an estimation of replacement cost
    b. an estimation of the maximum price possible
    c. an opinion made as of a particular date
    d. all of these

71. Estimating a property's value based on its future income for a specified number of years would be:
    a. the capitalization method
    b. an annuity method
    c. reversionary rights
    d. the straight-line method

72. The comparison method of appraising is:
    a. a simple method to learn
    b. used on vacant land
    c. not the desired method for income property
    d. all of these

73. Which of the following does not influence value?
    a. economic trends
    b. social trends
    c. government regulations
    d. cost

74. A property value would be adversely affected by:
    a. a neighborhood with similar values and income levels
    b. strict zoning enforcement
    c. deferred maintenance
    d. strong restrictive covenants

75. When appraising a commercial property, an appraiser would be least interested in:
    a. changes in use in the immediate vicinity
    b. the physical condition of the property
    c. the character of the neighborhood
    d. the original cost of the property

76. *Value* would be best described as:
    a. potential worth
    b. comparable recent sales price
    c. highest and best use
    d. present worth of future benefits

77. Value is best described as:
    a. cost
    b. price
    c. worth
    d. salability

78. Amenities are:
    a. elements of beauty, utility, and convenience
    b. interest payments
    c. elements of depreciation
    d. none of these

79. An example of unearned income would be:
    a. increased rents due to remodeling
    b. increased value due to more selective tenants
    c. increased income due to increased demand
    d. none of these

80. An appraisal is required:
    a. for a new subdivision in California
    b. for an FHA loan
    c. for any sale of housing
    d. all of these

81. Economic obsolescence would generally be considered:
    a. curable depreciation
    b. incurable depreciation
    c. a result of poor design or construction
    d. a result of age and wear and tear

82. Which of the following cannot be depreciated?
    a. bearing orchards
    b. a single-family house that is rented
    c. land used to raise alfalfa
    d. any of these

83. Actual rental income is best obtained by:
    a. checking the listing
    b. checking with the owner
    c. checking with tenants
    d. checking with the manager

84. The appraisal method that prices all labor and material in construction is:
    a. quantity-survey
    b. comparison
    c. capitalization
    d. unit-in-place

85. The most important factor for the average buyer of a home is:
    a. potential rent
    b. location
    c. architectural style
    d. floor plan

86. In appraisal of commercial property, the most important factor would be:
    a. the value of the improvements
    b. the location
    c. the sale price
    d. none of these

87. *Highest and best use* refers to:
    a. the greatest value of improvements
    b. the use that results in the greatest net
    c. the most beneficial use to the community
    d. none of these

88. An appraiser would be most interested in the:
    a. factors extraneous to the property
    b. price to be paid by the purchaser
    c. tax appraisal
    d. loan requested

89. As to the appraisal of a single-family dwelling, which of the following is true?
    a. Capitalization of income is the preferred method.
    b. The reproduction method is the preferred method.
    c. The market approach is accurate only with new homes.
    d. The cost approach can be used on new homes.

90. Excess land is defined as land:
    a. in excess of that used for comparable properties
    b. that does not add to the total property value
    c. not utilized by the improvements
    d. any of these

91. In appraising property with great amenity value, an appraiser would use:
    a. the reproduction method
    b. the comparison method
    c. capitalization
    d. none of these

92. Functional obsolescence can be created by:
    a. a land use not in conformance with the area
    b. an overimprovement
    c. deterioration of the driveway
    d. forces outside the property itself

93. Depth tables would be used by:
    a. surveyors
    b. an appraiser
    c. a municipal water district
    d. all of these

94. The relationship between a property and a prospective purchaser is known as:
    a. utility
    b. value
    c. contribution
    d. highest and best use

95. An appraisal is required for:
    a. a new FHA loan
    b. a new VA loan
    c. a probate sale
    d. all of these

96. To obtain a listing, a broker agrees to make a free appraisal of the property. As to this appraisal agreement, which of the following is true?
    a. It is void.
    b. The broker has violated the Real Estate Law.
    c. It is illegal.
    d. It is valid if it is an appraisal.

97. During an inflationary period, interest rates:
    a. drop and housing prices rise
    b. rise and housing prices drop
    c. and housing prices rise
    d. and housing prices drop

98. An accountant would be primarily interested in:
    a. market value
    b. book value
    c. exchange value
    d. assessed value

99. An appraiser who is concerned with the present worth of future benefits is likely using the:
    a. cost approach
    b. income approach
    c. market-comparison approach
    d. correlation method

100. Obsolescence would not include a:
    a. deteriorating neighborhood
    b. lack of closets
    c. need of painting
    d. bad design

101. In capitalization-of-income appraising, an appraiser need not consider management expenses when:
    a. the tenant provides management in lieu of rent
    b. the management is provided by a tenant
    c. the owner handles all management
    d. none of these

102. An area that would most likely maintain its value would:
    a. have income units mixed in among single-family housing
    b. have people of vastly different incomes
    c. be a new area requiring no down payments
    d. have people of similar incomes

103. In determining net income for use in the capitalization method of appraising, an appraiser would not be concerned with the:
    a. vacancy factor
    b. management costs
    c. property tax
    d. cost of borrowing money

104. Market value is best described as:
    a. the cost of a property
    b. what a property will bring at a sale
    c. the utility use to the owner
    d. none of these

105. A property owner can protect against economic depreciation by:
    a. proper property management
    b. scheduling all maintenance promptly
    c. both a and b
    d. neither a nor b

106. The cost that is most frequently overlooked in determining net income for capitalization appraising is:
    a. management expenses
    b. vacancy loss
    c. redecorating needs
    d. modernization expenses

107. The best appraisal would use:
    a. market comparison
    b. replacement cost
    c. capitalization of income
    d. all of these

108. The economic life of a frame dwelling is most nearly:
    a. 40 years   b. 60 years   c. 27 1/2 years   d. 19 years

109. Building a $200,000 home in a neighborhood of $70,000 to $100,000 homes is an example of:
    a. expanded value
    b. economic obsolescence
    c. progression
    d. functional obsolescence

110. Putting aside $1,000 a year in government bonds for five years to replace the roof is an example of:
    a. planned depreciation
    b. a sinking fund
    c. a contingency reserve
    d. a reserve for depreciation

111. A $200,000 new apartment house is to be depreciated over 40 years. The straight mortgage on it is due in 50 years for $100,000. The land is worth $10,000. When fully depreciated, the adjusted cost basis will be:
    a. $100,000   b. $200,000   c. $10,000   d. none of these

112. Capitalizing the net income and deducting the replacement cost of the improvements gives:
    a. the appraised value of the property
    b. the land valued
    c. the economic value
    d. the effective value

113. An appraiser would not obtain accelerated depreciation by using:
    a. the straight-line method
    b. the sum-of-the-digits method
    c. the 200 percent declining-balance method
    d. any of these

114. Functional obsolescence would not be caused by:
    a. surplus utility
    b. eccentric design
    c. lack of heating and cooling
    d. the proximity of a nuisance

115. By putting together four parcels of land, each worth $1,000, a property owner creates one large parcel worth $5,000. This process is known as:
    a. unearned increment
    b. assemblage
    c. growth
    d. appreciation of scale

116. To find a good comparable, an appraiser would be least interested in a sale:
    a. in another part of the city
    b. in an older neighborhood
    c. under distress conditions
    d. in which both the buyer and the seller were willing

117. The highest value would most likely be the:
    a. book value   b. loan value   c. assessed value   d. market value

118. Which value bears the least relationship to the market value?
    a. book value   b. exchange value   c. assessed value   d. loan value

119. It would be unethical for an appraiser to:
    a. appraise a property in which he or she has a disclosed interest
    b. charge an appraisal fee as a percentage of value
    c. both a and b
    d. neither a nor b

120. As to the replacement-cost method of appraising, which of the following is true?
    a. It tends to set the upper value of a property.
    b. It would be the method used for a library.
    c. It is good as to new improvements.
    d. all of these

121. Proper scientific appraisal can determine:
    a. the exact value at the time of appraisal
    b. the exact value at a future date
    c. both a and b
    d. neither a nor b

122. Which of the following values is always based on the price paid?
    a. utility value   b. market value   c. book value   d. exchange value

123. Which of these is not a method of providing for depreciation?
    a. straight-line
    b. sinking-fund
    c. obsolescence
    d. sum-of-the-digits (-years)

124. The major factor in determining the value of industrial land is:
    a. corner influence
    b. front footage
    c. square footage
    d. depreciation

125. A factor an appraiser would consider when appraising a building would be:
    a. square footage
    b. book value
    c. owner's depreciation
    d. all of these

126. When the demand for homes remains constant and the supply:
    a. remains the same, the value will decrease
    b. remains the same, the value will increase
    c. diminishes, the value will increase
    d. increases, the value will increase

127. Progression and regression in appraisal relate to:
    a. cost   b. change   c. appreciation   d. depreciation

128. A property is 15 years old, but an appraiser puts an age of 7 years on it since it has been kept up like new. This is an example of:
    a. economic age
    b. effective age
    c. physical age
    d. incorrect appraisal

129. The definition of *highest and best use* would contain which of the following phrases?
    a. net income
    b. effective gross income
    c. multiple properties
    d. income properties

130. A person engaged solely in the appraisal of real estate is required to:
    a. be a real estate broker
    b. be a real estate salesperson
    c. be an MAI
    d. none of these

131. Which of the following is the best example of functional obsolescence?
    a. massive cornices in an apartment building
    b. adverse zoning across the street
    c. a rotted mudsill
    d. decline of the neighborhood

132. The principle of substitution applies in:
    a. balancing out amenities
    b. finding an equal area
    c. substituting architectural styles
    d. all of these

133. A building can be leased as a post office or as a hardware store. Leased as a post office, the capitalization rate would:
    a. be lower than the rate used for the hardware store
    b. be higher than the rate used for the hardware store
    c. remain the same
    d. be dependent on the rental amount and not on the lessee

134. An appraiser is to appraise a store zoned for retail business only. As a retail store, expected income is $1,500 per month, but the property is leased on a long-term lease at $2,000 per month to a tenant who is using the store as a dry-cleaning plant in violation of the zoning. The appraiser should:
    a. refuse to make the appraisal
    b. make the appraisal using $1,500 per month as the estimated income
    c. make the appraisal using $2,000 per month, since there is a long-term lease
    d. use the reproduction approach, since the present income cannot be used

135. The statement "more buildings are torn down than wear out" is a definition of:
    a. physical deterioration
    b. functional obsolescence
    c. economic obsolescence
    d. none of these

136. The gross multiplier:
    a. is used primarily on single-family dwellings
    b. requires computation of all expenses
    c. is the best method for rental units
    d. may be expressed as an annual gross multiplier

137. A property is 40 years old. The present owner purchased it new and has depreciated it at 2 1/2 percent per year since then, leaving no allowance for salvage or land value. The building currently is appraised at $87,000, and the land under it is worth $200,000. The book value is:
    a. $287,000
    b. $40,000
    c. $287,000 minus depreciation
    d. zero

138. Cost represents a measure of _____ sacrifice either of materials or labor, and always represents a measure of _____ expenditure. Value, on the other hand, constitutes _____ worth of future benefits:
    a. present, present, present
    b. present, past, past
    c. present, future, present
    d. past, past, present

139. Such things as well-cared-for shrubbery and a fenced yard refer to:
    a. economic appreciation
    b. arrested depreciation
    c. the amenities of home ownership
    d. the stability of the neighborhood

140. Authorities say four agents contribute to gross income. Which of the following is not one of them?
    a. depreciation
    b. coordination or management
    c. capital
    d. land

141. A broker quotes an income figure based on 100 percent occupancy with no rental incentives given. The figure quoted is:
    a. net operating income
    b. gross scheduled income
    c. effective gross income
    d. bottom-line income

142. The subjective value of a parcel is:
    a. the exchange value
    b. the dollar value to buyer
    c. the use value to owner
    d. the loan value

143. The objective value of a parcel is most nearly:
    a. market value
    b. utility value to a seller
    c. book value
    d. loan value

144. As to the Inwood and Hoskold appraisal methods, which of the following is true?
    a. Inwood is an annuity method.
    b. Hoskold is a sinking-fund method.
    c. Both a and b are true.
    d. Neither a nor b is true.

145. Of the following reasons, which explains why replacement cost is better for new buildings than for old structures?
    a. difficulty in finding depreciation
    b. historical influence of structure on the neighborhood
    c. difficulty adjusting to 1907 materials prices
    d. the higher risks of insuring an older structure

146. A capital improvement to real property would:
    a. increase its value by the cost of the improvement
    b. increase the book value by the amount the appraisal is increased
    c. increase the book value by the cost of the improvement
    d. be written off in the year it is made

147. A commercial lot 150 feet deep loses the rear 50 feet because of condemnation.
    a. The value decreases by one third.
    b. The value per square foot increases.
    c. The front foot value increases.
    d. The lot value would not change.

148. The following are all good definitions of depreciation except:
    a. it is a loss of value from any cause
    b. it is due to wear and tear of investment property or property used in a trade or business
    c. it includes all of the influences that reduce the value of a property below its replacement cost if new
    d. it is always concerned with the intrinsic factors of property, never with the extraneous factors

149. Corner influence can most aid the value of:
    a. industrial property
    b. apartments
    c. retail stores
    d. single-family homes

150. Estimating total land value and adding the value of the improvements would:
    a. not be appropriate for newer construction
    b. be the best method for appraisal of a house
    c. tend to set the upper limit of value
    d. tend to set the lower limit of value

ANSWERS—CHAPTER 9 QUIZ

1. d. The rate is tied to risk, and since value by the capitalization method is determined by dividing rate into net, changing the rate changes the value.
2. b. The loss is $800 × 12 months = $9,600 per year; divide by the capitalization rate. $9,600 ÷ .08 = $120,000.
3. a.
4. b. Do not deduct principal payments to find net income.
5. b. Use a monthly gross multiplier of 140.
6. c. Since it is created by forces outside the property.
7. d. Price per installed unit.
8. d. Otherwise, it is a "wish."
9. a. The other neighboring properties significantly detract from the value.
10. b. Depth variance can have a significant effect on value.
11. d. Putting together several lots to form a large parcel of land.
12. d. To determine net income and capitalization rate.
13. a. The appraiser is interested in the cost to replace the structure now.
14. c. Willing seller and willing buyer.
15. d. Appraisal is based on cash value.
16. a. When no value is attributable to improvements, the property has exceeded its economic life.
17. c. It's based on condition, effective age, and construction.
18. d. And the easiest to use.
19. b. This method is most effective for new or service buildings.
20. b. A force outside the property.
21. c. Creates a replacement reserve.
22. d.
23. b.
24. a. Value remains the same.
25. b. Since it is the cost to replace minus depreciation plus the value of the land.
26. d. The other force is physical.
27. a. 5% of 300,000 = 15,000 net. $15,000 ÷ .08 = $187,500.
28. b. Value is based on possible use.
29. d. Or new structures.
30. b. The book value equals cost plus improvements minus depreciation.
31. a.
32. d.
33. b.

34. a. Answers b and c are the four elements of value.
35. c.
36. c.
37. c. Use the income capitalization method (it is an income property); $27,000 ÷ .085.
38. b. Monthly gross is $800 for the duplex.
39. d.
40. c. Member of Appraisal Institute.
41. a. A rising interest rate causes the capitalization rate to rise.
42. b.
43. a. This explains why "more buildings are torn down than wear out."
44. c. Used for comparables.
45. d.
46. c.
47. c. Divide the .09 rate into the net return for each use and subtract the cost of improvements to find the highest and best use.
48. a. $11,000 ÷ .11 = $100,000; $10,000 ÷ .10 = $100,000.
49. d.
50. a.
51. d. An appraiser uses economic life; an accountant would use 27.5 years. Both use straight-line depreciation.
52. a.
53. b. The post office lease is more secure—lower capitalization rate.
54. c.
55. a.
56. b. Land cannot be depreciated.
57. d. They should not affect the appraised value.
58. a.
59. c. Anticipated income.
60. a. Income property.
61. b. Won't pay more than necessary for an equally desirable property.
62. d.
63. d.
64. b. A previous opinion of value.
65. b.
66. c.
67. a. Profit is a return *on* your investment.
68. d.
69. c.
70. c.
71. b.
72. d.
73. d. Cost is the least important element of value.

74. c. The others keep the value up.
75. d.
76. d.
77. c.
78. a.
79. c. Not planned and without effort.
80. b.
81. b.
82. c. Land is never depreciated.
83. c. Because of lease concessions.
84. a.
85. b.
86. b.
87. b. Attributable to the land.
88. a. For economic obsolescence.
89. d.
90. d.
91. b. To balance the amenities.
92. b. Built-in obsolescence.
93. b.
94. b.
95. d.
96. d.
97. c.
98. b.
99. b. The capitalized value of future income.
100. c. This is physical depreciation; obsolescence can be functional or economic.
101. d. They are always to be considered.
102. d. Neighborhood cohesiveness.
103. d. Interest is not deductible in determining net for the capitalization approach, but it affects the capitalization rate.
104. b. With a willing buyer and a willing seller and a reasonable time to sell.
105. d. An owner can't protect against it because it is caused by forces outside the property.
106. a.
107. d. With different values attached to each method (correlation).
108. a. 27 1/2 years is for tax purposes.
109. d. Misplaced improvement.
110. b.
111. c. Land is not depreciated.
112. b.
113. a. The others are accelerated.
114. d. This is economic obsolescence.
115. b. The increase in value is a plottage increment.
116. c. The appraiser could adjust for the others.
117. d. The other values are likely less than market value.

118. a. No relationship to market value unless the property was just purchased.
119. b. An undisclosed interest would be unethical.
120. d.
121. d. All that is determined is an estimate as of a particular date.
122. c. Since it is cost plus improvements less depreciation.
123. c. Obsolescence is a cause of depreciation, not a method of providing for it.
124. c. Or size if location were given as an answer, it would be the best answer.
125. a. The owner's book value and depreciation don't affect value. The buyer's book value is based on the price paid and depreciates based on the portion of the total price allocated to improvements.

126. c. Supply and demand.
127. b. Change in value due to a house's placement in relation to values in the neighborhood.
128. b.
129. a. The highest net income allocated to the property.
130. d. There is a separate license.
131. a. Built-in obsolescence.
132. d. A person will not pay more for a property than a price at which he or she can purchase a similarly desirable and useful property.
133. a. Since the risk is lower.
134. b. Use the income that would be reasonably expected based on a permitted use.
135. c. The building exceeds its economic life.
136. d. It can also be expressed as a monthly multiplier (usually in cases of residential property).

137. d. The property is fully depreciated.
138. d.
139. c. Elements of utility, beauty, and convenience.
140. a. The other agent is labor.
141. b.
142. c. The others are objective.
143. a.
144. c.
145. a. It is difficult to determine accrued depreciation.
146. c.
147. b. Less valuable land was lost.
148. d. Economic obsolescence is a factor extraneous to the property.
149. c. More traffic and display area.
150. c. This is the cost approach, which sets ceiling on value.

CHAPTER 10

The Role of Escrow and Title Insurance Companies

ESCROW

Escrows are neutral depositories that handle the paperwork dealing with a real estate transaction. The escrow holder is agreed to by the buyer and the seller, and the agent cannot make a specified escrow a condition of the sale. Escrows balance out credits and debits for the parties and arrange settlement. They carry out the instructions of the buyers and the sellers and are bound by these instructions. They cannot change the instructions they receive or fill in blanks after the instructions are signed. They have a **fiduciary duty** (duty of trust) to both parties of the transaction. Since the escrow is the agent of both buyer and seller, only the buyer and seller are entitled to see the escrow instructions unless they have given their permission. The dual agency ends with the close of escrow, when the escrow agent has separate agency duties to deliver funds and documents to the parties. Only corporations may be escrows, and they must be bonded, although a broker may act as an escrow on his or her own sales or on sales in which he or she acts as a principal; a licensed attorney may also act as an escrow. Banks and savings and loan associations are exempt from licensing requirements. Escrows are licensed by the Corporations Commissioner.

The broker exemption is personal, so a broker cannot contract out any escrow duties to a third party. A broker cannot use a name that includes the name *escrow*. The broker must cause any trust deed to be recorded within one week of closing, or deliver it to the beneficiary with a written recommendation that it be recorded (delivery to the escrow holder is considered to be compliance). The broker must also see that both the buyer and the seller receive a statement as to the selling price within one month of closing. This is usually handled by the escrow.

Some of the duties an escrow agent would usually perform are as follows:

1. Order preliminary title search and report.
2. Obtain beneficiary statements from the lender to ascertain balances due on loans being assumed.
3. Prorate taxes, insurance, interest, rents, etc. (Taxes are prorated based on the present assessed value.)
4. Transfer insurance policies from the seller to the buyer.
5. Obtain deeds of reconveyance if refinancing is involved.
6. Draft grant deeds, trust deeds, notes, etc.
7. Obtain all necessary signatures.
8. Record all instruments.
9. Issue title insurance policies.
10. Disburse funds.
11. Issue closing statements to the parties.

To have a **valid escrow,** there must be:

1. A binding agreement between the parties.
2. Delivery of an instrument of conveyance and funds to escrow.

A **perfect escrow** exists when the escrow agent has received everything necessary for him or her to complete escrow. A **complete escrow** is an escrow in which all of the instructions have been met.

An escrow can be terminated by:

1. **Rescission:** The parties mutually agree to cancel.
2. **Expiration of the term of the escrow:** An escrow is to be completed by a specified date. If for some reason it cannot be completed as agreed upon, the escrow ends unless both parties agree in writing to an extension (amending escrow instructions). Some escrow instructions say that escrow will continue unless the parties cancel in writing.
3. **Full performance:** When escrow instructions have been signed by both parties, the escrow cannot be changed except by mutual agreement to amend the escrow instructions. A party may waive the performance of certain conditions as long as the waiver is not detrimental to the other party. The escrow company is personally liable if it violates the escrow instructions. When escrow instructions are signed after the purchase agreement, in the event of any ambiguity the escrow instructions (the later agreement) govern. Purchase contracts, such as the one included in Chapter 5, may constitute joint escrow instructions.

Escrow cannot close until funds held are **good funds** (cash or a check that has cleared). If an escrow fails to close, the escrow cannot turn funds over to either party without the approval of both parties. The wrongful refusal of a party to execute a release of funds (for one to four residential units where the buyer intends to occupy a unit) would entitle the aggrieved party to:

1. The amount of funds deposited in the escrow.
2. Treble the amount of escrow funds (but not less than $100 or more than $1,000).
3. Reasonable attorney fees.

The **Real Estate Settlement Procedures Act (RESPA),** discussed in Chapter 7, requires use of a uniform settlement statement and gives the borrower the right to inspect the statement the day before close of escrow. (The escrow must report the gross sale price to the IRS and the seller on IRS Form 1099.)

Loss of Funds

If funds are lost in escrow (embezzled) before the seller is entitled to the funds, the buyer would bear the loss. However, if funds are lost after the seller was entitled to the funds, then the seller would bear the loss as they would be seller funds.

Doctrine of Relating Back

The death of a grantor does not terminate a valid escrow or end the agency relationship. The delivery of the deed to the grantee is said to relate to (or take place upon) the grantor's deposit of the deed into escrow. This doctrine also cuts off liens against the grantor recorded after the deed was deposited in escrow.

Double Escrow

This is an escrow where one person is both buying and reselling the property, so that title never really vests in him or her.

Credits and Debits

In an escrow, the normal credits and debits are figured as follows:

Debit Seller

Existing liens being assumed
Money paid directly to the seller
Termite inspection and repair
Commission
Drawing of the grant deed
Notarizing of grant deeds
Reconveyance fees
Recording of the reconveyance
Escrow costs
Title policy (in Southern California)
Revenue stamps
New trust deed and note taken (recording)

Credit Seller

Purchase price
Balance in impound account
Prepaid insurance being assumed

Debit Buyer

Purchase price
ALTA or CLTA policy (extended-coverage policies)

Credit Buyer

Loans being assumed
Money paid directly to seller

Debit Buyer	**Credit Buyer**
Recording of deeds	Amount deposited with agent
Drafting of new trust deeds	New trust deeds given to seller
Notarizing of new trust deeds	

In addition to the normal credits and debits, the following are prorated and can be either debits or credits for the buyer or seller, depending upon the situation:

1. Rents.

2. Taxes.

3. Insurance.

4. Interest.

Prorating of costs is done as of the date the escrow closes. Prorating is done on the basis of a 30-day month and a 360-day year. The tax year is from July 1 through June 30. Interest is always paid in arrears; therefore, a house payment made on July 1 includes the interest for the month of June. The impound account is a fund collected in advance so that adequate money will be available to meet tax and insurance payments when they come due. **Recurring costs** are prepaid expenses such as taxes and insurance paid into a loan impound account. **Nonrecurring costs** are one-time charges on a closing statement.

Generally the risk of loss is on the seller until escrow closes. However, if possession is given to the buyer prior to close of escrow, the risk of loss passes to the buyer with possession. The buyer should obtain insurance coverage.

Escrow Statement Problem

Rules:

1. $2.50 will be charged for each deed drawn and for each combination of note and trust deed drawn.

2. A $3.00 recording fee will be charged for each deed and trust deed to be recorded.

3. Notary fees are $1.00 for each notarization required.

4. The seller will pay for a standard policy of title insurance.

5. The parties will split the escrow fees.

Problem:

1. The sale price is $46,500.

2. Two trust deeds are being assumed. The first trust deed balance is $31,808.93; the second trust deed balance is $5,218.27.

3. The seller is taking back a third trust deed in the amount of $5,000 as part of the purchase price.

4. Escrow costs are $163.80.

5. The commission due to the agent is 6 percent of the selling price.

6. The balance in the impound account is $2,311.47.

7. Closing is scheduled for October 15, 1996.

8. Annual taxes are $1,334.88, and they have not been paid for this year.

9. A fire insurance policy is being assumed by the buyer. It is a paid three-year policy effective November 15, 1994, and the premium was $247.32.

10. The purchaser gave the real estate salesperson a $1,000 check when he signed the deposit receipt.

11. The interest on the two trust deeds being assumed (monthly payments due on the first of each month) for the month of October is $215.98.

12. The buyer wants a California Land Title Association policy, which costs $87.35.

13. The standard policy of title insurance costs $137.15 and will be paid for by the seller.

14. Revenue stamps cost 55¢ for each $500 of seller's equity transferred.

Instructions:

Complete the escrow problem on your own paper. Show credits and debits for the buyer and the seller separately. After you are finished, check your results with those given here.

Escrow Statement

Seller		Debit	Credit
Sale price	(1)		$46,500.00
Balance of existing loans being assumed	(2)	$37,027.20	
Paid directly to seller			
New note and trust deed to seller	(3)	5,000.00	
Termite repair work			
Commission	(4)	2,790.00	
Drawing of papers ($2.50), notary fee ($1.00)	(5)	3.50	
Revenue stamps	(6)	10.45	
Reconveyance fee and recording reconveyance			
Recording of purchase money trust deed	(7)	3.00	
Pro rata fire insurance	(8)		89.31
Balance in loan trust fund (impound account)	(9)		2,311.47
Pro rata taxes	(10)	389.34	
Pro rata interest	(11)	107.99	
Escrow fee	(12)	81.90	
Title Policy	(13)	137.15	
Total		45,550.53	48,900.78
Check to seller		3,350.25	
		$48,900.78	$48,900.78

Buyer

Sale price	(1)	$46,500.00	
Balance of existing loans being assumed	(2)		$37,027.20
Paid directly to seller			
First, second, third new notes and trust deed to seller	(3)		5,000.00
Credit for loan proceeds			
Amount deposited with agent			1,000.00
Drawing of papers ($2.50), notary fee ($1.00)	(5)	3.50	
Recording of grant deed	(7)	3.00	
Pro rate fire insurance	(8)	89.31	
New fire insurance premium			
Balance in loan trust fund (impound account)	(9)	2,311.47	
Loan charges			
Pro rata taxes			389.34
Pro rata interest	(11)		107.99
Escrow fee	(12)	81.90	
ALTA and CLTA policy costs	(13)	87.35	
Total		49,076.53	43,524.53
Due from buyer to close escrow			5,552.00
		$49,076.53	$49,076.53

Explanation of Escrow Problem

1. The sale price is a credit to the seller and a debit to the buyer.

2. The sum of the loans being assumed is a debit to the seller (deduct from the sale price) and a credit to the buyer.

3. The new trust deed is a debit to the seller (used as part of the sale price) and a credit to the buyer.

4. The commission is 6 percent of the sale price and is paid by the seller.

5. The paper drawn for the seller is the grant deed, which is given to the buyer. The paper drawn for the buyer is the new third trust deed for $5,000. Since the buyer gives this deed, he or she must pay for its drafting. The party paying for drafting pays for the notary fee.

6. Revenue stamps are paid on the equity being transferred. Since $37,027.20 is being assumed, $9,472.80 is being transferred ($46,500 minus $37,027.20). Revenue stamps are $1.10 × 9 + $.55. Revenue stamps are a county tax and are paid by the seller ($1.10 per $1,000 of the seller's equity being transferred and $.55 for each $500 or portion thereof). When property is refinanced, revenue stamps are computed on the entire purchase price.

7. The seller pays to record the new trust deed given by the buyer, and the buyer pays to record the grant deed given by the seller.

8. Since the insurance is paid for in advance, it is a credit to the seller and a debit to the buyer. The policy costs $247.32, and since it is for 36 months, the cost per

month is $6.87. There are 13 months remaining, or a value of $89.31 for unused fire insurance.

9. The balance in the loan trust account is a credit to the seller and a debit to the buyer.

10. Taxes are paid on a tax year, July 1 through June 30. Since taxes have not been paid, the seller has occupied the property for 3 1/2 months without paying taxes. The seller is thus debited this amount and the buyer credited (since the buyer will have to pay the taxes for this period). Since $1,334.88 in taxes equals $111.24 per month and 3 1/2 months' taxes are involved, the figure is $389.34.

11. Interest is always paid in arrears; thus the November 1 payment, which the buyer will make, will cover the interest for the entire month of October. Since the closing is on October 15, the seller is debited a half-month's interest and the buyer is credited the same.

12. The escrow fee, according to the problem, was split between buyer and seller.

13. The standard policy of title insurance is paid by the seller, but the buyer pays for any extended-coverage policies he or she may desire, such as the ALTA policy, which protects the lender, and the CLTA policy, which protects the purchaser.

TITLE INSURANCE

Evolution of Title Insurance

Abstract of Title A summary of all recorded documents dealing with a property. (This is not necessarily a true picture of the chain of title, since documents may not all have been recorded.) An abstract does not guarantee good title. Attorneys studied the abstract and gave title opinions based solely on what was revealed in the abstract.

Certificate of Title The abstractor's opinion as to who owned the property and to what encumbrances it was subject (showed marketable title).

Guarantee of Title The abstract company actually guaranteed what it had stated. This was the beginning of the abstractor becoming an insurer.

Title Insurance Today

The **standard title insurance policy,** commonly referred to as the CLTA policy, insures that all risks are reported and insured against:

1. Forgery.
2. Lack of capacity.
3. Failure of delivery.

4. Tax liens.

5. Unknown spousal interests.

The standard policy does not cover defects known to the policyholder that were not disclosed to the insurer; easements and liens not shown by public records; rights of parties in possession; and things that, while not of record, could be ascertained by physical inspection, such as encroachment and incorrect survey. The standard policy also does not cover mining claims, water rights, or zoning limitations. The need for greater protection led to extended-coverage policies.

ALTA (American Land Title Association) Lender Policy   This policy, used to protect lenders, usually requires a survey. It expands the standard policy to include:

1. Rights of parties in possession.

2. Unrecorded liens (mechanics' liens that have not been filed).

3. Easements.

4. Claims that a correct survey or inspection would show.

5. Mining claims and water rights.

Policies to provide extended coverage to owners are also available. There are ALTA as well as CLTA (California Land Title Association) extended coverage policies. The **Standard Joint Protection Policy** is a single policy of title insurance that protects both the property owner and the lender.

No policies of title insurance insure against zoning, environmental laws, or defects known to the insured about which he or she fails to tell the insurer. When a deed is given by a minor, the title insurer will demand proof of emancipation.

Title insurance covers the named insured and his or her heirs only. A policy purchased by a previous owner offers no protection to the present owner. Title insurance is the best protection of title yet devised. In California it is used with a grant deed. Title insurance shows marketable title (title free from objectionable liens and encumbrances). To obtain title insurance, the owner must have a legal description on the deed (the address is not sufficient). The title insurance company must defend the owner in a legal action regarding title, and is liable for his or her loss up to the policy limits.

Preliminary Report   The computerized or microfilm records of the title company covering all property within a county are known as the **title plant.** After studying the records, the insurance company first issues a **preliminary title report,** which describes the property and encumbrances (the state of the title). It is *not* a policy of insurance. It is issued prior to the title policy, which normally is issued at the close of escrow.

Color of Title   This is no title at all, just an appearance of ownership. An example would be a person who receives and records a forged deed.

Cloud on Title   This is any condition discovered by a title search that could affect the title.

In Southern California, the seller normally pays for the standard policy of title insurance; in Northern California, the buyer normally pays. Extended-coverage policies normally are paid for by the buyer.

Rebate Law   Title companies and escrows must charge for their services and use their best efforts to collect. Rebates, kickbacks, or favored treatment are prohibited. Rebates to licensees from structural pest control firms and home protection companies are also prohibited.

CHAPTER 10 QUIZ

1. Which of the following may *not* engage in the escrow business?
   a. an individual who is not a real estate broker or attorney
   b. a bank
   c. a domestic corporation
   d. a foreign corporation

2. An escrow prorates based on _____ days in a year.
   a. 300   b. 360   c. 365   d. 370

3. In a buyer's closing statement, the selling price is:
   a. a credit to the buyer   c. a debit to the seller
   b. a debit to the buyer   d. none of these

4. A buyer's escrow statement would *not* show:
   a. the amount in the seller's impound account
   b. unpaid taxes
   c. the value of unused insurance
   d. points to be paid by the seller

5. The signed escrow instructions disagree with the prior purchase contract. As to the disagreement, which of the following is true?
   a. Parol evidence is admissible to discover true intent.
   b. The courts would have to decide what the agreement is.
   c. The purchase contract prevails.
   d. The escrow instructions prevail.

6. Which of the following, prorated, would be a credit on the seller's closing statement?
   a. prepaid insurance   c. both a and b
   b. prepaid rents of tenants   d. neither a nor b

7. Which of the following will not terminate an escrow?
   a. agreement of the principals   c. inability to meet a contingency
   b. the broker's order to terminate   d. none of these

8. A fire insurance policy cost $360 for three years. Six-and-a-half months after the insurance policy is taken out, the building is sold and the policy is assumed. On a closing statement:
   a. the insurance will be split using a short rate
   b. the seller would be debited $65
   c. the buyer would be credited $65
   d. the seller would be credited $295 and the buyer debited this amount

9. Which of the following is *not* a credit in a seller's closing statement?
   a. prepaid taxes   c. a standard policy of title insurance
   b. prepaid insurance   d. none of these

10. The closing statements the buyer and seller get from escrow:
    a. are acknowledged   c. are always different
    b. are identical   d. both a and b

11. An escrow agent is most likely to get into trouble if he or she:
    a. represents both parties
    b. accepts escrow instructions containing blanks to be filled in by him or her after escrow instructions are signed
    c. holds funds after close of escrow
    d. engages in a double escrow

12. In the absence of a closing date, the escrow should close:
    a. within 30 days   c. within a reasonable period of time
    b. within 60 days   d. escrow cannot close until a date is agreed upon

13. A buyer assumes a trust deed. On the buyer's closing statement, it would be shown as a:
    a. credit   b. debit   c. balance factor   d. none of these

14. In an escrow statement, the term *recurring costs* pertains to:
    a. title insurance fees
    b. insurance prorations
    c. impound account items
    d. recording fees

15. A broker gets a deal into escrow. After all papers are signed, both the buyer and the seller die. The escrow agent should:
    a. await the instructions of the heirs
    b. return all monies and cancel escrow
    c. await the decision of the broker
    d. continue with escrow

16. Possession in a real estate sale, in the absence of any agreement, should be given:
    a. prior to close of escrow
    b. at close of escrow
    c. within 30 days of close of escrow
    d. within a reasonable time

17. A 30-day escrow cannot be completed during the set time.
    a. The broker can extend the escrow.
    b. The escrow remains valid until completed.
    c. Both the seller and buyer must agree to an amendment of the escrow instructions or the escrow is canceled.
    d. It is a perfect escrow.

18. The broker's commission is normally paid:
    a. when the broker obtains a buyer ready, willing, and able to buy
    b. when funds are deposited in escrow
    c. when escrow closes
    d. none of these

19. Escrow would be automatically canceled by:
    a. the death of the buyer
    b. the death of the seller
    c. the request of the broker
    d. none of these

20. The term *binding contract and conditional delivery* describes:
    a. a valid escrow
    b. a complete escrow
    c. a perfect escrow
    d. none of these

21. A seller delivers a grant deed to escrow after escrow instructions have been signed. He asks that it be returned to him so that he can have an attorney check it.
    a. The escrow holder must return the deed if so instructed.
    b. The return of the deed constitutes rescission by the seller.
    c. The escrow holder cannot return the deed based on the seller's request.
    d. The request, to be honored, must be written.

22. Escrow companies are primarily under the jurisdiction of the:
    a. Real Estate Commissioner
    b. Corporations Commissioner
    c. state banking commission
    d. none of these

23. A broker can, without being licensed as an escrow, handle the escrows on transactions where he or she:
    a. acts as a principal
    b. represents the buyer
    c. represents the seller
    d. any of these

24. On a real estate closing statement, prepaid rent is always a:
    a. credit to the seller
    b. debit to the buyer
    c. debit to the seller
    d. none of these

25. An escrow company may:
    a. give rebates to brokers for sending business
    b. fill in blanks in the escrow instructions
    c. disregard instructions received from a broker after the escrow instructions are signed
    d. none of these

26. The Rebate Law:
    a. prohibits brokers from rebating commissions to nonlicensees
    b. prohibits all finder's fees
    c. requires escrows to treat brokers like everyone else
    d. all of these

27. An item such as "liens to be assumed by buyer" would be found in a seller's closing statement under:
    a. the credit column
    b. the debit column
    c. assumption costs
    d. none of these

28. An impound account would belong to:
    a. a trustee   b. a trustor   c. a beneficiary   d. none of these

29. A title company holding papers for an escrow is a(n):
    a. broker   b. agent   c. subagent   d. none of these

30. An escrow officer alters a deed after it has been signed to convey property other than agreed.
    a. The grantee gets title, but escrow is liable to grantor for damages.
    b. The title remains with the grantor.
    c. The deed conveys the property originally described, not the later modification.
    d. None of these is true.

31. Which of the following is false?
    a. A broker may sometimes act as an escrow.
    b. A broker may have a financial interest in an escrow company.
    c. Escrow companies are under the jurisdiction of the Corporations Commissioner.
    d. None of these is false.

32. Escrow closes on the 15th day of February (28 days). The seller receives $500 rent for the month of February. The seller:
    a. owes the buyer $250
    b. owes the buyer more than $250
    c. owes the buyer less than $250
    d. keeps the entire $500

33. Recording costs on an escrow would be paid by:
    a. the broker
    b. the party drafting the instrument
    c. the party receiving the instrument
    d. the county recorder's office

34. On an escrow the daily prorated charge for a three-year insurance policy costing $97.20 would be:
    a. 20 cents   b. 9 cents   c. 11 cents   d. none of these

35. A buyer would get the least protection from:
    a. an abstract
    b. a standard policy of title insurance
    c. a certificate of title
    d. a guarantee of title

36. A standard policy of title insurance covers:
    a. the rights of the party in possession
    b. incompetence of any of the parties
    c. zoning restrictions
    d. encroachment

37. An extended coverage policy of title insurance does not cover:
    a. encroachment   b. incorrect survey   c. easements   d. zoning

38. Title insurance is *not* available if:
    a. the deed does not include a legal description
    b. the lender is not located within the state
    c. the deed does not mention consideration
    d. all of these

39. A title insurance company is least likely to physically inspect property for:
    a. a standard policy
    b. an ALTA policy
    c. an extended-coverage policy
    d. none of these

40. To obtain marketable title, a person who is claiming his or her interest under adverse possession could:
    a. obtain a policy of title insurance
    b. obtain a quitclaim deed from the record owner
    c. start a quiet title action
    d. either b or c

41. The usual way for a buyer to ensure that he or she is getting marketable title is to obtain:
    a. an abstract
    b. a policy of title insurance
    c. a grant deed
    d. a warranty deed

42. *Title plant* refers to all records relative to real estate transactions in a:
    a. city   b. township   c. county   d. subdivision

43. A buyer would be protected against a right of a party in possession by:
    a. a standard title insurance policy
    b. an extended-coverage title insurance policy
    c. either a or b
    d. neither a nor b

44. The files of a title company of recorded documents on microfilm are known as:
    a. a grantor/grantee index
    b. a title plant
    c. the Torrens title system
    d. none of these

45. A sale takes place on January 1. There is $1,800 in the impound account. Proration would be:
    a. half to the buyer, half to the seller
    b. half to the buyer after expenses
    c. all to the buyer
    d. none of these

46. The exact history of conveyances and encumbrances affecting title to a property is called:
    a. an abstract   b. a title report   c. a chain of title   d. ownership

47. Which of the following is *not* covered by an extended-coverage policy of title insurance?
    a. defects known to the buyer
    b. a mistake in property line
    c. a deed that was never delivered
    d. a forged deed

48. A standard policy of title insurance does *not* cover:
    a. unrecorded liens
    b. incorrect marital status
    c. an incompetent grantor
    d. a forged document

49. A preliminary title report:
    a. describes the property and encumbrances
    b. provides interim insurance until a policy can be issued
    c. can be used in lieu of an escrow
    d. is issued to the buyer after close of escrow

50. On a closing statement, due and unpaid taxes would be:
    a. a credit to the buyer
    b. a debit to the seller
    c. both a and b
    d. neither a nor b

51. Closing is scheduled for May 20, 1996; the second property tax installment has been paid. On the buyer's closing statement, taxes are:
    a. a debit   b. a credit   c. an asset   d. a liability

52. A home is sold on August 31, with taxes being prorated.
    a. The buyer owes the seller for two months' taxes.
    b. The buyer owes the seller for three months' taxes.
    c. The seller owes the buyer for two months' taxes.
    d. The seller owes the buyer for three months' taxes.

53. *Impounds* refers to:
    a. indefeasible leases
    b. fixed rates of interest
    c. reserves
    d. all monies held in escrow

54. Who has primary responsibility for reporting sale information to the IRS?
   a. the seller   b. the buyer   c. the broker   d. the escrow agent
55. On a closing statement, an existing mortgage that is to be assumed by the buyer would be shown as:
   a. a debit to the buyer
   b. a credit to the buyer
   c. a debit to the seller
   d. both b and c

ANSWERS—CHAPTER 10 QUIZ

1. a. An escrow must be one of these or a corporation.
2. b. And 30 days in a month.
3. b. And a credit to the seller.
4. d. They would not affect the buyer.
5. d. Escrow is the later agreement.
6. a. The seller paid it in advance.
7. b. The broker is not a party to escrow.
8. d. Prorated at $10 per month.
9. c. But it could be a debit.
10. c. They have different credits and debits.
11. b.
12. c.
13. a. It balances against the sale price.
14. c. Taxes and insurance.
15. d. Unless representatives of the deceased agree to cancel.
16. b.
17. c.
18. c. But is earned when the buyer's offer is accepted.
19. d.
20. a.

21. c. Both parties must agree.
22. b.
23. d.
24. c. And a credit to buyer.
25. c. The broker is not a party to escrow.
26. c. Also applies to title insurers.
27. b. But is a buyer credit.
28. b. It contains prepaid taxes and insurance, which were paid by the trustor.
29. b. A dual agent of the buyer and the seller prior to closing. After closing, it has separate agency duties.
30. b. Alteration voids the deed.
31. d. All are true.
32. a. Prorated based on a 30-day month.
33. c. The party giving the instrument pays for drafting.
34. b. Divide by 36, then by 30.
35. a. Just a recorded history.
36. b. Insures grantor competency.
37. d. Zoning is not covered by any policy.
38. a.

39. a. Does not cover risks discoverable by inspection.
40. d.
41. b.
42. c.
43. b.
44. b.
45. d. The impound account belongs to the seller, but taxes and insurance are prorated.
46. c. Abstract shows recorded history.
47. a.
48. a. It covers liens of record.
49. a. And conditions of the policy the insurer will issue.
50. c. Since the buyer must pay the seller's obligation.
51. a. Taxes are paid through June.
52. c. Taxes are not yet due, so they are unpaid from June.
53. c. For taxes and insurance.
54. d. Reported on Form 1099.
55. d.

Landlord and Tenant Relations

Nonfreehold estates are leasehold interests. There are various types of leasehold interests, as well as various types of leases. The Statute of Frauds requires that leases for more than one year be in writing to be enforceable.

LEASEHOLD INTERESTS

Estate for Years This is an interest in real property for a fixed period. These are most common in commercial or industrial leases, where the estate ends with the lease. A lease for recreational property from June 1 to October 1 of the same year would be an estate for years, since it is for a definite fixed period.

Maximum Durations of Estates for Years

Agricultural leases	51 years
Residential property leases	99 years
Mineral, oil, and gas leases	99 years

Periodic Tenancy A periodic tenancy has no set expiration; it is a tenancy from period to period, such as week to week or month to month. (It automatically renews unless notice is given.) Automatic-renewal clauses in leases must be placed in large type just above where the lessee signs.

To terminate a periodic tenancy, either party gives a written notice to vacate. The notice period must be for the length of the rental period (but not less than 15 days). However, the notice period does have to exceed 30 days except when a tenant has been in the property for 12 months or more; in this case the notice must be for 60 days.

(Notice must be personally delivered or affixed to the property.) For mobile home parks, the notice period must be 60 days.

To raise the rent on a periodic tenancy, the tenant must also be given a 30-day notice. However, if the rent increase will result in a rent more than 10 percent greater than rent charged within the preceding 12 months, then the notice must be for 60 days.

Tenancy at Will   This estate extends for an indefinite period, and a tenant at will is entitled to at least 30 days' notice to vacate. In a tenancy at will, the tenant comes into possession with the permission of the landlord but without a tenancy agreement. An example would be a landlord giving possession to a prospective tenant prior to a lease agreement.

Tenancy at Sufferance   This is a tenancy created when a tenant holds over after expiration of a lease. No notice to vacate is required to terminate a tenancy at sufferance. A tenant at sufferance can be ejected much like a trespasser. If the landlord accepts rent from the tenant at sufferance after the lease expires, the tenant becomes a tenant from period to period, which requires notice to terminate.

LEASES

A verbal lease for one year or less is valid (this is an exception to the Statute of Frauds). The **lessor** is the landlord; the **lessee** is the tenant. To be valid, a written lease must be signed by the lessor. The lessee does not always have to sign the lease to be bound. The lessee can show acceptance of the lease after receipt of the lease by paying rent or taking possession of the premises. To be recorded, a lease must be acknowledged by the lessor.

Lease Requirements

A lease must:

- be written if for more than one year
- identify the leased premises
- identify lessor and lessee
- indicate rent
- indicate any time period (if other than periodic tenancy)
- be signed by lessor
- have competent lessor and lessee
- show any provisions for lease renewal in boldface type

Leases in Spanish

If a lease of more than one month was negotiated primarily in Spanish, or if the lessee requests it, the lessor must furnish a Spanish translation of the lease.

Security Deposits

The tenant is entitled to actual damages plus $600 in exemplary damages if the landlord, in bad faith, fails to return a security deposit within 21 days of regaining possession. In the case of a sale, the new landlord is jointly and severally liable with the selling landlord for repayment of the security deposit. The landlord can retain that part of the deposit required to repair damages, or to apply to rent owing. Security deposits that include the last month's rent for unfurnished units cannot exceed two months' rent; for furnished units the limit is three months' rent. Nonrefundable security deposits or cleaning fees are not allowed. Security deposits do not bear interest unless agreed to by the parties or required by local ordinance.

A nonrefundable applicant screening fee of up to $30 may be charged (a copy of credit report received must be given to the applicant upon request).

Duties of Landlord and Tenant

For residential leases, the landlord must keep plumbing, heating, and electrical systems in a safe operating condition; keep areas under landlord control in a proper and clean condition; and keep the premises free of pests and weathertight. The landlord must allow the tenant the **quiet enjoyment** of the premises. (Possession without interference of reasonable use.)

The tenant must pay rent on time, keep his or her unit clean, refrain from damaging or defacing the premises, dispose of garbage properly, use fixtures and appliances properly, use the premises only for the intended purpose, obey rules, give proper notice to vacate, return all keys, and leave premises in a clean condition. The landlord cannot prohibit a tenant from installing a satellite dish on an area controlled by the tenant.

Rental Offset   When a landlord fails to make obligated repairs, the tenant can make repairs and deduct actual out-of-pocket costs of up to one month's rent from the rent. This tenant remedy cannot be taken more than twice in any 12-month period.

Entry by Landlord   If there is no agreement as to entry, then the landlord may enter the premises if (1) the tenant consents to entry, (2) there is an emergency necessitating entry, or (3) the landlord has given reasonable notice (24 hours) to enter to make repairs or to show the property to prospective purchasers, contractors, lenders, etc.

Disclosure by Owner   The owner of a multiunit property must disclose to the tenant the names and addresses of all persons authorized to manage the premises or to receive notices. Leases and sale contracts must disclose that the California Department of Justice and local law enforcement agencies maintain a list of persons who must register as sex offenders and that there is a sex offender 900 number (**Megan's Law**).

Termination of Lease

A lease is terminated under any of the following conditions:

1. Failure of the landlord to give possession.

2. Failure of the landlord to make required repairs. (But the tenant can, after reasonable notice, make the repair and deduct the expense from the rent, providing repairs don't exceed one month's rent. This remedy is available twice in any 12-month period.) Residential leases have an **implied warranty of habitability.**

3. Failure of the tenant to pay rent as agreed.

4. **Destruction of the premises** (if there is no agreement to the contrary).

5. Use of the premises for illegal or unauthorized purposes.

6. **Breach** of any material condition of the lease.

7. **Eminent domain.** The taking of property by eminent domain terminates the lease (the tenant would generally also be compensated).

8. **Merger.** When a tenant buys the property, the lesser interest (lease) is merged into the ownership, so the lease is extinguished.

9. **Foreclosure** of a mortgage recorded prior to the lease, unless the mortgagee agreed to the lessee's priority right to possession.

Eviction for Nonpayment of Rent

1. **Three-day notice to quit or pay rent.** If the tenant fails to leave or pay rent within three days of receipt of notice, a court eviction is required.

2. **Unlawful detainer** (court eviction action). If the tenant fails to justify nonpayment of rent within five days, it results in forfeiture of the lease, damages assessed to the tenant, and a court order to vacate the premises.

A number of individuals have gone into business as **unlawful detainer assistants** helping tenants fight evictions. Because of abuses of the legal process, these assistants must now post a $25,000 bond and if landlords are awarded damges for the acts of unlawful detainer assistants, they can recover their damages from the bond.

Writ of Possession   Issued by court and given to sheriff for immediate possession.

Constructive Eviction   In every lease it is implied that the tenant shall have *quiet enjoyment* and possession. If the landlord deprives the tenant of quiet enjoyment of the premises, the tenant can consider the lease ended by what amounts to eviction. For example: A landlord who cuts off the water supply has created a constructive eviction. A landlord cannot willfully terminate any utility service to the tenant, subject to a $100-per-day penalty. Other examples of interference with quiet enjoyment would be making needless repairs, allowing other tenants to unreasonably disturb a tenant, and wrongful entry. The landlord must provide heating, plumbing, and weather protection and keep the dwelling pest free for it to be considered fit for human habitation.

Retaliatory Eviction   The landlord cannot retaliate with an eviction within 180 days of a tenant's complaint to the health department or other public agency, or for the tenant's activity in a tenant organization.

Lease-related Terms

Renewal of Lease A new lease.

Extension of Lease A continuation under the old lease.

Demise Transfer of a leasehold interest.

Gross Lease A lease with a fixed or *flat* rental (flat lease).

Net-Net-Net Lease Also known as a *net lease;* the tenant pays taxes and expenses and the landlord gets the net amount (a long-term lease).

Percentage Lease The lessor gets a percentage of gross income. This type of lease is used on commercial property. Generally, a business with a higher markup pays a higher percentage. Percentage leases should be coupled with a covenant to remain in business and a minimum rent payment.

Broker's Commission The commission for procuring a tenant is normally a percentage of the gross to be paid under the lease. On multiyear leases, the percentage may be greater for the first year and lower for later years and renewals. Property management contracts generally provide for a percentage of the gross and a minimum fee. On a percentage lease, the broker's commission is normally a percentage of the minimum rent for the lease, which is paid at the time the lease is entered into, plus a yearly payment based on a percentage of the amount that was received above the minimum rent (so it is a percentage of rent actually received).

Recapture Clause This is a clause in a percentage lease giving the lessor the right to take back the premises in the event that an anticipated volume is not reached.

Exculpatory Clause A *hold-harmless* clause in a lease, in which the lessee agrees to indemnify the landlord for any losses suffered because of the condition of the premises. Exculpatory clauses are not valid in residential leases.

Escalator Clause A clause in a lease that allows rents to rise or fall based on some determining factor.

Assignment and Sublease Unless a lease prohibits subleasing or assignments, the lessee can assign or sublease the property.

Assignment The transfer by a lessee of all his or her rights and interests under a lease to another.

Assignor Gives assignment and remains secondarily liable under the lease (if the assignee does not pay, the assignor is still liable).

Assignee Takes over the assignor's interest and is primarily liable under the lease. The assignee makes rent payments directly to the lessor.

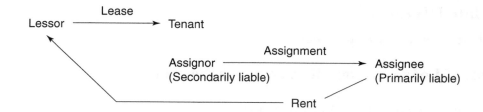

Sublease The lessee becomes a lessor by leasing to a sublessee. The lessee remains primarily liable under the lease and collects rent from the sublessee. The sublessee is liable to the lessee and not to the lessor.

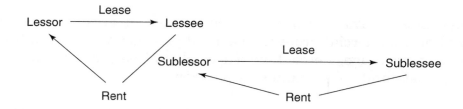

Sandwich Lease This is a lease between parties other than the original lessor and the party in possession. (This may also refer to the interest of the sublessor in any sublease.)

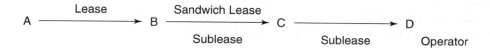

Surrender This is a mutual agreement of the parties to terminate a lease. It ends all obligations under the lease.

Abandonment When rent has been due for 14 days and there is reason to believe the tenant has abandoned the premises, a formal notice can be given. If the tenant fails to respond affirmatively, then the fact of abandonment is established. (If the tenant abandons personal property at the end of the lease, the landlord can dispose of it after statutory notice is given.)

Rent Control Rent control is considered a valid exercise of police power. However, when a tenant vacates a property, under most rent control ordinances the owner may establish a new rental rate without limitation.

While a landlord in rent-controlled areas may go out of business, the landlord cannot place the property in rental use again for two years. The landlord must provide a 120-day **Notice of Intent** to withdraw the residential rental from the market. If a tenant is at least 62 years of age or is disabled and has occupied the rental for at least one year, then the notice to remove the property from the rental market must be a one-year notice.

Mobile Home Parks and Leases

A tenant in a mobile home park is entitled to a 12-month lease upon request at the prevailing month-to-month charge. A copy of the **Mobile Home Residency Law** must be attached to all rental agreements and must be given annually to all tenants. Parks must provide 60 days' notice to terminate a periodic tenancy and can terminate only for specified causes. A 60-day notice is also required to increase rents.

A park can charge a security deposit of two months' space rent. The tenant can request return of the deposit if the tenant has paid rent promptly for 12 consecutive months. When a park is sold the seller must deposit in escrow an amount equal to the security deposits. Deposits held for more than 12 months must be refunded to any tenants entitled to refunds. The park need not pay interest on the deposit.

Parks having over 50 units must have a resident manager. Parks must allow tenant meetings to be held within the park. They cannot charge sales fees for services not rendered.

A park can require that a unit be removed upon sale of the unit only if it is 25 years old or older. A park owner who wants to sell the park must provide notice to the resident association not less than 30 days and not more than one year before making an agreement to sell or offering to sell.

A park cannot prohibit a homeowner from keeping at least one pet, subject to reasonable park rules.

CHAPTER 11 QUIZ

1. "Of definite duration" would most likely refer to:
   a. a life estate
   b. a periodic tenancy
   c. a nonfreehold estate
   d. an estate for years

2. A lessee notifies the lessor that he is going to vacate because the lessor raised the rent. By mutual written agreement, the lessee agrees to continue on a year-to-year basis at the new rent (paid monthly). Either party has the right to cancel by written notice prior to the beginning of the next year. This is:
   a. a tenancy at sufferance
   b. a periodic tenancy
   c. a tenancy at will
   d. an estate for years

3. The maximum lease on agricultural acreage is:
   a. 1 year
   b. 10 years
   c. 51 years
   d. 99 years

4. Although Mr. and Mrs. Sanchez's five-year lease has expired, they continue to live on the property and pay their rent semiannually. They have a:
   a. month-to-month tenancy
   b. periodic tenancy
   c. tenancy at sufferance
   d. tenancy at will

5. A tenant rents a summer cottage from June 1 to September 1. This is a(n):
   a. estate for years
   b. periodic tenancy
   c. tenancy at will
   d. tenancy at sufferance

6. A tenant at sufferance is a:
   a. tenant on a lease
   b. slum dwelling
   c. tenant on a month-to-month basis (with no lease)
   d. tenant who stays on after the lease expires

7. A rental house is located on a farm. The maximum legal lease is:
   a. 51 years
   b. 99 years
   c. 50 years
   d. 10 years

8. The landlord under a lease:
   a. increases the value
   b. subrogates his interests
   c. subordinates his rights
   d. cannot sell his rights

9. A sublessee could be described as a(n):
   a. tenant
   b. assignee
   c. owner
   d. assignor

10. A *gross lease* means the lessee pays:
    a. a percentage of the gross
    b. a percentage of the net
    c. all owner costs plus rent
    d. a flat rent

11. Which of the following is true with respect to the assignment of a lease?
    a. The original lessee is the sole party liable for the payment of rent.
    b. It is the same as a sublease.
    c. The original lessee would still retain a right to use the property for a limited time.
    d. The entire leasehold is transferred.

12. To maximize the income of a lessor as to commercial property with increasing desirability, the lessor should insist on a:
    a. gross lease
    b. percentage lease
    c. net lease
    d. long-term lease

13. A lease whereby the lessee pays the property tax is probably a:
    a. percentage lease
    b. net lease
    c. residential lease
    d. sandwich lease

14. A lessor gives a lessee a lease for two years. The lessee does not get around to signing it but moves in.
    a. The lease is valid though unsigned because of the lessee's partial performance.
    b. The lease is valid but unenforceable.
    c. The lease is invalid because of the Statute of Frauds.
    d. The lessee has a month-to-month tenancy.

15. Margaret leases Nathan's store for one year under a verbal lease. Margaret fails to take possession and indicates that she will not be bound by the lease.
    a. Margaret is liable under the lease.   c. The lease is illegal (because it is verbal).
    b. The lease is voidable.   d. The lease is unenforceable.

16. A tenant wishes to record her lease.
    a. She must have signed it.   c. It must have been signed by the lessor.
    b. It must have been witnessed.   d. All of these are true.

17. A lessee transfers all of his interests. The transferee would be the:
    a. sublessee   b. assignor   c. sublessor   d. assignee

18. Which of the following would pay the lowest percentage on a percentage lease?
    a. a music store   c. a prescription drugstore
    b. a furniture store   d. a supermarket

19. The highest percentage on a percentage lease would probably be paid by a:
    a. supermarket   c. shoe repair shop
    b. barber shop   d. parking lot

20. The term *demise* is related to which word?
    a. alienate   b. intestate   c. probate   d. executor

21. A landlord wished to evict four families who were behind in their rents but did not want to incur legal expenses. The landlord cut off the water supply to the tenants for 30 days. If a court later penalized the landlord for this action, the maximum penalty would be:
    a. $100   b. $400   c. $3,000   d. $12,000

22. A lease that does not involve the party in possession and the owner would be:
    a. an assignment   b. a sublease   c. a sandwich lease   d. both b and c

23. A lease prohibits assignment without the approval of the lessor. The lessee assigns the lease without approval. The assignment is:
    a. illegal   b. void   c. voidable   d. unenforceable

24. As to a lease, which of the following would be an implied covenant?
    a. term   b. rent   c. quiet enjoyment   d. none of these

25. Albert grants Frank an estate for a lesser period than Albert has. Frank has a:
    a. reversionary interest   c. remainder interest
    b. fee simple interest   d. leasehold

26. A tenant under a 10-year lease at $1,000 per month decides to go out of business. The premises currently are worth $1,500 per month. She would be best off to:
    a. assign the lease   b. sublet   c. rescind the lease   d. none of these

27. A lease clause that allows rent to fluctuate based on some stated criterion would be a(n):
    a. up-and-down clause   c. variable clause
    b. escalator clause   d. alienation clause

28. Gianni enters into a percentage lease as a tenant. His rent is likely based on a percentage of his:
    a. inventory   c. net income after taxes
    b. net income before taxes   d. gross receipts

29. An estate for years would be created by:
    a. operation of law   b. implication   c. express agreement   d. escheat

30. A tenant on a five-year lease abandons the premises. The lessor may not:
    a. sue for the balance due on the lease
    b. sue for the rent currently due
    c. rerent to mitigate damages
    d. lease for a lower rent than the previous tenant paid

31. A landlord can insist on a nonrefundable:
    a. cleaning deposit
    b. tenant screening fee
    c. security deposit
    d. none of the above

32. The efficiency of an office building would be measured by:
    a. ratio of rentable space to total space
    b. rents received
    c. length of leases
    d. the vacancy factor

33. Jones had not raised tenant Smith's apartment rent in 9 years. Jones notifies Smith that the rent, which was $600 per month, will be raised to $1,100. The notice of increased rent must be:
    a. for the length of the rent paying period
    b. 30 days notice
    c. 60 days notice
    d. a one year notice

34. What do residential tenants and owners of condominium units have in common?
    a. Both have an estate in real estate.
    b. Both have fee interest.
    c. Both have nonfreehold interests.
    d. both a and c

35. A lease does not specify when the monthly rent is due. It would be due:
    a. on the first of each month
    b. by the 10th of each month
    c. on the 15th of each month
    d. at the end of each rent-paying period

36. A lease failed to state its term. The lease would be:
    a. an estate for years
    b. a month-to-month tenancy
    c. a tenancy at will
    d. a tenancy at sufferance

37. To be recorded, a lease must be acknowledged by:
    a. the notary public
    b. the lessor
    c. the lessee
    d. either b or c

38. A landlord may not:
    a. charge a higher rent for the first month's occupancy
    b. change the tenant rules
    c. give a 30-day notice to vacate without specifying the reason
    d. do any of the above

39. A clause that relieves a landlord of any liability for injury to a tenant, would be a(n):
    a. exculpatory clause
    b. habendum clause
    c. dragnet clause
    d. escalator clause

40. A tenant who received permissive possession without a tenancy agreement, would have a:
    a. month-to-month tenancy
    b. tenancy at will
    c. tenancy at sufferance
    d. trespasser's interest

41. Jones has been Smith's tenant for 13 months on a month-to-month tenancy. To evict Jones, Smith must give Jones a:
    a. 3-day notice to quit
    b. 30-day notice
    c. 60-day notice
    d. one-year notice

42. In the question above, if Jones had only been a tenant for 6 months then the notice to vacate would have to be for at least:
    a. 15 days   b. 30 days   c. 60 days   d. one year

43. As to unlawful detainer assistants, they:
    a. cannot charge for services
    b. must post a $10,000 bond
    c. must post a $25,000 bond
    d. cannot advertise

44. Smith decides to evict Ms. Jones, who is confined to a wheelchair, because the income from the rent controlled unit is not sufficient. Smith wants to use the space for storage. His notice to vacate must be for:
    a. 3 days   b. 30 days   c. 60 days   d. one year

45. Mrs. Aaron, who lives in a mobile home park, has just purchased a dog as a companion. The park has notified Mrs. Aaron that she must vacate the park within 60 days or get rid of the dog since park rules clearly prohibit pets. Mrs. Jones:
    a. must comply with the notice
    b. should tell park management that she is entitled to a one-year notice
    c. can sue the park for retaliatory eviction
    d. is entitled to keep her dog subject to reasonable restrictions

ANSWERS—CHAPTER 11 QUIZ

1. d. By definition.
2. b. Tenancy is year to year.
3. c.
4. b. Six-month periods.
5. a. Tenancy is for a definite period.
6. d. Or who gives notice and fails to leave.
7. b. It is residential.
8. c. Of possession to the tenant.
9. a. Of the sublessor.
10. d.
11. d. But the assignor remains secondarily liable.
12. b. Income would increase with sales.
13. b. The lessee pays all expenses.
14. a. The lessee has accepted the lease by moving in.
15. a. A lease for one year or less is an exception to the Statute of Frauds.
16. c. And acknowledged.
17. d. The assignee is primarily liable on the lease.
18. d. Lower markup.
19. d. Up to 80 percent of gross.
20. a. It is a transfer (alienation) of a lease.
21. d. $100 per day for four tenants.
22. d.
23. c. At the option of the lessor.
24. c. The landlord will not interfere with tenant rights.
25. d.
26. b. And take advantage of the higher rent value.
27. b.
28. d. Never net, because there may be none.
29. c. Since it is for a definite period.
30. a. Can sue as rent becomes due.
31. b. Up to $30.
32. a.
33. c. Since rent increase is more than 10 percent.
34. a. Tenant has leasehold estate.
35. d. Although parties usually specify at beginning of each period.
36. b.
37. b. Lessor acknowledges before a notary.
38. a. This would be regarded as a nonrefundable deposit.
39. a. Unenforceable for residential leases.
40. b.
41. c. Since over 12 months as tenant.
42. b. Since less than one year tenant.
43. c.
44. d. Disabled or 62 years old and a tenant for at least one year.
45. d. One pet allowed in mobile home parks.

Land-Use Planning, Subdivisions, and Other Public Controls

URBAN GROWTH

Some metropolitan areas have grown to form an urban sprawl consisting of many communities. This is known as a **megalopolis.**

   Normally city growth follows a pattern or patterns.

- **Concentric Circle Growth** where a city grows out from a nucleus in all directions with land use based on distance from the center of the city.

- **Strip Development** where the growth follows an artery such as a river or highway as a relatively narrow but long development.

- **Axial Growth** where growth follows transportation arteries from the center of a city, much like the spokes of a wheel.

- **Sector Growth** where growth is from the center of a city in all directions but land use patterns resemble pieces of a pie.

- **Multiple Nuclei Growth** where a city grows from numerous centers rather than a single central area.

PUBLIC CONTROL AUTHORITIES

Planning Commission

Every city and county must have a Planning Commission, which is responsible for a long-term general plan. Zoning must generally be consistent with the adopted general plan (under the **consistency doctrine**). The general plan must include the following seven elements: land use, circulation, housing, open space, conservation, safety, and noise.

Local Building Inspector

This official issues building permits and enforces local and state codes. Wherever the local and state codes disagree, the more stringent version applies.

State Controls

State minimum standards of housing are set forth in the California Housing Act, which is part of the Health and Safety Code. Drainage, plumbing, water, and sewage are under the control of the state Department of Public Health, and are enforced by the local health officer.

ZONING

Zoning is local governmental control of land use (lot size, use, setbacks, height, etc.). It is an exercise of the **police power** of the state. There is no compensation for loss in value caused by zoning. Zoning is a **public restriction.** Zoning powers are given to local government by **enabling legislation,** which also gives the right to plan.

Zoning will not be upheld if it is arbitrary. It must be substantially related to the preservation or protection of public health, safety, morals, or general welfare. Zoning cannot be made retroactive (it cannot prohibit existing uses). If a **nonconforming use** was legal when it began, it will be allowed to continue, although a time period can be set for discontinuance. If the structure is destroyed or the use is discontinued, the nonconforming user has no right to start the use again. There are no standard zoning symbols, but generally:

> R1 = Single-family residence
> R2 = Duplex
> R3 = Apartments
> C = Commercial
> M = Manufacturing
> A = Agricultural

Down Zoning   A zoning change to a less intensive or more restrictive use, such as a change from apartment zoning to single-family residential use.

Cumulative Zoning   Zoning that allows more restrictive uses.

Noncumulative Zoning Zoning that allows only the use specified.

Exclusionary Zoning Zoning that excludes specified uses.

Inclusionary Zoning Zoning that requires specific inclusions such as a specific number of units for low-income housing.

Bulk Zoning Zoning for density by height, open-space, and setback requirements.

Incentive Zoning Zoning that provides a benefit if something is done, such as allowing greater density if a public plaza is included.

Spot Zoning Zoning in which one property or a small group of properties is zoned differently from the rest of the area. Spot zoning may be overturned by courts as being arbitrary.

Variance An exception to the zoning without actually changing the zoning. A variance does not allow a change in use, since this would be rezoning. Variances are normally given where strict adherence to the zoning would create a hardship. As an example, if zoning requires lots to have 9,000 square feet to build on, an exception might be made for a lot of 8,800 square feet that was subdivided prior to zoning.

Conditional-Use Permit A permit for a use not otherwise allowable under the zoning. The zoning ordinance must have considered the use and provided criteria for granting such permits.

Rezoning Changing the zoning of a parcel of land. Rezoning is an actual change in the master plan.

To change zoning (to obtain rezoning or a variance), a property owner petitions the city or county planning commission. Notices of hearings are sent to neighboring owners. The owner may appeal the planning commission's decision to the city council or county board of supervisors. Courts will override a decision only if it is arbitrary.

SUBDIVISIONS

A *subdivision* is the dividing of improved or unimproved land for the purpose of sale, lease, or financing into five or more parcels. It exempts out-of-state subdivisions, but covers California mobile home parks. The parcels need not be contiguous if they are reasonably related to each other.

Subdivided Lands Law

The Subdivided Lands Law is part of the Business and Professions Code, which is administered by the Real Estate Commissioner. Its purpose is to protect the public against fraud by requiring a **public report.** The public report sets forth complete facts about the subdivision (provisions for schools, utilities, improvements, financing, etc.). A buyer is not bound until he or she receives a copy of the public report, has an opportunity to read it, and signs a receipt that he or she has received it. The broker must retain the receipt for three years.

The law does not apply to parcels of 160 acres or more or to normal leasing of stores and apartments. Conveying a parcel to a government unit does not count as a division for the purpose of counting parcels. The law also does not apply to undivided interests (such as a tenancy in common) sold to 10 or fewer knowledgeable buyers who waive their protection under the Subdivided Lands Law. Out-of-state subdivisions sold in California do not require a public report.

Mechanics of the Public Report

1. The subdivider files with the Commissioner a **Notice of Intention** to sell or lease, as well as all pertinent information concerning conditions of the land and conditions of the sale.
2. The subdivider pays filing fees.
3. The subdivider complies with city or county control measures (under the **Subdivision Map Act**).
4. The Commissioner examines the property and issues or denies the public report. (If denied, the subdivider is entitled to a hearing.) The public report is good for five years from the date of issue.

A public report is not required on a subdivision in which each parcel will contain a completed residential structure and is located entirely within the boundaries of a city or for out-of-state subdivisions. A copy of the public report must be posted at the sales office, and copies must be available to the public upon request.

A **preliminary public report** may be issued upon receipt of the filing fee and completed questionnaire when everything is complete except for some particular requirement.

Use of Preliminary Public Report

1. A copy of the preliminary public report given to a prospective purchaser, who is given an opportunity to read it and sign a receipt, must be kept for three years. A copy must be posted at the sales office and be given to anyone requesting a copy.
2. The deposit of the prospective purchaser must be placed in a neutral depository (escrow).
3. Either the buyer or the seller may unilaterally cancel the purchase without penalty.
4. Although reservations and conditional offers can be taken, the sale cannot be completed until the public report is issued.

The preliminary public report expires one year from issuance, or upon issuance of the public report. Any of the following material changes in the subdivision must be reported to the Commissioner, and a new public report or an amended report may be required.

1. New ownership of the subdivision (applies also if one buyer of five or more lots wishes to sell one parcel).
2. Physical changes.
3. Changes in contracts.

Conditional Public Report   This report allows the parties to enter into a binding contract with funds placed in escrow, but the funds may not be released until the final public report is issued.

    The term for a conditional public report cannot exceed six months; it will be issued when the Commissioner believes that all conditions for the public report will be satisfied.

Desist-and-Refrain Order   The Commissioner can stop sales if he or she finds facts that would be ample grounds for the denial of a public report. (The subdivider has the right to a hearing.)

Blanket Encumbrance   If subdivision parcels have a blanket encumbrance, the subdivider must do one of the following in order to sell:

1. Provide a release from the blanket encumbrance.
2. Place any funds received in escrow to protect the buyer until a release is obtained.
3. Place the title in trust until the release of the land.
4. Furnish a bond acceptable to the Commissioner.

Violation   The penalty for violation of the subdivision law is a fine of up to $10,000 and/or up to one year in the state prison or county jail.

Types of Subdivisions

Standard Subdivision   Five or more improved or unimproved lots with no areas owned in common (the lot alone is sold).

Planned Unit Development (PUD)   Also known as a **planned development project.** This property contains five or more parcels, similar to a standard subdivision, but some areas are owned in common (for example, a community swimming pool). In a planned unit development, the title to the common area is normally held by the homeowners' association (in a condominium, each owner has an undivided interest in the common area as a tenant in common).

Stock Cooperative   Cooperative apartments of five or more units where apartment owners own stock in the owner's corporation. Each apartment owner has the right to occupy a unit under a proprietary lease. Cooperatives generally have sales restrictions in which buyers must be approved by the cooperative association. The right of occupancy can be transferred only with the shares in the corporation. The county assessor, upon written request, must separately assess the interests of the shareholders. Buyers financing a unit really borrow on their stock.

Community Apartment Project Buyers buy an apartment building (usually as tenants in common) with an undivided interest in the land and an exclusive right to occupy an apartment.

Condominium Project Also known as a **vertical subdivision.** A condominium project has five or more units. Owners own their own units or space. They have separate trust deeds and pay taxes separately. Common walls and public areas are owned in common with all other owners. Both community apartment projects and condominiums have provisions for maintenance and management. An owner cannot be held personally liable for tort injury relating to the common area if the association carries liability insurance up to a statutory amount.

Prior to resale, the owner of a condominium (as well as owners of other common interest developments) must provide the prospective purchaser with copies of the declaration of restrictions, bylaws, and articles of incorporation affecting the rights of the property offered for sale, plus a financial statement of the association including any delinquent assessments and costs. Failure to comply can result in $500 damages plus attorney fees.

Upon written request of an owner, the condominium association must supply within 10 days, a copy of the declaration of restrictions, bylaws, and articles of incorporation, plus a statement of delinquent assessments. (A fee can be charged.)

Condominium association rules cannot prohibit an owner from keeping at least one pet, subject to reasonable rules of the association.

Prior to converting existing residential property into a condominium, the developer must give tenants 180 days' notice, and the tenants must be given a 90-day option (from the date the public report is issued) to purchase their units under terms equal to or more favorable than those offered to the public. The tenants must also be given 10 days' notice of hearings. When existing lots in a mobile home park are to be sold as condominiums, a 12-month written notice must be given to the tenants, as well as a 15-day notice of approval hearings.

Time-Share Fractionalized ownership with a right of occupancy for a particular period of time. Time-shares are considered subdivisions if they consist of 12 or more time-share estates for five years or more. Purchasers of time-shares have a rescission right until midnight of the third calendar day after the agreement.

Copies of advertising must be submitted prior to issuance of the time-share public report. Any changes in advertising must be submitted prior to use.

Undivided-Interest Subdivision A subdivision in which the owners are tenants in common with other owners, with a nonexclusive right of occupancy. An example would be a campground or recreational-vehicle park owned by thousands of owners.

Purchasers of undivided-interest subdivisions have a three-day right of rescission after executing the contract.

Common-Interest Development (CID)   This is a subdivision with areas owned in common with other owners, such as planned developments, condominiums, stock cooperatives, and community apartments. It is a development with areas owned in common with the other owners, but owners have exclusive occupancy of their units. At the same time that the public report is provided, the purchaser in a common-interest development must be given a pamphlet entitled "Common-Interest Development."

Common Elements   These portions of the common areas are for the use of all owners, such as recreational facilities.

Limited Common Elements   These common areas of a subdivision are for the exclusive use of a designated owner, such as storage lockers or parking spaces.

The Subdivision Map Act

The Subdivision Map Act is part of the Government Code (separate from state subdivision law). It provides for city or county (local) control of the physical aspects of the subdivision.

For the purposes of the act, every division of land for the purpose of sale, lease, or financing is regarded as a subdivision (so a simple split into two contiguous parcels would be subject to Map Act approval). The purchaser of a parcel divided in violation of the act can rescind within one year of discovery of the violation.

The Map Act does not apply to:

1. Subdivisions in which each parcel is 20 acres or more and has road access.
2. Whole parcels of less than five acres where each lot abuts on a road.
3. Agricultural leases.
4. Time-shares, cooperatives, and undivided interests.

Procedure for Map Act Compliance

1. The subdivider prepares and files a tentative map with the local planning commission (showing property lines, topography, utilities, etc.).
2. The subdivider files certificates that all taxes and assessments have been paid or bonds posted.
3. The subdivider must make any changes requested and file a final map showing boundaries and numbers for each parcel and certificates (such as dedications for public purposes). An engineer must sign that the survey is proper and complete.

For subdivisions with less than five parcels, tentative and final maps are not required; however, the subdivider must submit a parcel map with designated parcels, and the surveyor must certify it for accuracy.

The following table indicates the differences and similarities of the Subdivided Lands Law (state control of subdivisions) and the Map Act (local control):

Subdivided Lands Law	Subdivision Map Act
Standard qualifying improved residential subdivisions within city limits are excepted	Included
Five or more lots or parcels	Two or more lots or parcels
A "proposed division" is included	Not included
No contiguity requirement	Land must be contiguous units
160-acre and larger parcels designated as such by government survey are exempt	No exemption for 160-acre and larger parcels
Community apartments are included	Same
Condominiums are included	Same
Stock cooperatives are included	Not included unless five or more existing dwelling units are converted
Leasing of apartments, offices, stores, or similar space in apartment buildings, industrial buildings, or commercial buildings is not included	Same
Long-term leasing of spaces in mobile home parks or trailer parks is included	Leasing or financing of mobile home parks or trailer parks are not included
Commercial and industrial subdivisions excluded	Included
Undivided interests are included	Not included
Expressly zoned industrial or commercial subdivisions are exempt	Included
Agricultural leases are included	Not included
Time-shares are included	Not included
Limited-equity housing cooperatives are included	Not included

Interstate Land Sales Act

Besides state control under the Subdivided Lands Law and local control under the Map Act, there is federal control under the Interstate Land Sales Act. This act is administered by the Office of Interstate Land Sales Registration (OILSR), a division of HUD. The act requires a developer to file a **development statement** setting forth the important details of the development with the Secretary of Housing and Urban Development for developments of 25 or more unimproved residential parcels of less than five acres each that may be promoted by mail or through interstate commerce.

A property report must be given to every purchaser. The California public report can be substituted for the federal report. The contract must contain a purchaser's **right to rescission** (seven days). Exempt from the act are cemetery lots and sales to developers. Purchasers have three years after discovery of fraud to bring legal action.

Environmental Impact Report (EIR)

Under the Environmental Quality Act of 1970, all subdivisions that have a significant effect on the environment must submit a report. A **negative declaration** is a statement that the development will not have a significant adverse effect on the environment, so that an environmental impact report would not be required.

Geologic Report

This is required for new real estate developments, or structures for human habitation, within 660 feet (1/8 mile) of either side of an earthquake fault (per the Alquist-Priolo Special-Studies Zone Act). The report is not required when three or fewer homes are constructed by a single builder. Also exempt are alterations not exceeding 50 percent of the value of a structure. Either the licensee as the agent, or the seller as the principal, must disclose to prospective purchasers that the property is located within a delineated special-studies zone, since a geologic report could be required prior to the issuance of a building permit.

Coastal Zone Conservation Act

This is a state act that strictly regulates coastal development. Land developments within approximately 1,000 yards of the Pacific coast require local agency approval. A developer can appeal to the state Coastal Commission.

Structural Pest Control Report

This is more than just a termite report; it covers all pests. It is required for VA and FHA loans; a copy is given to the owner and a copy is filed with the state Structural Pest Control Board, which must keep it on file for two years. Anyone may request copies of these reports. The California regulation applies to licensees whenever the buyer or lender requires a pest control inspection. The licensee must see that the report is delivered to the buyer and keep a record of his or her action.

EMINENT DOMAIN

Eminent domain is the power of *condemnation,* by which land may be taken for public use. Property owners are entitled to fair market value at the time the property is taken. Tenants are entitled to the value of their leasehold.

Eminent domain is *not* the exercise of police power, since there is no compensation for loss under exercise of police power. Police power cannot generally be delegated, but eminent domain not only can be used by governmental units but is also delegated to public utilities and to private schools. In some instances it can be given to a private individual. (A property owner can obtain an easement over the land of another for utilities by eminent domain.)

Severance Damage

When part of one's land is taken and this results in a loss of value of the remaining land, this damage is compensable. The California Relocation Assistance Law allows relocation expenses and certain other losses. The owner is not compensated for loss of profits and good will.

Inverse Condemnation

A landowner can, in some instances, force a governmental unit to buy his or her land if the government's action resulted in loss of the property's value (such as a new no-access highway making it landlocked, mistaken removal of topsoil so crops cannot be grown, etc.).

ANTIDISCRIMINATION LAWS

Unruh Act

Under the Unruh Act, business establishments (including real estate offices) cannot discriminate based on race, color, religion, ancestry, age, or marital status. (The act provides for actual damages plus punitive damages of $250 for each person subjected to discrimination.) The act also applies to discrimination against children in rentals and condominium sales. Age discrimination is allowable in senior citizen and retirement housing.

Rumford Act (California Fair Housing Act— Part of Government Code)

The Rumford Act applies to unimproved property intended to be used for residential purposes, as well as to improved residential property. This act prohibits discrimination on the basis of race, color, religion, sex, marital status, national origin or ancestry, or physical handicap. (The only exception is rental of a single room within the lessor's household.)

In the case of violations, the Fair Employment and Housing Commission can require the owner to rent the same or a like property to the person subjected to discrimination or award a civil penalty up to $10,000 ($25,000 if there has been a previous determination of discrimination). It is considered a violation of fair housing law for a broker to disclose the race of the purchaser to an owner. Complaints of violation of California fair housing laws should be made to the California Department of Fair Employment and Housing within 60 days of the violation.

Civil Rights Act of 1866

This act provides that all citizens shall have the same rights as white citizens to inherit, purchase, lease, sell, or hold real and personal property (the act applies to race only). There are no exceptions to this act. *Jones* v. *Mayer* (U.S. Supreme Court, 1968) was a landmark case that upheld the constitutionality of this act under the Thirteenth Amendment to the Constitution.

Federal Fair Housing Act (Contained in Title VIII of the Civil Rights Act of 1968)

Under this act, no one can refuse to sell or rent to another because of race, color, sex, religion, or national origin, and no real estate licensee may do so, regardless of his or her principal's direction. **Steering** (directing people to areas based on their race) is prohibited.

The act also prohibits **blockbusting**—inducing panic selling by representation that prices will fall because of minorities entering the area—as well as **redlining**—the refusal to insure or loan in an area.

The Fair Housing Amendment Act of 1988 extends protection against housing discrimination to persons with disabilities and families with children. (This protection extends to pregnant women.) Exempt from the discrimination-against-children provision are communities with at least 80 percent of the units occupied by at least one person 55 years of age or older. Also exempt are developments solely occupied by residents 62 years of age or older.

The act prohibits discrimination against persons with AIDS. Owners cannot refuse Seeing Eye dogs or support animals and cannot require an additional security deposit for renters with disabilities. Both physical and mental disabilities are included. While alcoholism is considered a disability, drug addiction is not a protected category.

Persons with disabilities must be allowed to alter the premises and common areas if necessary for their reasonable use. The landlord can require that the tenant agree to pay for restoration at the end of the tenancy if the alteration would not be appropriate for a nondisabled tenant. The tenant need not restore modifications made to common areas.

An **equal housing opportunity poster** must be prominently displayed in every broker's office. Failure to display the poster can shift the burden of proof to the broker should a complaint be made as to broker discrimination.

The Federal Civil Rights Act can be enforced by HUD, by the U.S. Attorney General, or by the individual subjected to discrimination. The aggrieved party has one year to file a civil lawsuit in state or federal court. Since California has its own fair housing laws, complaints usually are referred to the California Fair Employment and Housing Commission (within 60 days under the Rumford Act).

Americans with Disabilities Act

This act requires that places of public accommodation (offices, stores, restaurants, etc.) make their facilities accessible to persons with disabilities to the extent that such accessibility is readily achievable. The act also requires employers with 15 or more employees to alter the workplace for employees with disabilities unless such alteration would create an undue hardship on the business.

CHAPTER 12 QUIZ

1. Ken's petition for rezoning is rejected by the city planning commission. He:
   a. may appeal to the county planning commission
   b. may appeal to the court on the basis of hardship
   c. may appeal to the city council
   d. has no recourse other than to try again later

2. Which of the following is not upheld under the police power of the state?
   a. the Real Estate Law
   b. zoning
   c. eminent domain
   d. none of these

3. Every city, by law, must have:
   a. uniform zoning standards
   b. a uniform building code
   c. a planning commission
   d. a variance appeal board

4. An example of involuntary alienation would be:
   a. eminent domain
   b. zoning
   c. easement by reservation
   d. all of these

5. A *power granted by an enabling act* refers to:
   a. zoning
   b. eminent domain
   c. the Rumford Act
   d. none of these

6. As to zoning, which of the following is true?
   a. Zoning is never retroactive.
   b. Zoning takes precedence over deed restrictions.
   c. Aesthetic values are not an interest in the establishment of zoning.
   d. all of these

7. A report that allows a binding contract of sale of a subdivided parcel but will not allow funds to be disbursed would be:
   a. a preliminary report
   b. a public report
   c. a conditional public report
   d. any of these

8. Which of the following allows buyer cancellation?
   a. conditional public report
   b. public report
   c. preliminary public report
   d. any of the above

9. Which of the following is an example of police power?
   a. zoning
   b. building code enforcement
   c. health ordinance enforcement
   d. all of these

10. On a zoning map, "M" would most likely indicate:
    a. multiunit
    b. multiple use
    c. manufacturing
    d. mobile homes

11. A public report would be denied for:
    a. failure to show that parcels can be used for the purpose for which they are offered
    b. inability to demonstrate that adequate financial arrangements have been made for improvements
    c. inability to deliver title
    d. any of these

12. Subdividers may:
    a. sell lots prior to a public report if they agree to return money to purchasers upon demand
    b. make improvements prior to issuance of a public report
    c. change financing arrangements without approval
    d. print the public report in any manner or size of type they deem advisable

13. Nineteen tenants decide to purchase their apartment building as tenants in common with the right for each to occupy his or her unit. This would be a:
    a. condominium
    b. planned unit development
    c. cooperative
    d. community apartment project

14. The Subdivision Map Act requires:
    a. delivery of a copy of the public report to all purchasers
    b. insertion of release clauses when blanket encumbrances cover a subdivision
    c. subdividers to file tentative maps with the city or county planning commission
    d. all of these

15. In a condominium, which of the following could be owned in fee simple?
    a. the individual units
    b. the public hallways
    c. the outside yard
    d. all of these

16. Under the Subdivided Lands Act of the Business and Professions Code, the Real Estate Commissioner is concerned with:
    a. the layout and surfacing of streets
    b. the dimensions and placement of drainage and sewage disposal facilities
    c. financial provisions and arrangements to safeguard the vesting of title in the purchaser
    d. none of these

17. Condominiums have been increasing in popularity primarily because of:
    a. new lifestyles
    b. tax advantages
    c. land costs
    d. better loan terms

18. The Map Act allows subdivision control by the:
    a. corporation counsel
    b. Real Estate Commission
    c. local government
    d. state building inspector

19. The requirements of the Map Act need *not* be complied with for:
    a. California subdivisions sold in Arizona
    b. Arizona subdivisions sold in California
    c. both a and b
    d. neither a nor b

20. Taxes on a condominium apartment would be paid by:
    a. the owner of the apartment
    b. the board of governors
    c. the holder of the management contract
    d. the subdividers

21. A material change in a subdivision in regard to the public report would be:
    a. changes in lot or street lines
    b. changes in contracts used in sales
    c. changes in restrictions or rights
    d. all of these

22. A special-studies zone in proximity to a fault line would require the broker to:
    a. notify a purchaser prior to closing
    b. notify a purchaser prior to the offer
    c. obtain a new public report
    d. turn down any listing so affected

23. The Map Act requires:
    a. planning commission approval
    b. paved streets
    c. an adequate water supply
    d. all of these

24. The Map Act requires:
    a. submission of all advertising to the Real Estate Commission
    b. a public report to be issued
    c. the right to rescind by the buyer
    d. none of these

25. A farmer owns 120 acres, which he divides into five parcels to be leased for agricultural purposes. They are exempt from Map Act requirements if they contain:
    a. more than 20 acres
    b. 30 acres or more
    c. 40 acres or more
    d. any of these

26. Which of the following would be an offsite improvement?
    a. dwelling
    b. garage
    c. streets and curbs
    d. septic system

27. Which of the following is true?
    a. A public report cannot be used in advertising unless it is used in its entirety.
    b. A public report must always be supplied to advertising media.
    c. Both a and b are true.
    d. Neither a nor b is true.

28. The physical aspects of a subdivision are controlled by:
    a. the Real Estate Commission
    b. the city or county planning commission
    c. both a and b
    d. neither a nor b

29. A public report is good for:
    a. five years from the first sale
    b. five years from the date of issuance
    c. the length of time necessary to sell all lots
    d. none of these

30. A broker solicits only the longtime residents for listings in an area in which there had been recent sales to minority group members. The broker's action would be regarded as:
    a. steering   b. redlining   c. blockbusting   d. proper

31. A condominium unit owner owns separately:
    a. lawns and walkways
    b. common walls
    c. the common heating system
    d. none of these

32. A subdivider sells five lots to Frank, a dealer, who intends to immediately resell them, and five lots to Gwen, who is going to hold them for appreciation.
    a. Neither Frank nor Gwen needs a new public report.
    b. Gwen will need a public report only if she resells after the subdivider's public report expires.
    c. Frank will need a public report because he is a dealer.
    d. Both Frank and Gwen will need a new public report prior to their first sale.

33. A planning commission for each city and county is:
    a. required by statute
    b. made up of three members selected by the city council or board of supervisors
    c. required after the master plan is developed
    d. established when funds are appropriated

34. Violations of the subdivision law can result in a maximum fine of:
    a. $50   b. $500   c. $5,000   d. $10,000

35. Dedication under the Map Act takes place:
    a. when the final report is issued
    b. when the approved map is recorded
    c. when the preliminary report is issued
    d. upon filing of the tentative map

36. The subdivision law in California has the primary purpose of:
    a. preventing premature subdivisions
    b. obtaining the best land use
    c. community planning
    d. preventing fraud

37. A public report is required:
    a. prior to the sale of the fifth parcel in one year
    b. prior to the sale of the first parcel in a subdivision
    c. prior to any advertising
    d. prior to the issuance of a preliminary report

38. A condominium can be:
    a. residential   b. commercial   c. industrial   d. any of these

39. A requirement of the Subdivision Map Act is:
    a. submission of advertising to the local government unit prior to use
    b. preparation and filing of a tentative map
    c. approval of arrangements to safeguard buyer deposits
    d. providing purchasers with a copy of the public report before they are bound

40. *Jones* v. *Mayer* upheld the:
    a. Civil Rights Law of 1866
    b. Executive Order of 1962
    c. Civil Rights Act of 1964
    d. Civil Rights Act of 1968

41. A subdivider obtains a public report for five lots. He builds homes on each of the lots and leases them for five years. At the end of the lease he wishes to sell the homes.
    a. He requires a broker's license.
    b. He must get a new public report.
    c. Both a and b are true.
    d. Neither a nor b is true.

42. A subdivider must:
    a. furnish each buyer with a copy of the public report
    b. obtain a signed receipt from each buyer
    c. keep receipts on file for at least three years
    d. all of these

43. Breaking one parcel into two parcels would come under the regulation of:
    a. the Subdivided Lands Act
    b. the Subdivision Map Act
    c. both a and b
    d. neither a nor b

44. Which of the following comes under the jurisdiction of the Subdivided Lands Act?
    a. long-term leasing on mobile home spaces
    b. two or more contiguous parcels
    c. both a and b
    d. neither a nor b

45. A subdivider must comply with the Interstate Land Sales Act for subdivisions of:
    a. 5 or more parcels
    b. 25 or more parcels
    c. 50 or more parcels
    d. 100 or more parcels

46. Karen is going to subdivide for condominiums. She needs a public report if she is going to have more than _____ unit(s):
    a. one
    b. two
    c. four
    d. five

47. The Subdivision Map Act includes:
    a. 160-acre and larger parcels
    b. leasing mobile home spaces
    c. noncontiguous units
    d. none of these

48. Who can obtain a copy of the previous pest reports from the pest control board?
    a. the buyer
    b. the seller
    c. the broker
    d. anyone

49. Under the Subdivided Lands Act:
    a. parcels must be contiguous
    b. undivided interests are included
    c. agricultural leases are excluded
    d. all of these

50. The actions of the city planning commission:
    a. are recommendations only
    b. are advisory
    c. are binding rulings
    d. none of these

51. Individual ownership of a lot and common ownership of other areas would constitute a:
    a. standard subdivision
    b. planned unit development
    c. cooperative project
    d. condominium

52. A public report is not required for land located in:
    a. California and sold in California
    b. California and sold in Arizona
    c. Arizona and sold in California
    d. none of these

53. The Interstate Land Sales Act does not apply to sales:
    a. of cemetery lots
    b. of lots of five acres or more
    c. both a and b
    d. neither a nor b

54. Under the California Subdivided Lands Act, a subdivider who is not a resident of the state must submit an irrevocable consent that in the event of legal action against him or her, and if he or she cannot be located after a diligent search, a valid service may be made by delivering the process to:
    a. the Real Estate Commissioner
    b. the superior court in the county where the action occurs
    c. the state secretary of state
    d. the recorder in the county in which the land is located

55. In order to obtain a public report, a subdivider would not supply the Commissioner with:
    a. plans for utilities
    b. information on marketability of title
    c. financing arrangements
    d. plans of homes

56. A planned development project is a:
    a. fully improved subdivision
    b. subdivision containing areas owned in common
    c. community apartment project
    d. subdivision for which a final report has been issued

57. Building permits are issued by the:
    a. building inspector
    b. Real Estate Commission
    c. city or county planning commission
    d. board of supervisors

58. Giving real property for public use for Map Act approval is known as:
    a. inverse condemnation
    b. eminent domain
    c. dedication
    d. none of these

59. As to a public report, which of the following is true?
    a. Copies must be given to anyone upon request.
    b. A copy must be posted in the subdivision sales office.
    c. A public report may be renewed.
    d. All of these are true.

60. A subdivider must notify the Real Estate Commissioner if:
    a. he or she sells five parcels to one purchaser
    b. he or she makes physical changes in the subdivision
    c. he or she changes the contracts of sale
    d. all of these

61. The required elements of a general plan do *not* include:
    a. budget   b. safety   c. circulation   d. land use

62. Subdividers who wish to use a public report in their advertising:
    a. are prohibited from doing so
    b. may use any part of the public report so long as they reference the entire report
    c. may use the report only if they use it in full
    d. require special permission to use any portion for advertising purposes

63. A subdivider holding a down payment in trust for the purchase of a parcel covered by a blanket encumbrance is doing so for the benefit of:
    a. the beneficiary of the blanket encumbrance
    b. the Real Estate Commissioner
    c. the subdivider
    d. the purchaser

64. The planning commission, when administering the Map Act, would be concerned with:
    a. street width and traffic pattern
    b. drainage
    c. plans of homes
    d. both a and b

65. The Subdivided Lands Act covers:
    a. 12 or more time-shares of five years or more
    b. undivided interests
    c. both a and b
    d. neither a nor b

66. The office usually responsible for the enforcement of proper sewage and sanitation construction practices in a subdivision is:
    a. HUD
    b. the state Department of Health
    c. the local health office
    d. the Real Estate Commission

67. When an apartment building is converted to a condominium, the tenants must be given:
    a. 180 days notice
    b. a 90-day right to buy their unit
    c. both a and b
    d. neither a nor b

68. A negative declaration, when required from a developer as it pertains to an EIR, would:
   a. indicate a negative influence of the development on the environment
   b. indicate no negative influence of the development on the environment
   c. show whether the developer had a previous record of poorly designed subdivisions
   d. indicate a developer's financial status to protect purchasers from developers likely to file bankruptcy

69. A subdivider has a free-lot scheme. He or she is offering:
   a. lots free with the purchase of another lot
   b. a lottery with charges for transfer
   c. lots free as premiums
   d. free lots in order to get a subdivision started

70. Herman reads the Real Estate Commissioner's preliminary public report on an ordinary residential subdivision. He decides to buy a lot and gives the developer a $500 deposit, which the developer places in his trust account. The Real Estate Commissioner then issues the final public report. Upon reading it, Herman demands the return of his deposit. The developer must return:
   a. none of it   b. $250   c. $375   d. $500

71. A difference between the state Subdivided Lands Act and the Map Act is:
   a. for the Map Act the parcels must be contiguous
   b. long-term leases of trailer parks are not included under the Map Act
   c. both a and b
   d. neither a nor b

72. A disadvantage of a cooperative would be:
   a. owners cannot deduct tax payments made to the corporation
   b. owners could lose their equity if other owners fail to make their tax and loan payments
   c. owners' costs are greater than in a condominium
   d. all of these

73. The California Housing Act, which contains minimum code requirements, is found in the:
   a. state Contractor's Code   c. Uniform Commercial Code
   b. Fair Housing Act   d. Health and Safety Code

74. Under state subdivision law, a purchaser may rescind a contract to buy within a specified period in cases of:
   a. condominium sales   c. cooperative apartments
   b. time shares   d. none of these

75. In a new subdivision, who is responsible for installation of curbs, gutters, streets, and utilities?
   a. individual buyers
   b. the developer
   c. the city or county
   d. the planning commission

76. A buyer who reserves a home receives a copy of the preliminary public report. The buyer:
   a. may cancel the reservation at any time
   b. has the right to request that the deposit be placed in an interest-bearing account
   c. both a and b
   d. neither a nor b

77. The Subdivided Lands Act is part of:
   a. the Commissioner's regulations   c. the Business and Professions Code
   b. the Real Estate Code   d. none of these

78. The police power of the state can be invoked against the practice of discrimination in housing accommodation because of race, color, religion, or ancestry under the:
   a. Health and Safety Code   c. Penal Code
   b. Civil Code   d. Government Code

79. What does 🏠 stand for?
    a. California Fair Housing
    b. NAREB
    c. HUD
    d. Equal Housing Opportunity

80. The Federal Fair Housing Act of 1968 provides:
    a. low-income housing
    b. minimum construction standards
    c. low down payments for government housing
    d. equal housing opportunity for all

81. If a broker refuses to show or rent to parties because of race or color, the most likely thing to happen to the broker would be:
    a. a $250 fine for each party
    b. automatic revocation of his or her license
    c. a prison sentence
    d. no disciplinary action at all

82. The federal Fair Housing Act stems from:
    a. the First Amendment to the Constitution
    b. the Thirteenth Amendment to the Constitution
    c. the Rumford Act
    d. none of these

83. Violations of the Rumford Act are heard by the:
    a. state attorney general
    b. Real Estate Commissioner
    c. Fair Employment and Housing Commission
    d. superior court

84. Linda intends to build a six-foot fence around her property on the property line. She should check:
    a. local building codes
    b. zoning restrictions
    c. deed restrictions
    d. all of these

85. Zoning would most likely cover:
    a. construction standards
    b. CC&Rs
    c. escheat proceedings
    d. building setbacks

86. A master plan would not be concerned with:
    a. land use
    b. flood control
    c. sanitary problems
    d. deed restrictions

87. By accident, Edward's crops are sprayed by the city with a chemical that makes use of the land dangerous. He should:
    a. institute escheat proceedings
    b. start inverse condemnation
    c. either a or b
    d. neither a nor b

88. In the case of a violation of the Rumford Act, the Department of Fair Employment and Housing can:
    a. issue a cease-and-desist order
    b. invoke a $10,000 penalty
    c. invoke a $25,000 penalty if there was a previous violation
    d. any of these

89. A property owner, in listing his property, adds specific instructions that the property is not to be offered to anyone who is not a Caucasian, as the owner does not want to be the first to break the barrier to minorities in the neighborhood. The broker should:
    a. refuse to discuss the matter of the listing any further with the owner
    b. tell the owner that it is unlikely that a minority member could afford the property, so there is not a problem
    c. tell the owner to see another broker
    d. tell the owner to sell the property himself

90. The owner of a residential property found guilty of discrimination in the sale of his or her property may be required to:
    a. pay a civil penalty of $10,000
    b. sell to the offeror
    c. sell the offeror a similar property, if one is available
    d. any of these

91. The regulation of housing and construction in California is covered by the:
    a. local building code
    b. State Contractor's License Act
    c. state Housing Act
    d. all of these

92. The Americans with Disabilities Act applies to:
    a. drug addicts
    b. only physical disabilities
    c. both physical and mental disabilities
    d. both a and c

93. An area zoned for apartments allows single-family homes to be built because the zoning is:
    a. noncumulative
    b. cumulative
    c. exclusionary
    d. inclusionary

94. A broker ramped the front steps of her office, placed paper cups by the water cooler, and put a grab bar in the washroom in order to comply with:
    a. VAMA
    b. the 1988 amendment to the Civil Rights Act of 1968
    c. ADA
    d. the Rumford Act

95. A property owner may refuse to rent to a person who is:
    a. pregnant
    b. an alcoholic
    c. a drug addict
    d. blind and has a guide dog

96. A landlord may charge an increased security deposit for:
    a. tenants with disabilities who modify their units
    b. persons with guide dogs
    c. families with children
    d. none of these

97. Advertising a property located in a predominantly minority area only in a newspaper primarily read by that minority group would be:
    a. redlining   b. steering   c. blockbusting   d. legal

98. A white couple inquires about an ad for a home located in a minority area. The broker should:
    a. tell them it is a minority area
    b. suggest more suitable properties
    c. treat the inquiry in the same manner as an inquiry from a minority group buyer
    d. tell them the property is no longer available

99. A lender will not make loans in a minority area with a high crime rate. This action is:
    a. prudent   b. steering   c. redlining   d. blockbusting

100. An apartment house owner's ad violates the law if it states:
    a. no drinking allowed
    b. handicapped accessible
    c. no smoking
    d. adults preferred

ANSWERS—CHAPTER 12 QUIZ

1. c. Then he would go to the courts.
2. c. There is no compensation under police power.
3. c. And a general plan.
4. a. Involuntary taking of property.
5. a. And planning.
6. a.
7. c.
8. c. Reservation only. Deposit is refundable.
9. d. Health, safety, morals, and general welfare.
10. c.
11. d. Its purpose is to protect the public.
12. b.
13. d. They own as tenants in common.
14. c. The Map Act covers local control.
15. d. Fee simple is a degree of ownership. Areas can be owned in common but in fee simple.
16. c. The others are under local control.
17. c. Higher density housing.
18. c. City or county.
19. b. There is no local control in Arizona.
20. a.
21. d. The subdivider would need a new or amended report.
22. b. Geological hazards.
23. a.
24. d. These are all state requirements.
25. d. Agriculture excluded.
26. c.
27. a.
28. b. Under the Map Act.
29. b. It can be renewed.
30. c. Inducing panic selling.
31. d. All are commonly owned.

32. d. Due to the change in ownership.
33. a.
34. d. Plus one year in prison.
35. b. The dedication would also be recorded.
36. d. To protect the buyer.
37. b.
38. d.
39. b.
40. a. Decision of the U.S. Supreme Court, 1968.
41. b. The report has expired.
42. d.
43. b. Any division falls under local control.
44. a. Five or more.
45. b.
46. c. Five or more.
47. a. But they are exempt from the state requirement.
48. d. Records must be kept for two years.
49. b.
50. c.
51. b.
52. c. Out-of-state subdivisions are exempt.
53. c.
54. c. The rule is the same for a non-resident broker.
55. d. These are under local control.
56. b.
57. a.
58. c.
59. d.
60. d.
61. a. The other elements are housing, open space, conservation, and noise.
62. c.
63. d.
64. d.
65. c.
66. c.

67. c.
68. b.
69. b. A scam in which the transfer charge exceeds the value.
70. d.
71. c.
72. b. If they are paid by association.
73. d.
74. b. Also in cases of undivided interest subdivisions.
75. b. As a condition of approval.
76. c.
77. c.
78. d. Rumford Act.
79. d.
80. d.
81. a. Under the Unruh Act.
82. b. According to *Jones* v. *Mayer*.
83. c.
84. d.
85. d.
86. d.
87. b. Force the city to buy his land.
88. d.
89. a.
90. d. Under the Rumford Act.
91. d.
92. c.
93. b. More restrictive uses are allowed.
94. c. The Americans with Disabilities Act.
95. c. Not a protected group.
96. d.
97. b. Directing buyers based on race.
98. c. Brokers must treat everyone equally.
99. c. And illegal.
100. d. Discrimination based on familial status is prohibited; the owner may prohibit an activity but not the person, as in "no drinkers or smokers."

Introduction to Taxation

TAXATION

Taxes on real estate are **ad valorem,** meaning "according to value." Because of Proposition 13, real estate taxes cannot exceed 1 percent of the market value (up to 1 percent can be added to pay for bonded indebtedness) or increase more than 2 percent per year. The tax rate is set by the county board of supervisors, up to the maximum allowed by law. Tax is collected by tax collectors.

Property is reassessed only upon sale. Transfers bewteen spouses will not trigger reassessment. A buyer is required to file a change-of-ownership statement with the county tax assessor within 45 days of purchase. **Proposition 58** allows transfer of the principal residence plus the first $1,000,000 of other property between a parent and children without any reassessment. Proposition 193 extended this exemption from reassessment to grandparents transferring to grandchildren.

Proposition 60 allows homeowners aged 55 and older, as well as those severally and permanently disabled, to transfer their current tax assessment to a replacement residence in the same county within 2 years of the sale. **Proposition 90** extends Proposition 60 to other counties if the county has accepted Proposition 90.

The assessed value is the value placed by the county tax assessor and is based on market value. (The county assessor must assess the property by July 1 for the tax year.)

A property owner may file an objection if not satisfied with an assessment. Objections should be filed in early July. In July the local board of supervisors sits as a county board of equalization to hear these matters. Some larger counties have special **assessment appeals boards.**

The county tax assessors do not assess property of public utilities. Public utilities are assessed by the state Board of Equalization.

Supplemental Tax Bill

Because property is reassessed upon sale, a buyer will probably get supplemental tax bill(s) reflecting the new valuation increase for the period of ownership within the tax year of the sale.

Exemptions

Homeowner's Exemption on an Owner-Occupied Dwelling The homeowner's exemption is $7,000 of the assessed value. The homeowner must be a resident by March 1 and apply by April 15.

Veteran's Exemption The veteran's exemption is $4,000 of the assessed value. The veteran must apply by April 15. The same person may not use both homeowner's and veteran's exemptions. Veterans disabled due to war service have a $100,000 exemption ($150,000 if it is a limited-income household). There is also a $40,000 tax exemption to the unmarried surviving spouse of a veteran who died on active duty from a service-connected injury.

Postponement of Tax Taxpayers aged 62 and older with limited income can qualify to have the state pay the taxes and take a lien on the home. They may apply to the state controller. The tax is repaid when the property is sold or the taxpayer dies.

Tax Year

The tax year runs from July 1 through June 30. Real property taxes are due in two equal installments:

The first installment is due November 1; it is delinquent December 10 at 5 P.M.

The second installment is due February 1; it is delinquent April 10 at 5 P.M.

On January 1 of the year preceding the tax year, taxes become a lien on real property.

Tax Sale (Book Sale)

On or before June 8, the tax collector publishes a notice of intent to sell the property if assessments are not paid. The sale is made on or before June 30. This is a sale to the state (not open to bidders). The sale, known as a **book or stamp sale,** does not really affect the owner's right to use the property. It only sets the time running for a five-year period of redemption. To redeem, the owner must pay the taxes, interest, costs, and redemption penalties. If the property is not redeemed within five years, the property is deeded to the state.

As long as the state continues to own the property, the former owner can still redeem. The county tax collector manages the property after it is deeded to the state and can sell it at public auction. The tax collector sets the minimum bid, which is approved by the county board of supervisors. Sales are for cash. The purchaser receives a *tax deed,* and the former owner loses all redemption rights. A purchaser with a tax deed can obtain title insurance after one year. Since taxes are a priority lien, junior liens are wiped out by a tax sale.

Crops

Crops are not taxed as real estate, with the exception of fruit trees more than four years old and grapevines more than three years old.

Special Assessments

These are levied for the costs of specific local improvements. They are priority liens equal to property tax liens.

The **Street Improvement Act of 1911** is used for county and city improvements. Part or all of the cost of improvement may be paid within 30 days of completion, or the balance goes to bond (tax-exempt municipal bonds). (Charges are based on benefits received and are generally on a front-footage basis.)

Property tax liens are specific liens for that property, but IRS tax liens are general liens for all property of the debtor.

Mello-Roos Bonds

These bonds are issued by a special tax district created by either a developer or a municipality to finance streets, schools, sewers, or other construction. The home-owners in the district pay off the bonds. Purchasers must be informed of the presence of Mello-Roos bonds.

Personal Property Tax (Only Tangible Business Property Is Taxed)

Unsecured Personal Property Taxes

> *Due:* March 1.

> *Payable:* On assessment.

> *Delinquent:* After August 31.

Secured Personal Property Taxes

> *Due:* At the same time as the first installment of real estate taxes (November 1).

> *Delinquent:* September 1.

Federal Estate Tax

The marital deduction is 100 percent of the estate going to a surviving spouse. If the estate passes to other than a surviving spouse, there is a $700,000 exemption from estate taxes. This exemption increases in increments to $1,000,000 by the year 2006.

Federal Gift Tax

The yearly exemption is $11,000 per donee. The federal gift tax is taxed on the donor.

There is no state gift tax.

Federal Income Tax

Rents from real estate are taxed as ordinary income at the full tax rate. Tax rates rise with taxable income. The federal income tax is considered to be a progressive tax in that the percentage of taxation increases as income increases.

Deductions

Interest paid on a home-purchase loan for a primary residence plus one second home is tax deductible for a principal amount not exceeding $1,000,000. Interest on home-equity loans is deductible for loans up to $100,000. Property taxes are also a deduction for homeowners.

Capital Gains

A capital gain is a profit on the sale of a capital asset (real estate). Capital gains are computed by deducting a taxpayer's adjusted cost basis from the sale price. Adjusted cost basis is the original cost plus the value of improvements minus any depreciation that was taken:

$$\text{Adjusted cost basis} = \text{Original costs} + \text{Improvements} - \text{Depreciation}$$

Capital gains receive preferential treatment for income tax purposes. While gains for property held for one year or less are taxed as regular income, gains from the sale of property held for more than 12 months is taxed at a maximum rate of 15 percent. For lower income taxpayers (in 10 percent and 15 percent tax brackets), the gains are taxed at 5 percent. This rate becomes zero in 2008.

That portion of a capital gain attributable to depreciation taken is taxed at a 25 percent rate.

Universal Exclusion (Two-Year rule)

Taxpayers who have lived in their permanent residence for at least two years during the prior five-year period have an exemption from taxation as follows:

Married couples	$500,000
Single persons	$250,000

To arrive at the two-year period, the occupancy need not be continuous as long as it totals two years. A person can take this exemption every two years. Unmarried co-owners can each take $250,000.

Capital Losses A taxpayer can offset a gain in the year of the gain by a capital loss from the same year. However, a taxpayer cannot take a loss on his or her residence.

If a taxpayer has no loss to offset a gain in the year of the sale, the taxpayer may carry the loss forward using $3,000 of the loss each year.

Tax-Free Exchanges (Property Held for Business or Investment) By exchanging property, a taxpayer can defer capital gains. If cash or anything else of value is given as part of an exchange to even things out, then this part of the exchange (known as *boot*) is taxable.

To have a tax-free exchange, the exchange must be "like for like" (for example, income or investment property for income or investment property).

In a tax-free exchange, each party keeps his or her original cost base. It will be increased or decreased if the trade involves boot. The cost base is also increased or decreased based on the increase or decrease of the obligation being assumed in the trade (debt relief is considered to be boot).

Starker Exchange A *delayed* or *Starker exchange* is possible where the seller's proceeds remain in escrow to acquire the exchange property. For a delayed exchange, the property must be designated within 45 days of closing, and title transfer must be within 180 days of closing.

Installment Sales

Profit can be taxed in the year in which it is received, regardless of the amount received in the year of the sale. This applies to a maximum of $5 million in loans for installment sales. By spreading the tax over a number of years, the taxpayer may be in a lower tax bracket. Dealers, however, are taxed for the entire gain in the year of the sale.

Tax Shelter

Depreciation can be used to shelter profits (passive income) from real estate operations. If a taxpayer has an adjusted gross income of $100,000 or less, he or she can also use real estate losses to shelter up to $25,000 of active income (such as wages). For taxpayers having an adjusted gross income of $100,000 to $150,000, the $25,000 that can be sheltered is reduced by one dollar for every two dollars of income over $100,000. Persons considered to be real estate professionals can use passive losses to shelter active income without limit. (They must meet IRS criteria.)

Documentary Transfer Tax

Documentary stamps (revenue stamps) are a local (county) tax on the transfer of real estate. Notice of payment of the tax is normally entered on the deed. It does not apply to transfers of $100 or less. The tax is normally paid by the seller.

The tax rate is 55 cents per $500 of consideration, or fraction thereof. The tax is only on the seller's equity; if the buyer assumes a trust deed, the tax would not be computed on the amount assumed.

Example:

Sale price	$150,000
Existing loan assumed	−70,100
Seller's equity being transferred	$79,900

$79,900 ÷ $500 = 159.86. Since each fraction of $500 is treated as $500, the tax would be 160 × .55 = $88.

Example:

A property has a sale price of $150,000, the seller has a $70,100 loan, and the property is refinanced with a new loan. In refinancing, the existing loan is paid off, so the tax is on the entire purchase price regardless of any new loans. The tax is on the seller's equity; the seller is transferring the entire property at $150,000:

$$150,000 ÷ $500 = 300; 300 × .55 = $165$$

(Documentary tax must be divisible by $.55.)

Foreign Investment in Real Property Tax Act (FIRPTA)

To prevent foreign nationals from selling property and leaving without paying taxes, FIRPTA requires the buyer to withhold 10 percent of the purchase price unless the buyer certifies nonforeign status. (CAL FIRPTA requires the withholding of 3 1/3 percent for California taxes.) The withholding requirements do not apply to the purchase of a personal residence for $300,000 or less.

California Withholding

California requires buyer tax withholding from all sellers (not just foreign nationals) of 3 1/3 percent of the sales price. Excluded from the withholding requirement are:

1. Sale of a seller's personal residence
2. Sales under $100,000

The purpose of this withholding requirement is to give the state the tax money right away rather than wait until income taxes are filed.

CHAPTER 13 QUIZ

1. Which of the following is an *ad valorem* tax?
   a. sales tax   b. use tax   c. real estate tax   d. both a and c

2. Ralph builds a swimming pool at his apartment building in order to reduce his vacancy factor. For tax purposes, he may:
   a. deduct the cost of the pool as an expense in the year it was expended
   b. add the value of the pool to his depreciation for that year
   c. add the cost of the pool to his book value
   d. none of these

3. A prudent person would be interested in income taxes:
   a. when he or she first considers purchasing   c. after purchasing
   b. at the time the first income is received   d. after sale

4. The federal income tax would be best described as a(n):
   a. progressive tax   b. graduated tax   c. cumulative tax   d. *ad valorem* tax

5. You may gain a federal tax advantage by:
   a. depreciating income property
   b. taking proceeds of a sale over a number of years
   c. trading like for like
   d. all of these

6. For a tax-free exchange on Sharon's rental units, she should exchange for:
   a. a residence for herself having the same value
   b. smaller apartment units and take cash to balance out the trade
   c. an apartment unit of the same value with a lower mortgage
   d. an apartment unit of a greater value, and pay cash to balance out the trade

7. For tax purposes, Paul can depreciate:
   a. his urban residence   c. raw land held for appreciation
   b. his residence on his farm   d. a mature fruit orchard

8. Street improvements are assessed based on:
   a. *ad valorem* value   c. assessed value
   b. front footage   d. none of these

9. When a seller pays points, for tax purposes this would:
   a. be deductible as an interest expense
   b. be treated the same as a prepayment penalty
   c. increase the cost basis
   d. not be deductible

10. The term *tax shelter* is associated with:
    a. personal property tax   c. real estate tax
    b. sales tax   d. income tax

11. The second installment of the real estate tax is due:
    a. February 1   b. April 10   c. March 1   d. December 10

12. The California sales tax is:
    a. a tax on personal property   c. both a and b
    b. a tax on real property   d. an *ad valorem* tax

13. A veteran must apply for tax exemption by:
    a. April 15   b. March 1   c. June 1   d. December 31

14. A purchaser at a tax foreclosure sale obtains a:
    a. tax deed   c. state controller's deed
    b. warranty deed   d. sheriff's deed

15. Regina's city puts in a sewer line in front of her lot. She can expect a:
    a. general assessment
    b. special assessment
    c. tax rate increase
    d. all of these

16. A tax on the gross receipts of a broker would be a:
    a. business license tax   b. use tax   c. sales tax   d. none of these

17. The following are not exempt from real property taxation:
    a. growing crops
    b. grapevines 3 1/2 years old
    c. fruit trees 3 1/2 years old
    d. both b and c

18. The period for redemption for unpaid taxes is:
    a. five years from the date assessed
    b. five years from delinquency
    c. five years from the date of book sale
    d. five years from the sheriff's sale

19. *Boot* refers to:
    a. commercial or income property
    b. evictions
    c. sale of a business
    d. exchanges

20. A property owner's tax rate would be set by the:
    a. tax assessor
    b. tax collector
    c. county board of supervisors
    d. mayor

21. By use of a tax shelter, a taxpayer may:
    a. evade taxes
    b. defer taxes
    c. decrease his or her net spendable income
    d. increase his or her book value

22. A married couple sold the home they had lived in for three years and realized a $600,000 profit. What would they pay in taxes?
    a. $125,000
    b. $100,000
    c. $15,000
    d. nothing

23. Which of the following will have the least impact on property tax rates?
    a. compactness of the area
    b. amount of commercial property in the area
    c. homeowner's exemptions
    d. large amounts of vacant land

24. Gerald sells his residence for $200,000. He purchased it 12 months ago for $220,000. For tax purposes he has:
    a. a $20,000 loss
    b. a tax shelter
    c. a $20,000 capital gain
    d. no loss or gain

25. A disadvantage of corporations in relationship to taxes is:
    a. minimum tax rates
    b. double taxation because both corporate profit and dividends to stockholders are taxed
    c. both a and b
    d. neither a nor b

26. Harold sells a lot to Dick for $29,420. Dick assumes a first trust deed of $17,933. He gives Harold $1,000 cash and a second trust deed for the balance. The revenue stamps required are:
    a. $16.50   b. $12.65   c. $22.45   d. $19.80

27. The proposition that allows an elderly homeowner to transfer his or her cost basis to another home in the same county is:
    a. Proposition 13
    b. Proposition 58
    c. Proposition 60
    d. Proposition 90

28. Josie takes a $30,000 loss on operations of her apartment building. In the same year her total adjusted gross income is $152,000. How much of her other active income can be sheltered from taxes?
    a. $30,000   b. $25,000   c. $12,500   d. none

29. Clyde, age 53, sells his residence for $160,000. He purchased it for $40,000 18 years earlier. Clyde does not intend to buy another house. What portion of the sale price is taxable?
   a. $160,000   b. $120,000   c. $35,000   d. none

30. A veteran who is disabled due to military service has a property tax exemption of:
   a. $4,000   b. $40,000   c. $100,000   d. $150,000

31. A buyer purchased a home on April 15th. The taxes for the tax year had been paid, but the buyer received a tax bill anyway. This bill is known as a:
   a. revised statement of taxes   c. delinquency charge
   b. supplemental tax bill   d. transfer charge

32. The capital gains rate on a gain by a person in a 28 percent tax bracket is:
   a. 5 percent   b. 15 percent   c. 25 percent   d. 28 percent

33. A seller had owned an income property for 19 months. The tax on the capital gains upon sale, would be:
   a. 5 percent   b. 15 percent   c. 25 percent   d. 28 percent

34. To be eligible for the universal exclusion, a couple must have:
   a. owned the property for five years
   b. used it as a permanent residence for two years
   c. both a and b
   d. neither a nor b

35. A taxpayer, who has an adjusted gross income of $125,000, suffered a passive loss of $100,000. How much of his loss can be used to shelter active income?
   a. $100,000   b. $50,000   c. $12,500   d. none

36. A buyer does not have to withhold part of the purchase price from a foreign national seller when:
   a. the property is unimproved
   b. the broker failed to explain the withholding requirement
   c. it is a personal residence with a $250,000 sale price
   d. none of the above

37. Special assessments are assessed to each property owner based on:
   a. square footage   c. a prorated share per property owner
   b. benefits derived by the property owner   d. the assessed value of the parcel

38. An advantage to a seller of an installment sale is:
   a. tax avoidance
   b. the two-year rule
   c. the fact that boot is not taxable
   d. the payment of capital gains over the contract period

39. *Boot* in an exchange would be:
   a. mortgage relief   c. cash received
   b. unlike property received   d. all of these

40. Under the Street Improvement Act of 1911, how long does an owner have to pay the bill after receipt?
   a. 10 days   b. 30 days   c. 45 days   d. 90 days

41. The party responsible for reporting a sale to the IRS is the:
   a. seller   b. buyer   c. broker   d. escrow

42. The adjusted basis of a taxpayer's residence would be:
   a. cost plus improvements minus depreciation   c. cost
   b. cost plus improvements   d. cost minus improvements

43. The unadjusted basis of a taxpayer's residence, would be:
   a. cost
   b. cost minus improvements
   c. cost plus improvements
   d. cost plus improvements minus depreciation

44. The owner of an apartment building would have a number of tax deductions. Which of the following is not a deduction?
    a. interest paid on a mortgage
    b. monthly gardening costs
    c. depreciation
    d. cost to build a swimming pool

45. For income tax purposes, an income property owner cannot deduct:
    a. loss of income because of vacancy
    b. depreciation
    c. rental commissions paid
    d. management fees

46. The maximum gift a donor can give to each donee and be exempt from the federal gift tax is:
    a. zero   b. $1,000   c. $10,000   d. $11,000

47. A seller sold his residence in California for $400,000. How much must the buyer withhold for California tax purposes?
    a. nothing
    b. 3 1/3 percent of sale price
    c. 10 percent of sale
    d. $150,000

48. Under FIRPTA, how much must the buyer withhold from the sales price when the seller is a U.S. citizen?
    a. nothing   b. 1 percent   c. 3 1/3 percent   d. 10 percent

49. Which proposition allows a property to retain its tax base when it is transferred from parent to child?
    a. 42   b. 58   c. 60   d. 90

50. Three years ago a taxpayer had a large capital loss but no gain to offset it. How much of the gain is she allowed to use each year to shelter other income?
    a. $1,000   b. $3,000   c. $5,000   d. no limit

ANSWERS—CHAPTER 13 QUIZ

1. c. Taxed according to value.
2. c. And depreciate it.
3. a.
4. a. Rates increase with income.
5. d.
6. d. She pays the boot.
7. d. Fruit trees can be depreciated.
8. b. Generally.
9. c. It is treated as a sale cost, but buyer points are treated as interest.
10. d. To shelter income from taxation.
11. a. But is delinquent April 10.
12. a. Taxed on price, not value.
13. a.
14. a. A sheriff's deed is given at a creditor sale.
15. b.
16. a. Based on volume.
17. b. Grapevines under three years old and fruit trees under four years old are exempt.
18. c. The date of sale sets the five-year redemption period.

19. d. Unlike property in trade.
20. c. The assessor sets the value.
21. b. The taxpayer pays when the gain is realized.
22. c. $500,000 exclusion so 15% on $100,000.
23. c. The others are more significant.
24. d. There is no loss since the property is a residence.
25. b. Except Chapter S corporations.
26. b. $.55 per $500 of the seller's equity.
27. c. Proposition 90 applies to another county.
28. d. Her adjusted gross income is over $150,000.
29. d. He has a $250,000 exclusion.
30. c.
31. b. It will reflect the new assessment for the balance of the year.
32. b.
33. b. Over 12 months.
34. b. Can be taken every two years.

35. c. Up to $25,000, but it is reduced $1 for every $2 in adjusted gross income over $100,000.
36. c. $300,00 or less is exempt.
37. b.
38. d.
39. d.
40. b.
41. d.
42. b. Can't depreciate your residence.
43. a.
44. d. Would be added to cost basis and depreciated over life of pool.
45. a. It is neither income nor a deduction.
46. d.
47. a. Exemption for seller's residence.
48. a. FIRPTA applies only to foreign nationals.
49. b.
50. b.

Single-Family Homes and Mobile Homes

A homeowner in California owns his or her home an average of five to seven years. The average California resident lives in a home an average of two to three years (this figure includes tenants).

CONSTRUCTION DETAILS

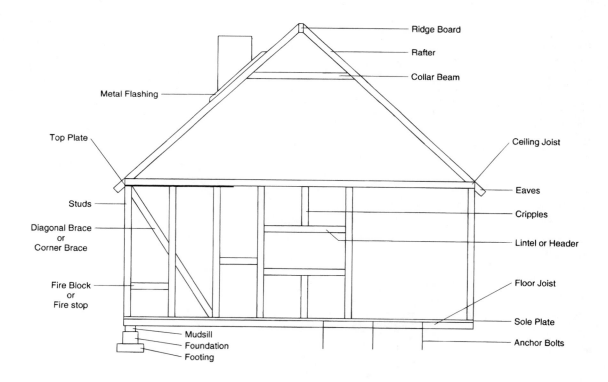

Distance between studs—16 inches (center to center).

Minimum crawl space (FHA)—18 inches.

   Entrance to crawl space—minimum 18 inches by 24 inches.

Minimum room size (FHA)—70 square feet. One room must have at least 120 square feet.

Minimum room height (FHA)—90 inches (normal room height is 96 inches). For the kitchen and bath, the minimum height is 7 feet.

Minimum stairwell width (FHA)—3 feet with one handrail.

Dark color—makes the room appear smaller.

Light color—make the room appear larger.

Reds are warm colors.

Blues are cold colors.

Better homes follow high ground.

Gently rolling hills are most desirable for subdivisions.

Long blocks are more economical because they provide more lots per acre.

Selected Real Estate Construction Terms

Adobe A type of soil.

Anchor Bolt A bolt holding a mudsill to the foundation.

Backfill Fill dirt replaced around the foundation.

Bearing Wall A wall that supports the structure. It would have a footing.

Benchmark A U.S. survey marker showing elevation.

Board Foot A measure of lumber $1' \times 1' \times 1''$ (144 cubic inches).

Bridging Criss-crossing boards between the floor joists to prevent twisting.

BTU (British Thermal Unit) The measure of heat required to raise the temperature of one pound of water by one degree Fahrenheit.

Casement Window A window on hinges that opens outward.

Circuit Breaker A safety device that breaks an electrical circuit when it becomes overloaded (replaces fuses).

Collar Beam A beam joining opposing rafters.

Commercial Acre The area of the land left over after deductions for streets (a commercial acre is less than an acre).

Compaction   Compression of soil. Compaction tests determine whether the soil will support a structure.

Conduit   A pipe (plastic or metal) that holds electrical wiring.

Coniferous   An evergreen tree having cones. The wood is regarded as soft wood.

Contour Lines   Lines on a topographic map showing elevation. When lines are close together, the slope is steep, but contour lines far apart indicate that the land is relatively flat.

Crawl Space   The space between the floor joists and the soil when the house is not built on a concrete slab.

Cripple   A short, vertical piece of a stud above or below an opening.

Cul-de-Sac   A dead-end street. Cul-de-sacs are desirable because they have no through traffic.

Deciduous   Trees that lose their leaves. The wood is considered hardwood.

Drywall   An interior wall treatment applied dry (plasterboard or paneling) as opposed to plaster.

Eaves   That portion of the roof extending beyond the exterior walls.

Elevation   A drawing on a builder's plan that shows views of the structure from the sides. This term can also apply to height.

Energy Efficient Ratio (EER)   Efficiency rating of heating and air conditioning units. The higher the EER, the greater the energy efficiency.

Expansion Joint   Soft insulation-like material placed between slabs of concrete to allow for expansion and prevent cracking.

Expansive Soil   Soil that expands with moisture.

Facade   The face or front of a structure.

Fire Stop   A short, horizontal board between studs in a wall.

Flashing (Counterflashing)   Metalwork in the roof around chimneys and vents and in valleys of the roof to prevent leaks.

Floor Space   Interior dimensions.

Footing   Concrete poured in the ground bearing the weight of the structure.

Foundation   The concrete support wall that rests on the footing.

Foundation Plan   The construction drawing showing footings, columns, piers, foundation and subfloor.

Frost Line   The depth to which frost penetrates the soil.

Furring   Wooden strips used to level a surface (usually a wall).

Gable Roof   A roof that has triangular vertical wall sections at its ends.

Gambrel Roof   A roof having a steep lower slope and a gentler upper slope (two slopes on each side); found on barns and Dutch Colonials.

Header   The beam over a window and door. Also known as a *lintel*.

Hip Roof   A roof on which all sides slope to the eaves.

HVAC   An acronym for heating, ventilating, and air conditioning.

Jalousie Window   A window made of short panes of glass that open and close like a venetian blind.

Jamb   The lining of a door or window frame.

Joists   Parallel horizontal beams that support the floor (floor joists) or ceiling (ceiling joists).

Key Lot   A rectangular lot having a number of other lots butting against one side; so called because it resembles the handle of a key. Key lots are undesirable for residential purposes because there are many neighbors and, thus, less privacy.

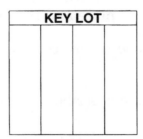

Kiosk   An open-sided structure such as a newsstand or a sales booth in a mall.

Lateral Support   The duty of a property owner to physically support the land and structures on the adjacent property.

Lath   The base upon which plaster is applied.

Lintel A horizontal beam or stone above a window or door. Also known as a *header*.

Livable Floor Space Interior dimensions of each room.

Mansard Roof A roof having two slopes on all sides with the lower slope being far steeper than the upper slope.

Mantel The facing around a fireplace.

Monument A survey marker.

Mudsill (Sill) The lowest board in the house (usually redwood or treated fir), which is anchored to the foundation upon which the house rests. Redwood is the best wood for mudsills because it resists rot.

Orientation The placement of the house upon the lot in relationship to exposure, views, etc.

Overimprovement An uneconomical improvement that would not be reflected in increased value.

Party Wall A wall on a boundary line maintained by both owners.

Penny A measurement for nails expressed by the small letter "d." The larger the penny, the larger the nail.

Percolation The ability of water to drain through the soil. Percolation tests are generally required for septic systems.

Pitch The degree of slope of a roof. A steep or high-pitched roof will last longer than a low-pitched roof because the water will run off faster.

Plat Map A subdivision map showing all lots in a subdivision.

Plate A horizontal board in a wall to which the studs are nailed. The two main plates in a wall are the sole (bottom) plate and the top plate.

Plot Plan A drawing of a lot showing how the improvements (structure, driveway, walks) will be oriented on the lot.

Potable Drinkable; a term used to describe water quality.

Purlin A horizontal board used to line up rafters.

R-Factor The resistance factor used to measure efficiency of insulation.

Rafter A diagonal support beam in the roof.

Ridge Board The board between the peaks of opposing rafters. It is the highest board in the house.

Riser   A vertical board between the treads in a staircase.

Sash   A window frame in which glass is set.

Septic Tank   A sewage disposal tank in which waste is decomposed by bacterial action.

Setback   Distance a structure must be from lot lines.

Sheathing   A wall, floor, or roof covering (generally plywood) nailed to studs, joists, or rafters over which a finished treatment will be applied. Wood shingles are attached to *open* or *strip sheathing* rather than to solid sheathing.

Siding   The exterior wall treatment (generally wood, hardboard, aluminum, or vinyl).

Soil Pipe   The pipe that carries the sewage from the house.

Square Footage   Exterior dimensions, excluding the garage. Two-story houses cost less per square foot than one-story houses because of the double use of the roof and the foundation. The larger the house, the lower the price per square foot, since the kitchen, baths, sewer, etc. are the same.

Stringer   The diagonal member in a staircase.

Studs   Vertical support members in a wall.

Subjacent Support   Physical support of the surface by owners of mineral and gas rights.

Termite Shield   Metalwork over the foundation to protect against termite infestation. The most destructive termite in California is the subterranean termite.

Topography   The physical surface (contour) of the land.

Treads   A horizontal board in a staircase; the part that is stepped on.

Truss   A single triangular roof structure that includes the rafters, ceiling joist, collar beam, and supporting braces.

Valley   An internal angle in a roof.

Vent   An air pipe allowing wastewater to flow from the structure.

Wainscoting   A wall treatment in which the lower half is treated differently from the remainder of the wall (generally paneled).

Water Pressure   Pounds of pressure exerted by water service. To determine adequate water pressure for a home, a simple test is to turn on taps then flush a toilet. If faucet flow materially decreases, then pressure is not adequate.

Water Table   The depth of percolating water in the ground.

ARCHITECTURE

Roof Styles

Gable roof

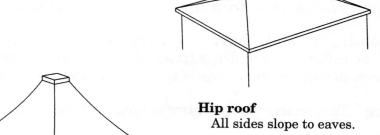

Hip roof
All sides slope to eaves.

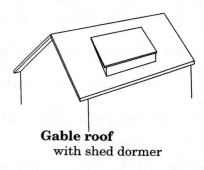

Victorian roof

Shed roof

Gable roof
with shed dormer

Gambrel roof
Found on barns and
Dutch Colonial homes.

Pyramid roof
All sides slope from one point
(no ridge line).

Mansard roof
(French style)

282

Home Styles

New England Colonial
A box-shaped two-story house with a center entrance, wood siding, and shutters.

Georgian Colonial
A brick two-story house with a center entrance and a hip roof.

Southern Colonial
A two-story house with pillars and shutters.

Dutch Colonial
A two-story house with a gambrel roof.

California Bungalow
A small one-story house with a low-pitched roof.

California Ranch
A one-story house with a low-pitched roof and a sprawling floor plan.

Spanish
A house with a tile roof and arches.

Cape Cod
A house with a second story above the eaves, a high-pitched roof, wood siding, and a large chimney.

French Provincial
A formal house with a high-pitched slate hip roof, a stone or brick exterior, and shutters.

Victorian
A house with ornate gables.

English Elizabethan
A house with a high-pitched slate roof, rough half-timbers, and a plaster exterior.

Monterey
A two-story house with a front balcony.

French Norman
A house having a tower as the main entrance and a steep roof.

English Tudor
A house with a high-pitched slate roof, a cathedral-like entrance, and a masonry exterior.

Mediterranean or Italian
A house with a tile roof, a stucco exterior, and rounded decorative work above the windows.

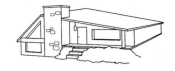

Contemporary
A house of modern design.

Mobile Homes (Manufactured Homes)

Mobile Home Sales

Licensees are authorized to list and sell mobile homes. A broker cannot, however, advertise a mobile home as being new. The mobile home must be in place and able to remain. If the mobile home is sold with a lot, then the lot must be properly zoned for mobile homes. A broker cannot represent that a mobile home can be moved unless the unit meets the requirements for transport on California highways. (The broker must reveal all equipment requirements.) The broker must also withdraw any advertisement on a mobile home within 48 hours of receipt of a notice that the mobile home is no longer available for sale. A broker may not have an office where two or more mobile homes are displayed for sale unless the broker is also licensed as a mobile home dealer.

The broker must cause all transfer documents to be delivered and is responsible for submission of documents and fees (if required) to the Department of Housing and Community Development (fees must be paid within 10 days of sale).

A broker may not indicate that there is no down payment if a second loan is to be arranged to cover the down payment. A broker also cannot prorate license or title fees unless the buyer and the seller agree to the proration.

Mobile homes installed for occupancy as a residence after July 1, 1980, or mobile homes for which the owner has allowed the registration to lapse for 120 days or more are subject to local property tax rather than vehicle tax. A pink slip is no longer used for mobile homes that are not subject to vehicle registration. If a new unit is attached to a foundation, it will be taxed as real property; if not, it will be taxed as personal property.

To transfer a mobile home to real property, the owner must:

1. Obtain a building permit.
2. Place the mobile home on a foundation.
3. Record a document showing that the mobile home has been affixed to a foundation.
4. Obtain a certificate of occupancy.

A licensee can be disciplined for:

1. Knowingly participating in the sale of a stolen mobile home.
2. Failure to provide for delivery of a properly endorsed certificate of ownership from the seller to the buyer (where applicable).
3. Submitting a check to the Department of Housing and Community Development that is dishonored.

Brokers have the same duty of a reasonably competent visual inspection and disclosures for mobile homes as they have for conventionally built housing.

A city or county is now precluded from prohibiting mobile homes on permanent foundations on residential sites.

CHAPTER 14 QUIZ

1. The highest board on a building is the:
   a. chimney cap   b. purlin   c. eave board   d. ridge board

2. A difference between a two-story house and a one-story house is that normally:
   a. the cost per square foot is greater on a two-story house
   b. the cost per square foot is greater on a one-story house
   c. a two-story house is more expensive than a one-story house
   d. a one-story house is more expensive than a two-story house

3. The beam over a window or door is known as the:
   a. door jamb   b. door joist   c. header   d. plate

4. When comparing a large house with a small house, which of the following applies?
   a. A large house costs more per square foot.   c. Size does not affect square-footage cost.
   b. A small house costs more per square foot.   d. None of these apply.

5. A mudsill would most likely be made of:
   a. steel   b. redwood   c. hemlock   d. pine

6. The woodwork around a door is known as the:
   a. lintel   b. jamb   c. sill   d. cripples

7. The easiest way to test for water pressure is to:
   a. open several taps and then flush a toilet
   b. turn on interior and exterior taps and notice the difference
   c. hold your hand over a tap and turn it on
   d. turn on a tap and check the water meter

8. A gambrel roof would be found on:
   a. barns   b. ranch houses   c. office buildings   d. factories

9. The sill is usually fastened to the foundation by:
   a. gravity   b. anchor bolts   c. epoxy   d. 10-penny nails

10. Shutters, a high-pitched slate hip roof, and stone construction would most likely be found on a:
    a. Dutch Colonial   c. Cape Cod
    b. Georgian Colonial   d. French Provincial

11. The term *cul-de-sac* refers to:
    a. a French architectural style
    b. an above-ground storm channel on the side of a street
    c. a type of street
    d. land rights

12. A window on hinges would most likely be a:
    a. double-hung window   c. glide-by window
    b. casement window   d. louver window

13. A roof on which all four sides slope to the eaves would be:
    a. a gambrel roof   b. a gable roof   c. a low-pitched roof   d. a hip roof

14. Which of the following is the most destructive to wood in California?
    a. boll weevil   c. wood worm
    b. subterranean termite   d. praying mantis

15. Studs are usually:
    a. 20 inches on center   c. 16 inches on center
    b. 90 inches on center   d. 12 inches on center

16. Drywall construction would *not* include which of the following?
    a. plaster   b. plasterboard   c. wood paneling   d. acoustical tile

17. A footing is:
    a. concrete blocks on which the house is constructed
    b. piles driven into the ground to support a structure
    c. the concrete laid across the foundation
    d. concrete poured in the ground on which the foundation rests

18. Ceiling height in a bedroom cannot be less than:
    a. 90 inches   b. 96 inches   c. 84 inches   d. 102 inches

19. Studs are contiguous to a:
    a. joist   b. rafter   c. plate   d. mudsill

20. Short pieces of vertical two-by-four above or below an opening are known as:
    a. studs   b. cripples   c. joists   d. fire blocks

21. That portion of the building which will spread its load directly to the soil is called the:
    a. footing   b. purlin   c. foundation   d. bearing wall

22. Beams supporting the floor are called:
    a. bases   b. studs   c. joists   d. collar beams

23. The fact that the interior and exterior walls feel the same temperature to the touch inside the house indicates:
    a. good circulation   c. poor insulation
    b. good insulation   d. lath and plaster construction

24. The boards covering the exterior studs or rafters are known as:
    a. insulation   b. siding   c. sheathing   d. bridging

25. Which of the following doesn't belong with the group?
    a. adobe   b. caliche   c. expansive   d. deciduous

26. Criss-crossed boards between floor joists are known as:
    a. bridging   b. diagonal bracing   c. fire stops   d. joists

27. The square footage of a house is normally figured by taking the:
    a. interior dimensions of the house
    b. interior dimensions of the house less partitions
    c. exterior roof line of the house
    d. exterior dimensions excluding the garage

28. The floor space of a house is normally figured by:
    a. adding to the square footage the patio and garage areas
    b. taking the interior dimensions of the house
    c. taking the cubic area enclosed by all walls
    d. taking the exterior measurements of the complete foundation

29. A party wall is:
    a. a wall dividing land owned by one person
    b. a wall on a property line maintained by both owners
    c. a bearing wall
    d. none of these

30. The purpose of a state contractor's license is to:
    a. protect against incompetent contractors   c. provide revenues
    b. eliminate the need for bonding   d. eliminate dishonesty

31. A bearing wall:
    a. would never have any doors or windows
    b. must run through the center of a house under the ridge line
    c. would be taken into consideration in remodeling
    d. would always be parallel to the rafters

32. Which of the following would *not* be contiguous?
    a. rafters and ridge board   c. joists and headers
    b. sole plate and studs   d. mudsill and anchor bolts

33. A soil pipe is:
    a. a drainage pipe
    b. a sewer pipe
    c. a used pipe
    d. any clay or porcelain pipe
34. The average person in California moves every _____ years.
    a. 2 to 3   b. 5 to 7   c. 4 to 6   d. 8 to 12
35. That part of the roof extending beyond the exterior walls is known as:
    a. the ridge   b. the eaves   c. flashing   d. fascia
36. Subflooring would be nailed to the:
    a. foundation   b. joists   c. studs   d. cripples
37. Which of the following does *not* belong with the others?
    a. gambrel   b. pitch   c. hip   d. penny
38. The most desirable land for a housing development would be:
    a. flat terrain
    b. gently rolling hills
    c. steep valleys and hills
    d. a 20-degree incline slope
39. Metalwork around chimneys and drains to prevent leaking is known as:
    a. a fire stop   b. flashing   c. waterproofing d. webbing
40. Which of the following are horizontal members in a wall?
    a. studs   b. cripples   c. joists   d. fire blocks
41. BTUs measure:
    a. power usage   b. value of insulation   c. thickness of a wire   d. heat
42. The term *potable* refers to:
    a. septic systems
    b. plumbing
    c. soil pipes
    d. quality for consumption
43. Percolation would be most likely considered in:
    a. floor plan arrangements
    b. septic system construction
    c. electrical installations
    d. heating system installations
44. Compaction would be most important in:
    a. building a home on a hillside lot
    b. setting density requirements for housing
    c. building a home on filled land
    d. selecting an architectural style
45. A four-story apartment building without an elevator would be a:
    a. flat
    b. walk-up
    c. tenement
    d. slum
46. Buildings getting new facades on a regular basis would most likely be:
    a. homes
    b. apartments
    c. commercial buildings
    d. industrial buildings
47. The vertical boards between the treads on each stair step are known as:
    a. risers
    b. stringers
    c. joists
    d. cripples
48. A percolation test determines:
    a. whether water is potable
    b. the level of absorption of water
    c. the ability of the soil to support a structure
    d. the elevation above the water table
49. *Wainscoting* refers to the:
    a. facade of a building
    b. waterproofing of a foundation
    c. lower three or four feet of an interior wall when finished differently from the rest of the wall
    d. lining on the inside of the eaves
50. The average homeowner in California moves every:
    a. 5 to 7 years   b. 2 to 3 years   c. 10 to 12 years   d. 3 to 4 years

51. In laying out a subdivision, the most uneconomical practice would be:
    a. street intersections at right angles
    b. curved streets
    c. long blocks
    d. short blocks

52. A nail is measured by:
    a. the inch   b. the pound   c. the penny   d. the metric system

53. Three-bedroom homes should have two baths because:
    a. families with over two children should have two bathrooms
    b. every house in the $100,000–$150,000 class should have two bathrooms
    c. health considerations demand it
    d. the buyers demand it

54. Building a house on a lot in such a way that the morning sun lights up the kitchen is known as:
    a. exposure   b. orientation   c. plottage   d. none of these

55. The housing market involves homes appealing to different economic groups; therefore, the market is considered to be:
    a. homogeneous   b. perfect   c. stratified   d. unstructured

56. Conditions pertaining most closely to the life of a wood-shingle roof would be:
    a. materials
    b. the pitch of the roof
    c. the location
    d. the size of the shingles

57. Which of the following would be a one-story house?
    a. Cotswold   b. Monterey   c. Garrison   d. California ranch

58. Which of the following would *not* be contiguous to a rafter?
    a. ridge board   b. ceiling joist   c. collar beam   d. all are contiguous

59. After a mobile home listing has expired, the broker has how long to cancel all advertising?
    a. must cancel immediately
    b. three working days
    c. 48 hours
    d. 72 hours

60. As to a new mobile home just installed for occupancy, which of the following is true?
    a. If it is attached to a foundation, it will be taxed as real property.
    b. If it is not attached to a foundation, it will be taxed as personal property.
    c. If it is sold with land, a licensee could have sold it.
    d. All of these are true.

61. The owner of a mobile home on wheels that is registered annually with the Department of Housing and Community Development installs new kitchen cabinets using bolts. The cabinets would be considered:
    a. a fixture   b. a chattel real   c. personal property   d. real property

62. A kiosk is a(n):
    a. dome frequently found on churches
    b. open-sided booth
    c. type of miter joint
    d. small vacation home

63. A single flat-plane roof that slants for rain runoff would be a:
    a. shed roof   b. gable roof   c. gambrel roof   d. dormer roof

64. The rental of lots in a mobile home park is under the jurisdiction of:
    a. the Real Estate Commissioner
    b. the Corporations Commissioner
    c. the state Department of Housing and Community Development
    d. HUD

65. *Conduit* refers to:
    a. water supply
    b. traffic flow
    c. electrical wiring
    d. heating systems

66. At least one room in a new house must be:
    a. a dining room
    b. at least 120 square feet
    c. earthquake resistant
    d. air conditioned

67. How many board feet are there in a board 2″ × 8″ × 12′?
    a. 2
    b. 16
    c. 32
    d. 64

68. The minimum ceiling height for a bath is:
    a. 70 inches
    b. 84 inches
    c. 90 inches
    d. 96 inches

69. A brass marker set by the U.S. Geological Survey showing elevation above sea level is known as a:
    a. lateral marker
    b. benchmark
    c. locator marker
    d. baseline marker

70. Fuses have been replaced in newer structures by:
    a. thermostats
    b. direct wiring
    c. conduit use
    d. circuit breakers

71. The purpose of using 6-inch studs rather than 4-inch studs in exterior walls is:
    a. greater strength
    b. the state building code
    c. the room for more insulation
    d. all of the above

72. Compaction is important as to:
    a. landfill
    b. setbacks
    c. multiple-family housing
    d. room size

73. A dark color:
    a. makes a room larger
    b. makes a room smaller
    c. can be either a or b
    d. neither a nor b

74. The diagonal boards supporting stairs are known as:
    a. stringers
    b. treads
    c. risers
    d. casing

75. Urban growth that follows main traffic routes outward from the city center would be:
    a. concentric circle growth
    b. multiple nuclei growth
    c. radial growth
    d. a megalopolis

76. A metropolitan area composed of cities that have grown together is known as a:
    a. megalopolis
    b. Gotham
    c. suburb
    d. planned community

77. The term HVAC stands for:
    a. a home vacuum system
    b. heating, ventilating, and air conditioning
    c. housing verification access code
    d. none of these

78. Open roof sheathing would be used with a:
    a. wood shake roof
    b. built-up roof
    c. asphalt shingle roof
    d. tile roof

79. The roof angle is measured by the:
    a. pitch
    b. rafters
    c. purlin
    d. shingle length

80. A broker noticed irregular mud lines from the ground to the siding on a home. This would be a likely indicator of:
    a. settling
    b. roach infestation
    c. subterranean termites
    d. a moisture problem

ANSWERS—CHAPTER 14 QUIZ

1. d. It sets the ridge line.
2. b. The same roof and foundation would cover double the square footage on a two-story house.
3. c. Or lintel.
4. b. The kitchen, grading, etc., are the same.
5. b. Or treated lumber to resist rot.
6. b.
7. a. See if the flow decreases.
8. a. And Dutch Colonials.
9. b.
10. d.
11. c. A circular dead-end street.
12. b.
13. d.
14. b. It makes mud tunnels.
15. c.
16. a. It is applied wet.
17. d.
18. a. And seven feet for the kitchen and bath.
19. c. The sole plate and the top plate.
20. b.
21. a.
22. c.
23. b. Little heat loss.
24. c. They are covered by siding.
25. d. The others are soil types. Deciduous refers to a hardwood tree (loses its leaves).
26. a.
27. d.

28. b.
29. b.
30. a
31. c.
32. c. They are on different planes.
33. b. Carries sewer waste.
34. a. Includes renters.
35. b.
36. b. Floor joists.
37. d. A nail measurement.
38. b. It breaks monotony without high costs.
39. b.
40. d. Between the studs.
41. d. A rating for furnaces and air conditioning.
42. d. Of water.
43. b. The ability of water to be absorbed into the soil.
44. c. The engineer tests for compaction.
45. b.
46. c. New exterior facing.
47. a. Multiple nuclei growth is from several points, sector growth is like pieces of a pie, and radial or axial growth is like the spokes of a wheel.
48. b. For septic systems.
49. c.
50. a.
51. d. The streets would take up more land.
52. c. Shown by the letter "d."

53. d.
54. b.
55. c. Market conditions vary by price range.
56. b. A greater pitch means longer life.
57. d. Ranches are one story.
58. d.
59. c.
60. d.
61. c. Since the mobile home is personal property.
62. b.
63. a.
64. c.
65. c. A pipe encasing wiring.
66. b.
67. b. 144 cubic inches per board foot.
68. b. Seven feet.
69. b.
70. d.
71. c.
72. a. To stabilize the soil.
73. d. It makes a room appear smaller.
74. a.
75. c.
76. a.
77. b.
78. a. To allow air circulation.
79. a.
80. c. Termite tunnels from the ground to the wood.

15

A Career in Real Estate

Real estate offers a career in which compensation is directly tied to performance. Salespersons work on a percentage of the total commissions earned on a transaction.

WHO NEEDS A REAL ESTATE LICENSE?

Basically, anyone doing anything in real estate for compensation must be licensed. This includes assisting someone in filing for the purchase of government land, as well as selling promissory notes secured by real estate.

A California licensee can sell property anywhere in the state of California. A California licensee can sell property located outside of California as long as all negotiations are conducted in California.

The following actions or persons do *not* require a license:

1. Dealing in one's own property.
2. Acting under an executed power of attorney (the person so acting is known as an attorney-in-fact).
3. Services rendered by an attorney-at-law while acting as an attorney-at-law.
4. A receiver or trustee in bankruptcy acting under a court order.
5. A trustee who sells property under a deed of trust.
6. Salaried employees of lending institutions.
7. Employees of a person who is a broker and has a management contract and are working under the direction of a licensed broker or salesperson.

8. A resident apartment manager (apartments of 16 or more units must have a resident manager.)

9. A condominium manager who only collects assessments and arranges maintenance (does not rent or sell).

10. Clerical workers. (An unlicensed secretary can quote prices and provide information contained on the listing to persons who inquire about a property.)

11. A cemetery lot salesperson.

12. A general partner in a limited partnership, providing that separate fees for real estate services are not charged.

13. Anyone, such as a hostess, who merely shows property and gives out brochures.

Salesperson's License

An applicant for a salesperson's license must be 18 years old, be honest and truthful, pass the examination with a score of 70 percent or better, be fingerprinted, and have a broker sign the application. He or she must apply for the license within one year following the examination date.

A salesperson is usually considered an employee of his or her broker. The salesperson is required to have a written, signed contract with his or her broker.

Even though the contract may claim to make the salesperson an independent contractor, the Department of Real Estate regards the salesperson as an employee of the broker.

If a salesperson is fired for a violation of the Real Estate Law, the broker must immediately notify the Department of Real Estate with a certified statement of the facts. Failure to do so can result in suspension or revocation of the broker's license.

The initial salesperson's license is really an 18-month conditional license. Within 18 months after issuance of the license, a salesperson must also complete two 3-college-unit classes, one of which must be Real Estate Practice. The second class must be one of the following:

General Accounting
Property Management
Real Estate Finance
Escrow
Mortgage Loan Brokering and Lending
Real Estate Appraisal

Business Law
Legal Aspects of Real Estate
Real Estate Economics
Real Estate Office Administration
Computer Applications in Real Estate

Failure to meet these requirements will result in automatic suspension of the salesperson's license.

The Federal Personal Responsibility and Work Opportunity Act denies public benefits, including professional licensing, to illegal immigrants. This applies to original and renewal real estate licenses. To implement this act, applicants for new and renewal licenses must provide proof of either U.S. citizenship or a legal alien status.

If a person is delinquent in family or child support payments, the Department of Real Estate can deny issuance or renewal of a real estate license.

Broker's License

An applicant for a broker's license must be 18 years old, be honest and truthful, have the experience and education required by law, and pass the examination with a score of 75 percent or better. A broker must maintain a definite place of business in California and must also be fingerprinted.

Experience A broker must have acquired two years' full-time experience as a salesperson or the equivalent within the previous five years. Graduation from an accredited four-year college can be substituted for the two years' experience.

Education Broker applicants must have completed eight college-level courses including:

Real Estate Practice   Legal Aspects of Real Estate
Real Estate Financing   Real Estate Appraisal

Accounting or Real Estate Economics (If the applicant completes both courses, only two courses from the following group are required.)
The remaining three courses must be selected from:

Real Estate Principles   Mortgage Loan Brokering and Lending
Real Estate Office Administration   Business Law
Advanced Legal Aspects of Real Estate   Property Management
Advanced Real Estate Appraisal   Escrows
Advanced Real Estate Finance   Computer Applications in Real Estate

An alien can obtain a California real estate license providing that a California resident can be a licensee in the alien's state of residence (reciprocity). Any nonresident licensee must consent to legal service upon the state Secretary of State (the licensee can be sued in California even if he or she can't be located within the state).

There is no limit to the number of times a person can take the real estate examination for either broker or salesperson. A person may reschedule his or her examination upon payment of a fee.

Brokers as Salespersons

A broker may obtain a saleperson's license without taking an examination. His or her broker's license continues to run in an inactive status but can be reinstated. A broker may also work for another broker as an associate broker.

Corporations as Brokers

Corporations can be licensed, but at least one officer must be a licensed broker (the chief officer responsible for real estate operations). At the time of corporate license application, background statements must be submitted for officers, directors, and persons having more than 10 percent of the corporate shares.

Partnerships

There is no real estate partnership license, but real estate partnerships can exist. Each partner in a real estate partnership who deals in real estate must be a licensee. A salesperson can now be a partner with a broker, but the broker is primarily responsible for the real estate acts of the partnership. If a nonlicensee is a partner with a broker, the nonlicensee cannot perform any act for which a license is required.

Splitting Commissions

There is only one agent and the broker is that agent. The broker can split commissions with or compensate:

- Salespersons working for the broker
- Another broker who aided in a transaction
- Another broker for a referral (even if in another state)

A broker cannot directly compensate a salesperson employed by another broker for an act that requires a real estate license.

Advance-Fee Brokers

These brokers collect fees in advance for advertising expenses in special magazines and papers devoted primarily to the sale of the property advertising. (They can't collect advance fees for normal newspaper ads.) The solicitation of advertisements for advance fees must be approved by the Real Estate Commissioner. The Commissioner has 10 days to approve or reject advertising. An accounting of expenses must be made to the principal within three months; the Commissioner may also demand an accounting. Funds must be placed in a trust account until actually expended. If funds are misapplied, the principal can recover treble damages.

Prepaid Rental Listing Service (PRLS)

An advance-fee rental agent requires a separate two-year Prepaid Rental Listing Service license (PRLS), but real estate brokers are exempt from the license requirement. The prospective tenant must be given a written contract (approved by the Department of Real Estate) not to exceed 90 days. The licensee shall refund in full the advance fee paid by a prospective tenant if the licensee does not supply a list of at least three rental properties that meet the prospective tenant's stated criteria within five days. Licensees must have the owner's permission to list a rental.

The agent shall return all over the first $50 of the advance fee upon demand of the prospective tenant if a rental is not obtained through the services of the agent and a refund is requested within 10 days of the expiration of the contract. Bad-faith refusal to return that portion of the deposit can result in damages not to exceed $500 in addition to actual damages. The contract must advise the potential renter (in boldface type) of the right to file a small-claims action for failure of the licensee to return all or part of the contract fee within 10 days of a request. The agent must confirm the availability of the property during the four-day period prior to supplying the information. (It is not a violation if the licensee checked availability from five to seven days prior to giving the information, if he or she made a good-faith effort to confirm it.) A $2,500 surety bond is required for each PRLS location.

Branch Office License

A special *branch office license* is required at each branch office. The licenses of the salespersons must be available for inspection at the broker's main office (not at the branch office where the salesperson may be working).

Mineral, Oil, and Gas License

No new licenses are being issued. A real estate licensee may handle a mineral, oil, or gas transaction (mineral, gas, and oil rights or leases) without a special permit.

Renewals

In order to renew a real estate license, the licensee must meet the continuing education requirements shown in the following table:

Continuing Education Requirements for Renewal Dates

Type of License	Initial Renewal on or after 1/1/96	Second and All Subsequent Renewals after 1/1/96 for "A" and "B" Licensees
A All licenses, broker and salesperson, except as provided in "B" below	• A total of 45 clock hours, which must include: (1) three-hour courses in ethics, agency, trust fund accounting and handling, and fair housing; and (2) at least 18 hours of consumer protection courses (The remaining 15 hours from consumer service or consumer protection courses)	• A total of 45 clock hours, which must include (1) a six-hour survey course covering the subjects of ethics, agency, trust fund accounting and handling, and fair housing; and (2) at least 18 hours of consumer protection courses (The remaining 21 hours from consumer service or consumer protection courses)
B Salespersons renewing for the first time after issuance of an original license	• Three-hour courses in ethics, agency, trust fund accounting and handling, and fair housing (a total of 12 clock hours)	

Restricted Licenses

After a hearing in accordance with the Administrative Procedures Act, a license may be revoked, suspended, or denied. A probationary license may, however, be issued. These licenses are restricted as to term (they are limited to a certain time period, such as six months), area of activity, and, for a salesperson, employment by a particular broker. These licenses can now be suspended without any further hearing, but a revocation requires a hearing. There is no automatic right of renewal or transfer with a restricted license. As a condition for a restricted license, the Department of Real Estate can order that restitution be made to any party damaged by the licensee's actions, as well as order the posting of a surety bond.

Disciplinary Action

The document that initiates a disciplinary action is known as the **accusation.** A hearing is held in accordance with the **Administrative Procedures Act.** The administrative law judge prepares a decision, which is sent to the Real Estate Commissioner, who can adopt it, reduce the penalty, or reject it.

The Commissioner may revoke, suspend, or deny licensing. Decisions of the Commissioner may be appealed to the courts, but the courts will overrule only if the decisions were arbitrary or capricious. (See Chapter 4 for a list of violations that can lead to disciplinary action.)

Suspension and Revocation

The Real Estate Commissioner can suspend without a hearing, within 90 days of issuance, any license obtained by fraud, misrepresentation, or deceit. When a real estate broker's license is revoked or suspended, the licenses of his or her salespeople are automatically canceled, although they may transfer their licenses to other brokers. The commission can require reexamination as a condition of reinstatement of a revoked license, and continuing education requirements must be met. The Real Estate Commissioner may require proof of honesty of an applicant.

Procedure for Transfer of a Salesperson's License

1. The former broker has three days to return the salesperson's license and sign the transfer application. (The three days also applies to termination of employment.) The broker *immediately* notifies the Commissioner. (A salesperson's real estate license is kept by the broker. The salesperson keeps only a pocket identification card, while the broker keeps the licenses, which need not be displayed.)
2. The salesperson crosses out the former broker's name on the license, puts in the new broker's name, and delivers it to the new broker.
3. A transfer application signed by the salesperson and the new broker must be sent to the Department of Real Estate within five days of new employment.

Broker's Use of a Fictitious Name

Use of a business name that does not contain the surnames of the principals is considered a *fictitious name.*

The broker must comply with the fictitious-name statute and advertise and file with the county clerk. The fictitious name shall appear on the broker's license. A fictitious-name statement expires after five calendar years. The licensee shall file a certified copy of the fictitious-name statement with the license application.

COMMISSION PAYMENTS

Commissions are usually a percentage of the sale price but can be a set fee or tied to a formula. Commissions can be anything of value (as agreed by the parties) but are usually paid in money.

The state labor commissioner, a member of the Department of Industrial Relations, handles commission disputes between brokers and their salespeople. (Disputes between brokers would be handled either by voluntary arbitration or through the courts.)

PROFESSIONAL REAL ESTATE DESIGNATIONS

AFLM Accredited Farm and Land Member. A professional designation of the Farm and Land Institute of the National Association of REALTORS®.

AMO Accredited Management Organization. A firm that meets the guidelines of IREM and has at least one CPM.

ARELLO Association of Real Estate License Law Officials. The Real Estate Commissioners of each state are all members of this organization.

ARM Accredited Resident Manager. A professional designation of IREM.

ASA American Society of Appraisers.

ASREC American Society of Real Estate Counselors.

CAR California Association of REALTORS®. Associated with the NAR.

CAREB California Association of Real Estate Brokers. Affiliated with NAREB.

CCIM Certified Commercial Investment Member. A professional designation of the REALTORS® National Marketing Institute.

CMB Certified Mortgage Banker. A professional designation of the Mortgage Bankers Association of America.

CPM Certified Property Manager. A professional designation of IREM.

CRB   Certified Residential Brokerage Manager. A professional designation of the REALTORS® National Marketing Institute.

CRE   Counselor of Real Estate. A professional designation of the American Society of Real Estate Counselors (ASREC), part of the NAR.

GRI   Graduate REALTORS® Institute. A professional designation of the CAR.

IREM   Institute of Real Estate Management. Part of NAR.

MAI   Member of Appraisal Institute. A professional designation of the Appraisal Institute.

NACORE   National Association of Corporate Real Estate Executives.

NAR   National Association of REALTORS®.

NAREB   National Association of Real Estate Brokers. An association of primarily African American real estate brokers founded in 1947.

Realtist   A designation for a member of NAREB.

REALTOR®   A designation for a member of the NAR.

REALTOR-ASSOCIATE®   A salesperson who is a member of the NAR.

RESSI   Real Estate Securities and Syndication Institute. Part of the National Association of REALTORS®.

RM   Residential Member. A professional designation of the American Institute of Real Estate Appraisers.

SIR   Society of Industrial REALTORS®.

WCR   Women's Council of REALTORS®.

BUSINESS OPPORTUNITIES

A real estate license allows the licensee to deal in business opportunities as well as in real estate. A business opportunity includes personal property and goodwill.

Goodwill

The expectation of continued public patronage. The price of goodwill can be computed as follows:

Price paid for goodwill = Price of business − Value of assets

Listings of business opportunities need not always be in writing (since real estate may not always be involved and the value may be less than $500). Listings should, however, be detailed as to what inventory and fixtures are included, as well as their condition and all terms of sale.

Purchase Contract

The purchase contract should indicate that it is subject to transferability of the lease as well as subject to the buyer obtaining all the necessary licenses and permits. There may be an attached list of fixtures included in the sale as well as a definite price or formula for the stock in trade of the business.

Send-Out Slips

A broker may not ask a prospective purchaser of a business to sign a *send-out slip* (a statement that the purchaser will deal only on properties disclosed through that particular broker) unless the broker has the authorization of the owner to do so.

Fictitious Names

A business frequently operates under a name that does not include the surnames of all the principals. Every business operating under a fictitious name must file a fictitious-name statement in order to be able to sue or enforce agreements under the firm name. The fictitious-name statement must be filed with the county clerk in the county where the business is located within 40 days of beginning business. Within 30 days of filing, it must be published in a newspaper of general circulation, in the county where the business is located, once a week for four weeks.

A fictitious-name statement expires at the end of five years, computed from December 31 of the year it was filed. A business wishing to abandon a fictitious name must file a statement of abandonment with the county clerk.

Bulk Sales Act

The purpose of the Bulk Sales Act, which is part of the **Uniform Commercial Code,** is to protect purchasers of a business against unsecured creditors of the former owner, as well as to protect the creditors from disposal of assets by the debtor. A **bulk sale** is any sale not in the course of normal business. For example, selling 10 pounds of nails may be a normal sale, but selling all the hardware in the store to one customer is not a sale in the normal course of business.

Requirements of the Bulk Sales Act

1. Record a notice of the sale with the applicable county recorder at least 12 business days before the sale is consummated.
2. Publish a notice of the sale in a newspaper of general circulation within the judicial district in which the property is located at least 12 business days before the sale is consummated.

3. Send by registered or certified mail a notice of the sale to the county tax collector at least 12 business days prior to sale.

The notice must include the name and address of the seller, all other business names and addresses used by the seller within the past three years, a statement that a bulk transfer is to be made, the description and location of the property, the time and place of the sale, and the name and address where claims are to be filed.

The purpose of recording and publishing a notice of the sale is to alert creditors of the vendor that the vendor is selling his or her business. If they wish to assert their rights against the property, they must do so prior to the sale. If the Bulk Sales Act is properly complied with, creditors who fail to come forward can go only to the vendor for payment and not to the merchandise.

Effect of Noncompliance   If the Bulk Sales Act is not complied with, the creditors of the vendor can treat the assets purchased by the vendee as still belonging to the vendor. That is to say, if they obtain a judgment against the vendor, they can reach the assets sold to the vendee. Therefore, it is primarily the responsibility of the *vendee* to see that the Bulk Sales Act is complied with, since he or she is the one adversely affected by noncompliance.

Sale at Auction   In the case of sale of a business at auction, it is the auctioneer's responsibility to see that the requirements of the Bulk Sales Act are met. If not, he or she can be held personally liable.

Franchising

Franchising is a form of investment where the franchisee has a right to engage in a business under a marketing plan of the franchisor.

Franchise Investment Law   The purpose of this disclosure, which is part of the Corporation Code, is to protect against fraud and the possibility that the franchisor will not fulfill his or her promises. The law requires a franchisor to provide a prospective franchisee with enough information so that he or she can make an intelligent decision. This information must be furnished at least 10 business days before the franchisee is bound. (Fees cannot be paid until close of escrow.)

To sell a franchise, the franchisor must register the sale with the state; he or she must also be one of the following:

1. A franchisor (a person owning a basic franchise).
2. A real estate broker or salesperson (a licensee may sell franchises).
3. A licensed corporate security dealer.

Exempt from registration are franchisors with a net worth of $5,000,000 or more with a minimum of 25 franchises in operation during the five years prior to the sale. Violations of the Franchise Investment Law can result in a fine of up to $10,000 and/or up to one year in jail.

Bill of Sale

A *bill of sale* passes title to personal property, whereas a deed passes title to real property. However, a bill of sale is not recorded. In a sale of a business, title to the stock and fixtures would pass by bill of sale. Leases are assigned on the leases themselves and are not transferred by bill of sale. Licenses are not transferred by bill of sale, because permission of the licensing authority is required.

A bill of sale must include the following:

1. The date.
2. The signature of the vendor (the vendee does not sign).
3. The name of the vendee.
4. A description of the property (an inventory may be attached).

ABC (ALCOHOLIC BEVERAGE CONTROL) ACT

This act is administered by the Department of Alcoholic Beverage Control. Alcoholic beverage licenses will be issued to persons 21 years of age or older, partnerships, fiduciaries, or corporations. An alien can also obtain a liquor license.

Licenses are limited in number and are issued for particular premises. Licenses issued for a specific location must be placed in use within 30 days of issuance. Fingerprinting is required, and application may be denied because of the moral character of the applicant or a disqualifying criminal record, or because the license is in the vicinity of a church, school, playground, etc.

A license is not a right; it is a privilege. It may not be pledged or otherwise encumbered.

On-Sale License A license to sell liquor that will be consumed *on the premises* (for example, a tavern).

Off-Sale License A license to sell liquor that will be consumed *off the premises* (for example, a package liquor store). Licenses for off-sale will not be allowed where there is an on-sale license.

General License A license to sell any alcoholic beverage, as opposed to a license to sell only beer and wine (beer or beer and wine license).

New License The fee for a new general on-sale or off-sale license is $6,000. A social or fraternal organization must have been established for at least one year to apply for a new license.

Selling Existing Licenses The resale price for any general license cannot exceed $6,000. (*Exception:* There is no limit on the price for a license five years old or older.)

In selling a license where the resale price is limited to $6,000, the price paid for fixtures must be reasonable, and the price paid for goodwill cannot exceed the average month's gross (figured over 12 consecutive months). The purpose of this is to prevent circumvention of the law. Limitations on prices for new licenses and prohibitions against moving new licenses are designed to limit speculation in liquor licenses.

In the sale of a business opportunity involving a license, escrow may not be closed until transfer of the license is approved.

Sales Tax

The sales tax applies to the sale of tangible personal property. The basic rate is 7 1/4 percent up to 8 1/4 percent. Taxing districts can add up to .5 percent to the state rate. The state Board of Equalization collects the sales tax from the retailer, who collects it from the consumer. Sales tax must be shown separately on receipts. The retailer is liable for the tax even if the retailer fails to collect it.

The penalties for failure to pay sales tax are as follows:

Failure to pay tax on time	10% penalty
Fraud in nonpayment	25% penalty
	35% total penalties possible

(So if, by fraud, a retailer fails to pay $1,000 in sales tax, he or she could be liable for up to $350 in penalties.)

Resale Certificate

A *resale certificate* allows a retailer to purchase goods without paying sales tax when the goods are to be resold. (Sales tax is collected only once, from the final customer.)

In the sale of a business, sales tax is not charged on the stock of merchandise held for resale, since the consumers will eventually pay when the merchandise is resold. Fixtures and other items not for resale (counters, trucks, displays, lighting, etc.) used to carry on a business are subject to the sales tax; therefore, in the sale of a business, a cash register would be subject to sales tax, but cases of perfume held for resale would not.

Successor Liability The purchaser of a business is liable for the sales tax collected by the previous owner but not remitted to the state. For his or her protection, the purchaser of a business should obtain a **clearance receipt** from the state Board of Equalization stating that the sales tax has been paid to a particular date.

Use Tax This fills a gap of taxing items to be used or stored in this state for which sales tax was not paid. The tax rate is the same as that of the sales tax. Payment of the use tax is the responsibility of the purchaser.

Business-Related Terms

Assets Items of value owned by a business. May include cash, stock in trade, paid-up rent, prepaid insurance, accounts receivable, etc. **Liquid assets** are cash or securities that can be readily converted to cash. **Illiquid assets,** such as real estate, are not readily converted to cash.

Liabilities   Debts owed by a business. May include liens, notes outstanding, accounts payable, etc.

Balance Sheet   Shows total assets and liabilities, therefore giving net worth at a particular point in time. It does not show whether or not a business is profitable.

Profit-and-Loss Statement   An operating statement for a period of time. It shows profit or loss, but not net worth.

Net Worth   Value of assets over liabilities.

Turnover   The number of times the stock of a business is sold during a period of time. *Example:* If the value of the stock at the retail price is $100,000, and the yearly volume is $1,000,000, the turnover rate is 10.

Gross   Total receipts.

Liquidity   The ability to pay debts when due. A ratio of current assets to current liabilities of 2:1 is considered safe. Cash and accounts receivable within one year are considered current assets. Liabilities due or payable within one year are considered current liabilities.

Scheduled Gross Income   Gross income based on 100 percent occupancy and no collection cost.

Adjusted Gross Income   Gross income adjusted for a vacancy factor and collection loss.

Debt-to-Income Ratio   The ratio of a borrower's total incurred debt to the borrower's gross income; an important loan criterion used by lenders.

Debt-to-Equity Ratio   This is the ratio of what a business owes in both long-term and short-term debt to the equity the owner has in the business. Equity is the value of the business assets minus liabilities. As a rule of thumb, this ratio should be between 3:1 and 4:1.

Gross Profit   Total sales minus the cost of the merchandise sold.

Net Profit   Total sales minus the cost of goods and all other expenses.

Net Spendable   See Cash Flow.

Markup   The percentage added to cost to determine the selling price. (It may also be expressed as a percentage of the selling price.)

Example:

Item costs $1 and sells for $2

Markup as a percentage of cost = 100%

Markup as a percentage of selling price = 50%

Cash Flow   That amount of money that remains as net spendable. Noncash expenses such as depreciation are not considered in determining cash flow.

Company Dollar   A term used in the real estate business to denote the portion of the commission earned that goes to the office (the broker) after paying salespersons and/or cooperating brokers.

Desk Cost   The company cost to keep each salesperson. It is the total operating overhead divided by the number of salespersons in the office.

Turn-Key Project   A complete construction package from site preparation to delivery of a structure ready for occupancy.

Property Insurance   Prepaid insurance is an asset. If an insurance company cancels a policy, it is **prorated** as to the refund, but if the insured cancels, he or she gets back less than a true prorated share. This is known as a **short-rate refund.** Because insurance is a personal contract, the insurer must agree to a policy assumption. Insurance policies customarily list all structures on a property. Policies provide for cancellation a specified number of days after notice by the insurer.

Coinsurance   Insurance under which the insured is required to carry a policy covering a percentage of replacement cost (usually 80 percent) to receive full coverage for a loss. If the insured carries less coverage, he or she receives only a percentage of the loss based on the coverage. Coinsurance is generally for nonresidential property.

CHAPTER 15 QUIZ

1. Phil pays the Department of Alcoholic Beverage Control $6,000.
   a. He is buying a general, off-sale, or on-sale license from a licensee.
   b. He is applying for a new general, off-sale, or on-sale license.
   c. Either a or b is true.
   d. Neither a nor b is true.

2. The *successor liability* of a business refers to:
   a. unpaid prior debts for inventory
   b. collected but unpaid sales tax
   c. pending lawsuits
   d. all of these

3. General liquor licenses less than five years old cannot be resold for more than:
   a. $6,000
   b. $500
   c. $10,000
   d. there is no limit on the sale price

4. Notice of an intended sale of a business is recorded and published a day prior to sale. The sale is:
   a. void as to the vendor's creditors
   b. illegal
   c. void
   d. none of these

5. A balance sheet shows:
   a. operational detail　　b. net worth　　c. profit or loss　　d. sale value

6. An advance fee is:
   a. prepayment of a commission
   b. a bonus to a broker to accept a listing
   c. prepayment of promotional costs in a paper or magazine devoted primarily to describing properties for sale
   d. prepayment of regular newspaper ads

7. The Bulk Sales Act is part of the:
   a. Commissioner's regulations
   b. Real Estate Code
   c. Uniform Commercial Code
   d. Corporation Code

8. The Franchise Investment Law requires:
   a. a franchisor to register sales
   b. disclosures in an offering prospectus
   c. both a and b
   d. neither a nor b

9. Licensees for on-sale and off-sale alcoholic beverage licenses must be fingerprinted, with the exception of:
   a. corporate officers having management duties
   b. partners having only slight management duties
   c. wives when the husband is also a licensee
   d. none of these

10. Which of the following would be concerned with obtaining a clearance receipt in the sale of a business?
    a. the vendor
    b. the lienholder
    c. the state Board of Equalization
    d. the vendee

11. Subtracting cost of merchandise from gross sales gives:
    a. net profit
    b. gross sales
    c. adjusted gross sales
    d. gross profit

12. A certificate of resale is:
    a. required from the merchant to avoid sales tax
    b. required by law when used goods are sold
    c. a limitation on personal property tax
    d. provided by the purchaser

13. You must have a sales tax permit if you are going to:
    a. engage in retail sales
    b. engage in wholesale sales
    c. either a or b
    d. neither a nor b

14. An alcoholic beverage license will be issued:
    a. for a location adjoining a public school
    b. for a location where it can be expected to cause traffic difficulties
    c. to a person who has no specific location where he or she intends to conduct business
    d. only after the licensee has been fingerprinted

15. An advance-fee rental agent must:
    a. be a real estate broker
    b. return all over the first $10 of the fee if a rental is not obtained
    c. confirm availability of rentals at least seven days prior to providing the information
    d. give a prospective tenant a written contract

16. A liquor license must be put in use within _____ days of initial issuance.
    a. 10   b. 30   c. 60   d. 90

17. Balancing a bank statement with an account is known as:
    a. auditing   c. reconciliation
    b. taking a trial balance   d. none of these

18. The term *liabilities of a business* refers to:
    a. balances of debtors   c. accounts receivable
    b. claims of creditors   d. prepaid insurance

19. After publication has been made of a sale, the earliest the business can safely be sold is:
    a. immediately   b. 5 days   c. 12 days   d. 30 days

20. To have any effect, a bill of sale must:
    a. be signed by the vendee   c. be acknowledged by the vendor
    b. describe the property   d. be acknowledged by the vendee

21. Colonel Cluck wishes to open franchise stores in California. They have had 25 franchises operating for five years in Arizona. Their net worth is in excess of $5,000,000. They must:
    a. register with the Corporations Commissioner
    b. post a $10,000 fidelity bond
    c. both a and b
    d. neither a nor b

22. Sales tax would *not* be collected on:
    a. fresh produce   c. groceries
    b. prescription medicine   d. any of these

23. A broker who uses a send-out slip:
    a. must have written permission from the prospective buyer
    b. must have written permission from the owner
    c. is violating the Real Estate Law
    d. none of these

24. An economics-conscious landlord would set rents based on:
    a. owner costs   c. replacement cost
    b. tenant income   d. market data

25. By checking a profit-and-loss statement, you would find:
    a. net worth   b. book value   c. operational results   d. none of these

26. As to the sale of a business in which the Bulk Sales Act requirements have *not* been met, which of the following is true?
    a. The sale is valid as to the buyer and the seller.
    b. Transfer is not enforceable by the parties.
    c. The sale is void.
    d. The sale is illegal.

27. The state Board of Equalization:
    a. appraises public utilities for property tax
    b. checks county assessors as to the uniformity of their assessments
    c. collects state sales tax
    d. all of these

28. An auctioneer who sells at auction and fails to comply with the Bulk Sales Act:
    a. is secondarily liable to creditors
    b. is personally liable to creditors of the vendor
    c. is an agent and as such is not liable unless he or she agreed to be personally responsible for compliance
    d. is liable only if he or she proceeded with the auction knowing of the noncompliance

29. A large feed wholesaler wishes to sell 100,000 pounds of bulk feed to a dealer. He or she should comply with:
    a. the Bulk Sales Act   c. both a and b
    b. the Franchise Investment Law   d. neither a nor b

30. The ABC will *not* issue an alcoholic beverage license to:
    a. a social or fraternal organization established two months ago
    b. a married woman
    c. an alien
    d. a seasonal resort

31. Which of the following cannot obtain an alcoholic beverage license?
    a. an unmarried woman   c. a minor
    b. a person with an arrest record   d. all of these

32. The capital turnover of a real estate investor is _____ that of the average vendor.
    a. about the same as   c. slightly less than
    b. slightly more than   d. much less than

33. State sales tax on the fixtures of a business being sold would never be:
    a. collected by the seller and remitted with his or her sales tax
    b. sent directly to the state Board of Equalization
    c. waived by the transferor
    d. all of these

34. A balance sheet would *not* show:
    a. accounts receivable   c. inventory
    b. operating expenses   d. value of fixtures

35. Property sold in a bulk sale would be transferred by:
    a. a financing statement   c. a bill of sale
    b. a bulk sales agreement   d. none of these

36. Sales taxes normally are required to be remitted to the state Board of Equalization:
    a. weekly   b. monthly   c. quarterly   d. when requested

37. A detailed listing of the physical assets of a business would be found in a(n):
    a. profit-and-loss statement   c. listing
    b. balance sheet   d. inventory sheet

38. Compliance with the Bulk Sales Act requires publication at least 12 days prior to the sale in:
    a. a paper of record
    b. a paper within the same county where the property is located
    c. a paper of general circulation within the judicial district where the property is located
    d. any of these

39. The financing statement for personal property in the sale of a business would most likely be filed with the:
    a. Department of Alcoholic Beverage Control
    b. secretary of state
    c. Real Estate Commissioner
    d. Bulk Sales Commission

40. The goodwill value of a business can be computed by:
    a. subtracting the value of stock, fixtures, and leases from the sale price
    b. subtracting net from the sale price
    c. $1.00
    d. none of these

41. A $6,000 fee is:
    a. the annual fee for a general on-sale license
    b. the annual fee for a general off-sale license
    c. both a and b
    d. neither a nor b

42. All of the following terms have something in common except:
    a. clearance receipt
    b. state Board of Equalization
    c. successor liability
    d. Real Estate Commissioner

43. Advance-fee broker advertising must be submitted to the Real Estate Commissioner _____ days prior to use.
    a. 5   b. 7   c. 10   d. 30

44. A liability of a business would be:
    a. uncollectable accounts receivable
    b. prepaid insurance
    c. value of fixed assets
    d. none of these

45. A real estate broker's ad must include:
    a. the name of the broker
    b. that the advertiser is a broker or agent
    c. the address of the broker
    d. either a or b

46. *Turnover* refers to:
    a. the number of times a business is sold
    b. the number of times an inventory is sold
    c. dollar volume
    d. none of these

47. The most reliable income figure for a grocery store that is for sale would be:
    a. the figure on the listing
    b. the figures from the owner's income tax returns
    c. the broker's estimate
    d. sales tax paid

48. An on-sale liquor license may be transferred:
    a. from person to person
    b. from premises to premises
    c. both a and b
    d. neither a nor b

49. The most important element of goodwill is:
    a. attitude of employees
    b. value of stock
    c. previous volume
    d. habit of patronage

50. The least important element of goodwill is:
    a. store policies
    b. knowledgeable and pleasant employees
    c. advertising history
    d. a modern store

51. Accounts payable on a balance sheet would show up as:
    a. a liability   b. an asset   c. both a and b   d. neither a nor b

52. A retailer can:
    a. show the sales tax separately when pricing goods
    b. absorb the sales tax
    c. set his or her own accounting period for remitting collected sales tax to the state Board of Equalization
    d. none of these

53. A valid bill of sale does *not* require:
    a. the vendee's signature
    b. documentary stamps
    c. a notary seal and recording
    d. any of these

54. One year ago, Judy received an on-sale general liquor license from the state. She wishes to sell to Greg. The most she can get for the license is:
    a. $500
    b. $5,000
    c. $6,000
    d. there is no limit

55. The notice required under the Bulk Sales Act need *not* include:
    a. the name of the seller
    b. a description of the property
    c. the sale price and terms
    d. the date and place of the sale

56. Accounts payable are in the same accounting category as:
    a. accounts receivable
    b. cash on hand
    c. prepaid insurance
    d. bank loans

57. The term *cash flow* refers to:
    a. the amount of profit on a rental
    b. the amount of money received
    c. the length of time it takes to recover on an investment
    d. the difference between receipts and all cash expenses

58. Which of the following would *not* be transferred by a bill of sale?
    a. goodwill
    b. fixtures
    c. lease
    d. stock in trade

59. Goodwill costs for an on-sale or off-sale general alcoholic beverage license less than five years old cannot exceed:
    a. $6,000
    b. average monthly sales based on the previous 12 months' sales
    c. $1,000
    d. none of these

60. Liquidity of a firm would be best described as the ratio of:
    a. cash to total indebtedness
    b. total assets to total liabilities
    c. current assets to current liabilities
    d. income to expenses

61. To be enforceable, listings of business opportunities:
    a. must always be in writing
    b. never have to be in writing
    c. do not always have to be in writing
    d. must be exclusive

62. Notice of intent to engage in the sale of alcoholic beverages must be posted on the premises for at least:
    a. 5 consecutive days
    b. 10 consecutive days
    c. 30 consecutive days
    d. 90 consecutive days

63. A business balance sheet might include all except:
    a. goodwill
    b. inventory
    c. gross sales
    d. accounts payable

64. Since there are county and state sales taxes:
    a. the state collects both and remits a portion to the county
    b. merchants must pay the state and county separately
    c. merchants may, at their option, pay the entire tax to the state Board of Equalization
    d. none of these, since there is no county tax

65. The maximum sale price for resale of a general off-sale license originally issued July 1, 1959, when the current owner has had the license for only one year, is:
    a. $600
    b. $6,000
    c. $1,000
    d. there is no limit

66. A business owner fails to remit $1,000 in collected sales tax in a timely manner. He is also guilty of fraud. The maximum penalty he can be assessed is:
    a. $350
    b. $500
    c. $1,000
    d. $50,000 and/or up to five years in prison

67. Jane purchases a car in Oregon and wishes to license it in California. She is going to be taxed. This tax based on value is:
    a. a sales tax
    b. a use tax
    c. an ownership tax
    d. none of these

68. The tax paid on fixtures by the purchaser of a business would be a:
    a. sales tax
    b. use tax
    c. franchise tax
    d. none of these

69. The stock in trade of a business is transferred by a(n):
    a. financing statement
    b. deed
    c. inventory list
    d. bill of sale

70. A listing of buildings and outbuildings would most likely be required for a:
    a. grant deed
    b. title insurance policy
    c. fire insurance policy
    d. land contract

71. A balance sheet would show:
    a. retail value of inventory
    b. wholesale value of inventory
    c. volume of sales
    d. operating expenses

72. The acid-test ratio for cash on hand (includes securities readily converted to cash) to current liabilities is:
    a. 1:1
    b. 1:5
    c. 2:1
    d. 1:2

73. The term *short-rate* describes an:
    a. insurance refund when the company cancels
    b. interest table for short-term loans
    c. insurance refund when the insured cancels
    d. none of these

74. If you were planning a suburban shopping center, one of the first things you would consider is:
    a. the purchasing power of the area
    b. the population
    c. competition
    d. location

75. Which of the following is true?
    a. A regional shopping center requires a population of 200,000 or more.
    b. A community shopping center would be supported by a population of 100,000 or less.
    c. A small neighborhood shopping center requires 7,000 to 18,000 population.
    d. All of these are true.

76. A right to use a marketing plan would be described as a(n):
    a. chain operation
    b. franchise
    c. license
    d. easement

77. The least desirable business in a shopping center would be a:
    a. sporting goods store
    b. supermarket
    c. real estate office
    d. drugstore

78. A use tax is:
    a. a listing on a sales price
    b. a form of income tax
    c. a tax on tenants
    d. none of these

79. An on-sale liquor license would *not* be issued to which of the following?
    a. a restaurant opened a year ago
    b. a bar opened six months ago
    c. a cafeteria opened six months ago
    d. a liquor store opened one year ago

80. In a sale of a business, sales tax would *not* be paid on:
    a. stock in trade
    b. fixtures
    c. both a and b
    d. neither a nor b

81. When a business is being sold, the term *successor liability* may become important. Real estate brokers know that this term involves certain obligations to the:
    a. Department of Alcoholic Beverage Control
    b. secretary of state
    c. Department of Corporations
    d. state Board of Equalization

82. The Franchise Investment Law could best be described as:
    a. a law that regulates franchisors' activities
    b. a disclosure law
    c. both a and b
    d. neither a nor b

83. To sell franchise opportunities, a person must be:
    a. the owner of a basic franchise
    b. a real estate broker
    c. a licensed corporate security dealer
    d. any of these

84. Accounts payable of a business would be:
    a. an asset
    b. a liability
    c. a prorated item for escrow
    d. none of these

85. As to a business, which of the following is false?
    a. assets minus liabilities = net worth
    b. income minus expenses = profit
    c. expenses plus profit = gross income
    d. gross income minus profit = net

86. A fictitious-name statement expires:
    a. five years from abandonment
    b. five years from recordation
    c. five years from December 31 of the year recorded
    d. none of these

87. A profit-and-loss statement would *not* include:
    a. operating expenses
    b. gross receipts
    c. interest charges
    d. value of fixtures

88. The license of a salesperson working at a branch office is held:
    a. at the branch office
    b. with the Real Estate Commissioner
    c. at the broker's primary place of business
    d. in the pocket or purse of the salesperson

89. For a fee, Thomas offers to assist Sara in leasing and/or purchasing federal land.
    a. Thomas cannot charge a fee.
    b. Thomas must be a broker.
    c. Thomas can charge a fee.
    d. Both b and c are true.

90. Terri does not require a real estate license if:
    a. she is an employee of a property management firm and rents apartments
    b. she employs a real estate salesperson to sell her property
    c. she charges a flat fee rather than a commission
    d. her commission agreements are verbal

91. A prospective renter paid $300 for a list of rentals. Since a rental was not obtained, the prospective renter asked for the return of the fee 7 days later. The agent must return:
    a. nothing   b. $25   c. $50   d. $250

92. An unlicensed secretary in a real estate office can:
    a. quote prices over the phone
    b. type listings and sales contracts for licensees
    c. hand out brochures
    d. all of these

93. Roland, a broker, makes a sale. His license is later revoked. After revocation, escrow is completed.
    a. A commission goes to the Real Estate Education Research and Recovery Fund.
    b. The seller does not have to pay the commission.
    c. The commission is split between the buyer and the seller.
    d. Roland gets his commission.

94. A real estate salesperson may *not:*
    a. take a listing for the broker
    b. take a deposit on the broker's listing
    c. agree in writing to work for a 1 percent commission
    d. accept a commission directly from another broker

95. A broker may *not*:
    a. employ licensed salespeople on a salary basis
    b. hire other brokers to work as salespeople
    c. hire unlicensed persons to solicit listings
    d. pay a commission to a broker in another state who sent him or her a client

96. Which of the following needs a real estate license?
    a. an attorney-in-fact selling property for his or her principal
    b. an executor of an estate disposing of real property
    c. an attorney taking a listing
    d. none of these

97. Real estate licenses are issued for:
    a. one year　　　b. two years　　　c. four years　　　d. life

98. To serve process on a nonresident California licensee, a person would serve upon:
    a. the Department of Real Estate　　　c. the California secretary of state
    b. the applicable district attorney　　　d. none of these

99. Robert, a developer who is unlicensed, hires Yvonne, a broker, to sell his property. While Yvonne is out of town, Robert shows property, quotes prices, and makes sales.
    a. Yvonne can be fined $500.
    b. Yvonne can be fined $50.
    c. Robert has violated the Real Estate Law.
    d. Neither Robert nor Yvonne has done anything wrong.

100. Which of the following is true?
    a. Every real estate broker must maintain a definite place of business in California.
    b. A salesperson's advertisements must include the broker's name.
    c. both a and b
    d. neither a nor b

101. To obtain a real estate broker's license under the law, which of the following is required?
    a. a verification　　　c. an affirmation
    b. a state civil service examination　　　d. a written examination

102. Walter, a broker in California, pays a commission to Rita, a broker in Wisconsin who sent him a client.
    a. Walter can be fined $450.　　　c. Both a and b are true.
    b. Walter can have his license revoked.　　　d. Neither a nor b is true.

103. A salesperson leaves a broker. The broker must notify the Real Estate Commissioner:
    a. immediately　　　c. before the broker's license renewal
    b. within five working days　　　d. not at all—it is the duty of the new broker

104. George manages and leases five separate properties for an out-of-state owner, getting an apartment furnished at one of the locations as part payment for the work.
    a. George needs a real estate license.
    b. George does not need a real estate license.
    c. George must be a CPM.
    d. Both a and c are true.

105. A salesperson's commission is paid by:
    a. the seller　　　b. the broker　　　c. escrow　　　d. the buyer

106. A licensee with a restricted license may be restricted by the Commissioner as to:
    a. the term and area of activity　　　c. the amount of commission
    b. the number of sales　　　d. none of these

107. A person passing the real estate examination must apply for a license within:
    a. one year of the examination　　　c. six months of the examination
    b. one year of notification of passing　　　d. six months of notification of passing

108. Which of the following indicates an organization of brokers founded in 1947?
    a. NAR   b. CAR   c. Realtists   d. none of these

109. *Turn-key project* refers to:
    a. a franchise sale
    b. a purchase and resale
    c. a resale before taking possession
    d. construction of a property from groundbreaking to completion

110. Dividing office overhead by the number of salespersons gives:
    a. broker dollar   c. company dollar
    b. desk cost   d. operational ratio

111. The *company dollar* refers to the:
    a. portion of the commission that the broker is entitled to
    b. gross commission less office overhead
    c. net income before taxes
    d. net income after taxes

112. Which of the following properties is likely to have the highest degree of liquidity?
    a. single-family residence   c. raw land
    b. residential income property   d. commercial property

113. What a person pays to develop a property is known as:
    a. price   b. value   c. assessment   d. cost

114. Which of the following incomes would be the highest?
    a. adjusted gross income   c. net spendable income
    b. scheduled gross income   d. adjusted net income

115. In considering a community shopping center, a developer would be most interested in:
    a. raw population figures   c. topography
    b. traffic patterns   d. purchasing power of the area

ANSWERS—CHAPTER 15 QUIZ

1. b. Since the money was paid to ABC.
2. b. The buyer is liable for the seller's obligation.
3. a.
4. a. But it is valid between the parties.
5. b. Assets and liabilities.
6. c.
7. c.
8. c.
9. d.
10. d. Because of successor liability.
11. d. For net profit, deduct all costs.
12. d. When the purchaser will resell the goods.
13. c.
14. d. A prerequisite.
15. d.
16. b.
17. c. Trust accounts are reconciled monthly.
18. b. Debts owed by the business.
19. c. Under the Bulk Sales Act.
20. b.
21. d. Colonel Cluck meets the registration exemption.
22. d.
23. b.
24. d. Supply and demand.
25. c. Income and expenses.
26. a. But void as to creditors.
27. d.
28. b.
29. d. Not a bulk sale.
30. a. Must be established one year.
31. c.
32. d. Likely less than 1.
33. c.
34. b. These are on a profit-and-loss statement.
35. c. Personal property.
36. c. But some businesses pay monthly or annually.
37. d.
38. c.
39. b.
40. a.
41. d. It is a one-time original fee to the state.

42. d. The others deal with sales tax.
43. c.
44. d. All are assets.
45. d.
46. b.
47. b. There is no sales tax on groceries.
48. c.
49. d.
50. d.
51. a.
52. a. It must be shown on the receipt.
53. d.
54. c. The license is less than five years old.
55. c. For a sale at auction, the price is unknown.
56. d. Both are debits.
57. d. Spendable cash.
58. c. Transferred on the lease.
59. b.
60. c. The ability to pay current debts.
61. c.
62. c.
63. c. This appears on the profit-and-loss statement.
64. a.
65. d. Since over five years old.
66. a. 10 percent for late payment and 25 percent for fraud.
67. b. The same amount as sales tax.
68. a.
69. d.
70. c.
71. b.
72. a. A business owner must be able to pay current obligations.
73. c. The seller should transfer the policy to avoid a short-rate refund.
74. a.
75. d.
76. b.
77. c. Does not help other tenants.
78. d.
79. d. Both on-sale and off-sale licenses will not be issued for the same premises.

80. a. Paid by the consumer.
81. d.
82. b.
83. d.
84. b.
85. d.
86. c.
87. d. This is on the balance sheet.
88. c.
89. d.
90. a.
91. d. Must return all over $50.
92. d.
93. d. He was licensed when he earned the commission.
94. d. Only from his own broker.
95. c. This activity requires a license.
96. c. The attorney is acting as a broker.
97. c.
98. c.
99. d. Robert is selling his own property.
100. c.
101. d.
102. d. The commission is a legal referral fee.
103. a. The deadline is five days for the transfer application.
104. a. He is a nonresident manager at four of the properties.
105. b.
106. a.
107. a.
108. c. A member of NAREB.
109. d.
110. b.
111. a.
112. a. Most readily sold.
113. d. What he has in it—price is what was paid.
114. b. Gross income based on 100 percent occupancy and collection.
115. d. Can the area economically support the center?

HELP OTHERS

We would appreciate your sending us an e-mail after you have taken your examination to provide us with the following information:

1. Material covered in your examination that you feel was not adequately covered in this text.
2. Any suggestions you have that will make the next edition more helpful for students.

Dr. William Pivar
e-mail: pivarfish@webtv.net

REVIEW TEST I

1. Fire insurance is a contract for indemnity. If proper coverage is received, the owner will:
   a. gain financially but not lose
   b. lose financially but not gain
   c. not gain or lose
   d. none of these

2. A promise made in exchange for the promise of another person would be:
   a. consideration
   b. a unilateral agreement
   c. unenforceable
   d. void

3. A rental security deposit would be reported on the lessor's income tax:
   a. in the year collected
   b. at the end of the lease
   c. in the year forfeited, if it is forfeited
   d. never

4. The major advantage of trading real estate as opposed to selling would be:
   a. avoiding commission
   b. higher prices are possible
   c. deferring taxes
   d. none of these

5. The cost-of-living index increases from 100 to 120. What effect does this have on the purchasing power of the dollar?
   a. lowers it 25 percent
   b. lowers it 20 percent
   c. lowers it 16.67 percent
   d. none of these

6. In order to protect against mechanic's liens, a lender might post a bond. The bond would be:
   a. 100 percent of the loan
   b. 75 percent of the estimated total cost
   c. 75 percent of the loan
   d. none of these

7. How much of the national wealth consists of real property?
   a. one-fourth
   b. one-third
   c. one-half
   d. two-thirds

8. Improved urban properties occupy approximately how much of the total U.S. land area?
   a. 1 percent
   b. 3 percent
   c. 6 percent
   d. 9 percent

9. After closing a transaction, a broker must cause the grant deed to be recorded within:
   a. 1 day
   b. 1 week
   c. 5 days
   d. 30 days

10. The ability to buy goods and services, to create and use real estate projects, and to build cities relates directly to which of the following?
    a. foreign trade
    b. consumer reaction
    c. government spending
    d. income receipts

11. A tree is overhanging Colleen's property. She can:
    a. cut the tree down
    b. remove overhanging branches
    c. either a or b
    d. neither a nor b

12. Which is *not* a direct building cost?
    a. materials
    b. subcontracts
    c. building permit
    d. labor

13. Cecilia, an investor, buys and sells 18 existing trust deeds in one year. She must:
    a. be a real property securities dealer
    b. be a real estate broker
    c. have a corporate securities license
    d. either b or c

14. A deed can be:
    a. assigned
    b. transferred
    c. foreclosed
    d. signed with an "X"

15. A major business cycle varies from 6 to 13 years, but major building cycles run from:
    a. 2 to 9 years
    b. 15 to 20 years
    c. 1 to 2 years
    d. 10 to 14 years

16. "The value of a home is only in the mind of the person" is an example of what kind of thinking?
    a. objective
    b. subjective
    c. alienation
    d. subordination

17. What is the first month's interest payment on a $25,000, 30-year, 9 percent loan if the monthly payments are $201?
    a. $100.50
    b. $187.50
    c. $175.00
    d. $34.50

18. Michael needs $5,000 to buy a new car. He owns a note secured by a $14,000 trust deed. Larry, a friend, says he will lend him the money if Michael will give him his note and trust deed as security. To complete this transaction according to the facts stated, which of the following would be needed?
    a. a hypothecation agreement
    b. a security agreement
    c. a loan discount agreement
    d. a pledge agreement

19. All of the following are considered theft in real estate except:
    a. signing the name of another without authorization
    b. removing security for a loan with intent to defraud
    c. conversion of trust funds
    d. carrying away fixtures

20. Which of the following may inspect the records in the county recorder's office without supervision?
    a. a bonded employee of a title company
    b. an employee of the county recorder's office
    c. a resident of the county
    d. anyone

21. A title insurance company might search the records of the:
    a. county recorder
    b. secretary of state
    c. federal land office
    d. all of these

22. A subdivider who needs money for site improvements and wants to pass on the cost of the improvements to the purchasers without placing a lien on the property could:
    a. sell capital stock
    b. issue bonds
    c. let the improvements go to bond
    d. both a and b

23. The relationship between a thing desired and a purchaser would be best described as:
    a. utility value
    b. cost
    c. value
    d. price

24. Kim's operating cost of his apartment building is 15.8 percent of his gross income, and his net income amounts to 20 percent. If he increases his rent 10 percent and gets a 10 percent vacancy factor, his net income will be:
    a. the same
    b. 10 percent less
    c. higher
    d. 1 percent less

25. Laura pays $96.25 over a seven-month period on a $2,500 straight note secured by a trust deed. The interest rate on the note is most nearly:
    a. more than 5 1/2 percent but less than 6 percent
    b. more than 7 percent but less than 7 1/2 percent
    c. more than 6 1/2 percent but less than 7 percent
    d. more than 6 percent but less than 6 1/2 percent

26. The primary reason for which the FHLBB was established in 1932 was to:
    a. control federally chartered S&Ls
    b. control state-chartered S&Ls
    c. provide a line of credit
    d. make low-income loans

27. A purchaser of income property would be least concerned with the:
    a. seller's book value
    b. terms of current leases
    c. financial strength of tenants
    d. deferred maintenance

28. The market data approach to valuation could be a poor value indicator when:
    a. the marketplace is undergoing rapid change
    b. there are numerous similar properties on the market
    c. there have been many sales of similar properties
    d. similar properties have been selling within a narrow range

29. When a tenant gives leased premises back to the lessor prior to the expiration of a lease, this is known as:
    a. surrender
    b. rescision
    c. novation
    d. abandonment

30. A landlord dedicates land to the county for a road. The landlord will get the land back if:
    a. consideration was not given for the dedication
    b. the county failed to maintain the road
    c. the county abandoned the road
    d never

31. Although it is clear that a note is to be interest-bearing, it fails to state the rate of interest.
    a. The legal rate would apply.
    b. It would be set at the maximum rate allowable.
    c. No interest can be charged.
    d. The rate would be 10 percent.

32. Real estate investments require:
    a. long-term gains
    b. debt and equity funds
    c. a stable economy
    d. all of these

33. A real estate broker's license is required if which of the following is done for compensation?
    a. assisting another in the purchase or lease of federal land
    b. soliciting borrowers for real estate loans
    c. buying, selling, or exchanging real estate sales contracts for others
    d. all of these

34. Franklin has a property worth $80,000 and a $49,000 first trust deed with a savings and loan. Mia agrees to buy the property for $1,000 down and a trust deed for $79,000. The trust deed includes an agreement that Franklin will continue to make the payments to the savings and loan. This type of trust deed/mortgage is called:
    a. an all-inclusive trust deed/mortgage
    b. an overriding trust deed/mortgage
    c. a wraparound trust deed/mortgage
    d. all of these

35. A creditor's action after judgment would be:
    a. notification of default
    b. attachment
    c. execution
    d. lis pendens

36. Sam sells Bob a house for $70,000. Sam's cost base was $40,000. After the sale, the house is assessed at $1,200 for a bond for street and sewer improvements. Bob's cost base is:
    a. $40,000   b. $41,200   c. $70,000   d. $71,200

37. Loans made by mortgage companies are generally:
    a. serviced by the mortgage company
    b. resold on the secondary mortgage market
    c. at below market interest
    d. both a and b

38. A waiver would best be described as a:
    a. bilateral agreement that returns the parties to a previous position
    b. bilateral agreement that leaves the parties as they are
    c. unilateral act that affects the position of both parties to a contract
    d. revocable act

39. A grant deed that does not specify any limitations on the grant would convey a:
    a. possessory interest only
    b. nonfreehold interest
    c. license
    d. fee simple interest

40. When an apartment building is converted to condominiums, the existing tenants must be given a period of _____ to purchase their units:
    a. 90 days from subdivision submission
    b. 90 days from public report issuance
    c. 120 days from public report issuance
    d. six months from notice to the tenants

41. A consideration of economic obsolescence would be:
    a. a leaking roof
    b. numerous partitions
    c. no parking for tenants
    d. oversupply

42. With respect to delinquent property taxes, which of the following is false?
    a. They constitute a specific lien as opposed to a general lien.
    b. On a foreclosure sale, property taxes take precedence over the first trust deed holder.
    c. The redemption period is terminated if the owner alienates the property.
    d. None of these are true.

43. Blind advertising is prohibited. It consists of:
    a. failure to state the location of the property
    b. failure to state the full name of the advertiser
    c. giving misleading information to get prospects
    d. failure to state that the advertiser is an agent

44. By dividing the net operating income by the price of a property, a buyer can determine the:
    a. capitalization rate
    b. adjusted basis
    c. adjusted gross income
    d. capital gain

45. A problem with personal property that makes ownership rights difficult to ascertain is that personal property can:
    a. be alienated
    b. be hypothecated
    c. become real property
    d. be pledged

46. An appraiser would understand that which of the following terms has many meanings?
    a. cost
    b. depreciation
    c. value
    d. appraisal

47. Which of the following is *not* directly involved in the secondary mortgage market?
    a. FNMA
    b. GNMA
    c. FHLMC
    d. FHA

48. Given the amount of interest paid, the rate of interest, and the time, which of the following formulas should be used to find the amount of principal?
    a. $P = \dfrac{I}{R \times T}$
    b. $P = \dfrac{R}{T \times I}$
    c. $P = \dfrac{T}{R \times I}$
    d. $P = R \times T \times I$

49. Bryan and Sandra signed a joint and several note, which is now delinquent. The payee can collect:
    a. all from Bryan
    b. all from Sandra
    c. from Bryan and Sandra
    d. any of these

50. In order to handle the collection on trust deeds for an owner, the broker must:
    a. be licensed as a real property security dealer
    b. have written authorization from the beneficiary
    c. post a bond
    d. all of these

51. The four elements of successful advertising are:
    a. attention, interest, desire, action
    b. location, price, size, design
    c. attention, interest, affordability, closing
    d. disclosure, location, price, desire

52. Who would be most interested in the Soldier's and Sailor's Civil Relief Act?
    a. the Real Estate Commissioner
    b. the county assessor
    c. a Vietnam veteran
    d. parties to a trust deed

53. The inside of a building is 20 feet by 30 feet and the walls on each side are six inches thick. What is the total square footage?
    a. 600
    b. 651
    c. 551
    d. none of these

54. A married woman buys a store and has beer for sale, which is consumed off the premises.
    a. She must apply for an off-sale liquor license.
    b. She and her husband must both apply for an off-sale liquor license.
    c. Her husband alone must apply for an off-sale liquor license.
    d. She needs no liquor license.

55. Which of the following is *not* personal property?
    a. a leasehold interest
    b. a chose in action
    c. an easement
    d. a trade fixture

56. In making real estate loans, a lender would be concerned with:
    a. reserves
    b. liquidity
    c. diversification
    d. all of these

57. The maximum tax reserves collectable under RESPA are:
    a. the estimated prorated taxes to the date of closing
    b. one-sixth of the annual estimated taxes
    c. the sum of a and b
    d. reserves are not allowed

58. As a hedge against inflation, an investor should consider:
    a. equity assets
    b. government bonds
    c. insurance annuities
    d. certificates of deposit

59. The meaning of the Latin term *et ux.* is:
    a. and wife
    b. and others
    c. and so forth
    d. none of these

60. Normally an investor would provide for the return of the investment in the:
    a. capitalization rate
    b. interest rate
    c. operational costs
    d. principal payments

61. A grant of an easement that does *not* specify easement location is:
    a. valid
    b. void
    c. voidable
    d. unenforceable

62. A prohibition against any "For Sale" signs in a restrictive covenant would be:
    a. valid, as it relates to appearance
    b. void, as an unreasonable restriction on alienation
    c. valid, if it applies uniformly
    d. valid, if it is also in conformance with the zoning

63. The expansion and contraction of an area's rental inventory would be determined by changes in:
    a. construction methods and costs
    b. prices and rents
    c. financing
    d. taxes and insurance

64. Joan is the recipient of a testamentary disposition, a house left to her by her uncle. Under these circumstances, the house is referred to as a:
    a. bequest
    b. legacy
    c. devise
    d. all of these

65. Which of the following actions of a property owner would *not* violate fair housing laws?
    a. encouraging tenants to solicit their friends as the exclusive means of filling vacancies
    b. requiring minority tenants to post larger property damage bonds than other tenants
    c. refusing to rent to singles and unmarried couples
    d. prohibiting children under the age of 12

66. A commercial corner lot measures 60 feet by 90 feet. The owner wishes to install a sidewalk 7 feet wide beyond the lot lines on both frontage streets. How many square feet of sidewalk will be installed?
    a. 1,220
    b. 1,580
    c. 1,099
    d. none of these

67. In the preceding question, if the sidewalk is four inches thick, how many cubic yards of concrete are required?
    a. 366
    b. 122
    c. 14
    d. 18

68. A standard-coverage policy of title insurance excludes from its coverage:
    a. delivery of the deed
    b. the trust deed of record
    c. special assessments
    d. prescriptive easements

69. The best prospect of a broker for an exchange is the:
    a. owner of a three-year-old residence
    b. owner of an older house
    c. original owner of a 40-year-old apartment building
    d. owner of a new apartment building

70. Which of the following deductions may Christine, the owner of a single-family residence, take on her federal income tax?
   a. interest on her home loan
   b. insurance on her home
   c. taxes on her home
   d. both a and c

71. The buyer on a sale of personal property would sign a:
   a. bill of sale
   b. security agreement
   c. trust deed
   d. pledge

72. As the depth of a commercial lot decreases:
   a. the front-foot value increases
   b. the front-foot value decreases
   c. the front-foot value is not related to depth
   d. the value of a lot decreases proportionately to the decrease in total square footage

73. A broker accepts four acres of land valued at $4,000 in lieu of a cash commission for a sale. Immediately after closing, the broker accepts an offer of $200,000 for the land. The broker:
   a. has made a secret profit
   b. must return the property
   c. must turn over the profit
   d. has not done anything wrong

74. Which of the following has first priority or is superior to the others?
   a. an assessment based on the Vrooman Street Act
   b. the one among these that was first recorded
   c. a homestead
   d. a first trust deed

75. According to the Statute of Frauds, certain contracts must be in writing, such as:
   a. the employment of a broker to sell the stock of a merchant
   b. the employment of a broker to solicit loans within the loan brokerage law
   c. a listing of a business opportunity
   d. any agreement not to be performed within one year

76. *Secured collaterally* refers to:
   a. a loan secured by another loan
   b. loans secured by personal or real property
   c. junior liens
   d. an all-inclusive loan

77. In inspecting the footing of a house, the building inspector notices diagonal cracks extending outward from a corner. This is usually referred to as:
   a. poor construction
   b. earthquake damage
   c. improper compaction
   d. settling

78. *Tender* is:
   a. performance
   b. an offer to perform
   c. money
   d. a valid contract

79. Alex and Agnes are joint tenants. Alex borrows on his interest, giving a lender a mortgage. Alex then dies.
   a. Alex's heirs and Agnes own the property as tenants in common.
   b. Agnes owns the property free of the mortgage.
   c. Agnes owns the property with the mortgage.
   d. The mortgagee owns the property.

80. Ellen, a widow, gives her property to her children and reserves the right to live on the property until her death. She has:
   a. a fee simple estate
   b. a life estate
   c. chattel real
   d. an estate in remainder

81. The Supreme Court has barred all racial discrimination in the sale or rental of property on the basis of:
   a. the Fourth Amendment
   b. the Fourteenth Amendment
   c. the Eighteenth Amendment
   d. none of these

82. In planning a new subdivision, the most important study would be:
    a. site analysis
    b. market analysis
    c. facilities analysis
    d. cost analysis

83. A tenant moves in and pays rent prior to receiving a written copy of a verbally agreed on three-year lease. The tenant would have a(n):
    a. estate at will
    b. tenancy at sufferance
    c. estate for years
    d. periodic tenancy

84. Who is entitled to possession when the taxpayer is in default on property taxes?
    a. the taxpayer
    b. the state controller
    c. the county tax collector
    d. the state treasurer

85. Which of the following can be regulated under the police power of the state?
    a. eminent domain
    b. water quality
    c. taxation
    d. none of these

86. In most commercial transactions, interest is computed by:
    a. government method
    b. the banker's method
    c. individual selection
    d. none of these

87. The maximum allowable renter deposit is _____ months' rent.
    a. two furnished, three unfurnished
    b. three furnished, two unfurnished
    c. two
    d. none of these

88. A contract can be described as a deliberate agreement between:
    a. two or more parties, upon legal consideration, to do or abstain from doing some act
    b. competent parties to do or abstain from doing some legal act
    c. competent parties upon legal consent to do or to abstain from doing some legal act
    d. competent parties upon legal consideration to do or abstain from doing some legal act

89. Most insurance company loans are made through:
    a. commercial banks
    b. savings and loan associations
    c. mortgage brokers
    d. mortgage companies

90. Most lawsuits involving sales in real estate are brought in:
    a. justice court
    b. the court of appeals
    c. superior court
    d. municipal court

91. When may a broker advertise property in an area into which minority people are moving, in a newspaper subscribed to primarily by members of that minority group?
    a. only if that property is also advertised in general-circulation publications
    b. only if he or she also advertises other properties from other areas in the same minority publication
    c. there are no restrictions
    d. never

92. Victor, a real estate agent, holds an option on a piece of property. He must disclose to the prospective purchaser that he is a(n):
    a. principal   b. mortgagor   c. agent   d. optioner

93. Harriet purchases a home for $100,000 and has a trust deed for $80,000. Because of inflationary trends, the value of the dollar decreases. This is of benefit to the:
    a. beneficiary   b. lender   c. trustor   d. trustee

94. Which of the following would be an incorrect amount for documentary transfer tax stamps?
    a. $366.30   b. $94.05   c. $178.95   d. $59.95

95. What is fraud?
    a. a promise made with no intention of keeping it
    b. suppression of truth by a person having knowledge or belief of a fact
    c. suggestion as fact of that which is not true by a person who does not believe it to be true
    d. all of these

96. Which of the following is *not* real property?
   a. mineral, oil, and gas rights
   b. air space over property
   c. shares in a real estate syndicate
   d. trees

97. Open sheathing is characteristic of:
   a. a foam roof
   b. asphalt tiles
   c. wood shingles
   d. all of these

98. Which of the following is an example of bulk zoning?
   a. height restrictions
   b. open-space requirements
   c. setbacks
   d. all of these

99. The tax assessment roll that shows the assessed value of all property would:
   a. establish equal tax assessments
   b. determine the tax base
   c. set the tax rate
   d. establish owner exemptions

100. Which of the following is most likely a case of incentive zoning?
   a. colonial-style architecture only
   b. retail stores on the first floor of an office building
   c. 40-foot setback
   d. only residential

101. A notice that commissions are negotiable must be included in:
   a. every sale or lease listing
   b. a listing of one to four residential units
   c. every sale listing
   d. none of these

102. Which date is most important to an appraiser?
   a. date of agreement
   b. date of close of escrow
   c. date of recordation
   d. date of appraisal

103. A deed transfer is void if:
   a. the grantor's name is fictitious
   b. the grantee is a fictitious name
   c. the grantee is nonexistent
   d. all of these

104. A deed restriction restricts an entire subdivision from using a residence as a business. The buyer tells the broker he is planning to use one room of his house as a barber shop.
   a. It is all right, since the entire block was rezoned this year to C-4.
   b. It will be all right if eight of the nine owners agree.
   c. It is all right as long as he has no employees.
   d. It is not all right, because of the deed restriction.

105. An appraiser measures the quality of income by the:
   a. rate of capitalization
   b. amount of income
   c. term of the lease yet to run
   d. age of the building

106. When correlating values obtained by the three methods of appraisal, an appraiser would:
   a. average the three values
   b. assign weights to each of the three values
   c. use the lowest value
   d. use the highest value

107. *Ethics* is most nearly defined as:
   a. honesty
   b. dealing with the law
   c. a broker's responsibility to the public, his or her principal, and other brokers
   d. agency responsibility

108. The rescission provisions of the Truth-in-Lending Act do *not* apply to:
   a. a first trust deed given for a home purchase
   b. construction loans
   c. both a and b
   d. neither a nor b

109. Which of the following loans would be least likely to require a down payment?
   a. FHA
   b. VA
   c. CAL-VET
   d. conventional

110. A maker of a negotiable instrument can defend against a holder in due course in case of:
    a. incapacity   b. forgery   c. a raised note   d. all of these

111. FNMA is involved primarily in:
    a. equal housing enforcement   c. secondary financing
    b. the secondary mortgage market   d. all of these

112. A lot is listed at $25,000. The broker finds a buyer at $22,000. The owner says she will take the deal if the broker lowers his 6 percent commission by 16 2/3 percent. The broker receives:
    a. $1,500   b. $1,320   c. $1,100   d. none of these

113. An executrix would be:
    a. the widow of the deceased   c. appointed by the will
    b. appointed by the court   d. none of these

114. Often a developer sets up a subdivision and places certain restrictions on each of the lots. Which of the following has experience shown that the developer is least likely to enforce?
    a. number of stories or total height   c. limitations on the square footage of each house
    b. limitations on the size of each lot   d. minimum dollars allowed for improving each lot

115. Enforcement of sanitary regulations in connection with sewage disposal in a subdivision is the responsibility of the:
    a. health officer   c. building inspector
    b. plumbing inspector   d. public works director

116. Bids (prices offered) at a private sale of estate property for court approval must be at least:
    a. 95 percent of appraisal   c. 90 percent of appraisal
    b. 80 percent of appraisal   d. 100 percent of appraisal

117. As to the value of a retail site, the most important factor is:
    a. parking   c. access
    b. the purchasing power of the area   d. the shape of the parcel

118. On foreclosure of a trust deed, the buyer gets:
    a. a sheriff's deed   c. a tax deed
    b. a trustee's deed   d. none of these

119. Which of the following is *not* required in a lease?
    a. a description of the property   c. the length of the lease
    b. rent paid in advance   d. the amount of rent

120. A 17-year-old single minor can likely purchase a home using a(n):
    a. CAL-VET loan   c. VA loan
    b. insured conventional loan   d. none of these

121. A mortgage is foreclosed. The mortgagor has one year to redeem. Possession most likely would be with the:
    a. mortgagee   b. mortgagor   c. court   d. sheriff

122. As to partnership income tax, which of the following is true?
    a. A partnership does not pay income tax.
    b. The partners each pay their own taxes on their shares of the profits.
    c. The partnership must file a tax return.
    d. all of these

123. To confirm information regarding title and description of real property, one should check with the:
    a. owner   b. county records   c. secretary of state   d. plat book

124. Which of the following loans would have a balloon payment?
    a. $58,000, 20-year loan at 6% with monthly payments of $415.54
    b. $100,000, 15-year loan at 8 3/4% with monthly payments of $999.45
    c. $50,000, 10-year loan at 6% with monthly payments of $410.12
    d. $49,000, 2-year loan at 6 1/2% with monthly payments of $2,182.77

125. Which of the following is *not* an encumbrance?
    a. easement in gross
    b. declaration of homestead
    c. mechanic's lien
    d. second trust deed

126. Under a(n)_____, the person occupying the property is primarily liable on the lease, but under a(n)_____ he or she is *not* liable to the owner.
    a. assignment, land contract
    b. sublease, assignment
    c. sandwich lease, assignment
    d. assignment, sublease

127. In order to be valid, restrictions must:
    a. be less restrictive than zoning
    b. be contained in a deed or a written agreement
    c. be contained in a deed
    d. run with the land

128. In a probate sale, the sale price is $12,000. The amount of a late overbid must be at least:
    a. $12,500   b. $13,000   c. $13,100   d. $13,500

129. Pat, Samantha, and Kelly hold possession of property in joint tenancy. Pat dies. Which of the following is correct?
    a. Samantha and Kelly hold possession as tenants in common.
    b. Samantha and Kelly hold possession as community property.
    c. Samantha and Kelly inherit Pat's share by right of succession.
    d. Pat's share terminated at his death.

130. Liquidity of a firm would best be described as the ratio of:
    a. cash to total debt
    b. total assets to total liabilities
    c. current assets to current liabilities
    d. income to expenses

131. Daniel purchases two lots for $6,000. He lists the lots with a broker to sell for 30 percent more than his cost. They do not sell right away, so he reduces the price 25 percent. After deducting the broker's 6 percent commission, how much is Daniel's profit or loss?
    a. –$50   b. –$501   c. –$560   d. +$43

132. Jean, an investor, purchases an apartment complex and does not occupy a unit. She is required to have a resident manager if the number of apartments is in excess of:
    a. 14   b. 15   c. 16   d. 20

133. A judgment takes priority over a homestead if:
    a. the homestead is abandoned
    b. the homestead is declared void
    c. the judgment is recorded first
    d. any of these

134. A buyer gives a seller $90,000 cash for a home and assumes a $7,000 bond assessment. The buyer's cost basis would be:
    a. $97,000   b. $90,000   c. $83,000   d. $80,000

135. What kind of a deed is issued to a person who is buying property previously sold to the state where the state has acquired title after five years?
    a. tax collector's deed
    b. warranty deed
    c. state controller's deed
    d. none of these

136. The Federal Fair Housing Law contains, in its preamble, words that are intended to eliminate discrimination (prejudice or bias) in housing and to:
    a. provide low-cost housing for all
    b. provide fair housing throughout the United States
    c. establish Fannie Mae
    d. none of these

137. Under the Truth-in-Lending Law, a buyer may rescind a loan:
    a. for business purposes
    b. made to purchase a home
    c. secured by furniture
    d. none of these

138. A broker is found guilty in superior court of making a secret profit in connection with a real estate transaction closed three years previously. The Commissioner may suspend the broker's license:
    a. upon receipt of a certified copy of judgment
    b. never, because of the time element
    c. never, because it was a civil case
    d. after a hearing

139. Priority of trust deeds would be based on the date:
    a. on the instruments
    b. of execution
    c. of recordation
    d. of loan application

140. Interest in property can be acquired by adverse possession and by prescription. When acquired by prescription, such interest:
    a. constitutes a right to pass over the land of another
    b. is for five years only
    c. constitutes legal title
    d. none of these

141. Ingrid lists her house with a broker. Roy makes an offer, which Ingrid accepts. Prior to execution of the deal, the value of the property increases 1,000 percent. Ingrid wants to rescind the deal. Based on the Statute of Limitations, how much time must pass before Roy loses his right to force a settlement?
    a. 90 days   b. one year   c. two years   d. four years

142. After Henry sells his farm to Frank, but before the title passes, Henry harvests the crops and sells them.
    a. Frank is entitled to reclaim the crops.
    b. Frank is entitled to the proceeds from the crops.
    c. Henry may keep the proceeds from the crops.
    d. None of these are true.

143. Arlene signs a purchase contract and gives a $500 deposit on August 10. The contract specifies that the seller has five days to accept or the deposit will be refunded. On August 11, Arlene changes her mind and asks for a refund of her deposit. What should the broker do?
    a. The deposit belongs to the seller, so he cannot refund it.
    b. He should put the deposit in his trust fund.
    c. He should give the refund to Arlene because the offer has not been accepted yet.
    d. He should give Arlene half of the deposit.

144. A property being appraised has two baths, while a comparable has three baths. In adjusting for the difference, the appraiser would:
    a. lower the value of the house being appraised
    b. raise the value of the comparable
    c. lower the value of the comparable
    d. raise the value of the house being appraised

145. An amortization table shows monthly payments for:
    a. principal only
    b. interest only
    c. both principal and interest
    d. principal, interest, taxes, and insurance

146. A lis pendens *cannot* be filed by:
    a. a prospective purchaser who has made an accepted offer
    b. a person who claims he or she has title
    c. a real estate broker for a claim of money due from the owner
    d. any of these

147. The best method for appraising a vacant lot for residential purposes is:
    a. construction cost
    b. market data
    c. income
    d. a combination of a and c

148. Which of the following does *not* belong with the others:
   - a. judgment
   - b. attachment
   - c. mechanic's lien
   - d. easement

149. The cost basis of a property after an exchange would be based on:
   - a. the cost basis of the trade-in property
   - b. boot given or received
   - c. neither a nor b
   - d. both a and b

150. The process of determining marketable title is:
   - a. a title search
   - b. a title report
   - c. an abstract
   - d. title insurance

1. c.
2. a. Also, it is a bilateral contract.
3. c. It belongs to the lessee until it is forfeited. However, prepaid rent is taxed in the year it is received.
4. c.
5. c. It now takes $6 to do what $5 did before; so each dollar is worth one-sixth less.
6. c. The bond to remove a mechanic's lien is 150% of the lien.
7. d.
8. b.
9. b. Business & Professions Code, Section 10141.5.
10. d.
11. b. But she can't kill the tree.
12. c. An indirect cost.
13. b. Eight or more in one year.
14. d. A deed is used only once. If it is signed with an "X," witnesses are required.
15. b.
16. b.
17. b. 9 percent of $25,000 divided by 12.
18. d. Giving personal property as security for a loan. A loan secured by another loan is collaterally secured.
19. a. This is forgery, but not necessarily theft.
20. d.
21. d.
22. c. Such as Mello-Roos bonds.
23. c.
24. d. Add 10% to the rent, then cut the whole by 10%.
25. c. Interest is $13.75 per month; 10% of $2,500 for one month is $2.08, so $13.75 ÷ $2.08.
26. c. The Federal Home Loan Bank Board established a pool of money for savings and loans.
27. a.
28. a.
29. a. It ends all obligations under the lease.
30. c. Since it was given for a particular purpose.
31. a. At the legal rate of 7 percent.
32. b. Down payment and borrowed funds.
33. d. Business & Professions Code, Section 10131.
34. d.
35. c.
36. d. The cost of improvement increases the cost base.
37. d.

38. c. It leaves them as they are.
39. d.
40. b. At the best price and terms to be offered.
41. d. A force outside the property.
42. c. Selling does not affect the five-year redemption period.
43. d.
44. a.
45. c.
46. c. Market, assessed, loan, etc.
47. d. The FHA insures loans.
48. a.
49. d. Since both are jointly and separately liable.
50. b.
51. a. AIDA (acronym).
52. d. Since the beneficiary cannot foreclose if the reason for the trustor's delinquency is service in the armed services.
53. b. Use exterior dimensions for square feet.
54. d. She needs an off-sale beer and wine license.
55. c. Easements are real property.
56. d.
57. c. Also applies to insurance.
58. a. Such as real estate.
59. a. *Et al.* means "and others."
60. a. Add depreciation to the capitalization rate.
61. a. The grantor can determine a reasonable location.
62. b. (Also free speech.)
63. b. Supply and demand.
64. c. Answers a and b deal with personal property.
65. a.
66. c. $60' \times 7' + 97' \times 7'$.
67. c. The sidewalk is 1/3 foot thick, so $1,099 \div 3$ = total cubic footage; divide by 27 to get cubic yards.
68. d. Would require inspection.
69. c. Since the owner would have to pay significant taxes to sell.
70. d.
71. b. The seller signs a bill of sale.
72. b. But the per-square-foot value increases.
73. d. Unless the broker failed to make disclosure of all facts known.
74. a. Tax assessments take priority over other liens.
75. d. The question asks what the Statute of Frauds requires to be in writing.
76. a.
77. d.
78. b. Legal tender is money.

79. b. Alex's interest transfers free of debt.
80. b.
81. d. Thirteenth Amendment.
82. b. Demand factors.
83. d. The lessor must sign the lease to bind the lessee.
84. a. Until the tax sale.
85. b. Health.
86. b. 30-day month, 360-day year.
87. b. Cannot be nonrefundable.
88. d. Mutuality, consideration, competent parties, and legal purpose.
89. d.
90. c.
91. b. Otherwise the ad constitutes "steering."
92. a. And a licensee.
93. c. Paying back with cheaper dollars.
94. c. Not evenly divisible by $.55.
95. d.
96. c. Personal property, or chattel real.
97. c.
98. d. Limiting density.
99. b.
100. b.
101. b.
102. d. An appraisal is a present valuation.
103. c. The grantee must be real.
104. d. And the broker must disclose this to the buyer.
105. a. Risk affects rate.
106. b.
107. c. Also an application of the Golden Rule.
108. c. Both are exempt.
109. b. A down payment is not needed for a VA loan unless it is required by the lender.
110. d. All are considered real defenses, as opposed to personal defenses such as fraud, which cannot be raised against a holder in due course.
111. b. Buying and selling existing loans.
112. c. The regular commission of 6 percent on a $22,000 sale would be $1,320; reduced by 1/6 = $1,100.
113. c. Not necessarily the widow.
114. d. Difficult to ascertain.
115. a. The local health officer enforces state and local requirements.
116. c.
117. b. Relates to location.
118. b. Since it is a trustee's sale.

119. b.
120. a. Age exception for veterans.
121. b. Normally, the mortgagor remains in possession during the redemption period.
122. d.
123. b.
124. c. Would not be amortized. Total payments are less than the loan.
125. b. A homestead is not regarded as an encumbrance.
126. d.
127. b. And be recorded.
128. c. 10 percent higher on the first $10,000 and 5 percent higher on the balance.
129. d. Samantha and Kelly take Pat's share by right of survivorship as joint tenants.
130. c.
131. b. Listed at $7,800, reduced to $5,850; deduct commission of $351 = $5,499; net loss of $501.
132. b. If the number is *16 or greater*.
133. d.
134. a.
135. a. Tax sale.
136. b. Equal opportunity.
137. d. All are exempt. Rescission rights last till midnight of the third business day after the agreement if the loan puts a lien on your house.
138. b. The Commissioner has only three years to bring action.
139. c.
140. a. An easement.
141. d. Four years on a written contract.
142. c. Crops are personal property.
143. c. The buyer can revoke the contract prior to acceptance.
144. c. Adjust comparable based on property being appraised.
145. c. Principal plus interest payments.
146. c. The broker has no right in the property.
147. b.
148. d. The others are liens.
149. d.
150. a. This is the process.

REVIEW TEST II

1. The largest repository of savings in the United States is held by:
   a. banks
   b. savings and loan associations
   c. mutual funds
   d. insurance companies

2. *Surplus utility* would be an example of:
   a. progression
   b. functional obsolescence
   c. physical deterioration
   d. economic obsolescence

3. For preparing the federal RESPA Disclosure statement, the maximum fee that can be charged is:
   a. nothing
   b. $25
   c. one-half of 1 percent of the loan
   d. 1 percent of the loan

4. When an African-American prospect makes an offer, does the broker breach ethics by telling the seller that the prospect is African American?
   a. No, because the broker has a duty to tell the principal about all material facts.
   b. No, because the broker's primary duty is to the seller.
   c. Yes, because it should not matter.
   d. Yes, because it is a violation of the Unruh Act.

5. Which of the following is a cost of home ownership?
   a. land appreciation
   b. amenity value
   c. improvement appreciation
   d. interest lost on the owner's equity

6. According to the Code of Ethics for REALTORS®, the real estate business is an honored profession and citizens of the United States can best be served in ownership and:
   a. making a substantial profit
   b. building homes and other buildings
   c. buying and selling property
   d. the wise utilization and wide distribution of land

7. Under the Civil Rights Act of 1968, if parties feel they were discriminated against, they should:
   a. file action in local court for indefeasible rights and actual damages
   b. file criminal action in local and state courts
   c. file criminal action in federal court
   d. file civil action in federal court

8. Which of the following is a subdivision?
   a. turning a duplex into a condominium
   b. selling ten 36-day time-shares in a single condo unit
   c. both a and b
   d. neither a nor b

9. Disclosure laws require a broker to inform a buyer that:
   a. the seller has AIDS
   b. African Americans live next door
   c. there was a brutal murder in the house six years earlier
   d. none of these

10. A few Chicano and Asian families recently moved into a neighborhood. A broker gave his salesperson instructions to canvass the neighborhood, but not to solicit the Chicano and Asian landowners because they were recent purchasers and the broker felt they would not want to list their homes for sale. The broker's action was:
    a. redlining
    b. unlawful
    c. blockbusting
    d. both b and c

11. A utility company has an easement to erect telephone lines. The easement is:
    a. appurtenant and affirmative
    b. personal and negative
    c. in gross and affirmative
    d. in gross and prescriptive

12. Which of the following is *not* a conservation easement?
    a. a solar easement
    b. a prohibition against future development
    c. a requirement that land remain in its present state
    d. a negative easement that prohibits a landowner from change in land use

13. Deed restrictions on the use of land are *not* permissible:
    a. unless they promote the public health, safety, and welfare
    b. if they are based solely on aesthetic considerations
    c. if they become an unreasonable burden on the landowner
    d. for any of these reasons

14. An estate for years is created by:
    a. an implied contract
    b. an express contract
    c. operation of law
    d. both b and c

15. Alicia performs her duties for John as his agent in real estate transactions in an unethical manner. John did not instruct her to perform in this manner but, after learning of her conduct, does nothing to prevent her continuing. This is an example of:
    a. the principle of estoppel
    b. ratification
    c. waiver
    d. none of these

16. Calvin is purchasing Joanna's property. Joanna holds a $64,000 VA loan. Calvin conditions the purchase "subject to assuming the VA loan." In the event of default:
    a. Calvin and Joanna are equally liable
    b. Calvin is primarily liable
    c. Joanna is primarily liable
    d. Calvin has no liability

17. Most fire insurance policies have clauses in their contracts that call for cancellation:
    a. at any time
    b. a specified number of days after notice of cancellation
    c. because of unusually high losses of the insured
    d. after notice of cancellation and acceptance by the insured

18. Scott gets a VA loan approved. He tells Martha, the salesperson, that he is short of money and wants to borrow $250 to cover closing costs. Martha:
    a. can lend her own money to save the deal
    b. must notify the lender first
    c. must get Scott to negotiate a second trust deed in her favor
    d. may not lend the money

19. It is least likely to be a violation of the Real Estate Law for a broker to rebate a portion of the commission to a(n):
    a. salesperson who is licensed for another broker
    b. unlicensed party who aided in the sale
    c. principal to the transaction
    d. unlicensed party who obtained the listing for the broker

20. Insurance can be described as:
    a. placing chance in the hands of a professional risk company
    b. trading an uncertainty for a certainty
    c. purchasing a specified amount of coverage for a specified amount of time
    d. all of these

21. The most commonly used appraisal method to evaluate land is:
    a. the developmental method
    b. the residual method
    c. the allocation approach
    d. the market-comparison method

22. As to the cost method of appraising, which of the following is false?
    a. It is hard to apply, since it involves complicated procedures.
    b. It is used in computing real estate values of public utilities.
    c. It is used in new residential homes.
    d. It gives computed results of lowest value.

23. The transfer of an estate for years, estate for life, or estate at will is termed a:
    a. devise
    b. demise
    c. conveyance
    d. certificate of clearance

24. An African-American couple walks into a real estate office. The salesperson should:
    a. show six homes in a white neighborhood
    b. show six homes in an African-American neighborhood
    c. show six homes in both neighborhoods
    d. treat them like everyone else

25. When rent is prepaid, how is it classified in the accounting procedures?
    a. accrued income to the lessor
    b. accrued expense to the lessee
    c. deferred income to the lessor
    d. deferred income to the lessee

26. The least important factor in a sale leaseback is:
    a. the seller's book value
    b. the cost to replace
    c. the loan value
    d. the lease payment

27. All of the following are considered to be contracts except:
    a. a mortgage
    b. an open listing
    c. an escrow agreement
    d. a deed

28. Which of the following positions requires the highest use of knowledge in accounting procedures and practices?
    a. appraiser
    b. CPW
    c. escrow officer
    d. real estate salesperson

29. Erich, an appraiser, has a 5 percent interest in a property he is asked to appraise. The customer says this interest is so minor that it won't affect the appraisal. Erich should:
    a. appraise the property and not mention his interest
    b. appraise the property and mention the 5 percent interest in the appraisal
    c. refuse the appraisal and let someone else do it
    d. none of these

30. A lender, yielding to the arguments of a borrower for a 1/2 percent concession in interest, agrees to take a 2 percent equity. This is a:
    a. packaged loan
    b. shut-in loan
    c. participation loan
    d. management loan

31. An owner gives false information to a buyer about the age of a property and its size in the presence of the broker. The broker should:
    a. keep silent
    b. notify the owner to remain silent in the future
    c. correct the owner in private
    d. immediately give the correct information to the buyer

32. In computing the unspecified maturity date of a conventional construction loan, the time for repayment generally begins:
    a. on the date funds are placed in escrow
    b. on the date of the note
    c. on the date of the first disbursement
    d. in accordance with the purchase contract

33. A buyer must disclose to a seller:
    a. the reason for the purchase
    b. that the price asked is too low
    c. that the seller is mistaken as to zoning
    d. none of the above

34. How many days does a broker have to place a cash deposit in escrow or a trust account?
   a. 30 days
   b. 10 days
   c. 3 days
   d. the next working day

35. Maura enters into a contract with a person she does not know; she has no reason to know that the person previously has been declared incompetent. The contract is:
   a. void
   b. valid
   c. voidable by the incompetent party only
   d. voidable by either party

36. Termite inspections are filed with the:
   a. state Housing Department
   b. state Department of Health
   c. state Structural Pest Control Board
   d. none of these

37. The classical definition of ownership of land is that one owns:
   a. all of the land below and some of the sky above
   b. all of the sky above and some of the land below
   c. all of the sky above and all of the land below
   d. some of the land below and some of the sky above

38. To get an FHA appraisal, an owner would:
   a. have the lender apply for a conditional commitment
   b. contact an approved FHA appraiser
   c. apply to the FHA
   d. none of these

39. After the owner leases all 10 units in a building on long-term fixed rentals, the interest rates rise dramatically.
   a. The owner's equity decreases.
   b. The owner's equity remains constant.
   c. The value of the building increases.
   d. None of these are true.

40. A city park would be owned by the city in:
   a. severalty
   b. joint tenancy
   c. tenancy in partnership
   d. tenancy in common

41. A right that exists between two parties, each of whom under an independent contract owes the other a debt, would be:
   a. a double contract
   b. a setoff
   c. an eleemosynary contract
   d. all of these

42. Hank, a builder, constructs a backyard pool for Elsa. Not being paid in full, he files which of the following liens?
   a. a general lien
   b. a voluntary lien
   c. a specific lien
   d. none of these

43. All of the following are liens on real estate except:
   a. an easement
   b. an attachment
   c. a judgment
   d. delinquent taxes

44. A corporation seal on a deed means the corporation:
   a. owns title
   b. has given authority to the person signing
   c. both a and b
   d. neither a nor b

45. Not buying a house because you feel the price is too high is an example of the principle of:
   a. contribution
   b. substitution
   c. anticipation
   d. change

46. In the absence of custom or an agreement to the contrary, rent is due:
   a. as stated
   b. at the end of each period
   c. in advance
   d. at the termination of tenancy

47. A loan in which the lender shares in the profit would be:
   a. a rollover or renegotiable loan
   b. a reverse mortgage
   c. a SAM
   d. a GPM

48. An individual owning a large apartment complex would decide on rent prices through the:
    a. capitalization approach
    b. market-comparison approach
    c. cost approach
    d. double-declining-balance approach

49. A corporation is *not* permitted to take title of California real estate as a joint tenant because of its:
    a. centralization of control in a board of directors
    b. ability to use a fictitious name
    c. perpetual existence
    d. right to be foreign or domestic

50. A real estate broker refuses to negotiate a commission. The broker:
    a. is subject to revocation of license
    b. is subject to suspension
    c. either a or b
    d. none of these

51. A lot has 1,320 feet on its south boundary. The west boundary is perpendicular to the south boundary and is 660 feet. The north boundary is parallel to the south boundary and is 1,980 feet. The northeast and southeast corners of the lot are joined by a straight line. What is the total acreage of the lot?
    a. 40 acres   b. 62 1/2 acres   c. 37 1/2 acres   d. 25 acres

52. The person who would install a conduit in a new home would be:
    a. a plumber   b. a carpenter   c. a bricklayer   d. an electrician

53. In order to incur a late charge for a loan on a single-family dwelling, the payment must be:
    a. 7 days late
    b. 10 days late
    c. more than 10 days late
    d. more than 14 days late

54. Real property is sold on credit and the seller retains legal title. The instrument the seller would use would be a:
    a. bailment
    b. security agreement
    c. real property sales contract
    d. trust deed

55. To take action against a licensee, the Real Estate Commissioner must take action within _____ of the violation.
    a. six months   b. one year   c. three years   d. there is no time limit

56. In depreciating a 10-year-old commercial building for tax purposes:
    a. a salvage value must be considered
    b. 39 years would be used for depreciation purposes
    c. the owner can use either straight-line or 175 percent declining-balance depreciation
    d. both b and c

57. Clyde gives a trust deed on his property to Ramona. Clyde then signs a 20-year lease with Adam, who spends a considerable sum renovating the premises for his use. Ramona forecloses on the trust deed because Clyde did not pay on the trust deed. Ramona orders Adam from the premises.
    a. Adam does not have to leave because his lease is valid.
    b. A buyer always takes subject to the rights of a tenant; therefore, Adam can stay.
    c. Both a and b are true.
    d. Neither of these is true.

58. An insurance company encourages commercial policy holders to carry adequate coverage by requiring:
    a. coinsurance
    b. a rider
    c. a special endorsement
    d. a prorated policy

59. As to real estate, which of the following is true?
    a. Like any product, real estate can readily be sold from "samples."
    b. An advantage of land as an investment is that it can be depreciated.
    c. A real estate sale usually involves at least two sales.
    d. The location of real estate affects the availability of financing.

60. An owner gives an exclusive-right-to-sell listing to Polly, a broker; an exclusive-agency listing to Kurt, another broker; and an open listing to Susan, a third broker. Susan sells the house and collects a commission while the other listings are still in effect. As to Polly and Kurt:
   a. both are entitled to a split of the commission
   b. the owner will have to pay them a second commission
   c. they are each entitled to a full commission
   d. only Polly is entitled to a full commission

61. A defeasance clause in a mortgage provides for:
   a. the right of the mortgagee to foreclose
   b. the release of the mortgage upon payment of the note
   c. mortgage protection against unrecorded liens
   d. the assumption of the loan

62. Helga is getting a second mortgage on her house for $4,000 from a mortgage company. What are the maximum loan costs she may incur?
   a. 10 percent of the loan   c. $200
   b. 15 percent of the loan   d. $390

63. On a $40,000 short-term loan at 9 percent interest, the borrower pays total interest of $1,200. The loan is for:
   a. 2 1/2 months   c. 4 months
   b. 3 months   d. 4 1/2 months

64. A tenancy by the entirety differs from a joint tenancy as to:
   a. survivorship
   b. termination by the conveyance of one owner
   c. ability to will an interest
   d. right of possession

65. The clause in a deed that defines the extent of the estate granted is known as the:
   a. defeasance clause   c. alienation clause
   b. habendum clause   d. subordination clause

66. Sex discrimination in housing is outlawed in sales and rentals under:
   a. the Civil Rights Act of 1866   c. the Thirteenth Amendment to the Constitution
   b. the Civil Rights Act of 1968   d. RESPA

67. Recording has the effect of all *but:*
   a. creating the presumption of delivery
   b. setting the priority of liens
   c. providing constructive notice to all of the interest
   d. providing actual notice of the interest

68. Upon execution of a judgment, the deed given would be a:
   a. warranty deed   c. trust deed
   b. tax collector's deed   d. sheriff's deed

69. Paige offers the S 1/2 of the NW 1/4 of the NE 1/4 of Section 21 for sale through Richard, a broker, at a list price of $350 per acre. Richard presents Cathy's offer of $6,100 to Paige. Paige accepts Cathy's offer provided that Cathy pays Richard's 10 percent commission of the offer price. How much less than the original list price does Cathy actually pay?
   a. $270   b. $280   c. $290   d. $330

70. A broker who sells mobile homes but is not licensed as a mobile home dealer may *not:*
   a. advertise "no down payment" if a second loan will be arranged to cover the down payment
   b. have an office where three mobile homes are displayed for sale
   c. both a and b
   d. neither a nor b

71. Recording is *not* required for a:
   a. notice of default   c. notice of completion
   b. trustee's deed   d. grant deed

72. Two people suffered a loss from a single transaction involving a real estate licensee. One person obtained a $20,000 judgment against the licensee, which was uncollectable. The Recovery Fund paid the $20,000. The second person has now commenced a lawsuit asking for $80,000. If the second person is successful and the real estate licensee cannot pay, the liability of the Recovery Fund will be:

a. $80,000   b. $40,000   c. $20,000   d. zero

73. The total number of cubic feet of space contained in the building shown is:

a. 24,000
b. 12,000
c. 18,000
d. none of these

16'
8'
30'   50'

74. A person would contact the Real Estate Commissioner to:
   a. decide a commission dispute
   b. arbitrate a claim against a broker
   c. report fraud by a real estate salesperson
   d. any of these

75. Property values are going down because of a changing neighborhood, and there is a mass exodus of whites. A broker takes listings under these circumstances and does the following solicitation:
   1. Advertises "Sell your property fast before you lose equity."
   2. Offers whites a lower commission rate to sell their property.
   Which of these violates the federal Fair Housing Law?
   a. (1)   b. (2)   c. (1) and (2)   d. neither (1) nor (2)

76. A major disadvantage of home ownership is:
   a. leverage of investment
   b. loss of liquidity
   c. appreciation
   d. all of these

77. Wally purchased his home four years ago for $100,000. Since then property values have gone up 10 percent each year. Based on this increase, the present value of his home should be:
   a. $140,000   b. $180,000   c. $146,410   d. $131,100

78. A grandfather clause would provide for:
   a. lineal descent
   b. a change in zoning
   c. the continuation of a nonconforming use
   d. restrictions as to use

79. The last lot in a subdivision sold for over twice the price of the first lot. This is an example of the principle of:
   a. change
   b. supply and demand
   c. conformity
   d. progression

80. A listing is signed by the owners but not by the broker. The listing:
   a. is void
   b. is a bilateral contract
   c. has placed the broker's license in jeopardy
   d. is likely a unilateral contract

81. A corporation could hold title as:
   a. tenancy by the entirety
   b. joint tenancy
   c. community property
   d. a partnership

82. *Upset price* refers to:
   a. a value set for tax purposes
   b. the minimum acceptable price
   c. sales price in excess of the listing price
   d. the price received at auction

83. A mortgage broker's fee would customarily be paid by:
   a. both the lender and the borrower
   b. the lender
   c. the borrower
   d. the seller

84. John sells a property for $190,000 with the buyer assuming the $190,000 mortgage. John's cost basis is $150,000. The $40,000 difference between the cost basis and the property indebtedness would be treated by the IRS as:
   a. a taxable gain to John
   b. a nontaxable gain
   c. a loss
   d. neither a gain nor a loss

85. ☑ stands for:
   a. square root
   b. square feet
   c. an unknown quantity
   d. within the boundaries

86. A broker has received an accepted offer on a 10-acre parcel. The broker has just learned that the buyer has been buying up land in the area at a much higher price than the seller agreed to take. The broker should:
   a. notify the seller as to the facts
   b. recommend that the seller breach the contract
   c. do nothing, because the seller is obligated to convey
   d. do nothing, because the agency has been completed with the procurement of the buyer

87. A nonprofit women's organization has developed housing to meet the needs of unmarried mothers. They will give preference to unmarried mothers by the size of the family. As to these rentals, which of the following is true?
   a. They are all right as long as the group is nonprofit.
   b. They are proper because they violate no laws.
   c. They would be violating the Equal Credit Opportunity Act.
   d. They would be violating the Civil Rights Act of 1968.

88. In taking a listing, the broker *appraised* a property. This was proper:
   a. because it falls within the real estate law
   b. if the broker was also a licensed or certified appraiser
   c. if the broker did not directly charge for the service
   d. both a and c

89. A purchaser of a condominium files a declaration of homestead. Since she has made no payments to the homeowner's association, a lien is filed. The lien is:
   a. unenforceable because of the homestead
   b. enforceable if the owner has greater equity than the homestead exemption
   c. collectable as if there were no homestead filed
   d. void, as homestead interests are not subject to liens

90. As the property tax increases, the value of rent-controlled property will:
   a. increase in the amount of the tax increase
   b. increase by a greater amount than the tax increase
   c. decrease by the amount of the tax increase
   d. decrease by a greater amount than the tax increase

91. "It would *not* be an appurtenance" describes:
   a. a right of egress
   b. mineral rights
   c. water rights
   d. trade fixtures

92. A planning commission would customarily regulate all *but:*
   a. streets
   b. land use
   c. construction methods and materials
   d. parks and playgrounds

93. In computing replacement cost, compute the cost to replace:
   a. the identical structure
   b. the identical structure using modern materials
   c. an equally desirable property with the same utility value
   d. the most economical structure having the same utility value

94. The Real Estate Settlement Procedures Act applies to:
   a. agricultural loans
   b. second trust deeds
   c. unsecured personal loans
   d. none of these

95. An action for payment of a commission under an exclusive listing must be started within:
   a. three years of the listing
   b. one year of the sale
   c. four years of earning the commission
   d. three years of earning the commission

96. It would *not* be a violation of the Real Estate Law to:
   a. use the term *REALTOR®* or *Realtist* without authorization
   b. claim a commission if the exclusive listing did not have a termination date
   c. violate the confidentiality of information received in a governmental capacity
   d. fail to tell a buyer that the seller would accept less

97. Gloria sells a home to Dale under a real property sales contract. Dale includes in his payment an amount for taxes. Gloria, who is *not* a real estate licensee:
   a. may use the money until the taxes are due
   b. can credit the tax payment to the principal due
   c. must hold the payments in trust to pay the taxes
   d. may leave the money in her personal account as long as her balance does not go below the trust funds

98. Ron, a salesperson, brings to a seller an offer for the exact listing amount and terms from a African-American prospect. Unknown to Ron, his broker shortly thereafter brings the seller an offer from a white prospect for less money. The seller rejects both offers. The seller later sells the home at the listing price through Ron to a neighbor, who says he is buying to keep the neighborhood white. Who is blameless?
   a. Ron
   b. the broker
   c. the white prospect
   d. the neighbor

99. The Federal Reserve has increased the money supply. The reason for the increase would probably be:
   a. to increase unemployment
   b. to fight inflation
   c. to fight a recession
   d. all of these

100. Truth-in-Lending creditor disclosure statements need *not* be made by a:
   a. real estate broker who arranges credit
   b. creditor who extends credit on real estate transactions no more than five times a year
   c. creditor extending credit on consumer transactions no more than 25 times a year
   d. any of these

101. When a topographical map has contour lines close together, it indicates:
   a. level land
   b. rivers
   c. plateaus
   d. a steep grade

102. A tenant on a 20-year fixed-monthly-rent lease buys the property from the owner. To increase working capital, the former tenant later sells the real property to an investor. After the sale, the investor gives the tenant a 30-day notice of a rent increase.
   a. The rent increase is improper, since it is a valid lease.
   b. The tenant lost the lease by merger.
   c. The lease must have been recorded to be valid.
   d. None of these are true.

103. Tom owns a lot free and clear, valued at $30,000, on which he plans to construct a commercial building and lease it for 25 years at an annual rent of $65,000. Maintenance and operating costs are estimated at $11,000 per year. If an 8 percent net return is expected on the total investment, what will be the cost of the improvements?
   a. $675,000   b. $645,000   c. $595,000   d. $435,750

104. Every real property sales contract must include all except:
   a. a legal description
   b. a statement of the number of years to pay it off
   c. the existing encumbrances if any
   d. the basis for the tax estimate

105. The Federal Reserve Board raises the discount rate to its borrowers. This would:
   a. reduce interest rates
   b. raise interest rates
   c. reduce the money supply
   d. both b and c

106. A lender under a prior unrecorded trust deed would take priority over:
   a. a subsequent recorded judgment lien
   b. a subsequent recorded gift deed
   c. both a and b
   d. neither a nor b

107. *Profit à prendre* refers to:
   a. crops
   b. capital gains
   c. depreciation
   d. phantom income

108. Which of the following provisions in a deed would be enforceable?
   a. The property is not to be resold but shall remain with the grantor and his or her heirs in perpetuity.
   b. The property shall not be resold to anyone other than Caucasians.
   c. The property may be used only for religious purposes.
   d. The property may be occupied only by males.

109. An investor purchases two lots at $6,000 each and divides them into three lots, which he sells at $4,800 each. His percentage of profit is:
   a. 10 percent
   b. 12 percent
   c. 20 percent
   d. 24 percent

110. To find information as to the thickness and width of a foundation footing, you would check the building's:
   a. specification list
   b. foundation plan
   c. elevations
   d. plot plan

111. An owner of a triplex valued at $150,000 with a $120,000 trust deed against it wishes to exchange it for a fourplex valued at $270,000 with a $216,000 trust deed against it. How much cash will she need to pay?
   a. $54,000
   b. $30,000
   c. $24,000
   d. none of these

112. The gross rent multiplier is determined by:
   a. multiplying price times rent
   b. dividing sales price by gross rent
   c. dividing sales price by net
   d. none of these

113. Who is most likely to pay for mutual mortgage insurance?
   a. a CAL-VET loan applicant
   b. a conventional loan applicant
   c. an FHA loan applicant
   d. all of these

114. A single loan for $100,000 was divided between two lenders with one taking the first $70,000 and the other taking the second portion of $30,000. This would be a:
   a. participation mortgage
   b. sharing appreciation mortgage
   c. piggyback loan
   d. soft money loan

115. Property management fees would generally range from:
   a. 1 to 5 percent
   b. 1 to 10 percent
   c. 5 to 20 percent
   d. 7 to 15 percent

116. An unrecorded deed:
   a. gives constructive notice
   b. can pass good title
   c. requires buyer occupancy
   d. all of these

117. The Government Code of the State of California contains a statement that prohibits discrimination due to race, color, religion, marital status, national origin, or ancestry. Discrimination in which of the following areas would be a violation of the code?
   a. vacant housing accommodations
   b. unimproved real property to be used for a home
   c. multiple housing units
   d. any of these

118. A property manager should *not* be compensated:
   a. for rentals
   b. for a percentage of the gross
   c. for supervising repairs
   d. by receiving kickbacks on materials and services

119. A subordination clause in a trust deed benefits:
   a. the trustor
   b. the trustee
   c. the beneficiary
   d. none of these

120. The term *kiosk* refers to:
   a. a financing scheme
   b. an open-sided booth
   c. a house of worship
   d. an architectural style

121. Stephen's cost basis on a property he paid $300,000 for is now $118,000. He trades it free and clear for another free and clear property (without boot) that is worth $500,000. His cost basis on the new property is:
   a. $118,000   b. $300,00   c. $500,000   d. none of these

122. Francine inherits property. Her cost basis is:
   a. the decedent's cost
   b. the decedent's book value
   c. the fair market value at the time of the decedent's death
   d. none of these

123. An investor might prefer a straight mortgage to an amortized mortgage because of:
   a. the greater loan
   b. greater leverage
   c. lower payments
   d. lower interest

124. An easement in gross:
   a. is attached to a person, not a property
   b. must have a definite termination date
   c. is always a negative easement
   d. all of these

125. Which of the following could a tenant regard as constructive eviction?
   a. the lessor making alterations that make the premises unsuitable for the purpose leased
   b. the lessor making constant needless repairs that interfere with the lessee's peaceful possession
   c. the lessor leasing the premises to others while the premises are occupied by the tenant
   d. all of these

126. The premium for title insurance would be paid:
   a. monthly with the mortgage payment
   b. annually
   c. upon issuance of the title policy
   d. by the subdivider for subsequent holders

127. A purchaser is buying under a zero-interest loan. As to the purchaser's income tax, which of the following is true?
   a. None of the payment is deductible.
   b. A portion of the payment is deductible as imputed interest.
   c. That portion of the purchase price in excess of fair value is imputed as interest and taxed to the purchaser.
   d. Both b and c are true.

128. By recording a notice of delinquency, a junior lienholder would be notified when the trustor gets more than _____ behind in payments.
   a. one month
   b. three months
   c. four months
   d. six months

129. A purchase agreement requires a structural pest control report. Who is responsible for the report being given to the purchaser?
   a. the purchaser
   b. the broker or the seller
   c. the termite control company
   d. none of these

130. When a property has an assessment lien against it, the price asked by an owner is usually:
    a. plus the lien amount
    b. minus the lien amount
    c. based on the lien being paid by the seller
    d. none of these

131. A buyer, before closing, asks the broker for permission to enter a vacant house to make minor repairs. The broker should:
    a. ask the buyer to deposit the balance of the purchase price in escrow
    b. present the request to the owner
    c. refuse the request
    d. allow the buyer to enter

132. An easement holder does *not* own any land. The easement would be:
    a. personal   b. appurtenant   c. negative   d. void

133. The building-residual method of appraisal is used to determine the value of the:
    a. land alone
    b. building alone
    c. building and land
    d. unearned increment

134. To protect against inflation, a buyer can purchase:
    a. trust deeds
    b. government bonds
    c. equity assets
    d. certificates of deposit

135. Without the knowledge or consent of the other joint tenant, one joint tenant conveys her interest to a third person. Upon her death:
    a. the remaining joint tenant holds title in severalty
    b. the grantee and the surviving joint tenant hold title as joint tenants
    c. the grantee and the surviving joint tenant hold title as tenants in common
    d. none of these

136. Gwen is appraising a building that rents for $750 per month. She discovers that the slightly smaller structure next door that rents for $600 per month just sold for $66,000. Using this as her only data, she would say the building is worth:
    a. $66,000   b. $82,500   c. $77,800   d. none of these

137. An owner does not receive a copy of the exclusive-right-to-sell listing she signed. The owner, believing this relieves her of any obligations, sells the property herself while the listing is in effect.
    a. The listing is invalid and the broker is liable to be disciplined.
    b. The listing is valid but the broker is liable to be disciplined.
    c. The listing is valid and the broker has done nothing wrong.
    d. The broker is not entitled to a commission but cannot be disciplined.

138. A 17-year-old divorcée wishes to sell real property. A broker:
    a. can accept the listing
    b. cannot accept the listing because she is a minor
    c. cannot accept the listing because only a man can be emancipated
    d. can accept the listing only if she has a guardian

139. An owner cannot use an unlawful detainer action against a tenant who:
    a. refuses to pay rent
    b. holds over after the tenancy expires
    c. violates lease provisions
    d. exercises the lease option but fails to make payments

140. A property manager would *not:*
    a. handle new leases
    b. arrange for repairs
    c. solve tenant disputes
    d. prepare depreciation schedules for owners

141. The cash down payment on a purchase of real estate is known as:
    a. a float   b. a margin   c. equity   d. leverage

142. Which of the following *cannot* be considered an example of constructive eviction?
   a. The landlord uses threats and profanity against the tenant.
   b. The landlord refuses to make required repairs and properly maintain the property.
   c. The landlord makes excessive and needless alterations and additions to the property.
   d. The property has been condemned under the principle of eminent domain.

143. Appraisal standards are set forth in the:
   a. real estate law   b. USPAP   c. CPA   d. MAI

144. Due to inflation, the capitalization rate of a property changes from 8 percent to 10 percent. The value:
   a. goes up 25 percent   c. goes up 20 percent
   b. goes down 25 percent   d. goes down 20 percent

145. High turnover of salespeople in a real estate office would most likely be the result of:
   a. not enough advertising   c. too low a commission structure
   b. not enough good listings   d. lack of supervision and training

146. A loan broker made a $6,000, 5-year, second trust deed. The maximum that can be charged the borrower in both costs and commission is:
   a. $990   b. $1,200   c. $1,290   d. $1,600

147. Cost basis would *not* be affected by an owner's:
   a. principal payments   c. operational costs
   b. interest expenses   d. any of these

148. When advertising a property for sale:
   a. the broker's licensed name must be shown
   b. the broker's licensed name and address must be shown
   c. the salesperson's licensed name must be shown
   d. none of these

149. When is a *lis pendens* effective?
   a. while the action is pending   c. until judgment is rendered
   b. until dismissed by the court   d. all of these

150. What is the definition of "unadjusted basis"?
   a. original cost   c. original cost plus improvements equal losses
   b. original cost minus losses   d. initial down payment

ANSWERS—REVIEW TEST II

1. d. Insurance policies and pension funds.
2. b. Built-in.
3. a.
4. c.
5. d. An opportunity cost.
6. d. Preamble to code.
7. d. Relief is available—injunction, a restraining order, or actual damages.
8. d. 5 or more except time-shares, which are 12 or more.
9. d.
10. d. He still solicited based on race (blockbusting).
11. c. There is no adjoining dominant tenement, and it is to do an affirmative act.
12. a.
13. c. The court will remove them if they become unreasonable.
14. b. Since it is for a definite period of time.
15. b. By failing to act, he ratified the acts.
16. b. Because of the assumption, Joanna retains secondary liability.
17. b. Normally five days after notice.
18. d. A buyer cannot borrow the down payment for FHA or VA loans.
19. c. This is not a violation if disclosed.
20. d.
21. d.
22. d. It gives highest value.
23. b. Transfer of a leasehold.
24. d.
25. a. As soon as it is received, not when it is due.
26. a.
27. d. A deed is a completed transfer.
28. c. Requires accounting knowledge of debits and credits.
29. b.
30. c. The lender shares in the profits.
31. d.
32. b. But the interest does not start accruing until the borrower receives the money.
33. d. Buyer has no disclosure duties.
34. c. Otherwise it could be commingling.
35. a. Since one of the parties has been declared incompetent.
36. c.
37. c. "Classical," not modern.
38. a. An approved lender.

39. a. The capitalization rate would increase.
40. a. The city owns it alone.
41. b. Each can set off the claim against the payment due.
42. c. A mechanic's lien is a specific lien.
43. a. An encumbrance, not a lien.
44. b. Presumption.
45. b. Like property is priced less.
46. b. But is normally agreed to be paid in advance.
47. c. Sharing-appreciation mortgage.
48. b. What others are charging for similar units.
49. c. Therefore there is no survivorship.
50. d. No violation of law.
51. d. 1,320′ × 660′ is half of a 40-acre parcel; and a triangle 660′ × 660′ is half of a 10-acre parcel.
52. d. A hollow pipe containing wiring.
53. c. There is a 10-day grace period.
54. c. Or land contract.
55. c. Except in the case of fraud, in which case the limit is three years or within one year of discovery of the fraud.
56. b. 27 1/2 years for residential property.
57. d. The trust deed was prior to the lease, so the junior interest is wiped out by foreclosure.
58. a. The insured must carry a specified percentage to be fully reimbursed for loss.
59. c. The buyer was a previous seller and/or the seller will be a buyer.
60. c.
61. b. (Time = interest earned ÷ principle × rate.)
62. d. 5 percent or $390, whichever is greater.
63. c. Since the monthly interest is $300.
64. b. A joint tenancy for husband and wife where neither spouse can convey a separate interest.
65. b. Also known as a "to have and to hold" clause.
66. b. The 1974 amendment.
67. d. Provides constructive notice.
68. d. One year after the sale.
69. c. The property = $6,710, or $290 less than the list price.
70. c.
71. d. Good between the parties.

72. d. Liability is $20,000 per transaction and $100,000 per licensee.
73. c. Compute the square footage of the front (length by width), then multiply by depth (a right triangle contains half of a rectangle).
74. c.
75. c. Blockbusting.
76. b. Real estate is illiquid.
77. c. $110,000 after the first year, $121,000 after the second year, $133,100 after the third year, and $146,410 after the fourth year.
78. c. Old rules apply.
79. b. A decrease in supply.
80. d. An open listing.
81. d.
82. b. Usually at auction.
83. c.
84. a. It is treated as if he received it.
85. b. Found on builders' plans.
86. a. Duty of disclosure.
87. d. Discrimination as to sex and marital status.
88. b. Only appraisers appraise.
89. c. An assessment lien takes priority over homestead rights.
90. d. Since net is reduced and value is determined by capitalizing the net.
91. d. They don't go with the land.
92. c. Regulated by the building department.
93. c. Using modern methods and materials.
94. d. First trust deeds for one to four residential units.
95. c. The Statute of Limitations is four years from the date due for written contracts.
96. d. Disclosure would violate the fiduciary duty.
97. c. Impounded funds under a contract of sale must be kept in a trust account.
98. c. The others clearly violated the law.
99. c.
100. d. All are exempt.
101. d. And contour lines far apart indicate level terrain.
102. b. When the tenant purchased the property, lesser interest (the lease) was merged into the ownership.
103. b. $65,000 − $11,000 = $54,000; $54,000 ÷ .08 = $675,000; $675,000 − $30,000 = $645,000.

104. d. Needed only if the payment includes taxes.
105. d. To fight inflation.
106. c. Neither is considered a purchaser for value.
107. a. A right to crops from the land of another.
108. c. The others violate the Civil Rights Act of 1968 or unreasonably restrain alienation.
109. c. He paid $12,000; he sold the property for $14,400; his profit was $2,400; $2,400 ÷ $12,000 = 20 percent.
110. b.
111. c. $30,000 equity versus $54,000 equity.
112. b.
113. c. This is FHA insurance.
114. c.
115. b.
116. b. Between the parties.
117. d. The Rumford Act applies to an improved or unimproved property used or intended to be used for residential purposes.

118. d. A breach of fiduciary duty as well as a secret profit.
119. a. The trustor can use the property as security for a priority lien.
120. b.
121. a. The cost base remains the same unless it is adjusted by boot.
122. c.
123. c. Interest-only payments.
124. a. No dominant tenement.
125. d.
126. c. One-time premium.
127. b.
128. c.
129. b.
130. c.
131. b.
132. a. Easement in gross.
133. b.
134. c. Such as real estate.
135. c. The transfer ended the joint tenancy.

136. b. $66,000 ÷ 600 = 110 (monthly gross rent multiplier); $750 × 110 = $82,500.
137. b. Failure to give a copy does not void the contract.
138. a. She is emancipated.
139. d. This is a buyer, not a tenant.
140. d. This is a function of an accountant.
141. c. Equity capital.
142. d. This would be actual eviction.
143. b. *Uniform Standards of Professional Appraisal Practice.*
144. d.
145. d.
146. c. Costs of $390, commission of 15 percent or $900.
147. d.
148. d. Can use "broker" or "agent."
149. d.
150. a. Adjusted basis would be cost plus improvement minus depreciation.

REVIEW TEST III

1. In a deflationary period:
   a. the value of the dollar rises
   b. the value of the dollar falls
   c. profits increase
   d. the gross national product increases

2. Henry sells his principal residence for $85,000. He originally purchased it for $79,000, but has spent $7,200 on improvements. For tax purposes Henry has a:
   a. $6,000 gain
   b. $7,200 loss
   c. $1,200 loss
   d. none of these

3. A condition subsequent would be eliminated by:
   a. renunciation by the grantee
   b. a subsequent resale
   c. merger of ownership
   d. none of these

4. An indefeasible contract would be one that:
   a. has been executed
   b. provides for exceptions
   c. is unenforceable
   d. cannot be voided

5. There are five acres in the triangular parcel between J and K streets. The distance between the streets is:
   a. 1,089 feet   b. 652.77 feet   c. 400 feet   d. 812.75 feet

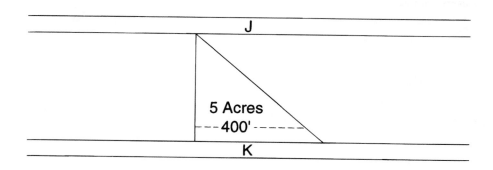

6. A loan for a longer term would have:
   a. higher loan payments
   b. a lower interest rate
   c. lower total loan costs
   d. greater total loan costs

7. The Uniform Commercial Code tends to modify or make uniform which of the following:
   a. the Uniform Sales Act
   b. the Negotiable Instrument Law
   c. both a and b
   d. none of these

8. The amortization period would most likely be subject to change on an existing _____ loan.
   a. VA   b. conventional   c. CAL-VET   d. FHA

9. As to brokers' trust accounts, which of the following is true?
   a. They can be kept in separate interest-bearing accounts.
   b. If not otherwise requested by the owner, they must be kept in demand deposits.
   c. The account must be insured by the FDIC.
   d. All of these are true.

10. A legal description would least likely appear on a:
    a. deed
    b. title insurance policy
    c. tax statement
    d. preliminary title report

11. Putting a new loan on real estate to buy another property is known as:
    a. leverage
    b. trading on equity
    c. arbitrage
    d. none of these

12. A comparable property has two baths, but subject property has 1 1/2 baths. In using the market-comparison approach, the appraiser would:
   a. disregard the slight difference
   b. increase the sale price of the comparable property
   c. decrease the sale price of the comparable property
   d. increase the value of the subject property

13. When there have been no similar sales and a property produces no income, an appraiser would likely use the:
   a. cost approach
   b. market-comparison approach
   c. gross multiplier
   d. income approach

14. Forecasting would be applicable to:
   a. the cost approach
   b. the income approach
   c. the comparison approach
   d. none of these

15. A notice of a transfer under the Bulk Sales Act would *not:*
   a. identify all creditors
   b. set forth terms of sale
   c. both a and b
   d. neither a nor b

16. A Realtor states, "If you sell this property in two years, you will be able to triple your money." Four years after buying the property, it is worth no more than when the buyer purchased it.
   a. The Realtor is guilty of puffing and can be disciplined.
   b. The buyer cannot rely on the self-serving statement of the broker.
   c. The broker can be disciplined.
   d. The broker is not subject to discipline.

17. An investor buys a property with $10,000 down and assumes a 6 percent loan. The investor sells the property on a land sales contract for the same price and down payment. She expects to make money on:
   a. volume
   b. arbitrage
   c. trading on her equity
   d. foreclosure

18. Liquidated damages can exceed 3 percent of the sale price in the case of:
   a. five residential units
   b. the buyer's nonintention to occupy
   c. a commercial building
   d. all of these

19. In selling mobile homes, a broker advertises "no down payment." A down payment is required because it is being covered by a separate loan. The statement is:
   a. proper since there is 100 percent financing
   b. unlawful—a second loan cannot be used to make the down payment
   c. proper since it is not illegal
   d. expressly forbidden by the Real Estate Law

20. A bank loans Chen $85,000. Part of the loan agreement calls for Chen to keep $8,000 of the loan fund on deposit with the bank for the life of the loan. This is an example of:
   a. spreading
   b. prepayment balance
   c. compensating balance
   d. declining balance

21. The principle that housing passes down to lower economic groups is known as:
   a. Schwabe's law
   b. filtering down
   c. supply and demand
   d. correlative user

22. Which of the following would *not* be a blanket encumbrance?
   a. a mortgage over two condominium units
   b. assessment bonds on all the property in a subdivision
   c. a promotional note
   d. both b and c

23. In the case of points being paid by a borrower, which of the following is true?
   a. The effective rate of interest would exceed the nominal rate.
   b. The nominal rate of interest would exceed the effective rate.
   c. The nominal rate would remain identical with the effective rate.
   d. The nominal rate would increase proportionally to the increase in points.

24. Off-site improvements would include:
    a. streets   b. sewers   c. street lighting   d. all of these

25. An important economic characteristic of real estate is its:
    a. immobility   b. measurability   c. beneficial use   d. permanence

26. A broker may use money in his or her trust account to:
    a. provide advances to salespeople against commissions
    b. make repairs on buildings managed by the broker
    c. pay office operational expenses
    d. none of these

27. The distance between the SE corner of Section 13, T5N, R4E, SBBL&M and the NW corner of Section 7, T4N, R5E, SBBL&M would be:
    a. 6 miles   b. 5 miles   c. 4 miles   d. none of these

28. Which of the following would *not* be constructive notice?
    a. a stranger in possession
    b. telephone poles across the property
    c. knowledge of an unrecorded deed to a stranger
    d. a recorded deed to a stranger

29. The most important reason for an increase in housing demand would be:
    a. an increase in savings   c. growth in the number of household units
    b. an increase in population   d. economic growth

30. An adverse user would obtain marketable title after:
    a. five years' open and notorious use
    b. paying the taxes for five years
    c. five years' open, notorious, and hostile use as well as paying the taxes
    d. a decree in his or her favor in a quiet title action

31. A master plan would *not* include:
    a. land uses   c. existing and proposed roads
    b. parks   d. existing and proposed utility rates

32. A *red flag* refers to:
    a. a condemnation notice
    b. a cited code violation
    c. anything that should alert an agent to a possible problem
    d. the date interest begins

33. A dragnet clause in a mortgage would cover:
    a. future contingencies   c. future advances
    b. additional parties   d. additional property acquired by the mortgagee

34. To be considered an independent contractor for IRS purposes, a salesperson needs to do all of the following except:
    a. be licensed as a salesperson
    b. have his or her pay related to sales success
    c. have a written contract stating that he or she is an independent contractor
    d. be free from a broker's supervision

35. A rectangular piece of property has 200 feet on one side and an apartment building that is worth $193,600, which is the equivalent of $4.40 per square foot for the lot. What is the front footage?
    a. 110 feet   b. 220 feet   c. 440 feet   d. 880 feet

36. Which of the following is *not* an estate in real property?
    a. a leasehold   b. a remainder   c. a reversion   d. an easement

37. A *gore* refers to:
    a. damaged property   c. a property of low value
    b. a triangular parcel of land   d. a parcel that cannot be built on

38. A bilateral contract in which both the offeror and the offeree are grantors would be:
   a. an exchange   b. a land contract   c. a mortgage   d. a sublease

39. The terms *good, valuable, adequate,* and *sufficient* refer to:
   a. income   c. broker's fees
   b. consideration   d. exclusive-right-to-sell listings

40. A conservative lessor under a sale leaseback would likely want a:
   a. level-payment gross lease   c. percentage lease
   b. net lease   d. short-term periodic tenancy

41. Advertising that must be submitted to the Commissioner for prior approval would include:
   a. subdivisions with common areas   c. subdivisions in unincorporated areas
   b. advance fees   d. condominium conversions

42. Ahmad invested $7,000 in a trust deed. His return for 90 days was $210. His rate of return was:
   a. 9 percent   b. 11 percent   c. 12 percent   d. 14 percent

43. The value of a home would be least affected by its:
   a. demand   b. rental income   c. location   d. floor plan

44. A purchaser of a condominium requests a copy of the CC&Rs and the association bylaws. These must be provided within:
   a. 5 days   b. 10 days   c. 21 days   d. 30 days

45. In establishing a capitalization rate, a person would be least interested in:
   a. prevailing interest rates   c. risk
   b. return on investment   d. taxes

46. A major disadvantage of a real estate investment is loss of liquidity. This can be offset by:
   a. amortization   c. leverage
   b. depreciation   d. all of these

47. A person is likely to be taxed for a gain when:
   a. trading up   b. trading down   c. giving boot   d. none of these

48. Albert gives Charles a grant deed to a property that Albert has no interest in. Charles records the deed. This is known as:
   a. a wild document   c. forgery
   b. conversion   d. subordination

49. An advantage that renting has over home ownership would be:
   a. tax write-offs   c. mobility
   b. equity buildup   d. depreciation

50. A safety clause protects a broker in a(n):
   a. land contract   c. deposit receipt
   b. exclusive-right-to-sell listing   d. lease option

51. A dwelling unit occupying one floor of a building is known as a:
   a. walk-up   b. flat   c. condominium   d. penthouse

52. "For Deposit Only" on the back of a check is a(n):
   a. restrictive endorsement   c. blank endorsement
   b. qualified endorsement   d. open endorsement

53. Real estate inflation would be of greatest benefit to:
   a. real estate lenders   c. real estate salespeople
   b. real estate borrowers   d. none of these

54. The Federal Reserve Board intends to tighten the money supply. What action might it take?
   a. raise the amount of reserves required for member banks
   b. raise the discount rate for member banks
   c. sell government bonds on the open market
   d. all of these

55. A right to buy a property at a yet-undetermined price in which the seller has an option *not* to sell would be:
   a. a lease option
   b. a right of first refusal
   c. either a or b
   d. neither a nor b

56. To avoid a taxable gain, a person would most likely trade his or her apartment for:
   a. stocks and bonds of equal value
   b. an apartment having a smaller encumbrance
   c. an apartment of lesser value
   d. an apartment with a greater encumbrance

57. Expressing the present value of projected income as an annual rate would be known as:
   a. the internal rate of return
   b. arbitrage
   c. trading on equity
   d. none of these

58. A holdover clause in a lease reduces the likelihood of:
   a. a tenancy at sufferance
   b. an estate for years
   c. a periodic tenancy
   d. a tenant committing waste

59. By planning a salvage value of $50,000 on a commercial building, the owner would:
   a. increase income tax liability
   b. decrease income tax liability
   c. lower the property value
   d. increase the property value

60. To determine the accrued depreciation on a building he or she is contemplating purchasing, a person should contact:
   a. the owner
   b. an appraiser
   c. the county recorder
   d. an accountant

61. An option does *not* become a binding contract on both parties until the:
   a. expiration of the option period
   b. option is signed by both parties
   c. consideration is paid
   d. option is exercised

62. Lenders, in considering loans, use the term *MPR*. This means:
   a. maximum percentage rate
   b. minimum property requirements
   c. minimum percentage rate
   d. none of these

63. The federal Fair Housing Act is also known as:
   a. Title VIII
   b. the Uniform Fair Housing Act
   c. the Civil Rights Act of 1964
   d. the Civil Rights Act of 1866

64. A debtor holding equitable title would be:
   a. the vendee under a real property sales contract
   b. a trustor who has given a trust deed
   c. both a and b
   d. neither a nor b

65. An argument between two users of water from the same source would most likely be before the:
   a. county planning commission
   b. federal district court
   c. Department of Water Resources
   d. board of supervisors

66. A plot plan would indicate:
   a. setbacks
   b. elevations
   c. subdivision layout
   d. none of these

67. Licensing and certification of appraisers is under the:
   a. Business, Transportation, and Housing Agency
   b. Department of Real Estate
   c. Department of Corporations
   d. secretary of state

68. The market-comparison method would have the least validity:
   a. when used for commercial property
   b. when applied to raw land
   c. in a thin market
   d. in a period of rapid change

69. When the purchasing power of the dollar _____, the price of housing _____, although the value may remain constant.
    a. decreases, increases
    b. increases, increases
    c. decreases, decreases
    d. none of these

70. *Unearned increment* refers to:
    a. income not realized
    b. income increase due to forces outside the owner's control
    c. income decrease due to better management
    d. income due to more careful tenant selection

71. Which of the following would a person's books *not* show as an expense?
    a. vacancy factor
    b. collection expenses
    c. management costs
    d. none of these

72. A person endorses a check but does not guarantee payment. The endorsement is:
    a. qualified
    b. in blank
    c. restrictive
    d. invalid

73. The state acquired title to an owner's land by escheat. How long must the state wait before it can dispose of it?
    a. one year
    b. three years
    c. five years
    d. there is no waiting period

74. Which of the following is *not* deducted in determining net spendable income?
    a. interest payment
    b. tax payment
    c. depreciation expense
    d. insurance payment

75. A listing distributed by a multiple listing service would most likely be:
    a. a net listing
    b. an open listing
    c. an exclusive-agency listing
    d. an exclusive-right-to-sell listing

76. After executing the contract, the purchaser of an interest in an undivided-interest subdivision has the right to rescind for:
    a. 24 hours   b. 3 days   c. 7 days   d. 14 days

77. A seller wrongfully refuses to release escrow funds to the buyer when the seller is unable to deliver clear title. A court could award the buyer:
    a. return of the amount deposited in escrow
    b. reasonable attorney fees
    c. treble the escrow funds but not more than $1,000
    d. all of these

78. A railroad company divides three sections into 20-acre parcels. Sixteen parcels are sold for $4,000 each. The remaining ones are sold for $5,000 each. The total price received is:
    a. $84,000   b. $164,000   c. $464,000   d. none of these

79. Large land developers prefer suburban areas because of:
    a. lower land costs
    b. better transportation
    c. better planned community development
    d. all of these

80. A *walk-up* refers to:
    a. a drive-in restaurant
    b. agricultural land
    c. an apartment building
    d. a trailer home

81. Simply signing your name on the back of a check is known as:
    a. a blank endorsement
    b. a special endorsement
    c. a qualified endorsement
    d. a restrictive endorsement

82. In purchasing an income property, you would be most concerned with:
    a. the price paid by the owner
    b. depreciation taken by the owner
    c. the owner's book value
    d. present leases

83. A 90-by-60-foot building is to be carpeted. Sixty percent of the square footage will be covered at a cost of $6 per square yard. The cost of the carpeting will be:
   a. $32,400   b. $3,600   c. $19,440   d. $2,160

84. During a period of time, the sum of all the products and services of our nation make up:
   a. the gross domestic product
   b. the gross national income
   c. net economic welfare
   d. net national product

85. The terms *expansion, recession, depression,* and *revival* refer to:
   a. business   b. real estate   c. the stock market   d. the bond market

86. An accountant and an appraiser are both interested in depreciation.
   a. The accountant would be interested in straight-line depreciation.
   b. The accountant would be interested in accelerated depreciation.
   c. The appraiser would be interested in straight-line depreciation.
   d. All of these are true.

87. A Realtor belongs to a syndicate and lists a piece of property he thinks is of value to the syndicate. He tells the seller that the syndicate is buying it, but not that he is a member. The seller learns the facts and refuses to sell. The Realtor sues for his commission. The judge would most likely:
   a. give the Realtor his commission
   b. revoke the Realtor's license
   c. find for the seller
   d. fine the Realtor $10,000

88. Roger agrees verbally to buy Pamela's farm. Roger gives Pamela $100 down and builds a new house and barn and improves the fences. Pamela doesn't want to sell now at the old price.
   a. Pamela does not have to sell because of the Statute of Frauds.
   b. Pamela must sell. The verbal agreement is enforceable because of possession, improvements, and partial payment, which is an exception to the Statute of Frauds.
   c. Roger's only remedy is damages.
   d. Pamela does not have to sell, but Roger can remove all of his improvements.

89. There are five units in a condominium complex. They sold for the following prices: $13,500, $14,800, $15,200, $16,500, and $17,500. The annual common maintenance cost of the complex amounts to $1,900. Each of the owners is supposed to share in proportion to his or her condominium value. What is the nearest monthly share for the owner of the $13,000 unit?
   a. $32   b. $28   c. $36   d. $44

90. In the absence of an agreement to the contrary, all of the following may be freely assigned except:
   a. an option   b. a lease   c. a mortgage   d. a fire insurance policy

91. Return *on* investment is taken care of by profit, while return *of* investment is taken care of by:
   a. depreciation
   b. rents
   c. taxes
   d. appreciation

92. Leo owns a three-quarters-of-an-acre piece of property with a depth of 110 feet. He buys a piece next to his, two-thirds the size of his with the same depth, for $1,400. He divides the two properties into lots, each with an 82.5-foot frontage. He sold the lots for $750 each. The sale price was a 50 percent profit over what the property cost him. What did he pay for the first piece of property?
   a. $1,600   b. $3,100   c. $850   d. $2,800

93. EER would be considered in regard to:
   a. environmental requirements
   b. air conditioning and heating
   c. tax-deferred exchanges
   d. property tax assessments

94. The recording of an instrument that transfers or encumbers real property has all of the following effects except:
   a. giving notice of the contents of the instrument
   b. creating the presumption of delivery
   c. preventing the creation of wild documents
   d. giving the instrument priority over subsequent recorded instruments

95. Lots A, B, and C sell for $39,000 together. Lot B is priced at $6,400 more than Lot A, and Lot C is priced at $7,100 more than Lot B. Lot A's price is:
   a. $13,000   b. $6,366.66   c. $5,433.33   d. can't compute

96. A buyer purchases two lots for $6,000. He lists the lots with a broker to sell for 30 percent over his cost. They do not sell, so he reduces the price 25 percent. Deducting a 6 percent commission, how much is his profit or loss?
   a. −$50   b. −$501   c. −$560   d. +$43

97. In a subdivision, the Real Estate Commissioner has primary regulatory authority over which of the following?
   a. alignment of streets
   b. financial arrangements to complete community facilities
   c. drainage
   d. none of these

98. A rider is:
   a. an additional party to an instrument
   b. an amendment to an insurance policy
   c. an ambulatory instrument
   d. none of these

99. Dennis wills Greenacres to Ruby with the condition that she marry before title vests. This is a:
   a. condition precedent
   b. condition subsequent
   c. covenant
   d. none of these

100. A road contains five acres along the south boundary of a section. The road is:
   a. 12 feet wide   b. 35 feet wide   c. 41 feet wide   d. 18.67 feet wide

101. A disadvantage of a deed in lieu of foreclosure is that it:
   a. is quick
   b. eliminates junior liens
   c. fails to eliminate junior liens
   d. is costly

102. As to options, which of the following is true?
   a. No consideration is necessary.
   b. They are not valid if consideration is less than $10.
   c. Consideration does not have to be paid, as long as it is recited in the option.
   d. A valid option is possible even though the consideration is less than $10.

103. Morris gives Joyce, a broker, the deed to his house as security for a loan. Morris defaults on the loan.
   a. Joyce can treat Morris as a tenant and evict him by an unlawful detainer action.
   b. Morris can immediately be ordered out, as he has no interest in the house as owner or tenant.
   c. Morris has a period of time to redeem his property.
   d. Both a and b are true.

104. Under the California Subdivided Lands Act, subdividers who are *not* residents of the state must submit an irrevocable consent that in the event of legal action against them, and if after diligent search they cannot be located for the service of process, a valid service may be made by delivering the process to the:
   a. secretary of state
   b. Real Estate Commissioner
   c. recorder in the county in which the land is located
   d. superior court in the county where the action occurs

105. Zoning that requires a developer to include low-income housing would be:
   a. exclusionary   b. inclusionary   c. incentive   d. cumulative

106. In a seller's market, a motivated seller would least likely accept an offer:
   a. that requires seller financing
   b. contingent on the sale of the buyer's house
   c. contingent on the buyer obtaining a 70 percent loan within 30 days
   d. contingent on the house getting a clean bill from the termite inspection

107. A provision in a listing includes a purchase right. The broker informs the owner that she will buy the property. To do so she must:
    a. present any offers she has received
    b. obtain the seller's consent to exercise her option
    c. disclose all known facts to the seller
    d. all of these

108. An owner must obtain the permission of the lender to:
    a. agree to restrictive covenants
    b. agree to a boundary change
    c. grant an easement over the property
    d. do any of these

109. An acquired legal privilege or right of use or enjoyment, short of an estate, which one may have in the land of another is known as:
    a. an easement
    b. riparian rights
    c. a devise
    d. a leasehold

110. An appraisal using the approach used by contractors that is comprehensive and detailed and includes provisions for materials, labor, overhead, and profit would be:
    a. the quantity-survey method
    b. the unit-in-place method
    c. the index method
    d. the comparison-residual technique

111. Metalwork in an internal valley of a roof would be:
    a. flashing
    b. gutters
    c. downspouts
    d. none of these

112. All liens are:
    a. specific
    b. general
    c. encumbrances
    d. none of these

113. In taking a listing, it is proper practice for the broker to:
    a. accept the listing at the price the owner wants
    b. raise the owner's asking price to include the commission
    c. agree to list at a greater price than any competitor
    d. ascertain the seller's reason for listing

114. On a multiyear commercial lease, the broker's commission is usually:
    a. a flat negotiated fee
    b. a set percentage of the total lease
    c. a percentage of the first month's rent
    d. a percentage of the first year's rent, a percentage of the next year's rent, etc.

115. A disadvantage of a conventional loan compared with a government-insured loan for a borrower is:
    a. lower interest
    b. a lower loan-to-value ratio
    c. greater security
    d. longer terms

116. To depreciate real estate, it must be:
    a. paid for
    b. encumbered
    c. improved
    d. none of these

117. A buyer purchases a new house, and as part of the transaction a trust deed is given to the lender. A later search of the county records would show a trust deed signed by:
    a. the grantor to the grantee
    b. the lender to the trustee
    c. the trustee to the trustor
    d. the trustor to the trustee

118. Joel moves into a deserted farmhouse and makes improvements. The owner finds out and has him ejected. Joel wants the return of his newly hinged doors and cabinets.
    a. He can get them back.
    b. The owner gets title to the improvements.
    c. He can get them back only if their removal does not damage the property.
    d. None of these are true.

119. A person who wishes to use leverage:
    a. keeps investing assets in government bonds
    b. buys income property with a low down payment
    c. buys property for cash
    d. none of these

120. James sells property to Bernice. Bernice takes possession but does not record her deed. James learns of this and immediately sells to Ryan. Ryan records his deed. In a court of law the decision most likely to be rendered would be:
   a. Ryan wins because he recorded the deed
   b. Ryan wins because he had no notice
   c. Bernice wins because she was in possession
   d. Ryan wins because he purchased the property first

121. A seller needs to disclose to a buyer the fact that the property is in a(n):
   a. area of potential flooding
   b. high fire hazard severity zone
   c. seismic hazard zone
   d. any of the above

122. The most difficult appraisal task is to determine the:
   a. economic life
   b. capitalization rate
   c. net income
   d. chronological age

123. A standard policy of title insurance protects against:
   a. rights of parties in possession
   b. unrecorded easements
   c. zoning restrictions
   d. forging in the chain of title

124. The following is equal to one acre:
   a. 1/640 of a section
   b. 1/23,040 of a township
   c. 43,560 square feet
   d. all of these

125. In California, life estates are *not* created by which of the following?
   a. will   b. law   c. grant   d. gift

126. Which of the following would be an estate of inheritance?
   a. a leasehold estate
   b. an estate for years
   c. a life estate
   d. a fee simple

127. Personal property can be:
   a. hypothecated   b. alienated   c. pledged   d. all of these

128. Which of the following acts of a landlord would be unlawful?
   a. requiring six references of every lessee
   b. requiring cosigners for single lessees
   c. requiring security deposits for all leases
   d. requiring lessees to sign occupancy rules

129. A difference between mechanic's liens and judgment liens is that:
   a. mechanic's liens must be recorded to be valid
   b. mechanic's liens not enforced within a particular period of time are lost
   c. mechanic's liens are based on statutory rights
   d. none of these

130. An old deed may use the term "vara," which is:
   a. a land grant   b. a measurement   c. 10 hectares   d. a life estate

131. In the average house, the section below the foundation is called the:
   a. slot   b. filling   c. footing   d. none of these

132. Under the Street Improvement Act of 1911, an owner has how long to pay the assessment before going to bond?
   a. 30 days   b. 60 days   c. 90 days   d. 120 days

133. After application of the homeowner's exemption, the taxable value of a home assessed at $80,000 would be:
   a. $7,000   b. $78,250   c. $73,000   d. none of these

134. A prospective African-American buyer wants to see a house. The broker has been told not to show the house while the owner is away. The broker cannot locate the owner. The buyer threatens to notify the real estate board if the broker refuses to show the property. The broker should:
   a. refuse to show the property
   b. ask the local board to arbitrate
   c. contact HUD
   d. show the property

357

135. If demand is constant:
    a. prices increase if supply increases
    b. prices increase if supply decreases
    c. prices remain constant
    d. prices are not related to supply

136. Which of the following is *not* community property during a marriage?
    a. the husband's acquired pension rights
    b. an inheritance received by the husband
    c. earnings of the wife during the marriage
    d. earnings of the husband

137. The maximum legal commission that can be charged for the sale of a house is:
    a. 6 percent   b. 10 percent   c. 15 percent   d. there is no limit

138. A real estate purchase contract always contains what type of clause?
    a. alienation   b. exculpatory   c. forfeiture   d. execution

139. The first action by a subdivider would be to:
    a. check the zoning
    b. obtain the property
    c. analyze the market
    d. comply with the Map Act

140. The maximum interest a private seller can charge on a second trust deed he or she receives as part of the purchase price is:
    a. the legal rate   b. 10 percent   c. 18 percent   d. there is no limit

141. Everett, age 71, sells his home for $125,000 and moves to an apartment. Assuming he paid $25,000 for his home 30 years earlier, his taxable gain is:
    a. $100,000   b. $28,000   c. $25,000   d. zero

142. As to the law of agency, which of the following is true?
    a. The broker can renounce the agency.
    b. The owner can revoke the agency.
    c. Both a and b are true.
    d. Neither a nor b is true.

143. A salesperson is fired because of an illegal act. The broker's act of informing the Real Estate Commissioner of the firing is:
    a. unethical   b. conditional   c. unconditional   d. arbitrary

144. As to loan broker loans, which of the following is true?
    a. Commissions are regulated for all loans.
    b. They can require credit life and disability insurance.
    c. Balloon payments are never allowed.
    d. None of these are true.

145. The gross multiplier is inaccurate for appraisal since it does *not* consider:
    a. amenity value
    b. net income
    c. location
    d. depreciation

146. The term *PMI* refers to:
    a. Professional Management Institute
    b. private mortgage insurance
    c. point margin indicator
    d. property

147. Mutual mortgage insurance:
    a. pays off the lender if the borrower dies or becomes disabled
    b. makes payments for the borrower should the borrower be in default
    c. protects the borrower against title defects
    d. covers lender losses because of foreclosure

148. Liquidation of liability for a loan in equal increments or installments is:
    a. amortization   b. conversion   c. acceleration   d. conveyance

149. A broker negotiates a hard-money loan in the sale of a property. As used in this statement, *hard-money* most nearly means:
    a. a trade   b. a security agreement   c. a secondary loan   d. cash

150. Which of the following is most nearly an antonym of *intestate?*
    a. probate   b. will   c. administrator   d. demise

ANSWERS—REVIEW TEST III

1. a.
2. d. A tax loss is not recognized on the sale of a person's residence.
3. c. The reversionary-rights owner and the fee owner would be the same person.
4. d. A defeasible contract can be voided.
5. a. Divide the total area of the rectangle ($10 \times 43,560 = 435,600$) by the known dimension of 400 feet.
6. d. Borrowing for a longer period, but a lower payment.
7. c.
8. c. If the interest rate increases, the borrower can keep the same payment by extending the term.
9. d. If the owner of the funds so requests, they can be kept in a separate interest-bearing account.
10. c. Would show the tax parcel number.
11. b. Using equity funds to pyramid holdings.
12. c.
13. a.
14. b. Forecasting future income.
15. c.
16. d. It is fraud and not puffing because it was a statement of fact. The time to bring action would be three years or within one year of discovery of the fraud.
17. b. On the interest differential.
18. d. The 3 percent limit applies to one to four residential units intended as the buyer's residence.
19. d.
20. c. It results in higher interest for available funds.
21. b.
22. b. They would be specific liens on individual properties.
23. a.
24. d.
25. c. The others are physical characteristics.
26. b. From the property rent income held in trust.
27. c.
28. c. This is actual notice.
29. c.
30. d. Or a deed from the former owner.
31. d.

32. c. Such as water stains on the ceiling.
33. c.
34. d. Broker must supervise salespeople.
35. b. $193,600 = $4.40 per square foot; $193,600 \div \$4.40 = 44,000$ square feet; divide the area by the known dimension—$44,000 \div 200 = 220$.
36. d. While it is real property, it is not an estate.
37. b.
38. a.
39. b.
40. b. Guaranteed net.
41. b.
42. c. $\$210 \times 4 = \$840$ per year. $\$840 \div \$7,000 = 12\%$.
43. b.
44. b. Of the request.
45. d. Used to determine the net, not the rate.
46. c. Low down payment.
47. b. Would likely receive boot.
48. a. Outside the chain of title.
49. c.
50. b.
51. b.
52. a. Restricts further endorsement.
53. b. They can repay loans with cheaper dollars.
54. d.
55. b.
56. d. If the person receives debt relief, it is considered boot, but he or she can give boot (to increase the cost base).
57. a.
58. a. Higher rent discourages holding over.
59. a. Since the building would depreciate less.
60. b. Actual, not book, depreciation.
61. d.
62. b. For FHA loans.
63. a. Of the Civil Rights Act of 1968.
64. c. Neither holds legal title.
65. c. Disputes are normally sent to them for a hearing by the court.
66. a. Orientation on the lot.
67. a. By a separate appraisal department (Office of Real Estate Appraisers).
68. c. A thin market means few sales.
69. a.
70. b. Such as a demand increase.

71. a. It is not an expense; it is lack of income.
72. a. Without recourse.
73. d. Since the state has *acquired* the land.
74. c. Deduct only cash expenses to determine net spendable.
75. d. Although it could be any kind of listing.
76. b.
77. d.
78. c. $640 \times 3 = 1,920$ acres; $1,920 + 20 = 96$ parcels; $(16 \times \$4,000) \div (80 \times \$5,000) = \$464,000$.
79. a.
80. c. Without an elevator.
81. a. "To the order of" is a special endorsement.
82. d.
83. d. $90 \times 60 = 5,400$ square feet; 60% of $5,400 = 3,240$ square feet $\div 9 = 360$ square yards; $\$6 \times 360 = \$2,160$.
84. a.
85. a. Parts of the business cycle.
86. d.
87. c. The seller won't have to pay a commission and can void the sale.
88. b. Doctrine of estoppel.
89. b. The total of the five units = $77,500; $\$13,500 \div \$77,500 = 17.42\%$. $17.42 \times \$1,900 = \$330.09$ annual cost; $\$330.98 \div 12 = \$27.58$ monthly.
90. d. Requires the consent of the insurer.
91. a.
92. a. 3/4 acre = 32,670 square feet; 2/3 of $32,670 = 21,780$ square feet; total 54,450 square feet. $54,450 \div 110 = 495'$ frontage (divide the total area by the known dimension to find the other dimension); $495 \div 82.5 = 6$ lots; $6 \times \$750 = \$4,500$ or 150% of the cost of $3,000; since one parcel cost $1,400, the other cost $1,600.
93. b. Energy efficiency rating.
94. c. A wild document is an instrument outside the chain of title.
95. b. (Lot A) + (Lot B + $6,400) + (Lot C + $13,500) = $39,000; $\times$ 3 lots + $19,900 = $39,000; 3 lots = $19,100; $\$19,100 \div 3 = \$6,366$ for Lot A; $\$6,366 + \$6,400 = \$12,766$ for Lot B; $\$12,766 + \$7,100 = \$19,866$ for Lot C.

96. b. $6,000 × 1.30 = $7,800; $7,800 − 25% = $5,850; $5,850 × .06 = $351; net is $5,499; loss of $501.
97. b.
98. b.
99. a. Future vesting of title.
100. c. Divide the known dimension into the total area: (5 × 43,560) ÷ 5,280.
101. c. Intervening liens would have been wiped out by foreclosure.
102. d. There must be some consideration that has actually been paid.
103. c. A deed given as security is treated as a mortgage.
104. a. As must nonresident licensees and foreign corporations.
105. b.
106. b. This would tie up the sale for a longer period of time.
107. d.
108. d. All could affect value.
109. a.
110. a.
111. a.
112. c. But not all encumbrances are liens.
113. d.

114. d. The percentage generally declines.
115. b. Requires greater down payment.
116. c. Since land is not depreciated.
117. d.
118. b. They are fixtures; the court might allow an innocent improver to remove improvements, but this is not the case here.
119. b. Uses other people's money.
120. c. Possession is also constructive notice.
121. d. All are included in the *Natural Hazard Disclosure Statement.*
122. b. Determining effective age is also difficult.
123. d.
124. d.
125. b. In some states, a widow has a legal life estate in the home of her deceased husband (dower).
126. d.
127. d.
128. b. Marital status discrimination.
129. c. And judgments are based on court decisions.
130. b. Approximately 33 inches (Mexican).

131. c.
132. a.
133. c. Because of the $7,000 exemption.
134. a. The reason has nothing to do with race.
135. b.
136. b. Separate property.
137. d. Negotiable.
138. d. The contract must be signed.
139. c. Is there a need?
140. d. Exempt from usury (seller carryback financing).
141. d. Universal exclusion.
142. c. But he or she could be liable for damages.
143. c. Mandatory.
144. d. All are incorrect.
145. b.
146. b. Reduces lender risk on conventional loans.
147. d. FHA insurance.
148. a.
149. d. Rather than seller financing, which is "soft money."
150. b. *Intestate* means "without a will." (Antonym means opposite.)

The Language of Real Estate

Note: It is strongly recommended that students read through this section at least once during each week of study. This glossary contains many terms not covered in the text. They are included because at times they have appeared on state license exams, although they are not commonly tested.

Note: Words ending in *-or* normally indicate givers, while words ending in *-ee* generally indicate receivers.

Abatement A method of termination of a nuisance.

Abstract A recorded history of a property (abstracts of all recorded documents).

Abstractive method An appraisal method used to find comparable land value. The value of improvements is deducted from comparable sales, and the remainder is the value attributed to the land.

Abstract of judgment A condensation of a court judgment which, when recorded in the county where the property of the debtor is located, becomes a lien on the property.

Abut To border on or to touch.

Accelerated depreciation Any method of depreciation that allows a greater rate than the straight-line method.

Acceleration clause A clause in a note giving the lender the right to demand the entire balance owed upon the happening of some event.

Acceptance The agreement of the offeree that forms the binding contract.

Access right The right of an owner for ingress and egress.

Accession Acquiring property because it has become joined with other property (such as fixtures).

Accommodation party A third person who signs a negotiable instrument to give it strength.

Accord and satisfaction Acceptance of a different consideration than had been agreed to. This is common where there is a disputed claim and one party accepts less than the agreement calls for.

Accredited management organization See *AMO.*

Accretion Addition to land from buildup of soil or action of water.

Accrued depreciation The difference between the replacement cost new at the present time and its present value.

Accusation The first action of the real estate commissioner in instituting a hearing against a licensee.

Acknowledgment A declaration made before a notary by an individual that he or she has, in fact, executed (signed) a document.

Acquisition Act of procuring property.

Acre A measurement of land equal to 43,560 square feet or 208.7 feet by 208.7 feet.

Action *in personam* Legal action against a person.

Action *in rem* Legal action against a property.

Ademption The disposal of a property before death that revokes any disposition made by a will.

Adjustable-rate mortgage See *ARM.*

Adjusted cost basis Cost plus improvements minus deductions taken for depreciation.

Adjusted gross income Gross income adjusted for a vacancy factor and collection losses.

Administrative procedures act An act that covers procedures for hearings by administrative agencies, such as hearings for revocation, denial, or suspension of real estate licenses.

Administrator A man appointed by a probate court to administer the estate of the deceased. (A woman would be an administratrix.)

Adobe A type of soil (also a type of brick).

Ad valorem A tax according to value (such as real estate tax).

Advance commitment A lender's prior agreement to provide permanent financing after construction is complete.

Advance fee A fee charged by a business-opportunity broker for advertising (the ad must be in a publication primarily devoted to the sale of property).

Adverse possession Holding property adversely to the owner's right. Title can be obtained by adverse possession.

Affidavit A written statement sworn under oath.

Affirm To ratify or verify.

Affirmation A solemn statement before a court by a person whose religion prohibits him or her from taking an oath.

Affirmative easement An easement that allows the holder of the dominant tenement to use the land of the servient tenement.

After-acquired title A title or interest acquired by a grantor after he or she has conveyed the property.

Age-life tables Appraiser's tables that show economic life for various types of structures.

Agency A relationship between a principal and an agent whereby the agent is empowered to act for the principal.

Agency coupled with an interest An irrevocable agency in which the agent has an interest in the subject property.

Agent One who represents another.

Agreement of sale A written contract setting forth the conditions of sale.

Air rights The right of a landowner to reasonable use of the air space above the property.

Alienation Transfer.

Alienation clause A type of acceleration clause requiring the existing loan to be paid if property is transferred. Also known as a *due-on-sale clause.*

All-inclusive trust deed (mortgage) See *Wraparound trust deed.*

Allodial tenure An ownership system in which ownership is complete except for some rights held by the government.

Alluvium Soil deposited by action of water (accretion).

ALTA (American Land Title Association) An extended-coverage policy of title insurance to protect the lender.

Amend-escrow instructions A change in escrow instructions, such as an extension. Both parties must sign.

Amenities Satisfaction derived from living in a home, such as the beauty, privacy, etc. that contribute to the quality of life.

AMO (Accredited Management Organization) A firm that meets the guidelines of the Institute of Real Estate Management (IREM) and includes at least one Certified Property Manager (CPM).

Amortization Payment of a debt on an equal-installment basis in which the last payment liquidates the obligation.

Anchor bolt A bolt used to anchor the mudsill to the foundation.

Ancillary probate A probate in a state other than the domicile state in which the deceased owned property.

Annexation Adding to, such as a city adding additional land.

Antimerger clause A clause that provides that the senior lienholder retains lien priority in the event of a merger should there be a deed in lieu of foreclosure. While a foreclosure of a senior lien wipes out junior liens, a deed in lieu of foreclosure would leave the junior liens intact if this clause were not in the trust deed.

Appraisal An opinion of value.

Appreciation A rise in value.

Appropriation of water Diverting water to one's own use. The appropriator, after doing so for a period of time, obtains a continuing right (the right of prior appropriation).

Appurtenance Something that belongs with another thing and goes with it (such as a house with land).

Appurtenant easement An easement right that transfers with the dominant tenement.

APR (annual percentage rate) Expressed as simple interest considering loan costs.

Arbitrage Making money on an interest difference (buying at one interest rate and selling at a higher rate).

ARM (adjustable-rate mortgage) A mortgage whose rate is tied to an index such as the T-bill rate.

Artificial monument A manmade point on a metes and bounds description, such as an iron stake, road, canal, or building.

As is A statement intended to mean that the purchaser will not hold the seller liable for any problems. Its use is considered unethical unless it refers to a specific problem that the purchaser is aware of.

Assemblage The act of bringing together two or more contiguous parcels to form a larger parcel.

Assessed value A value placed for tax purposes.

Assessment The amount of tax levied.

Assets Property owned by or owed to a business.

Assignment The turning over to another of a person's rights in property.

Assignment of rents Transfer of the right to collect rent. This is often included in trust deeds, allowing the beneficiary to collect the rents when the trustor is in default.

Assignor One who assigns to another.

Assigns/assignees Those to whom property has been assigned.

Assumption Taking over an obligation of another and agreeing to pay.

Assumption fee Fee charged by a lender to allow assumption of loan.

Attachment Seizure of property before a judgment under court order to make sure it will be available after judgment. An attachment lien is good for three years.

Attest To witness a document.

Attorney-in-fact One who operates under a power of attorney. Not necessarily a licensed attorney.

Attornment A tenant's agreement to pay the new landlord and the landlord's agreement to honor the lease. A tenant will often enter an attornment agreement with a lender to be protected in case the prior trust deed is foreclosed.

Attractive nuisance doctrine A doctrine according to which an owner is liable for unsafe conditions to child trespassers if children are likely to be attracted.

Avulsion Tearing away of land by action of water.

Axial growth Fingerlike growth in all directions from the center of a city following highways, rivers, etc.

Backfill Dirt filled in around an excavated foundation.

Bailment Giving possession of personal property for some purpose but retaining title (such as renting a trailer or leaving shoes for repair).

Balance sheet A document that shows net worth by listing assets on one side and liabilities on the other.

Balloon payment A final installment payment greater than the preceding payments; it is needed to pay the debt in full.

Baltimore method An appraisal method for a corner commercial lot in which the value of the corner lot is said to be equal to the sum of the values of the lots on each side of it.

Band-of-investment method A method of finding an average capitalization rate to use for appraising.

Banker's interest Interest based on a 30-day month and a 360-day year.

Bankruptcy A legal procedure whereby a person can eliminate his or her unsecured debts (to eliminate secured debts, one must surrender security). A person cannot go bankrupt more than once every six years.

Bargain-and-sale deed A deed, given for consideration, that does not contain any warranties other than that the grantor has not harmed or clouded the title.

Baseboard A narrow board placed against the wall at the floor around the perimeter of a room.

Base line An east-west surveyor's line used to locate property.

Base shoe or molding Molding used in conjunction with the baseboard.

Batten Wood strips used to cover joints (as in board-and-batten siding).

Beam A heavy horizontal structural member.

Bearer paper An instrument made out "to bearer" or to "cash." No endorsement is necessary to negotiate it.

Bearing wall A wall that also supports the building.

Benchmark A location marker placed by a government survey showing elevation.

Beneficiary One who is benefited by a trust, or the lender under a trust deed.

Beneficiary statement A statement by a lender as to the condition of a trust note (the balance).

Bequeath To give by will.

Bequest Personal property that is given by will.

Betterments Improvements to real estate.

Bilateral contract A promise made for a promise.

Bill of sale A written instrument passing title to personal property.

Binder Insurance coverage given by an agent prior to issuance of policy.

Blank endorsement Signing name only on back of negotiable instrument. No further endorsements are required.

Blanket mortgage One encumbrance covering several separate properties.

Blended interest rate A rate of interest greater than the previous rate but less than the prevailing rate. It is used in refinancing and loan assumptions.

Blind advertisement An ad that fails to state that the advertiser is a broker or agent. (An abbreviation, such as *Agt.* or *Bro.*, is acceptable.)

Blind pool A syndication in which the property to be purchased will be selected after the money is raised.

BLM (Bureau of Land Management) The federal bureau that controls federal land.

Blockbusting The illegal procedure of inducing panic selling based on the fear of minority groups entering the area.

Board foot A measurement for lumber. One foot by one foot by one inch, or 144 cubic inches.

Book value The value at which a firm carries an asset on its books (cost plus improvement expenses minus depreciation).

Boot Additional money or unlike property given to even up a trade of property.

Bracing Diagonal boards added for rigidity (located in corners).

Bracketing See *reconciliation*.

Breach The breaking of an agreement or law.

Bridging Diagonal boards nailed between joists.

Broker A person employed as an agent for real estate dealings. Only a broker can employ a salesperson.

364

BTU (British thermal unit) A unit of heat measurement. One BTU equals the amount of heat needed to raise the temperature of one pound of water by one degree fahrenheit. It is used to measure the capacity of heating units.

Budget loan A loan with payments that include taxes and insurance.

Building line The setback for building.

Building paper Tar paper used as a vapor barrier in the walls and on the roof.

Build-up method See *Summation method.*

Bulk Sales Act Part of the Uniform Commercial Code. It requires recording and publication of sales not in the course of usual business.

Bulk zoning The use of zoning to control density with setbacks, height, and open-area requirements.

Bullet loan A short-term unamortized loan.

Bundle of rights Includes all rights that are incidental to ownership (such as the right to sell or lease).

Bureau of Land Management See *BLM.*

Buy-down loan A loan in which the seller pays the lender so that the lender will provide the purchaser with a loan at a lower rate of interest.

Buyer's market A real estate marketplace where there are more sellers than buyers.

Bylaws Corporate rules that include the authority of officers.

Caliche A type of soil.

California Association of REALTORS® See *CAR.*

California Housing Finance Agency (CHFA) A public agency that sells tax-exempt bonds to raise funds for low-interest housing loans for low- and moderate-income borrowers.

California Land Title Association See *CLTA.*

CAL-VET loans Loans made to California Veterans; administered by the California Department of Veterans Affairs.

Capital assets Physical assets (land, buildings, and equipment).

Capital gain Profit from the sale of a capital asset.

Capitalization method An appraisal method based on the income of a property.

Capitalization rate A percentage of return that is divided into net income to arrive at value.

Capital loss Loss from the sale of a capital asset.

CAR (California Association of REALTORS®) The state organization of the National Association of REALTORS®.

Casement window A window on hinges that swings outward.

Cash flow The amount of cash left over from gross receipts after cash expenses (does not consider paper expenses such as depreciation).

Casing Wood trim around doors and windows.

Caveat emptor "Let the buyer beware." The old rule is now being replaced with duties on the seller.

CC&Rs Covenants, conditions, and restrictions.

CCIM (Certified Commercial Investment Member) A designation earned by a member of the Commercial-Investment Real Estate Institute, which is a part of NAR.

Certificate of eligibility A certificate given by the VA to a veteran as to loan eligibility.

Certificate of Reasonable Value (CRV) A VA loan appraisal.

Certification of title An opinion of title showing liens.

Certified appraisal A written appraisal in accordance with standards required by law.

Certified Property Manager See *CPM.*

Chain A surveyor's measurement equal to 66 feet.

Chain of title A history of the actual conveyances from the original patent to the present owner.

Chattel An archaic term for personal property.

Chattel mortgage A mortgage on personal property.

Chattel real A personal property interest in real property (a lease).

Check A 24-mile-square area formed by correction lines on government surveys. This is also known as a quadrangle.

Chronological age The actual age of a structure.

Circuit breaker A safety device that shuts off electricity in the event of an overload (used instead of a fuse).

Clapboard Overlapped horizontal board siding.

Clearance receipt A receipt from the State Board of Equalization for the sale of a business, certifying that the sales taxes have been paid to a certain date.

Closing statement The final accounting statement for a real estate transaction.

Cloud on title Anything of record that may create any possible doubt as to marketability of the title.

CLTA (California Land Title Association) The organization that developed the standard form of title insurance for buyer protection.

Codicil An amendment to a will.

Coinsurance Requires that insurance be at least 80 percent of the replacement value. If the insured carries only a percentage of the required coverage, then the insured gets only that percentage of any loss (generally for nonresidential property).

Collar beam A horizontal beam connecting opposite rafters.

Collateral Property given as security for a loan.

Collaterally secured Describes a loan secured by other loans, such as in mortgage warehousing.

Collusion Agreement to defraud or to perform an illegal act.

Color of title An appearance of having title but actually not having title at all.

Commercial acre The net remainder of an acre after deduction of land for streets, walks, etc. (less than 43,560 square feet).

Commercial paper Bills and drafts used in lieu of currency in a business.

Commingling Failure to properly segregate the personal funds of a licensee from funds entrusted to the licensee as an agent.

Commission An agent's percentage for successfully completing a sale, lease, etc. For tax purposes, it is treated as an expense of the sale or lease.

Commitment A pledge or promise. For example, a loan commitment is a promise to make a loan.

Common area An area of common interest owned by all owners in a subdivision.

Common elements Those portions of the common areas for the use of all the owners (see *Limited common elements*).

Common-interest development (CID) A subdivision with areas owned in common with other owners, such as planned developments, condominiums, stock cooperatives, and community apartment projects.

Common law The unwritten law of England carried over into U.S. statutes.

Community apartment project Two or more units where each tenant has an undivided interest in the entire building plus the right to occupy a particular unit.

Community property Property acquired during marriage that is owned equally by the husband and the wife.

Community property with right of survivorship Community property type that cannot be willed.

Compaction Packing soil to support a building load. Important where fill material has been used.

Company dollar The broker's share of commission dollars earned (expenses would be deducted to determine the broker's net income).

Compensating balance A lender requirement that a borrower maintain a portion of the loan in a low-yield account with the lender. It serves to raise the effective rate of interest.

Compensatory damages Damages awarded to make up for a loss suffered or to compensate for the damages.

Complete escrow An escrow in which everything required to be done has been completed.

Completion bond insurance Bond that obligates insurance company to complete construction if the builder defaults.

Compound interest Interest paid both on previously accumulated interest and on principal.

Concentric-circle growth Urban growth in a circular pattern from the city center.

Conclusion The final estimate of value set forth in an appraisal.

Condemnation The process of taking of private property for public use. Also a declaration that the property is unfit for use.

Condition precedent The passing of title is not accomplished until the condition has been fulfilled.

Condition subsequent The reversion of title to the previous owner upon the happening of some event.

Conditional commitment A promise to make a loan of a specified amount to a buyer yet unknown, providing his or her credit is okay.

Conditional sales contract A sales contract for personal property in which the buyer obtains possession, but the seller retains title as security.

Conditional-use permit Permission for a use not allowable by the zoning, but provided for under special permission.

Condominium A subdivision in which there is individual ownership of the units themselves, but joint ownership of common areas.

Condominium declaration The document that establishes the condominium.

Conduit A metal or plastic pipe containing electrical wires.

Confession of judgment The debtor agrees to a judgment by voluntary admission.

Conforming loan A loan that meets Fannie Mae and Freddie Mac purchase criteria.

Conservation easement An easement granted by a landowner that prohibits future development (the land is to remain in a natural state).

Conservator A person appointed by the court to handle the property of one who is unable to handle his or her own affairs.

Consideration Something of value given in exchange for a promise, act, or property.

Consistency doctrine The requirement that cities and counties bring their zoning into conformance with the general plan.

Constructive eviction An act of a landlord materially affecting a tenant's quiet possession which entitles the tenant to consider the tenancy at an end.

Constructive notice The notice given by recording or occupancy. Although the parties are not actually notified, it serves as notice.

Constructive severance When crops are sold, they are considered to be personal property even though they have not been physically severed.

Consumer goods Goods used for personal or household purposes rather than in production.

Consumer price index See *CPI*.

Contiguous Adjoining or actually touching.

Contingent remainder A remainder interest in property that will vest only if some contingency is met.

Contour lines Lines on a topographic map. When the lines are far apart it means that the land is relatively flat.

Contract An agreement enforceable by law.

Contraction period A period in which real estate prices hit their low point; it follows a recession period.

Controlled business arrangement Broker-controlled service provider that operates as separate business but broker shares in profits.

Conventional loan A loan neither guaranteed nor insured by the government. It is made by a lending institution.

Conversion Taking the property of others and converting it to one's own use.

Convertible mortgage A mortgage that can be changed to another loan type.

Conveyance Transfer of property.

Corner influence Additional value of commercial property because of a corner location.

Cornice Ornamental stonework on top of a wall or building.

Corporation A legal entity created by law (an advantage of a corporation is no personal liability of stockholders for debts of the corporation).

Corporeal rights Possessory rights in real property.

Correction lines Surveyor's lines used to compensate for the curvature of the earth in government surveys. Their use results in some townships not containing 36 squares miles and some sections of less than 640 acres.

Correlation See *Reconciliation*.

Correlative user The right of a landowner to use underground percolating water.

Cost approach A method of appraisal that takes the cost to build today minus accrued depreciation plus the value of the land.

Cotswold A two-story English stone cottage.

Counterflashing (flashing) Metalwork mounted around the chimney and vents to keep out rain.

County board of supervisors Sets the tax rate, sits as the County Board of Tax Equalization for assessment appeals, and also hears zoning appeals.

Covenant A promise. When recorded, it runs with the land and binds subsequent owners.

CPI (consumer price index) An index that reflects inflation. Long-term leases are often tied to the CPI.

CPM (Certified Property Manager) A member of the Institute of Real Estate Management of the NAR.

Crawl space The air space between the ground and the floor for homes not built on concrete slabs. The minimum height is 18 inches. The minimum size of the access hole is 18 inches by 24 inches.

CRB (Certified Real Estate Brokerage Manager) A designation conferred by the REALTORS® National Marketing Institute of the NAR.

CRE (Counselor of Real Estate) A member of the American Society of Real Estate Counselors.

Creditor One to whom something is owed.

Cripple A short vertical piece of two-by-four above or below an opening.

Cross-default clause A loan provision in which default on one loan constitutes default on the other loans of the trustor.

CRV See *Certificate of Reasonable Value.*

Cul-de-sac A dead-end street ending in a circle. It is desirable for homes because it is subject to little traffic.

Cumulative zoning Zoning that allows more restrictive uses.

Curable depreciation Depreciation that can be corrected within reasonable limits of expense. If not, it is incurable.

Curtail schedule A loan schedule showing payments and amount that principal is reduced by each payment.

Curtesy A common-law right a husband has in his wife's estate. Not valid in California.

Damages The amount of injury suffered for which the injured party can recover from the wrongdoer.

Datum plane A surveyor's level plane that shows elevations.

Debenture Bonds issued by a corporation without any security.

Debtor A person who owes money.

Deciduous trees Trees that lose their leaves, as opposed to coniferous trees.

Declaration of homestead A recorded document giving a person an exemption from unsecured liens. It is filed on the home by the owner at the time he or she is living in it.

Declaration of restrictions Restrictions recorded by the subdivider to cover all the parcels.

Declining-balance depreciation An accelerated method of depreciation used for tax purposes.

Dedication Giving real property free of charge to a public body. Under common law, the dedicated land belongs to the dedicator, but exclusive use is given.

Deed A written instrument conveying title to real property.

Deed in lieu of foreclosure A deed given by the trustor to the beneficiary. (It might not wipe out junior encumbrances.)

Deed of reconveyance A deed given by the trustee to the trustor when the trustor has paid up the trust note. Recording the deed of reconveyance removes the lien.

Default Failure to meet an obligation.

Defeasance clause A clause in a mortgage or trust deed that provides for the release of the lien upon payment.

Defeasible estate An estate that may be lost on the happening of some event (condition subsequent).

Deferred maintenance Needed maintenance that has not been performed.

Deficiency judgment A judgment obtained when foreclosure sale of the loan security does not satisfy the entire debt.

Degree A measurement for angles. Each degree is 1/360 of a circle. A degree may be broken down into minutes, which are 1/60 of a degree.

Demise Transfer of a leasehold interest.

Demographic study A study of the social and economic makeup of the people in an area (by age, sex, marital status, income, etc.).

Department of Housing and Urban Development See *HUD*.

Deposit receipt Now known as a purchase contract and receipt for deposit. It is an offer to purchase given by the buyer and accepted by the seller.

Depreciation A loss in value of property.

Depth table An appraiser's table for finding the additional value attributable to additional depth of a property.

Dereliction Land created by permanent recession of water.

Descent Passing of property to an heir.

Desist-and-refrain order An order by the Real Estate Commissioner to stop a violation of the Real Estate Law.

Desk cost The complete office overhead apportioned to each salesperson; overhead divided by the number of salespersons.

Determinable fee An estate that automatically ends on the happening of an event.

Development method An appraisal method used to determine land value in which the cost to develop an improvement is deducted from the value the property would have if it were so improved, leaving the value of the land.

Devise A transfer of real property by will.

Devisee A person who receives under a will.

Devisor A person who gives by a will.

Direct endorsement program A program in which lenders are able to process FHA insurance applications without prior approval of the FHA.

Directional-growth area An area in which residential sections are spreading from the city.

Discounting a loan Selling a loan for less than the value owed.

Discount loan A loan in which the interest is deducted in advance from the proceeds.

Disintermediation The sudden withdrawal of savings from banks and savings and loan institutions.

Disposable income Income left after taxes.

Distribution The apportionment and division of an estate to the heirs under probate.

Documentary stamps A county tax on the equity over $100 transferred in a real estate transaction. The tax is 55 cents per $500 or portion thereof.

Domiciliary probate Probate in the state where the deceased lived.

Dominant tenement The estate that has the use of the land of another under an easement.

Donee A person receiving a gift.

Donor A person who makes a gift.

Double escrow Use of one escrow by an individual to both buy a property and resell it. It is used by dealers and speculators.

Double-hung window A window that slides up and down.

Dower A wife's right in her husband's estate under common law. Not valid in California.

Down zoning A change in zoning to a more restrictive use, such as a change from commercial to residential zoning.

Dragnet clause A clause extending a deed of trust to cover past and future obligations between the trustor and the beneficiary.

Drywall An interior wallboard treatment other than plaster (which is applied wet).

Dual agency An agency in which the agent represents both the buyer and the seller.

Due-on-sale clause See *Alienation clause.*

Duress Unlawful constraint in which a person is forced to act. Duress may be a threat or actual violence.

DVA (Department of Veterans Affairs) Guarantees VA loans.

Earnest money Money given with an offer.

Easement A right of a landowner to use the land of another for a special purpose.

Easement by necessity An easement granted when both tenements were formerly under one ownership and no other access is possible.

Easement in gross A right of someone who is not a land owner to use the land of another (there is no dominant tenement).

Eaves The part of the lower roof that projects beyond the walls.

Economic life That period for which a property gives a financial return attributable to the improvements and not the land.

Economic obsolescence A decline in value or depreciation caused by forces outside the property itself.

Economic rent Anticipated rental income based on comparable rentals in the market-place.

Economies of scale Savings resulting from increased production.

EER See *Energy efficiency ratio.*

Effective age The age placed by an appraiser on a structure based on actual condition, not chronological age.

Effective gross income Gross income minus the vacancy factor and collection losses.

Effective interest The actual interest rate considering loan fees, etc. (The *nominal rate* is the rate stated.)

EIR See *Environmental impact report.*

Elder abuse law Requires broker to notify authorities if it appears that fraud, theft or undue influence has influenced an elderly person as to a transaction.

Ejectment A legal action to oust a trespasser or encroacher.

Eleemosynary Charitable.

Elevation Views of a structure from various sides found on builder's plans.

Ellwood tables An appraising method to determine the capitalization rate.

Emancipated minor A minor who is allowed by law to contract as an adult.

Emblements Cultivated crops (a tenant has the right to take the crops after the tenancy has ended if they are the product of his or her labor).

Eminent domain The right of government to acquire private property for public or quasipublic use. The owner is compensated for value at the time the property is taken.

Enabling legislation Laws that give powers to government units such as zoning authorities.

Encroachment A form of trespass in which a building or improvement is placed on or over the land of another.

Encumbrance Anything affecting title or use, such as liens, easements, and covenants.

Endorsement Signing of one's name on the back of a negotiable instrument.

Energy Conservation Retrofit Law The seller is obligated to pay for any retrofitting required for energy conservation.

Energy efficiency ratio (EER) The efficiency rating of appliances, water heaters, furnaces, and air conditioners.

Environmental impact report (EIR) Required for all projects that may have a significant effect on the environment. It is required under the Environmental Quality Act of 1970.

Equal Credit Opportunity Act A federal act prohibiting discrimination in credit.

Equitable title Right of a trustor and vendee under land contract to obtain legal title.

Equity A person's financial interest in property; the difference between its value and what is owed against it. The term also means "justice" or "what is right."

Equity of redemption The right of a mortgagor to redeem his or her property after foreclosure. The time limit is one year in case of foreclosure by court action when the sale is for less than the balance owing.

Erosion Wearing away of land by action of water.

Escalator clause A clause in a contract or lease providing for adjustments in costs upward or downward.

Escheat The reversion of property to the state when a person dies without either a will or heirs.

Escrow A neutral depository for documents and funds to carry out instructions in a real estate transaction.

Estate An interest in property.

Estate at will An estate that can be terminated without notice by either party (not valid in California).

Estate for life A freehold interest that a person has in property for the duration of his or her life or someone else's life. The person's interest is not inherited by his or her heirs but either reverts to the grantor or goes to someone having a remainder interest.

Estate for years An interest for a definite period of time (such as a lease for a specified period).

Estate of inheritance An interest that may be inherited.

Estoppel A doctrine whereby a person is barred from raising defenses when, by previous statements, he or she induced another person to act to his or her own detriment.

Estovers A tenant's reasonable right to use timber from the premises for fuel, fences, etc.

Et al. "And others."

Ethics Principles of conduct toward others. (The REALTORS® Code of Ethics comes from the NAR.)

Et ux. "And wife."

Eviction Dispossession by process of law pursuant to a court judgment.

Exception in deed Exclusion of a part of the property from a grant.

Excess land Land that does not economically contribute to a property value (more land than can be utilized).

Exchange value The value in terms of other goods that could be obtained for the property.

Exclusionary clause A clause in a deed excluding part of the property from the grant.

Exclusionary zoning Zoning that excludes specified uses.

Exclusive-agency listing A listing whereby the agent is entitled to a commission if anyone other than the owner procures a buyer.

Exclusive-right-to-sell listing A listing whereby the agent is entitled to a commission if the property is sold by anyone during the listing.

Exculpatory clause A clause in a contract excusing one party for injuries that may result. Frequently inserted by lessors in leases.

Execute To sign or to complete.

Executed contract A contract that has been performed.

Executing judgment Having the sheriff collect on a judgment by going against the property of the debtor.

Executor A man named by will to administer the estate of the deceased. (A woman would be an executrix.)

Executory contract A contract that has not yet been fully performed.

Exemplary damages Damages in excess of the actual loss, awarded for the purpose of punishment (punitive). They are awarded when the damage was willful or outrageous.

Expandable home A home designed for future expansion.

Expansion joint A fiber joint in concrete to prevent cracking.

Express contract A contract that is stated (written or verbal) rather than implied.

Extension of lease Continuing under the old or existing lease, as opposed to renewal of the lease, which would be a new lease.

Facade The front of a building.

Fair Credit Reporting Act An act that allows a person access to information in his or her credit file and the right to have information corrected. It also allows a person to insert his or her own statement in the file. If denied credit because of an unsatisfactory report, the borrower must be so informed.

Fair market value The amount that would be paid by a willing, informed buyer to a willing, informed seller.

Fannie Mae (Federal National Mortgage Association, or FNMA) A private corporation that sets the market in FHA and VA loans by buying and selling existing loans.

Farm Home Administration (FmHA) This agency guarantees loans made by private lenders and insures loans that are made and serviced by the agency. No points are allowed on loans made by the agency, and preference is given to veterans. The agency provides assistance to farmers and others living in rural areas where financing is not available at reasonable terms from private sources.

FDIC (Federal Deposit Insurance Corporation) Insures bank and savings and loan deposits.

Federal Home Loan Bank (FHLB) A bank that lends to member savings and loan associations.

Federal Home Loan Mortgage Corporation See *Freddie Mac.*

Federal Housing Administration See *FHA.*

Federal Land Bank System A government agency that makes long-term farm loans.

Federal National Mortgage Association See *Fannie Mae.*

Federal Reserve The federal agency that regulates the U.S. money supply and interest rates.

Fee An estate of inheritance.

Fee simple The highest possible form of ownership. There is no time limit; it can be transferred or inherited.

Felon A person convicted of a felony.

Felony A crime punishable by imprisonment or death.

Feudal tenure A system in which title was with the crown but lesser interests of use were granted to vassals.

FHA (Federal Housing Administration) The federal agency that insures housing loans.

FICO score A credit scoring system devised by Fair Isaac and Company used by most lenders.

Fictitious mortgage A mortgage that is recorded and is to be referenced by other mortgages. Its sole purpose is to set forth terms and conditions.

Fictitious name A name that does not include the surname of every principal.

Fiduciary A person in a position of trust and loyalty.

Filtering down The tendency of housing to pass to lower and lower income groups.

Financing statement A notice filed by a lender with the secretary of state to give public notice of a security interest in personal property.

Fire stop A solid board or wall to prevent fire from spreading.

Firm commitment A loan commitment made when the borrower is a known person, as opposed to a *conditional commitment.*

FIRREA (Federal Financial Institutions Reform, Recovery and Enforcement Act) Requires state licensing and certification of appraisers for federally related loans.

First right of refusal See *Right of first refusal.*

Fiscal year A business year, as opposed to a calendar year.

Fixture An item of personal property that has been so affixed to realty as to become part of the real estate.

Flag lot A lot behind another lot having a long easement or driveway that resembles the handle on a flag.

Flood plain Land adjoining waterway that is prone to flooding.

Floor space Interior square footage.

FMHA See *Farm Home Administration.*

FNMA See *Fannie Mae.*

Footing Poured concrete at the bottom of a foundation that spreads the building load to the soil.

Forecasting Used in the income approach to estimate future net income.

Foreclosure A procedure whereby property used as security for a loan is sold to pay the debt in the event of default.

Foreclosure by action Foreclosure through the courts (there is the possibility of a deficiency judgment).

Foreshore Land lying between the high and low water marks.

Forfeiture Loss of money or property because of failure to perform.

Foundation The supporting part of a building (masonry substructure).

Foundation plan Construction drawing that shows footings, piers, foundation slab, etc.

Four-by-fouring The illegal practice of breaking up parcels into four parcels and then having the buyers again break each of these into four more parcels.

Franchise A marketing plan to which a person is not otherwise entitled.

Franchise Investment Law A part of the Corporation Code that prohibits the sale of franchises where there is a likelihood that the franchisor's promises will not be fulfilled or where fraud is present.

Fraud Intentional trickery or deceit used to induce another to act to his or her detriment.

Freddie Mac (Federal Home Loan Mortgage Corporation) Deals in the secondary mortgage market.

Freehold An interest in land either for life or in fee simple.

Free-lot scheme A lottery in which lots are given away (everybody wins) but a large charge is applied for transfer expenses. Free-lot schemes are no longer allowed.

Front foot A linear measurement of a lot, determined by the footage on its street side.

Frost line The depth to which frost penetrates in the ground. Building footings are placed below the frost line.

Fructus industriales Cultivated crops and trees (personal property).

Fructus naturales Naturally growing plants and trees (real property).

Functional obsolescence Obsolescence due to the design or construction of a building (built-in obsolescence).

Funding fee A fee paid by a veteran to the VA for a VA-guaranteed loan.

Fungible Describes goods that are like and can be replaced by measure, such as oil and corn.

Furring Strips of wood applied to a wall to give the wall a smooth finish prior to paneling or other treatment.

Gable roof A roof in which two sides slope and meet at the top.

Gambrel roof A roof with a steep lower slope and a flatter upper slope (as on dutch colonials and barns).

Gap loan A short-term loan. It usually covers the gap between the construction loan and permanent financing.

Garnishment A legal seizure of funds or property of a debtor.

GDP (gross domestic product) The total of all goods and services produced by a nation during a year.

GEM (growing-equity mortgage) A mortgage with increasing payments in which the increases apply to the principal.

General license A license for the sale of all alcoholic beverages; either off-sale or on-sale, but not both.

General lien A lien against all property of a debtor (such as a judgment lien).

General power of attorney Power given by a principal to his or her agent to do anything that the principal can do; as opposed to a power for a specific purpose.

General warranty deed A deed in which the grantor warrants the title against claims of all others. See *special warranty deed*.

Geodetic survey A United States government survey.

Gift *causa mortis* A gift made in contemplation of death. Treated for inheritance-tax purposes as being part of the deceased's estate.

Gift deed A deed in which the only consideration is love and affection.

Ginnie Mae (Government National Mortgage Association, or GNMA) Provides special assistance for federally aided housing projects.

Girder A horizontal beam that supports the joists.

GNMA See *Ginnie Mae*.

Good faith estimate Estimate of closing costs required by RESPA.

Good funds A term used by escrows to designate cash or checks that have cleared. Escrow funds cannot be disbursed until they are good funds.

Goodwill The value given to the expectation of continued public patronage.

Gore A triangular piece of land.

Governmental loan A loan made by a conventional lender with a government guarantee or insurance.

Government National Mortgage Association See *Ginnie Mae*.

Government survey A method of describing property measuring from base lines and meridians.

Grade The ground level or slope.

Graduated lease A lease providing varying rents based on changes that might occur.

Graduate REALTORS® Institute See *GRI*.

Grandfather clause A clause that permits or exempts existing things but applies to new ones. A grandfather clause would prohibit retroactive zoning.

Grant A transfer.

Grant deed A common deed of transfer in California.

Grantee A person who receives title.

Granting clause A clause in a deed indicating that title is passing.

Grantor A person who transfers title.

Gratuitous agent An agent who undertakes agency duties without compensation.

GRI (Graduate REALTORS® Institute) A professional designation that requires seminar attendance and courses of study (administered by the state REALTORS® Association).

Grid A chart used by a lender in evaluating the property, the area, and the borrower.

Gross domestic product See *GDP*.

Gross income Total income before deductions.

Gross lease A lease with a flat or fixed rental rate (flat lease).

Gross multiplier A rough appraisal method in which the yearly or monthly gross income is multiplied by a multiplier, which gives an approximate value for a property.

Gross profit Gross sales minus the cost of the merchandise sold. Gross profit does not deduct overhead.

Ground lease A lease of land only.

Ground rent That portion of the rent attributable to the land alone.

Groundwater Underground water that is not flowing.

Growing-equity mortgage See *GEM*.

Guadalupe Hidalgo The treaty that ended the Mexican War in which the United States agreed to recognize the property rights of Mexicans.

Guarantee of title A guarantee by the abstractor based entirely upon recorded documents. It has been replaced by title insurance.

Habendum clause The granting clause of a deed. It defines the extent of ownership transferred and sets forth any exceptions or reservations.

Hard-money loan A loan in which actual cash changes hands.

Header A beam placed over a window or a door to spread the load.

Hectare A metric land measurement of 10,000 square meters, or approximately 2.47 acres.

Hereditaments Anything that can be inherited.

Highest and best use The use that provides the greatest net return to the building and/or land.

Hip roof A roof with all sides sloping to a top ridge.

Holder in due course A person who takes a negotiable instrument that is good on its face for value, without notice of any defenses of the maker and before it is overdue.

Hold-harmless clause An exculpatory clause in which a party agrees to make good any loss suffered by the other party (generally because of the condition of the property).

Holdover clause A clause in a lease providing for sharply increased rent should the lessee fail to vacate at the end of the lease. Instead of becoming a tenant at sufferance, he or she becomes a tenant on a periodic tenancy.

Holographic will A handwritten and signed will (no witnesses are required).

Homestead A home on which a declaration of homestead has been filed.

Homestead exemption $50,000 for a single person, $75,000 for a head of household, and $125,000 for those over 65 or disabled. It applies to unsecured creditors.

Homologous Of the same kind or structure.

Hoskold sinking-fund method A sinking-fund method of capitalization in appraising.

HUD The U.S. Department of Housing and Urban Development.

Hundred percent location The best retail location within an area.

Hypothecate To give something as security without giving up possession (borrowing on one's furniture or one's home).

Illegal Actually in contradiction to an existing law.

Illusory contract An agreement that is not legally binding on a party, so that there is no contract at all.

Implied agency An agency that is implied by the actions of the parties although not specifically agreed to.

Implied contract A contract that is not expressly stated but is implied by the actions of the parties.

Implied easement (easement by necessity) An easement that is implied when the grantor conveys land to the grantee that is landlocked by other land of the grantor. The grantee has an implied right of access over the grantor's land.

Impound account An account kept by the lender to provide funds for taxes and insurance. The borrower's payments include funds for this account. The fund actually belongs to the borrower and not the lender.

Imputed interest Interest that is implied. The IRS will assign an interest if the rate is too low or not stated.

Incentive zoning Zoning requiring that the ground floor of office buildings be devoted to retail stores.

Inchoate Incomplete. This is said of a right not yet perfected.

Income approach An appraisal method whereby net income is divided by a capitalization rate to estimate value.

Incompetent A person who, because of his or her age or mental capacity, lacks the ability to contract.

Incorporeal rights Nonpossessory rights in real estate, such as rights to rents and easements.

Increment An increase in value.

Indefeasible Not voidable.

Index lease A lease in which rent is tied to an index, such as the cost-of-living index or the wholesale-price index.

Informal description A description of real property by the name and address of the owner (not a legal description).

Ingress/egress A way of entering and leaving property.

Injunction A court order to cease or desist from performing an act.

Institutional lender A financial intermediary that pools the money of its depositors to make loans (includes banks, savings and loan associations, and life insurance companies).

Instrument A legal document.

Integration clause Contract cannot be altered by prior or contemporaneous parol evidence.

Interest Money charged for a loan.

Interest rate Percentage that the interest charged bears to the loan.

Intermediation Depositing of funds into savings institutions.

Internal rate of return A sophisticated formula that determines the present value of projected income expressed as an annual rate.

Interpleader action An action in which, when two or more parties claim an interest in property held by a third person, that third person can ask the court to determine the rights.

Interstate Land Sales Act A federal disclosure act for undeveloped property sold in interstate commerce.

Inter vivos A between-the-living conveyance; as opposed to testamentary transfer.

Intestate Without a will. The estate passes to the heirs of the deceased based on their relationship.

Inundation Covered by floodwater.

Inverse condemnation A process whereby a property owner forces a governmental unit to buy his or her property when, by its action, it has wrongfully restricted his or her use.

Involuntary conversion An involuntary exchange, as in condemnation or destruction by fire and obtaining of insurance proceeds.

Involuntary lien A lien imposed without the agreement of the property owner (such as a tax lien).

Inwood compound-interest method Use of annuity table in appraising property (prior to computers).

Irrevocable Incapable of being changed.

Irrigation district A quasi-political subdivision created under the law to provide water for an area.

Jalousie window A type of window with glass slats, like a venetian blind.

Jamb The lining of a door or window frame.

Joint liability Liability whereby each person is equally liable for the entire amount.

Jointly and severally Together and separately.

Joint tenancy A tenancy whereby several owners having rights of survivorship who took title at the same time by the same instrument have equal interest and equal rights of possession.

Joint venture A partnership created for one particular undertaking.

Joist A horizontal beam supporting a floor or ceiling.

Judgment The final order of a court.

Jumbo loan A home loan for an amount that exceeds Fannie Mae and Freddie Mac home loan purchase limits.

Junior lien A subordinate lien.

Jurisdiction The area in which a court or officer has authority.

Key lot A lot having on its side the rear yards of a number of other lots. Considered undesirable for residential purposes.

Key money Money paid for the lease (in addition to rent).

Kiosk An open-sided, usually free-standing structure, often in a mall or parking lot.

Laches Loss of rights because of unexcusable delay in bringing an action.

Land contract A contract in the sale of real property whereby the seller retains title and the buyer obtains possession. (It is used for Cal–Vet loans and when the buyer has a very small down payment.)

Land-residual method An appraisal method in which the income attributable to the improvements is deducted from the total income to determine the income attributable to the land alone. This income is then capitalized to determine land value.

Lateral support The physical support that a landowner must provide to the property of his or her neighbors (deep excavation could endanger a neighbor's property).

Lath Wood, metal, or gypsum board used as a base for plaster.

Lease A tenancy contract between a landlord and a tenant.

Legacy A gift of personal property (usually money) by will.

Legal description A description of real property relating to government surveys, recorded maps, or metes and bounds.

Lessee A tenant who receives a lease.

Lessor An owner who gives a lease.

Leverage Use of other people's money to make money by purchasing property with a low down payment.

License A privilege to use the land of another; unlike an easement, it may be revoked.

Lien An encumbrance that makes the property security for the debt (trust deeds, mortgages, mechanic's liens, taxes).

Life estate An estate that does not terminate until the death of a named party.

Like for like An exchange of similar property to postpone capital gains taxes.

Limited common elements Common areas in a subdivision for the exclusive use of designated owners, such as storage lockers and designated parking areas.

Limited liability company A company offering limited liability but fewer restrictions than an S corporation.

Limited partnership A partnership in which some partners are inactive and are liable only to the extent of their investment.

Link A standardized surveyor's measurement; 7.92 inches.

Lintel A beam or stone over a door or window.

Liquidated damages Damages agreed in advance at the time of entering into a contract that are to be paid if the agreement is breached. (These are normally used when actual damages are difficult to ascertain; they will not be enforced if they are so unreasonable that the court determines they are a penalty.)

Liquidity The position a person has as to cash or assets readily converted to cash. Real estate is considered a nonliquid asset.

Lis pendens A notice of a pending lawsuit.

Listing A contract between an owner and a broker authorizing the broker to procure a buyer or a tenant for an agreed compensation.

Littoral rights Waterfront property owners' rights to water from a lake, sea, or ocean.

Livable floor space The interior dimensions of each room.

Livery of seisin A common-law ceremony for delivering title (a key or a handful of dirt is used to symbolize title passing).

Loan-to-value ratio The percentage that will be lent based on the value of the property.

Lock-in clause A clause requiring full interest to be paid if the loan is prepaid. (It is normally used when interest is added on to the amount borrowed.)

Longitude and latitude Longitudes are north-south meridians, and latitudes run parallel to the equator. Both are measured in degrees, minutes, and seconds.

Louver An opening with horizontal slats set at an angle for ventilation.

LS Used in lieu of a seal. It is an abbreviation for *locus sigilli,* which means "place for seal."

MAI A designation of a member of the appraisal institute.

Maker A person who signs a note or instrument and is primarily liable.

Mansard roof A roof with sloping sides but flat on top.

Map Act The act that gives local control of the general layout of streets, lot sizes, and other physical aspects of a subdivision.

Marginal land Land where the financial return barely pays for the effort expended.

Marginal tax rate The income tax rate applied to the highest dollar of income.

Margin of security The difference between the amount of the mortgage and the appraised value of the property.

Marketable title Merchantable title, free from objectionable liens and encumbrances.

Market approach (comparison approach) An appraisal method in which value is based on sales of similar property.

Market price The price paid regardless of the circumstances of the sale.

Market value The price a willing buyer would pay to a willing seller.

Markup The percentage added to the cost to determine the selling price.

Material fact Any information that would likely affect a person's judgment.

Maturity A term used in property management to designate a stable income (also, the time at which a debt is due).

Meander lines Surveyor's lines showing the borders of a body of water.

Mechanic's lien A lien by a contractor, subcontractor, or material supplier for work or materials supplied to a property.

Megalopolis A growing together of cities in a vast urban sprawl.

Mello-Roos bonds A bonding district set up by a developer to place improvement costs on purchasers.

Menace A threat of harm (makes a contract voidable by the person threatened).

Merger The absorption of one right into another.

Meridian A surveyor's north-south line intersecting the base lines. In locating land from government survey, measure from these intersections.

Mesne The mean or middle between two extremes. (The mesne high-tide line would be halfway between the highest high-tide mark and the lowest high-tide mark.)

Metes and bounds Measurement of land by measurements and boundaries setting forth all of the boundary lines.

Mile 5,280 linear feet.

Mill 1/10 of a cent or 1/1,000 of a dollar. Written as .001.

Minimum property requirements (MPR) Minimum requirements for an FHA loan.

Minor Any person under the age of 18.

Mitigation of damages An injured party's duty to keep the damages as low as possible.

Molding Wood strips used on a building for ornamental outline.

Monument A fixed surveyor's marker used to locate property.

Moratorium A delay in the performance of a legal obligation or payment of a debt, usually authorized by law. A construction moratorium would stop new construction.

Mortgage A security device whereby the borrower retains title but gives a lien and a note to the lender (the property is hypothecated).

Mortgagee One who receives a mortgage as security for a loan or a debt.

Mortgage loan correspondent A company or individual in the business of arranging the sale of existing loans.

Mortgage note The instrument reflecting the mortgage debt. The mortgage is security for the mortgage note.

Mortgage warehousing Interim financing in which a mortgage company makes loans that later are taken over by an insurance company or other permanent lender. They may borrow on these loans.

Mortgage yield The actual return on the mortgage to the lender.

Mortgagor An owner of property who gives a mortgage.

MPR See *Minimum property requirements.*

Mudsill (sill) Perimeter boards anchored directly to the foundation on which the rest of the house is built. (Redwood is preferred because it resists rot.)

Multiple listing Usually an exclusive-right-to-sell listing which is given out to a group of brokers with rights to sell (a cooperative listing).

Multiple nuclei growth City growth from a number of separate points.

Muniments of title Documents showing the historical evidence of title (deeds).

Mutual mortgage insurance (MMI) FHA insurance that is paid by the borrower.

Mutual savings banks Lenders located in northeastern states that can make government-insured or -guaranteed loans anywhere in the country.

Mutual water company A water company organized by users to supply water at reasonable rates. Stock is issued to users.

Naked title Legal title only, such as the title given to a trustee under a trust deed in which the trustee has no rights of possession.

NAR National Association of REALTORS®.

NAREB National Association of Real Estate Brokers.

Narrative report A comprehensive and complete appraisal report.

National Flood Insurance Act Makes flood insurance available to communities that have developed a flood protection program.

National Housing Partnership (NHP) An arrangement whereby the government buys a 25 percent interest in a local project and the government and the developer are partners.

Natural monument A natural point on a metes and bounds description, such as a rock, tree, or river.

Negative amortization A loan in which the payments are insufficient to pay the interest, so that the unpaid balance is increasing.

Negative declaration A declaration that a development will not have a significant effect on the environment. (An environmental impact report would not be required.)

Negative easement An easement that prohibits the servient tenement from some use of the land.

Negative fraud Fraud by failure to disclose negative facts.

Negotiable Capable of being transferred or negotiated in the normal course of business.

Neighborhood The area of social conformity in which a property is located.

Net listing A listing in which the broker retains all money received over the agreed sale price as his or her commission.

Net-net lease A lease in which the tenant pays for everything except taxes and insurance.

Net-net-net lease A lease in which the tenant pays taxes and all expenses, so the lessor is guaranteed a net amount.

Net operating income (NOI) The net income before debt service (principal and interest). It is the gross profit minus operational expenses.

Net profit Profit after all expenses other than taxes on the profit.

Net spendable Same as cash flow. The balance left over from income after cash expenses.

Nominal Stated or named.

Nominee A new person who is designated to perform on a contract. Not an assignee, as the named party is totally relieved of performance.

Nonconforming loan A loan that fails to meet Fannie Mae and Freddie Mac purchase criteria.

Nonconforming use A use prior to zoning that is not in conformance to the zoning.

Noncumulative zoning Zoning that allows only the use specified. (See *Cumulative zoning*.)

Nonfreehold estate An estate for years or a leasehold interest.

Noninstitutional lender A lender other than a bank, savings and loan, or insurance company. Generally they charge higher interest rates.

Nonjudicial foreclosure Foreclosure under the sale provision of a trust deed or mortgage.

Note A signed instrument acknowledging a debt and promising to pay.

Notice of abandonment A formal way to end a homestead declaration. A homestead is also abandoned by its sale.

Notice of cessation A notice filed when construction is halted. It sets the period for filing mechanic's liens.

Notice of completion A notice filed by the owner for the purpose of setting the time limit for filing mechanic's liens.

Notice of default A notice issued under a deed of trust; it sets the three-month period for the trustor to make payments.

Notice of intention The first subdivision filing with the Real Estate Commissioner.

Notice of nonresponsibility The notice recorded and posted by an owner within 10 days of discovering unauthorized work on his or her property; it is a way to avoid liability.

Notice to quit A notice to a tenant to vacate rented premises.

Novation The substitution of a new agreement or party for an old one.

Nuisance An objectionable use of property so that it interferes with the rights of others.

Nuncupative will An oral deathbed will; no longer valid in California.

Objective value The actual sale price paid.

Obligatory advances Loan advances made by the lender that he or she is obliged to make as construction progresses.

Obsolescence Loss in value due to reduced desirability. (See *Functional obsolescence* and *Economic obsolescence*.)

Occupancy permit A permit required by the building department that states that a new structure may be occupied.

Office procedures manual Sets forth commissions and operational procedures of a real estate office.

Off-sale license A license to sell alcoholic beverages to be consumed off the premises.

Offset statement A statement by the holder of lien as to the status of the lien (the amount owed).

Off-site improvements Improvements such as street, curb, gutter, walks, etc., outside lot boundaries.

On-sale license A license to sell alcoholic beverages to be consumed on the premises.

One-stop shopping A broker offering all service providers needed at the broker's location.

Open-end mortgage A mortgage that provides that the borrower can obtain additional money during the term of the loan up to a stated limit.

Open listing A listing in which the broker has a nonexclusive right to sell. More than one open listing can, therefore, be given at the same time.

Open mortgage A loan that can be prepaid without penalty.

Option A right given for a consideration to enter into a purchase or contract (a contract to make a contract).

Optionee The person receiving the option.

Optionor The person giving the option.

Order paper An instrument made out to a specific person requiring his or her signature to negotiate.

Orientation The placement of a structure on a lot with regard to sun, wind, etc.

Origination fee An advance fee, such as points, that is paid to the lender in order to obtain the loan.

"Or more" clause A clause allowing prepayment of a note without penalty.

Ostensible agent A person who has the appearance of being an agent.

Outlawed Describes a claim that cannot be maintained because of the expiration of the time allowed by the statute of limitations.

Overhang That portion of the roof which extends beyond the walls.

Overimprovement Spending more for improvement than return or sale price would justify.

Packaged loan A loan covering personal property as well as real property.

Paramount title Title that is superior to all others.

Parol evidence rule The rule that verbal evidence may not be used to modify an otherwise complete written agreement as to the sale of land.

Parquet floor A hardwood floor laid in squares.

Participation loan An agreement whereby a lender receives a share of revenue or profits besides the interest in the loan.

Partition action A court action to sever a joint ownership.

Partnership Two or more people engaged in a joint business as principals.

Party wall A common wall on a property line for the use of both parties. Both owners are responsible for its cost and maintenance.

Par value The face value or price at which securities are issued.

Passive loss A paper loss from depreciation.

Pass-through certificate An investment certificate backed by a pool of Ginnie Mae insured mortgages. The principal and interest paid by the borrower are passed through to the certificate owner.

Patent An original conveyance of title from the government.

Penny A measurement term applied to nails, abbreviated by the letter "d." The larger the penny, the larger the nail.

Per autre vie A life estate based on the life of a third party rather than on the life of the life tenant.

Percentage lease A lease in which rent is determined as a percentage of the gross receipts. It normally contains a minimum rental, as well as a covenant to remain in business.

Perchlorate A highly toxic substance from munitions and propellants that can get into the water system.

Percolation The ability of water to flow through soil. Percolation is important as to septic tanks and is determined by percolation tests.

Perfect escrow An escrow in which all documents and funds have been deposited so that the escrow is ready for completion.

Perimeter heating Baseboard heating with registers located around the outside wall.

Periodic tenancy Rental from period to period, such as week to week or month to month, as opposed to a rental for a definite period, which would be an estate for years.

Personal defense A defense that is good only against the original holder by the maker of a negotiable instrument (such as fraud).

Personal property Movable property; that which is not real property.

Personal Responsibility and Work Opportunity Act Federal law that limits professional licensing to persons who can prove legal residence in the U.S.

Per stirpes Inherited by right of representation.

Physical description An informal land description based on the land's relationship to other properties.

Physical deterioration Depreciation caused by age and use.

Pier A concrete vertical column used for support of floor joists.

Pitch The degree of incline of a roof.

PITI A payment that includes principal, interest, taxes, and insurance.

Planned development project A subdivision that contains areas owned in common.

Planning commission A body appointed by supervisors or the city council to make long-term plans. Counties and cities must have one.

Plat A plan or map of a subdivision.

Plate The horizontal board against which the vertical studs are nailed (at top and bottom of a wall).

Pledge A deposit of personal property with a creditor (pawn broker) as security for an obligation.

Pledgor One who gives a pledge.

Plot plan An architectural drawing of a lot showing the location of the structures.

Plottage Joining of two or more parcels to form a larger parcel that has a greater value than the sum of the individual values. (The increase in value is the plottage increment.)

Plywood Laminated wood sheets (cross-grained) to give greater strength.

PMI (private mortgage insurance) Used to insure conventional loans where there is a low down payment.

POB Point of beginning on a metes and bounds description.

Pocket listing A listing that a broker does not share with other brokers.

Point A percentage of a loan given to the lender for the privilege of receiving the loan. It makes up for a lower interest rate (one point equals 1 percent of the loan).

Police power The power of the state to enforce order, safety, health, morals, and general welfare. No compensation is given an individual from the taking or limiting of his or her property use under police power.

Ponding Depressions in flat areas where pools of floodwater accumulate.

Potable Drinkable.

Power of attorney A written authorization given by an individual to another to act for him or her. It may be for specific purposes or in general.

Predatory lending Illegal and abusive lending practices such as refinancing without benefit to the borrower and making loans beyond borrower's ability to make the payments.

Preliminary notice A written notice by a contractor that work may be subject to a mechanic's lien. It is given within 20 days of first supplying labor, materials, etc.

Prepaid rental listing service Rental service that charges for a list of rentals.

Prepayment penalty A penalty for paying off a note prior to its maturity.

Prescription Obtaining an easement by adverse use.

Presumption A legal inference that is considered fact unless disproved.

Prima facie Evidence that, if not rebutted, is sufficient (evidence good upon its face).

Primary financing First trust deeds and mortgages.

Primary mortgage market The making of first and second trust deeds and mortgages by lenders to borrowers.

Principal The employer of an agent.

Principle of anticipation Value will change based on anticipated future uses.

Principle of balance Value is created and maintained when there is a proper mix of land use so as to obtain the highest and best use for a site.

Principle of change Values do not remain constant.

Principle of competition When unusual profits are being made, new competition will enter the market and reduce the profit.

Principle of diminishing returns As demand is met, new units will bring a lower return.

Principle of integration and disintegration Property goes through phases of development; integration, equilibrium, and disintegration (growth, stability, decline).

Principle of substitution A person will not pay more for a property than it would cost for a similar property.

Principle of supply and demand The greater the supply, the lower the value; the greater the scarcity, the higher the value.

Principle of surplus The net income of a property, after deducting for labor, management, and capital; it would be based on the land.

Prior appropriation The priority right of the first user of water over later users from the same source.

Private mortgage insurance See *PMI*.

Privity of contract The direct relationship between contracting parties.

Probate The court procedure for disposing of a deceased's estate. Its purpose is to carry out the wishes of the deceased and to protect the creditors of the deceased.

Procuring cause The proximate cause. A broker is the procuring cause if his or her efforts are the foundation of negotiations for a sale.

Profit-and-loss statement An operating statement for a period of time showing financial results of profit or loss.

Profit à prendre The right to take crops or other profit from the soil or land of another.

***Pro forma* financial statement** An estimated financial operating statement in which there is no real experience, such as for a building to be built.

Progression An increase in value of a home due to being located in an area of more expensive homes.

Promotional note A note used to finance a subdivision prior to the first sale.

Proprietary lease A lease from the cooperative to the tenant providing for the occupancy of a unit.

Prorate To apportion based on the actual time to the date of sale (taxes, rents, etc.).

Proximate cause The cause that led in a natural and continuous unbroken sequence to a sale (or lease).

Psychic income The value of the feeling of pride and independence that the sole owner of a property has.

Public Housing Administration A federal agency involved in low-rent housing projects.

Public report A report that must be given by the Real Estate Commissioner prior to the sale of a subdivision.

Puffing A statement of opinion given in normal sales talk and not a warranty.

Punitive damages See *Exemplary damages*.

Pur autre vie A third person on whose life a life estate given to another is based.

Purchase-money mortgage A trust deed or mortgage given by the buyer to the actual seller to partially finance the sale, or a loan by a lender to finance a purchase.

Purchase saleback (purchase leaseback) An agreement in which a lender buys a property upon completion and sells it back to the builder under good terms, or leases it to him or her.

Purlin A horizontal support between common rafters.

Pyramiding Refinancing property that has appreciated in value in order to buy additional property.

Qualified endorsement An endorsement "without recourse" that holds the endorser free from claims by subsequent holders if the maker defaults.

Quantity-survey method An appraisal method used to find the cost of new construction based on separate estimates for each item (such as carpentry, and electrical work).

Quarter round A molding shaped like one-fourth of a circle.

Quasi contract A contract that the law implies.

Quiet enjoyment The right of an owner to use his or her property without interference.

Quiet title A court action to determine ownership or remove a cloud on a title.

Quitclaim deed Deed covering whatever interest the grantor has, without any warranties.

Racial steering The illegal practice of directing minorities to particular areas.

Radial growth See *Axial growth*.

Radiant heating Heating whereby heat radiates out from hot coils, as opposed to forced-air heating, in which hot air is blown.

Rafter A diagonal beam supporting the roofing.

Raised note A note on which the amount due has been wrongfully changed.

RAM (reverse-annuity mortgage) A mortgage in which the lender makes regular payments to the borrower. The loan is not paid back until the property is sold or the borrower dies.

Range A vertical row of townships measured east and west from the meridian.

Range line A north-south line that forms the east or west boundary of a township.

Ratification Approval of an act or contract by a principal after the fact when the principal's agent acted beyond his or her authority.

Ready, willing, and able buyer One who is fully prepared, financially able, and willing to make the purchase.

Real defense A defense that is good against even a holder in due course, such as forgery or a raised note.

Real estate board A local organization of brokers and associates (salespeople). It is affiliated with the National Association of Realtors and the California Association of Realtors.

Real estate investment trust A trust consisting of 100 or more investors, in which property is conveyed to a trustee who manages it. They are under the jurisdiction of the Corporations Commissioner.

Real Estate Settlement Procedures Act See *RESPA*.

Real property Land and that which is attached to and goes with it.

Realtist A member of NAREB.

REALTOR® A member of the NAR.

Rebate law Requires a title company to charge equally for services and make honest efforts to collect (no preferences or rebates to brokers are allowed). It also prohibits licensees from receiving rebates from home protection firms.

Recapture The rate at which the principal invested is returned.

Reconciliation The use of all three appraisal methods where the appraiser applies different weights to each method.

Recurring costs Impound account costs for taxes and insurance.

Red flag Anything that would alert an agent to a possible problem concerning a property.

Redlining An illegal practice in which lenders formally or informally refuse to lend in high-risk areas.

Reformation An action to correct a mistake in a deed or contract.

Regression A decrease in value of a home because homes of lower value are in the area.

Regulation Z See *Truth-in-Lending Law*.

Rehabilitation Repair without design changes.

Reintermediation Return of deposits to savings institutions after being previously withdrawn.

Relating back Title is said to relate back to the date the deed is given to the escrow. The purchaser has priority as to intervening liens (prior to closing), if the lien creditors knew of the escrow.

Release clause An agreement in a blanket encumbrance to release individual properties from the encumbrance upon payment of an agreed sum.

Reliction See *Dereliction*.

Remainder interest That estate which vests after the termination of a prior estate, such as a life estate.

Remodeling Changing a building (interior or exterior).

Renewal of lease Replacement of an old lease with a new one.

Rent Consideration for use of property.

Rent skimming The illegal practice of collecting rents and not applying rents to debts secured by the property during the first year after purchase. Also collecting rent for property not owned.

REO (real estate owned) Foreclosed property held by a lender.

Replacement cost The cost to replace a structure with another having the same utility and desirability (not necessarily an exact reproduction).

Reproduction cost The cost to exactly reproduce a structure.

Request for notification of default A request filed by second lienholders so that they will be notified of any foreclosure action on a prior lien, giving them an opportunity to protect their interests.

Rescision of contract Annulment of a contract by mutual agreement of the parties.

Reservation Retaining a right, such as an easement, at the time of deeding property.

RESPA (Real Estate Settlement Procedures Act) A lender disclosure act applying to the first trust deed on one to four residential units.

Respondeat superior The doctrine that principals and employers are liable for actions of agents and employees within the scope of the agency or employment.

Restoration Return of a building to an original condition.

Restricted appraisal report Short-letter report.

Restricted license A probationary real estate license issued to a party whose license has been denied, revoked, or suspended.

Restriction An agreement whereby the owner of property is prohibited from certain use of his or her property (such as minimum size of a home or no more than two dogs).

Restrictive endorsement "Pay to the order of John Doe *only*." This type of endorsement limits further negotiation.

Revenue stamps A documentary tax stamp on the equity being transferred.

Reverse-annuity mortgage See *RAM*.

Reverse mortgage A mortgage whereby the mortgagor borrows against his or her equity in property by receiving monthly payments.

Reversionary interest The interest the original transferor of property has in the property upon the happening of some event such as the death of a life tenant.

Rezoning Changing the zoning for an area, as opposed to a variance, which only grants an exception to the zoning.

R factor A heat-resistance factor used to measure insulation.

Rider An amendment to an agreement (usually in an insurance policy).

Ridge board The board at the peak of the rafters that forms the ridge line. It is the highest board in a house.

Right of correlative user A landowner's right of reasonable use of underground percolating water.

Right of first refusal A provision in a lease that gives the lessee the right to meet any sales offer that the owner wishes to accept. It is also known as a "first right of refusal."

Right of way The privilege of passing over the land of another.

Riparian right The right of a landowner to the reasonable use of water on, under, or adjacent to his or her property.

Risers The upright boards in stairs, between the treads.

Rod A surveyor's measurement; 16 1/2 feet.

Rollover mortgage See *RRM*.

RRM (renegotiable-rate mortgage) A short-term mortgage in which the lender agrees to rewrite the loan when it is due, at the prevailing interest rate.

Rule against perpetuities Prohibits trusts or other interests that will not vest for more than 21 years after the death of a person now living.

Rumford Act A California fair housing law that prohibits discrimination in residential housing.

Safety clause A clause in a listing that protects the broker as to his or her commission if the owner sells to one of the broker's customers within a stated period after the expiration of the listing.

Sale leaseback An agreement in which the owner sells property and leases it back from the buyer. This lowers the capital investment required for a business.

Sales tax A tax on retail sales based on a percentage of the sale.

Salvage value The value (if any) for salvage after an asset has ended its useful life.

SAM (shared-appreciation mortgage) A mortgage in which the lender either provides a lower rate of interest or helps in the down payment in exchange for a percentage of the appreciation in value.

Sandwich lease A lease interest between the original lease and the current lease.

Sans An exclusionary word meaning "without." It may be used on a deed to exclude property.

Sash A wood or metal window frame containing the glass.

Satisfaction Discharge of a mortgage by payment. It is given by the mortgagee to the mortgagor.

Scheduled gross income Gross income based on 100 percent occupancy at scheduled rents.

Schwabe's law Lower-income groups pay a greater percentage of their income for housing than do higher-income groups.

Seal An impression made to attest to the authenticity of a signature; not required in California.

Seasoned loan A loan with a history of payments.

Secondary financing A loan given for a junior encumbrance (second trust deed).

Secondary mortgage market The resale market for existing loans.

Secret profit Undisclosed profit by a licensee.

Section A one-mile-square parcel of land containing 640 acres. There are 36 sections in a township.

Sector growth City growth pattern where uses of land extend outward in a pie pattern.

Security Any investment in which the investor has no management control.

Security agreement An agreement between a debtor and a lender or seller whereby the latter retains a security interest in personal property of the debtor (under the Uniform Commercial Code).

Security interest An interest in property to secure a debt; a lien.

Seisin Possession under a freehold interest.

Self-contained report A comprehensive appraisal report containing detailed analysis and photographs.

Seller's market A real estate marketplace in which there are more qualified buyers than sellers.

Send-out slip An agreement in which a broker gets a prospective purchaser to agree to deal only through him or her, for which the broker supplies a list of businesses for sale.

Separate property Property that is separately owned and not community property. It is acquired prior to marriage or by gift or inheritance.

Septic tank A tank in which sewage is liquified and then drained off into the soil.

Sequential notice Constructive notice based on priority of recording.

Servient tenement An estate that is used by another under an easement.

Servitude A charge or burden against land, such as an easement.

Setback The distance that structures must be from lot lines.

Severalty ownership Ownership by one person.

Shared-appreciation mortgage See *SAM*.

Sheathing A covering, usually plywood or composition board, over studs or roof rafters. A finished exterior treatment is applied over the sheathing.

Sheet flooding Storm runoff down an incline that is not in a water course.

Sheriff's deed A deed given by the sheriff after a sale to satisfy a judgment.

Sherman Anti-Trust Act Federal law that prohibits anticompetitive practices.

Short rate An insurance refund based on less than an actual prorating of the time. It is normally given when the insured cancels.

Short sale A sale whereby the lender agrees to accept less than the sale proceeds for a debt because the sale price is less than the amount owed.

Siding Exterior wall covering.

Sill A board resting on the foundation that supports the rest of the house. It is also called a mudsill.

Sinking fund A fund set aside so that it, plus accrued interest, will pay for replacement of a depreciating asset.

SIR Society of Industrial REALTORS®.

Situs Location preference based on economic reasons (proximity of other uses).

Sky lease A lease of space above a parcel.

Slander of title False statements disparaging an owner's title.

Soil pipe A pipe carrying sewage from a house.

Soldier's and Sailor's Civil Relief Act An act that prohibits foreclosure of mortgaged property while the owner is in military service and for three months thereafter, except by court order.

Sole (sole plate) A horizontal two-by-four on which the studs rest.

Span The distance between supports.

Special agent An agency in which the agent is limited as to specific acts.

Special assessment A charge against real estate for an improvement benefiting the property (streets, sidewalks, etc.), as opposed to general taxes for normal government.

Special endorsement Endorsement on a negotiable instrument to a named individual.

Special warranty deed A deed that warrants title only against defects arising during the grantor's ownership.

Specific lien A lien that applies to a specified property only.

Specific performance A legal action to compel a party to perform his or her agreement.

Split-rate interest One interest rate for the land and another for the improvements.

Spot zoning Zoning of a parcel of land that is not in conformance to surrounding zoning.

Square footage Exterior dimensions of a house, excluding the garage. May be shown as ☐.

Stagflation A period of no economic growth, coupled with inflation.

Standard subdivision A subdivision of improved or unimproved lots without any areas being owned in common.

Stand-by commitment A lender's agreement to make a loan in the future to a builder at agreed-upon terms.

Stare decisis The principle that courts should follow previous decisions.

Starker exchange A delayed exchange that qualifies for tax deferment.

State Board of Equalization Collects sales tax, oversees county assessors, and appraises public utility property.

State Labor Commissioner, Department Of Industrial Relations Handles settlement of commission disputes between brokers and their salespeople.

Statute of Frauds Provides that certain contracts must be written to be enforceable (contracts that can't be performed within one year, or that involve personal property of $500 or more).

Statute of Limitations Sets forth the time in which legal action must be started or the right will extinguish (for written contracts, four years).

Statutory management An arrangement whereby either spouse can manage community property.

Steering The illegal practice of directing prospective buyers to areas based on their race.

Stock cooperative project A project in which each stockholder has a right to occupy a unit and owns stock in a corporation that holds title.

Straight-line depreciation Deducting an equal sum each year as an expense so that the entire cost of an asset will be depreciated.

Straight note A note in which only interest is paid. It is an unamortized loan with the entire amount payable on the due date.

Street Improvement Act of 1911 The most widely used act for street improvements. The cost of assessment against each parcel must be paid (part or all) within 30 days of completion of the work, or it is put on the bond. The owner pays the assessment in equal installments during the term of the bond.

Strip development A line of commercial structures along a business street.

Studs Vertical two-by-fours in the walls and partitions.

Subagency An agency established through another agency.

Subdivision Land divided into five or more parcels of under 160 acres for the purpose of sale, lease, or financing.

Subjective value What it is worth to a seller to keep and use a property.

Subject to mortgage Buying real estate knowing of an encumbrance but not agreeing to pay it. The buyer must, of course, pay to avoid foreclosure; but if the property is foreclosed, no deficiency judgment is possible, as opposed to assuming the loan.

Sublease A lease given by a lessee to another.

Subordinate Junior to another encumbrance.

Subpoena Legal process requiring a witness to appear.

Subrogation Substitution of one party for another. In an accident, the insurance company, after paying the injured party, can now sue the party causing injury in his or her place.

Successor liability The liability of a purchaser of a business for collected but unremitted sales tax.

Summary appraisal report A short-form report where appraiser checks blocks and fills in blanks.

Summation method A method used to establish a capitalization rate by making adjustments to a safe rate.

Sum-of-the-digits depreciation An accelerated method of depreciation for tax purposes.

Supplemental property tax bill An additional tax bill sent out to the new owner when a property is sold because property is reappraised upon sale.

Surety One who guarantees the performance of another.

Surface water Water that is flowing but is not in a defined channel.

Surplus Value of assets over value of liabilities.

Surplus productivity After deducting the income attributable to labor, capital, and management, the surplus income would be attributable to the land.

Surrender A mutual agreement of the parties to terminate a lease.

Survey The process of measuring land.

Survivorship The right of joint tenants to the interests of other joint tenants upon their deaths.

Swing loan A short-term loan usually made when the borrower has purchased a new home but has not yet closed the sale of his or her old home.

Syndicate A limited partnership or corporation for investment purposes. The investors have limited liability.

Table funding The practice of naming the licensee rather than the lender as beneficiary to a loan. It is not allowed for property secured by a dwelling or for unimproved property. Can also mean a face-to-face closing where the funds are transferred in exchange for the deed.

Tacking on Adding a previous owner's period of use to obtain the statutory period of use for an easement by prescription or title by adverse possession.

Take-out loan Permanent financing taken out after construction financing.

Tandem plan A Ginnie Mae support plan for below-market loans to low-income buyers. Ginnie Mae reimburses Fannie Mae for buying these loans at par value on the secondary mortgage market.

Tax deed Given by the tax collector at auction.

Tax roll The assessed value of all taxable property. It shows the tax base.

Tax sale Sale of a property because of failure to pay taxes.

Tax shelter Having a book loss, such as depreciation, which can offset or shelter other income from taxation.

TD See *Trust deed.*

Tenancy at sufferance A tenancy in which the tenant holds over after the expiration of the lease.

Tenancy at will A tenancy in which no advance notice is required to end the tenancy. In California, 30 days' notice must be given in order to evict.

Tenancy by the entirety A form of joint tenancy between husband and wife which neither spouse can break by conveyance (not valid in California).

Tenancy in common Ownership by two or more people of an undivided interest without the right of survivorship. Interests do not need to be equal.

Tender An unconditional offer to pay a debt or perform in full.

Tenements Rights that pass with the land.

Tentative map The first subdivision map submitted to the planning commission. This is the first step in complying with the Map Act.

Termination statement A statement filed with the secretary of state by the lender to remove a personal property lien from the financing statement.

Termites Insects that feed on wood. The most dangerous termites in California are subterranean termites.

Termite shield Metalwork mounted under the mudsill on the foundation to keep termites out.

Testamentary trust A trust set up by a will.

Testate Dying with a will.

Testator A person who makes a will.

Three-day notice A notice to quit or pay rent, which is the first step in eviction.

Threshold A beveled board under a door.

Tidelands The land between the high- and low-tide lines (property of the state).

Tier A horizontal row of a township measured north and south from the base line.

387

Time is of the essence A statement making prompt performance mandatory.

Time-share Fractionalized ownership with a specified period of use. It is used for resort properties. Time-shares are considered subdivisions if there are 12 or more time-share estates for five years or more.

Title Evidence of ownership that is passed by deed.

Title insurance Insurance written by a title company to an owner guaranteeing market ability.

Title plant (data plant) The file of all recorded documents within a county.

Topography The changing surface elevations of land.

Torrens title system An obsolete system of recording in which a registrar issued certificates of title.

Tort A wrongful injury.

Township A six-mile-square parcel of land located by government survey.

Township line An east-west line forming the north or south boundary of a township.

Trade fixtures Personal property annexed to real estate for the purpose of carrying on a business or trade. They may be removed by the owner prior to the expiration of the lease.

Trading on equity Borrowing money on real estate at a rate lower than can be obtained by the use of the money.

Treads The horizontal boards of stairs.

Trespass Wrongful entry on the land of another.

Trim Finish woodwork and moldings.

Truss A rigid roof member joined together in one piece, forming roof joists, rafters, and diagonal supports.

Trust deed (TD) A deed given by the trustor to the trustee as security for a loan.

Trustee One who holds trust property for another.

Trustor One who gives a trust deed (the buyer or borrower).

Truth-in-Lending Law Also known as Regulation Z of the Consumer Credit Protection Act. It is a disclosure law that allows borrowers to know the cost of borrowing and the annual percentage rate (APR).

Turn-key project A complete construction package from site preparation to completion ready for occupancy (ready to turn the keys over to the owner).

Turnover The number of times an inventory sells in a year.

Twisting Misstatements of fact to induce a person to cancel one policy of insurance and take out another (generally illegal).

Ultra vires An act beyond the power of a corporation.

Unadjusted basis Original cost.

Underimprovement An improvement that fails to achieve the highest and best use for a property.

Undivided-interest subdivision A subdivision in which owners are tenants in common with other owners with a nonexclusive right of occupancy. An example would be a campground or recreational vehicle park owned by thousands of owners.

Undue influence Taking unfair advantage because of another's distress or weakness based on the nature of the relationship (such as between a nurse and a patient).

Unearned increment An increase in value of real estate not due to any effort or improvements of the owner.

Uniform Commercial Code (UCC) Sets standard commercial laws. The UCC has been in effect in California since January 1965.

Uniform Gift to Minors Act An act whereby a deposit of money or securities in a separate account for a minor is a completed gift for tax purposes, but the donee is guardian for the minor and can use the gift freely and even transfer it to third parties.

Uniform Simultaneous Death Act An act whereby if a husband and wife die in the same mishap and there is no evidence that they died other than simultaneously, then their property is treated as if the wife outlived the husband as to her property and as if the husband outlived the wife as to his property (one-half to the wife's heirs and one-half to the husband's heirs for community property).

Unilateral contract A promise in exchange for an act. It is accepted by the performance of the act.

Unit-in-place method An appraising method in which the cost of each component is separately priced (concrete, windows, etc.).

Unlawful detainer A legal eviction proceeding in which the tenant is ordered to appear in court.

Unmarried Formerly married person.

Unruh Act An act that prohibits a broker from discrimination based on race.

Upset price The minimum acceptable price (used at auctions).

Urban blight An economically declining area; a rapidly depreciating area, such as a slum area.

Urban property City property.

Use tax A tax on personal property purchased elsewhere to be used in the state. Plugs loopholes in state sales tax laws.

Usury A rate of interest on a loan above the maximum allowed by law.

Utility value Useful value.

VA See *DVA*.

Valid Good and enforceable.

Valid escrow An escrow in which an agreement has been reached and conditional delivery of transfer agreements (deeds) have been made to escrow.

Valley The internal angle formed by two sloping roof surfaces.

Valuation An estimation of worth.

Vara A Mexican land measurement equal to approximately 33 inches.

Variable-rate mortgage (VRM) A loan in which the interest rate rises or falls in accordance with an indicator of market interest, such as the prime rate.

Variance An exception to the zoning, as opposed to rezoning, that changes the zoning.

Vendee A buyer.

Vendor A seller.

Veneer Thin sheets of wood used for surfaces.

Vent A pipe used to provide air for drainage.

Verification A sworn statement under penalty of perjury as to the correctness of the contents of an instrument.

Vested Describes a present or sure interest that cannot be revoked.

Vested remainder A future interest that is bound to happen, such as a remainder interest when someone else has a life estate.

Veterans Administration See *DVA*.

Void Having no force or effect.

Voidable Capable of being nullified but good until then.

Voluntary lien A lien placed on property intentionally by the owner.

VRM See *Variable-rate mortgage*.

Vrooman Street Act (1885) An act that authorized cities to finish streets and issue bonds.

Wainscoting Lining the lower portion of a wall differently from the rest of the wall.

Waive To relinquish rights. A waiver is a unilateral act that leaves the parties as they are.

Walkup A multifloor apartment without an elevator.

Warehousing The practice of mortgage companies of putting together portfolios of loans to be sold in packages. They generally borrow on these loans.

Warranty deed A deed whereby the seller warrants the title. (In California a grant deed coupled with title insurance is used.) See *General warranty deed* and *Special warranty deed*.

Waste Destruction, injury, or failure to repair by a tenant for years or a tenant for life.

Water table The depth at which water can be found.

Wild document An instrument by someone who really has no interest in the property. It is outside the chain of title.

Wraparound trust deed (all-inclusive trust deed) Taking a second loan for the amount of the first and second trust deeds. The borrower makes the entire payment to the second trust deed beneficiary, who pays first trust deed.

Writ of possession Immediate possession given by the sheriff in an eviction (requires a bond).

Zero-interest loan A loan in which the seller buys down the interest rate to zero (usually a short-term loan).

Zone An area in which use is restricted for a particular purpose.

Zoning City or county regulations as to use of various areas.

Index

Quiet title action, 16, 42
Quitclaim deed, 17, 22

R

Range lines, 12
Ranges, 11–12
Ratification, 56
Real estate commission, 63, 67
Real Estate Investment Trust, 184
Real estate license, 292–297
Real Estate Settlement Procedures Act, 151–152, 220
Real Estate Transfer Disclosure Statement, 63, 64–66, 104
Real property, 2–3
Rebate law, 226
Recapture clause, 237
Reconciliation, 202
Recording, 2, 20, 21–22, 144
Recovery fund, 67
Recurring costs, 221
Red flags, 63
Redlining, 150, 255
Release clause, 145
Reliction, 5
Remainder depreciation, 199
Remainder interest, 23
Rent control, 238
Rent skimming, 142
Replacement cost, 195
Reproduction cost, 195
Resale certificate, 303
Rescission, 153, 250, 252
Reserve for replacement, 200
Residential leases, 235–236
Restricted appraisal report, 202
Restricted license, 297
Restrictive covenants, 43
Restrictive endorsement, 138
Retaliatory eviction, 236
Retention of records, 88–89
Return of deposit, 95
Reverse mortgage, 146
Reversionary interest, 23
Revocation of offer, 79
Rezoning, 247
Right of correlative user, 4
Right of first refusal, 89
Right of prior appropriation, 4
Right of survivorship, 24
Riparian rights, 4
Risk of loss, 220, 221
Rod, 14
Rollover mortgage, 146

Roof styles, 282
Rumford Act, 254

S

Safety clause, 82
Salespersons, 57
Salespersons license, 293, 294
Sales tax, 303
Sandwich lease, 238
Satisfaction of mortgage, 139
Scheduled gross income, 304
S corporations, 28
Seal, 21
Seasoned loan, 148
Secondary financing, 177
Secondary mortgage market, 177
Secret profit, 58
Section, 12, 14
Sector growth, 245
Securities, 184
Security agreement, 145
Security deposits, 235
Self contained report, 202
Seller Financing Disclosure, 105, 153, 154–156
Seller's agent, 58
Send-out slips, 300
Separate property, 18, 26
Septic system disclosure, 105
Servient tenement, 40–41
Severance damage, 254
Sharing-appreciation mortgage, 147
Sheet flooding, 5
Shelly v. *Kraemer,* 43
Sheriff's deed, 22–23
Sherman Anti-trust Act, 69
Simultaneous death, 19
Sinking fund, 200
Smoke detectors, 105
Soft money loan, 146
Solar Shade Act, 41
Special assessments, 267
Special endorsement, 138
Specific lien, 44
Specific performance, 81
Specific power of attorney, 56
Spot zoning, 247
Standard parallels, 12
Standard subdivision, 249
Standby loan, 149
Stare decisis, 2
Starker exchange, 269
State comptroller's deed, 19
Statute of Frauds, 20, 80, 81, 223
Statute of Limitations, 43, 81, 141
Statutory liens, 44